A Sourcebook
for Elementary Science

Second Edition

A Sourcebook
for Elementary Science

Second Edition

Elizabeth B. Hone

Professor of Education
San Fernando Valley State College

Alexander Joseph

Professor and Chairman, Division of Science and Mathematics
John Jay College, City University of New York

Edward Victor

Professor of Science Education
Northwestern University

Under the general editorship of **Paul F. Brandwein**

 Harcourt Brace Jovanovich, Inc.

New York / Chicago / San Francisco / Atlanta

COMPILATIONS:

Chapter bibliographies by Mrs. Margaret H. Miller, Supervisor of Elementary Libraries, Los Angeles City Schools

End-of-book bibliographies by Mrs. Dulcie I. Blume, Coordinator of Curriculum Materials, Alameda County School Department

Audio-visual materials list by Donald Lundstrom, Coordinator of Science, Alameda County School Department

Devices depicted in Figs. 11-4 and 11-7 were suggested by M. Lyons, Los Angeles City Schools.

COVER PHOTOGRAPH and those on pages 1, 71, 233, and 305 are drawn from the materials of the Elementary Science Study of the Education Development Center, Newton, Massachusetts.

ILLUSTRATIONS:

Acknowledgments and copyrights for illustrations begin on p. 455.

ISBN: 0-15-582855-X

Library of Congress Catalog Card Number: 74-145651

Printed in the United States of America

Preface

to the First Edition

The teaching procedures offered in this book have proved of value in many elementary science classrooms throughout the country. Certainly the book presents more techniques, demonstrations, projects, field trips, and suggestions than any teacher would need in any year. Many of the procedures are intended for use by the teacher alone; others are to be used by groups of children; still others are intended to stimulate individual investigations by groups or individuals. Some are simple in execution; some are moderately difficult; some are complex; a number may be considered too advanced for the majority of elementary-school students.

Children, differing as they do in needs, aptitudes, and attitudes, are idiosyncratic in their patterns of life and interests and in what they make of them. Since methods of teaching are, and do, indeed, remain personal inventions, each teacher will select the procedures that are applicable to his or her pupils or special school situation. The procedures are meant therefore simply as the raw materials from which a lesson, or part of it, may be constructed.

The authors—out of their experience in the elementary science classroom and in the training of elementary science teachers—have included techniques and procedures useful not only for the full range of elementary science classrooms (grades 1–8) but also for the variety of individual students who make up classes. These reflect the complete scope of the scientist's way: observing, thinking, imagining, developing "models," clarifying problems, inventing hypotheses and theories, discussing, reporting—all involved in designing experiments, all giving the fabric of science its special warp and woof.

This volume is one of a series of three sourcebooks; the others are *Teaching High School Science: A Sourcebook for the Biological Sciences,* by E. Morholt, P. F. Brandwein, and A. Joseph (Harcourt Brace Jovanovich, 1958), and *Teaching High School Science: A Sourcebook for the Physical Sciences,* by A. Joseph, P. F. Brandwein,

E. Morholt, H. Pollack, and J. F. Castka (Harcourt Brace Jovanovich, 1961). The three offer science teachers in elementary, junior high, and senior high schools a full review of demonstrations, field methods, and laboratory procedures in science.

The purpose of the authors is clear: to be of service to their colleagues, teachers of children.

PAUL F. BRANDWEIN

to the Second Edition

In the nine years since publication of the first edition of this sourcebook, it has become clear that it accomplished the purpose to which the authors originally dedicated it: to be of service to their colleagues, teachers of children. It remained only to improve the work, the better to fulfill its purpose. The authors have accomplished that in this second edition.

PAUL F. BRANDWEIN

Contents

1

Animal Life

page 1

2
Insect Life

page 21

3
Plant Life

page 49

4
Minute Worlds

page 71

5
The Air

page 82

6
Water

page 96

7
Weather and Climate

page 112

8

The Earth's Surface

page 127

9

The Stars and Planets

page 145

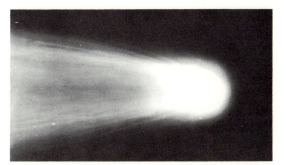

10
Chemistry for Children

page 173

11
Life Processes

page 188

12
Fibers and Cloth

page 204

13
Housing

page 212

14
Sound

page 222

15
Light and Color

page 233

16
Fire

page 255

17
Heat

page 268

18
Magnets and Magnetism

page 290

19
Electricity

page 305

20
Communications

page 331

21
Atoms and Radioactivity

page 343

22

Machines and Engines

page 358

23

Flight

page 383

24
Gravity and Space Travel

page 398

Hand-feeding a rabbit in the classroom.

1 Animal Life

Whether one teaches in a rural or urban school, there will be opportunities to care for animals in the classroom. If the class topic is "the farm," a child may bring a pet duck for the day; a study of nutrition may be made much more meaningful by the observation of white rats (obtainable from a hospital or test laboratory); and, if school regulations permit, an injured wild animal may be brought in for treatment and temporary observation. Some communities have a junior museum with an organized animal loan service for schools; a few school systems have their own service. Children who own pets or whose parents own pet stores will have helpful suggestions for the care of animals in the classroom.

MULTIPURPOSE ANIMAL CAGE

Whether wild or domestic, an animal in the classroom can best be housed in a cage large enough for a rabbit or cat, yet that can be folded when not in use. The cage should be of a metal that permits thorough scrubbing and rinsing in laundry bleach solution. (It is important that classroom equipment can be readily cleaned by the children.) A water fountain that provides fresh water on demand and seldom needs refilling, and a debris-catching metal tray that can be cleaned easily, must also be provided in the "cage" home. For dogs and rabbits, a 3-foot-square cage is preferable; 2 square feet is enough for guinea pigs, hamsters, and white rats.

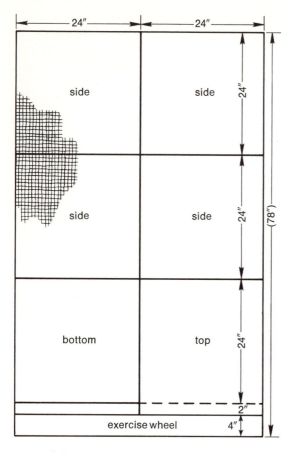

FIGURE **1-1** Cutting pattern for animal cage. Dashed line indicates where top is to be folded to make overlap. Construction of "exercise wheel" (lowermost portion of screening) is described in Fig. 1-3.

The cage is made of about seven feet of 48-inch-wide screening or wire mesh (cage screening of $\frac{1}{2}$- to $\frac{3}{4}$-inch mesh is available in rolls 36 to 48 inches wide) and a piece of galvanized sheet iron or aluminum (both resistant to corrosion) about 28 inches square. Also needed are about three dozen clips (generally obtainable from pet stores) or some bell wire, and about one dozen alligator clips (available from hardware stores, these clips are superior to wood pins which absorb odor and may be chewed by the animal). The necessary tools are: tin-snips, a ball-peen hammer, and side-cutting pliers. Where clips are used instead of bell wire, special pliers (or auto mechanic's pliers) will be needed to close them.

Unroll the wire mesh and cut it in half, making two 24-inch-wide strips. Trim any protruding wire ends with side-cutting pliers, and then cut five 24 × 24-inch squares from the strips (Fig. 1-1). Trim these squares closely, as before, and fasten four together to form the sides of the cage, using clips or wire at intervals as shown in Fig. 1-2. The fifth square forms the bottom and is fastened along only one edge to make a kind of hinge that permits opening and folding (Fig. 1-2). Cut a piece for the top (Fig. 1-1) with enough overlap (about 2 inches) to make it secure when bent down over the side. As with the bottom, fasten the top along one edge to permit folding. Attach a water bottle to the outside of the cage with the tip of its tube inside the cage (Fig. 1-2).

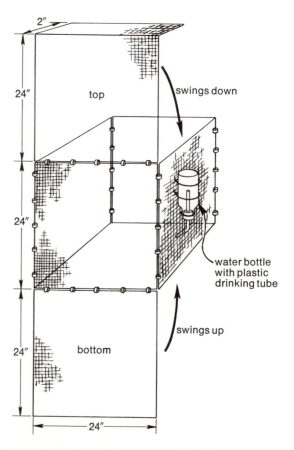

FIGURE **1-2** Animal cage assembly. With top and bottom open, cage folds for compact storage.

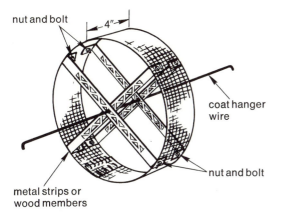

nut and bolt

4"

coat hanger wire

nut and bolt

metal strips or wood members

FIGURE **1-3** Animal exercise wheel. Made from wire mesh used in multipurpose cage construction (Figs. 1-1, 1-2).

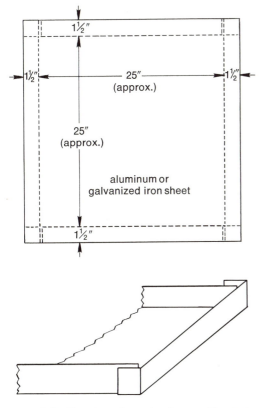

1½"

1½"   25"   1½"
(approx.)

25"
(approx.)

aluminum or
galvanized iron sheet

1½"

FIGURE **1-4** Tray base for animal cage. Metal sheet is folded along single dashed lines, cut at double dashed lines. Lower figure shows appearance of completed corners.

An exercise wheel may be made from a 4 × 48-inch piece of screening, as shown in Fig. 1-3. The screening forms the tread, which is braced by four members made of metal or wood strips (such as are found in toy construction sets) through which the coat hanger axle passes to hook onto the sides or across a corner of the cage.

To make the tray in which the cage is set, fold the sheet metal at the cage corners (see Fig. 1-4); then hammer the metal flat, using a block of wood as a form.

Fasten the top and bottom to the sides by placing alligator clips along the three open (unhinged) edges of the two parts. Then set the cage in the tray base. When the cage is occupied, weight the top to prevent the animal from pushing his way out or from tipping the cage.

Assemble the water fountain using a medium-sized pill bottle, a one-hole stopper, and a plastic tube; mount as shown in Fig. 1-2. The stopper can be made by drilling a cork with the blunt end of a rattail file; the business end of the file will help to smooth the hole. The fountain should be checked daily to see if it is flowing properly; it will probably not need to be cleaned and refilled more than once a week. The air pressure principle involved here may lead the children into a new area of questions and investigations (see Chapter 5).

Cage Furnishings and Housekeeping

Heavy glass ash trays are excellent containers for most foods; cardboard boxes serve well for dry foods. (Because the feeding habits of different animals are remarkably varied, in most cases it is best to offer the widest imaginable selection of foods, but in *small* amounts. *Do not overfeed.*)

Nothing promotes sickness in animals as quickly as putrefying food, dirty water, and foul quarters; any odor from classroom pets may be evidence of poor housekeeping. Daily removal of uneaten foods and of soiled bedding is a minimum essential. Softwood shavings or sawdust in the debris tray to absorb odors and a weekly washing in laundry bleach solution will keep the cage sweet-smelling.

Most animals should have a nest box to shelter them from drafts, especially if the cage is on the floor. (The difference between readings from two thermometers—one on the floor and one close to the ceiling—will demonstrate the need for this to the children, as will the flickering of a candle flame in different parts of the room.) In schools that are unheated over weekends, it may be necessary to take the animals home or to cover their cages with cloths or blankets. Electric heaters have been used in some schools during harsh cold waves.

Animals also need a dark retreat for rest as well as shelter. Cardboard is less sturdy than wood for a nest box, but it can be frequently replaced. For smaller animals, the entrance hole should be near the top of the box, creating a dark nest or chamber below, preferred by birds and mammals alike. Because of this predilection in animals, bird boxes with doorways drilled at the bottom often remain vacant.

MAMMALS

Almost any small pet that can be safely kept at home can be kept at school. Never confine any animal for long periods. About two weeks is the maximum except when training white rats for pets or keeping animals for nutritional experiments. If the fur of a mammal is in poor condition, try adding a small amount of vitamin A and/or milk of magnesia to the diet. Provide plenty of food for wild pets; wild animals do not usually overeat, and there is nothing more pitiable than a half-starved, caged animal. Feed baby animals with a doll nursing bottle, and use the smallest opening possible to avoid strangling from too rapid feeding. (Milk bubbling from the nostrils is a sure sign of strangling.)

One way of bringing animals not otherwise permitted at school into the classroom is to have a "pet day,"[1] during which each child who brings a pet may tell about feeding, cleaning, and training it.

[1]Greve, Anna M., "Let's Have a Pet Show," *Natl. Humane Review*, Vol. XXXI, No. 5, May, 1943, pp. 18–20.

Rabbits

A tame rabbit may be permitted the freedom of the classroom. This is good for both rabbit and children, since rabbits need exercise and children need to become accustomed to animals. (Wild rabbits sometimes carry the disease tularemia and should not be kept as pets.) In a mild climate, or in spring and fall, the rabbit can live in an elevated outdoor cage safe from dogs and cats. In the classroom, he needs a cardboard box shelter (which can be replaced when sanitation demands) where he may retreat and rest. (Cut an opening in one end of the box for an entrance.) For overnight and weekend quarters, the 2- or 3-foot-square multipurpose mesh cage (Figs. 1-1 to 1-4) is adequate, though it would be cramped for a full-grown rabbit over a more extended period.

Rabbits need heavy, non-tippable containers for food and water. A rack or manger for green food can be made from wire screening and attached low and to one side of the cage. All animals choose one spot in a cage or room for excretion. Once this choice has been made, spread newspaper in that area, changing it frequently. A dirty pen, damp food, and poor ventilation may soon produce a sick rabbit. In such a case, take the animal immediately to a veterinary.

Never lift rabbits by the ears; pick them up by the loose shoulder skin, at the same time supporting the hind quarters with a gloved or cloth-protected hand to guard against their long hind claws.

White Rats

For the elementary classroom white rats are preferable to white mice since they smell less "mousey" and are larger, making them easier for children to pick up. White rats also move less quickly than guinea pigs and are less inclined to bite than hamsters. They are usually available from hospital or medical research laboratories, which are usually glad to have the school return parents and progeny at the year's end. Keep rats in the multipurpose cage equipped with the exercise wheel (Figs. 1-1 to 1-4) and see that they are clean and comfortable. They should be amply (but not over-) supplied with a varied diet, which can include a bit of anything that humans eat; now and then give them some green twigs to gnaw. Rats may be washed, although a more natural method of cleaning can be achieved if they have a small sand box in which to rub any grease from their fur.

The gestation period in the rat is about three weeks. When the female is near the end of her pregnancy, the male should be removed to another cage. If he remains present at birth, the female may kill her newborn young. The mother will use partially shredded newspaper or paper toweling to make a nest.

The young begin to open their eyes and grow hair in 16–18 days, but they should stay with the mother 21–24 days. Then, because prolonged nursing will weaken the mother, begin weaning the babies by feeding them milk, bread soaked in milk, and lettuce. A few drops of cod liver oil on bread should be given twice a week. When the young are a month old, they may have the same food as the adults—that is, bread, bread and milk, lettuce, carrots, sunflower seeds, etc. If one offers small quantities of each food, the rats will select those that best meet their requirements.

Baby rats may be picked up as soon as their eyes are open if it does not seem to worry the mother. Condition her to accept your handling by slow gentle movements, talking to her and feeding her a bit of carrot or chocolate as you return her young to her. The young rats can be gentled by a little quiet fondling at first, which may become more frequent as they cease to show fear. Talk softly meanwhile, scratching them behind the ears and eventually under the chin. Show children how to pick up a rat without squeezing, yet with gentle firmness so the animal is not afraid of falling. Since all animals fear nothing so much as close physical restraint, even semi-domesticated white rats must become accustomed to handling gradually. Always move deliberately, never hurriedly or nervously, with any animal.

Gerbils

Mongolian gerbils, introduced into the United States in 1954, have rapidly gained popularity as admirable adjuncts to classroom and laboratory. They are clean and gentle, multiply readily, and (in contrast to hamsters) are active in the daytime. Because of their many virtues, gerbils are now available at pet stores in most states.

A mated pair of gerbils need space for movement and privacy, rest, and the raising of their young. They are crowded in anything smaller than a 10-gallon aquarium. A less expensive shelter is a terrarium, which should be no less than twelve inches high and have a minimum floor area of 200 square inches. A top of $\frac{1}{4}$- to $\frac{1}{2}$-inch mesh wire in a stout wood frame will offer protection from cats, while providing ventilation. Since gerbils are burrowing animals, wire mesh floors can make their feet and noses sore; a glass bottom covered with a generous layer of sand allows tunneling. A layer of several inches of pine chips or commercial litter over the sand provides bedding. Since gerbils excrete scarcely any urine, the bedding stays clean and odorless, and need be changed no more than every fortnight. If there are babies, do not change the bedding until they are weaned—usually about a month after birth.

Although desert gerbils can absorb water from their food, as do kangaroo rats, in captivity they prefer to drink minute amounts from an inverted water bottle (Fig. 1-2). Gerbils in the wild live on grains and grasses, seeds and roots. They should be provided with fresh sweet hay in abundance and offered a variety of generally "crunchy" foods, such as seeds, cereals, hamster or dog kibble, and, for a daily total of about one tablespoon, bits of apple, celery, carrot, fruit, lettuce, and other greens. Use sunflower seeds when training gerbils to eat from the hand, but in moderate amounts to avoid excess weight. (Keeping a record of the gerbils' food preferences could be a project for children.) Offering foods sparingly helps to keep quarters cleaner.

Gerbils demonstrate their rodent kinship by inveterate gnawing. If their incisors are not thus ground down, they will have to be nipped back

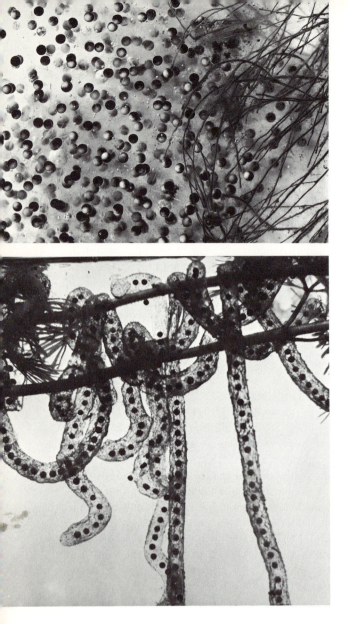

FIGURE **1-5** At top, frog egg mass; below, strings of toad eggs.

by a veterinarian so that the animal will not starve because it is unable to close its mouth and chew. Some pet store owners provide gerbils with softwood blocks soaked in salt water. Cardboard tubes or egg cartons will suffice for free-lance chewing. (An increase in such chewing may indicate pregnancy.)

Grown gerbils are between a rat and mouse in size. Males are usually heavier and darker, with a tapered tufted contour near the base of the tail. The female's rear is rounded with the two openings adjacent. Single gerbils or two of the same sex do not flourish. Unless they are already a mated pair from the same litter, a male and female must be introduced gradually. Put them in the same cage but separated by a wire partition until they are used to each other's smell.

The gerbil gestation period is 24–25 days, and litters average five pups (record when the young are born). If hidden in one of the extensive tunnels dug by the gerbils, babies may be detected by their faint chirruping. Nursing females need fluids from a daily supply of green foods and potato or apple peelings, but do not give them soft fruits. After 20 days, the infants' eyes open; when ten to twelve weeks old, the young should be separated from the parents and caged together. At two or three months old, they will begin pairing. Gerbils are monogamous and a mating pair should be moved to their own quarters.

AMPHIBIANS

The development of a dark spot in a mass of frog eggs into a tadpole and then into an adult frog is one of the perennial wonders of spring.

Played for the children, "Voices of the Night," a Cornell University recording of amphibian voices, will produce comments that provide a guide to the children's concepts of amphibians and life cycles. Amphibian eggs may be found in the spring in ponds and other still water. Toad and salamander eggs are laid in strings of jelly; frog eggs in masses of jelly (Fig. 1-5). The jelly serves as the tadpole's first food when it emerges from the egg; later it feeds on green scum or algae. The day before obtaining the eggs, bring in enough pond water and green scum to float them and to feed the newborn once they arrive. Measure and record the outdoor water temperature at the time of collection.

Keep the eggs in a covered glass container to reduce evaporation and protect them from chalk dust and other toxic matter. If additional water is needed, distilled water (available in most communities from a local bottling firm) should be used. If it is necessary to use tap water, let it stand several days. Keep the eggs in a relatively cool place exposed to some sunlight, but not enough to overheat the water. Normal room temperature with little variation should keep the water about the right hatching temperature.

From egg to frog usually takes about three months, although this varies from species to species. Some species—bullfrogs, for example—require two years to mature. Watching the legs appear is always interesting. (Do all four emerge at the same time?) Study of the whole developmental process offers an opportunity to help children acquire an understanding of the prenatal changes that take place in all animal species. (Greenlee[2] gives a delightful description of how a first-grade class met the problem of hatching salamander eggs and at the same time taught the science consultant a great deal about young children!)

A small amphibian will be comfortable in a moist woodland terrarium (Chapter 3). Since a tiny spring peeper or treetoad can scale the walls of a glass container or terrarium, keep the cover tightly closed. (A male peeper in a comfortable environment may "peep" softly when the room is still.)

Thin rocks built into a miniature "grotto" or formed into a rough wall in one end of a terrarium or aquarium furnish a cool retreat that amphibians such as frogs and toads will favor. Amphibious animals need a shallow glass or enamel dish in which to "muddle" and soak their skins. The dish must be cleaned and refilled daily, and animals should be able to enter and leave it unaided.

A frog or toad can be induced to eat an insect or a bit of hamburger or earthworm dangled before it. Children will be astonished to see the speed with which the tongue, attached at the front of the mouth, flicks out and gathers in the offering.

[2] Greenlee, Julian, *Better Teaching Through Elementary Science*, William C. Brown Company, 1954, p. 1 *ff*.

REPTILES

Turtles

Larger turtles (except snappers, of course) are one kind of animal that can be allowed to roam the classroom when children are present. Toy turtles and some larger species need shallow enamelware or glass dishes in which they can soak. A good turtle diet includes most insects, bits of hard-boiled egg, earthworms, meal worms, lettuce, and fruit. Some turtles like a small amount of chopped meat or canned fish. (A diet limited to ant eggs will induce blindness and eventual death.) Desert tortoises are vegetarians, but need a wide variety of food to remain healthy in captivity. Mud turtles feed underwater, as do many water turtles. Water turtles are carnivores. Land turtles are usually vegetarians. All uneaten food should be removed promptly.

Almost all turtles will attempt to hibernate for part of the winter and should be provided with a dark, cool place for this purpose. The duration of hibernation depends upon the latitude (actually the mean average temperature, generally corresponding with latitude): for instance, a turtle at latitude 40° will hibernate about six months; one at 60° for a shorter time. On emerging, they may look somewhat wasted, especially around the necks. If they refuse food, they may have to be force-fed. This usually requires two people: one to hold the animal, and one to pry open the beak (with a blunt tool) and stuff in the food. Do not overfeed.

In the interest of good conservation return the turtle to its habitat after a brief sojourn at school. Children should understand that it is cruel to paint a turtle since its back is composed partly of living tissue. The children can estimate the age of a living turtle from the major growth rings in each scale. Growth rings can also be seen in fish scales through a strong magnifying glass or a low-power microscope (Fig. 1-6).

Snakes

Small snakes appropriate to the classroom—garter, green, DeKay's—can be housed in a box

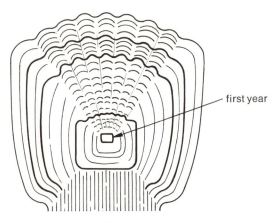

first year

FIGURE **1-6** Magnified growth rings on a fish scale (above) and (at right) growth rings on a turtle shell. Each broad ring represents a year's growth.

(Fig. 1-7) constructed from a wooden crate. Replace one side with a glass pane that slides in grooves cut into close-fitting wooden members nailed to the box. (Ready-grooved wood is available at lumber yards.) The slits in the box sides can be covered with tape. Snakes should be provided with a heavy shallow water dish; a glass ash tray may be used. They also need a branch on which to climb and a rock or bark under which to hide. During shedding time these rough surfaces will enable them to work loose from their old skins. Like other animals in the classroom, snakes must have a shady place available; a piece of curved tile or a fragment of flower pot will suffice. They also need *some* sunshine because their metabolism is influenced by air temperature; they will become sluggish if they are too cold. Do not expose the snake to direct sunlight for long, however; a rattlesnake can literally cook to death in minutes on a surface above 100°F.

Large snakes, if brought to school at all, should only remain a few days. It is not necessary to feed them during this period. Smaller snakes and the young of large species should be offered worms, grubs, insects, and bits of chopped meat, which should be dangled before them since they accept only live or moving food. Most snakes feed irregularly.

Never keep poisonous snakes in an elementary classroom. It is wise not to pick up a snake until its nonpoisonous nature is clearly established; a copperhead covered with roadside dust may not, at first, show its typical markings. However, there are very few poisonous species in the United States.

Lizards

Children often bring to school the little green or brown lizards sold at circuses and carnivals as chameleons. They will require living food such as flies, moths, and meal worms—not the sugar water that is often prescribed. Chameleons, also called the Carolina anolis, will sometimes eat very ripe bananas. It is possible for pet lizards to catch their own food if they are housed in a cage covered with a mesh large enough to admit flies. (Set the cage on the window sill, but not in continuous sunlight.) Horned toads prefer ants and can catch their own from an ant colony. A trail of sugar or grease will lead the ants to the cage.

Lizards may be kept in a cage similar to the

one described in Fig. 1-7. Like snakes, they will become sluggish unless they are kept relatively warm. Optimum temperature for lizards is 80°F; it should not drop below 65°F. A heat lamp shining on one end of a fairly large cage will provide an overall range of temperatures from which the lizards can select those most congenial to them.

A potted plant should be placed in the cage to give the lizard something to climb. Like snakes, lizards like bark, branches, and rocks, and need a heavy shallow water dish. To insure that their skins absorb moisture, the plant and the lizard can be sprayed at the same time with lukewarm water about once a week. The lizard may also be held in a dish of water, in which case the children will almost be able to see the skin soak up moisture like a blotter.

BIRDS

Caged birds, such as canaries, can thrive in the classroom if they are properly fed and cleaned. The principal problem will be exercising the bird.

It is recommended that parakeets or other members of the parrot family not be brought to school. They are susceptible to a virus disease, psittacosis, which is communicable to humans. It is possible to keep members of the parrot family (in subtropical areas only) if there is a place outside the school where the birds will be safe from cats and other predators.

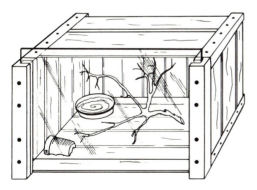

FIGURE **1-7** Observation box for snakes.

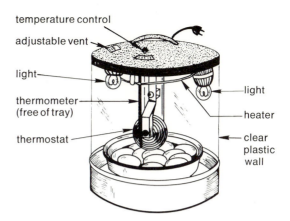

FIGURE **1-8** Commercial display incubator for use in classroom.

Wild baby birds that are occasionally brought to school may have to be force-fed. To do so, open the beak gently and put the food (pellets made of equal parts of raw hamburger, hard-boiled egg, and pablum)[3] in the back of the throat with forceps or tweezers. The food must touch the swallowing center on the back of the tongue. Keep the chick in a warm place in a cup or berry basket containing shredded paper.

Children enjoy letting ducks, chickens, and other pets "make tracks" on newsprint or painting paper spread on the floor. Dip the animal's feet in any water color tempera and let it walk across the paper; then thoroughly rinse its feet.

Chicken Incubator

Watching chickens hatch in the incubator of a commercial hatchery can be a profound experience for children.

An electric incubator (Fig. 1-8) with a capacity of 12–20 eggs is available for classroom use, but one can be made (Fig. 1-9) of readily available materials. Needed are a short lamp cord; an electrical socket and bulb; a piece of asbestos paper; a wall thermometer; a thermostatic switch; a cake pan about 8 × 10 inches; and a piece of $\frac{1}{4}$- or $\frac{1}{2}$-inch wire mesh about

[3] Walker, Ernest, *First Aid and Care of Small Animals*, Animal Welfare Institute, New York, 1955, p. 45.

12 × 14 inches. Also needed are two cardboard cartons: one about 10 × 10 × 14 inches, the other about 12 × 12 × 16 inches (or large enough to enclose the former and still leave some space for paper to be stuffed between the two boxes for insulation).

Cut one end from the small box. Then cut a square window in the large box which is slightly smaller than (and in a side corresponding to) the open end of the inner box (Fig. 1-9a). Pack the space between the boxes with shredded newspaper or other insulating material and line the

inner box with aluminum foil. Pass the wires to the light bulb through a hole in the sides of both the inner and outer boxes (Fig. 1-9a).

Cut a hole in the top of the inner box large enough to accommodate a clothespin. Using the clothespin, attach the wires of the bulb (Fig. 1-9b) to the underside of the box top so that the bulb hangs free. Connect the thermostatic switch to *one* of the wires leading to the bulb (Fig. 1-9c).

Fit a pane of glass over the window, taping all edges for safety. Use a double thickness of 1½–2-inch adhesive to make a flap along the top edge (Fig. 1-9a). Staple this flap to the box to form a hinge so the window can be opened. Paint the inner surface of the cake (water) tin to inhibit rusting. Bend the wire mesh so that it fits above the tin and place both in bottom of box.

Fasten thermometer and thermostat to a wall of the inner box. Use a light bulb of a wattage that keeps the box temperature near 103°F. Three or four ¾- to 1-inch holes plugged with corks can help to regulate the heat level. (Remove corks to lower the temperature and replace them to raise it.)

Once an even 100°F temperature can be maintained, put a dozen fertile eggs into the incubator. (A chicken farmer may show the children how he "candles" eggs to determine fertility, or children can make their own egg candler of a tin can with a light bulb inside and a hole slightly smaller than the long axis of the egg cut in the can. Internal changes may be seen by holding eggs against the hole.) After three days remove one egg and crack it just enough to slip its contents into a shallow dish. The heart beat of the three-day embryo should be discernible. Repeat every three days to let children observe the development (Fig. 1-10).

Eggs should be turned daily and water kept in a pan underneath the wire platform to maintain viable humidity. Chicken eggs take 21 days to hatch. One day after the chicks have hatched begin to reduce the incubator temperature a few degrees a day until room temperature is reached. The incubator can then serve as the chicks' home until they are about three weeks old. To allow them to go in and out at will, cut out one wall

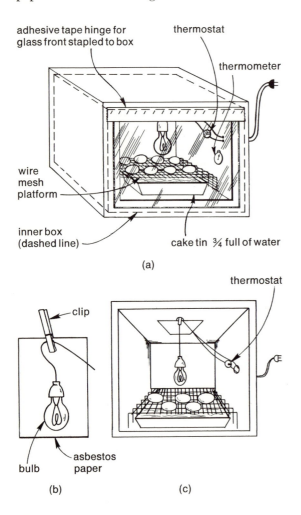

(a)

(b)   (c)

FIGURE **1-9** Classroom incubator. Consult with high school science teacher or local poultryman for specifics and supplies.

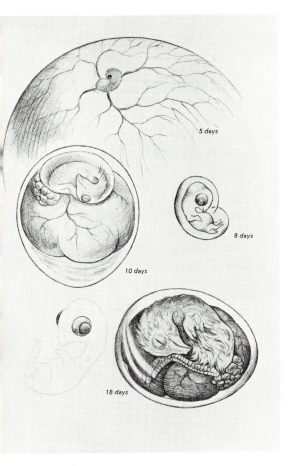

5 days

8 days

10 days

18 days

FIGURE **1-10** Chick embryo at various stages of development.

of the box two inches above its bottom, cover this opening with cloth tacked to the carton, and provide a ramp or runway of wood or metal. Surround the carton with a 12-inch-high fence of wire mesh or screening. A sheet of lightweight metal under the incubator and runway may be quickly removed and hosed off. Chick mash as well as dishes for food and water can be purchased at a feed store.

FISH AND OTHER WATER LIFE

A temporary fish tank can be made of a wide-mouthed gallon jar or old-fashioned glass candy

and cookie jars, or an open-topped glass brick. Globes are easily tipped over and tend to distort one's view of the fish. They also restrict both the area of water surface essential for absorption of air and the area available for shelter and exercise. With respect to capacity of the vessel, the aquarist's rule of thumb is: one gallon of water for one fish.

Most tropical fish require a water temperature that is relatively high and constant, necessitating use of a heater and thermostat. Heating equipment for aquariums is available from mail-order houses or from local pet shops, which can also provide fish, fish food, aquarium plants, snails, and washed sand for the tank bottom.

In the long run, good tanks usually cost less than inexpensive ones. The first step in preparing a tank is to wash it with soap and *warm* water. (Hot water may loosen the aquarium cement.) Rinse the tank several times in cold water and fill it two-thirds full. Pond, stream, or rain water is best for filling a tank because it may contain microorganisms, which multiply and become fish food. Moreover, unlike tap water, untreated water does not contain chlorine, which is poisonous to plant and animal life. If tap water is used, it should stand at least three days to allow the chlorine to escape and any lime that may be present to settle out. Then cover the bottom of the tank with an irregular layer of coarse sand (not beach sand) or gravel. If the sand is not bought, it can be prepared by stirring it in a detergent solution, rinsing it, and then baking it in an oven to kill mold. Aquariums stay cleaner and require less frequent addition of water if they are kept covered.

A few sprigs of Sagittaria, Elodea, Vallisneria, Cabomba, or Myriophyllum are useful for absorbing the carbon dioxide expelled by the fish. The first three listed are particularly valuable as sources of oxygen. After waiting 24–48 hours for the water to reach room temperature, imbed water plants one-inch deep in the sand, anchoring them with pebbles, which should first be boiled. Let the stems trail; they will rise as water is added. Remove broken or discolored leaves. If plants do not thrive, replant them in a sand layer

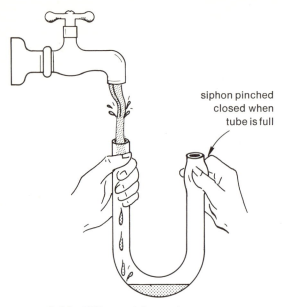

FIGURE **1-11** Filling a siphon tube.

FIGURE **1-12** A balanced aquarium.

is used in the laboratory.) A few 18-inch lengths of plastic or rubber tubing of $\frac{1}{2}$- to $\frac{3}{4}$-inch diameter will be useful for daily removal of debris from the tank. Before allowing children to do this chore, one should have them practice using a dip tube to remove loose dirt from the bottom of a jar. Some children know the principle of siphoning liquids. Fill the tube as shown in Fig. 1-11 or by immersion. When a tube is filled, pinch the ends while it is transferred into position.

After siphoning the water into the tank, let the aquarium stand until the water clears, then add the fish and one snail per gallon of tank capacity. (Snails control algae—water plants—and remove dead matter.)

Early-morning sunlight from an eastern exposure is desirable for an aquarium. If the aquarium is placed on the window sill, the resultant growth of algae may be reduced by fastening dark paper to the side facing the window. Do not place the aquarium near radiators.

Water that evaporates from the tank can be replaced without frightening the fish or dislodging plants by pouring it over a plate. The children may think of ways to calculate the amount of water that evaporates and ways to reduce the evaporation (that is, by covering the tank). The question of how fish can have enough air with the tank covered can lead to the fact that the plants produce oxygen (Fig. 1-12). (See p. 61.) Thus, too, a fish tank can be used to illustrate

spread on top of rich soil which, in turn, rests on a bottom layer of sand. Lay a piece of paper over the plants and gently siphon water into the tank. (The paper keeps the plants from being washed out of place and reduces roiling of the water.) The use of the siphon here is a fine way to illustrate air pressure at work (Chapter 5). (Children will enjoy playing at siphoning with drinking straws. They can use the straws as dip tubes by closing the top end with a finger to pick up a few drops of water just as a glass pipette

The label in the figure reads:

siphon pinched closed when tube is full

FIGURE **1-13** Model of life in $\frac{1}{2}$ inch of pond water, magnified 100 times, shows one-celled plants and animals and more complex forms. The plants range from the higher Utricularia (stem proceeding from *left center* to *right top,* with many bladder-like traps) and Elodea (*right center* to *top right* with tapering leaves) to the green algae Spirogyra (slender stalks at *left*), and Closterium (a desmid, crescent-shaped, appearing over the Utricularia stem in the *center*). The animals include the tiny bell-like protozoans Vorticella (*left center*), rotifers, fairy shrimp (bubble shape at *bottom center*), Hydra (large tentacled form bending from *bottom center* to *bottom right*), and a watermite egg (*center left,* with nucleus).

the major scientific concept that, under ordinary conditions, matter may be changed but not destroyed. The carbon dioxide which living creatures give off is used by the aquarium plants to make their food sugars in the presence of sunlight. (See Chapter 3.)

A small inexpensive dip net will facilitate handling the fish. Usually fish can be "poured" into the tank from a container, but if it is necessary to touch them, moisten the hands first.

Goldfish and Guppies

Because of their hardiness, goldfish are the most practical choice for a classroom aquarium, especially in view of the low temperatures that may prevail in classrooms over winter weekends. In the goldfish, children may readily observe the phenomenon of accommodation to environment—the streamlined form and smooth covering for easy passage through the water; the fins for propelling, balancing, and steering; the gills for extracting oxygen from the water. Also noteworthy is the light-gathering part of the eye (rounder than in land animals) and the lateral line, a faint horizontal row of spots the length of the body, a kind of sonar system instead of external ears.

Many useful questions can be answered by direct observation of the goldfish. Which fin does what? Does the goldfish rest on the bottom or near the surface? Can it stay still without moving a fin? Does it tend to float? If so, why? The action

of a fish's air bladder can be illustrated with a small capped bottle or corked vial in which some air is trapped. Vary the amount of trapped air to show how a fish can alter its buoyancy.

Of the tropical fish, guppies are the most durable. They are inexpensive and breed almost too easily. Unlike most fish, guppies are born alive, the eggs hatching inside the female's body. The male, smaller and usually more brightly colored, may have to be put into a separate tank to prevent his eating newborn fry. Guppies require a water temperature of 60–70°F.

Local Varieties

Small native fish found in local streams or ponds and suitable for a classroom aquarium are dace, perch, and stickleback. Tadpoles are also appropriate, but crayfish should be much smaller than the other varieties if depopulation of the tank is to be avoided.

Fish "breathe" to live just as do higher animals, although they use their gills. Continuous opening

FIGURE **1-14** Cattails.

and closing of the mouth and movement of the gills are aspects readily noted by children. Water continually passing over the gills carries oxygen for absorption by the blood, which at the same time gives up carbon dioxide to the water. In this exchange, much like that taking place in the human lung (Chapter 11) or that of other animals, the fish obtains the oxygen necessary for it to live. Children may closely examine the gills of a fish brought into the classroom. (Rinse the fish in dilute ammonia to remove odor.) They will note that the gill tissue is bright red because the skin is extremely thin to permit the blood to come close to the surface. To demonstrate the presence of carbon dioxide, place some goldfish briefly in clear lime water (see p. 180). The carbon dioxide given off by the fish will quickly cloud the lime-water. (See Chapter 10 for the carbon dioxide test.)

To demonstrate that there is air (and hence oxygen) in water, draw some tap water and let it stand in glass containers. In a relatively short time, air bubbles will form on the inside of the glass container. In a more graphic exercise, heat some water and let it stand until it is cool. Draw an equal amount of fresh water. The temperatures of the water in the containers and in the aquarium should not differ by more than two or three degrees. Place a goldfish in each jar and watch them carefully. The fish in the water that had been heated will come to the surface in order to breathe the oxygen that is beginning to diffuse into the water. (Watch that the fish in the airless water does not suffocate.) The children may note the analogy with problems of air and space travel caused by the very narrow range of environments from which humans secure the oxygen necessary for life. (See p. 408.)

The oxygen absorbed at the surface is supplemented by oxygen given off by the water plants in the aquarium when the sun's energy starts their "food factories" (Chapter 3). Thus, bubbles of oxygen will form at the tops of the leaves of water plants (such as Elodea or Anacharis) put in a container of water on a sunny window sill. Observing the search for balance between aquarium plants and animals moves children toward the larger concept of the interrelationships between all life and its environment.

LIFE IN THE LITTORAL ZONE

Geological evidence appears to substantiate the Biblical description of the face of the earth as once covered with mists. As the mists condensed and fell as rain, water collected in the depressions on the earth's surface. Some primitive cells began to form in the warm shallow waters of these ancient seas. Since the moon's and sun's gravitational pull created tides then as now, these primitive cells (probably not too different from single-celled water plants and animals today) were alternately left stranded and then inundated. Those that withstood the alternate drowning and dessication survived. Probably the odds for survival were greatest for the forms on the very edge of the tide zone. These reproduced in kind. Possible mutants that could withstand greater extremes moved further away from the water to become exclusively land-dwelling. Concepts of primitive life at the edge of the sea may be developed in children by having them collect, culture, and study the life in a drop of water (Fig. 1-13).

Scarcely a natural community exists that does not include remnants of water-life communities. Children are the first to know the nearest pond, stream, slough, or marsh. Field trips to these areas can be most instructive. Equipment for such trips is described under *Water Insects* in Chapter 2.

During the field trip, look for the boundaries between the various communities in and around the water. Most collecting will occur in the shallow water close inshore; here sun and light reach to the bottom. The warm water favors a wealth of life both visible and invisible. This shallow zone is characterized by emergent plants such as cattails which grow with their feet in the water and their heads in the air (Fig. 1-14). Under water, the stems of these plants are covered with algae, which provide food for swarms of minute crustaceans, plant-eating worms, and smaller water beetles. Here is a complete community of interdependent plants and animals found only in this shoreline zone.

Farther out, where the water is knee-deep, is the zone of floating-leaved plants, such as water lilies, duckweed, spatterdock, pondweed, and eelgrass. Usually the bottom is soft mud, which boils up around one's feet. The mud makes poor walking, but provides a rich pantry for the myriad forms of animal life usually present. The undersides of the lily pads are floating hatcheries for the eggs of water insects and snails.

A dip net should bring up a host of carnivorous insect forms. The plant stems provide anchorage for (in addition to the algae mentioned above) countless fresh water sponges, bryozoans, moss animals, and the snails or worms that feed upon the green slime. These smaller forms, in turn, are food for larger pond animals such as fish, amphibians, frogs, toads, salamanders, and reptiles such as the black (nonpoisonous) water snakes common to the Northeast.

Thus, larger forms of animal life live on plants or on smaller forms, which, in turn, ultimately live on plant life. Children can observe and describe the food chains of which each form they collect is a link. (See Fig. 1-15.) All animal life ultimately depends on plant life because animals cannot organically manufacture their own food.

LIFE IN THE SEA

The ocean floor has higher mountains and deeper canyons than anything we can see on dry land. In adaptation to these variations in depth, pressure, and light, life in the ocean has developed in myriad forms, shapes, and sizes. For example, the food of some of the largest creatures, the whales, is made up of the smallest creatures, the plankton (microscopic plants and animals). Kipling's delightful fantasy "How the Whale Got His

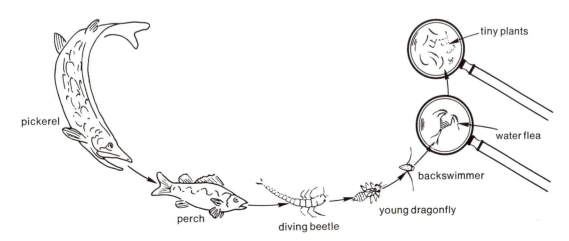

pickerel   perch   diving beetle   young dragonfly   backswimmer   water flea   tiny plants

FIGURE **1-15**   Part of a typical food chain.

Throat,"[4] read aloud, will precipitate discussion and research. Children may want to construct a cardboard-box diorama illustrating life in the sea, or to find out which forms of sea life move in schools and why. Marine mammals such as whales, dolphins, porpoises, seals, sea lions, sea cows, and sea otters have particularly interesting habits and interrelationships with other animals including man.

To illustrate the relationship between land and sea life forms, immerse chicken bones and sea shells in strong vinegar or better, dilute hydrochloric acid (obtainable from a drugstore or a high school chemistry teacher) and let stand for several days. Both the shells and bones should become soft and rubbery because the lime has been dissolved by the acids. The outside of the shell may not feel as limp as the inside.

Small samples of rough coral tested with acid will show that the bony skeleton of the coral animal is also largely lime. These tiny animals, like many other marine forms, tend to live in groups for protection. The coral reef islands which dot the South Pacific are really cemeteries of the coral animal built up by years of deposition of their bodies. The hard parts of other marine creatures such as mollusks have a similar composition; the seawater all about them contains in solution the lime from which their shells and outer covering are made.

TIDEPOOL ANIMALS

For children living near the sea coast, a small marine aquarium may be the capstone to a trip to a beach or tidal flats. In the interest of conservation, no more than one or two small specimens of the common species, such as clams, hermit crabs, sea anemones, starfish, scallops, and some salt-water fish, should be collected to stock the aquarium.

The salt-water tank should be clean, leak-free, and located in a cool place. Cover the bottom with sea sand and a few barnacled rocks. Water may be brought from the ocean or be synthetic brine. Sea salts in cloth bags (available from scientific supply houses) should be dissolved according to directions. Avoid contact between brine and brass, copper, or zinc.

Tidepool animals will not survive overnight without an aerator. Common aerators for freshwater tanks are suitable if more than one per tank (usually two) is used. Specimens will survive for a considerable period in a cool, aerated tank.

Even a superficial consideration of sea life will suggest comparisons with life in a pond—that is, communities within a community. Life in a tidepool is very different from the plant and animal life on a sandy beach or life along a muddy shore or tidal estuary. The offshore shallows also represent a different community. Children should be led to see that transitions between saltwater communities are sharper than those between freshwater life zones. Because of the rigorous conditions, animal forms, being more adaptable, predominate over plant forms in marine zones. Observation of this phenomenon can lead to discussion and research into the world's population explosion and food problems. With respect to the latter problem, the sea is achieving great prominence as a source of protein. The production of beef protein requires many acres of land and expensive labor for processing. The production of fish protein is less costly because of the extensiveness of the sea and its countless beds of algae and animal plankton, which need no cultivation or irrigation. The children may have read of government experiments in growing algae as a protein source. Agar from dulse (seaweed) is often sold at the drugstore. However we must adjust ourselves to its taste. The class can apply the protein test (p. 189) to agar and other sea products.

Representatives from government agencies for fish and game conservation are often available to give illustrated lectures and answer questions to help children understand modern "fish farming"—for example, controlling the Great Lakes lamprey, building farm ponds, finding schools of fish by radar.

[4] Kipling, Rudyard, *Just So Stories*, The Macmillan Company, 1954.

SUGGESTED PROJECTS

1. Find out the difference between hibernation and estivation. (Temporary hibernation may be induced by subjecting animals to short periods of artificial low temperature. Zoologists use this method with reptiles in photographing normally rapid motion. The concept of animal adaptation to environmental changes may be introduced by discussion of this phenomenon.) Children may also be interested in an investigation of why temporary hibernation has been considered for astronauts on long space voyages.

2. Make flannel board drawings of phases of amphibian metamorphosis. Let the children arrange these in cyclical order. (Experiences with animal life cycles may be used to introduce concepts of the genetic code or of like producing like.)

3. Examine the eye covering in a cast snake skin. Consider the relationship between your observation and accounts of snake blindness and irritability during shedding. Read about the elliptical pupils of poisonous snakes. Observe rather than collect snakes in their habitats.

4. By research and observation, distinguish between fact and fancy about snakes, bats, and the like. See Burnett, *op. cit.*, pp. 49–50, astrological superstitions; pp. 74–77, snake tales.

5. Examine samples of hair (fur) under magnification. Distinguish outer guard hairs from soft underfur and determine the function of each. (Hair is not the same all over an animal's body, being thinner near the skin and in places where it would be too bulky otherwise.)

6. Make a feather collection and consider the different functions of the various kinds. (Wing feathers are adapted primarily for flying, breast feathers to insulate against cold, and back feathers to shed water.)

BIBLIOGRAPHY

(**P** indicates recommended for primary grades, **I** for intermediate grades, **U** for upper grades.)

Adrian, Mary, *Fiddler Crab*, Holiday, 1953. Life cycle of common species at tide line along the beach. **I**

Andrews, Roy Chapman, *All About Whales*, Random, 1954. Information about different species of whales, written in a lively, anecdotal style. **U**

Bendick, Jeanne, *The First Book of Fishes*, Watts, 1965. Information about where fish live, the parts of a fish, reproduction, migration, families of fishes, and unusual fishes. **U**

Besser, Marianne, *The Cat Book*, Holiday, 1967. All about cats—family, history, personality, physical make-up, and relationships with people. **I**

Bethell, Jean, *How to Care for Your Dog*, Four Winds, 1964. Explains basic care including feeding, bathing, and training. **I**

Blough, Glenn O., *Bird Watchers and Bird Feeders*, McGraw-Hill, 1963. Follows the seasons; items such as bird menus, feeders, migration, banding, and necessary equipment for a beginning ornithologist discussed. Illustrated with water colors. **I**

Broekel, Ray, *True Book of Tropical Fishes*, Children's Pr., 1956. Information and suggestions for setting up and maintaining home aquaria. **I**

Brown, Vinson, *How to Make a Home Nature Museum*, Little, Brown, 1954. Specifics by an expert. **J**

——, *How to Make a Miniature Zoo*, Little, Brown, 1956. Includes care and feeding of animals, birds, and insects. **U**

Buck, Margaret W., *Pets from the Pond*, Abingdon, 1958. Detailed suggestions for setting up fresh-water aquaria for local forms of life. **U**

——, *Small Pets from Woods and Fields*, Abingdon, 1960. Concise text and fine illustrations. **U**

——, *In Ponds and Streams*, Abingdon, 1955. Intriguing account of fresh-water life. **I**

Buehr, Walter, *World Beneath the Waves*, Norton, 1964. An account of the most recent research, in areas such as desalting ocean water, sea crops, the effect of sea currents on weather. The important work done at Scripps Institute of Oceanography is briefly described. **U**

Carson, Rachel, *Sea Around Us*, ed. by Anne Terry

White, Golden Pr., 1958. Modern classic adapted for children. Many dramatic illustrations and informative diagrams included. **U**

Carter, Katherine, *True Book of Oceans*, Children's Pr., 1958. Ocean tides, currents, and zones of animal life. **I**

Chenery, Janet, *The Toad Hunt*, Harper & Row, 1967. Two small boys learn about the differences between toads and frogs, after discovering and observing turtles, salamanders, and polliwogs. **P**

Clemons, Elizabeth, *Tide Pools & Beaches*, Knopf, 1964. Lucid text and clearly-drawn pictures make this an excellent introduction to the identification of sea animals and plants. Invaluable to the beginning collector of seashore treasures. Safety precautions are stressed. **U**

Collins, Henry Hill, Jr., *Junior Science Book of Turtles*, Garrard, 1962. The structures, life cycles, and habitats of representative members of the turtle family; illustrated. **I**

Conklin, Gladys, *I Caught a Lizard*, Holiday, 1967. Briefly covers toads, salamanders, and other small pets in story form. Emphasis is on return to the natural habitat after observation. Fine pastel illustrations. **P**

Coombs, Charles, *Deep-Sea World; the Story of Oceanography*, Morrow, 1966. Covers the formation of oceans, deep-sea exploration and its future, and the submersibles "Alvin," "Turtle," and "Trieste I and II." **U**

Cooper, Elizabeth, *Science in Your Own Back Yard*, Harcourt, 1957. Back-yard exploration leads to a wealth of science experiences. The experiments are simple, and the materials easy to obtain. Interesting and well written. **U**

Cousteau, Jacques, and Frederic Dumas, *Silent World*, Harper & Row, 1953. Ocean tides, currents, and zones of animal life. **U**

Darby, Gene, *What Is a Fish?* Benefic, 1958. Typical structure and function. Simple concepts of adaptation and survival. **P**

———, *What Is a Turtle?* Benefic, 1959. One of an interesting and well-illustrated series. **P**

Darling, Louis, *Penguins*, Morrow, 1956. Many interesting facts about these strange birds. **I**

Earle, Olive L., *The Octopus*, Morrow, 1955. Simple, basic information of this marine animal and related forms. **I**

———, *Strange Companions in Nature*, Morrow, 1966. Some symbiotic and parasitic relationships found in land and sea animals are discussed with clarity. **U**

———, *Strange Lizards*, Morrow, 1964. Odd creatures from various parts of the world described by the author-artist. Lively drawings. **I–U**

Engel, Leonard, *The Sea*, adapted by the editors of Silver Burdett from a volume in the Life Nature Library. Silver Burdett, 1964. The same exceptionally fine color photographs that illustrate the original volume. The text has been shortened and simplified. **U**

Epstein, Samuel, *Junior Science Book of Seashells*, Garrard, 1963. Similar to others in this series in format and useful for identification purposes. **I**

Gallup, Lucy, *Spinning Wings*, Morrow, 1956. Life story of a black tern. **I**

Gans, Roma, *Birds Eat and Eat and Eat*, Crowell, 1963. Simple, concise text; well illustrated. **P**

Gaul, Albro, *Wonderful World of the Seashore*, Appleton, 1955. Interdependence of marine plant and animal life. **I**

George, John L. and Jean, *Dipper of Copper Creek*, Dutton, 1956. Outstanding life story of western water ouzel or dipper bird. **U**

Goldin, Augusta, *The Bottom of the Sea*, Crowell, 1966. Clear, simple description of the bottom of the sea, its cliffs, mountains, canyons, and volcanoes. The scientists' tools, as well as the facts learned about the underwater world are explained by text and informal illustrations. **I**

———, *Ducks Don't Get Wet*, Crowell, 1965. Two simple experiments, brief text, and illustrations explain why ducks are "waterproof." The unique habits of some ducks in the water and in the air are described. **P**

Harris, Louise D., *Little Red Newt*, Little, Brown, 1958. Life history of red eft salamander and pond ecology. **P–I**

Hausman, Leon, *Beginner's Guide to Fresh Water Life*, Putnam, 1950. Simple pocket guide. **I**

Hawes, Judy, *Shrimps*, Crowell, 1966. The physical characteristics, life cycle, and habits of shrimps. **P**

Hess, Lilo, *Sea Horses*, Scribners, 1966. Large photographs bring the exotic sea creature to life in this appealing book. Clear directions are given for keeping the sea horse in an aquarium. **I**

Hogner, Dorothy, *Snails*, Crowell, 1958. Structure and habits of common mollusks. Suggestions on fresh- and salt-water aquaria. **I–U**

———, *Earthworms*, Crowell, 1953. Directions on

how to make a classroom or school yard earthworm farm. **I**

———, *Odd Pets*, Crowell, 1951. Directions for the care of many outdoor animals. Photographs are useful for identification. **U**

Hoke, John, *First Book of Snakes*, Watts, 1952. Myths versus facts about common snakes. Includes directions for making cages. **I**

Holling, Holling C., *Pagoo*, Houghton Mifflin, 1957. Life cycle of a hermit crab and a close-up of the teeming life in a tide pool. Accurate and detailed marginal drawings and lavish full color illustrations. **U**

Huntington, Harriet E., *Let's Go to the Seashore*, Doubleday, 1941. The small creatures that live in the sea, on the seashore, and under the rocks at the bottom of the sea are described and excellently detailed in photographs. **P**

———, *Let's Go to the Brook*, Doubleday, 1952. Plant and animal life along a brook. **P**

Hurd, Edith T., *Starfish*, Crowell, 1962. Informs beginning readers about starfish that might be found on the shore; describes their habitat and briefly outlines their life cycle—how starfish eat, grow, and propagate. **P**

Hylander, Clarence, *Sea and Shore*, Macmillan, 1950. Information about marine life on east and west coasts. Many photographs and detailed sketches are helpful for identification. **U**

Jacobs, Lou, *Wonders of an Oceanarium; Marine Life in Captivity*, Golden Gate, 1965. Behind-the-scenes view of marine life in captivity in Marineland of the Pacific. Many excellent black and white photographs. **U**

Jordan, Emil Leopold, *Hammond's Pictorial Library of Pets, Plants, and Animals*, C. S. Hammond & Co., 1958. Clearly presented with many color illustrations, including five double-page maps showing geographic origins. A good index. **U**

Kumin, Maxine, *Eggs of Things*, Putnam, 1963. An easy-to-read story of two little boys who bring home from a pond some egg clusters that eventually hatch out. **P**

———, *More Eggs of Things*, Putnam, 1964. A sequel to *Eggs of Things*. Eggs that the children find at the seashore hatch out a rare kind of sea turtle. **P**

Lauber, Patricia, *The Friendly Dolphins*, Random, 1963. A clearly written, straightforward account of the evolution and history of the dolphin, emphasizing the intelligence and usefulness of the species

to scientists working on sonar systems and animal communication. Illustrated with photographs and drawings. **I**

Lubell, Winifred and Cecil, *In a Running Brook*, Rand McNally, 1968. A good descriptive study of the fishes, amphibians, insect larvae, crustaceans, planariums, and aquatic vegetation. **I**

Meshover, Leonard, *Guinea Pigs That Went to School*, Follett, 1968. Photographic story of a first grade and its two guinea pigs, which produce two more. **P**

Morgan, Alfred, *Aquarium Book for Boys and Girls*, Scribners, rev. ed., 1959. Setting up an aquarium using native local materials. **I–U**

Parker, Bertha M., *Pebbles and Sea Shells*, Harper & Row, 1959. Another of the excellent Basic Education Series, with simple text and a wealth of attractive colored pictures. Introduction to basic concepts in geology and marine biology. **I**

Pels, Gertrude, *Care of Water Pets*, Crowell, 1955. Excellent sourcebook on setting up and maintaining water life projects. **I**

Posell, Elsa, *True Book of Whales and Other Sea Mammals*, Children's Pr., 1963. Very brief text and many clear drawings provide an easy-to-read introduction. **P**

Russell, Solveig P., *Which is Which?*, Prentice-Hall, 1966. Animals that are often confused are juxtaposed and compared. Included are butterflies and moths, monkeys and apes, alligators and crocodiles, toads and frogs. **I**

Selsam, Millicent, *Benny's Animals*, Harper & Row, 1966. A simple lesson in the classification of animals. Illustrated. **P**

———, *Let's Get Turtles*, Harper & Row, 1965. Excellent information about the care and feeding of turtles in story form. **P**

———, *When an Animal Grows*, Harper & Row, 1966. How gorillas, lambs, sparrows, and ducks grow and are protected by their parents. **P**

———, *Plenty of Fish*, Harper & Row, 1960. A story about two goldfish and the little boy who learns about fish from them. **P**

———, *See Through the Lake*, Harper & Row, 1958. Cross-section of life cycles in a lake. **I**

Ubell, Earl, *The World of the Living*, Atheneum, 1965. Overview of biology emphasizing the needs, characteristics, and problems of survival common to all living things. Excellent black and white photographs. **I**

Uhl, Melvin J., *About Eggs and Creatures that Hatch from Them*, Melmont, 1966. How eggs are hatched and cared for by fish, reptiles, amphibians, birds, and insects. ❙

Wormser, Sophie, *About Silkworms and Silk*, Melmont, 1961. The device of a classroom situation used to describe how to hatch and raise silkworms. Also covers the manufacture of silk and the silk industry. ❙

Zim, Herbert, *Corals*, Morrow, 1966. Illustrated discussion of various species, locations, and physical characteristics of the tiny reef-building corals, whose activities have changed and continue to change the face of the globe. ❙

Forepart of a grasshopper, showing the armor-like carapace or exoskeleton, an antenna, legs, mouth, and a large faceted eye.

2 Insect Life

Children learn about themselves by studying other living things. They become absorbed in watching insects and learn to observe, thus practicing a part of the methods of science. They begin to see interrelationships between insect, plant, and other animal life, and between these and the climate and seasons. They begin to develop an understanding of the great biological principle of interdependence between organisms and environment.

Generally, the best insects for study are those that the teacher and children find. Of the nearly 750,000 *identified* species, only the most common insects, those likely to be brought to school, are briefly considered below. A librarian can recommend general and specific references for children and adults.

CARE OF INSECTS

Some of the children will be proud to handle and care for the insects. Moreover, they will find and collect insects in almost limitless quantity and variety. In the warm days of early fall (September is the best month in temperate zones), bring in one or more insects in a plastic container. A brace of crickets that feel enough at home to chirp during a quiet interlude will loose a flood of discussion. Soon the classroom will not want for live study material.

Making crickets (or any insects) comfortable in the classroom promotes close observation of how insects live, which may be reinforced by research or reading. Ideally, learning how to care for insects precedes their capture.

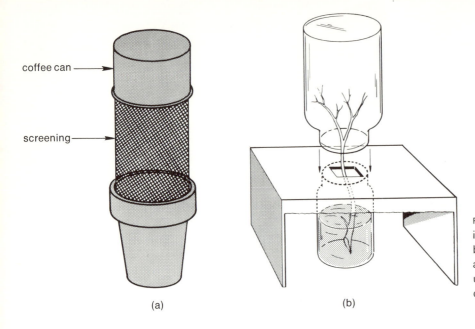

coffee can

screening

(a)

(b)

FIGURE **2-1** Cages for large insects. (a) The wire mesh may be safer than the lamp chimney around young children. (b) The upper jar rests on a cut-down carton for better stability.

Cage for Large Insects

Large insects can be kept in a strawberry basket cage of plastic mesh or in a big flowerpot fitted with a roll of wire mesh or stiff cellophane and capped by a coffee can (Fig. 2-1a). Put a plug of grass or clover in the bottom of the can.

A temporary cage can be made from an ice cream or cereal carton, with window screening (cut with garden scissors) stapled in place over an observation window cut in the carton. A wire kitchen strainer may serve as the cover. Because such a container does not have the natural humidity that is provided in the cricket cage by evaporation from soil and plants, it is suitable only for temporary quarters.

Grasshoppers, walking sticks, praying mantises, and the like will be comfortable in a cage made from two pint jars, one inverted over the other, in which a bunch of grass and twigs is set in water (Fig. 2-1b).

Terrarium Garden

To make a terrarium garden for insects, use a terrarium or aquarium or a gallon jar with cover. Spread an inch of fine gravel over the bottom, scatter a few small pieces of charcoal on the gravel, and then add a layer of soil, a layer of sand, and another layer of garden soil. (The carbon will prevent the soil from becoming sour by absorbing waste gases; a few pieces of limestone will help neutralize soil acidity.) Now plant grass seed, mixed whole bird or chick feed, corn, oats, or any of the grains. Put crickets, katydids, or grasshoppers into the container. Sprinkle enough water on the soil to keep it moist, but not soggy. If caterpillars are used, bring in some of the plant leaves on which they are found. Put the leaf stems into the soil, or into a pill bottle sunk into the soil so the mouth of the bottle is flush with the surface. Praying mantises, spiders, and other insect-eaters should be kept apart from the others.

Cages adapted to the needs of specific insects are described under the relevant headings.

Hatching Box

Insect eggs or egg masses need a container that permits observation and provides shelter for the emerging insects. A cardboard box with a hole in the side just large enough to insert the neck of a vial, bottle, or tube is suitable for this. When the insects emerge they move out into the glass bottle or tube where they can be seen.

PREPARING AND MOUNTING INSECTS

Children can collect many different kinds of insects in a weed patch by use of an old net curtain or netting in the manner of fishermen seining in shallow water. With the net stretched along the edge of the weed patch, the children on the end move in and quickly fold the curtain into a small roll. The curtain is then slowly unrolled and insects that remain sticking to it are popped into containers. Small plastic boxes and containers are much safer for collecting than glass jars. Caution children to free stinging insects (for example, bees, wasps, hornets). Children may have seen flies that resemble bees; point out that the resemblance helps them survive since many predators will avoid the combative bee.

For individual collection of fast-moving insects, children can use nets made from a wire coat hanger, an old net curtain, and a broomstick (Fig. 2-2). The net should taper to a point and be long enough to fold over to entrap the insect.

Insect Anesthetics

For close examination, insects can be temporarily anesthetized with carbon dioxide. Generate car-bon dioxide (CO_2) gas from a mixture of vinegar and baking soda (see Fig. 16-7) or from a lump of dry ice in a bottle. Place insects in a test tube or bottle from which carbon dioxide gas has displaced water. When the insects become quiet, it will be possible to examine closely structures such as a bee's stinger, a hornet's jaws, the antennae of a moth, the wings of a butterfly, or spider spinnerets. The insect usually recovers within a few minutes. Cooling insects by putting them in a refrigerator for a brief time will slow their movements to allow closer study.

Killing Jar and Relaxing Jar

Screw-top pint jars or any wide-mouthed jars will do as a killing jar. Place a wad of cotton in the bottom and cover it with a disc of blotting paper or perforated cardboard, or with strips of paper laid on each other to form a mesh. Soak the cotton with cleaning fluids containing carbon tetrachloride or about an ounce of rubbing alcohol. The alcohol will kill most insects except moths and butterflies. (*Do not use potassium cyanide in the elementary classroom!* Caution children against direct inhalation of fumes from cleaning fluid.) Put the insects into the jar and screw the cover on tightly, leaving it on until the insects are dead.

A dead insect is usually very dry and stiff and must be relaxed before it can be mounted. To do this, prepare another jar in the same way as the killing jar, but use a small sponge dampened with water instead of the wad of cotton. When the insect's body is flexible and its legs can be moved without breaking, transfer it to the spreading board (see below).

Spreading Board

Made flexible in the relaxing jar, the insect is fastened to the spreading board to dry in the position required for mounting. Commercial spreading boards are not expensive (see appendix list of supply houses). In making one, the main requirement is material that pins will penetrate

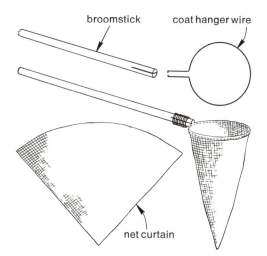

FIGURE **2-2** Homemade insect net.

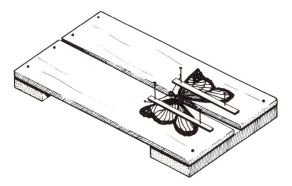

FIGURE **2-3** Insect spreading board. To avoid damage to delicate parts, pins are passed through cardboard strips laid on the wings. Note tapered slot.

easily, such as soft wallboard. Two 2 × 12-inch strips of wallboard are aligned to form a narrow slot (Fig. 2-3). To accommodate different-sized bodies, the slot should taper gradually from a width of $\frac{3}{4}$ to $\frac{1}{4}$ inch.

Mounting-boxes

Cigar boxes are suitable for mounting insects such as beetles and grasshoppers. Be sure to include a moth ball or lump of paradichlorobenzene (moth crystals). The traditional glass-covered Riker mount, or a shallow container such as a hosiery box is suitable for moths, butterflies, and other broad-winged insects. Prepare the cigar box

with a layer of corrugated paperboard fitted into its bottom. For the hosiery box, cut out all but a narrow margin of the cover and replace it with cellophane; fill the box nearly to the top with absorbent cotton. Common pins are often too thick and too short for mounting most insects. Instead, use long, slender insect pins (obtainable from a biological supply house) passed through the insects (as shown in Fig. 2-4) and into the bottom of the cigar box. The label bearing the insect's name, the date and locality of collection, and other data should be placed on the pin just below the insect (Fig. 2-4). For mounting in the hosiery box, simply arrange the insects on the cotton with labels beside each specimen and pin the cover in place.

A "Berlese" Funnel

A good hand glass or low-power microscope will disclose an astonishing variety of animal life in most soil. To separate insects from soil, place a cup or two of leaf mold (well-rotted woods soil or garden soil from under shrubs) in a paper funnel under a 100-watt bulb overnight (Fig. 2-5). A piece of screening across the bottom of the funnel will keep soil from falling through. Place a jar of alcohol underneath the funnel to preserve insects that drop through. Since soil insects shun light and heat, they will burrow down through the soil and fall through the screening.

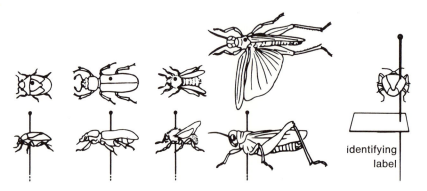

FIGURE **2-4** Method of mounting insects on pins. In upper row, heavy dots indicate position of head of pin. Because the small printing required on labels may be difficult for children, numbered tags corresponding to a numbered list may be substituted.

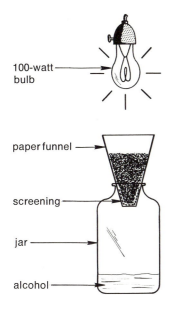

100-watt bulb

paper funnel

screening

jar

alcohol

FIGURE **2-5** A Berlese funnel. A larger funnel will collect more light to drive out the soil organisms.

NON-FLYING INSECTS

Ants

Ants can be found almost any time and any place, even in a city. Medium-sized ants are best for classroom study. Ants are generally black, "red," brown, or parti-colored. Ants of different colors may be found in the same nest. For example, ants with a rust-red head and thorax, and brown legs and abdomen may be in the same colony as black or ash-colored ants. These last may be the slaves of the brown species, having been stolen as larvae or pupae from another nest and reared as part of the brown-ant colony.

Ants, like bees, are social insects; they are always found living together. Wasps, bumblebees, and many other forms are solitary insects. A seeming exception, the "velvet ant," a solitary scarlet speck occasionally seen bustling along the floor of the desert, is really a wingless wasp, a solitary insect.

Ants are found in a variety of homes. The largest species often build a hill or mound com-posed of a bushel or two of small pieces of plant debris. Some ants make tunnels in rotten logs. Carpenter ants tunnel in the wood of living trees; their homes are indicated by small telltale piles of wood dust at the foot of the tree. (The wood dust is finer and smaller in amount than that produced by woodpeckers.) Most ants make labyrinthine tunnels underground. Those with tunnels under a flat stone have a cozy nursery for their young; the stone will hold the sun's midday heat through the night. If it is too warm in the daytime, the nurse ants carry the young deeper into the ground. In winter, the whole colony lives deep under ground, well below the frost line.

Observation nests If you find a colony under a stone, carefully replace the stone to avoid frightening the ants away before a classroom nest is prepared. The simplest kind of ant nest for school observation is a screw-top (quart or gallon) glass jar. Place a block of wood or a tall narrow empty can in the center of the jar to make a hollow core. Fill the jar about three-quarters of the way up with sandy garden soil. Leave room for some soil from the ant hill and the ants, and place a small water dish or sponge just under the cap so that the soil is kept moist (Fig. 2-6). Wrap dark paper around the jar when not observing the ants, since they will tunnel into the interior if continuously exposed to light. Keep the jar in a relatively warm place, but not in direct sun-

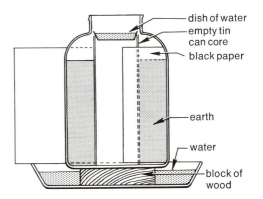

dish of water
empty tin can core
black paper

earth

water

block of wood

FIGURE **2-6** Screw-top jar ant nest. The core helps make ant tunneling more readily seen by keeping ants from penetrating far below surface.

shine. To keep ants from escaping, set the jar on a wood block in a pan of water.

An ant maze can be made from a pair of window panes and modeling clay (Fig. 2-7a). Lay one pane on a block of wood which rests in a shallow pan of water. Make clay labyrinths with clay "walls" about one square inch in cross-section, as shown in the figure, and add a sponge. Cover the labyrinths with the second window pane, which can be lifted for feeding or watering the colony. The glass should be covered with dark paper when the ants are not being observed.

An ant observation frame, similar to an observation hive, is made from a pair of window panes set vertically in wooden blocks (Fig. 2-7b). Rout out two channels in the wood slightly wider than the thickness of the glass plus a $\frac{3}{4}$- to 1-inch wood strip, four of which are placed at the edges of the panes to hold them apart. The frames and strips are nailed and taped together at the sides and bottom, the top strip being left unattached so that it can be lifted out. Use $1\frac{1}{2}$-inch masking or cloth tape cut so that it laps itself at the corners. (See Fig. 3-8.) Drill three small ($\frac{1}{2}$-inch) holes in the top strip; these holes should be corked except when introducing food (see below) or water through them. Use a medicine dropper to avoid giving too much water. Nests should be filled with moistened sandy soil (about three-quarters full in the case of the vertical nest), preferably from the nest in which the ants are found. Commercial nests complete with inhabitants are available from large department stores or scientific supply houses.

Food As do many other classroom animals, ants need a varied diet in very small amounts. Uneaten food should always be removed before more is added. Offer bread or pastry crumbs, sugar water, honey, fruits, bacon, other insects, vegetables, and seeds. Ants swallow only food that they have chewed and reduced to liquid form. The ant's relatively large abdomen is for storage of this liquid nourishment. Usually the food gathered is carried back to the nest to feed the growing larvae, or grubs.

Collecting Materials for collecting ants are a garden trowel, a large piece of old bedsheet or other white cloth or paper, and two narrow-necked plastic bottles with stoppers. Lift off the stone cover of the nest and lay one of the bottles flat on the ground. Guide about 100 ants into the bottle and stopper it securely. If a colony is to last more than two or three weeks, a queen is necessary. Dig rather deeply and spread the soil on a white cloth or paper; look for one ant much larger than the rest—the queen. (The queen is merely an egg-laying machine, not the ruler of the colony.) Guide her into the second bottle, along with some of the earth in which she is found.

The colony tends to last if it also contains many

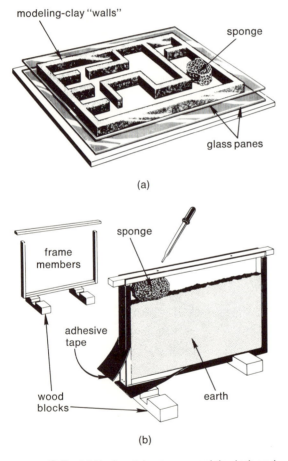

FIGURE **2-7** (a) Horizontal ant maze or labyrinth and (b) vertical ant nest. These observational frames, if large enough, are adaptable for use as observation beehives. (See Fig. 2-22.)

immature ants. As many of these as possible should be collected in a shoe box or similar container. Ant eggs are so small they are almost impossible to find except with a hand lens. The grubs or larvae look like translucent rice grains, pointed at one end, or like miniature crook-neck squashes. The cocoons, which contain the pupae, are the third stage in ant metamorphosis. They are yellowish, about the size of wheat seed, and are commonly sold as food for small turtles.

The soil from the old nest and the immature ants should be put into the new home first; then the workers, and lastly, with care, the queen. Once the nest is settled and the queen begins laying, the nest may be unplugged or removed from the pan of water. If the nest is placed near some opening to the outdoors, the workers will come and go freely for the entire year.

Castes There may be as many as eight castes in an ant hill. Except for the queen and the drones, who provide the continuation of the species, the most important caste is the workers; the first eggs the queen lays in a new nest hatch into workers. Nurse ants constantly move pupae between upper and lower nurseries, depending on the temperature. Food gatherers stop en route to pass a mouthful of liquid nourishment to a fellow worker. The myriad tunnels in an ant nest are the work of the builders. As in any communal living, cleanliness is essential, and some workers seem to have the special task of carrying refuse to a heap in a corner of the nest far from the brood.

Behavior of soldier ants, who guard the entrance of the nest, may be seen by introducing an ant from another nest. The soldier will rear on its hind legs, throw its formic acid toward the intruder, and close in, trying to cut him in two with its jaws. If an ant is removed from the nest and returned after a few days, the ant on guard will carefully examine the returnee with his feelers. It is said that ants depend on their sense of smell to recognize other members of their nest.

One interesting group of workers is that which herds ant "cows," called aphids or plant lice (Fig. 2-8). (See also pp. 28–29.) Aphids secrete a sweet juice, sometimes called "honeydew," favored by

FIGURE **2-8** Aphids, aphis, or plant lice. These tiny (about $\frac{1}{8}$ inch), innocuous looking insects are a scourge to plants. Some species are mealy white, some juicy green, tan or brown.

ants. By stroking the aphids with their feelers or antennae, the ants "milk" their "cows" of the sweet juice. Usually where one finds aphids on outdoor plants, one finds ants climbing or descending the stem. In winter some kinds of ants carry aphids underground, where they suck the roots of plants and provide the ants with a year-round supply of "milk." Leaf cutter ants cut and carry underground bits of green leaves, which rot and form leaf mold. The mushrooms upon which the leaf cutters feed grow in this leaf mold.

Much remains to be discovered about the habits of ants. For instance, although investigators believe ants recognize each other by a sense of smell and apparently communicate with their feelers, no one has proved it. We suspect, but do not really know, that the sense of smell enables ants to find their way back to the home nest.

Winged Ants and Termites

Occasionally one encounters a cloud of what appear to be winged ants. They are the queen and the male ants of the nest who have grown wings and are on their nuptial flight. One of the males mates with the queen, who then returns to the nest where she sheds her wings and starts the egg-producing process. All species of ants do this, but sometimes the winged forms are not ants but the queen and males from a termite colony.

FIGURE **2-9**   An ant lion (about ¼ inch) and the pits it makes in fine, dry sand.

Although termites at first glance look like pale, thick-bodied ants, they belong to an entirely different insect order. Termites are the only organisms known to reduce wood cellulose directly. They are able to do this because their intestines harbor protozoa capable of digesting the wood pulp of the termite diet. All winged termites as well as all winged ants are either male or female; the workers are sexless. Termites are found almost everywhere. Living termites should be handled carefully lest some escape in the school building, for they do great damage by boring into the wooden parts of structures. Samples of such damage may be available from local contractors or insect exterminators.

Observation frame   To observe termites at work, imbed a block of soft wood about 2 inches thick in a pan of damp soil. Drill one or two holes in the wood. Drop the termites into the holes and plug the holes with soil. Cover the sides of the block with glass panes, and seal the top with tape or a strip of glass.

Ant Lions

In dry, pulverized soil along a roadside or stream, one may notice a series of miniature craters or pits (Fig. 2-9a). These are made by the larval form of an insect that looks like a small dragonfly. These ant lions (Fig. 2-9b), also called "doodlebugs," lie in wait at the bottom of the pit for whatever unwary creature may tumble in. To determine which pits are occupied, use a grass stem or fine twig to start a few grains of sand tumbling down from the rim of the pit. If this causes a twitch at the bottom, the pit is occupied. To catch the trapper it is necessary to take a large scoop of soil quickly from around the crater. Even then one must look sharply, for the ant lion's soft, oblong body is coated (in effect, camouflaged) with sand and dust. Put them in a jar or empty aquarium partly filled with fine, powdery soil, and offer ants and other such small insects as food.

Aphids

There are over 8000 forms of aphids. Most common of these "drops of sap on legs" are the green aphid, almost the color of the plant, and the woolly aphid, whose body is covered with tiny cottony filaments. Aphids are slow-moving creatures that settle on the stem or leaf of a plant and live by sucking sap through their bill or sucking tube. Some ants draw a sweet secretion ("honeydew") from their aphid cows or carry aphid eggs underground for the winter. (See above under *Ant Castes.*) In the spring the ants carry the eggs to a plant stem or leaf where the eggs will hatch. Children may notice ladybugs among the aphids on a plant, for ladybugs and their larvae eat aphids. Commercial growers use ladybugs to combat aphids in their orchards and truck gardens.

Spraying insecticide on plants infested by aphids often has no effect on the insects. An experiment to investigate this phenomenon is useful in illustrating something about aphids in particular and insects in general. Use two twigs of comparable size about equally infested with aphids. Add a teaspoon of mineral oil or kerosene to a quart jar of *warm* soapy water. Shake thoroughly and spray one twig with the oil–water emulsion. Enclose the branch in a plastic vegetable bag tied at the bottom. Clean the spray gun thoroughly and spray the second twig with any kind of insect spray designed for insects that injure plants by chewing (for example, rosebugs, Japanese beetles, potato bugs). Cover this twig too with a plastic bag. In a day or two, there should be very few aphids on the branch sprayed with the oil–water emulsion. Because aphids are not chewing insects, but suck their food from the interior of the plant, they cannot be destroyed by poisons that are merely deposited on the surfaces of the plant. The oil–water emulsion is not a poison, but acts simply by clogging the spiracles (Fig. 2-12) or breathing holes along the aphids' sides so that they suffocate. Hence, the second twig, sprayed with a *poison* insecticide should show no reduction in aphid population. This twig—in effect, *unsprayed*—can be used to illustrate how rapidly aphids multiply. A question for the class might be: What would happen to the plant population if aphids multiplied unchecked? An interesting investigation would be to estimate the number of eggs in insect egg cases—e.g., those of the praying mantis. If say 50% of insects did not eat other insects, the insect population would be overwhelming. Study of the labels of insecticide containers will corroborate that poisons are used against chewing insects, and suffocants against the sucking types. It also offers an opportunity to stress safety in storage and handling of insecticides.

Cockroaches (Croton Bugs)

Cockroaches deserve our attention for their history if not for their habits. Cockroaches with 4-inch wing spread have been found fossilized in rock layers 200 million years old and fossil roaches identical to our modern pests have also been found. Their survival in abundance today is evidence of a durable and adaptable organism. The name, Croton bug, derives from the fact that the first serious roach infestation in New York City occurred about the time of the opening of the Croton Reservoir aqueduct to the city.

City children living in older buildings can usually catch roaches for observation, or a pest exterminator may supply some. Keep the roaches out of direct sunlight in a large glass jar with secure screw-top. The bottom of the jar should be damp at all times. As with ants, keep the jar enclosed in an opaque covering when the insects are not being watched. Put in some strips of newspaper, toweling, twigs, or bits of bark for the insects to hide under. Feed the roaches small amounts of table scraps. The female carries eggs in a small brown capsule at the end of her body until she finds a place to lay them. If the children find a capsule, have them imbed it in damp sand or cotton in a smaller jar with tight cover. Later, they can watch the young emerge and the changes as they mature.

Silverfish (Lepisma)

This curious insect, often seen scuttling about the bathroom floor or in the tub, is a living fossil, and represents a primitive group. It has no eyes and is harmless. It may eat the starch in the dried paste of book bindings.

Cricket

Cricket cage A cricket cage (Fig. 2-10) may be prepared as follows: plant a plug of fresh grass or clover in a small flower pot set in a saucer of water. Imbed firmly in the soil a glass lamp chimney or a roll of clear acetate or fine wire mesh. (Lamp chimneys are usually available from hardware stores; clear acetate is safer but more easily tipped over; wire mesh reduces visibility.) Cover the top of the chimney with cheesecloth. If you keep tree crickets, add a twig on which they can climb.

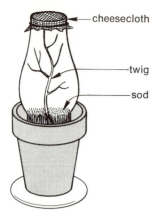

FIGURE **2-10** Cricket cage.

Children may find by trial and error what crickets like to eat. Place a pair or more of crickets in a flower-pot cricket cage on a sunny window sill, keeping the sod moist, but not soggy. If the food, shelter, and temperature are to their liking, the insects may chirp during a classroom lull.

Keeping crickets in the classroom may lead to the collection and observation of other "musicians"—the katydid, the cicada, and the tiny, but loud-voiced, tree cricket.

Make rough blackboard sketches of the detail of a male cricket's file and scraper (Fig. 2-11a). Female crickets are identified by the long ovipositor (Fig. 2-11b).

Grasshopper

Arrangements for keeping crickets, katydids, and the praying mantis will work for their relatives—the grasshoppers. Do not put grasshoppers into a terrarium planted with choice small plants for they will consume the foliage.

Most children already know a good deal about grasshoppers—for example, the grasshopper's ability to jump, which they might estimate and then measure in relation to his size. Many children know it is easier to catch grasshoppers in the early morning, and a few may know that this is related to the low temperatures prevalent in morning hours. Grasshoppers, like snakes and frogs but unlike humans and other warm-blooded animals, do not have a constant body temperature. The body temperature of these cold-blooded animals is usually only a few degrees higher than the air temperature.

Children may wonder how grasshoppers survive the winter. If they have noticed the long ovipositor of the female, they may be able to determine that grasshoppers live in the egg stage until spring.

Eventually, the children should bring in reports of or actual grasshoppers showing greater differences in size than of appearance. The smaller forms without fully developed wing covers are the nymphs, or immature grasshoppers. There is no resting (or pupal) stage in grasshoppers.

FIGURE **2-11** (a) Male cricket, vibrating file and scraper on raised wing covers. (b) Female cricket, showing ovipositor.

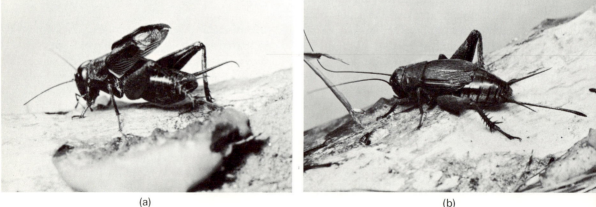

(a)

(b)

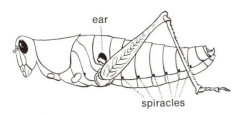

FIGURE **2-12** The grasshopper's ear (tympanic membrane) is behind the leg at the seventh or ninth somite (body segment). Wings and forelegs are omitted from this drawing.

Chill (refrigerate) or anesthetize some grasshoppers with CO_2 (see p. 23) to permit the children to look carefully at the body parts—the leg mechanism with its extraordinary leverage for jumping, the feet with the toe pads of sticky hairs which permit climbing the side of a glass container.

The grasshopper's face is a cartoon of solemnity. The great compound eyes give it 180° vision, useful in avoiding becoming breakfast for a bird or small mammal. (Some insects have as many as 30,000 simple eyes compounded in one eyepiece.) The grasshopper's ear and breathing pores should also be identified (Fig. 2-12), the latter being located just above a lengthwise suture or crease that opens and closes like an accordion bellows as the insect breathes.

In addition to all its other defense mechanisms, the grasshopper, as most children have experienced, can nip and also, it secretes "tobacco," a bitter and evil-smelling brown liquid.

Praying Mantis

The praying mantis was introduced to the United States as a control measure. It is generally found in coastal regions. Relative of grasshoppers and cousin to the walking stick, the mantis illustrates the effectiveness of insect camouflage. If you see a stick move, it may well be the praying mantis (Fig. 2-13). Although the praying mantis is related to grasshoppers, they are its favorite food, which it catches by lying in wait, its stout front legs poised to pounce. Often a green color like a katydid or tree cricket, the mantis is hard to find

FIGURE **2-13** Praying mantis, so named for the reverent stance it takes when poised to prey upon other insects.

unless it moves, which it does slowly and with dignity, as befits an insect three to five inches long when full grown. If one is to keep a mantis in the schoolroom, it will be necessary to catch live insects to feed it.

Like the grasshopper, the mantis has an incomplete metamorphosis—that is, there are only three stages in its life history. Children may find its large egg mass in a weed patch. Put the mass into the terrarium or gallon jar with sod on the bottom. Put in twigs on which the young can climb Since several hundred hatch from one egg mass, the children will realize that, as with other insects, there is overproduction to allow for high mortality. (If the jar is not covered with fine screening or netting, the room will soon be filled with tiny mantises as the warmth promotes hatching.) Keep a few mantises for observation and free the rest. Feed them fruit flies and other small insects. The carnivorous and some-

Non-flying Insects **31**

times cannibalistic mantis is one of the reasons the world is not overrun with insects: do not put two in one jar with no other food.

Worms and Larvae

Earthworms Children can dig up earthworms from the school garden or collect them from the ground surface after a heavy rain. Quite literally, earthworms go quietly about improving the earth. (They may also be used as winter food for classroom frogs, toads, snakes, and turtles.) To illustrate the way in which these "little plough-men," as Darwin called them, improve the soil, put three alternating layers of moistened dark soil (loam or leaf mold) and light-colored soil or sand into two wide-mouth gallon jars. Put earthworms on top of the soil of one jar and wrap this jar with a sheet of dark or black paper. The worms, which normally avoid light, will then tunnel at the periphery of the soil mass, where they can be seen, as well as in the center. In a few days, dark tunnels should begin to appear in the sand layer; eventually the soil in the jar containing worms will be quite thoroughly mixed, while that in the other jars remains unchanged (Fig. 2-14). Thus, earthworms bring up subsoil and take down topsoil, contributing inestimably to soil fertility and hence to human welfare. The soil may be

(a)

FIGURE **2-15** (a) Leaves of the red mulberry and (b) the sassafras, with which it is often confused. Most of the other varieties of mulberry have glossy green leaves without the characteristic notch. (Note also the differences in venation.) Nonfruiting varieties are often grown for shade and as a source of silk-worms (c), shown on facing page.

(b)

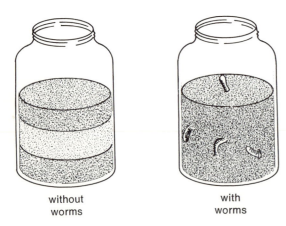

without worms   with worms

FIGURE **2-14** Demonstrating churning of soil by earthworms. Jar at left, without worms, shows layers of soil undistributed.

(c)

Meal worms Meal worms are useful in that they provide a live food supply, especially during winter, for reptiles or amphibians that hibernate briefly in a warm classroom. Their partial metamorphosis from larval to adult (beetle) form will contribute to children's concepts of life cycles. Meal worms are usually available at pet or feed stores. A few may be kept in a quart or half-gallon glass jar partly filled with wheat bran, bran flakes, and/or cornmeal, with a bread crust or small chunk of apple or carrot added occasionally. Punch air holes in the jar's tin cover or cover the jar mouth with cloth or netting. Keep in a *warm, dark* place. For faster multiplication of the worms, divide the supply into two containers, one to be left undisturbed for breeding, one to be used for pet food.

Silkworms Silkworms require mulberry leaves for food. (More than one variety of mulberry grows in the United States, and any medium-sized tree with *some* mitten-shaped leaves—see Fig. 2-15—may be a mulberry.) Silkworm eggs may be ordered in early spring from a scientific supply house (see Appendix). Keep the eggs in a refrigerator until the mulberry leaves are well out. Then bring the eggs to room temperature, keeping a few fresh leaves on hand for the moment the tiny larvae begin to emerge. Silkworms (Fig. 2-15c) will never leave their food supply, and should be fed daily, *including weekends;* most children will be pleased to perform this chore. Both eggs and leaves, as well as the silkworms, when they emerge, may be kept in an open box-top on a table or window sill (not in hot sun). Since silkworms eat only the margins of leaves, supplies can be extended by cutting leaves into pieces; they should be blotted dry. Osage orange or lettuce leaves may serve as a *temporary* substitute for mulberry leaves. Covering the silkworm container with a piece of windowpane or clear plastic sheet reduces evaporation from the leaves. Wilted leaves and debris should be removed before adding fresh ones, or coarse wire mesh or netting may be laid over the old leaves and the silkworms will crawl up through it to the fresh leaves.

When the silkworms have matured, they stop

seen to pass through the earthworms as they tunnel through it. They have no teeth, but have a remarkable gizzard which grinds and pulverizes the soil they take into their systems. Commercial worm farms use ground olive pits and walnut shells as worm feed; anglers give their worms small amounts of coffee grounds and cornmeal. Where tunnels against the glass permit watching earthworms in their holes, they can be seen holding onto the top of the hole with the tip of the tail, moving in a circle searching for food, and pulling bits of leaves into their mouths with the upper lip. When not observing the earthworms, replace the black covering around the jar.

Early in the mixing process, worm castings of digested pulverized soil may be seen on the surface. This pulverizing of soil particles makes minerals and other plant nutriments more soluble and, hence, more readily available for plant use, so that beans planted in pots of such "wormy" soil will produce a more abundant growth than beans planted in ordinary school garden soil.

Why one finds worms above ground after a downpour can be determined by a simple experiment: Pour into the worm jar more water than its soil can accommodate; the worms will come to the top of their tunnels for air. Be ready to rescue them from drowning by moving them to new quarters.

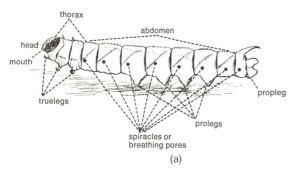

FIGURE **2-16** Tomato worm or sphinx caterpillar; (a) drawing showing external anatomy; (b) the caterpillar; (c) "brown jug" chrysalis; and (d) the moth stage.

feeding and begin moving their heads from side to side. They are preparing to spin their cocoons and should be placed in an open shoebox containing twigs to which they can anchor the cocoons. Some use plastic tubes such as toothbrush containers, or pint or half-pint transparent plastic food containers but these must contain

FIGURE **2-17** Leaf-miner "tracks" in white oak leaves. There are many varieties of this insect, each specialized to a specific plant.

some rough object or surface to which the cocoon may be attached. To make observation of the cocoon-making easy, the plastic tubes can be wedged into holes in the sides of a shallow box so that they project from it. To examine the silk fibers, boil a few cocoons in order to kill the larvae within. With a needle or tweezers and magnifying glass, tease free and gently unravel the end of the silk thread with which the cocoon was spun. About ten days after spinning of the cocoon, moths will begin to emerge and mate. To raise silkworms in another season, set aside some eggs under low refrigeration as described above.

Woolly Bear (Isabella Tiger Moth Larva)

Often during autumn, children may bring in a furry, brown and black caterpillar, usually called the "woolly bear." An old belief, now disproved, was that the width of the woolly bear's bands of color was an indicator of the severity of the winter. This caterpillar is unusual in that it normally spins its cocoon in April or May. The moth that emerges is somewhat nondescript. Because of its late cocoon-spinning, a woolly bear should be kept outdoors in a box to protect it from storms. Keeping it indoors in a warm room can kill it by disrupting the normal course of its temperature-related metamorphosis.

(c)

(d)

Tomato Worm

In late summer, one can find among tomato plants the tomato worm, a green caterpillar about thumb-size. The color and diagonal white body stripes suggest leaf veins; the camouflage is most effective when the tomato worm is on the midrib of a broad leaf such as that of the tobacco plant. These giant larvae of the sphinx moth are also called hornworms because of a fierce-looking but harmless "horn" at the tail end.

The spiracles or breathing holes (Fig. 2-16) are easily seen. Each pair of these holes opens into a network of tubes whose diameters diminish with distance from the spiracle. These tracheal tubes carry oxygen through the body.

After four weeks of voracious feeding, the caterpillar pupates into a hard, mahogany-hued chrysalis. The sheath protecting the beak of the developing adult forms a neat "handle," giving rise to the nickname, "little brown jug."

Although butterflies generally emerge from chrysalises and moths from cocoons (see above), in this case the adult is a grey moth with five pairs of yellow spots along the tapered body.

Leaf Miner and Leaf Roller

Sooner or later children will bring in examples of the work of the leaf miner and leaf roller. The familiar "serpentine mine" (Fig. 2-17) is made by the former, the tiny grub of a $\frac{1}{4}$-inch moth that lays its egg on the leaf. The grub spends its entire life until it pupates between the top and bottom surfaces of a leaf, proof that leaves, however thin and papery, are composed of layers of cells or chambers. The insect that causes leaf-rolling is very selective, each species using only a specific variety of leaf. When the egg first hatches, the tiny grub first feeds on the underside of the leaf. Then, when it is still almost too small to be seen, it folds or rolls one edge of the leaf down to make a kind of nest for itself. No one knows how this tiny creature accomplishes such a relatively Herculean task.

Spiders

Spiders, like crustaceans, insects, and other groups, belong to the great arthropod phylum of over 640,000 species. Arthropods have segmented external skeletons and appendages, which must be shed periodically to accomodate growth. Spiders are not insects, but are arachnids, a group that includes scorpions, horseshoe crabs, daddy longlegs, mites, and centipedes. True insects have a head, thorax, abdomen, and six legs; spiders have eight legs and two body parts—the abdomen, and the head and thorax fused. One may correlate science and beginning fractions with a

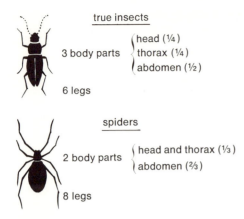

true insects

3 body parts

head (¼)
thorax (¼)
abdomen (½)

6 legs

spiders

2 body parts

head and thorax (⅓)
abdomen (⅔)

8 legs

FIGURE **2-18** Fractional relationships of body parts in insects and spiders.

simple drawing of a spider and an insect to illustrate the differences in the proportional relationships of their parts (Fig. 2-18). The figure suggests the greater bulk or weight of a true insect compared to that of a spider of about the same size; a spider is "all legs."

Of all the structures made by lower animals, the great radial web of the orb weaver is the most outstanding in design and workmanship, and the outer "cables" of the spider's web are analogous to the cables of suspension bridges. By close observation, the children may discover that the spider walks on its own web without getting caught by using the radial threads; only the encircling threads are sticky.

Grass spiders build another kind of web, a funnel-shaped structure spread out among the grass stems. At the mouth of the funnel, out of sight, sits the weaver waiting for some hapless insect to cross the web. A light touch at the edge of the funnel may bring the spider rushing out if the intruders keep out of sight and are not heavy-handed.

The beautiful little crab spider hides among flower petals. Among the lemon lilies they are an almost invisible color match.

Other spiders catch their prey by running or jumping. One of these, the wolf spider, has such long legs and is so timid that it usually runs out of sight before it can be seen clearly; another, the little jumping spider, is delightfully ugly.

The trapdoor spider is known to observant children who explore the foothills and arroyos of southern California. These spiders are insignificant looking, medium-sized, and without the tiny hairs that make most spiders appear so formidable, but their burrows are works of art. The trap door of the burrow has an inner lining of silk to which the spider clings in order to keep the door closed. From above, these entrances look much like part of the surrounding earth and it takes sharp looking to find one, although they are common in certain sections of adobe overlay.

The only poisonous spider in the United States is the black widow, the danger of which tends to be greatly overrated. The black widow is a medium-sized spider, glossy black, with a red marking shaped like an hourglass on the abdomen. Immature females are brown with a red "hourglass" on the *back*. (Shiny black spiders should be overturned to check for the telltale "hourglass.")

Spider bites, like those of many insects, tend to cause irritation unless neutralized with an alkali such as dilute household ammonia. An infected spider bite is due usually to infectious organisms already present on the skin when the spider punctures it. As a precautionary measure, always wear gloves when working in a garden clearing rubbish from under shrubs, moving old lumber, etc. In common with all spiders, the

FIGURE **2-19** Individual insect cubicles for one-day close observation. (See also Fig. 3-9.)

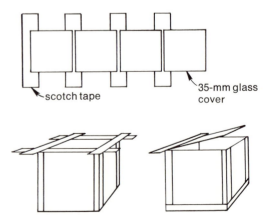

scotch tape

35-mm glass cover

FIGURE **2-20** Left to right, worker, queen, and drone bees. Each has a different function, which is reflected in its anatomy and size.

FIGURE **2-21** A bumblebee in its pollinating role. When it enters the flower to obtain nectar, some of the pollen grains (particles on its body) from a flower visited earlier will adhere to the pistil of this flower.

black widow seeks only to avoid contact with the larger animals.

Tarantulas are the hairy, large, timid spiders found (among other places) in the subtropical sections of the United States. They may be kept for a while, but eventually should be released outdoors. They are not poisonous and are excellent insect controllers. The hairs that make spiders such as the tarantula appear so fearsome serve as antennae.

Since spiders are solitary insects, even to the point where females will devour their mates and their young, they should be kept for observation in the classroom in individual containers. Any small, unbreakable jar or plastic container will do. However, it should be large enough to hold some soil to absorb moisture and provide the humidity the creature needs. For any of the orb-weaver spiders, put in a branch upon which they can weave a web. Children may enjoy improvising a web with thin grocery string. They may find silvery patches called "fairies' pocketbooks" on the undersides of stones. These are spider egg cases; slit open they disclose many tiny eggs.

Spider observation cage An observation cage (Fig. 2-19) for small spiders may be made from six 2 × 2-inch squares of cover glass for 35-mm. color film. Available in quantity from camera stores, the glass can be taped together to form a cube. The cage contains enough air for a week for small spiders. Do not keep insects or any other creatures in the classroom for more than a week or two. Make a point of freeing classroom crea-

tures and returning them to collection area before the children lose interest.

FLYING INSECTS

Bees

Much of the preceding section on ants applies to bees, which are also highly organized, social insects (Fig. 2-20). Not all bees are social insects, however, the carpenter and bumblebees (Fig. 2-21) being solitary.

Observation hive An observation hive (Fig. 2-22) with an opening to the outside can be a year-long source of interest and information to children. Begin with a standard frame (obtainable from a beekeeper) and build the "beehive" around it. The hive is set up at the classroom window with egress to outdoors through the slot. (Check local ordinances to be sure there is no prohibition of beekeeping.) Enlist a local beekeeper to help set up the observation hive. Watching a beekeeper hive a swarm is an unforgettable experience.

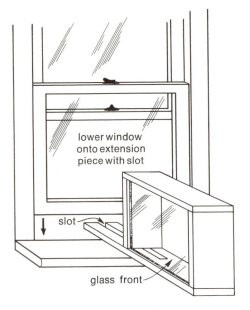

FIGURE **2-22** Observation beehive in place in a classroom.

FIGURE **2-23** A hornet (a) and its nest (b) and a mud dauber wasp (c) and its nests (d). This hornet like the yellow jacket has a rather heavy waist and folds its wings like a fan so they do not obscure its body.

Children should observe, draw, and read about insect stinging and biting organs. Consult school health personnel and reference materials for correct treatment of insect bites and stings.

Wasps and Hornets

As with bees, some species of wasps and hornets are solitary and some are social insects.

The mud dauber (Fig. 2-23a), a common solitary wasp, may be distinguished by its shiny black body, threadlike waist, and iridescent wings, which fold beside each other over its back. It lays its eggs in tubular cells that it makes of mud and saliva and attaches to the undersides of window ledges, eaves, and other sheltered spots. Each tube is about 1 inch long, smooth inside and rough outside. The wasp fills each tube with spiders paralyzed by its sting, deposits one egg (which will hatch into a grub that feeds on the spiders), and seals the tube. When found, a tube may be empty or may contain a silken cocoon or fat white grub and half-eaten spider, or it may be nearly full of spiders and have a wasp egg at the top of the tube—depending on what stage of its life cycle (metamorphosis) the wasp has reached.

(a)   (b)

Look for mud wasp nests near water. In the early summer, watch the edges of pools or puddles for the many little holes from which the wasp draws its clay or mud.

There are about 70 species of mud wasps in the United States. Some, such as the potter wasp or jug-builder, provision their nests with caterpillars instead of spiders. The jug-builder uses animal hairs to reinforce her nest cells.

Yellow jackets and white-faced hornets (Fig. 2-23a) are wasps that live as social insects. They may be regarded as the original papermakers, for both make nests of chewed wood pulp. These nests, a marvel of construction, are fastened at the top to a tree branch or similar support and have the entrance near the bottom. Of the two, the yellow jackets make a somewhat finer-textured paper. The wood pulp is made of bits of wood pulled off fences or boards and laid on in thin layers. Depending on the wood source, the layers may have different color.

Sometimes a windstorm brings down one of these wasp apartment houses. It deserves careful and close examination. Check first to be sure the former adult inhabitants have departed. (Yellow jacket bites can be toxic to some individuals; allergic reactions are not uncommon.)

Butterflies and Moths

Care of chrysalises and cocoons Whether bought from a dealer or found outdoors, chrysalises and cocoons must be kept in an environment that approximates outdoor humidity. Moths or butterflies kept in dry heat may die or emerge imperfect or misshapen. Keep them in a terrarium or in a quart jar with sod. Cover the jar with wire screen or netting and keep the sod moist. Since the cocoon or chrysalis will mold if it lies directly on the moist earth, suspend it in mid-air from a thread or twig. Cocoons and chrysalises found during the fall and winter and properly cared for will illustrate for the class how butterflies issue from a naked chrysalis whereas a moth may issue from a cocoon that encloses a chrysalis (Fig. 2-24).

As soon as the inhabitant shows signs of emerging, such as splitting of the pupa, transfer the chrysalis or cocoon to a container large enough for the insect to spread its wings to dry. A resting twig will help. When the insect has emerged, add a wad of cotton soaked in sugar water. Watch to see if the insect unrolls its long tongue to feed.

Some children will probably try to catch some

(c)

(d)

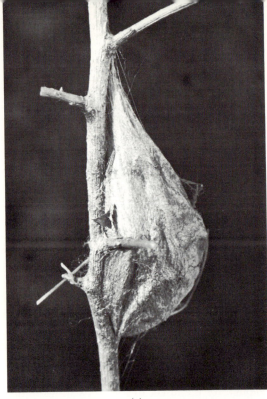

(a)

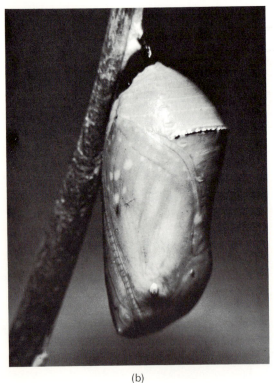

(b)

(c)

(d)

FIGURE **2-24** (a) Moth cocoon, about $2\frac{1}{2}$ inches long; (b) butterfly chrysalis, about 1 inch long; (c) moth antennae; and (d) butterfly antennae. Actual size of the latter is always much greater than antennae of moths.

of the larger, brightly colored species of butterflies and moths. They should be told that such delicate creatures are generally damaged too seriously for mounting unless captured in a net and carefully handled. In any case, the children can infer (from its fragility and its dependence on season-related food such as flower nectar) that a butterfly's life span is short. The differences between the antennae of moths and butterflies can also be seen: Butterflies have two long antennae, usually coiled like a spring; moth antennae are shorter and feathery in appearance (Fig. 2-24).

A toy microscope will disclose the scales that make up the color in a butterfly's wings.

Monarch Butterfly

The butterfly that one notices sailing along high in the air at various seasons is the Monarch (Fig. 2-25). A native of tropic America, it follows its food plant, milkweed, northward in the spring. Toward fall large flocks of Monarchs drift southward, spots of color high in the sky. In its caterpillar stage, the Monarch feeds day and night on milkweed only, attaining a length of about 2 inches and maturing in about eleven days. The caterpillar is green with yellow and black stripes and has long whiplike appendages—two in front and two behind—which lash the air and frighten away parasites. The adult Monarch, which emerges after a pupation of about twelve days, has wings that are copper-colored on the upper surface and yellow with black veins and white-spotted borders on the undersurfaces. Since birds find its taste offensive, it can fly safely at a leisurely pace, without the rapid dodging movements characteristic of most butterflies.

Clothes Moth

It is not the tiny flying moth but the larva that makes holes in wool and fur garments. Making a list of different ways of controlling such insect pests can be an informative exercise. One may also enlist the advice of school health personnel in compiling a list of home antidotes for insect poisons.

Dragonfly

Dragonflies hatch from eggs laid in the water (pp. 15, 46, 47). Some children will know the insect by the name "darning needle."

Firefly

Fireflies are of interest to scientists because of their ability to produce cold light. The eastern form glows at night; the western does not. Like many members of the beetle family, the firefly

has two pairs of wings. The outside wings form a hard protective cover for the animal. The inside wings are soft and thin and fold up when the insect is not flying. Firefly larvae live in the ground and are often known as wire worms.

Fruit Fly

Because the fruit fly has a very short life cycle it is particularly well suited to use in experiments requiring observation through many generations of a species. It is also useful in illustrating the astonishing rapidity of insect multiplication. All that is needed is a pint jar plugged with absorbent cotton (Fig. 2-26), a bit of crumpled paper or rag, and some overripe bananas and/or grapes. Place the fruit inside the jar, cover, and set it in a warm room (not sunlight) until fruit flies appear. Most fruit will have eggs in it from which the pupae should emerge in a day or two. They will feed about a week before pupation and will be visible on the crumpled paper or rag. In three to five days, the pupae change to adults. Females are larger than males and have a slightly broader abdomen with small lines across the end; males can be distinguished by a black-tipped abdomen. A hand glass may be necessary to make sex differentiation. The adults mate soon after they emerge. Subsequent generations of fruit flies can be raised quickly by use of another habitat jar. For closer observation, place fruit flies in stoppered test tubes partially wrapped in foil. The flies will move into the part that is open to the light. A daily count of the number of flies in the jar during one week will probably show an increase in the population. If the children can estimate the rate of increase and project it for a month or a year, the figures will show that if insects multiplied unchecked this would soon be a world of insects.

Insects that Cause Plant Gall

Insect galls on plants are so common that children are bound to ask about them. Galls illustrate the high degree of adaptation of certain insects to certain plants. For example, the insect that causes the oak apple (a gall) is not the one that causes

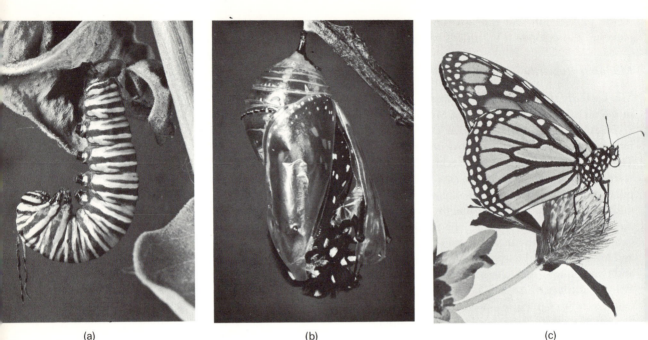

(a)   (b)   (c)

FIGURE **2-25** Stages in the life cycle of a Monarch butterfly. (a) Caterpillar feeding on milkweed. (b) The adult Monarch emerging from the chrysalis. (c) The adult butterfly, its wingspread about four inches.

the willow cone gall or the goldenrod stem gall. In each case, however, the insect deposits an egg in the plant tissues. The egg hatches and the larva begins to eat its way out. Apparently, it secretes a substance into the surrounding plant tissues that irritates them so that they begin to enlarge almost like a tumor, forming a kind of constantly expanding house around the creature responsible for it. Green galls cut open will generally disclose an inhabitant; dry brown galls will generally be found vacant. A tiny hole can usually be found through which the tenant escaped to the world of free flight.

Houseflies

Houseflies are our most dangerous insect because they are the most frequent carriers of disease. To illustrate this, prepare two to four sterile Petri dishes of nutrient agar (obtainable from a high school biology teacher or hospital laboratory). Put a housefly into one of the Petri dishes. While it is walking around on the layer of agar, have

a child cough several times into another dish and quickly re-cover it. Wipe a pencil over the surface of the third dish and re-cover it. Keep the fourth dish covered as a control. Remove the fly

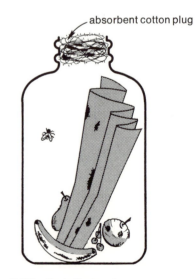

absorbent cotton plug

FIGURE **2-26** Fruit fly hatchery.

from the first dish and label all four with wax crayon or an adhesive label. Seal all the dishes with tape and put them in a warm dark place for a week. Then compare the resulting bacteria and mold colonies (see p. 77).

Mosquito

Next to the housefly, the mosquito is probably most harmful to man. However, this is true only in subtropical and tropical latitudes, where malaria and yellow fever are common. It has been said that 250 million of the world's inhabitants suffer from malaria. In Los Angeles, which is one of the largest cities in the United States and is in subtropical latitudes, the park department puts Gambusia fish (similar to guppies) into its ponds. These limit mosquito breeding by eating mosquito wigglers (larvae), which develop in stagnant water (Fig. 11-2). Put some wigglers (and some of the water in which they are found) in each of three jars. Hold aside one jar as a control. Sprinkle a drop or two of light oil on the water in the second jar. Put a goldfish or tadpole in the third jar as the wigglers begin to change into adults. The children may thus witness on a small scale two methods of controlling mosquitoes—chemical and ecological, respectively.

Water Insects

Children may enjoy watching aquatic insects change from the larval to the adult form. This change occurs most frequently in late spring along brooks where the water runs slowly, in ponds, or in swampy places, particularly where there are plants growing in the water. A kitchen strainer lashed to an old broom handle makes a fine dip net. A white enamel pan may be useful for spreading the catch so that one can readily select the specimens to be kept. These go into small bottles of water and the remainder are returned to the brook or pond. Encourage the children to collect small plastic containers, which can be easily carried in a canvas knapsack. Take along a clean gallon can for pond water in which to keep the specimens; they will feel more at

home and will find food in it that cannot be seen without magnification.

In the classroom the "catch" may be kept in a fresh-water "aquarium" similar to that described in Chapter 1. For water insects, the

FIGURE **2-27** (a) Damsel fly larva; note visible gills (tail appendages). (b) Damsel fly adult; this insect has a slenderer, more brilliantly colored body than the dragonfly, and its folds its wings together over its back when resting, whereas dragonfly rests with its wings outspread as if in flight.

(a)

(b)

(a)

FIGURE **2-28** (a) May fly larva, showing feathery lateral gills. (b) May fly adult, showing characteristic curved body, not straight as in damsel and dragon-flies.

(b)

aquarium need be nothing more elaborate than a gallon jug: Wash the jar and put an inch layer of sand on the bottom. (Do not use ocean beach sand; the salt in it is fatal to fresh-water life.) In this layer, imbed roots of the native water plants (for example, Utricularia, Spirogyra, Nitella) you may find on a collecting field trip. Hold the roots down with pebbles or gravel. Add a gallon of pond or brook water, tilting the

FIGURE **2-29** The backswimmer, which gets its name from the direction of its movement.

FIGURE **2-30** Caddis worm cases. The insects make these chambers of such materials as (a) shells, (b) pebbles, (c) sticks and leaves.

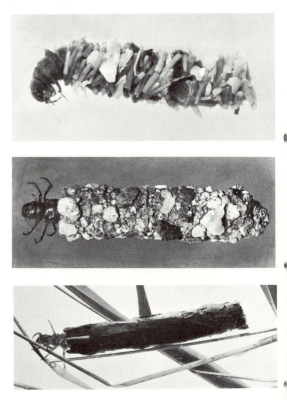

aquarium jar in order to avoid roiling the bottom with a direct flow of the pond water. Fill the jar to within a couple of inches of the top. If jam jars are being used to make individual insect habitats, fill these to within an inch of the top. Set the large or small aquariums in a north or east window and let the water settle and clear. Add a slanting stick and a rock (both partly out of water) for perching and hiding.

The catch may include larvae of damsel flies (Fig. 2-27) or May flies (Fig. 2-28). If these pupate into adult form, the aquarium in which they are kept will need a top of netting or cloth to keep emerging adults from flying off. Most of these larvae are equipped with gills and use the air dissolved in the water. While fish gills are usually at the head end, the gills of water insect larvae are usually toward the tail end. Some, like the young whirligig beetle, have feathery gills along the sides of the body. Young diving beetles do not have gills, but have a breathing tube at the rear of the body; this means they must "come up for air." Water beetles also come up for air, but, like the water spiders, they take some back down with them by trapping a bubble of air under each wing cover.

Two interesting and active insects look much alike: the water boatman and the back swimmer (Fig. 2-29). The back swimmer does just that and the water boatman uses a pair of legs like oars.

Like aphids, these water insects suck food through their beaks. Water boatmen suck fluids from plants, and back swimmers from other small creatures in the water.

Water insects are very speedy and many species have protective coloration. Water striders offer a beautiful example of such coloration, their bodies being dark above and pearly white below. The color of the lighter underparts offsets the darkening effect of ground shadow, making the insect less visible to predators below. For an explanation of how water striders walk on the water see p. 106, Chapter 6.

The way the dragonfly larva moves about the bottom is a good example of jet propulsion in nature. If the water is clear, it may be possible to see the insect draw water into an opening at the rear (within which the gills are located) and then expel the water (comparable to exhalation in an air-breather). The sudden expulsion of water makes the young dragonfly shoot forward.

On field trips, collect tiny freshwater snails and sponges that cling to rocks, in addition to water insects. Also suitable are the tiny chambers of stone or sticks that the caddis fly larvae build for themselves (Fig. 2-30) and which may be found under rocks in streams. You may find a

FIGURE **2-31** (a) Dragonfly larva, or nymph. (b) Dragonfly adult.

(a)

(b)

dragonfly nymph (Fig. 2-31); certainly you will find the cast skin of these nymphs, split open along the back and still clinging to the rock on which the dragonfly emerged to dry and spread its iridescent wings in the sun. That anything so dainty as a dragonfly could hatch from such a grotesque as the nymph is one of the surprises of fresh-water study.

SUGGESTED PROJECTS

1. Count the number of times a black cricket chirps in fourteen seconds. Add 40 to find the approximate air temperature. (The higher the air temperature, the faster the chirps; low temperatures slow metabolism and "music.")

2. Obtain reference material on insect control from pest control firms.

3. Read and report on the story of how gulls saved crops in Salt Lake City from annihilation by grasshoppers. Look for a picture of the statue erected to commemorate the event.

4. From observation and study, develop a pictorial report of insect warfare. (A study of insecticides might conceal the importance of insect control by insects.)

5. Compare the whitish cave crickets sometimes found in a cellar with common black field crickets.

Although structure is similar, difference in pigmentation reflects difference in environment.

6. Make an exhibit of insects grouped by size, color, or other criteria.

7. Soak paper fibers from a hornet's nest and spread them to dry on blotter or felt cloth. Compare fibers with those of handmade paper.

8. Using fine string, construct an orb weaver's web.

9. Collect earthworms after a rain, spread them on damp paper towels, and describe what may be seen. Determine how the earthworm moves. (See Comstock in end-of-book bibliography.)

10. Compare domesticated silkworms and their cocoons and moths to the stages of metamorphosis in American silkworm moths such as the Cecropia, the Polyphemus, and the Promethea.

BIBLIOGRAPHY

(**P** indicates recommended for primary grades, **I** for intermediate grades, **U** for upper grades.)

Bartlett, Ruth, *Insect Engineers,* Morrow, 1957. Collection and indoor observation.   **U**

Blough, Glenn O., *Discovering Insects,* McGraw-Hill, 1967. A boy entomologist makes an insect location map of his back yard. Experiments and discoveries, many open-ended, are suggested. Clear illustrations. **I**

Bronson, Wilfrid, *Beetles,* Harcourt, 1963. Various beetles, their growth and development, and adaptation to environment are described. Numerous detailed life-size pencil drawings and useful information on collecting, preserving, and exhibiting.   **U**

Coggins, Jack, *Nets Overboard! The Story of the Fishing Fleets,* Dodd, Mead, 1965. The various methods of commercial fishing described and illustrated. Information about the food resources of the world for the present and the future.   **U**

Conklin, Gladys, *The Bug Club,* Holiday, 1966. Useful pointers for young naturalists on collecting, observing, raising, and exhibiting bugs, and organizing a bug club. Good line drawings, bibliography, and list of supply houses are included.   **U**

———, *I Like Caterpillars,* Holiday, 1958. Describes various kinds of caterpillars. Vivid, dramatic illustrations.   **P**

De Seyn, Donna, *Termite Works for His Colony,* Holiday, 1967. Simple text and good illustrations.   **I**

Dodge, Natt N., *Poisonous Dwellers of the Desert,* Southwest Monuments Assn. Pop. Ser. No. 3, Santa

Fe, New Mexico. Photographs and brief descriptions of common arid-region insects and other creatures. **I**

Dupre, Ramona Stewart, *Spiders*, Follett, 1967. Anatomy, life cycles, and habits of several kinds of spiders introduced through colorful illustrations and brief text. **I**

Earle, Olive L., *Crickets*, Morrow, 1956. Life cycles of different common forms. Directions for keeping as pets. **I**

Goldin, Augusta, *Spider Silk*, Crowell, 1964. Basic information on spiders and their habits. Detailed color illustrations. **P**

Goudey, Alice, *Red Legs*, Scribners, 1966. Simple text and graphic drawings tell the life cycle of the red-legged grasshopper. **I**

Hawes, Judy, *Fireflies in the Night*, Crowell, 1963. Presented in simple and informative, artistic illustrations. **P**

————, *Ladybug, Ladybug, Fly Away Home*, Crowell, 1967. Attractive easy-to-read account of how California orange trees were saved by ladybugs. **I**

Hogner, Dorothy, *Butterflies*, Crowell, 1962. Descriptions of the anatomy of the butterfly, its food, habitat, and life cycle. Well illustrated with numerous black and white drawings. Includes a chapter on raising caterpillars. **I**

————, *Spiders*, Crowell, 1955. Covers physiology, life cycle, and web spinning, and how spiders differ from insects. **I**

Hopf, Alice, *Monarch Butterflies*, Crowell, 1965. Instructions for observing, propagating, banding, and photographing butterflies, illustrated with black and white drawings and clear diagrams. Contains a bibliography, a list of suppliers, and an index. **U**

Hussey, Lois J., and Catherine Pessino, *Collecting Cocoons*, Crowell, 1953. Collection, identification, and indoor care of cocoons and larvae. **I**

Hutchins, Ross E., *Insects: Hunters and Trappers*, Rand McNally, 1957. For young naturalists; lively text and excellent photographs **I**

Lavine, Sigmund, *Wonders of the Hive*, Dodd, Mead, 1958. Sourcebook for use with an observation hive. **I**

————, *Wonder of the Spider World*, Dodd, Mead, 1966. The good spiders do for man and their place in ancient legends. Clear photographs. **U**

McClung, Robert M., *Caterpillars and How They Live*, Morrow, 1965. Describes different kinds of caterpillars, their body structure, habits, life cycle, defense mechanisms, and usefulness to man. One chapter is devoted to raising caterpillars, their cages, and care. **I**

————, *Green Darner: The Story of a Dragonfly*, Morrow, 1966. Ecology and habitat of the common large dragonfly. Excellent treatment of nymphal stage. **U**

————, *Tiger: The Story of a Swallowtail Butterfly*, Morrow, 1953. Annual cycle of a common butterfly; well illustrated. **P**

Politi, Leo, *The Butterflies Come*, Scribners, 1957. Annual migration of monarch butterflies at Monterey peninsula, California. **I**

Poole, Lynn, *Fireflies in Nature and Laboratory*, Crowell, 1965. A wealth of information about luminescent insects in legend, history, and nature; recent research on fireflies; and possible application of bioluminescent materials in space exploration. Directions for collecting specimens. **U**

Sears, Paul M., *Firefly*, Holiday, 1956. Life cycle of the firefly and related insects. **I**

Selsam, Millicent, *The Bug That Laid the Golden Eggs*, Harper & Row, 1967. A group of children find eggs and try to identify them using an insect book, a magnifying glass, more collected specimens, and an appeal to the Natural History Museum. A neighbor scientist helps, but the identity is never discovered. Clear photographs and diagrams. **P**

————, *Questions and Answers About Ants*, Four Winds, 1967. Includes information about feeding habits, mating, and stages of growth, division of work within a colony, and instructions for setting up and caring for an ant colony. Clear, precise illustrations. **I**

————, *Terry and the Caterpillars*, Harper & Row, 1962. A clear, easy-to-read description of the life cycle of the cecropia moth—from caterpillar to cocoon to moth to egg and back to caterpillar. Attractive color illustrations show the stages of development. **P**

Shenefelt, Roy D., *Insects in Our World*, Whitman, 1964. Some of the topics covered: What is an Insect? The Parts of the Insect. Insect Homes. How Insects Live Together. Enemies of Man. Friends of Man. Starting an Insect Collection. Profusely illustrated with full-color drawings and clear black and white diagrams. **U**

Shuttlesworth, Dorothy E., *Story of Ants*, Doubleday, 1964. Emphasizes the variety of ant types to be found in a colony. Illustrations of the highly magnified insects are detailed and carefully tinted. **U**

————, *Story of Spiders*, Garden City, 1959. Good on webs and web construction. I

Simon, Hilda, *Exploring the World of Social Insects*, Vanguard, 1962. Nine kinds of ants, four of bees, six of wasps, and the most common of the termites are introduced in a way to stimulate personal observation. Lists of scientific names and life-size drawings. U

Sterling, Dorothy, *Insects and the Homes They Build*, Doubleday, 1954. One of the best; excellent text and illustrations. I

Swain, Su Zan Noguchi, *Insects in Their World*, Garden City, 1955. Insect collection, identification, and observation. Well described and beautifully illustrated. U

Tee-Van, Helen D., *Insects are Where You Find Them*, Knopf, 1963. Short descriptions of the lives, habits, and environments of 50 insects. Exceptionally good black and white illustrations. The chapter devoted to insects in legend, literature, art, and music includes some unusual material. U

Tibbetts, Albert B., *First Book of Bees*, Watts, 1952. Mine of information on types of bees and their work; how to remove a sting. I

U.S. Dept. of Agriculture, Publications on various aspects of entomology. U

Several of the insectivorous plant, Venus's flytrap, common to the southeast coast of the United States.

3 Plant Life

Many children do not think of plants as living things that, like all living things, must adapt or perish. Ultimately all animal life depends upon plants; even man cannot yet duplicate the process—photosynthesis (p. 61)—by which a common dandelion, using sunlight, makes its own food out of elements in the air, water, and soil. A discussion of the origin of food will soon lead children to the realization that all of man's daily diet (except some water and salt) comes directly or indirectly from plants. Social studies can be enriched by a bulletin board exhibit of plant foods, using a large stylized plant made of construction paper. To the different plant parts—each a different color—attach yarn leading to food packages or cans processed from plant roots, stems, leaves, etc. Parts of plants used in industry

—for example, lumber—may be pointed out similarly. A 3-D bulletin board might effectively illustrate subjects like "The Garden in the Grocery Store" and "The Garden in the Dry Goods Store."

A five-minute walking trip around school grounds can indicate where plants grow best. Children may note in what kind of soil the most plants are found—and the fewest; that few or no plants grow in thoroughfares where the soil is packed hard; that most plants grow along fences, where there is little wear and tear and more moisture.

A few house plants can make a classroom more attractive, and the presence of even one plant can lead to discussion of many productive questions: Why do we think plants beautiful? What if foliage were red instead of green? Why are plants green rather than some other color? The last can lead directly into the subject of photosynthesis (below) and into the study of light, color, and wave length (Chapter 15). The moisture and oxygen that plants release also make a room more healthful and comfortable. (In the average steam-heated classroom, a gallon of water must evaporate daily to maintain a constant 50% humidity.)

SELECTION AND CARE OF CLASSROOM PLANTS

The knack of successful plant growing in school is not necessarily the hereditary possession of a favored few. This "knack" is often only a reflection of their genuine curiosity about and interest in plants such that, for instance, they will be quick to note that a plant "looks" dry before this lack becomes critical. Since plants are relatively slow to show the effect of neglect, the relationship of cause and effect may not be apparent to the unschooled observer.

Ready-grown Plants

Select plants that fit the classroom climate and exposure; for example, geraniums, spring bulbs, and other flowering plants need a sunny window. African violets will do well with a north or east exposure. Philodendrons and most of the shadelovers, which do well in a terrarium, also grow best in a north or east window. (A first-grade class that had struggled for weeks with the problem of surplus algae in its aquarium finally discovered, by the process of elimination, that the tank was placed where it got too much sun.)

Given information on a classroom's exposure and its average temperature and average light intensity, a neighborhood florist or nurseryman should be able to help in selecting plants. Children helping to plan for schoolroom plants will be astonished by the differences in light intensity to be found in the average schoolroom. Readings may be made with a foot-candle meter (available through school health authorities) or a photo light

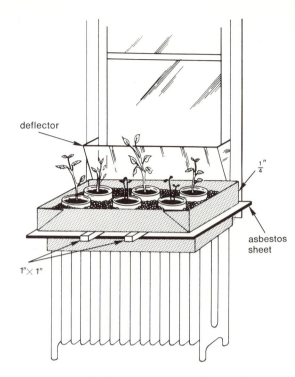

FIGURE **3-1** Pebble tray mounted on radiator in front of window equipped with a deflector.

meter (possibly available through parents). Note the variations, too, for readings taken at different times of the day. (These observations and records may correlate with the study of latitudes and seasons discussed in Chapter 9.) Temperature readings should also be taken at various hours and in various parts of the room. To demonstrate the extremes of temperature that may prevail in a room, take simultaneous readings from a pair of identical thermometers, one on the floor and one near the ceiling.

While a window sill location may offer abundant sunlight for plants, it also may impose rigorous climatic extremes on them. In cold weather the plant may be exposed both to blasts of cold air from an open window and to waves of hot dry air from radiators, which are often situated close to windows. When windows are left open at the bottom, plants may be protected from cold air by plate glass or plastic air deflectors (Fig. 3-1). On very cold nights, insulate the plants by covering the window with several layers of newspaper.

Room climates may be improved for both plants and people by using a pebble tray (Fig. 3-1). This may be made in the same manner as the tray for the pet cage (Chapter 1)—from thin rust-resistant galvanized iron or from medium-weight sheet aluminum. Measure the window sill or other space for the pebble tray. Add 8–9 inches to each dimension in order to have a tray about 4 inches deep (Fig. 3-1). Bend up the edges with pliers or a vise, forming a "pig's ear" folded back to seal the corners. Flatten the folded edges with a hammer. If the pebble tray is to be placed on a radiator, insulate it from heat by standing it on some 1×1-inch wood blocks that rest in turn on several layers of thin asbestos sheet. Sprinkle on the bottom a thin layer of pebbles and a few bits of charcoal which will absorb acids produced by decaying organic matter. Arrange potted plants as desired and fill in around them with small pebbles or vermiculite to the level of the tray's top. Sprinkle the planted tray until, by probing with the finger tips, about $\frac{1}{2}$ inch of water can be felt on the bottom. By capillary action (Chapter 6) the water rises around the pebbles so that the pots are always moist, but not soggy. Recording the amount of water needed in changing weather or seasons may develop in the children concepts of evaporation and humidity in relation to weather (Chapter 7). At the end of each school year, clean the pebble tray and repaint it with metal paint in preparation for the next season. Aluminum trays need no painting.

In overheated indoor winter environments, plants tend to dry out quickly. Indoor plants should be watered thoroughly and then permitted to dry out before being watered again. Dried out soil will be light brown and dry—but not bone dry—to the touch. (The "feel" of soil and its weight are better indicators than color; soil should contain enough moisture to feel cool.) If the plant goes too long without water, the cells lose their normal turgidity or fullness and the plant begins to look slightly limp. If allowed to become very limp, the plant, even if it does not

succumb, will require days, or even weeks, to go through the process of sloughing off the damaged tissue and putting out new growth.

The usual method of watering plants from above is less successful than bottom watering. In the latter method, pots are immersed to the rim in water in a dishpan, pail, or other container. (The soil surface should not be underwater.) Within an hour or two, after the plants soak up the water they need and the soil looks and feels moist, pots are removed and set in saucers to drain. (Plants in the pebble tray are, of course, bottom-watered.) If it is not possible to set pots in water, water from above until water ceases to soak in.

Since bottom watering is possible only for plants in porous clay pots, the pots should not be painted, and decorative china or glass pots should be used only as outside containers for porous pots. Decorative florists' foil should be removed from pots to let air get to the roots.

To determine the amount of water used by a plant such as philodendron or other indoor plants that grow in water, insert the plant's stem in water in a glass container. With a grease pencil or crayon, mark the water level each day on the outside of the container. Prevent evaporation by sealing the top of the container with foil held on with a rubber band and pressed tightly about the plant stem and over the mouth of the vessel. A more accurate apparatus for measuring water loss in plants (Fig. 3-2) employs a small funnel, some rubber tubing, two plastic or glass drinking tubes, and paraffin or modeling clay. Seal a geranium cutting into one tube with clay or paraffin, adding water daily through the funnel and recording the amount necessary to maintain the water level in the tube.

At least once a month, transfer all potted plants to the nearest sink or dishpan and thoroughly rinse off the foliage in order to remove dust and dirt, which clog the pores, or stomata, on the leaf surfaces. (Chalk dust is particularly harmful.) Use a tissue or a soft small rag; a small sprayhead is also excellent for this purpose. To illustrate that plants need to breathe, smear petroleum jelly lightly on both sides of a leaf. Do not detach the

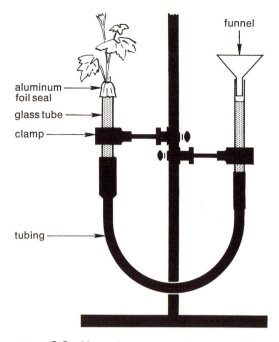

aluminum foil seal

glass tube

clamp

tubing

funnel

FIGURE **3-2** Measuring amount of water used by a plant by use of a potometer.

leaf from the plant. After a day or two the leaf will wilt because the stomata are plugged. Some leaves will wilt even if coated on only one side. Plants in the pebble tray can be rinsed off on the spot, without moving. Some plants, such as a sweet potato vine will benefit from rinsing as frequently as daily or bi-weekly. Washing also tends to keep down infestations of such insects as the red spider. An infestation of aphids may be discouraged by a light soap spray, bubbles of which literally suffocate the aphids. Dead foliage, which tends to harbor pests, should be removed. (Live aphids may be saved for ladybugs in season. The latter are used on a commercial scale to control aphids and other pests.) Children may also have an opportunity to observe common black ants "milking" their green aphid "cows" (see Chapter 2).

Since some plant pests are so minute as to multiply in force before becoming noticeable, the undersides of leaves should be examined regularly with a magnifying glass. A florist or nurseryman can identify and advise on how to deal with pests.

Plants from Seed

Growing plants from seed may help to enrich social studies, in that children can experience, on a small scale, some of the problems and practices of the farmer. If the season and daily temperature range permit, exterior window sills may be utilized. Sills too narrow to accommodate seed beds can be extended by a simple plank shelf laid across brackets (simple iron corner-braces will do) attached to the exterior wall (Fig. 3-3a) or by a shelf resting half on the sill and half on wooden legs (Fig. 3-3b) extending to the ground. (Drainage holes should be drilled in the horizontal surface.)

Seed beds, or flats, can be made from shallow wooden fruit crates 3–4 inches deep. Tighten the corners with a few additional flat-headed nails. Drill a number of small holes in the bottom (good drainage reduces rotting) and use a soil made up of equal parts of sand, loam, and leaf mold—the standard greenhouse potting mixture.

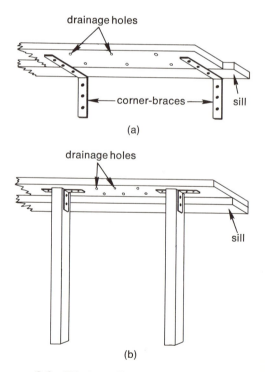

drainage holes

corner-braces — sill

(a)

drainage holes

sill

(b)

FIGURE **3-3** Window sill extensions: (a) plank shelf attached to wall; (b) leg-supported type.

Planning for spring planting will reveal the existence of microclimates around the school. What part of the school grounds is the warmest, which the coldest? Note newspaper records of daily temperatures and precipitation. If it is too early in the season for flats to be put outdoors and there is no room in the school building, plant seeds in cigar boxes, clay flower pots, or waxed food containers. With an ice pick or other sharp tool, punch drainage holes in the bottom of the cigar box and waxed containers. Do not use glass containers. Seeds planted in cans usually do not thrive: the soil is either dry or soggy unless one has punched drainage holes with a small nail. Try planting the same kind of seeds in soil that is kept dry, in soil kept moist, and in soil kept soggy. Soggy soil keeps air from the seedlings while dry soil brings them no moisture. It may be necessary to start the seeds with normal good treatment before showing the effects of air or water deprivation.

Soil Select the best soil by testing several kinds and mixtures, making test plantings of lima beans, radishes, oats, or other quick germinators in soil samples from local sources—for example, sand from the kindergarten sandbox, a nearby construction site, a fresh-water beach, or the school playground; topsoil from the school garden or a neighboring garden or window box; and humus from beneath school shrubs or from nearby woods. Test soil from the center of a lot as well as from its borders or hedgerows, and from a roadcut or excavation. Collect topsoil from the thin dark layer on top as well as from the subsoil layer just below and plant seed in at least two containers of each soil sample. Identify the contents of each with wooden tongue depressors or ice cream sticks thrust into the soil. Treat all samples alike as to planting procedures, watering, etc.

The water-holding characteristics of different soils may be tested as shown in Fig. 3-4 (see also Chapter 6). Children may notice that water runs very quickly through sand, whereas clay tends to hold moisture almost too well. With equal amounts of water and fresh soil samples, use the can-jar system to determine which soil

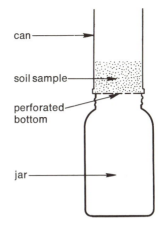

FIGURE **3-4** Arrangement for testing soil samples for water-holding and runoff characteristics.

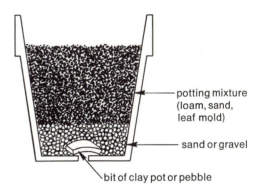

FIGURE **3-5** Clay pot properly prepared for seed planting.

retains the most water and which the least, recording run-off time.

Plant a few of the seeds used in the test plantings (above) in components of the standard potting mixture (above)—sand, loam, leaf mold, and peat—or in mixes of different proportions of the components and have children observe the differential effects (on growth) of the different soils.

Planting techniques The following general planting techniques with clay pots are applicable to plantings in other containers. Soak clay pots in water just before use since a dry pot will draw moisture out of the soil and away from the seeds. Knead or work enough water into the soil to form a soft (not muddy) ball that holds its shape in the open hand. Fill the pot or container with soil and then tap it until the soil particles settle to within about 1 inch of the top (Fig. 3-5). Spread seeds on top of the soil. (Too many induce rot, and too few will not allow for "duds" or casualties; follow instructions on the packet.) Cover the seeds with $\frac{1}{2}$ to $\frac{3}{4}$ inch of soil, firming it with the bottom of a milk bottle, can, or the like. Soil that is loose and full of air spaces allows sprouting seeds to dry too quickly.

A pane of glass or a sheet of plastic covering the seed containers produces a miniature hotbed to keep seeds warm and moist until they have germinated. Seeds may also be covered with a light cloth or board, which is removed as soon as the seedlings show above ground.

Small seeds and baby plants may be washed out of the ground by overzealous watering. Sprinkle lightly with a toy watering can or a rubber squeeze sprinkler. Where possible, water seeds in clay pots from below (see above).

In many states, seeds are available to schools free or in inexpensive packages. Follow planting directions carefully. Use quick germinators such as beans, corn, and radishes. Very small seeds are hard for children to handle. The directions on the packages may also provide useful reading experiences: Many include maps of the United States showing when to plant according to region. Most quality seeds guarantee a high percentage of germination, offering an opportunity for an incidental lesson in calculating percentages.

A rag-doll seed tester may be made to check germination time and the percentage of viable seeds. To make the tester, mark off strips of sheeting or cheese cloth in 5- to 6-inch squares. Spread seeds in the center of each square—15–20 of one kind per square—label, and cover with another cloth strip. Roll up whole strip and secure with string or rubber bands. Dampen and set on end in a dish of shallow water or in a plastic bag. Periodically unroll and record results.

Wheat and oats will grow well on a window sill farm, especially if a little clay (even art clay) is well mixed into the soil to help retain water. For comparison, any of the above-mentioned seeds, mixed bird seed, or some chick feed (whole,

not ground) may be sprouted on a plastic sponge set in a saucer of water indoors. Once the seeds have sprouted, they should be transplanted into earth if the seedlings are to survive. A pleasant outdoor activity can be the transplanting of sunflower seedlings to borders of playgrounds or home gardens for fall and winter bird-feeding. In most transplanting, some root hairs (see below under *The Parts of Plants*) are destroyed and later replaced by new ones. It is important to destroy as few as possible to minimize shock to the plant.

There are two ways of watering transplants. Either transplant seedlings into holes prepared for them, fill with soil, then with water, or fill holes with water, set in the plants, and fill around roots with soil. In either case, firm seedlings in place with the hands.

Seeds sown in flats can be handled much the same way as those in pots. Firm seeds into the soil with a ruler or flat stick, label the rows, and water with a fine spray from above. It is better to water thoroughly every two or three days than a little every day. Frequent light sprinkling tends to draw moisture out of the ground by capillary action (Chapter 6). This is one of the reasons the farmer cultivates lightly in warm weather, for compacted soil loses its moisture much faster than soil whose top layer is loose or mulched. This can be seen in miniature in a sugar lump sprinkled with powdered sugar. Liquid will quickly move up through the lump by capillary action from one particle to another but will slow almost to a stop at the powdered sugar (Chapter 6).

Cultivate the window sill farm in order to control weeds and retain subsoil moisture. Use toy hoes or rakes, but dig lightly and well away from roots of seedlings. Periodic thinning can offer an opportunity for children to observe the development of the root system. In some plants—for example, alfalfa—the root system may be much larger than the part above ground. Children may work in pairs with a magnifying glass for close study and diagramming of root hairs. The tiny root hairs absorb water and minerals from the soil into the plant; the root proper functions as a passageway or pipeline and as an anchor for the plant (see below).

To see the progressive development of an entire plant, sow bean or corn seeds every two or three days for two weeks. Then uproot the resultant plants and arrange in order of development. Annual flowers may also be grown from seed; but for quick blooms, it is probably worth the expense to get seedlings for transplanting.

Bulbs and Cuttings

Many plants can be grown from cuttings and portions of plants. A pineapple top cut $\frac{1}{2}$ inch below the base of the leaves will sprout spring green in winter if planted as shown in Fig. 3-6. Rex Begonia can be grown from leaf cuttings. Cut leaves at junctions of the large veins underneath and peg surface-down with toothpicks in damp sand or special soil. Roots should sprout at the slits. A glass dish inverted over the plant will keep it moist. Strawberry plants can be propogated by pegging down the stolons, or runners, with hairpins. When new growth has taken root, snip the connecting stolon. Miniature greenhouses for rose or geranium cuttings can be made by placing the cutting in sand and covering with a glass or a plastic bag.

Bulbs and sweet potato or avocado may be forced in nonporous containers. Imbed bulbs in enough pebbles to keep the plant from tipping over when full height and keep the water level just above the roots—no more or less. To determine whether all parts of the plant grow at an

FIGURE **3-7** Sweet potato suspended in water for sprouting.

equal rate, mark the growing tip with India ink at close intervals. Have children check whether the intervals remain the same. (Better-quality bulbs, like more expensive seeds, often justify the additional expense in stronger blooms.) The sweet potato and avocado are suspended in water (Fig. 3-7), the latter broad end down. Rudimentary buds, nodes, or eyes indicate the end of the sweet potato that should be up. Set in the dark to stimulate root growth before top growth. Keep water at original level.

MINIATURE OUTDOOR ENVIRONMENTS

A terrarium is a container for terrestrial life, just as an aquarium is for water life. A terrarium may be set up in a wide-mouthed gallon jar, a leaky aquarium, or a glass box constructed for the purpose. A glass globe tends to distort the interior view, and holds few plants.

Pickle-jar Terrarium

A wide-mouthed jar makes a small but sturdy terrarium. A wooden or cardboard box cradle (Fig. 3-8) or plaster of Paris base will keep it from rolling. Prepare a foundation layer of woodland soil or leaf mold, some sand for drainage, and

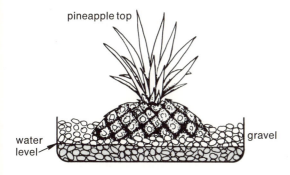

FIGURE **3-6** Method of planting pineapple tops for winter sprouting. Vegetables such as carrot, onion, and turnip may also be used.

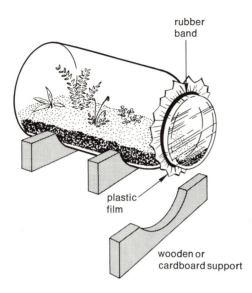

FIGURE **3-8** Pickle-jar terrarium.

a few pieces of charcoal to go in the bottom. Beginners tend to use too much soil, making the terrarium too heavy and leaving too little room for plants; use only enough to imbed plants and cover their roots. Moisten the soil before spreading it in the container. In larger containers, contour the soil into a miniature hill. To minimize weight, use an aluminum foil pie plate as a hollow core for the hill. Plant small, compact woodland shade plants such as moss, ferns, wintergreen, and the like. When obtaining the plants, include some soil. Take no more than one plant from each group, leaving the rest to spread and eventually fill the gap. One's back yard may supply tiny ferns, baby tears, wandering Jew, or other shade-loving plants and of course, the local florist or dime store will have an assortment of small plants in pots. Miniature ivy and the philodendrons are the best investment. Buy only the smallest pots and remove the plants by tapping the inverted pot while holding a finger on either side of the plant stem. It may be necessary to push from the bottom through the drainage hole. In any case, endeavor to keep soil intact around roots. Set plants out in a balanced design. If using moss, plant with the green side out. Imbed a water dish with its edge level with the soil sur-

face. (A glass custard cup is about the right size lake for the miniature landscape.) Set in the plants, covering roots completely and firming in place. Remove any bruised or broken leaves, trimming with scissors to make a clean cut. Wipe the inside of the glass clean with paper toweling. Wet down the earth with a sprinkler and close the jar mouth with plastic wrap—not the metal cover. A lens from a hand glass may also be taped to the mouth of the jar to provide magnification as well as a seal.

After its initial watering, a terrarium should never have to be watered: Moisture evaporating from the plants and the water dish condenses on the inside and precipitates—a model of the water cycle (Chapter 6). The first day or two after it has been made, the terrarium will be so foggy or dewy one will scarcely be able to see into it. In this case, remove the cover and clean the inside glass surfaces. It may be necessary to refill the water dish in proportion as moisture is removed. Be sure to remove moldy plants and to keep the glass clean. Succulents such as the sedums, ice plant, and the like, which will mold in a moist woodland terrarium may be used in a desert terrarium.

For a desert terrarium, plant miniature cactuses and other thick-leaved plants in a 1- to 2-inch foundation layer of sand or sandy loam. Cover the opening of the container with screening, and place where it will receive some sunlight. Water sparingly. (A gallon-jar terrarium is too small to house desert animals, except as temporary quarters.)

A marsh or bog terrarium should have a foundation of wet, acid peat soil, with such typical wet-foot plants as sphagnum, sedges, and pitcher plants (see p. 66). Insect-eating plants are of particular interest.

Glass-box Terrarium

A larger, though inexpensive, terrarium can be constructed from six panes of standard window glass (four oblong panes for top, bottom, and two sides, and two square panes for the ends), a cake or cookie baking sheet as a base, and two rolls

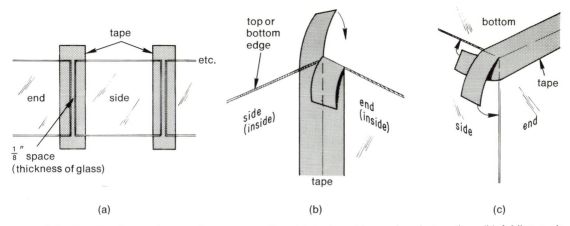

(a)   (b)   (c)

FIGURE **3-9** Details of steps in terrarium construction: (a) taping sides and ends together; (b) folding ends of tape over edge and against inside surfaces of glass; (c) taping bottom to sides and ends. Omitted from c for clarity is the tape that would hold end to side and bottom to side.

of $1\frac{1}{2}$-inch cloth or plastic adhesive tape to bind the glass edges (Fig. 3-9). (While children can make a pickle-jar terrarium either individually or in teams, this larger terrarium may require that they work in "committees"—one to obtain materials, others to do construction, for planting, care, and the like.) If the cake or cookie tin cannot accommodate the standard-size glass, make a tray base from a sheet of medium-gauge aluminum (Fig. 3-10) at least $2\frac{1}{2}$ inches larger than the bottom glass all around. The glass may also be bought cut to fit the cake tin. (Allow for the thickness of the glass in overall measurements.) If a nonaluminum cake tin is used, paint it to prevent rusting. Smooth the edges of the glass with emery paper or sandpaper.

Assemble the sides and ends as shown in Fig. 3-9a, using pieces of tape that extend about $1\frac{1}{2}$ inches beyond each edge of the glass, and leaving a space of about the thickness of the glass between the panes. Split the overhanging ends of tape and press to glass. Half the width of tape attached to the first piece of glass is left unattached to accommodate the outer edge of the last (fourth) pane. When ready to make this attachment, set up the four pieces so they make a hollow rectangle (Fig. 3-9c). Place this rectangle edge down on the bottom and apply four tapes as before, with half the width of each tape

pressed to the bottom glass and half to the bottom edge of a side or end. Lap overhanging tape ends at the corners. Lay the covering glass on top after binding with tape all four edges as well as the top edge of the sides and ends. Such binding improves safety (by covering the sharp edges of the glass) and improves the fit of the cover. (One need not be concerned about air in the terrarium; plants give off enough oxygen to satisfy the needs of the few creatures that may be kept in it.) Set the completed glass box (Fig. 3-10) into the aluminum tray or the cookie sheet. Put in a thin foundation layer of pea gravel mixed with char-

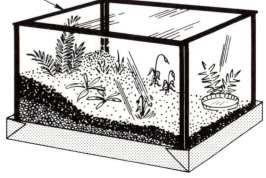

FIGURE **3-10** Completed terrarium.

coal fragments. Then add a $\frac{1}{2}$ inch of sand followed by a 2-inch layer of loam and leaf mold mix. Plant as with the pickle-jar terrarium (above), although the water dish should be larger. A lightweight aluminum foil pie plate (to hold water for moisture by evaporation) can be bent to fit into the corner.

A moist woodland terrarium of this size provides a comfortable habitat for small snakes, frogs, toads, turtles, and salamanders or newts. Large specimens will disarrange and tramp down the miniature landscape. A bit of lichen-covered bark or rotting wood will please salamanders. Frogs and toads favor a cool smooth stone, and snakes like to rub against bark or climb on twigs.

The live food needed by amphibians can be obtained by sweeping an insect net through the grass or weeds outdoors or from an indoor fly trap. Do not put snails in a terrarium, for they will chew up the plants; they may be kept in a separate quart-jar "snailery." The insect-eating bog plants such as the sundew and pitcher plant can be observed at first hand by setting up a bog terrarium of sphagnum, wild cranberry, and other such bog plants.

THE PARTS OF A PLANT

To emphasize that plants are more than what is visible above ground, that they have an organic unity and are related to an environment, ask children to show you one in a vacant lot or weed patch. Accept as a plant only one that has been pulled from the ground *whole*—leaves, stem, and roots, and with some soil still clinging to the latter. This is a plant—a complete organism, still showing the soil that is part of its environment and without which the plant is no longer a total organism and will soon die.

Roots and Geo- and Hydrotropism

Root systems are often enormously extensive. Alfalfa roots have been known to penetrate over 100 feet in dry soil. Children can compare the root system of a weed and the part above ground.

The roots of any leguminous plants (alfalfa, clover, lespedeza, etc.) will show very small knobs or nodules. These contain nitrogen gas-fixing bacteria, which extract nitrogen from the air. (Nitrogen, potassium, and phosphorus are the elements most essential to plants.) Without heat or noise, these microbes can accomplish what it takes many hundreds of kilowatts of electricity to accomplish at huge industrial plants. Compare seed growth in pots of soil into which some nodules have been mixed and growth in soil without these nitrifying agents.

Roots provide a passageway for water and minerals to move up into the plant. Close examination of roots, even without a magnifying glass or low-power microscope, will disclose the tiny root hairs through which the molecules of soil minerals in solution diffuse into the root proper and then into the xylem (Fig. 4-6) or water-conducting cells. Have children compare the growth of transplants with root hairs stripped off and of transplants with root hairs undisturbed. Children can also see the bundle of stringy water-conducting tissue in the center of mature root vegetables such as parsnips and beets.

Roots also anchor plants. In digging up weeds, children will notice how firmly some are held in place by their root system and why other kinds are easy to uproot. One may note, too, the shallowness of the root systems of trees blown over in storms.

Whole plants may be grown from roots. Although white potatoes are really underground stems, the sweet potato is a root, and a luxuriant, attractive room plant may be grown from it by placing the butt end in water and keeping it in a warm, dark place (atop a water heater, for example) until rootlets are well developed. It should then be moved into the light in gradual stages over a period of days. If the container is too wide, keep the potato partly out of water as shown in Fig. 3-7. (Daily sprinkling will hasten sprouting.)

To grow plants from such root vegetables as beets, carrots, turnips, onions, and parsnips, cut an inch or two from the tops, trim back any foliage, being careful not to injure new central growth, and imbed the tops in gravel or vermiculite in a shallow dish. Maintain a half-inch water level on the bottom. Green sprouts will soon emerge. A carrot "basket" can be made by hollowing out the center of a large fleshy carrot (Fig. 3-11). Fill the hollow with water and suspend the carrot. When the "basket" sprouts, it is ready to transplant into soil.

Geotropism and hydrotropism The parts of plants always behave as they must if the plant is to thrive: Stems grow upward, roots always downward. To see how plants respond to gravitational pull (geotropism), line the sides of six tumblers or clear plastic containers with blotting paper. Fill the tumblers with peat, cotton, sawdust, or the like. Slip bean, corn, or radish seeds between the glass or plastic wall of the container and the blotter. Keep a half-inch of water in the bottom of each tumbler. As soon as the seeds begin to sprout roots and stems, lay two tumblers on their sides, and invert two (taped or covered with cloth or screening to keep the contents from falling out). In a few days check the direction of the roots, then return one tumbler of each experimental pair to the control or normal posi-

tion. In a few days, again note direction of root growth. The changes in direction of root growth are *positive*—toward the earth; negative response to gravitational pull can be seen in the action of the stems of three medium-sized potted geranium plants manipulated in the same way.

A third investigation of plants' geotropism requires two squares or panes of glass the same size, some damp cotton or blotters, and fast-germinating seeds. Cover one glass with blotters or cotton, on which place seeds about 1 inch apart. Cover with the second glass and tape together as shown in Fig. 3-12. Set on edge in $\frac{3}{4}$ inch of water in a glass casserole or other container. When the roots show, rotate the glass "sandwich" a quarter turn to the left or right (as one faces its wide surface) so that it stands in the water on an edge adjacent to the one originally in the water. Observe the roots' response in a few days. Return to the original position in three or four days and the roots will reverse themselves.

Plants also exhibit a positive *hydrotropism*, growing *toward* water. To show this, cut two adjacent sides from a half-gallon milk carton, lay the carton on one of its remaining sides, and replace one side with a sheet of glass (Fig. 3-13). With an ice pick, punch a few small drainage holes in the side that is now the bottom; then spread a thin layer of sand and/or gravel in the bottom. Fill three-quarters with plotting soil and plant seeds along one end, close to the glass.

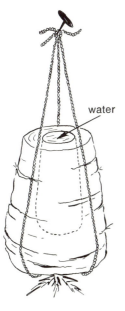

FIGURE **3-11** Carrot basket.

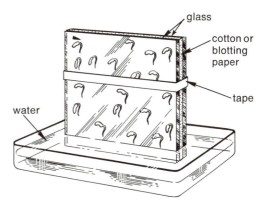

FIGURE **3-12** Arrangement with germinating seeds, showing geotropism.

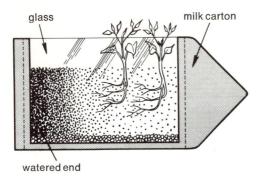

glass   milk carton

watered end

FIGURE **3-13** Root growth demonstrating hydro-tropism.

Water only the end of the box away from the seeds. When the seeds have sprouted, observe how the roots grow toward the water. (Covering the glass with dark paper will stimulate root growth.) Hydrotropism can also be illustrated as follows. Imbed a small clay pot in the soil in the center of the glass-sided container described above. The pot should be unpainted, and the bottom drainage hole corked. Keep the pot partly full of water and plant seeds at both ends of the container close to the glass. The roots will be seen growing toward the water source (the pot) in the middle.

Stems

The function of plant stems is less obvious to children than that of leaves and roots. Stems generally support the leaves, flowers, and fruit of a plant putting the leaves in a position to absorb sun light; trapping solar energy for photosynthesis or food-making (see below). Stems also carry solutions of nutriments from the roots to the upper parts. Although celery stalks are part of the leaf rather than the stem, the following investigation, "patriotic celery," may illuminate the latter aspect. Using celery with yellowing leaves, place one stalk in clear water, one in red food color solution, and one in blue, and leave for a few hours in bright sun. Then note the change in the leaves. (This may also be done with lettuce leaves or white carnations.) A cut across celery left in solution should reveal that celery

"strings" are really the "pipes" or conducting tissue. Repeat the first investigation with one stalk of celery divided in thirds at the bottom, each segment in a different one of the three solutions (Fig. 3-14). Using celery or carnations and one color solution, cut one stalk at right angles and one obliquely. Which transports liquids most quickly? (Fresh-cut stems provide better transport of fluids than dry—and hence, partially sealed—cuts; an oblique cut provides more absorptive surface.) Trimming flower stems under water prevents interference (from air bubbles) with passage of fluids in the tubes.

Jewelweed (*Impatiens*), the fresh-water, stream-side plant, if held up to the light, will show the fibrovascular bundles or plant "pipelines" in the stem.

The trunks of trees are essentially the stems of big plants. Like trees, plants with tough stems are often perennials rather than annuals, which

FIGURE **3-14** Celery stalk split to stand in three different colored solutions.

live but a season. The age of a tree is recorded in its stem—in the annual rings of cells produced through a growing season. The trunk of a discarded Christmas tree may be cross-sectioned quickly with a hand saw, providing tree ring samples for the class. Fish scales under low-power magnification also show growth rings; a turtle shows growth rings in each individual scale, particularly along the marking of the upper shell, or carapace (Chapter 1).

Leaves and Photosynthesis

To show that plants need sun, lay a board over grass. After a week or two, remove the board and compare the color of the covered grass with that of the grass around it. Children may observe how long it takes for the grass that was under the board to turn green again. On class trips, perhaps to a nearby vacant lot, children can compare the display possibilities of weeds with tall stems and those without stems, noting how the rosette arrangement of the leaves, common to low-growing plants, maximizes exposure to light. Also noteworthy is how few leaves of a shrub or small tree are shaded by the others. Leaves grow on a stem in an arrangement that tends to allow the most light for each leaf; the arrangements are alternate (one leaf at a node); opposite (two leaves opposite each other at a node); or whorled (three or more leaves at a node).

Leaves are essentially the "factory" portion of the plant, using solar energy in a process, called photosynthesis, by which they manufacture starch. (Analysis of the word *photosynthesis* into its parts, and discussion of associated words—such as *photography* and *synthetic*—may afford the basis for a dictionary lesson.) In the process, the chlorophyll of the green plant cells traps solar energy, which is used to effect a combination of carbon dioxide (from the air) and water to produce starch and oxygen, which the plant gives off. (By absorbing carbon dioxide, plants tend to keep its concentration in the atmosphere stable.)

To demonstrate starch in leaves, boil some leaves from a geranium or Golden Beta Yellow coleus plant (that has been in sunlight for several days) for a few minutes in water in a glass vessel. Warm the softened leaves in a glass vessel half full of ethyl alcohol. To avoid igniting alcohol fumes, heat the alcohol in a water bath (as shown in Fig. 3-15) or with an electric immersion heater or a hot plate.

The chlorophyll, soluble in alcohol, should be extracted completely from the leaves in about five minutes. (For thick leaves repeat the process with fresh alcohol.) Wash the blanched leaves, spread them flat in open Petri dishes, and add enough iodine solution (one drop of iodine to 300 cc. of water) to cover them. After several minutes (usually 2–5, but as long as 15) rinse off the iodine solution and hold the leaves up to the light. The blackish areas indicate the presence of starch.

It may be useful to show the starch-iodine reaction first by adding iodine solution to starch paste in a test tube. To make the role of light in starch-making more graphic, cover (Fig. 3-16) portions of one of the leaves to be tested with thin cork, carbon paper, or aluminum-foil discs for a few days before the leaves are taken from the plant. The covered portions will show little or no starch reaction.

The oxygen byproduct of photosynthesis can be demonstrated by setting water plants (either native or pet-store kinds or both) in a tumbler

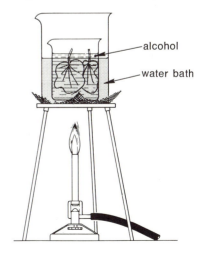

FIGURE **3-15** Apparatus for removing chlorophyll from green leaves.

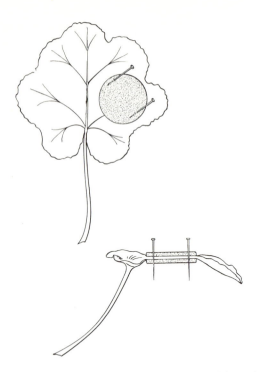

FIGURE **3-16** Method of covering leaf with thin cork, carbon paper, or aluminum foil disks.

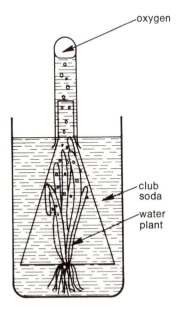

FIGURE **3-17** Method of collecting oxygen given off by plant.

of water on a sunny window sill. The bubbles that appear on the plant are, of course, oxygen. This may be tested for with the laboratory test for oxygen (Chapter 10) or as follows (Fig. 3-17). Place a water plant in soda water (club soda) to provide carbon dioxide. (Allow the soda water to stand open $\frac{1}{2}$ hour before using.) Put the vessel containing the plant in sunlight and invert a glass funnel over the plant. Fill the funnel tube with water. Fill the test tube with water and invert over the funnel tube. The bubbles of oxygen from the plant will rise and collect in the test tube. Light an end of a wooden applicator, blow out the flame quickly, remove the test tube, and insert the glowing tip of the applicator. The oxygen in the tube should relight the flame.

In those parts of the country where autumn is announced with a defiant splash of color, children may become very conscious of tree leaves. A fine display can be collected easily. Leaves may be preserved for a time by ironing them between two layers of waxed paper (covered with newspaper to absorb excess wax) or by dipping them in melted paraffin. (Caution: Never melt paraffin over direct flame; use a double boiler or water-bath arrangement over slow heat.) The leaf may also be glued to tagboard and covered with clear "contact" paper.

At the end of each leaf stock (petiole) is a corky layer that seals off the leaf from the parent tree. Close examination will disclose a knobby bundle of scars where the food and water "pipes" entered the leaf.

A discussion of what would happen if leaves did not fall can be instructive. Children may share experiences concerning the weight of snow, and speculation on what snow would do to leaves, and whether deciduous trees could bear the weight of snow if they kept their leaves. Some may have noticed how rigid and often upturned are the branches of most deciduous trees (see below), while Christmas tree (coniferous) branches are limber and more often horizontal, so that they can bend without breaking to drop a load of snow.

Freeze some soil to illustrate how winter locks water away from plants.

Flowers and Seeds

In the higher plants, flowers are the reproductive structure that usually enclose the fruit and/or seeds, the latter containing the actual embryo plant.

In general children should be encouraged to look at flowers rather than to collect them. After determining the scarce varieties, which should be left to grow, have children collect and press a few common flowers or weeds, spreading one of each kind on a 3 × 5 card. Cover completely with clear cellophane tape in order to retain color and form. (Entrancing art work may emanate from a study of common weeds.)

As seed planting is associated with spring, so seed gathering comes with fall. The children may construct a display of seeds from the grocery or pet store. Fall is the season for collecting wild seeds such as burdock or sticktight seeds. Dragging a cloth through a weed patch, will often produce a number of varieties. Store the seeds in cellophane bags marked with location and general description of plant and possible identification. Children will often recognize bases on which to sort seeds—for example, according to the ways seeds travel (by air, water, wind, animals, gravity, etc.). Analogies can be drawn between fliers' parachutes and the mechanics of distribution of airborne types such as dandelion seeds; maple seeds whirl earthward like the blade of a helicopter. The "parachute" material making up the "itching powder" in sycamore seed balls should be examined and discussed. The number of seeds in a ball might be estimated and then counted. Other plants that produce multiple seeds as survival "insurance" may be found. One should call children's attention to the economy of arrangement and beauty of design of seeds in a milkweed or jacaranda (subtropical tree) pod. Also noteworthy is the elastic attachment of seeds in the magnolia "cone," which lengthens as the seed ripens, permitting it to swing and scatter farther from the parent tree.

FIGURE **3-18**   (a) Pistillate and (b) staminate blossoms of the pussy willow.

(a)   (b)

The embryo plant lies within every seed with its food supply (cotyledons). Soak corn, peas, and bean or pumpkin seeds overnight and with the fingernail remove what was the hard outer coat. Then remove the cotyledons and plant the embryo (preferably in planter mix). Have children consider the considerable energy needed to split the hard coat and push the new plant up through the ground (see p. 52).

A temporary seed box may be made from a half-gallon milk carton as described above, under *Geotropism and Hydrotropism* (Fig. 3-13). Plant seeds at different depths against the glass. Keep the glass covered with dark paper or cloth, and cover the box with cellophane to retain moisture until seeds have sprouted. Record the time required for seeds at different depths to send shoots up to ground level. Plant other seeds at normal depth in the rear of the seed box, and periodically dig up one or two seedlings to observe development. A partially sprouted avocado seed, suspended broad side down in water, and kept in a warm, dark place and watered regularly, will develop roots when it should be transplanted to soil. (See under *Plants from Seed*, above, for other details of planting seeds.)

TREES

Some plant study activities are more easily motivated in fall than at other seasons. Early September days at school may be quite warm, making school seem all the more confining to children who have had three months of freedom. Outdoor tree study may reduce restlessness in addition to broadening understanding and appreciation.

A useful exercise is to bring in one leaf or small branch each from five to ten selected trees, and have teams of two to three children find the tree from which each leaf was picked. When all trees have been located and leaves or branches matched, the class may then make the rounds together to give each team a chance to prove its "match" and impart other details about its tree. (Such a tree-matching game would, of course, be limited to the school grounds or some small area where children can be supervised and safe from traffic hazards.)

As children learn to identify trees around the school, they may wish to make a plant map of the school grounds. This might lead to suggestions for further planting, especially for a mulberry tree to provide food for silkworms in spring (Chapter 2). In the East, fall is a very good time for transplanting trees and shrubs. The National Audubon Association provides lists of shrubs and trees containing fruits attractive to wild birds.

The tree-matching activity may be reinforced by the making of blueprints (Chapter 10) of a tree leaf. Spatter-printing and sketching are also enjoyable ways of becoming familiar with tree leaves. Sketches should be dated and filed for comparison with sketches to be made in winter or spring. (For forms of leaf distribution on the twig see above under *Leaves and Photosynthesis*.) Twigs such as those of the pussy willow, forced indoors in late winter, may sprout roots. These should be put in soil, making sure to trim the cut ends under water to reopen food- or water-conduction tissue sealed by exposure to air. Pussy willow catkins under a magnifying glass should show flowers (Fig. 3-18). All trees have two kinds of flowers or two kinds of parts to each flower. Look for male and female flowers on evergreens. (The scent of fragrant tree flowers such as Norway maple set on an open window sill may draw bees.)

Coniferous Trees (Evergreens)

The evergreens are cone-bearing (coniferous) trees. Green evergreen cones brought indoors will dry, allowing the seeds to drop out. Have children observe the "wing" on each seed and the "nest" or special place for each seed on the bract scales (Fig. 3-19). Compare the naked seeds typical of cone-bearing trees to the enclosed seeds of flowering plants. The Angiosperms, or enclosed-seed plants, represent the most recent and dominant stage of plant evolution.

Most dry, open evergreen cones take on a polished appearance if heated in a very low oven (about 150°F). (They should be placed on news-

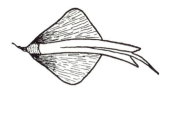

FIGURE **3-19** Bract scale and seed from a Douglas fir.

paper to catch excess pitch.) The polished look is due to the fact that the heat brings the resin to the surface.

The fact that evergreen needles are really leaves should be made clear.

Deciduous Trees

Deciduous trees (those that shed their leaves periodically) reveal their true shape in winter. Weather permitting, children can sketch outlines of the same school yard trees they drew in early fall (see p. 64). Buds, bud scales, leaf scars, and bundle scars observed in the fall should be re-examined in the winter.

WATER PLANTS

Many plants grow wholly or partly in water. Algae, which make up the scum in an unbalanced aquarium (Chapter 1) or in a pond, generally occur as green cells (Chapter 4) singly or in chains. Common algae are desmids and spirogyra (Fig. 3-20). The single celled dia-

FIGURE **3-20** Common types of algae: (a) and (b) desmids, single-celled species, occur in a variety of shapes; (c) spirogyra, a filamentous species composed of cells linked in chains.

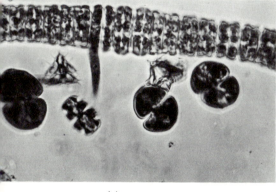

(a)

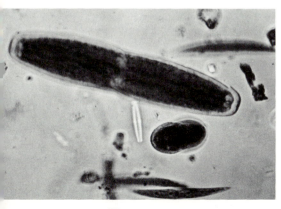

(b)

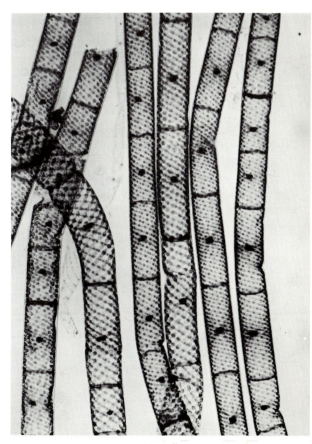

(c)

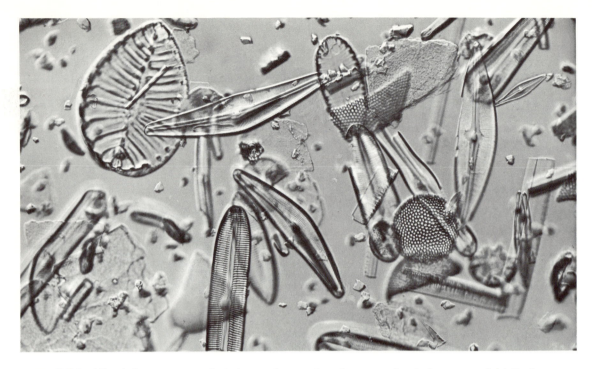

FIGURE **3-21** Mixed diatoms, one-celled plants whose cell walls are made of glassy material (silica).

toms (Fig. 3-21), generally transparent or light amber, occur in a wide variety of forms. In large masses they make brook beds and water weeds golden brown.

Children may preserve seaweed, especially the filamentous or branched forms, by mounting them on paper. Float the seaweed in a shallow pan and slip white drawing paper under it. Separate the strands of seaweed, center them on the paper, and drain off water. The gelatin in the seaweed makes it adhere to the paper as it dries.

Eelgrass and pondweeds live completely in water and send leaves near the surface for light (for photosynthesis). Cattails have their stems in the water and their leaves in the air. Duckweed (Fig. 3-22) and giant kelp float free on the surface. Water lilies and arrowroot have surface leaves and submerged stems. The leaves of the water lilies grow in a mosaic arrangement (Fig. 3-23) that gains maximum exposure to sunlight. Children may consider why stomata (see above) are not found on the undersurface of lily pads.

The insect-eating habits of bog plants such as sundew and pitcher plant can be observed at first hand in a bog terrarium (see above).

Though not water plants, liverworts (Fig. 3-24a) and mosses, which grow in mat-like clusters, are generally found close to the edges of streams or in other damp and shady places. The more highly evolved mosses can grow further away from water. Though they will not grow in a terrarium, liverworts can be grown as shown in Fig. 3-24b.

NONGREEN PLANTS

There is a whole array of plants that do not have the all-important green matter, chlorophyll. Therefore, like animals, they are dependent upon other plants (or animals) for food. Some are parasitic, surviving on living tissue and many are saprophytes, deriving food-energy from dead plant tissue.

These nongreen plants range from microscopic one-celled yeast and even smaller bacteria cells to molds and mildews visible through a hand glass (Chapter 4). Mushrooms and fungi, the giants of the species, are still rather small compared to green plants, with their more highly developed vascular structure and adaptation for reproduction. Mushrooms, in common with molds, reproduce by spores. Spores are minute bodies sometimes acting as a resting stage, carrying the plant over hard times. Bacteria reproduce by fission or splitting, although they form spores when conditions for growth are not normal. Bacteria are usually spread in the spore stage.

Although mold is regarded as undesirable in the home, if it were not for molds and bacteria there would be no formation of organic material to rebuild the soil. Leaves would fall and never disintegrate into leaf mold, or humus. To prove that spores of molds and other plants are floating about, try growing mold gardens on bread. Exposing them to air as little as possible, place one slice of bread in a sandwich bag (and keep in a dark place) and one slice in a covered box or dish where it will get light or sunlight (as on a

FIGURE **3-22** Duckweed, small floating plants with dangling rootlets.

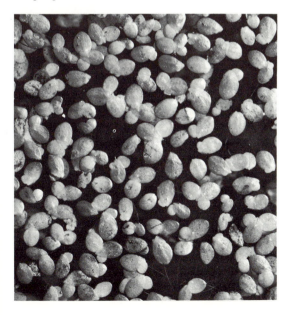

FIGURE **3-23** Lily pads, showing mosaic leaf arrangement.

window sill). Expose a third slice of bread to air in the classroom for half a day and then put in a warm dark place. Place a fourth slice in an *open* saucer or box top and allow it to dry out. Since dampness, warmth, and the absence of light promote the growth of mold, a flourishing mold garden should eventually develop on the third slice of bread. Examine with a hand lens or microscope. It may be necessary to rerun the experiment because it is difficult to place the first and second slices in containers without momentary exposure to mold spores and other bodies in the air.

To illustrate the principle of infection, pierce a moldy spot on some decayed fruit with a needle first sterilized in flame or alcohol. Then pierce the skin of unblemished fruit with the same needle. Put the fruit in a warm, dark, damp place and check daily to see if mold forms where the needle pricked the good fruit.

(a)

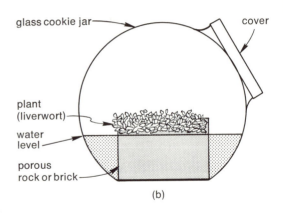

glass cookie jar —— cover

plant (liverwort) ——

water level ——

porous rock or brick ——

(b)

FIGURE **3-24**   (a) Liverwort. (b) Liverwort "in captivity."

Bacteria, like molds, are ever-present in the air. Some cause disease, while others are useful and necessary to mankind. Though very similar to one-celled primitive animals, or protozoans, bacteria are nevertheless nongreen plants. Bacteria gardens for classroom study may be grown using Pyrex Petri dishes and nutrient agar solutions, sterilizing the agar by heating in the Petri dish in a pressure cooker. Observations and conclusions about bacteria may also be drawn from solid media such as white potatoes. Sterilize by boiling a pair of Mason or screw-top jars big enough to accommodate the potatoes. Have two children—one with carefully washed hands and fingernails, and the other with dirty hands and fingernails—peel one potato each. The child with clean hands must not even touch the doorknob until the potatoes have been peeled and placed inside the jars with covers sealed. Place both jars in a warm dark place and observe daily. (It would be advisable to prepare cultures in several jars.) The potato peeled by the more casual subject should develop a mass of mold and bacteria colonies (and promote considerable hand-washing). Interest in colonies of microorganisms may develop from laying a hair on a slice of potato or letting a fly walk over the potato before it is placed in the jar.

FIGURE **3-25**   Diagram of pond plants. In the background are the emergent water plants: 1, pickerel weed; 2, cattails; 3, bulrush; 4, burreed; 5, water plantain; 6, arrowhead. In the foreground are the floating-leaved plants: 7, lily pads; 8, hornwort; 9, spatterdocks; 10, eelgrass; and 11, pondweed. Also in the foreground are the submerged plants: 12, Riccia; 13, bladderwort; and 14, water milfoil.

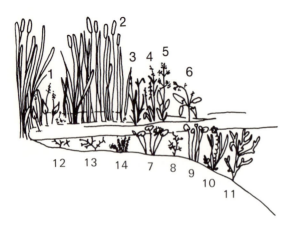

PLANT ZONES

Characteristic plants are indicators of life zones or belts. In the mountains, the vegetation and associated animal life changes as the altitude changes. (The main determinant appears to be mean average temperature.)

Children can sketch or map the plant zones around the nearest body of water. A mural in cross-section could show how plants continually invade or infiltrate water (Fig. 3-25). Eventually, living plants and plant debris will choke up a small pond, and the overflow water will eventually seek another depression, where the process of plant succession will be repeated.

The plant and associated animal zones found with changes in altitude—as on a mountain—can be shown by inserting, in slits cut into a large, shallow stiff-paper cone, bits of plants characteristic of the various altitudes, which can also be marked on the cone.

SUGGESTED PROJECTS

1. Note which plants florists keep out of their window. (They are probably the shade-lovers such as fern and philodendron.)

2. Plan for spring-flowering bulbs. (Bulbs for indoor forcing are usually advertised by Thanksgiving. Reading planting directions and writing for bulbs and materials offer language lessons. Consult a local nurseryman for details.

3. With a hand glass, sort and examine a teaspoon of mixed seed. Illustrate the range in size of seeds from coconut, say to pansies.

4. Collect and examine perennial weeds that grow through the winter in green rosettes close to the ground. (Often found in places such as vacant lots are yarrow, mullein, Queen Anne's lace, field daisies, dandelions, St-John's-wort, and Pennyroyal.)

5. Test soils for alkalinity or acidity. Use litmus or inexpensive soil-testing kits available from a nursery or from science supply houses. (Soils from such places as swamps and moist woodland will usually show an acid reaction; normal soils tend to be slightly alkaline.)

BIBLIOGRAPHY

(**P** indicates recommended for primary grades, **I** for intermediate grades, **U** for upper grades.)

Baker, Samm, *The Indoor and Outdoor Grow-it Book*, Random, 1966. Clear, concise information and instruction on growing plants. Large drawings illustrate the simple materials and experiments. **U**

Barr, George, *Research Adventures for Young Scientists*, McGraw-Hill, 1964. Science concepts arranged in ten categories. Experiments suggested. **U**

Blough, Glenn O., *Discovering Plants*, McGraw-Hill, 1966. Analysis of the parts of a plant from the roots up. Drawings enhance the text and illustrate the easy experiments. **U**

———, *Tree on the Road to Turntown*, McGraw-Hill, 1953. Interrelations in nature illustrated by life cycle of an oak tree. **I**

———, *Wait for the Sunshine*, McGraw-Hill, 1954. The concept of photosynthesis; illustrated. **P**

Bulla, Clyde, *Flowerpot Gardens*, Crowell, 1967. Twenty plants suitable for flowerpot gardens are described, with simple directions for their selection and care. **U**

Bush-Brown, Louise, *Young America's Garden Book*, Scribners, 1962. Gardening as a science is discussed; extensive charts and lists of plants are included, and projects suggested. **U**

Collier, Ethel, *Who Goes There in My Garden?*, W. R. Scott, 1963. Scientific concepts relating to seasonal changes and the interrelationships of soil, sun, water, insects, and plant life. **P**

Cooke, Emogene, *Fun-Time Window Garden*, Children's Pr., 1957. Growing house plants from slips and seeds. **I**

Cooper, Elizabeth, *Insects and Plants; the Amazing Partnership*, Harcourt, Brace & World, 1963. Stimulates independent observation. Well illustrated with clear drawings. **U**

Darby, Gene, *What Is a Tree?*, Benefic, 1957. Tree physiology and development. **P**

Dickinson, Alice, *First Book of Plants*, Watts, 1953. Good section on physiology. Some experiments. **I**

Downer, Mary L., *The Flower*, W. R. Scott, 1955.

Cross section shows step-by-step changes in the seed; illustrated. **P**

Earle, Olive L., *Strangler Fig and Other Strange Plants*. Morrow, 1967. Introductory material covering exotic forms of plants in partnership with other forms of life. Clear illustrations. **I**

Farb, Peter, *The Forest*, Silver Burdett, 1964. Simplified and shortened adaptation from the Life Nature Library volume of the same title. **U**

Goldin, Augusta, *Where Does Your Garden Grow?*, Crowell, 1967. Important concepts of good and poor soil, what makes topsoil, and what humus is. Plants that grow in both kinds of soil are described. **I**

Hammond, Winifred, *The Riddle of Seeds*, Coward-McCann, 1964. Seeds and their importance to man. Includes projects and suggested experiments. Encourages use of scientific methods. Illustrated with photographs and diagrams. **I**

Hutchins, Ross E., *Lives of an Oak Tree*, Rand McNally, 1962. Sprouting, growth, maturing, and death and decay of an oak tree. Well illustrated. **U**

Jordan, Helene, *How a Seed Grows*, Crowell, 1960. Clear and amusing illustrations, and easy text with instructions for a home demonstration. **P**

————, *Seeds by Wind and Water*, Crowell, 1962. A very simple introduction to plant life, emphasizing the mobility of seeds of various plants. **I**

Kirkus, Virginia, *First Book of Gardening*, Watts 1953. Detailed information. **I**

Learner, Sharon, *I Found a Leaf*, Lerner, 1964. Identifies twelve common trees by the texture and outline of their leaves. Unusual, with distinctive art work and creative approach to science. **U**

Lubell, Winifred, *Green Is for Growing*, Rand McNally, 1964. Information on many kinds of plant life—algae, moss, ferns, grasses, wild flowers, vines, shrubs, and trees. **I**

Milne, Lorus and Margery, *Because of a Tree*, Atheneum, 1963. Introduction to ecology stressing the interdependence of plant and animal life. Diverse trees such as the palm, the sugar maple, the redwood, the bald cypress, and the suguaro are included. **U**

Poole, Lynn, *Insect-Eating Plants*, Crowell, 1963. Venus' flytraps, the sundews, the bladderworts, pitcher plants, and some fungi are described. Directions for obtaining specimens and growing them in a terrarium included. Many black and white illustrations. **U**

Riedman, Sarah R., *Naming Living Things; The Grouping of Plants and Animals*, Rand McNally, 1963. Principles of biological classification according to organic likenesses and differences explained with examples and illustrations. **U**

Selsam, Millicent, *Milkweed*, Morrow, 1967. Growth and reproduction of the milkweed plant. Animal-plant relationships and possible uses of the plant discussed. An outstanding presentation of plant fertilization. **I**

————, *Plants that Move*, Morrow, 1962. The author's earlier titles, *Play with Leaves and Flowers* and *Play with Vines*, reissued in a single volume with one page of additional material on seeds. **I**

————, *Play with Plants*, Morrow, 1949. How to grow plants indoors from roots, stems, leaves, and seeds. **I**

————, *Play with Seeds*, Morrow, 1957. Development and dispersal of seeds from various plants. Simple experiments suggested. Illustrated and indexed. **I**

————, *Play with Trees*, Morrow, 1951. How a tree grows, how to grow a tree, and how to recognize each kind by its shape, bark, buds, and leaves. Illustrated. **I**

————, *Seeds and More Seeds*, Harper & Row, 1959. A boy learns by experimentation what seeds are, how they grow, where they come from, and how they are dispersed. **P**

Stefferud, Alfred, *The Wonders of Seeds*, Harcourt, 1956. Examines the formation, structure, and germination of seeds. The work of plant breeders. Activities suggested. **I**

Sterling, Dorothy, *The Story of Mosses, Ferns, and Mushrooms*, Doubleday, 1955. Remarkable microphotos and clear, strong text about less familiar plants. **I**

Wall, Gertrude W., *Gifts from the Grove*, Scribners, 1955. The story of citrus growing, processing, and transportation. **I**

Webber, Irma E., *Bits that Grow Big*, W. R. Scott, 1949. Growth of plants from seeds and cuttings. Experiments illustrate growth factors. **P**

————, *Travelers All*, W. R. Scott, 1944. Plant dispersal. **P**

————, *Up Above and Down Below*, W. R. Scott, 1943. Plant dispersal and root development. **P**

Wood, Dorothy, *Plants with Seeds*, Follett, 1963. Abundant illustrations show a variety of plants, including the grasses, trees, vegetables, fruit, and berries. **I**

Zim, Herbert, *What's Inside of Plants?*, Morrow, 1952. Elementary botany. **I**

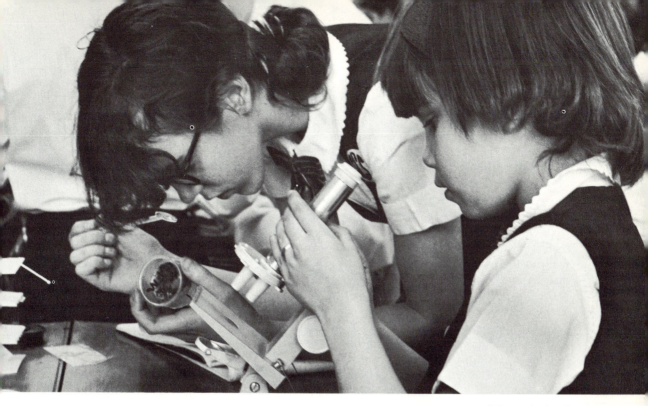

Using a simple microscope.

4 *Minute Worlds*

A provocative exercise for children is to imagine how things would look to Lilliputians in a grassroot jungle. The breathing pores or spiracles of a grasshopper (Fig. 2-12), for example, minute pests on indoor plants and animals, and bud scales and leaf scars of twigs in winter may be seen best with a hand glass. Use of magnifying glasses and a microscope adds a dimension to classroom science and can lead into an interest in magnification and the microscopic world in general. Inexpensive plastic magnifying glasses can be purchased in variety stores.

SIMPLE MAGNIFIERS

An optometrist may provide convex lenses from which the children can make magnifying glasses, or one may use a pair of discarded eyeglasses made to correct farsightedness. To make a magnifier, fill one lens to the brim with water. Cover with a second lens and tape the two together at the rim with cellophane tape (Fig. 4-1), leaving only a small hole as shown in the figure. Fill the remaining space with a medicine dropper, and seal. Type, such as that in a newspaper, can be magnified by viewing it through a drop of water placed on it. (Cover the paper with plastic-film wrap to keep the water from soaking into it.) The transparent lens center, cut from the eye of a pig or other animal (available from a local butcher), will work in the same way. A large hand magnifying glass is always useful in the classroom. The common tripod magnifier and hand lens often used by botanists are difficult for young children to focus.

MICROSCOPES

Glass-Bead Device

A working model of the original microscope invented by Leeuwenhoek can be made in the classroom (Fig. 4-2). Needed are a $2 \times 3 \times \frac{1}{4}$ inch sheet of plywood or other wood, a piece of soft wood, a 2- or $2\frac{1}{2}$-inch-long $\frac{6}{32}$ machine screw, some wood screws or small nails, and a solid glass bead. A pound of such beads, available from scientific supply houses, the local high school chemistry department, or a laboratory, will provide hundreds of simple lenses of great magnifying power. Suitable plastic (Lucite) beads, $\frac{3}{8}$ inch in diameter, are also available at a cost of about $11 per hundred. Drill a $\frac{1}{4}$-inch-diameter hole as shown in Fig. 4-2. Force one of the glass beads into this hole, with the flatter faces of the beads parallel to the front and back of the board. Cut a 1-inch cube of soft wood, drill a $\frac{1}{8}$-inch hole $\frac{1}{4}$ inch from one edge, and attach it with nails or screws as shown. Thread the screw or bolt into the $\frac{1}{8}$-inch hole. Put a drop of pond or aquarium water on the end of the screw, place the lens to the eye, and adjust the screw until algae or microscopic protozoans in the water can be seen. Filed to a point, the screw can be used to hold nontransparent objects for examination.

Selection and Use of Instrument

A good low-power ($100\times$ magnification) microscope (Fig. 4-3) is usually a better investment than the so-called toy microscopes. (The magnifi-

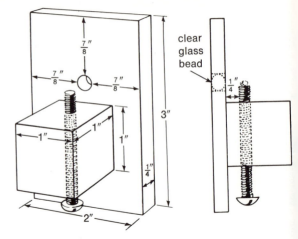

FIGURE **4-2** Front and side views of glassbead microscope.

cation of which a microscope is capable can be ascertained by multiplying the figure (followed by an $\times$) on the eyepiece by that—also followed by an $\times$—on the objective. A biology teacher can be helpful in the selection of one. Projecting the eyepiece image on the ceiling or on a side screen (described below) will permit the whole class to participate in use of the microscope.

Many children *can* be taught the use and care of a microscope for individual viewing. For such use, place the microscope on a window sill, where the mirror under the stage can pick up strong daylight, but not direct sunlight. It may be safer to use the microscope on a table with a desk lamp as light source. In either case, adjust the substage mirror until it reflects the light so that it is visible through the eyepiece as a bright circle. Place a glass slide (Fig. 4-4), or any small piece of glass, on the stage (Fig. 4-3), making sure the material to be examined is *directly* under the lens. Most beginners place too much material on the slide, producing opacity. Use of the merest shred of material or focusing on its edge gives best results. Slowly and carefully lower the lens with the focusing knob (Fig. 4-3) until the objective *almost touches* the slide. Focus by turning the knob to *raise* the lens slowly until the image is sharp. Never attempt to focus by lowering the lens; always start by bringing the lens *close* to the

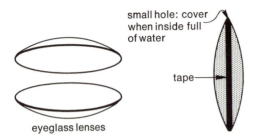

FIGURE **4-1** Water-drop lens. When filled with water, close-fitting eyeglass lenses or other convex glasses blend light rays to produce magnification.

material on the slide, and then raise it to focus. After focusing, readjust the mirror for maximum light. Clean slides either by breathing on them and wiping with a soft cloth, or by wiping with a cloth saturated with rubbing alcohol.

MATERIAL FOR MICROEXAMINATION

Green Plants

Beginners are often disappointed by what they can see with a microscope because they try to look at material which is too thick or too large. Plant cells may be seen to advantage in a tiny,

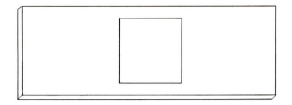

FIGURE **4-4**   Glass slide with cover glass in center. The cover glass may be round.

thin piece of onion skin. To obtain a slice suitable for viewing, make a razor cut anywhere on the onion. Starting from the cut, peel off the thinnest possible layer. With a tweezer or needle, place the onion on a slide and, with a medicine dropper, add one drop of water. Lower a cover slip (Fig. 4-4) onto the water. If cover slips are not available, do not use water, but replace the specimen every ten to fifteen minutes with a fresh one. If the piece in focus is sufficiently thin, rectangular or brick-like cells will be visible. The pieces of onion skin may be stained with a drop of dilute iodine solution or food coloring. About five minutes after staining, each cell nucleus, a small round body, should become visible.

Microprojector

If a lantern-slide projector is available, a microscope can be adapted as a microprojector at no cost (Fig. 4-5). Remove the eyepiece lens from the microscope and the front lens from the projector. Focus the light beam from the projector on the microscope mirror. Place a slide on the stage and adjust the mirror until a spot of light shows on the ceiling or, depending on the arrangement, on a screen that is on a wall, freestanding, or part of a carton, as shown in Fig. 4-5. (The carton, necessary if the room cannot be darkened, is opened at one end, the four flaps braced open to act as a shadow shield, and a translucent screen of tracing paper or tracing cloth attached across the opening. The carton can be placed on the teacher's desk, with the screen facing the class.) Adjust the position of the projector until the cone of light from it just fills the mirror. (Check this by tapping a cloud of chalk

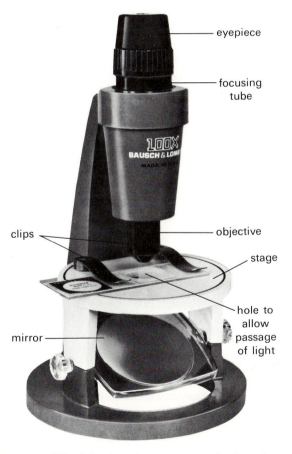

FIGURE **4-3**   A beginner's microscope. Such an instrument, with a magnification of 100–200–300 X, may be purchased for about $20.

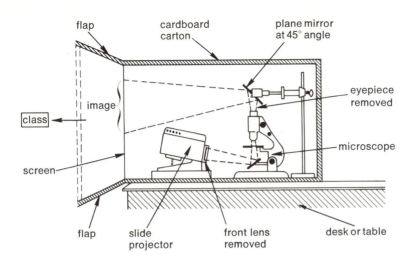

FIGURE **4-5** Microprojector shown for use in daylight. Without the cardboard container, the same projector can be used to throw an enlarged image on a wall or free-standing screen (or, without the plane mirror, on the ceiling) in a darkened room.

dust from a blackboard eraser to make the cone more readily visible.) Then focus on the specimen, using the low-power objective. A clear enlarged image will be visible on the ceiling or screen.

Leaves Kalanchoe or peperomia plants, carried by most florists, show interesting leaf structure under a microscope. (Although Kalanchoe is preferable, either plant will do.) Tear a leaf in half. Some of the lower layer will adhere to the underside, or skin, of the leaf. Remove this with tweezers and place on a slide. With careful focusing, one may see the stomata (Greek, "little mouths") through which air enters and leaves a leaf. Each stoma is made up of two lip-like parts

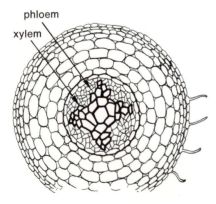

FIGURE **4-6** Carrot conducting tissue, which may be seen with aid of a microscope.

called guard cells. In dry weather the stomata are only slight parted, limiting loss of water (see Chapter 3).

Microscopic examination of stomata from two plants of the same species, but one unwatered for a week, will show those of the watered plant open, and those of the dry plant closed.

The microscope shows skin cells, but no stomata, on the top surface of Kalanchoe leaves. Water lilies have stomata on the upper surface only, which is functional for reasons that children may be able to deduce. Grasses have them on both sides of the blade. Most plants have stomata on the underside of the leaf.

Roots Using a razor blade, make an exceedingly thin cross section of a carrot. Under a microscope, one can see the tubes or conducting tissue (Fig. 4-6) that carry water and minerals up (xylem tissue) and food down (phloem cells).

Spores The spore cases of ferns are interesting brownish structures found on the underside of the fronds in summer and fall. Under magnification these spore cases look very different from the way they appear to the naked eye. Individual spores are so small that they are hard to observe under low magnification. Plants related structurally to ferns, such as ground pine, horsetail, or scouring rush, shake out a yellow powder when the spore cases are mature, and are worth a closer look. Spores from the strange-looking horsetail have an interesting projectile device wrapped around

Courtesy Carolina Biological Supply Company

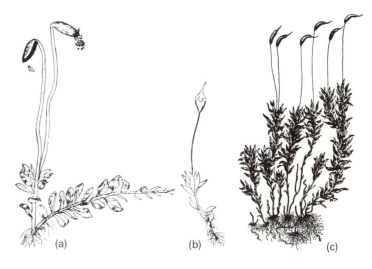

FIGURE **4-7** *Polytrichum* (left) and three common mosses related to *Polytrichum* (below): (a) *Mnium affine;* (b) *Physcomitrium pyriforme;* (c) *Catharinea undulata.*

(a) (b) (c)

them, which can be seen in magnification. When weather is right for the spores to germinate, this structure uncoils and propels the spore as far as possible from the parent plant.

Primitive green plants such as mosses, liverworts, and lichens bear spores instead of seeds. Under magnification the fruiting bodies are interesting and different: Polytrichum, or haircap moss (Fig. 4-7), for example, carries its spores in a bell-shaped cap that has an opening that locks and, when it is time for the spores to scatter, works like the top of a pepper shaker. Liverworts are often found along streams. The odd-shaped fruiting bodies (Fig. 4-8) called gemmae cups grow in the center of the leaf-shaped thallus.

Aquarium plants A balanced aquarium may be a rich source of microscopic plant life. Green scum on the sides of the tank or in the water is composed of the primitive green plants called algae. Under the microscope they may appear as threadlike plants composed of chains of boxlike cells. The tiny green bodies in the cells are chloroplasts, which contain chlorophyll. Most

FIGURE **4-8** Liverwort, showing parasol-like antheridia from which spores drop into gemmae cups (at center).

pond scum contains more than one kind of green alga and some interesting single-celled plants called diatoms (Fig. 3-21), which look like amber.

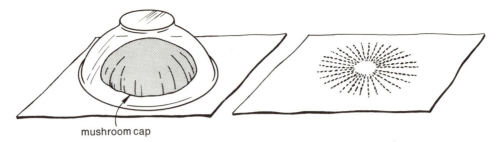

mushroom cap

FIGURE **4-9** Obtaining mushroom spore prints. At left, the covered cap; at right, the spore print.

Motion engendered by life processes is visible inside the leaves of aquarium plants such as *Elodea* and *Vallisneria*. To view this protoplasm in motion inside the living cells, warm a slide in lukewarm water, dry it, and place a leaflet in the center. Add a drop of lukewarm water and a cover slip. The chloroplasts should be visible streaming slowly around inside the cell.

Nongreen Plants

Many species of the nongreen plants (see Chapter 3), which have no chlorophyll, have features that are well-suited to study by microscope or other magnifier—for example, the spore print of a common mushroom, which can be seen well with a hand magnifier. To study the spore print, break off the stem and place the cap, gills down, on a piece of white paper. (With white-spored varieties, use black or brown paper for visual contrast.) Cover with a glass or other bowl for 24–28 hours, then gently remove cover and cap. The spores should have fallen out of the cap to form a radial design (Fig. 4-9) on the paper. The tiny round dots—the spores—are the primitive equivalents of seeds in green plants.

Molds Molds may usually be found growing on dead organic matter (see Chapter 3). The common bread mold (*Rhizopus nigricans*), examined with a hand lens will show a branching system of myceliae, threadlike structures, branches of which extend downward into the food substance and upward to support the spore structures by which the mold reproduces.

Yeast In examining yeast cells, the question of what makes bread rise may come up. It can be answered by the children through an experiment using the main ingredients listed in bread recipes.

Using containers of the same size (for example, pint-sized plastic food containers), introduce into each: water (in a proportion of about nine parts to one of sugar by weight), flour, sugar, and yeast in equal amounts and in the following combinations (which the children may suggest): flour-water, sugar-water, yeast-water, flour-sugar-water, flour-yeast-water, and sugar-yeast-water. If warm water is used, bubbles should soon appear in the mixtures containing yeast; the yeast-sugar mixture should show the most change. In about two hours, a drop of this mixture examined under the microscope should show cells budding (Fig. 4-10) to form new cells. (Use one yeast cake

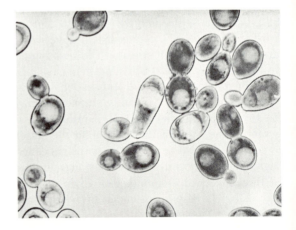

FIGURE **4-10** Yeast cells budding after standing in warm sugar-water solution. The cells are usually colorless.

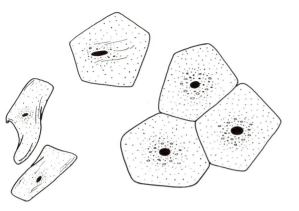

FIGURE **4-11** Epithelial cells from the lining of the mouth.

for each mixture for fast action. The mixtures without yeast will show no change.)

Bacteria Bacteria, like molds, are ever-present in the air but invisible except when in large colonies. Thus, while bacteria *colonies* and growing yeast are easily seen, individual yeast or bacteria cells require high-power magnifications—up to 1000 ×. Bacteria colonies are slick-looking patches of yellow-orange or other bright-colored growth in contrast to those of mold, which are generally furry-looking and black, white, or grey.

A school doctor or nurse may be able to provide slides of common disease bacteria. That boiling kills most bacteria may be inferred from the fact that a few drops of egg white dropped into boiling water coagulate almost immediately. Egg white, like bacteria, is mostly protein. One can also show this by examining a drop of water from a fish tank under a microscope. Note the tiny protozoans (see below), then boil some water from the same tank and examine a drop; the microorganisms will be dead (no movement).

That all bacteria are not harmful can be made clear by microscopic examination of the amazing nitrogen-fixing bacteria, which can be found in the small lumps or nodules on the roots of any leguminous plants such as clover, alfalfa, or peas. It would be useful to refer at this point to the role of the wonder-plant *Penicillium* (from which penicillin is derived) and related microorganisms in the control of other microbes.

Animal Tissue

Human cells Cells from the human body offer another interesting subject for microscopic examination. A safe, readily available source of body cells is the lining of the mouth. Rub the inside of the cheek with the tip of a sterile tongue depressor (available from a school nurse) and then touch the tip to the center of a slide. Use a medicine dropper to stain the slide with iodine dissolved in water. Under the microscope one should see epithelial cells, which compose the epithelium, the layer of tissue covering the inner and outer body surfaces. The cells are irregular pentagons, as shown in Fig. 4-11.

With the cooperation of school health personnel and the permission of parents, one may make blood smear slides of the children's own blood. (It is illegal and unsafe to have children prick their own fingers for the required blood sample.) Since unstained smears show only red cells, it is necessary to use Wright's, the standard stain, or food coloring. When stained and examined under the microscope, the slides will show larger white cells (or disease fighters) as well as the small, circular red cells and blood platelets (Fig. 4-12).

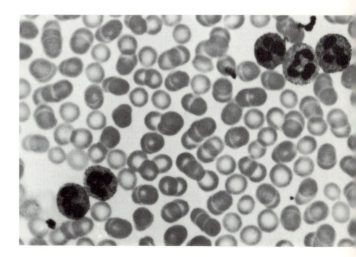

FIGURE **4-12** Human blood, stained with Wright's stain. The many small circular bodies are red cells; the five large dark bodies with complex nuclei are white cells; the three small dark bodies are clusters of blood platelets.

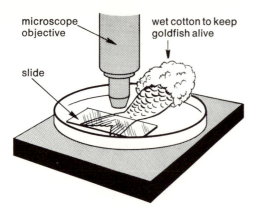

microscope objective

wet cotton to keep goldfish alive

slide

FIGURE **4-13** Observation of blood circulation in the capillaries of a goldfish tail.

Circulating blood To observe circulating blood and living cells in the tail of a goldfish, wrap the fish in wet cotton and place it in shallow water in a glass or plastic saucer (Fig. 4-13). Focus the microscope on the tail, which should have a slide laid across it. The many criss-crossed tiny tubes, or blood capillaries, should be visible. Some of the red corpuscles coursing through the blood vessels will move in one direction, some in another. Because the microscope lens reverses everything (see Chapter 15), the blood that seems to move away from the tail is really moving toward it. This is arterial blood coming from the heart. Blood moving in the opposite direction is traveling through veins back to the heart.

Protozoa Most balanced aquariums contain microscopic one-celled animals, called protozoans, and more complex forms, such as the fairy shrimp, or hydra (Fig. 4-14a). These animals are usually near the food, which sinks to the bottom of the tank. Using a dip tube or medicine dropper bring up water from the bottom of the aquarium and put a drop on a slide. One may see, in addition to the hydra, protozoans such as amoebae, paramecia, and vorticellae (Fig. 4-14b, c, d) as well as single celled or filamentous algae. Under the microscope an amoeba looks like a dab of jelly. Its margins will be seen to bulge, and the cytoplasm flow in the direction of the bulge until the whole animal moves into the bulge. Amoebae

"flow" around their food and reproduce by dividing. Visible in the common slipper-shaped protozoan shown in Fig. 4-14c are two contracting vacuoles, one at either end of the body. Its whole body is covered with *cilia* which it uses for propulsion. The *Euglena* (Fig. 4-14e), which may also be visible, is a borderline case between plant and animal and is classified as both alga and protozoan. It moves by lashing its whip-like *flagellum* appendage.

Instead of using water from a balanced aquarium for a source of protozoans, one may prepare a "hay infusion" culture. To do so, boil about a quart of water. (If it is pond or spring water, the culture may also include some microscopic plants such as filamentous algae and diatoms.) As it comes to a boil, add a handful of timothy hay. Allow it to cool and add five grams of uncooked rice or wheat grains. Let stand undisturbed in semidarkness for a week, at which time a dark area should be visible around the grains of rice. With a dip tube, suck up a drop and spread it on a slide under the microscope.

To start other colonies, put rice grains in another jar of cooled boiled water. Add a dropper of solution from the bottom of the first jar. If pond water is available, compare the kinds of microscopic inhabitants in it with those from the hay infusion. Protozoan cultures are also available from biological supply houses (see Appendix). As in the study of bacteria and molds, one may note (but not overemphasize) the role of protozoans in disease.

Crystals To draw parallels between the worlds of physical and biological science, use the microscope to observe crystals of Epsom salts, table salt, or granulated sugar. Gradually add the salts to half a glass of hot water until no more will dissolve. Dip a paint brush in the solution and "paint" a slide. With the microscope one may watch the crystals form as the water evaporates.

FIGURE **4-14** (a) The hydra, a fresh-water relative of the jellyfish; (b) amoeba; (c) paramecium; (d) the vorticella; (e) euglena.

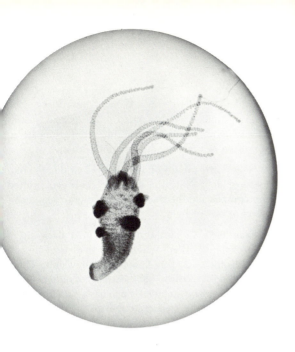

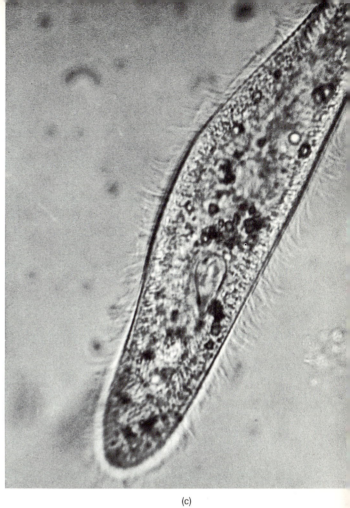

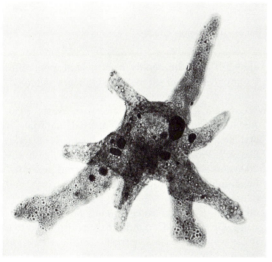

(c)

(e)

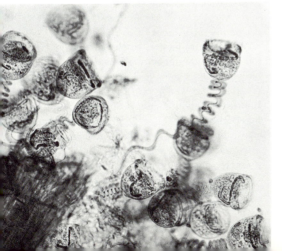

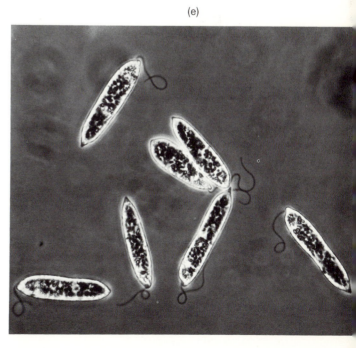

SUGGESTED PROJECTS

1. Examine many familiar objects under magnification—for example, the print in newspapers or books, fabrics, pieces of wood, sugar, soda, a pencil point, etc.

2. Fit a hand glass into a mailing tube or a tube of thick paper. Insert a second hand glass the same size, cutting a slot for the handle so that it can be slid up and down to focus with magnification through the stationary glass. If the second glass is smaller, fit it into another tube smaller than the first and move the smaller tube instead of the glass.

3. Examine a ruler through lenses of different power. For example, with a lens power of 8, a line $\frac{1}{8}$-inch long will appear to be 1-inch long.

4. Under the microscope, examine fingerprints made by using thick washable paint or an ink pad. Determine whether all are different, then study the pattern of skin on the fingers under magnification.

5. Newspaper pictures under magnification are composed of dots. Note the similarity between printed photographs and the way television pictures are composed of bits of light.

6. Examine a radiant watch dial in a dark closet under magnification. When one's eyes become adjusted to the dark, tiny flashes will be visible. These are caused by the fission of the atoms of radiant paint used to coat the watch dial. Each flash is an exploding atom; there is, of course, no danger.

BIBLIOGRAPHY

(**P** indicates recommended for primary grades, **I** for intermediate grades, **U** for upper grades.)

Beeler, Nelson F., *Experiments in Optical Illusion,* Crowell, 1951. How the eye works. **I**
———, *Experiments with a Microscope,* Crowell, 1957. How to grow and study microorganisms. Structure and use of microscopes. **U**
Beeler, Nelson F., and Franklyn M. Branley, *Experiments with Light,* Crowell, 1958. Experiments to explain characteristics of light and principles of optics in lenses, microscopes, and other optical instruments. **U**
Cosgrove, Margaret, *Wonders under a Microscope,* Dodd, Mead, 1959. How to use a microscope. What to look for and how to make and stain slides. **I**
Epstein, Samuel, *Grandpa's Wonderful Glass,* Grossett & Dunlap, 1962. Two children make discoveries about nature when they learn to use a magnifying glass. **P**
Headstrom, Richard, *Adventures with a Hand Lens,* Lippincott, 1962. Fifty investigations that should lead to many more as children learn what to look for. Many detailed black and white drawings. **U**
Kelly, Patricia M., *Mighty Human Cell,* Day, 1967. How human cells live, grow, and multiply. Describes cells in general and specialized cells. Clearly written; new vocabulary in italics. **U**
Kohn, Bernice, *Our Tiny Servants: Molds and Yeasts,* Prentice-Hall, 1962. Several types and their uses,

among them the molds from which penicillin, streptomycin, and other antibiotics are obtained. Illustrated and indexed. **U**
Lewis, Lucia Z., *First Book of Microbes,* Watts, 1955. Accurate, simple, interesting factual material. **I**
Lietz, Gerald S., *Junior Science Book of Bacteria,* Garrard, 1964. The advances in bacteriology in the 300 years since bacteria were discovered presented in simple terms. Illustrated with drawings and diagrams. **I**
Lindemann, Edward, *Water Animals for Your Microscope,* Crowell, 1967. A guide to organisms that live in the water. Discussed by species with each section followed by microscope experiments. **U**
Neurath, Marie, *Too Small to See,* Sterling, 1957. Everyday objects seen through a hand glass. **P**
Payne, Alma, *Discoverer of the Unseen World: A Biography of Antoni Van Leeuwenhoek,* World, 1966. An introduction to the man who laid the foundations for modern protozoology and microbiology. **U**
Perry, John, *Our Wonderful Eyes,* McGraw-Hill, 1955. Information about light and sight, eye structure and function. **I**
Pinney, Roy, *Collecting and Photographing Your Microzoo,* World, 1965. How to collect, raise, study, preserve, and photograph microorganisms. Clear

instructions on equipment, materials, and suppliers. Excellent photographs. **U**

Rogers, Frances, *Lens Magic,* Lippincott, 1957. Story of glass. History of scientists who experimented with microscopes and telescopes. **I**

Schatz, Albert, and Sarah Riedman, *Story of Microbes,* Harper & Row, 1952. A comprehensive account of the role of microbes in everyday life. Several simple experiments. **U**

Schwartz, Julius, *Through the Magnifying Glass,* McGraw-Hill, 1954. Things to look at under magnification with suggestions for further investigation. **I–U**

Selsam, Millicent, *Greg's Microscope,* Harper & Row, 1963. Observing familiar things through the microscope. In story form, and based on principles of teaching science in the primary grades. **P**

————, *Microbes at Work,* Morrow, 1953. The role of microorganisms in soil, food, and the body. Experiments using household equipment. **U**

Showers, Paul, *A Drop of Blood,* Crowell, 1967. What blood is and its importance. Clear and graphic illustrations. **I**

Showers, Paul, *Your Skin and Mine,* Crowell, 1965. The appearance, the function, and the care of the skin. **P**

White, Anne Terry, *Secrets of the Heart and Blood,* Garrard, 1965. The work of the blood in the body, the action of the heart, the body's reactions to injuries, and some important medical discoveries. **U**

Yates, Raymond F., *Fun with Your Microscope,* Appleton, 1953. Excellent handbook for the science-prone. **U**

Parachutists float to earth supported only by the air on which the canopies of their parachutes rest

5 *The Air*

Air is a mixture of many gases, although mostly of oxygen and nitrogen, which make up about 99% of the air—about 21% oxygen and about 78% nitrogen. The remaining 1% includes carbon dioxide and the inert gases—helium, neon, argon, xenon, and krypton. Helium is a very light gas used to lift dirigibles and balloons. It is also mixed with oxygen in place of nitrogen to make "artificial air" used in hospitals and by deep-sea divers. Neon will be well known to children for its use in red "neon" electric signs. Argon is used in electric light bulbs, since, being inactive, it does not readily combine with other elements (see Chapter 10) and so helps prevent the filament in the bulb from decomposing and burning away.

Air also contains varying amounts of water vapor (depending upon weather conditions) and tiny solid particles such as dust and pollen. The particles can easily be illuminated with a beam of light from a flashlight or filmstrip projector in a darkened room. (A ray of sunlight will also show this.) To increase the number of particles visible, have one of the children ruffle his hair vigorously near the beam of light, shake a jacket, sweater, or coat near the beam, or clap two chalkboard erasers together. One may also examine (with a hand magnifying glass or a microscope) the dust that accumulates on a sheet of white paper left for several days in a quiet part of the classroom.

AIR VOLUME

Because air is invisible, children are often unaware that it is a substance and that, like any other substance, it occupies space. To illustrate this, flatten a large, sturdy plastic bag. (Not the kind used for onions or potatoes; these have small holes in them.) Then fill it with blocks of wood or other bulky material, demonstrating how the bag bulges out.

Empty the bag and refill it with water so that it bulges again. Finally, empty the bag again and, gripping it at one side of its mouth, quickly move it through the air. When the bag fills with air, hold it tightly at the neck so that the air will not escape. Call attention to the fact that the bag bulges out just as it did with the other real (but visible) materials.

Also, have a child run across a playground holding in front of his body a square of cardboard, the size of a newspaper (or a double sheet of newspaper opened up). Then have the child run across the playground again without the cardboard. Point out that, when moving, one must push air out of the way and that, because the sheet of cardboard presents more surface, the child carrying the cardboard has more air to push out of the way, and so runs more slowly or with more effort.

Also useful to emphasize that air has substance is the following investigation. Press a crumpled paper napkin or paper towel into the bottom of a glass tumbler so that it remains there when the tumbler is upended. Lower the tumbler, mouth down, to the bottom of an aquarium or large glass jar almost filled with water (Fig. 5-1). (The water will compress some of the air and rise part of the way into the tumbler.) Then lift the tumbler straight out of the water. Keeping it upside down, dry the edges. Then remove the paper napkin and show that it is still dry. Because the tumbler was not empty, but filled with air, the water could not rise all the way into it.

Bubbles under water make the same point. These can be produced with an "empty" bottle lowered into water and then tilted, or by squeez-

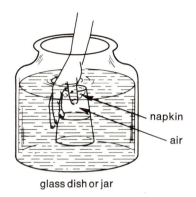

glass dish or jar

FIGURE **5-1** Air preventing water from rising all the way into a tumbler.

ing (under water) a hollow rubber ball with a hole in it or a rubber syringe bulb.

Another way of making air's presence visible: Cover the mouth of a jar of water with cardboard or glass and invert the jar into a pan or dish containing water. Remove the cardboard when the mouth of the jar is below the surface of the water and let the jar stand inverted in the pan. Tilt the jar and place the tip of a medicine dropper under it. Squeeze the bulb of the medicine dropper and watch the bubbles of air move to the top of the jar. Refill the dropper with water and repeat the process several times. Call attention to the fact that as more and more air enters the jar, it occupies space, forcing some of the water out of the jar.

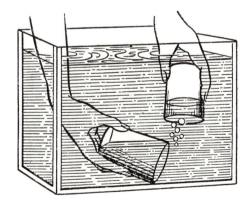

FIGURE **5-2** Transferring air from one glass tumbler to another under water.

To transfer air from one glass tumbler to another (Fig. 5-2), let one tumbler fill with water in an aquarium or large glass jar almost full of water. Then, with its mouth down, hold the tumbler just below the surface of the water.

Lower the second tumbler into the aquarium with its mouth down, bringing its edge under the edge of the tumbler full of water. Then slowly tip the tumbler of air so that air bubbles rise directly into the tumbler of water, where the accumulating air will displace the water.

AIR WEIGHT (PRESSURE)

We live at the bottom of an ocean of air that is at least 500 miles deep. Earth's gravity pulls the air to it, just as it does everything else on earth. Therefore, air has weight. A basketball or football weighed when inflated and again when deflated can demonstrate that air has weight. Use of a sensitive scale or balance can help make the difference graphic.

Although air does not seem to weigh much when compared to other materials, an ocean of air 500 miles deep weighs a great deal. The great weight of air above us exerts a pressure at sea level of 14.7 pounds on each square inch of surface. Point out that one does not notice this pressure because it is exerted equally on the inside and outside of the body. The body doesn't collapse under the weight of the air because of the many inner air spaces. (At very high elevations air pressure is so slight that the body fluids of mammals, if unprotected—as with astronauts' pressure suits—would vaporize.)

To give impact to the idea of air pressure, children need experience with square inches and 15-pound weights. For example, display a square inch of colored paper pasted on the middle of a large white sheet of paper, or estimate 15-pound weights—say of books—and check these on a scale. Or cut out enough inch squares of paper to cover the palm. At 15 pounds per square inch calculate the amount of air pressure on an outstretched hand—about 200 pounds on that of an average sized, middle-grade child. Air

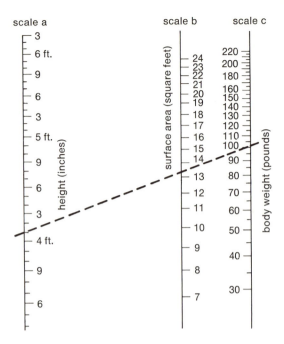

FIGURE **5-3** Nomogram for calculating surface area from height and weight.

pressure is equal in all directions—up, down, and sideways—and is balanced by pressure within the hand. Fig. 5-3 may be used to calculate total air pressure on the body as follows. Draw a straight line between the height, on Scale A, and the weight on Scale C. Note where this intersects Scale B (surface area). Multiply the indicated square feet of body area (in this case, about $13\frac{1}{2}$) by 144, to yield the surface area in square inches. Multiply again by 14.7 or 15 (pounds per square inch) to yield the total air pressure on the body. For the example shown in the figure the calculation for a child 50 inches tall, with a weight of 100 pounds is: $13\frac{1}{2} \times 144 = 1944$; 1944×14.7 = about 28,577 pounds.

The pressure of moving air, as from a fan or pump, is familiar to most children. The pressure of stationary air can be demonstrated in several ways, as follows.

Place a heavy book upright on an empty paper bag and blow hard into the bag. The pressure of the air will cause the book to topple. This can also be demonstrated with a long balloon and a tin can.

One can also demonstrate air pressure as follows. Lay a stick about 2 feet long, 1–2 inches wide, and no thicker than a wooden ruler, on a table with about 8 inches extending beyond the table edge. Cover the part of the stick on the table with two or three sheets of newspaper. Smooth the paper down and, with a hammer or a baseball bat, strike the extended end of the stick sharply. The stick will break because of the weight of the air on the large surface presented by the newspaper. (Inertia, the tendency of a body at rest to stay at rest, is also acting on the stick, tending to keep it from flipping up.)

Under ordinary conditions, air pressure is exerted equally in all directions, demonstrated by the fact that soap bubbles are spherical (if not deformed by air currents). The pressure of the air inside the bubble is acting equally in all directions, as is the air outside the bubble.

This can also be shown with a funnel whose wide end is covered with a piece of rubber from a balloon. Glue or tie the rubber so that it fits snugly. Remove some air from the funnel by sucking at the narrow end, slipping a finger over it to maintain the partial vacuum thus formed. The rubber will then curve inward because the pressure of the air outside the funnel is greater than the air pressure inside. No matter in which position the funnel is held—upward, downward, or sideward—the rubber remains curved inward because the pressure of a gas (air in this case) is exerted equally in all directions.

Like most solids, liquids, and gases, air expands when heated and contracts when cooled. Experiments showing this effect, together with convection currents, are taken up in detail in Chapter 17.

The pressure of the air can be measured; this is taken up in detail in Chapter 7.

Vacuum "Pressure"

When air is removed from a space, leaving nothing in its place, the resulting "empty space" is called a *vacuum*. (Because it is almost impossible to remove all the air, vacuums are only *partial*.) Whenever a vacuum is produced, a difference in air pressure results. This difference in air pressure can be used to move things and produce other effects.

In the seventeenth century, Otto von Guericke, mayor of Magdeburg in Germany, performed an ingenious experiment demonstrating the effect of a vacuum. Two large iron hemispheres, each resembling half a rubber ball, were constructed so that air could be pumped out of the hollow sphere that resulted when they were joined. When von Guericke removed most of the air from the hemispheres, thereby creating a considerable vacuum within the sphere, teams of eight horses on each side were unable to separate the hemispheres.

With most of the air removed from the spheres, there was little air pressure on the inside surface, while, on the outside, atmospheric pressure of about 15 pounds of air was being exerted on each square inch of surface, of which there was a total of about 1200 per hemisphere. (Calculating the total pressure can be a useful arithmetic exercise.) When air was readmitted to the sphere, and air pressure on the inside and outside equalized, the hemispheres parted easily.

Children can, in effect, repeat von Guericke's experiment with two small sink plungers. Moisten the surfaces of both cups (to help seal out the air) and have a child hold the handle of one against the floor or wall. Push one cup against the other to force the air out of both cups (Fig. 5-4). Then have two children try to pull the plungers apart.

Pour a glass of water into a large, clean can with a screw cap. With the cap off, heat the can on an electric hot plate. Boil the water vigorously until steam escapes through the opening. Remove the can from the hot plate (*Caution: It is hot.*) and cap it quickly. The can will collapse and

FIGURE **5-4** Demonstrating effect of a partial vacuum with two sink plungers.

twist out of shape as it cools. If pressed for time, the same effect can be obtained by pouring cold water over the hot can to hasten cooling.

Point out that, before the experiment, air was both inside and outside the can and that heating and subsequent cooling removed the air inside, lowering or reducing the inside air pressure and allowing the greater air pressure on the outside of the can to crumple it. Heating then cooling reduced air pressure as follows: When the water boiled, steam was formed. The steam, occupying space, pushed out some of the air. When the cap was replaced and the can allowed to cool, the steam condensed, leaving less *air* in the can. (The rapid cooling with cold water caused the steam to condense more quickly.)

The effect described above can be accomplished simply with a bicycle-type vacuum pump available from scientific supply houses. (An ordinary bicycle pump may be used if the valve at its base can be reversed.) Connect the pump as shown (Fig. 5-5), using a one-hole rubber stopper that fits the opening in the can, a short piece of glass tubing in the hole, and heavy rubber or plastic tubing running to the pump. Then simply pump the air out of the can. With less air in the can, the air pressure inside becomes lower and the can collapses under the pressure of the air on its outside surfaces.

Still another way employs a 15- to 20-foot piece of rubber or plastic tubing. Attach the tubing (Fig. 5-6) in the same manner as the vacuum pump, using a rubber stopper and a short piece of glass tubing. Fill the can with water,

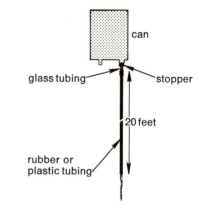

FIGURE **5-6** Evacuating air from a can by use of a long length of water-filled tubing.

put in the stopper with tubing attached, and fill the rubber tubing with water. Fold back the free end of the rubber tubing so that the water will not run out. (A spring-type clothespin can be used as a clamp.)

Place the can on the sill of an upper-floor window with the rubber tubing hanging down to the ground below. When the clamp is released, enough water will run out of the tubing to cause the can to collapse. As the water leaves the can, an empty space in which there is virtually no air (a vacuum) is created. With little or no air pressure on the inside of the can, the external air pressure again causes the can to collapse. (This, in turn, allows more water to flow out, thereby creating a new vacuum, which causes the can to collapse a bit more.)

Children will enjoy the demonstration of vacuum pressure in which a hard-boiled egg is put into a milk bottle. Peel a hard-boiled egg that is slightly larger than the mouth of a milk bottle. Light a twist of paper and, while it is still burning, drop it into the milk bottle and quickly set the peeled egg into the mouth of the milk bottle (Fig. 5-7). Almost as soon as the flame goes out, the egg goes through the neck of the bottle with a loud report.

The burning paper uses some of the oxygen from the air in the bottle and also drives some air out through expansion. With less air in the bottle and, thus, lower air pressure, the air pres-

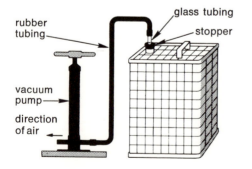

FIGURE **5-5** Evacuating air from a can with a bicycle-type pump.

sure on the outside of the bottle is greater and pushes the egg into the bottle.

To remove the egg, tip the bottle so that the narrower end of the egg rests in the neck. Pressing the mouth firmly against the mouth of the bottle, blow hard into the bottle. This will force air into the bottle until the air pressure inside is greater than that outside, pushing the egg out.

The same demonstration can be done with a partially peeled banana. Leave about two-thirds of the banana unpeeled and insert the peeled end in the bottle mouth. The banana will end in the bottle, completely peeled.

The sink plunger can also be used to illustrate the effects of a partial vacuum in another way: Moisten the rubber cup and press it down firmly on a stool or chair until most of the air in the cup is expelled. The stool can now be lifted with the plunger. Point out that forcing the air out of the cup forms a partial vacuum inside and that greater air pressure on the outside holds the cup firmly to the stool.

Many toys and gadgets use suction cups. One such is the dart gun, which shoots darts that have suction cups instead of points. Some automobile ash trays, which attach to the dashboard with a suction cup, can be used for demonstration in class. Because water evaporates rapidly, try mineral oil or petroleum jelly to seal out the air, and the suction cup will remain attached longer.

Have a child drink some soda (colored) or lemonade through a clear plastic or glass straw.

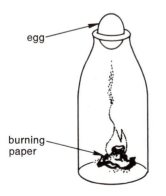

FIGURE **5-7** Arrangement in which a partial vacuum forces an egg into a bottle.

Sucking on the soda straw removes some of the air in it, creating a partial vacuum inside. The air on the surface of the soda, exerting a greater pressure than the air inside the straw, pushes the liquid up the straw. Putting one's tongue quickly to the top of the straw while drinking will make the straw a dip tube (see p. 12). If the straw is inserted into a one-hole rubber stopper fitted tightly into the bottle (or if modeling clay is packed tightly around the straw), it will be impossible to draw the soda up the straw, since no air can enter the bottle and push the soda up the straw.

A partial vacuum is responsible for the action of a medicine dropper, too. When the bulb is squeezed, some of the air is forced out of the dropper, creating a partial vacuum in it and allowing the pressure of the air on the surface of the liquid to push it up into the dropper.

Interaction with Water

The effect of air pressure on water makes possible some interesting demonstrations:

Fill a glass tumbler or bottle with water. Place a square of cardboard over the mouth of the tumbler. While holding the card against the tumbler, invert it. When released, the cardboard will not fall because the weight of water pushing down on it is more than balanced by the pressure of the air against the outer side of the cardboard. (Do this demonstration over a sink or pan.)

Stretch a double layer of cheesecloth over the mouth of a bottle and fasten securely with a rubber band or string. Fill the bottle with water by pouring it through the cheesecloth. Quickly invert the bottle. The pressure of the air prevents the water from flowing out because the interstices of the cheesecloth are small enough so that the effect of surface tension (see Chapter 6) comes into play. The air is thus presented a network of skin-like surfaces (a separate one at each opening in the mesh of the cheesecloth) against which it can exert its pressure. The bottle can be filled through the cheesecloth because the stream of water filling it does not occupy the whole opening, thus leaving a space through

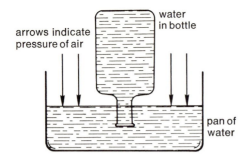

arrows indicate pressure of air

water in bottle

pan of water

FIGURE **5-8** Air pressure preventing bottle of water from emptying into pan.

which the air in the bottle can escape past the entering water.

Place a bottle or tumbler in an aquarium or large pan of water. When the bottle is full, lift it (open end down) until it is nearly out of the water. The water will not run out of the bottle because, to do so, the surface of the water in the pan would have to rise (from the addition to it of the water in the bottle). It cannot rise because of the pressure of the air on it (Fig. 5-8).

Another demonstration of how air pressure interferes with pouring liquids is as follows: Place a glass or plastic funnel in a narrow-neck bottle and pack clay tightly in the space between the funnel and the neck of the bottle. Slowly pour water into the funnel. The water will not run into the flask because the tube of the funnel does not provide enough room for the air to be vented. As a result, the air in the bottle prevents the water from running in. If a hole is punched through the modeling clay, the water will run in freely as the air escapes through the hole.

With this information, children may be able to explain that water gurgles and spurts when it is poured out of a narrow-neck bottle because air, entering as the water pours out, gurgles as it goes through the water and slows or stops it as it is coming out.

Everyday experiences illustrate this phenomenon: A can of fruit juice with only one hole will pour with difficulty or not at all. Punch a second hole in the can and it will pour out easily, the air entering the second hole presses down on the surface of the juice with as much force as it pushes on the juice emerging from the first hole. This allows the juice to pour of its own weight.

This effect can also be shown quite clearly with a glass dip tube or transparent straw. Holding a finger over one end, lower the tube into a glass of colored water. Very little water will enter the tube because the tube is filled with air that cannot escape. Removing the finger allows the air inside the tube to escape as the water in the tumbler moves up into the tube. Put a finger over the tube and lift it out of the water. Air pressure acting at the bottom of the tube prevents the water from running out. (See discussion of vacuums above.) Remove the finger once more and the water runs out: The air is now pressing down on top of the tube with just as much force as the air pressing up at the bottom; the water then falls of its own weight.

Air pressure enables men to work under water. To show how this is possible, float a cork in an aquarium or a large, half-full jar. Place a glass tumbler, mouth down, over the cork and press the tumbler down to the bottom. The pressure of the air in the tumbler will prevent water from filling the tumbler and wetting the cork. Large-scale devices using the same principle are called diving bells or caissons. In these steel devices, men work safely and are kept dry at the bottoms of lakes or oceans.

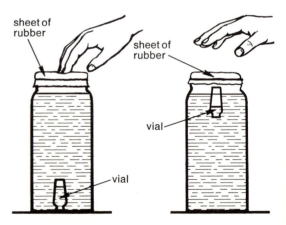

FIGURE **5-9** A Cartesian diver; at left, with pressure applied to rubber diaphragm; at right, with pressure released.

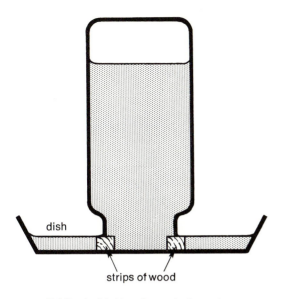

FIGURE **5-10**   A drinking fountain for pets.

Continuous pumping of fresh air into these caissons maintains the oxygen supply as well as the pressure that keeps the water from entering the caisson at the edge that rests on the river or ocean bottom.

Children can have fun with a Cartesian diver, which can be made as follows. Fill a tall glass jar almost full of water. Then partly fill a small, straight-sided vial with water and turn it upside down in the water in the jar. Hold a piece of cardboard or glass or a finger over the mouth of the vial when placing it in the jar. If the vial sinks to the bottom, it contains too much water; if it floats with the bottom above the water, too little water. The aim is to have the vial float upside down with its bottom about level with the surface of the water in the jar. Vary the amount of water in the vial until it floats in the desired position. Then stretch a piece of a balloon tightly over the mouth of the tall jar, securing it with a rubber band or string. When the sheet of rubber is pressed, the vial sinks to the bottom of the jar (Fig. 5-9); when it is released, the vial rises. Pressure on the rubber sheet compresses the air in the jar. The compressed air presses on the water, forcing it into the vial, the air in which becomes compressed. With more water in the

vial, it becomes heavier (water weighs more than air) and sinks. When pressure on the rubber is released, pressure on the water returns to normal, and the (compressed) air in the vial can expand and push out the extra water. The vial then rises to its original position. It is possible to adjust the balance finely so that pressure against the glass sides of a capped bottle completely filled with water will produce the same effect.

Drinking fountains for pets utilize air pressure. To make one, fill a wide-mouthed jar with water, cover the top with cardboard, and set the jar, open end down, in about an inch of water in a deep pie dish. Replace the cardboard with two small strips of wood about $\frac{1}{4}-\frac{1}{2}$-inch thick so that the jar rests on the strips of wood (Fig. 5-10).

When water is removed from the dish (children can suck some out with a straw), water from the jar will take its place. At the same time, large bubbles of air will occasionally move up into the jar, replacing the water that flowed out. Children may have noticed the same action in office water containers.

A simple demonstration of vacuum effect can be done with a balloon and a Pyrex flask or Pyrex baby bottle. Heat a small amount of water in the flask until the water boils. Then remove the flask from the heat and quickly stretch the opening of the balloon over the mouth of the flask. As the flask cools, the balloon will turn inside out, ending inside the flask. The partial vacuum formed by boiling the water allows air outside to push the balloon into the flask and even to inflate it.

FIGURE **5-11**   Making a balloon larger by reducing the air pressure around it.

A balloon can also be enlarged by a vacuum action around it. Needed are a large bottle, a one-hole stopper to fit, a short piece of glass tubing passed through the stopper, a piece of rubber tubing attached to the outer end of the glass tube, and a balloon. Partially inflate the balloon and close its neck with a rubber band. Put the balloon in the jar, stopper the jar tightly, and have a child suck air repeatedly from the jar (Fig. 5-11). (When the child stops for a breath, squeeze the tube closed to prevent air from going back into the jar.) The balloon will become larger as a partial vacuum is formed in the jar; the air inside the balloon pushes against the inner surface of the balloon.

Breathing involves vacuum action, too. In breathing, the diaphragm contracts and the chest muscles raise the chest and rib cage upward and outward, increasing the volume of the chest cavity. The air already present in the lungs expands to occupy this larger space, reducing the air pressure in the lungs. The higher external air pressure pushes air through the nose or mouth into the lungs. How we inhale and exhale is explained more fully in Chapter 11.

MOVING AIR

Lift a book cover and, holding the book near a child's face, close the cover suddenly. The puff of air the child feels on his face should help make graphic the idea that air is all around the book and that, when the book cover is closed, it pushes the air. This moving air will easily blow away a small crumpled piece of tissue paper placed in front of the book.

Have children make a paper fan by folding a piece of paper into narrow strips. When fanning themselves, they are moving air and thus creating a wind. Point out that the blades of an electric fan cause the air to move quickly and thereby create a strong wind.

Children can make a pinwheel of a 6 square-inch piece of heavy paper or cardboard. Draw two diagonal lines joining the corners (Fig. 5-12). Cut along each diagonal to within an inch of the

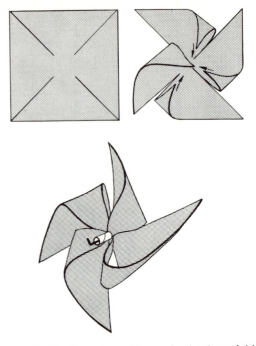

FIGURE **5-12** Steps in making a pinwheel, useful in showing the effect of moving air.

center. Bend every other corner so made so that each lies over the center. Push a pin through the center; then push the pin into a pencil eraser. Children can blow on the pinwheel, hold it in front of an electric fan, or run with it held before them. In each case, it is moving the air that turns the pinwheel. To make a toy windmill, push the pencil holding the pinwheel through an empty paper milk carton.

Call the children's attention to the wind as it rustles leaves, causes a flag to wave, and makes clothes on a line flutter and flap.

When air moves rapidly, air *pressure* is affected. Where the forward speed of the moving air stream is high, the air pressure at the sides tends to be low.

A strip of paper held in front of an electric fan bends *away* from the fan because the whirling blades tend to compress the air, creating a zone of high pressure. Held in back of the fan, the paper strip bends toward the blades, because the air pushed out in front of the fan was drawn from behind, creating a partial vacuum (see above).

A *vacuum* cleaner has a motor that drives a fan. The high-pressure area is in the region of the bag, in which the dirt is collected. The low-pressure area is in the nozzle and the hose. Here air rushes in with such force that it carries the particles of dirt with it.

Children can perform many experiments to show the effect of fast-moving air streams. In each case, the fast-moving air stream creates a low air pressure on one side, so that the relatively greater air pressure on the other side (or sides) then pushes toward the side with the lower.

Suspend two ping-pong balls or other spheres from a support one or two inches apart (Fig. 5-13). Have a pupil blow air through a straw between them. They will come together because the fast-moving stream of air creates an area of low pressure on their facing sides and the higher-pressure air on the outer surfaces pushes them together.

To demonstrate an aspect of the principles of moving air that has aerodynamic applications, hold one end of a sheet of paper between the fingers. Holding it at mouth level, blow over the top of the sheet (Fig. 5-14). The paper will rise. Point out that here again the fast-moving air stream moving over the top of the paper creates

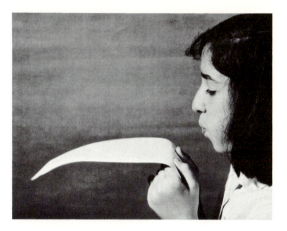

FIGURE **5-14** A rapidly moving air stream across the top of a paper makes the paper rise.

a low air pressure zone, allowing greater air pressure underneath the paper to push it up. The wing of an airplane is shaped to maximize this same lifting effect. (See Chapter 23.)

The following activities illustrate a principle of moving air streams discovered by the scientist, Bernoulli, called Bernoulli's principle.

Bend down one inch of each end of a piece of paper about 8 inches long and 4 inches wide so that the paper forms a bridge. Place the bridge on a table and blow hard under it. The bridge will cling tightly to the table.

Draw diagonals to find the midpoint of a 3-inch square card and put a pin through it and into the hole in an empty thread spool, so that the card is at the bottom of the spool (Fig. 5-15).

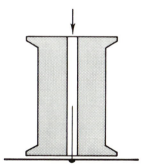

FIGURE **5-15** Spool and card used to demonstrate Bernoulli's principle. Arrows indicate direction of air flow.

FIGURE **5-13** An air stream moving rapidly between two bodies—in this case, apples—makes them swing toward each other.

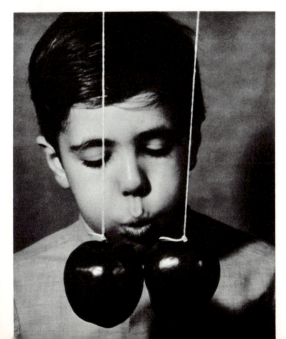

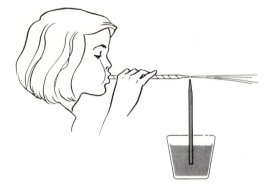

FIGURE **5-16** A simple sprayer made of two drinking straws.

Holding the card lightly against the spool with the finger, blow through the spool hole. Then remove the finger, continuing to blow. The card will cling to the spool. Have the children note that the stream of air flows out rapidly between the bottom of the spool and the card, producing a low-pressure zone in this space.

The same process can be illustrated with a ping-pong ball in a glass or clear plastic funnel. Holding the funnel broad end up, blow hard into the stem. The ball will not blow out of the funnel but clings closely to it. Invert the funnel and, holding the ping-pong ball with the fingers, blow hard into the stem. Remove the hand while continuing to blow. The ball will remain in the funnel.

An inflated rubber balloon (tie the neck tightly) placed in the air stream of an electric fan that it is facing straight up will remain in the stream. The pressure of the surrounding air is greater than the air pressure of the stream.

Place one of two soda straws (slightly flattened at one end) in a tumbler of colored water. Place the other straw at right angles to the first (with flattened ends together) and blow hard through the horizontal straw (Fig. 5-16). The water level in the vertical straw will rise. If the stream of air is strong enough, the water will rise to the top of the vertical straw and spray out. Point out that blowing a stream of air rapidly across the top of the straw lowers the air pressure inside

it. The air on the surface of the water in the glass then pushes the water up the straw, where the fast-moving air stream breaks the water up into a spray. This is the way an atomizer or insect and paint spray gun works.

Have a child hold a 2- or 3-square-inch piece of cardboard in front of a lighted candle (Fig. 5-17a) and blow hard toward the cardboard. The flame will move toward him because the air stream will be directed over, under, and around the card, producing a low-pressure area behind it, into which the higher-pressure air moves, pushing the flame before it. If he does the same with a teardrop-shaped cardboard (Fig. 5-17b) (pointed end toward the candle), the air flows smoothly along the side of the "teardrop," meets at the candle, and blows the flame away from him or extinguishes it.

Point out that autos, trains, planes—vehicles that travel at high speeds—often have this teardrop, "streamlined" shape. This helps to reduce air resistance and the turbulence at the rear of

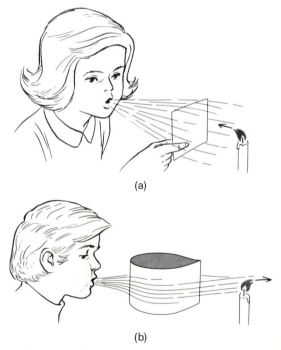

(a)

(b)

FIGURE **5-17** (a) Blowing against card creates a low-pressure area, indicated by direction of candle flame; (b) streamlining produces opposite effect.

the vehicle by creating air streams moving in opposite directions, as in Fig. 7-17b.

APPLICATIONS OF AIR

Air in various forms is very helpful to man. Wind helps dry clothes and drives windmills. Fan-driven air cools us and our engines.

Compressed air is useful in caissons or diving bells (above), in underwater diving, in air brakes, submarines, door checks, whistles, and pneumatic tools (such as the riveter, hammer, drill, and sand blaster), and to inflate such things as tires, footballs, and basketballs.

Differences in air pressure such as are involved in partial vacuums are utilized in the soda straw, medicine dropper, atomizer, spray gun, and lift pump.

Children can make a "gusher" using compressed air. Push the narrow tip of the glass tube from a medicine dropper through a one-hole rubber stopper. Attach to the large end of the glass tube a rubber or plastic tube long enough to reach almost to the bottom of a bottle (Fig.

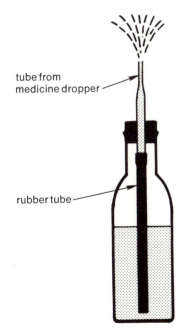

tube from
medicine dropper

rubber tube

FIGURE **5-18** A "gusher" fountain.

FIGURE **5-19** Transferring water from one container to another with a siphon. Arrow indicates direction of flow.

5-18) half full of water, into which the stopper (with tubes attached) should be pushed firmly. Have a child blow as hard as he can into the bottle. When he removes his mouth from the top of the dropper, the water gushes out of the tube. Point out that the child blew air into the bottle and compressed it. When he removed his mouth and thus released the pressure, the compressed air pushed against the water and forced it up the rubber tube and medicine dropper.

A siphon emptying a container of water can be a fascinating spectacle for children. Fill one of two glass jars with water and place it on a table. Place the second jar on a chair, so that it is lower than the other. Fill a 15- to 20-foot piece of rubber tubing with water. Do this by holding the tube so that it forms a U. Hold one end of the U under a faucet and let the water run until it flows out of the other end of the tube.

While pinching both ends of the tube tightly, place one end in one jar and the other end in the second jar (Fig. 5-19). Release the ends of the tube.

Water will flow from the jar on the table to the jar on the chair. Point out that because there is more water in the long arm of the rubber tube than in the short arm, gravity acts more on the former, and the water runs out, leaving a partial vacuum in the tube. The pressure of the air on the surface of the liquid pushes the liquid up the short arm of the rubber tube and over into the longer arm. In this way, the water is transferred continuously from one jar to the other.

The siphon can also be started without filling the tube with water. Simply put one end of the tube in the jar of water and suck the air from the lower end of the tube, creating the partial vacuum in the tube.

A siphon fountain can be made as follows: Fit a glass bottle or flask with a two-hole rubber stopper. Insert the glass tube of a medicine dropper through one hole and through the other, a short piece of glass tubing that extends about an inch above the stopper. Attach about 1 foot of rubber tubing to the medicine dropper and about 3 feet to the glass tube (Fig. 5-20). Fill a large glass jar with colored water. Put one rubber tube in the jar of colored water on the table and the other in the empty jar on the floor. Pour a little

water into the bottle, insert the stopper with tubes, and invert the bottle.

To start the siphon, suck on the end of the longer tube until water begins to flow. Quickly drop the tube into the lower jar. A fountain will play up against the bottom of the bottle. If the fountain will not start, try again with a little less water in the bottle.

Help the children to understand that when the water runs down the long rubber tube, a partial vacuum is formed in the bottle. Air pressure on the colored water in the jar pushes up into the bottle, whence it runs down the long rubber tube.

AIR IN WATER

Some air is dissolved in water. To demonstrate the presence of air in water, let a glass of cold water stand in a warm place for an hour or so. Tiny bubbles of air will appear on the sides of the tumbler. Or heat some cold water in a beaker. Bubbles of air will appear and rise to the surface long before the water begins to boil. Heating the water drives off the air dissolved in it. Air is more soluble in cold water than in hot water.

Many animals and plants that live in the water get their air directly from the water. (See Chapters 1 and 3.)

AIR IN SOIL

Soil also contains air. To demonstrate, fill a wide-mouthed glass jar about half full of soil. Add water; bubbles of air, originally present between the soil particles, will rise to the surface.

A few skeptics may feel that, because water also contains air, the bubbles may have come from it rather than from the soil. The objection can be met by repeating the experiment using cold water that has been recently boiled. Boiled water, on standing, will show no evidence of air bubbles since all the air was driven off by the boiling.

A building brick placed in a large container of water will give off air bubbles; point out that many materials are porous and contain air.

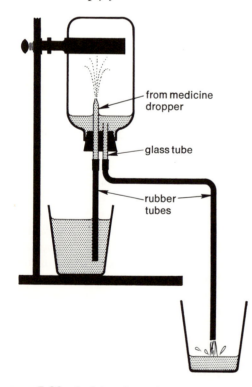

from medicine dropper

glass tube

rubber tubes

FIGURE **5-20** A siphon fountain.

SUGGESTED PROJECTS

1. Show the class an "empty" bottle and ask if the bottle is really empty. Lead into the question of whether air is real and occupies space.

2. Have children help originate and set up an experiment to prove that air has weight.

3. Encourage discussion of evidences of the presence, pressure, and movement of air from their everyday experiences: for example, the hiss of air entering a vacuum-packed can (especially coffee cans) as it is opened; the sound of compressed air escaping from a tire or the pump hose when tires are being inflated in a service station; the sensation of being drawn into the bottle when drinking from one without removing the mouth to allow air in; the difficulty of closing a close-fitting cabinet or closet door rapidly.

4. Analyze the phenomena (3) with respect to cause.

5. Discuss why space capsules become hot as they re-enter the atmosphere.

6. Have children speculate on why it is easier to boil water at high altitudes.

BIBLIOGRAPHY

(**P** indicates recommended for primary grades, **I** for intermediate grades, **U** for upper grades.)

Chester, Michael, *Let's Go to Stop Air Pollution,* Putnam, 1968. Causes, measuring devices, some of the dangers, and means of alleviation. **U**

Fenton, Carroll and Mildred, *Our Changing Weather,* Doubleday, 1954. Weather and its causes. **I**

Feravolo, Rocco, *Easy Physics Projects: Air, Water and Heat,* Prentice-Hall, 1966. Forty-eight experiments: 16 on air, 19 on water, and 13 on heat. Lists materials—all easily available—gives simple directions and clear explanations of the concepts involved. Clearly illustrated with line drawings and black and white illustrations. **I**

Friskey, M. R., *The True Book of the Air Around Us,* Children's Pr., 1953. Simple treatment of air and its properties. **P**

Larrick, Nancy, *See For Yourself,* Dutton, 1952. Simple experiments on air and water.

Newell, Homer E., Jr., *Window in the Sky,* McGraw-Hill, 1959. The upper atmosphere, with special emphasis on composition, density, pressure, temperature, and radiation. **U**

Parker, Bertha M., *Air About Us,* Harper & Row, 1958. Comprehensive description of properties of air. **U**

Piltz, Albert, *What Is Air,* Benefic, 1960. Characteristics of air, layers of atmosphere, and its importance to plant and animal life, combustion, and transportation. **I–U**

Pine, Tillie S., *Air All Around,* McGraw-Hill, 1960. Pictures about the nature of air and the ways it is used. Some easy experiments. **P**

Stambler, Irwin, *Breath of Life: the Story of Our Atmosphere,* Putnam, 1963. The earth's atmosphere and composition, and a description of the techniques used to gather such facts. Well illustrated with photographs. **U**

Stockard, Jimmy, *Experiments for Young Scientists,* Little, Brown, 1964. Simple Experiments (with safety rules and illustrations) that demonstrate scientific principles and facts concerning air, water, light, sound, simple machines, and electricity. **I**

Stone, A. Harris, *Take A Balloon,* Prentice-Hall, 1967. Fundamental ideas in physics and chemistry, including information on pressure. Open-ended approach. **U**

Wolfe, Louis, *Wonders of the Atmosphere,* Putnam, 1962. Contains a chapter on methods for controlling air pollution. Illustrated with photographs. **U**

Typical form produced at the surface when water displaced by the impact of a drop begins to flow back.

6 Water

Water, a compound of two invisible gases, is probably the most important compound on earth. A man can live 40 days without food, but only four without water. Water can seem the most changeable, obvious, devastating, and most enhancing of substances. A host of opposites describe its properties, most of which are taken for granted in our daily lives. What if there were no water on this spaceship, Earth? (The fuel cells that produce electricity for astronauts in space capsules provide water as a by product of the energy reaction.) The question could provoke an interesting discussion with older children. Younger children may be most aware of water in its role in weather; in fact, most accounts of weather are really descriptions of water in one form or another.

Water, like other matter, has weight and occupies space. Since weight is a measure of gravitational pull, how does water behave in response to the pull of the earth? Children can learn much about the shape and direction of running water by watching the way it runs out of a sink drain: Does it drain any faster when an air hole appears in the middle of the draining water? Careful observation will answer these and other questions. Cardboard held against the sink edge while the water is running from the tap will show a pattern of splash marks. The children can determine if the marks are the same whether the water runs slowly or fast.

Water, like other liquids, takes the shape of its container. Children may pour water from a pitcher into a sink or from one container to another and observe the shape and fall of the flow. Watching the pattern of waterflow from a dish drainer at home can also be instructive.

The sound of water running from a hot-water tap will change when the water begins to run hot. Children may note the sounds of water being poured into containers of different shapes and the change in the sound of boiling water as the pan begins to boil dry.

At sea level, water freezes at 0°C (32°F) and boils at 100°C (212°F). These limits will vary slightly depending on the amounts of impurities dissolved in the water. This difference can be shown graphically by having children compare the temperatures at which pure water and salt water freeze and boil.

EVAPORATION AND CONDENSATION

Where does water come from? Where does it go? Does it ever come back? Children's concepts of the evaporation–condensation cycle may be clarified in a number of ways: "Paint" (with water) two hand prints or figures of the same size on a chalkboard. Fan one and time the difference in evaporation between the two. (Make sure that the prints or figures are widely separated so that the fanning does not affect both prints.) Hold 2 teaspoons of water at the same level, heat one, and observe from which spoon the water disappears faster. Wet a handkerchief or piece of muslin and spread it on the blackboard to dry. Note which doll clothes hung on a line dry first—those in sun or those in shade. Spray water from an atomizer and observe how the water particles "disappear" (as they slip between the air molecules). Observe how the balance of a wet mop shifts as the mop dries out (Fig. 6-1). Compare the rate of evaporation of water from a pop bottle and an open saucer. (Begin with equal amounts of water, which may be tinted with food coloring to make the evaporation easier to observe.) A useful question for children is whether water evaporating into the air disappears for good. A simple investigation to help children

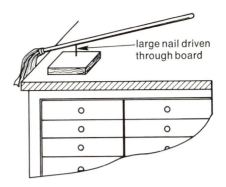

FIGURE **6-1** Loss of water (by evaporation) from the mop rope upsets the balance.

understand the "disappearance" of water can be done with two glasses. Put a drop of water into one glass and tape the other (mouth-to-mouth) to it. Stand the resulting *sealed* chamber in sunlight or near a warm radiator. When the drop of water has "disappeared," stand the chamber in about an inch of ice water. After about fifteen minutes have the children observe the "returned" water (the condensed vapor).

The classroom aquarium may also serve in the investigation of evaporation. By recording the amount of water added in order to keep the water level constant, one can calculate the amount evaporated daily—from the tank as a whole, and then from each square inch of surface. Have the children note whether the amount evaporated changes at different seasons. (Discussion of the word *evaporate* may help develop word skills and illuminate the meaning of such forms as prefixes.)

To demonstrate, further, that the amount of surface, or area, of liquid exposed to the air also affects the rate of evaporation pour equal amounts of water into a narrow-necked bottle and a wide-mouthed bottle. Let the bottles stand open overnight; then remeasure the amount of water in each. There will be less water in the wide-mouthed jar.

Moisture in the air, or humidity, affects the rate of evaporation. Wet thoroughly some cloth fastened on an embroidery hoop. Then wet two spots of equal size on the chalkboard as above.

Cover one spot with the embroidery hoop covered with the wet cloth. The open spot will evaporate first because the wet cloth on the embroidery frame also evaporates, and moist air accumulates under the hoop, making it difficult for the wet spot on the chalkboard to turn into water vapor and, thus, evaporate. Children will recall how difficult it is for perspiration to evaporate on a warm, muggy day when the humidity is high and the air is already full of water vapor.

Different liquids evaporate at different speeds. To show this, again wet spots of equal size on the chalkboard, but use water for only one and duplicator fluid or rubbing alcohol for the other. Note how quickly the duplicator fluid or alcohol dries.

Some solids evaporate without melting. Dry ice is converted directly into a vapor without melting, as are moth balls. Icicles and even snow will evaporate in weather too cold for melting.

The connection between evaporation and cooling may be experienced by dipping a finger in rubbing alcohol, then allowing it to dry. Water requires an enormous amount of energy to become vaporized. One hundred calories (units of energy; see p. 193) are required to raise the temperature of 1 gram (a quarter-teaspoon) of water 100°C. Over five times more energy is needed to vaporize, or launch in air, the molecules making up the water. Water converted into vapor expands 1800 times—the energy basis of "steam"-driven machines and other devices. When water vapor in clouds condenses into rain, the energy released may be apparent in the violence of the storm or in the rise in air temperature following a rain. A refrigerator makes ice cubes by removing heat from water. This heat is usually given off from cooling coils exposed at the back of the refrigerator.

To illustrate water's immense capacity to absorb heat, boil away 1 teaspoon (4 grams) of water using a stout plumber's candle as the heat source. Measure the amount of candle used and the time required to vaporize the water.

On a summer day, a cubic mile of air may hold 150 million barrels of water, all put there by evaporation, or vaporization. To gain some concept of the vast quantity of water molecules forever floating overhead, calculate the number of buckets or gallons of water in a barrel. Weigh a gallon of water and, to illustrate the enormous weight of water raised by evaporation, have a child lift a bucketful a few steps up a stepladder or staircase.

Earth's hydrosphere includes water in earth's ocean of air as well as on earth's surface. Children can see from a globe that the earth is seven-eighths ocean. The oceans and smaller bodies of water make up a great reservoir that provides much of earth's 30,000 cubic miles of annual rainfall. Over 97% of this watery harvest returns to the sea. Of the remaining 3%, surface fresh water, most is locked in ice, leaving only 0.4% available for potable water supplies. Evidence suggests that the available water in earth's atmosphere is a constant, sent aloft by evaporation, condensing as rain perhaps on other lands in other centuries. Writing an account of the imagined travels of a drop of water (through time *and* space) might be a stimulating project for a child.

The Water Cycle

The endless cyclical transformation of water from liquid to gas and back again may be illustrated in many ways. On cold mornings, for example, as the room temperature begins to rise from the weekend or overnight low, moisture will condense on the cover of a classroom terrarium (p. 57) forming drops which, when large enough, will make a kind of pocket rainfall. Breathing on the chalkboard or window pane produces a damp spot where moisture from the lungs condenses. A cool tumbler held over boiling water soon fogs up as the vapor condenses. "Raindrops" will fall from the bottom of a metal pan of ice held with kitchen tongs over boiling water. Classroom "crops" can be watered with indoor "rain" as follows (Fig. 6-2). Support a cookie sheet or metal serving tray of ice on two chairs or stools so that it is above the seedlings, on the floor. Place an electric hot plate and a teakettle of water to one side, with the kettle spout directed at the bottom of the tray or cookie sheet. The

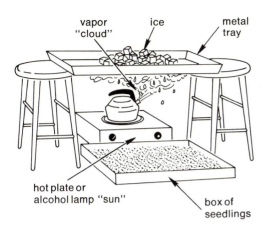

FIGURE **6-2** Producing "rain" in the classroom.

vapor will condense on the cold underside of the tray and rain on the crops beneath.

A model of the complete water cycle from evaporation to condensation to precipitation and around again can be made of a Florence flask and a Pyrex measuring cup. Place one-half glass of boiling water in the cup, pour ice water into the flask, and place it as shown on top of the cup (Fig. 6-3).

To make a "cloud" in the classroom, hold ice cubes in a metal tea strainer over "steam" escaping from a teakettle spout. Children can summarize their concepts of the process with the aid of placards lettered with the words (one per placard): cold, heat, water, and cloud, with *water* on the reverse of the *cloud* placard. Children wearing *water* placards come in contact with those wearing *heat* placards and reverse their *water* placards to read *cloud*. *Cloud* meeting *cold* air turns back to rain *water*. A dramatic way to relate concepts of water's change of state to the speed and density of distribution of its molecules is to have children (each representing a molecule of water) stand bunched tightly within an area marked on the floor by a chalk line or rope. To illustrate the effect of the application of heat energy, have them jump up and down in place briefly. The resultant spread of the "molecules" beyond the original chalk line (from the inevitable collisions and rebound) will be quite clear. Similarly, the molecules of gas that make up air,

when heated, move faster and farther apart (Chapter 16). However, humid air is less dense than dry air because of the *dilution* of air's gas molecules (av. mol. wt., 24) by water molecules (mol. wt., 18).

On *clear* nights dew falls (or, rather, *forms*) on grass much as it forms on a glass of iced drink on a warm day: The moisture condenses because with the fall in air temperature, the water molecules lose heat energy and slow down, ultimately coming to rest on surfaces, where they collect and form droplets. A discussion of dew and how to produce it in the classroom appears on p. 119, Chapter 7.

During nights of high humidity (see Chapter 7), water transpiring through leaf stomata (p. 51) trickles down, and collects at the leaf margins like a fringe of dew drops. This *water of guttation* can be distinguished from dew (water condensed from the atmosphere) by collecting droplets on a glass slide and letting them dry. Dew "distilled" of air is practically pure; water moving through plant cells carries sugar and minerals, visible as a whitish residue on the slide after the water has evaporated.

Distillation

A classroom still will extend children's concepts of condensation and water purification. With either of the arrangements shown in Fig. 6-4, one can remove food color, ink, vegetable coloring, or other impurities from the water. In the teakettle arrangement, ballast the jar with weights taped to its lower sides, and add ice to the water

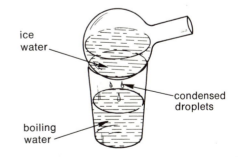

FIGURE **6-3** Illustrating the water cycle with a Florence flask and a measuring cup.

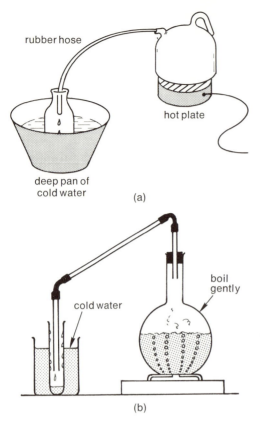

FIGURE **6-4** Removing impurities from water by distillation.

to hasten vaporization. (Children may wish to propose explanations for the colorlessness of the water condensing in the jar.) Distillation purifies water because, in vaporizing, water subdivides into minute particles (molecules) many thousand times smaller and *lighter* than the particles of coloring, dirt, or bacteria, which are, therefore, left behind in the boiler. Water may also be cleansed by chemicals and filtration (p. 102).

Pilots are advised that, if downed in arid country, they can collect water by lining a shallow pit with plastic sheet on which dew will condense overnight and collect at the bottom. A more elaborate device, a solar still, may be constructed as shown in Fig. 6-5. The piece of garden hose must be cut in half lengthwise (to form a trough) and attached to the frame under the bottom edge of the slanted pane, where it will catch the distil-

led water and drain it into the cup. After putting salt water into the pan, tape the edges of the glass panes together.

SOLID WATER

Like all other forms of matter, water contracts as it cools: its molecules slow down. *But,* below 39°F water expands, becoming (volume for volume) lighter. To verify this, leave a milk carton brimful of water in a freezer overnight. The top will pop up because in solid form water has about 9% greater volume. More dramatic proof may be had using a screw-top glass jar instead of a carton. (Select one of a size to fit into a larger jar or plastic container.) Fill as before, screw on the top, and place upright in the refrigerator. By morning the smaller jar will have been shattered by the expansion of the frozen water. If water turned into ice with no loss of weight, like most solids, it would sink in its own *melt* instead of staying on top, and every pond and lake would soon freeze to the bottom. Class discussion of the possibilities inherent in this could be stimulating. Compare the position of ice cubes in an iced drink to paraffin or fat that is partially liquefied by heat.

Salt's effect on ice can be demonstrated in a simple investigation. Using candy or kitchen thermometers, compare the temperatures of plain ice

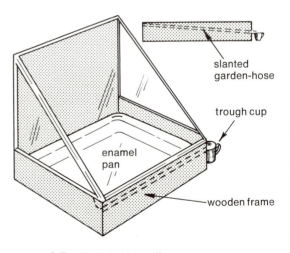

FIGURE **6-5** Model solar still.

water and a salt-ice mixture. Children may infer from this the reason salt is applied to highways in freezing weather.

Frost crystals formed on windows in very cold, dewy weather demonstrate the same laws of crystallization as snow. A cloud of vapor from boiling water introduced into a very cold area, as in a freezer, might freeze and precipitate as snow crystals.

WATER AND LIFE

The earth's *average* annual harvest of rain and snow would cover its entire surface with three feet of water. If all this water were available, the per capita daily supply would be 22,000 gallons. However, two-thirds of this precipitation evaporates or runs off to the sea. Of the remainder, 70% is transpired through plants or evaporates from the soil. A plastic bag placed around well developed plants and in sunshine will demonstrate transpiration and evaporation. Fasten the bags around the stem with tape or wire plant-ties. Water droplets condensing inside the bags must have transpired from the plant leaves. Use of bags large enough to envelope plants *and* containers will show the added effect of evaporation from soil.

To observe water moving through plants, set celery or rhubarb stalks in colored solutions (see p. 60). Try this also with flowered plants such as hyacinth, daisy, yarrow, or Queen Anne's lace. (Water as a vehicle for plant nutrients is discussed below under *Water as Solvent*.)

All organisms, whether plant or animal, are composed of cells, and cell protoplasm is 50% water. Green corn is 78% water. For every pound of living plant cells it produces, a corn plant uses nearly 370 pounds of water; to produce a pound of dry corn cobs or stalks, 500 pounds of water. Green timber is 65% water; plant leaves, 95%; roots, 90%; potatoes, 78%; and apples, 80% water.

The predominance of water in apples or potatoes may be illustrated by weighing some sections before and after setting them aside to dry. A shorter-term demonstration consists in heating the sections in an open vessel while holding a pane of glass or a dry tumbler (upside down) above the vessel. Moisture condensing on the cool glass surface must have come from the food. Repeat with other types of food, cooling and drying the glass each time. Corn meal, oatmeal, or bran flakes yield little or no moisture, yet it is possible for mealworms to grow and multiply on these foods (p. 33). Like desert kangaroo rats and a few other animals, they do so by utilizing water formed by the chemical breakdown and recombination of elements in their food.

The human body is about 70% water. To maintain this equivalent of eight buckets or fifteen gallons of water requires a daily intake of *two* gallons. Representing these facts pictorially may lead children to the preparation of a class project on water in living things, which can, in turn, involve number relationships: How many glassfuls in two gallons? How many glasses of liquid do you drink in a day? Such data, kept by each child, can be used to determine a class average of liquid intake. The average, likely to be short of two gallons per child, may raise the question of where the body gets the difference. The source has been indicated above for typical vegetable foods; other typical sources are: bacon, 22% water; beef, 62%; eggs, 65%; fish, 80%; and milk, 87%. Children may enjoy predicting the approximate water content of other foods; the school nurse or dietitian can probably provide verification.

Purification of Water Supplies

The present average daily per capita water consumption in the United States for all purposes is about 65 gallons; in large cities, about 100 gallons. But industrial uses of water increases this figure to nearly 1800 gallons. What is their source and how is water made safe to drink? Why water is not sterilized by boiling can be demonstrated by having children compare the taste of tap water and of water that has been boiled and cooled. Boiled water has a flat taste because the boiling has driven off much of the dissolved air. (More prohibitive than taste is the *cost* of boiling to sterilize water.) Examination of a freshly drawn glass of tap water and one of boiled water will soon show air bubbles in the glass of tap water.

Most urban water supplies are purified by the use, in trace amounts, of chemicals such as chlorine. To observe the effect of chemicals on bacteria in water supply, add to a test tube half full of water three or four drops of iodine solution and (to represent bacteria protein) five to six drops of egg white. After 20 minutes the egg white will be coagulated as if it had been boiled. Home disinfectants such as household bleach or Lysol may be tried in place of the iodine.

The coagulation process used by many municipalities for purifying water may be demonstrated using a tall bottle of muddy water. Add a few crystals of alum plus a tablespoon of ammonia. Stir and let settle. Alum forms a jellied mass which carries dirt particles with it as it settles.

Also used is filtration, in which the water is passed through beds of sand, crushed stone, and other materials in which particles in the water become trapped. Coagulation and filtration, while they make water cleaner, cannot alone always make it safe to drink because bacterial contaminants (Chapter 4) may remain.

Although clear water may not be pure, pure water is usually clear and colorless. Many water supplies must be filtered as well as chlorinated. An inverted oil-lamp chimney makes a fine filter (Fig. 6-6) as does a milk carton with a number of small holes punched in the bottom and covered

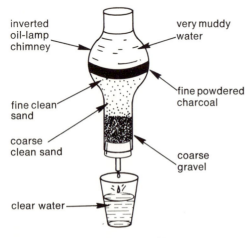

FIGURE **6-6** Oil-lamp chimney filter.

inverted oil-lamp chimney

very muddy water

fine powdered charcoal

fine clean sand

coarse clean sand

coarse gravel

clear water

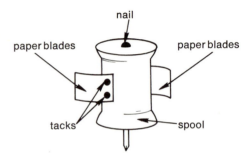

FIGURE **6-7** Model water wheel.

nail

paper blades

paper blades

tacks

spool

with a paper towel folded to fit inside the carton. Test different filtering materials—such as gravel, sand, and/or pulverized charcoal—by filtering very muddy ill-smelling water (the smell is usually a by product of the growth processes of bacteria, algae, and other water organisms) through layers of different materials and of varying thickness.

WATER POWER

Abetted by earth's downward pull, water is forever at work, changing and degrading the face of the land. Where the earth's rock layers are tipped or bent or formed of resistant igneous rocks, waterfalls often form. Water wheels, powered by falling water, can provide energy for operating machinery. Thus, places along running streams often become nuclei for settlements—for example, Fall River, R. I., and other cities along the "fall line" between the Atlantic coast piedmont region and coastal plain.

A model water wheel is easily made from a spool, three pieces of stiff paper, thumbtacks, and a nail. Use two thumbtacks as shown (Fig. 6-7) to attach one end of each paper vane to the spool. Use the nail as a horizontal axle for the spool, which will turn if held under the water from a spigot.

Pressure

Work is the moving of an object through a distance. Water at work can be shown with a tire pump to which an outdoor faucet is connected by a piece of rubber tube. Opening the faucet slowly, watch the water pressure lift heavy objects tied to the pump handle. An everyday object that uses this hydraulic lift is the barber chair, although the fluid used is oil, not water.

How water pressure lifts water to the upper stories of buildings by gravity flow can be shown as follows. Near the bottom of a quart milk carton, punch a hole large enough so that one end of some rubber tubing will fit into it snugly. With the other end of the tube in a plastic or glass container, fill the carton with water. The children may note the difference in the rate of flow into the collecting jar according to the height at which the carton is held. Thus the water will seem to run "uphill" as long as the milk carton "reservoir" is held at least as high as the outlet. The greater the height of the source, the better the water pressure; this can be readily demonstrated with a can having two holes punched in its side at different heights, as shown in Fig. 6-8. The jet of water from the lower hole will extend further than that from the upper hole.

Buoyancy

Buoyancy is another useful property of water. Since water is 775 times heavier than air (at sea level), water has a correspondingly greater force of buoyancy, or upward pressure, than air. The principle can be demonstrated in several ways. An ice cube or a piece of wood held under water will bob to the surface when released, because the weight of the cube or piece of wood is less than the weight of the water *displaced*—that is, the water that would occupy the space were the object not there. To make this principle of *displacement* graphic, put a pound of sand in a tin can in a pan of water. Mark the 1-pound water line on the can with a grease pencil or wax crayon. Add a second pound of sand and mark the new waterline. With the can empty, children can experience the pressure necessary to push the can down to the marked levels. With its 1- and 2-pound marks, the can can be used as a scale to weigh other objects.

Fill several bottles or jars of different sizes with

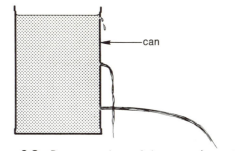

FIGURE **6-8** Demonstration of increase in water pressure with depth.

sand until they are of equal weight. Set the bottles in a pan of water. The smallest bottle will float lowest in the water since it displaces the least water although it weighs as much as the other bottles. Larger vessels can carry heavier loads because they have more volume under water, and hence displace more water. Water buoys an object that weighs less than the weight of the water displaced by the object.

Make a toy boat of heavy-duty metal (tin or lead) foil. Float it in water, then fold and pound it into a tight ball, which will sink because the ball has much less *volume* in relation to weight than the toy boat. A steel ship has high volume and low density in comparison to the steel of which it is made.

Weigh a piece of tin sheet with a spring balance. Bend the sides of the sheet to form a floating tray and mark *inside* (with a grease pencil) the position of the water line on the *outside* of the tray. Remove the tray from the water and fill it with water to the level marked. Pour off the water and weigh it; its weight will equal that of the tray. The amount displaced by the tin sheet was much less than when it was made into a tray. Thus an object which is heavier than water can float if it is shaped so as to displace water equal to its own weight. An object which is lighter than water sinks only far enough to displace its weight in water. An ocean liner displaces as much water as it weighs, hence its description in terms of tons of displacement. To weigh a goldfish, fill a jar brimful of water and set in a light, shallow pan. Carefully slip the fish into the jar. The water displaced should equal the weight of the fish. Children may want to read the story of Archimedes' use of the principle of buoyancy to determine the relative proportions of gold and an adulterating metal in a king's crown.

The more closely packed the molecules of a substance, the more it is apt to weigh. (Children may wish to verify that water weighs $62\frac{1}{2}$ pounds per cubic foot or approximately 1 pound per pint.) To build concepts of density in relation to floating, fill each of several uniform-size cans with a different substance—such as soil, soap powder, sawdust, cotton—and weigh. Although all the cans have the same volume, each will have a different weight. Children may try to predict which substance will float, and which not. Substances sink if they have greater density than water.

Different liquids have different densities—that is, the weight of a volume of one liquid differs from the weight of an equal volume of another liquid. Thus alcohol is less dense, or lighter, than water, and molasses is denser, or heavier than water. (The density of water, taken as one, is used as the standard unit in expressing densities of other substances.) Compare the weights of like volumes (such as a gallon or quart) of water and syrup, oil, kerosene, milk, etc.

Just as balloons are supported by air, sea plants and animals are supported by water. Whales, the largest living mammals, move about easily in water. Such large sea-dwelling animals may suffer injury when removed from water because of the absence of bodily support.

Water pressure is so great at great depths that it constitutes a major problem of underwater exploration. A *Cartesian diver* (Fig. 5-9) illustrates how a nice balance between air and water pressure can be utilized. Needed are a flat-sided pint bottle, a medicine dropper, a balloon, and a fragment of vinyl tile. Fill the bottle to the neck with water, as shown. Cut out the figure of the "diver" from the vinyl tile and fasten it to the medicine dropper, head down. Draw water into the dropper until it floats upright in the neck of the bottle. (To achieve this balance may require some delicate adjustment.) When the dropper neither sinks nor rides too high, stretch a piece of the balloon over the mouth of the bottle. If the air and water in the dropper are in proper balance, the "diver" will descend whenever the rubber membrane is pressed. In doing so, the air in the bottle neck is compressed. Transmitted to the water, this increased pressure upsets the air–water balance in the dropper (more water, less air) and the increased weight (of the additional water) sends the diver to the bottom. Releasing pressure on the rubber reverses the process and allows the diver to rise.

How submarines use similar phenomena to dive and ascend can be illustrated with a simple model (Fig. 6-9). Needed are a bottle, a candle, a two-hole rubber stopper, and some glass and rubber tubing. Insert a short piece of glass tube in one hole of the stopper and a longer one that reaches well into the bottle when the stopper is in place. Attach a 3-foot length of rubber tubing to the longer tube. To balance or "trim" the bottle (which serves as the submarine hull), bal-

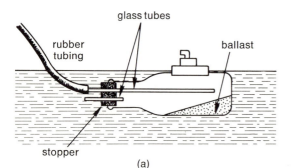

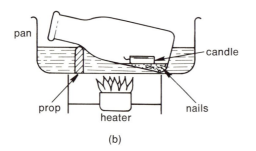

FIGURE **6-9** (a) Model "submarine" assembled and (b) method of preparing wax ballast.

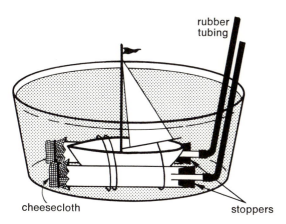

FIGURE **6-10**   Model of a salvage device for raising sunken ships.

last with nails and paraffin by inserting them into the bottle and laying it on its side in a pan of water. Heat the water until the wax melts. When cooled, the wax ballast will remain in place. An optional touch is a conning tower fashioned of sponge rubber and glued to the bottle as shown in the figure. Placed in a pan of water with stopper and tubes in place and the long tube open, the "submarine" will settle to the bottom. The descent can be stopped at any level by pinching the tube closed. Blowing into the tube makes the submarine rise. (Using colored water will make it easier to follow what happens within the model in the process.) The model rises when the air forces out a volume of water equal in weight to the model.

The same principle is used in raising sunken ships. Needed to illustrate this are two large-diameter plastic tubes, a small nonfloating model boat or one with a hole in its hull, two one-hole rubber stoppers, two short lengths of glass tubing, and some rubber tubing and cheesecloth. Assemble the large tubes, stoppers, and tubing as shown (Fig. 6-10), covering one end of each tube with a double layer of cheesecloth held on with rubber bands or cord. As shown in the figure, tie the two tubes (representing the pontoons used in actual salvage) to the "wreck" and submerge whole assembly in a pan of water. Blow the water out of the tubes. (The cheesecloth subdivides the

relatively large opening into openings small enough for the air pressure within to prevent the water from reentering.) As the tubes surface, they will bring the "wreck" with them. Keep the rubber tubing pinched with a clothespin to retain air in the plastic tubes.

A simple device (Fig. 6-11) for measuring water pressure requires a small plastic funnel, a toy balloon, about 3 feet of rubber tubing, and a clear glass or plastic drinking straw. Stretch a piece of the balloon over the mouth of the small funnel and fasten it securely with plastic tape. Attach one end of the rubber tubing to the funnel tip and the other end to the glass or plastic tubing. Anchor the tubing to white cardboard with thin wire or cord, bending the rubber tubing to form one leg of a U, with the glass or plastic tube as the other leg. (For greater permanence, the tubing can be mounted on wood.) Remove the funnel from the rubber tubing and introduce water tinted with food coloring until the glass tube is half full. Replace the funnel and lower it into an aquarium or bucket of water. As the funnel is lowered, the water will push with

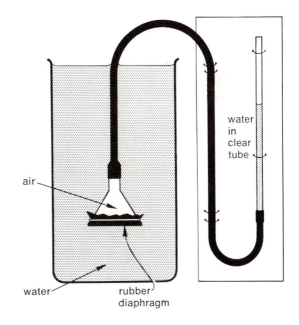

FIGURE **6-11**   Water pressure or depth indicator.

greater and greater pressure against the rubber membrane, which, in turn, will push the air in the tube, and then the column of colored water in the clear tube, making it rise. One of the devices used by submarines to determine their depth below the surface works on the same principle.

Capillarity and Surface Tension

Another interesting property of water and other liquids is *capillarity*, the tendency of liquids to rise in small tubes and in the small passages in porous material. This can be shown with two plates of glass. (For safety, bevel their edges with emery or sandpaper.) Spread a film of water over one plate, lay the other against it, and secure with rubber bands. Keep the plates slightly separated at one edge with cardboard tags (Fig. 6-12) and set in a dish of water. Have the children note how the water rises highest where the plates are closest together. Capillarity is the product of *adhesion* and *cohesion*. The former is the attraction between *unlike* molecules and can be seen operating in any thin glass vessel containing water. Because molecules adhere better to glass than to other water molecules, the water climbs slightly at the edge (adjacent to the glass surface). Cohesion, the attraction of *like* molecules, tends to act to draw along other water molecules (so that the layer of molecules adhering to the glass is not just one molecule thick). The total weight

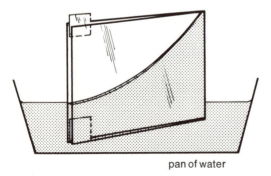

FIGURE **6-12** Water rising by capillarity between two glass plates.

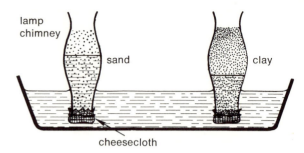

FIGURE **6-13** Water rising through sand and through clay.

of water drawn up is balanced by the *surface tension*, the tendency of the surface molecules to draw together—also a product of cohesion. Thus, the smaller the tube, the higher the level of liquid, because surface tension is smaller in a smaller surface. Capillarity is at work in the human circulatory system, in sponges, lamp wicks, soil, blotters, and in many other types of porous materials.

A film of water molecules climbs through soil aggregates in much the same way that colored water will "climb" a lump of sugar. In warm weather, to reduce evaporation of this water when it reaches the surface, gardeners loosen the top layer of soil by hoeing or cover it with loose mulch. The cultivating breaks up the capillary tubes that have formed in the soil, sealing them off, and the mulch produces the same effect by blanketing them. Thus, the colored water that climbs readily through the sugar lump will climb through pulverized sugar piled atop the lump.

Water does not rise with equal speed through all kinds of soil. This can be seen by filling one lamp chimney with sandy soil and one with clay soil (Fig. 6-13), partially closing the bottoms with netting or cheesecloth, and placing both in a pan of water.

Cohesion of water molecules is what enables insects such as water striders (p. 45) to walk on the water. The same property of water permits a steel needle or razor blade—though nearly eight times the weight of water—to float on the surface. Water can similarly bear objects full of holes such as plastic mesh baskets. If a basket is lowered gently onto water, one may observe how the water bulges like little pillows through the openings.

Molecular cohesion in water molecules and the resultant phenomenon of surface tension may be explored further by investigating the behavior of water drops. Provide each of several small groups of children with a square of waxed paper, a drinking straw, a toothpick, a small dish of colored water, and a paper towel. Use the straw as a pipette to make water drops on the waxed paper, dividing or merging the drops with the toothpick. In a row of drops of graduated size, one can see that the smaller the drop the more nearly spherical, for, while surface tension remains the same in all the drops, the volume of water enclosed in the larger drops is greater and presses out against the skin-like surface of the drop with greater force; hence the tendency of the larger drops to spread at the bottom. To see how the drop acts as a lens, lower it gently onto one letter of print. The delicate elastic membrane of water's surface tension is also responsible for soap bubbles.

How a touch can break a surface-tension film can be shown with a wire-mesh kitchen strainer coated with cooking oil. Allow water to trickle gently down the side of the sieve until there is about $\frac{1}{2}$ inch in the bottom. Examination of the bottom of the strainer with a hand lens will show what holds the water in. The water, while it sags through the mesh, does not penetrate it until a touch of the finger breaks the surface film (of oil).

Thermal Properties

Of all naturally occurring substances, water has the greatest capacity to absorb and hold heat energy. This is why it takes a hot fire to boil water for coffee, or why hot soup cools slowly. Another related property of water is its ability to absorb or release considerable heat energy without much change in its own temperature.

From direct experience and/or from the study of geography, children may be aware that large bodies of water tend to stabilize the climate of adjacent land. Working in teams, children can study this effect. Needed for each team are a pair of wall thermometers that show the same reading, a glass of water, and access to sunlight (or a radiator) and a refrigerator. Have the children put one thermometer in the water and leave one in the air, setting both aside in a closet until they again show the same reading. Then put both in sun or above a hot radiator for three minutes. Record and diagram the readings obtained and once again set both thermometers in a closet until they show the same readings. When they do, put them in a refrigerator for three minutes and again record the results. As the investigation will show, water absorbs and holds heat energy better than air; thus, land near water tends to have more equable climate.

To investigate heat transfer and temperature rise in water, heat a wooden-handled soldering iron, then plunge it into a pan of water. Use a floating baby's bath thermometer to check water temperature before and after inserting the hot iron. Note the temperature drop when the iron is removed. (Before the advent of the white man's metal cooking pots, Indians cooked with bark vessels or baskets over open fires. The vessels did not burn because their kindling temperature was well above 212°F, the boiling point of water. Thus, water in a container made of folded paper, and placed on a wire mesh stand above heat, will boil before the paper kindles.)

WATER AS SOLVENT

To illustrate water's exceptional power as a solvent, dissolve small quantities (equal amounts) of such household staples as sugar, salt, and soda in hot water. Compare the rates at which solution takes place in other liquids such as oil, vinegar, milk, alcohol, and kerosene.

The peculiarities of the saturated solution can be demonstrated by gradually adding sugar or salt to a small quantity of water until no more will dissolve. Pour the solution into shallow dishes, across which short lengths of white cotton string have been laid. As the solution evaporates, crystals of solute will form along the string. Copper sulfate, alum, or "hypo" (usually available from a local druggist) treated in the same way will produce larger crystals. A piece of string may also be suspended (with a weight such as a nail tied to the end) in a deeper container such as a peanut butter jar. Children will undoubtedly enjoy growing rock candy crystals. To do this, add 2 cups of sugar to a cup or more of boiling water. Stir until dissolved, and cool. Suspend a clean string in the solution and leave undisturbed until crystals have grown large. If a string of rock candy is added to another sugar solution, the crystals will grow larger.

Nearly all parts of the country have some rock formations that show evidence of the dissolving action of water. In limestone regions, water may have dissolved out caves or potholes in the rocks. The salts that are dissolved out of the rocks and find their way to the ocean account for the saltiness of the sea. Classroom chalk is a powdered, compressed form of a kind of rock that is usually a combination of limestone and gypsum (plaster). Crush some chalk in water and mix. Pass the result through filter paper, until the filtrate appears clear. If the fluid is boiled away or allowed to evaporate, however, there will be a white, powdery residue—that part of the chalk that went into solution.

Dissolve lime tablets obtained from the drugstore. Filter until clear. Also procure a small quantity of phenolphthalein solution from the drugstore. Adding a few drops to the clear limewater turns it red. Nothing happens when the phenolpthalein is added to some pure tap water.

Put a crushed lump of sugar into a glass jar and a whole lump in another container. Add equal amounts of water to both. Since more surface is exposed in the crushed lump, it dissolves faster.

As may be seen from examination of their labels, many household products contain water. Many contain elements that may be recombined to form water. For example, water drops should condense within a cool tumbler held over heated oil. (For safety, heat the oil in a waterbath or double boiler.) Hydrogen and oxygen gas released from the oil recombine as water.

A kitchen is a fine place to observe and investigate the uses and properties of water. Listing kitchen activities dependent upon water may be instructive. The preparation of many dishes would be impossible without water or some liquid—such as milk—largely water.

Water is the main vehicle for the removal and redistribution of dirt. Dirt is usually considered as tiny particles of solids bound to surfaces by a film of fats and greases. From the investigations into surface tension (above) it is clear that water alone would be a poor agent for dissolving and removing the fat binder. Soaps emulsify (see p. 176) or loosen the fat binder so that water can then flush out and bear off the dirt. Detergents, now more popular than soap for some kinds of cleaning, act by lowering the surface tension of the water, so that it penetrates more readily, surrounding the dirt particle with a film of water and, thus, separating it from the surface to which it is attached.

"Pure" water is more a figure of speech than fact, even in the case of double-distilled laboratory water, which also contains minute traces of dissolved substances. Rainwater, naturally distilled from clouds, collects gases and dust from the atmosphere in its fall. An important reagent thus formed from rainwater is weak carbonic acid (H_2CO_3), a compound resulting from the absorption of carbon dioxide (CO_2) molecules by the rain, and their chemical combination with water molecules (H_2O). Acting on surface and subsurface rock, this common chemical can dissolve enough minerals from limestone and some other earth materials to make the resulting water "hard." Hard light-colored crusts in teakettles and other vessels used for boiling water are the telltale residue of water with much mineral in solution. If local water comes from wells, samples may be tested in the classroom for hardness. Fill several test tubes or other glass vessels with equal amounts of water, each from a different source. Add a drop of liquid soap to each. Plug the opening with the thumb and shake the tube until suds appear. Record the number of drops necessary to make suds lasting half a minute. Repeat, testing different forms of soap and soap preparations.

While dissolved minerals make water hard, these same materials in solution constitute nutrients carried to living cells in plants and animals by the water. Indeed, water is a chief determinant of the ecosystem of an area. Distribution of desert plants and associated animal life is closely related to available precipitation. Weeds and the attendant insect population of a vacant lot can often reflect, in a kind of microcosm, how population and distribution of water supply are related.

Investigations into chemical gardening (hydroponics) will help develop an understanding of the role of water in bearing nutrients to plants. (The feeding of indoor plants with nutrient solutions is now quite common.)

Ground water saturated with minerals in solution is responsible for the beautiful crystal formations that every rock collector hopes to find. (For classroom crystal-making see p. 108.)

CONVECTION IN WATER

Convection currents such as are at work in the ventilation of rooms and in changing weather also occur in water. These currents can be made visible in a test tube $\frac{2}{3}$ full of water by adding a drop of food color while holding the tip of the tube over heat. The color particles, denser than water, first fall to the bottom, then stream toward the top (where the water cools), then fall, rise again, and so on as heating produces currents of warm water that rise, drawing along the color particles.

Thus, like air, warm water rises and cool water descends, producing convectional currents. To see this clearly, fill a quart jar and a tumbler with ice water and another jar and tumbler with warm water. Add blue food color to the tumbler of ice water and another color to the tumbler of warm water. Slowly pour the tumbler of ice water into the jar of warm water, and the glass of warm water into the jar of ice water. Conclusions drawn from the investigation described on p. 94 should make it possible for children to predict that the blue (and, hence, cool) solution holds the most dissolved oxygen. (In a cool solution, the oxygen molecules lack the speed necessary to escape the fluid.) Raising water temperature from 32°F to 77°F decreases oxygen content more than 40%: For this reason goldfish in boiled water (the boiled water should be kept closely covered as it cools) will surface for air more often than fish in freshly drawn water.

Convection currents also explain the spring and fall "overturn" in fresh-water bodies—that is, the movement of bottom water to the top and vice versa. The mechanism, in a frozen lake, for example, would be as follows. The temperature of water directly under the ice is 0° while that at the bottom is around 4°. As the ice melts in spring and the water warms to 4°, it sinks (causing overturn) because it becomes more dense than the water below it. (Water becomes *more* dense as it warms from 0° to 4°, and *less* dense above 4°.) As the surface water warms above 4°, density becomes lower, stopping any further descent of water.

With the first cold weather, the temperature of the surface water drops below that of the deeper waters, increasing the density of the former and producing another overturn as the cooler and denser water sinks. The convection currents so formed return organic nutrients to depleted parts of the water column of the lake.

Fathoms below the warm Gulf Stream is a cold current flowing in the opposite direction. (The cooling water molecules of the Gulf Stream slow down and pack more closely together, and the resultant denser water sinks to the bottom.)

Investigations into water may enrich and extend children's vocabulary by the acquisition of such terms as the derivatives of the root word *hydro*—viz., hydrant, hydroplane, hydrosphere, etc. A glossary of terms might include picture definitions of buoyancy, cohesion, evaporation, transpiration, precipitation, and the like.

SUGGESTED PROJECTS

1. Boil 2 inches of water in a saucepan. Cool and remeasure. Heat and carefully remeasure the depth of the water. Set the pan in ice, wait several minutes, and again remeasure.

2. Put an egg into a pot of fresh water; then add salt until the egg floats. Have children consider whether the load (or Plimsoll) lines on ships would be the same for fresh as for salt water.

3. Make flannel board drawings to illustrate the water cycle.

4. Study a globe or world map and decide what percentage is covered with water.

5. The phenomenon of surface tension permits the delightful pastime of blowing soap bubbles. Encourage children to discover whether different kinds of soap or differences in strength of solution make any difference in the size of the bubbles.

6. Have children determine the composition of household bleach (from container labels).

7. Do a study of municipal water purification. (Some public water supply agencies offer explanatory literature.)

8. Let children discuss and do research to determine whether water is a chemical. A mineral?

BIBLIOGRAPHY

(**P** indicates recommended for primary grades, **I** for intermediate grades, **U** for upper grades.)

Bate, Norman, *Who Built the Dam?* Scribners, 1958. Concept of current and control. Pictures depict construction of hydroelectric dam. **I**

Bauer, Helen, *Water: Riches or Ruin,* Doubleday, 1959. The case for conservation of natural resources. Illustrated with photographs, line cuts, diagrams, and maps. **U**

Black, Irma S., *Busy Water,* Holiday, 1958. Water cycle. **P**

Blough, Glenn O., *Not Only for Ducks: The Story of Rain,* McGraw-Hill, 1954. Water cycle, seed germination, and frog life cycle. **P**

Boys, C. V., *Soap Bubbles and the Forces Which Mold Them,* Doubleday, 1959. Work of a nineteenth century scientist. Part of a fresh approach to the study and teaching of physics. **U**

Branley, Franklyn M., *Floating and Sinking,* Crowell, 1967. Through experimentation the reader learns about buoyancy. Precise illustrations. **I**

Buehr, Walter, *Water: Our Most Vital Need,* Norton, 1967. Concise and lucid explanation of water in our lives—the need for it, its many uses, its conservation, protection, and production. **U**

Carlisle, Norman, *The True Book of Rivers,* Children's Pr., 1967. A brief and simple explanation of how rivers are formed, used, and kept clean. **P**

Carlson, Carl Walter, *Water Fit to Use,* Day, 1966. Concentrates on America's water needs and pollution. Discusses the international problem of a growing population and a shrinking water supply. **U**

Carrick, Carol, *The Brook,* Macmillan, 1967. From rain to rivulets to brook to river to pond and, finally, to the sea. Water color illustrations, large type. **I**

Cocannouer, Joseph A., *Water and the Cycle of Life,* Devin-Adair, 1958. In story form: the importance, use, and control of water. Extensive glossary. **U**

Feravolo, Rocco, *Easy Physics Projects: Air, Water and Heat,* Prentice-Hall, 1966. Forty-eight experiments—16 on air, 19 on water, 13 on heat. Lists materials—all easily available—gives simple directions and clear explanations of concepts involved. Clearly illustrated. **I**

———, *Junior Science Book of Water Experiments,* Garrard, 1965. Hydrological cycles, underground water, and water pressure. Easy experiments clarify the concepts. **I**

Green, Ivah, *Water: Our Most Valuable Natural Resource,* Coward-McCann, 1958. Water—its sources, movements, benefits, and problems. **U**

Pine, Tillie S., and Joseph Levine, *Water All Around,* McGraw-Hill, 1959. All kinds of water in various forms. Simple experiments. **P**

Riedman, Sarah R., *Water for People,* Abelard-Shuman, rev. ed., 1960. Water—where it comes from, where it goes, how it works, how it changes, why it grows scarce, how we can get more. Illustrated, indexed. **U**

Rosenfeld, Sam, *Science Experiments with Water,* Harvey, 1965. Introduction to physics; clear explanations of physical laws and easy experiments demonstrate underlying principles. Illustrated with drawings and photographs. Includes a section on laboratory apparatus, study questions and answers, glossary, bibliography, and index. **U**

Schloat, G. Warren, Jr., *The Magic of Water,* Scribners, 1955. Simple experiments to help children understand the source and uses of water. **I**

Stockard, Jimmy, *Experiments for Young Scientists,* Little, Brown, 1964. Simple experiments (with safety rules and illustrations) demonstrate scientific principles and facts concerning air, water, light, sound, simple machines, and electricity. **I**

Tresselt, Alvin, *Rain Drop Splash,* Lothrop, 1954. Raindrops to puddles to ponds to rivers to sea. **P**

Van Dersal, W. R., and E. H. Graham, *Water for America,* Walck, 1956. Picture story of water conservation. **U**

Winchester, James H., *Wonders of Water,* Putnam, 1963. Historical, scientific, and economic significance of water. Describes Scripps Institute of Oceanography experiments for the conversion of sea water and the use of icebergs. **U**

Satellite view of clouds reflecting the spiral movement of the winds of a hurricane

7 Weather and Climate

Understanding of weather and climate should be approached through many simple investigations building ideas of matter and energy, of the great cycle of evaporation–condensation, and of convection currents in earth's ocean of air. Study of climate and weather can begin on school grounds. A great deal can be learned by studying temperature, pressure, and humidity changes that occur around the "elfin forests" of school shrubbery, the grassy prairies of a school lawn, and the "paved deserts" of school playgrounds.

As a first step in a close look at the forces involved in the ocean of air in which we live, it will be convenient to map the school grounds—to inventory the terrain and pinpoint weather study stations. Divide a large sheet of paper into squares representing units (1 foot, 10

feet, etc.) appropriate to the children's grasp of relative scale and to the size of the school grounds. Teams of two or three children can measure and draw small sections, which can be transposed to a large master map. The map need not be too detailed (Fig. 7-1), but should show the outlines of buildings, boundaries, and the general locations of such elements as shrubbery, trees, playground, lawn, etc. Each child can then make on graph paper his own copy of the master map.

TEMPERATURE

Primary-grade children enjoy reading a room thermometer especially if this is part of the duties of a "window monitor" in charge of room ventilation. Giant-size thermometers make the reading easier, as does a "thermometer" made of tagboard, chart paper, and a long zipper (Fig. 7-2). Sew or glue the zipper to the tagboard and paint the metal strip and handle with red nail polish or lacquer. A narrow strip of unmarked graph paper attached alongside the zipper allows children to add the calibrations and special markings. The strips should be removable so that each new class can be offered the same challenge. As interest grows, it may be useful to install an outside thermometer (away from direct sunlight) for reading, recording, and comparing indoor and outdoor temperatures over an extended period.

To make a model thermometer, fill a flask or a narrow-neck bottle with water colored dark red with food coloring. Insert a long, thin, glass or plastic tube in a one-hole rubber stopper and fit the stopper tightly into the mouth of the flask (Fig. 7-3). Adjust the amount of water in the flask so that when the stopper is inserted, the colored water will rise about half way into the tube above the stopper. Make two slits in an unruled index card and slide the card over the tube. Mark on the card the level of the water in the tube. If

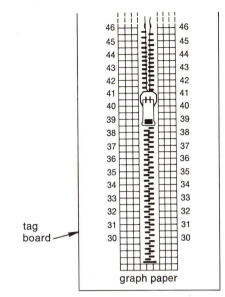

FIGURE **7-2** Zipper "thermometer," with graph-paper strips.

the room temperature rises, so will the water in the tube (the warming water expands). Calibrate the marks on the scale of the index card with the readings on a standard thermometer.

Directions for making other kinds of thermometers are given in Chapter 17.

Relation to Plant Life

Accurate temperature readings taken through the year in selected spots on school grounds can offer insight into the relation between temperature and light and plant growth. Why do some shrubs, for example, flourish on the south side but not on the north side of buildings? Answering such a question requires several inexpensive thermometers that show the same readings at the time of purchase. Have children make ground temperature readings on the lawn, the school garden, the bare playground, under shrubs and trees, above the sidewalk, one foot inside or outside the eaves of the building, and at four walls (facing in different directions) of the school building. Repeat at different hours and seasons being careful to shade the bulb when making readings in sunlight. Record, on the small maps (Fig. 7-1) of

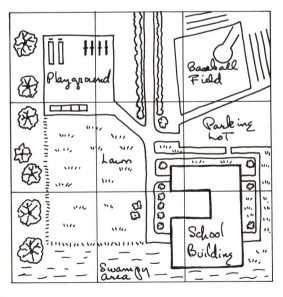

FIGURE **7-1** Typical master sketch map of school grounds.

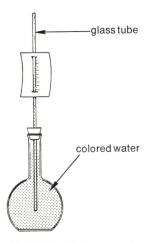

FIGURE **7-3** Model liquid thermometer.

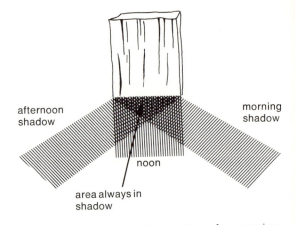

FIGURE **7-4** Typical shadow pattern for morning, noon, and afternoon.

school ground locations, air temperatures taken daily at the same time of the day.

Ground temperature readings are made by placing thermometer bulbs on the ground. For subsurface readings, slip the thermometer into a 3-inch slot in the soil, press the soil close around the bulb, and read as soon as the liquid stops moving.

Snow often insulates and protects plants and animals against very low temperatures. To illustrate, take readings at different depths in snow with a thermometer fastened to the end of a yardstick or, if the snow is too deep, to a broom handle or a piece of doweling marked off in inches.

Relation to Light

Temperature records will soon disclose a relationship between temperature and light. Place stones or stakes to mark the borders of shadows cast by a school ground tree, a building, etc. Drive a shingle into the ground and note the area covered by its shadow at mid-morning, noon, and afternoon (Fig. 7-4). The shade is permanent where the shadows intersect. Children may observe whether there is any difference between the plant or animal life in areas of permanent shade, partial shade, and permanent light.

A photographic light meter will show surprising variations in readings from one part of a school ground to another. Since meters are sensitive instruments, easily broken by careless handling or a sudden fall, only the owner or teacher should use it. Children can record the light readings, which should be made as follows. Aim the meter at a sheet of white paper mounted at different stations. Hold the meter about 1 foot from the paper and take several readings from different angles, until a position is found that gives a median reading. Use this same position for other readings in other places. It might be informative to make readings of the same place at different times of the day.

AIR PRESSURE

Next to the thermometer, the most useful instrument for a classroom weather station is a barometer, which shows changes in air pressure. A simple barometer can be made of a milk bottle or a milk carton with its top cut off (Fig. 7-5). Warm the carton or bottle in hot water (to create a partial vacuum in the vessel), and stretch a section of toy balloon over the top, securing it with rubber bands or tape. Glue a broomstraw or drinking straw to the rubber with a small piece

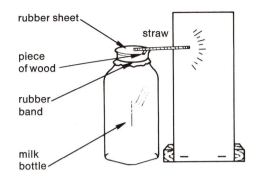

FIGURE **7-5**   Milk-carton barometer.

of wood beneath it as shown. When the air pressure increases, the rubber diaphragm and the attached wood-and-straw indicator move down; when pressure decreases, they move upward. Draw divergent calibration lines on cardboard with a pencil box protractor and fix the scale behind the tip of the straw. Children can check for correspondence with daily barometric pressures reported in the news.

A barometer can also be made from a small can. Make two small holes in the can, remove the contents, wash the can, and stand it in hot water. Although it is preferable to seal the holes with solder or epoxy cement, they may be sealed with chewing gum or hot wax. Attach the can to a wooden base about $3 \times 20 \times \frac{3}{4}$ inches, as shown in Fig. 7-6, (available at a model airplane shop), a small cork, and some Tinkertoy sticks. Cement a cork to the center of the top of the can. To one side mount, in a hole drilled in the wood base, a $\frac{1}{4}$-inch dowel or a stick from a construction toy. The dowel may also be

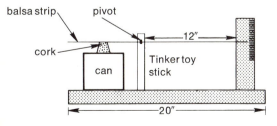

FIGURE **7-6**   Barometer made of metal can.

mounted in a hub (such as are found in many construction toy sets) glued to the base. Attach a thin ($\frac{1}{8}$ inch) balsa wood strip to the stick by means of a common pin or extremely fine nail. The strip must move freely on the pin, and one end of it should rest on the cork. Place a cardboard scale, calibrated as shown in the figure, behind the other end of the strip.

MOISTURE

Most children are aware only of extremes in the amount of moisture in earth's ocean of air. On warm damp days, a glass of ice water is soon coated with moisture condensed from the atmosphere (not through the glass!). "Snow" may be seen on refrigerator coils and "frost" on a glass container of dry ice. Children may have come to school through fog on cool damp days or enjoyed startling experiences with static electricity on cool, dry days.

Humidity

In estimating fire danger, the Forest Service keeps close watch on minor humidity changes. Fire lookout stations daily weigh a standard-sized cube of kiln-dried wood after it has been exposed to air. On damp days the cube, having absorbed some of the moisture, is heavier. When the air is dry, the wood loses moisture to the air and weighs less. The lower the humidity, the greater the fire danger.

Anyone who develops photographic film knows how dry film can curl unmanageably. To exploit this characteristic as an indicator of relative humidity, tack a strip of 35-mm. or other film to an old ruler or calibrated stake (Fig. 7-7). Distribute the film sticks in different areas. In an hour or more, note how far the film has curled or uncurled in each location.

Blue cobalt chloride paper from the druggist hung in various parts of the school grounds will indicate relative humidity by the time required for the paper to change from blue to gray-white

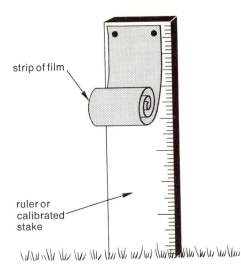

FIGURE **7-7** Photographic film used as a moisture indicator.

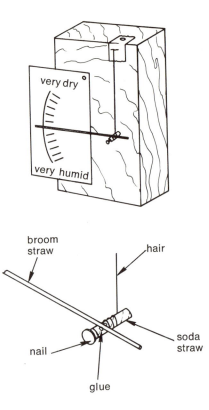

FIGURE **7-8** Human hair hygrometer.

or pink. Try at different times of day and on different days, and at varied sites such as under a rock or piece of bark or in the mouth of a culvert. (When not in use, the paper should be stored in a well-closed bottle together with a drying agent such as calcium chloride or silica gel.)

A hair hygrometer, to measure the amount of moisture in air, can be made of human hair (Fig. 7-8) or of catgut (Fig. 7-9). For the former, use a strand of brunette human hair, about 10 inches long, washed thoroughly in hot, soapy water, rinsed in cold water, and allowed to dry. Cut a 1-inch piece from a soda straw. (Use a sharp razor blade to avoid flattening the straw.) Glue one end of a 5-inch broomstraw to the piece of soda straw.

Put a long, thin nail through the piece of soda straw and drive it into a (12-inch) block of wood near one end, as shown in the figure. Fasten one end of the hair to a piece of cellophane tape about 2 inches long by piercing the tape about 1 inch from its end and passing the hair through the hole to the gummed side of the tape. Glue the other end of the hair to the piece of soda straw. When the glue has dried, turn the soda straw a few times to wind part of the hair around

it in the direction shown in the figure. Attach the cellophane tape to the top of the piece of wood so that the hair is taut (and prevented from rubbing against the wood by the lower inch or so of the tape) and the broomstraw horizontal. To prevent the tape from loosening, press it down firmly at the top of the block of wood and insert thumb tacks. Tack an index card to the wood on the side near the broomstraw.

When the air is dry, the hair will contract and the broomstraw pointer will turn up. When the air is humid, the hair will become moist and expand, relaxing and allowing the weight of the broomstraw to turn it down.

To calibrate the hygrometer, put it into a pail and cover the pail with a towel that has been soaked in very hot water. The relative humidity in the pail will quickly reach 100%, and the broomstraw will move down as the hair stretches. After 20 minutes remove the hygrometer and mark the position of the broomstraw as 100% relative humidity. Allow some time for the pointer to return to a normal position, then calibrate other positions on the index card by using a commercial hygrometer or a wet-and-dry bulb thermometer (see below).

To make a catgut hygrometer, suspend a musician's catgut string from any simple wooden stand (Fig. 7-9) and attach the other end to the base by means of a rubber band passed through a hole in or tacked to the base. A toothpick pushed through the gut acts as a pointer as the gut twists or untwists according to variations in moisture in the air. Glue or tack to the base a circular scale drawn on a 3 × 5 card. Note and record daily the position of one end of the toothpick, marking also the humidity as reported in the news. After a month, the calibrations for the string hygrometer should be fairly accurate. During the winter, steam-heated classrooms will show about 25% relative humidity. Readings should also be made outdoors—on a window sill,

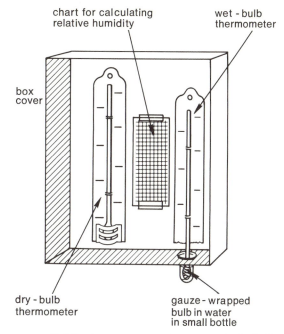

FIGURE **7-10** Arrangement of wet- and dry-bulb thermometers for determining relative humidity.

for example. Do not leave the instrument in the rain or snow.

Relative humidity is the amount of moisture in the air stated as a percentage of (relative to) the maximum amount of moisture that air can hold (without precipitation) at a given temperature. The higher the temperature, the greater the amount of moisture a given volume of air can hold. One can determine relative humidity with a wet- and dry-bulb hygrometer. Needed to make one are two identical, inexpensive wall thermometers, a shallow cardboard box cover, a small vial or pill bottle, and a small piece of gauze. Remove the bulb guard of one thermometer and wrap the bulb with gauze. Mount both thermometers in the box cover (Fig. 7-10) and fix the pill bottle (filled with water) in a hole in the box lid edge so that the gauze-wrapped bulb extends down into the water. As water moves up the gauze (as in a wick, by capillary attraction) the thermometer will register a drop in temperature. (A copy of the humidity table (Table 7-1) may

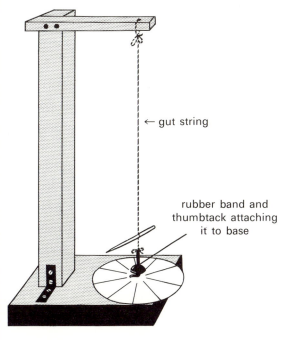

FIGURE **7-9** Catgut string hygrometer.

be positioned between the thermometers.) Fanning the wet-bulb thermometer will produce (by evaporation—see p. 97) a further drop in the temperature it records. When this no longer occurs, note the difference between the wet-bulb and the dry-bulb (open to the air) thermometer readings. To calculate relative humidity, find the wet- and dry-bulb temperatures in the chart (Table 7-1); the figure at the point of intersection of the columns in which the temperatures appear is the relative humidity. For example, a dry-bulb thermometer reading of 72°F, when the wet-bulb thermometer reads 64°F indicates a relative humidity of 65% (shown in boldface figures in the table).

A more accurate measurement of humidity can be obtained with a wet- and dry-bulb thermometer arrangement on a sling (Fig. 7-11). To do

Table 7-1   RELATIVE HUMIDITY   Chart Based on Wet- and Dry-Bulb Thermometer Readings

Wet-bulb temperature	Dry-bulb temperature (°F)									
	62	64	66	68	70	72	74	76	78	80
42	8	4								
44	16	11	7	3						
46	24	18	14	10	6	3				
48	32	26	21	16	12	9	5	3		
50	41	34	29	23	19	15	11	8	5	3
52	50	43	36	31	25	21	17	13	10	7
54	59	51	44	38	33	28	23	19	16	12
56	69	60	53	46	40	34	29	25	21	18
58	79	70	61	54	48	42	36	31	27	23
60	89	79	71	62	55	49	43	38	33	29
62	100	90	80	71	64	57	50	44	39	35
64		100	90	80	72	**65**	58	51	46	41
66			100	90	81	73	65	59	53	47
68				100	90	82	74	66	60	54
70					100	91	82	74	67	61
72						100	91	82	75	68
74							100	91	83	75
76								100	91	83
78									100	91
80										100

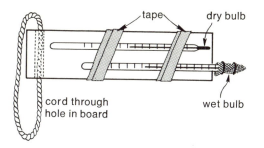

FIGURE **7-11** Sling psychrometer for accurate measurement of relative humidity.

this, securely attach two wall thermometers to a narrow board with several turns of strong tape. Cover one bulb with wet gauze. Loop a strong cord through a hole near the top of the board. Holding the psychrometer by the cord, whirl it overhead for two minutes, and then note the difference between the wet- and dry-bulb readings. To find the relative humidity, use Table 7-1 as described above.

Dew and Frost

The temperature at which water vapor will condense from air is called the dew point. This temperature will vary, depending upon how much water vapor is in the air (that is, the humidity). The higher the relative humidity the less the air has to be cooled to produce condensation; thus the water vapor condenses out at a relatively high temperature, and the dew point is relatively high. Conditions are often ideal for formation of dew in the spring and the fall because the days are warm (and water evaporates readily, filling the air with water vapor) and the nights are cool. Warm summer air can hold four to five times as much water as frosty fall and winter air.

To produce dew, fill a shiny metal can half full of water; add ice cubes and stir. Soon a thin film of tiny droplets of dew will form on the outside of the can. The tiny droplets will gradually come together to form larger droplets. In the summer, the humidity may be so high that the water vapor will condense without the addition of ice. In the winter, however, the humidity may be so low that

salt will have to be added to the cold water and ice in order to get the water vapor in the air to condense.

The temperature of the can's contents at the moment the droplets of water begin to form is the dew point. The dew point can be arrived at by slowly adding small pieces of ice to the can of water, while stirring the contents with a thermometer, whose reading can be checked the moment the first thin film of water appears. (Do not breathe on the sides of the can when watching for dew; the water vapor in one's breath will condense on the can and distort results.)

Frost can be made by filling a tall, shiny metal can with firmly packed alternate layers of cracked ice and table salt, each ice layer twice as thick as the salt layer. Some dew may form on the sides of the can and then freeze, but frost will also form as the temperature of the air immediately surrounding the can falls to below freezing and the water vapor in the air condenses *directly* into tiny crystals of ice.

Fog and Clouds

Clouds form when warm moist air rising from the earth meets cooler air at higher levels (temperature generally is about one degree F cooler for each 300 foot rise in altitude) and the water vapor condenses (on condensation nuclei such as dust or other particulate matter) from the air to form clouds. A fog is really a cloud at ground level.

To "make" a fog, place a large ice cube in the mouth of a milk bottle a quarter full of hot water (Fig. 7-12). Holding the bottle up to the

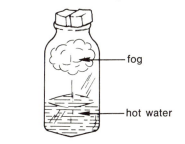

FIGURE **7-12** "Fog" in a milk bottle.

sunlight or a lamp will make it easier to see where the warm moist air, rising from the hot water, meets the cold air around the ice cube to form a fog.

Rain

The amount of moisture in the air depends upon several variables, such as temperature and air pressure. These variables also determine the amount of rainfall by determining condensation and one of its results—rain.

To determine such things as why rain varies—from a drizzle to a downpour—and whether all raindrops are the same size, investigators are now using high-speed photography and other specialized equipment. Children can study raindrops by observing the "tracks" that drops make in trays of soft powder or flour set outdoors briefly during rainfall. Raindrops may also leave tracks as splash marks (p. 135).

By direct observation of clouds, children may make three-dimensional "pictures" of them from cotton, paste, and blue paper. These may be categorized into major types—for example, cirrus, stratus, cumulus. "Contrails," also visible in the sky, occur when vapor in the hot exhaust gases of high-flying jet planes condense in the cold air usually present at high altitudes.

U.S. Weather Bureau statistics show rainfall figures for most locations and daily newspapers usually include some data on local precipitation. Keeping their own records will give children a chance to gain a concrete concept of local rainfall patterns and of how seasonal patterns are related to what people do and how they live.

A way of producing a local "rainstorm" in the classroom is described in Chapter 6, p. 99 and Fig. 6-2.

Snow, Sleet, Glaze, Hail

In winter, when the humidity is low, the air may be cooled to the point where condensation and precipitation take place below the freezing point. Then snow instead of rain is formed. To examine snowflakes, catch some on a soft, dark wool cloth,

cold window glass, microscope slides, or cold metal. (Small snowflakes are best because they are individual while the larger are usually clusters of smaller flakes.) Using a magnifying glass, children may note that all snowflakes have six sides; no two are alike.

Raindrops that form in air temperatures above freezing, but then fall through layers of air colder than 32°F, freeze and fall as sleet. Glaze is a coating of ice that forms when rain freezes after it reaches the ground.

Hail, also a form of frozen rain, is usually formed in the summer during a thunderstorm when there are strong upward currents of air within the thundercloud. These upward currents will often blow the raindrops up into a layer of air where the temperature is below freezing. The raindrops freeze into tiny pellets of ice which, if it is snowing in this layer of air, will become coated with snow. The pellets then fall back into warmer air where they become coated with rain. These water-coated pellets of ice may be blown up into the layer of below-freezing air again where the coating of water freezes to form a layer of ice over the original pellets. This process may be repeated several times, the hailstones becoming larger each time.

A hailstone quickly cut through with a sharp knife may reveal the layers of ice (and snow), like rings in an onion, showing just how many times the original raindrop was blown upward into the cold air and then fell back into warmer air.

Frost

Frost is not frozen dew nor is snow frozen rain. Both are formed of water vapor that has condensed (the former on a surface, the latter in air) directly as a *solid*, not first as water. To make frost, use a can stripped of its label similar to the one used to determine dew point (above). Pack the can with a mixture of two parts ice and one part salt. The can will soon become frosted. To investigate the role of salt in lowering the freezing point of water (to 25°–20°F) one can have the children make ice cream. (The school cafeteria manager may provide ice cream mix as well as several empty No. 10 cans.) Use smaller cans to hold the mix; the larger, ice and salt (and the small cans). One can also use plastic pill bottles (for the mix) and plastic insulated cups for the ice and salt.

Measurement of precipitation An effective rain gauge can be constructed of a 4-inch (top diameter) funnel placed in a 2-inch-diameter bottle with a ruler pasted to it and that, in turn, placed in a gallon glass jar (Fig. 7-13). With apparatus of these proportions, 4 inches of water collected in the bottle equals 1 inch of rain per square inch of surface. Thus, 1 inch of water collected in the olive bottle indicates a $\frac{1}{4}$-inch rainfall. Any water overflowing into the larger jar should be poured into the smaller and included in the measurements. Set the apparatus on the school roof or, if that is not accessible, wired to a stake on an open, grassy lawn. Keep records over a period of months, both for spring and fall, and compare with weather bureau data for the same period.

Measure snow depth immediately after a snowfall by pushing a ruler or yardstick into the snow where drifting or blowing has not taken place. Divide the depth by 10 to get a rough estimate of the number of inches of rain that would have fallen instead.

To convert snowfall accurately into the equivalent rainfall, collect falling snow in a tall can and measure the depth with a ruler. Bring the can indoors, cover the top with a piece of cardboard, and let the snow melt slowly to keep loss by evaporation to a minimum. Then measure the melted snow to get the equivalent number of inches of rainfall.

WIND

That wind is moving air can be made tangible for children quite simply: by directing an electric fan onto their faces and by pointing out the rustling of the leaves of a plant put near the fan.

Wind is a result of unequal heating of the earth's surface by the sun. To illustrate one of

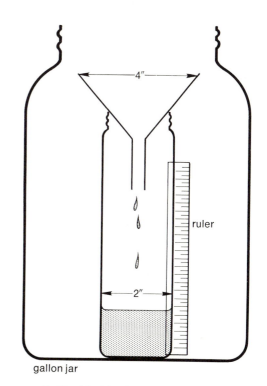

FIGURE **7-13** Model rain gauge.

the ways this occurs, put equal amounts of soil into each of two boxes and place both boxes in the sunlight, one laid flat so that it receives slanted rays from the sun, and the other propped up so that the sun's rays strike it directly. Insert a thermometer the same depth in each box of soil. Take temperature readings every ten minutes. The soil that receives the direct rays of the sun, hence the warmer, can represent the earth's equatorial region, which receives direct rays, while the rays received in the northerly and southerly latitudes are more slanted. The air above the earth in these regions will be heated correspondingly unequally.

Winds are convection currents like those described in Chapter 17, but on a large scale. The air over heated areas becomes warmed, expands and (volume for volume) becomes lighter. It rises, therefore, and cooler, heavier air comes in and replaces it.

Land and sea breezes (onshore and offshore winds) are produced similarly. One can demon-

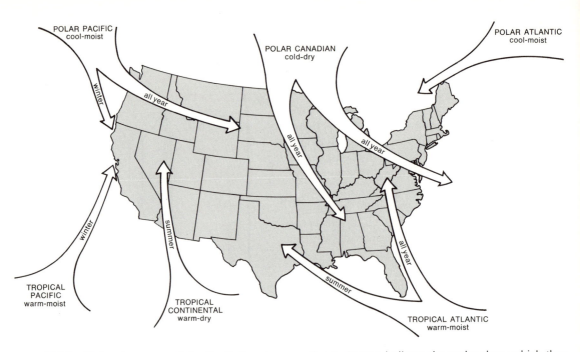

FIGURE **7-14** Major air masses of the North American continent. Arrows indicate the paths along which they commonly move and interact.

strate this by putting some dry soil in a tumbler and filling another of the same size to the same level with water. Place a thermometer in each tumbler and keep the tumblers in a shaded spot until their temperatures are the same. Then set both tumblers in direct sunlight, noting their temperatures every fifteen minutes. The soil will warm more rapidly than the water. In the same manner, in the afternoon and early evening land has heated up more than a neighboring ocean or lake. The air above the land becoming warmer than the air above the lake, rises, and the cool air above the water moves in (onshore breeze) from the water. At night and in the morning, when the land has cooled more than the water, the process is reversed.

To demonstrate how continual winds can dry out land, fill two flowerpots with soil dug up immediately after a rain. See that both pots, with their contents, weigh the same. Place one in a protected spot, say a closet, the other directly in front of a small electric fan. Reweigh both at the end of the day.

Air Masses and Fronts

The rotation of the earth causes the winds on earth to swerve. Generally, winds moving north or south are deflected to their right in the northern hemisphere and to their left in the southern hemisphere. A chalkboard drawing showing the motion and direction of the major wind belts (available in most geography texts) can lead to discussion of how the belts are formed. Information on discoveries of new jet streams in the atmosphere of the earth may be found in reports on studies made during the 1957–1958 International Geophysical Year.

A chalkboard relief map of North America and Mexico on which are shown the six major air masses that affect weather in the United States (Fig. 7-14) can be useful, as can information concerning their seasonality.

Children can watch for the appearance of fronts, using the weather forecast as a guide and keeping a record of the weather conditions that prevail from the time it begins to move in until it has passed. A useful supplement to this would be a chalkboard representation of the structure and dynamics of cold and warm fronts (Fig. 7-15), showing the kinds of clouds and precipitation that are formed in each case.

Using newspaper weather maps covering a period of two weeks, children can (1) note the progress of cold and warm fronts across the country; (2) predict the kinds of weather changes the appearance of each front might bring (check against the actual weather conditions that ensued); and (3) locate highs and lows on a weather map and compare the kinds of weather found in the corresponding regions. Also draw chalkboard diagrams showing (by means of arrows) the tendency toward clockwise rotation of high-pressure centers and the counterclockwise direction of lows in the northern hemisphere (Fig. 7-16). In the case of low-pressure masses, the phenomenon has as its basis the fact that the lowest air pressure in a low is at its center. As a result, air of higher pressure blows toward the center and, because of the earth's rotation, moving air in the northern hemisphere is deflected to the right, making the inward-blowing air travel in a counterclockwise direction. In the case of

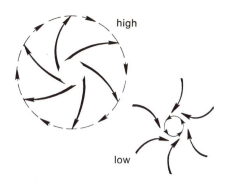

FIGURE **7-16** Direction of movement in high- and low-pressure air masses.

a high, the opposite conditions prevail, the highest air pressure being at the center, so that the air blows outward and so on.

Measuring the Wind

To make a wind vane, cut two large arrows exactly the same size from a piece of heavy cardboard, making sure that the tail is much larger than the head (Fig. 7-17). Staple the two arrows together at the edges of the head and the tail. Remove the rubber bulb of a medicine dropper and seal the pointed tip by placing it in the edge of a gas flame or the flame of an alcohol lamp, then rotating the dropper slowly and steadily. Let the closed tip cool for at least five minutes, then place the arrow across the edge of a ruler and determine the point where it balances. Insert the medicine dropper between the two pieces of cardboard at this balancing point and staple the edges of the body of the arrow.

With wire cutters, cut a straight piece of wire from a coat hanger and file one end of the piece to a sharp point. With friction tape, fasten the wire, point-up, to a strong piece of wood; then place the open end of the medicine dropper over the sharp point of the wire. Nail small strips of wood marked with the cardinal compass points onto the upright so that children can determine the wind direction easily. Use a magnetic compass when erecting the wind vane in order to orient it properly.

Because the tail is larger than the head, it will

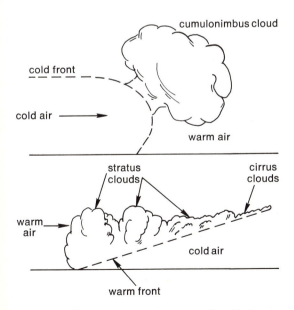

FIGURE **7-15** Dynamics of warm and cold fronts.

react more to the pressure of the wind. As a result, when the wind blows, the vane will swing around until it points into the wind (toward the direction from which the wind is blowing).

An anemometer measures wind speed. One suitable for the school ground can be made as follows. With nails or screws, fasten the centers of two pieces of wood about $15 \times \frac{1}{2} \times \frac{1}{4}$ inch to make an equal-armed cross (Fig. 7-18). At the center, where the wood pieces cross, bore a hole just large enough for the glass part of a medicine dropper to pass through and so that the lower of the two pieces will rest on the lip of the dropper. Tack a paper cup (brightly painted) to each end of the pieces of wood.

Seal the tip of a medicine dropper and prepare and mount (on a piece of wood) a wire as described above in the directions for making a wind vane. Slip the two fastened pieces of wood over the dropper (it may be necessary to use friction tape above and below the hole to prevent the pieces

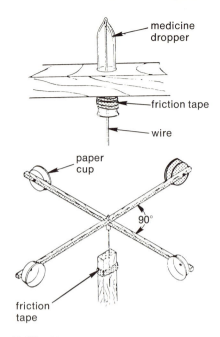

FIGURE **7-18** Model anemometer.

of wood from slipping off the dropper) and place the dropper over the wire.

To calibrate the anemometer, hold it outside the window of a moving car on a calm day where there is no traffic and the road is smooth and level. With the car moving steadily at 5 miles an hour, count the number of turns the anemometer makes in one minute. (Use a watch with a second hand.) The colored cup will make it easier to count the turns. Repeat the count at 10 and at 15 miles an hour. Using these three counts, a graph can be made from which one can read the wind speed on the basis of the number of revolutions per unit of time. A quick but rough approximation of wind speed (in miles per hour) can be made by dividing by 10 the number of revolutions made in one minute.

WEATHER STATION

Children can set up their own weather station using many of the instruments described above. Weather maps can be obtained from the nearest weather bureau or from the Superintendent of

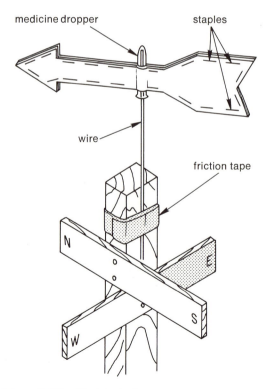

FIGURE **7-17** Model wind vane.

Documents in Washington, D.C. Weather forecasts can be posted on a school bulletin board and might include a small chart comparing children's predictions with official weather forecasts.

Children can keep a daily weather chart for a month, recording observations (made about the same time each day) of the following: date and time, temperature outdoors, air pressure, humidity, direction and speed of the wind, condition of the sky, and kind and amount of precipitation. In the column describing the condition of the sky, a small circle can be blacked in to an extent corresponding to the amount of sky covered with clouds.

SUGGESTED PROJECTS

1. Using cotton, glue, and blue construction paper, model cloud forms from life. This can be an outdoor class activity for children working in pairs or small groups. Select only major cloud types, such as cirrus, cumulus, stratus, and nimbus. Identify from government cloud charts, photos, and text illustrations.

2. Correlate changes of shadow patterns over a month with changing sunrise and sunset time as given in the daily newspaper.

3. Investigate the "life zone" theory propounded by government naturalists who discovered that certain species of plant and animal life in Western mountains were distributed in a pattern that seemed related to the mean average temperature for the year. In connection with this, make a large, paper, cone-shaped mountain and insert cutout picture of appropriate plants and related animal life at upper, middle, and lower levels. *Up the Mountain* (juvenile) by Betty Morrow, and *Life* (p. 96–7) (adult) by George Gaylord Simpson are recommended references.

4. Children with ability in numbers can report with audiovisual aids on the arithmetic involved in weather recording. For example, the relative areas of funnel and collecting can in a rain gauge.

5. In addition to daily records, a special exhibit or collection of weather in the news might include information about weather radar, weather satellites, Coast Guard weather ships, Navy hurricane patrol, weather reports for commercial flying, samples of U.S. Weather Bureau teletype reports, and facsimile weather map transmittal.

6. Study and report on wind belts of the earth as compared to jet streams in the upper air (stratosphere).

7. Investigate how hurricanes are formed, tracing the general path of hurricanes in the northern hemisphere, listing the most destructive ones, comparing their forward and circular speed, and describing the work of "hurricane hunters" in locating and charting the hurricanes.

8. Distinguish between hurricanes that form in the East in the late summer and fall, and tornadoes that form in the Midwest in the spring, noting their similarities and differences, the destructiveness of such storms and safety precautions that should be taken.

9. Collect pictures of unusual weather conditions or unusual happenings that were influenced by the weather, and determine their causes.

BIBLIOGRAPHY

(**P** indicates recommended for primary grades, **I** for intermediate grades, **U** for upper grades.)

Adler, Irving and Ruth, *Storms*, Day, 1963. The causes and effects of various types of storms briefly described. Illustrated with photographs and diagrams. **I**

Adler, Irving, *Weather In Your Life*, Day, 1959. Theory of ice ages; cloud seeding. **U**

Antoine, Tex, *Wonders Of The Weather*, Dodd, 1962. By the television weatherman. **U**

Barr, George, *Research Adventures for Young Scientists*, McGraw-Hill, 1964. Various science concepts are arranged in ten categories. Experiments suggested. **U**

Bell, Thelma, *Snow,* Viking, 1954. Types of snowflakes, their formation, and snow's effects. Beautiful illustrations. **I**

Bendick, Jeanne, *The Wind,* Rand McNally, 1964. Basic information about the wind in simple and concise terms. Clear cartoon-type illustrations. **I**

Branley, Franklyn M., *Flash, Crash, Rumble, and Roll,* Crowell, 1964. An easy-to-read text which provides an introduction to the subject. Illustrations and helpful diagrams. **P**

————, *Snow Is Falling,* Crowell, 1963. Brief, easy-to-read text and clear drawings explain the nature of snow, its uses and hazards. **P**

Gallant, Roy A., *Exploring The Weather,* Garden City, 1957. A readable, informative book on weather phenomena and the study of meteorology. Maps, diagrams, charts, and pictures. Bibliography. **U**

Hicks, Clifford, *The World Above,* Holt, Rinehart and Winston, 1965. Informal account of the characteristics of the earth's atmosphere, microclimate, and the universe beyond the earth. A chapter on air pollution. **U**

Podendorf, Illa, *True Book of Weather Experiments,* Children's Pr., 1961. Easy book with suggestions for simple experiments. Clear illustrations. **P**

Polgreen, John, *Thunder and Lightning,* Doubleday, 1963. A simple account of seven kinds of lightning and the weather conditions that produce them. Clear text and well-drawn color illustrations. Two pages of teacher material are included. **P**

Schneider, Herman, *Everyday Weather and How It Works,* rev. ed., McGraw-Hill, 1961. Many ideas for simple instruments and experiments. **I**

Spar, Jerome, *The Way of the Weather,* Creative Educational Society, 1962. A detailed, yet simple, account of all phases of weather. **U**

Spilhaus, Athelstan, *Weathercraft,* Viking, 1951. Directions for assembling and operating a home weather station made with inexpensive materials. **U**

Rugged terrain of Augustine Island, Alaska, with one of the area's active volcanoes in the distance.

8 The Earth's Surface

Not all schools have a view of mountains, but there are few schools that are not near one or more of the other major land forms—hills, valleys, or plains. Others may be near wind-built sand dunes; river-built bars, deltas, or flood plains; or water-carved land forms, such as canyons, arroyos, draws, washes, caves, and cliffs.

All too often the study of geography and how it affects people is only an abstraction. Home geography and the way it has determined the location of the town or of business or homes is sometimes ignored for a study of distant lands. A school might, for example, have been located on a hill to obtain adequate drainage, or local topography may have determined the size and shape of the school grounds. In touring local

neighborhoods or discussing the locations of children's homes, have them note the kinds of land surface on which the various buildings stand. Consider whether geography has affected the layout of streets in the city or town. Watch for road cuts where one may see exposed the tilted layers of bedrock of which the hills are formed. These layers were once horizontal, since they were deposited as sediments settling out of the water that may have covered an area. To see how far from horizontal the rocks have been warped, hold a jump rope or clothesline level against the rock (Fig. 8-1). (To level the line, use a "pop" bottle half full of water, as farmers sometimes do in laying out lines of uniform elevation for contour plowing.) Other examples of local rock structure

FIGURE **8-1** Tilted rock layers in contrast to a horizontal line. The line may be leveled by use of a bottle half-full of water, as shown.

may help children see today's landscape as the result of many stages in the endless cycle of erosion, deposition, and uplifting of the earth's crust.

FORMATION OF MOUNTAINS

The bending of rock layers by which mountains were formed took hundreds or thousands of centuries. Sometimes pressure was so great that rock layers were bent into A-shaped *anticlines* or S-shaped *synclines* (Fig. 8-2), the formations often visible in road cuts. To simulate the mountain-making action that took place in the cooling, shrinking earth, spread a sheet of kitchen foil on a desk or table and push with fingertips from each end of the sheet toward the center. Resultant wrinkles represent hills and mountains. (Set the crumpled sheet into a sink or tray and sprinkle it with colored water to depict the accumulation of water in a watershed.) Or push, in the same manner, a stack of construction paper made up of several different colored sheets, each color representing a different rock stratum. The layers will arch or hump up like hills and mountains.

Thin layers of colored sponge rubber or layers of colored modeling clay that is not too soft may also be used. Press the clay layers between two boards, continuing until layers "crack" under pressure.

Mountain-making by the lifting forces resulting from imbalance of land masses can be shown with a batch of dough. Knead the dough well, then spread it in a thin, even layer in a pie tin. Press down on the dough with the hands held apart about one handbreadth. The dough will rise between the hands. The pressure of the hands simulates the effect of an unbalanced land mass, which causes the rising of parts of the earth. Except for movements occurring in volcanic action ("mountains in a hurry") and in earthquakes, crustal movements occur in slow motion on the order of thousands or hundreds of thousands of years.

To help build concepts of the great weight of closely-packed dirt, have children guess the weight of a plastic bag of garden loam, of sand, and of a third filled with leaf mold. Verify weights with household scales or perhaps with scales in the school nurse's office. Estimate the weight of a cubic foot of soil, then dig it out and weigh it.

The immense weight of accumulated sediments carried to the sea by the rivers can cause shifting and faulting in nearby areas. This can be illustrated using a platform balance. Place a book and/or a pile of paper on each side of the scale to represent layers of sediment. On one side place a pan of water to symbolize oceans and on the other a pan of rock and soil representing mountains. Balance carefully, then transfer just one teaspoon of earth to the "ocean." Note how easily the balance between continental land masses or blocks and ocean bottom blocks is disturbed. Such imbalance may cause faulting, even earthquakes.

A model of a seismograph, the device used to detect and record earthquake waves, may be made of a cardboard box, a cup hook, stiff wire or a metal coat hanger, and a soft pencil, pen or, preferably, a felt-tip marker, as shown in Fig. 8-3. With the box standing on a table, draw the strip of paper slowly through the slot while children jump on the floor nearby or jostle the table. The pen will record the disturbance.

Faulting

Earthquakes are the outer sign of the shifting of great masses of the earth's crust. During earthquakes, the rock masses slip past each other along cracks formed earlier by bending of the layers of rock—like the layers of modeling clay under heavy pressure (see above). These cracks or breaks in rock layers are called *faults*. Sometimes the heat generated by the friction of sliding rock layers is so great that the areas of contact are partly melted. The resultant patches of smooth or slick-looking rock surface are called "slickensides," and should not be confused with glacial polish, which is the result of the smoothing effect of glaciers as they moved slowly across the underlying land.

The school sidewalk may illustrate faulting. If erosion has undermined part of the foundation,

the walk may have dropped or tilted to one side. If a slab has cracked, one side may be higher than the other. Similarly, when rocks become pushed up into mountain ranges, the stresses are so great that one side of the fault may become much higher than the other. Thus, Mt. Whitney, the highest peak in the contiguous 48 states, lies just west of Death Valley, the lowest point on the continent.

Volcanic Action

Needed for a simple, safe, and effective method of illustrating volcanic action are detergent or soap powder, a funnel, and a bicycle pump (Fig. 8-4). Moisten the soap powder and model it around an inverted funnel to simulate a volcanic cone. Heap dry powder[1] around the mouth of

[1]The practice of using asbestos for this purpose should be avoided; asbestos dust, once inhaled, remains permanently in the lungs and can cause serious illness.

FIGURE **8-2** Rock layers formed into anticlines, left and synclines, right. The latter is a result of shifts in the Earth's crust at the famous San Andreas fault, in California.

the cone. Insert the pump base into the bottom of the cone and pump air through. The stream of air will scatter the powder in much the same way erupting volcanic gases spew powdered pumice and ash over surrounding terrain.

Wells, Geysers, and Lakes

The question why some wells must be deeper than others to strike water may be useful. Water percolates through soil particles until it reaches a depth where the soil aggregates can hold no more. This saturated layer is called the water table and will occur at depths that vary with the soil profile. A classroom model of a surface well can be made of a dishpan, gravel, and a tin can with top and bottom removed. Cover the bottom of the pan with 3 to 4 inches of gravel; press the tin can down into the gravel until it touches bottom. Remove gravel from inside the can and add water to the gravel outside the can. As the water rises through the gravel, it will rise to the same height inside the can or "well." Water from such wells is usually lifted or pumped to the surface. Water "seeks its own level" in this case

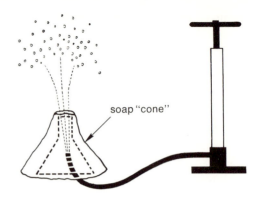

FIGURE **8-4**   Model volcano.

because earth's gravitational pull is the same inside and outside the miniature well.

With the glass top off, water will boil up through the central tube of a percolator much as (and for the same reasons) it does in the geysers of Yellowstone and other hot springs. (For safety, keep the heat low while observing the spurts of boiling water.)

To demonstrate why artesian wells flow without pumping, fill a funnel and 2 to 3 feet of flexible tubing with sand as shown in Fig. 8-5. The sand and funnel represent a porous layer enclosed in nonporous rock, and the glass tube, attached to one end of the flexible tubing, represents a well shaft. Holding the tube higher than the funnel, fill the latter with water tinted with food coloring for better visibility. Slowly lower the glass tube until the water in it is at the same level as in the funnel. Lower the tube further (over a bucket) and the water will flow at the same time as it sinks in the funnel—"seeking its own level."

One can construct a model of an artesian well in an empty terrarium or aquarium (Fig. 8-6). Make a hill of soil over a plastic cone or container. Add a layer of pebbles, to represent porous rock, and a layer of modeling clay, the latter incomplete near the top of the "hill." (Paraffin may be used in lieu of modeling clay.) Test whether the top layer (clay) makes a watertight seal against the glass walls of the tank by pouring water over the clay, observing whether any leaks

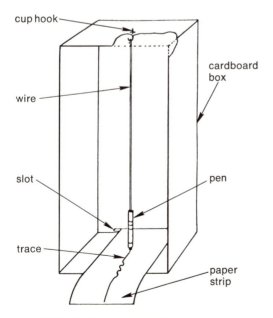

FIGURE **8-3**   Model seismograph.

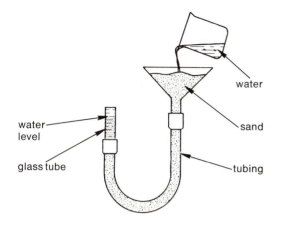

FIGURE **8-5** Device to demonstrate movement of water in an artesian well.

through. Then pour or siphon out the water. The construction represents a mountainside composed of three layers of rock. Drill a "well" at the base of the "hill" by pushing a $\frac{1}{2}$-inch rod or dowel through the clay layer. Into this hole set an inverted medicine dropper tube, pressing the clay around the tube.

Pour water into the porous layer at the top. When the porous layer fills with water, water will spurt out of the medicine dropper. In much the same way, in mountains where layers or rock are upturned and open on the surface under the soil, rainwater and melting snow find their way into layers of permeable, or porous rocks located between nonporous (impermeable) rocks

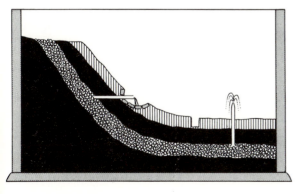

FIGURE **8-6** Model of spring and artesian well showing permeable layers, or aquifers.

(the clay layer in the model). Some artesian wells must be pumped because the water pressure is too low to force the water up the pipe.

In glaciated country may be found small, round, deep lakes formed where a huge chunk of ice broke off the glacier and was imbedded in soil and gravel carried by the glacier. When the ice melted, the resultant depression became a lake. Children can imbed a chunk of ice in sand or sawdust, noting the depression it leaves when it has melted.

ROCKS AND MINERALS

Rock is composed of minerals. Minerals in different combinations and proportions produce different rocks. Granite rock, for example, is made up of three kinds of minerals: quartz, feldspar, and mica. The rock, mica schist, is made up of mica, aluminum silicate, and occasional tiny garnets. An analogy may be made with the variety of baked goods produced by varying ingredients, proportions, baking times, and temperatures. Minerals often occur in crystalline form. To discover the unique character of different crystals, examine salt, sugar, and other granular materials under magnification (Chapter 4). Have children observe and diagram the appearance of crystals grown from saturated solutions of sugar, salt, borax, alum, epsom salts.

Most children like to collect rocks but need guidance in it. Use of containers such as papier-mache egg boxes or plastic egg containers encourages organization of the collections. The name or site of collection can be written inside the cover.

Fist-sized rock specimens may be stored in a cigar box sectioned off with cardboard egg separators. Interest in local geography may be motivated by use of a road map and colored ribbon running from the rocks and minerals collected to the place of collection indicated on the map.

All rocks in the earth's crust may be grouped, according to the mechanism of their origin: igneous (heat-made), sedimentary (deposited, by water or wind), and metamorphic (changed by heat and pressure). The table below, showing basic materials and typical rocks produced from them by the three principal mechanisms, suggests the close interrelationships that make it difficult for geologists to classify some specimens; for example, limestone subjected to sufficient heat, pressure, and chemical changes may be metamorphosed into marble (see p. 133).

Igneous Rock

Geologists believe that the oldest rocks are igneous. The rocks in the bottom of the Grand Canyon were once molten and were probably formed when the earth cooled billions of years ago. Igneous rocks such as pumice, lava, and obsidian are usually associated with volcanic action, and were brought to the surface during eruption or squeezed up through weak places in the bedrock, spreading out between the layers to form a *dike*. The Hudson River Palisades were once a molten volcanic mass that squeezed up between layers of red Jersey sandstone to form columnar basalt cliffs. To illustrate how molten magma moves, squeeze soft clay or flour paste from one end of a small plastic bag to the other, then puncture the tightly rolled bag near the top with a pin. The contents squirt out much as molten rock erupts through the cone of a volcano.

Igneous rock, particularly that of volcanic origin, is further classified as extrusive and usually characterized by great weight or density and compact, fine-grained crystalline structure. (Instrusive, coarse-grained igneous rocks like gran-

ites and pegmatites intrude or squeeze between crustal layers, but cool and harden below the surface; they are later exposed by faulting and erosion.) Pumice and lava are the exceptions, having been extruded with much attendant hot gas, then cooled relatively quickly. Obsidian, the handsome, black, volcanic glass, was valuable for barter among the Indians, who used it to make arrowheads because of its glasslike conchoidal fracture planes. Obsidian has the same basic chemical composition as commercial glass—silicon dioxide (sand).

Granite, abundant everywhere, is probably the rock most commonly used in buildings and in road construction. It is composed of three minerals: quartz, the glasslike translucent crystals that can scratch glass; mica, the black or clear, shiny, flaky crystals; and feldspar, pinkish crystals with flat, rectangular faces like the facades of modern skyscrapers.

Sedimentary Rock

To illustrate how sediments are laid down, partly fill a jar with water and add a half-cup each of gravel, sand, garden loam, and local subsoil. Cover the jar and shake it thoroughly; then allow the soil to settle. By the next day the material should have settled, the heaviest at the bottom, the sand next, and the finer and lighter particles in successive layers up to the lightest (Fig. 8-7). Highway engineers test soil samples in much the same way in order to predict the behavior of the soil on which they build roads, bridges, and buildings.

Basic Material	Variety of Rock		
	Sedimentary	Metamorphic	Igneous
gravel	→ conglomerate	→ quartzite conglomerate	
sand	→ sandstone	→ quartzite	
clay mud	→ shale	→ slate, mica schist	
lime mud	→ limestone	→ marble	
peat	→ soft coal	→ anthracite (hard coal)	
		gneiss ←	granite
		greenstone ←	basalt

Models of sedimentary rock can be made by mixing small amounts of cement, lime plaster, and sand in water in discarded milk cartons. Cement and water produce a kind of shale; lime plaster, and water a limestone that reacts like natural limestone to chemical tests; and sand, cement, and water a synthetic sandstone. The cartons can be peeled off after each mixture hardens. (In nature, the hardening of sediments into rock takes hundreds of centuries.) The "sediments" can be made readily distinguishable by adding colored chalk and fragments of flower pots to some of the layers. (Pulverize the chalk and pot fragments by hammering a cloth wrapped around them.) Fossils are nearly always found in sedimentary rock; a fossil-bearing layer can be made by adding bits of shell from the seashore or the banks of fresh-water creeks, where racoons leave little piles of mussel shells.

Most cement sidewalks are a kind of artificial conglomerate or pudding stone. Some slabs include water-worn or rounded pebbles. Those that include angular fragments simulate conglomerate *breccia* (Italian, meaning "broken"). Older cities offer slate sidewalks for examination; slate is metamorphosed shale.

There are some simple tests for sedimentary rocks: shale has an earthy or oily smell; sandstone shows tiny grains of glass quartz; the calcium carbonate in soft limestone bubbles in vinegar. (The bubbling will be more rapid if the vinegar is concentrated by heating or by allowing the water in it to evaporate for several days.

Metamorphic Rock

Some very common rocks were so changed by the intense heat, pressure, and chemical action deep within the earth that they are quite different from their original sedimentary or igneous character. For example, some granite was subjected to such pressure that the dark mica crystals became aligned, forming banded gneiss, which looks almost sedimentary. On closer inspection, gneiss will be seen to have a much harder, more crystalline structure than the typical sedimentary rock.

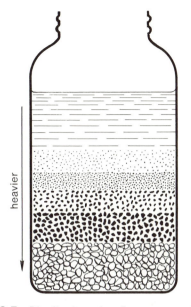

FIGURE **8-7** Distribution of sediments according to particle size after mixture of gravel, sand, garden loam, and subsoil has been allowed to settle.

Mica schist, especially common through parts of New England, is metamorphosed from a soft shale that contained many flakes of clear (sometimes black) mica. Marble is metamorphosed limestone, originally a soft sedimentary rock. A tombstone-maker may be a good source of chips of marble, granite, and other rocks for testing or for a starter collection of rocks.

Mineral deposits Hydraulic mining depends on gravity and the relatively greater weight and density of the valuable minerals as compared to the ore. This can be illustrated by mixing a small quantity of sand, clay, bits of bricks and metal such as tacks, nails, bits of wire, solder, and lead sinkers in a jar partly full of water. When the jar is shaken, the heavier materials sink to the bottom.

To answer the question of why oil is found most often in sand layers, apply a drop of oil to a pile of pulverized gravel, sand, pebbles, clay, shale, shells, and so forth. The one that absorbs and holds the oil most readily—the sand—is the one most apt to be the material of which the oil-bearing layer is formed.

EROSION

Erosion, the wearing away of the earth's surface, is a result of the action of many agents working together or singly: water, wind, plants, animals, glaciers, and marked temperature changes.

By Water

Gutters near the school should be watched for evidences of erosion. During or right after a rain, collect water running in the gutters and set aside to settle in glass or plastic containers. Try to get samples from different gutters and compare for possible differences in the amount and kind of sediment. If there is soil in the gutter after a rain, establish whether the particles tend to be heterogeneous or sorted into relatively uniform sizes (see below) and whether any larger flotsam is being fragmented as it is washed along. Children who have set up a rain gauge (Chapter 7) may recognize a relation between the amount of sediment and debris and the amount or intensity of rainfall.

Sidewalks at the foot of sloping lawns often show an accumulation of fine topsoil. This is evidence of sheet erosion, more insidious than gullying (below) because the topsoil is eroded so gradually that the loss is not usually observed and checked before gullying actually begins. Many farm pastures begin to look bare and rocky where overgrazing has exposed the soil to sheet erosion. If unchecked, the process carries the fine topsoil to the foot of the slope until, ultimately, the steepest spots begin to gully.

Children may examine the fine soil washed out into the grass along school sidewalks or curbing or at short cuts worn across a corner. Where the particles of soil are graduated in size, there has been a sifting action by the water: the swifter a current of water, the heavier the particles it can carry. Water running at twice the speed necessary to roll a 1-pound rock will move a 64-pound boulder. As the current slows, the heavier particles are dropped. Thus, the lightest particles travel the farthest, being the last to be dropped. Children may also find signs of sheet

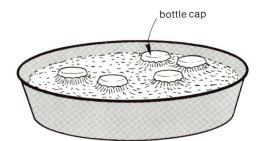

FIGURE **8-8** Pedestal erosion illustrated by bottle caps embedded in sand and sprinkled with water.

erosion around the roots of playground trees, evidence that the present school ground soil level is lower than when the trees started growing.

Any water running over bare, sloping soil is apt to carry off finer soil, leaving coarser, less fertile ground. In such places, one may find stones or pebbles atop little pillars of finer soil that are held in place by the stones. These structures are miniatures of the great sandstone buttes of the southwest. Such pedestal erosion can be simulated by using containers such as the pie tins with perforated bottoms used in splash erosion studies (p. 135). Fill the tins level with firmly packed soil. Imbed bottle caps or pebbles in the surface and sprinkle with water. Soon soil pedestals will be left under the caps and pebbles (Fig. 8-8).

There are usually many signs of gullying in raw land around new school buildings and grounds until planting and seeding take hold. To graphically demonstrate this variety of erosion, mark the head and widest parts of a large gully with stakes. After a rainstorm, check whether the gully has advanced. The sifting action of flowing water (see above) may be demonstrated by the distribution of rocks and pebbles, strewn along the main channel of the gully, and by the miniature delta or flood plain that often forms at the mouth of a gully. A crooked channel with smaller gullies branching from it and miniature cliffs and caves in the side walls may indicate where more readily dissolved or eroded material was located. Where water swirled around a rock or other obstruction, there may be an islet held in place by tough grass, demonstrating the ability of root networks to slow or prevent erosion. There may still be a pool of water in a low place along the channel and debris along the bank. The kind of debris and where it has lodged may show the presence of objects more resistant to the force of the water. Children can estimate the amount of soil removed in the gullying, and discussion of where the soil has gone can be productive. They can also test the differences between soil from the gully channel and that from the sides and top by planting beans in samples of each and observing which produces the best plants.

Evidences of another kind of erosion—splash erosion—may be found following a rain along the base of buildings where mud may have splashed against the walls. Children may easily feel the soil splashed up during a rain on the walls of frame buildings. Splash sticks may be driven into the ground (leaving about 15 inches above ground) in such selected areas as the lawn, under deciduous or evergreen trees, under the eaves of buildings, in a school garden, on a baseball diamond, and under shrubs. One can see the differences in amount and height of splash (according to the location of the stake) by simulating rain with a watering can held at the same height and distance from each stake. Verify the differences by noting the splash marks left by an actual rain.

Splash erosion can be studied with old tin or aluminum-foil pie plates. Punch holes in the plates and line with paper toweling. Fill nearly level with fine, dry soil. Weigh, and set out just before a rain in the same areas chosen for the

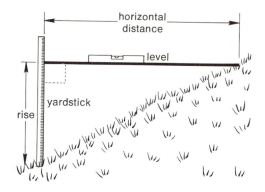

FIGURE **8-10** Method of determining slope.

splash sticks. After the rain, allow soil in the plates to dry, then weigh again to determine how much of the soil in the plates has been washed away by the rain. Using another set of soil-filled plates, compare the effect of a watering can with that of the rain.

Function of slope and soil cover To illustrate the relationship between slope and erosion, cut one end from each of several shoeboxes (Fig. 8-9) and line the boxes with aluminum foil so as to form a spout at the open end. Add some soil and raise the closed end of one box an inch and of another, 3 inches. Sprinkle the boxes with a measured amount of water and note the difference in run-off and sediment according to slope. Determining slope (a 1-inch rise in 100 inches is a 1% slope) provides good exercise in calculating percentages. A 20-inch square seed flat raised an inch on one side, for example, will have a 5% slope ($\frac{1}{20} \times 100$).

To determine the slope of land, use a small carpenter's level and two sticks held at right angles to each other, one end of the horizontal stick resting on the ground, as shown in Fig. 8-10. Level the horizontal by shortening or lengthening the vertical as necessary. Then divide the length of the vertical by the length of the horizontal and multiply the quotient by 100.

To show how swift-running water forms a canyon, allow water to pour rapidly onto soil or sand piled near a hose bib or in a long shallow carton outdoors. A deep "river bed" will form. As the water flows the length of the carton, it

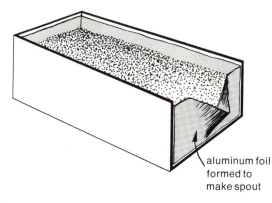

FIGURE **8-9** Shoebox erosion tray.

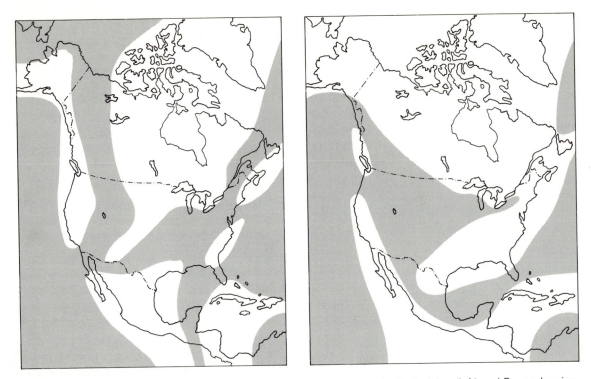

FIGURE **8-11** Position of the sea in North and Central America during the Ordovician (left) and Pennsylvanian (right) periods. The sea is shown in gray.

will slow down and deposit a "delta" made up of the silt it has cut away. If the water is allowed to flow slowly and the carton of soil is tilted to form a gentle slope, the water will follow a course resembling an "old" river, with meanders, or sinuous curves. If the volume of water is increased, the shallow "river" will flood; old rivers usually have such flood plains. Sprinkling a "mountain" of sand with "rain" will produce such a flood plain at the base of the mountain.

Children may wish to model of sand, soil, or clay a stream or gully they have seen. Their exhibit might include a bank cut by water, exposed tree roots, a sand bar, silt deposits, or water-worn pebbles. To construct land forms such as a hill, spread plaster of Paris over a mound of crumpled newspaper. When dry, cover with a thin layer of soil. Water sprinkled over this will flow down, carrying soil along. The sorting action of water may again be seen here.

To illustrate the relationship between erosion and soil cover, prepare several shoe boxes as described above (Fig. 8-9) and put soil with leaves and twigs in one box, plain soil in another, and sod in a third. Using a sprinkler-head watering can or a clothes sprinkler, apply equal amounts of "rain" to each box and compare run-off. A touch of realism may be provided by planting a "forest" of shrub seedlings in one box and a "burned forest" (charred sticks and ash) in another.

The effectiveness of terracing and contouring, used around the world to conserve water and hold soil in place, can be demonstrated by dashing water on a blackboard and delaying the downward flow of the water with strips of wet toweling pasted across its path.

Miniature outdoor gullies "laced" with rows of pebbles will show the beginnings of miniature terraces of topsoil after a rain.

In addition to carrying visible particles of rock

and soil, eroding water also transports materials in solution. Many of these substances ultimately reach the oceans. An interesting recent development is the idea that we can "mine" seawater and the sea's bottom for all the elements that have been carried down in solution. For example, magnesium has been discovered in quantity on the ocean bottom, bromine is being taken from seawater, and salt has been taken from the sea over the ages. Seawater boiled off in an old pan should leave a residue of tiny crystals, which is mainly salt. Chemical tests would find traces of many other minerals. Fig. 8-11 shows the position of the sea in North and Central America half a billion years ago; sediments deposited then are now mined for valuable minerals.

How salt can be removed from the sea by evaporation can be illustrated as follows. Add a tablespoon of salt to a quart of hot water in an open saucepan. After children taste the solution, boil it 10–20 minutes, then cool and have them taste it again. The fact that it is saltier can lead the children to other experiences of evaporation, as from an aquarium (Chapter 1). The boiling and tasting process can be continued until only the salt crystals remain in the pan.

By Wind, Plants, and Animals

While the earth's surface is constantly changed by rain and running water, wind, plants, and animals may also be agents of change. Wind erosion is caused not by moving air but rather by the dust and grit wind carries. City buildings cleaned by sand blasting are illustrative of the mechanism of wind erosion. Some desert rock formations are believed to have been carved by the abrasive force of wind-driven sand. This can be illustrated by showing how a fan (wind) moves soil in a shallow box or pan but has little effect on an identical box of soil covered with grassy sod.

Although plant cover normally deters erosion (above), some plants function as erosion agents. Rock lichens (Fig. 8-12) are active rock-breakers or soil-formers; their spores sprout the thready root-like rhizomes, which penetrate the tiniest crevice or irregularity in rock. As the plant clings

and grows, it retains water, which in winter expands, cracking and splitting the rock and allowing the rhizomes to penetrate deeper. As detritus (rock debris) accumulates, larger masses can grow and soil formation (from the detritus and plant fragments) accelerates as larger plants gain foothold. Lichens may be found near the ground on the cool side of old buildings. The masonry underneath should show marks of etching by the rhizomes of these plants.

The penetration of hard, rock-like material by plants can be shown as follows: Place bean or other seed sprouts on the smooth surface of a slab made by allowing plaster to harden in a grease-lined cardboard or wooden box. Cover with moist paper toweling and keep in a terrarium or other humid container. After a few

FIGURE **8-12** Lichen (magnified about eight times) growing on rock.

days, have children note what the rootlets have done to the slab surface. Plant action can be illustrated, too, by planting bean seeds in about one inch of soil overlying a small piece of polished marble. Water the seeds and, after a few weeks, dig up the marble. Chemicals produced by cell growth will have etched a pattern on the polished surface of the marble.

Sidewalks cracked and heaved by roots are also evidence of plants acting as erosion agents. To discover the strength of germinating seeds, fill a small glass jar of beans brimful of water. Screw cover on securely and leave overnight. (Because the expanding seeds will crack the jar, enclose it in a canvas sack or metal container.)

Erosion along the joints of stone or brick steps, on weathered stone foundations of buildings (compare with those of new construction), and on weathered or lichen-covered cemetery markers is a product, at least in part, of the continuous, ever present process of erosion by plants.

Earthworms, continually pulverizing lower layers of soil and bringing it to the surface for use by plants, are important animal agents of erosion. The "castings," their undigested solid wastes, may be readily seen on the surface, especially after rain. What happens to coarse soil particles passed through their gizzards is illustrated by what they do to certain hard foods on earthworm "farms": Some earthworm farmers feed walnut shells and olive pits, which, in a surprisingly short time, are pulverized into the finest garden soil (Chapter 1). Other burrowers such as woodchucks and gophers also aid in the total amount of soil overturn. In digging, they bring rocks and coarse soil to the surface for further erosion by weathering and fragmentation (below).

By Temperature (Expansion and Contraction)

Expansion and contraction due to alternate heat and cold is an important erosion force, producing cracking of the surface of rock and enlarging fissures. Children who have seen the expansion joints, or spaces, between concrete highway slabs or between the ends of sections of railroad track may relate them to this erosion phenomenon. Sidewalk cracks not caused by tree roots may have been caused by expansion–contraction. To demonstrate how a sudden cold rain can affect a sun-baked sidewalk, cast three 2-inch slabs of cement (mix cement with equal parts of sand and water) in shoeboxes or milk cartons, which can be peeled off when the cement hardens. The next day, place one slab outdoors; heat one (with candles, Sterno, or other heat source), then sprinkle with cold water; and refrigerate the third and then pour hot water over it. Cracking should result from expansion–contraction in the case of the second slab and contraction–expansion in the third.

The expansive force of freezing water is a supplementary factor in erosion caused by expansion–contraction. To illustrate, freeze water in a milk container with push-up top or in a screw-top jar kept in a heavy canvas bag or other safe container for glass splinters. Water as a solid occupies about one tenth more space than it does as a liquid. Freezing water can split great trees with the crack of a pistol shot on a still cold night.

In climates where freezing temperatures occur, cracks photographed in autumn may show, when re-examined in spring, that they have been enlarged or extended by winter frost. In mountains, water freezing between rock layers or cracks may start a rock slide of loosened fragments.

SOIL

Erosion of the earth's crust contributes to the formation of soil. Rocks rubbed together or "sandpapered" will produce a kind of soil, which may be tested by comparing the growth of plants in such soil and in soil made of equal parts of sand, loam, and humus. It is clear that soil containing decayed or decaying vegetable and, perhaps, animal matter, in addition to finely divided rock, is better for plants.

Place rocks in a half-filled jar of water. The jar should be "stout" and the rocks neither too numerous nor too heavy. Children can shake the

FIGURE **8-13**
Soil "snakes":
at left, sandy soil;
center, silty soil;
and right, clay soil.

jar a few minutes each day, observing how quickly the process makes "soil." A local nurseryman or U.S. Department of Agriculture soils technician can give information on how to make soil.

Careful examination of some soil (use of a cubic foot gives good experience in measurement) will reveal a surprising "table of contents." To do this, use a gardener's flat spade to make a straight-sided hole (in order to calculate the cubic foot readily). Spread each shovelful of soil on paper and separate it into piles of pebbles, roots, sticks, and the like. Sowbugs, earthworms, or other animal life may be put into plastic pill bottles or other small containers. When the soil is partly dry, sift it through sieves of increasing fineness. A square of screening of $\frac{1}{2}$-inch, $\frac{1}{4}$-inch, or $\frac{1}{6}$-inch mesh will serve. With each screening, make separate piles of partly disintegrated plant or animal debris. Place the screenings in paper bags with a record of data—tentative identification, particle size (coarse-screened, fine, etc.), moistness of soil, depth of soil sample—for later classroom study.

Most surface soils are mixtures of particles of various sizes. Probably there are large and small stones. Usually sand grains can be seen with a magnifying glass; fine silt particles, often present, can be seen only through a microscope. A soil composition analysis might also show such things as bits of plant and animal remains, which become humus. Each of these soil elements has a

function and a distinctive feel—sand grains feel gritty; dry silt feels like flour or talcum powder and becomes smooth and slippery when wet; dry clay feels harsh, wet clay sticky. (Clay cements larger silt and sand particles together, and humus not only cements larger particles but also prevents clay particles from compacting.) Soil scientists use this method for testing soil by the feel, rolling it between their fingers and pressing it between the palms of their hands. In this way they have come to divide soils into four kinds according to the size of predominant particles: gravels, sands, loams, and clays. Loams—mixtures of sand, silt, and clay in fairly equal proportions—are good for plants.

One may make a quick analysis of soil as follows: With soil samples about equally moist (there should be enough moisture for all the particles to adhere when squeezed together, but no water should drip out), roll a ball of each sample the size of a big marble. Experiment until samples are just moist enough to shape into a snake-like roll (Fig. 8-13). Soils that make smooth rolls that hold their shape probably have high clay content; rolls that crack in several places are probably made largely of sandy soil.

A lump of moist garden soil or florist's potting soil breaks into smaller lumps very much like bread crumbs. Like bread crumbs, soil aggregates (Fig. 8-14) have holes or pores big enough to see with a simple magnifying glass. House and garden plants often sicken or die because these all-important spaces become compacted, preventing the free flow of air and water to the roots. Coarse sand promotes good drainage and the maintenance of spaces in soil aggregates.

Soil Profiles

Where three or more feet of soil has been dug away, as for a road cut or an excavation, at least two natural layers should be distinguishable—topsoil (dark) and subsoil (light). The thin, dark topsoil layer, in which grow virtually all the plants on earth, is often difficult to see because it is overhung by the roots of plants and by fallen debris. Subsoil is usually too poor in organic material and too tightly packed to promote healthy plant growth. Children can test this by sprouting seeds in samples of topsoil and subsoil from the same location.

It takes about 300 years for an inch of productive topsoil to form; children may be interested in relating local topsoil depth and local history.

Water-holding Properties

To determine the presence of moisture in soil, fill (about two days after a rain) uniform-sized paper containers with samples of soil from a grassy plot, from beneath shrubbery or trees, from a weedy area, from a garden, and from a bare section of a baseball diamond. Label the containers as soon as filled, record their weight, and set containers in a warm dry place. Stir soil and weigh daily. Where there is no change in weight for a few days, the soil may be considered dried out. Note the order in which the soil samples dried and calculate the percentage of moisture by dividing the loss of weight in each sample by the dry weight of the soil and multiplying by 100. Soil samples from pasture, crop land, or woods should also be tested.

The water-holding properties of soil vary with the proportions of its components. Needed to test this property are several glass jars of the same size and an equal number of a diameter slightly greater than that of the tops of the jars. Baby food jars and frozen juice cans are especially suitable (Fig. 3-4). With a slender nail or nail-punch, make half a dozen holes in the bottom of each can. To each can (each half-full of soil from a different area in the school vicinity), add half a cup of water. Children may note the times at which water starts to drip (and finishes dripping) from the various cans. The same procedure may be repeated with sand, clay (from a local clay bank or from pieces of an old clay pot pulverized by hammering), loam from a garden, and humus or leaf mold from the woods. (The sand, clay, and humus may be mixed in different proportions and combinations, and the samples retested for water retention. Sawdust may be

FIGURE **8-14**
Soil aggregates
of various sizes.

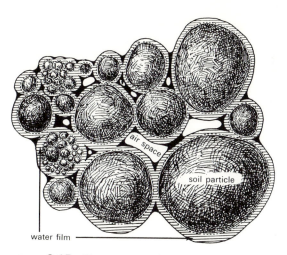

air space

soil particle

water film

FIGURE **8-15** How water and air are held in soil by soil particles (enlarged).

tried in place of humus.) Water slips rapidly through sandy soil, which is apt to erode quickly; it drips slowly through humus or organic matter, showing the importance of such material in the retention of rain and its consequent slowness of erosion. (How the particles composing a soil hold water by capillary action is shown in Fig. 8-15. Capillary action is discussed in Chapter 6.) The low permeability of clays makes rain run off high-clay soils, so that areas at a lower elevation than clay deposits tend to be washed more heavily by rains. Thus, soil samples acting like clays may come from an area prone to sheet erosion and gullying.

Water penetrability of soils may be studied as follows: Remove both ends of soup cans, leaving smooth edges. Press the resulting cylinders into the soil to the same depth in selected spots. Fill to the brim with water and record the time required for all the water to penetrate the ground.

Compaction

The differing pressures necessary to force the soup-can cylinders into the ground illustrate that soils differ in the compaction of their grains or particles. Children can recheck the phenomenon with a pencil or pointed length of dowel, noting how moisture and the amount of organic material in the soil influence the ease with which the ground can be penetrated and whether there is any relation between plant cover, erosion, water retention, and compaction.

SUGGESTED PROJECTS

1. Encourage children to make a small rock collection—say, a half-dozen or dozen samples of common rocks labeled and/or displayed in a cigar box or egg carton. A gravel pit or recent road cut make good sources.

2. List earth materials found in or around school; these might include chalk, clay pots, graphite, copper, iron and steel, porcelain, china, glass aluminum, slate.

3. With a hand glass, examine sand particles, salt, quartz or calcite crystals, and common feldspar crystals. (Note the cleavage planes in the latter.) Snowflakes (on dark cloth) or refrigerator ice crystals may also be examined. (Snowflakes, of course, are water crystals, and water is a mineral.)

4. Using a classified telephone book, list local industries depending primarily or secondarily on earth materials, and visit some for samples to display. Make a field trip, if possible, to a local quarry or builders' supply store.

5. Make a land-classification map of the nearest hill. (Soil conservation agents of the Department of Agriculture may provide necessary information.)

6. On white paper or toweling, have children separate and examine earth from a pasture or vacant lot.

7. Children can discuss and develop a chart showing the cycle of change from rocks into soil and vice versa.

8. How vacant is a vacant lot? The question can be answered by dividing a class into small teams, each team being responsible for making a close study and detailed report of everything it can find in an assigned sector.

9. In urban locales, children may find miniature examples of major geographical land forms on school grounds. The geology of local building stones, sidewalks, and curbstones can be reported and much may be observed by close study of the area between sidewalk and curb.

10. Fill a quart screw-top container about ⅔ full and add soil until water just overflows. Cover and shake well. As contents settle, sketch the proportions of different layers (sand, gravel, loam, clay) on a card laid against the side of the container. Samples from different locales may be compared and the following questions considered: Which layer has the largest particles? The finest? What is the major component of the sample?

11. After weighing dry leaves, pine needles, and grass together in a metal bucket, burn them in the bucket and reweigh. Discuss the results with reference to the importance of organic material in soil.

12. Older children can photograph local stream bank erosion or other evidence of gullying and develop a picture story on the subject.

BIBLIOGRAPHY

(**P** indicates recommended for primary grades, **I** for intermediate grades, **U** for upper grades.)

Adler, Irving, *Dust,* Day, 1958. Source and structure of particles in air. Economic value of dust. **U**

Ames, Gerald, *The Earth's Story,* Creative Educational Society in cooperation with the American Museum of Natural History, rev. ed., 1962. An introduction to geology, with photographs. **U**

Baumann, Hans, *The Caves of the Great Hunters,* Pantheon, 1954. A true story of boys who discover an Ice Age cave. Photographs. **U**

Bendick, Jeanne, *The Shape of the Earth,* Rand McNally, 1965. The earth, its composition, size, rotation, configuration, and principal features. Problems of flat map-making are briefly discussed. **U**

Brown, Vinson, and David Allan, *Rocks and Minerals of California and Their Stories,* Naturegraph Co., 1957. Guide for the amateur rock collector. **I**

Buehr, Walter, *Underground Riches: The Story of Mining,* Morrow, 1958. A brief survey with helpful diagrams and drawings. **U**

Colby, Carroll B., *Soil Savers,* Coward-McCann, 1957. Story of the U.S. Soil Conservation Service. **U**

Collins, Henry Hill, Jr., *The Wonders of Geology,* Putnam, 1962. Clear, concise descriptions of the earth's surface as it is affected by running water, ice, wind, heat, and other influences. **U**

Comfort, Iris T., *Earth Treasures: Rocks and Minerals,* Prentice-Hall, 1964. The origins of rocks—igneous, sedimentary, and metamorphic—with descriptive examples of each kind. Includes rock identification, crystals, caves, semiprecious stones, metals, fossils, and rock hunting. **U**

Crosby, Phoebe, *The Junior Science Book of Rock Collecting,* Garrard, 1962. An introduction to rocks and their collection. Illustrated with two-color drawings and diagrams. **I**

Fenton, Carroll L. and Mildred A., *Rocks and Their Stories,* Garden City, 1951. How to study, identify, and collect most important kinds. **I**

Gans, Roma, *The Wonder of Stones,* Crowell, 1963. A stimulating introduction to geology. **P**

Geology, Boy Scouts of America Merit Badge Series, 1953. Information and ideas adapted to children. **U**

Goetz, Delia, *Islands of the Ocean,* Morrow, 1964. The formation of islands, the plant and animal life peculiar to different types of islands, and the adaptations that human inhabitants make when they live on them. **I**

Hamilton, Elizabeth, *The First Book of Caves,* Watts, 1956. What caves are; how plants, animals, and man use them; and how to explore them in safety. **U**

Hamilton, Lee David, *Century: Secret City of Snows,* Putnam, 1963. An account of Century City, the Army's polar icecap station in Greenland. Findings in meteorology and geology and their implications for future world-wide weather conditions, explained in terms of ice ages past and future. Highly technical. Illustrated with photographs. **U**

Hogner, Dorothy, *Earthworms,* Crowell, 1953. Background information and suggestions for raising earthworms. **I**

Holden, Raymond, *Famous Fossil Finds: Great Discoveries in Paleontology.* Dodd, Mead, 1966. Included are chapters on Andrews' dinosaur eggs, the La Brea tar pits, the mammoth, giant sloth, and early man. **U**

Holsaert, Eunice, and Robert Gartland, *Dinosaurs,* Holt, Rinehart and Winston, 1959. The story of the thunder lizards. **P**

Irving, Robert, *Volcanoes and Earthquakes,* Knopf, 1962. A concise explanation of the causes of earthquakes and volcanic action. Well illustrated with diagrams. **U**

Keene, Melvin, *The Beginner's Story of Minerals and Rocks,* Harper & Row, 1966. Selecting and identifying rock specimens. Useful too for its simplified charts and index. **U**

Knight, David C., *Let's Find Out About Earth,* Watts, 1968. An overview, simply written, of the earth and its relationship within the solar system. Clear diagrams. **I**

Kieran, John, *Natural History of New York City: A Personal Report After Fifty Years of Study and Enjoyment of Wildlife Within the Boundaries of Greater New York,* Houghton Mifflin, 1959. **U**

Lauber, Patricia, *Dust Bowl: The Story of Man on the Great Plains,* Coward-McCann, 1958. Changes on the plains before and since the first settlers. Present conservation practices. **I**

———, *Junior Science Book of Volcanoes,* Garrard, 1965. How a volcano starts, kinds of eruptions, and some of the famous volcanoes of the world. Detection and measurement of earthquakes and work of volcanologists are described briefly. **I**

Laubell, Winifred, *In a Running Brook,* Rand McNally, 1968. A brook and its small inhabitants. Poetic yet accurate. **U**

Martin, Charles, *Monsters of Old Los Angeles,* Viking, 1950. Authentic account of Pleistocene animals trapped in the La Brea tar pits. **I**

Matthews, William H., *Exploring the World of Fossils.* Children's Pr., 1964. The science of paleontology, including how to become a fossil hunter and how to care for specimens. **U**

Matthews, William, *The Story of the Earth,* Harvey, 1968. The earth as a planet. Treats also minerals, rocks, volcanoes, earthquakes, mountain building, weathering, erosion, fossils, and earth history. **U**

Parker, Bertha M., *Soil,* Harper & Row, 1959. 36pp. Properties and uses of soil. **U**

Podendorf, Illa, *The True Book of Pebbles and Shells,* Children's Pr., 1954. For the young collector, a help in identification. **P**

———, *The True Book of Rocks and Minerals,* Children's Pr., 1958. A simple introduction to rock formation with examples of each kind. Illustrated. **P**

Pough, F. H., *All About Volcanoes and Earthquakes,* Random, 1953. Occurrence and causes, with description of some spectacular ones, and how man can protect himself from them. **U**

———, *Field Guide to Rocks and Minerals,* Houghton Mifflin, 1960, 3rd ed. A detailed description of many common minerals, with a complete explanation of collecting. **I–U**

Pringle, Laurence, *Dinosaurs and Their World,* Harcourt, 1968. A history of the dinosaur period telling what dinosaurs were, how they were discovered, and where their skeletons may be seen today. For the beginning paleontologist. **U**

Reed, W. Maxwell, *The Earth for Sam,* Harcourt, rev. ed. by Paul F. Brandwein, 1960. Comprehensive survey of earth science. Many exceptional illustrations. **U**

Ross, George Maxim, *The River,* Dutton, 1967. Process of growth from a small trickle of snow until it finally empties into the ocean. **I**

Schneider, Herman and Nina, *Rocks, Rivers, and the Changing Earth,* W. R. Scott, 1952. Story of the earth, accompanied by suggestions for interesting activities. **I**

Selsam, Millicent, *Birth of an Island,* Harper & Row, 1959. The history of a barren volcanic rock in the South Seas from its beginning to its life as a base for a community of plants and animals. **I**

Shuttlesworth, Dorothy E., *The Story of Rocks,* Garden City, 1956. Suggestions to the collector for finding, classifying, storing, and exhibiting rocks and minerals. Illustrated in color. **U**

Sibley, Gretchen, *La Brea Story,* Ward Ritchie Pr., 1968. The history of the La Brea pits in California from the time of the mammoths, mastodons, and giant ground sloths. Illustrated. **U**

Sootin, Harry, *The Young Experimenters' Workbook; Treasures of the Earth,* Norton, 1965. Simple experiments with rocks, minerals, soil, and water clearly presented, carefully illustrated. Cautionary instructions are included. Bibliography, glossary, and index appended. **U**

Sterling, Dorothy, *Story of Caves,* Doubleday, 1956. Cave sculpture, writings, and stories of cave animals, including some derived from various ancient legends. I

Weaver, Dolla Cox, *For Pebble Pups*, Chicago Natural History Museum, 1955. A collecting guide for junior geologists. U

White, Anne Terry, *All About Mountains and Mountaineering*, Random, 1962. The world's great mountains and the men who attempted to scale them. U

————, *Rocks All Around Us*, Random, 1959. The formation of rocks and the geological story behind each. Poetic, with few technical terms. I

Wise, William, *Monsters of Today and Yesterday*, Putnam, 1967. A brief account of the characteristics and habits of three monsters of long ago—giant beaver, saber-toothed cat, and lion—contrasted with several monsters of today. I

Wyler, Rose, and Gerald Ames, *The Story of the Ice Age*, Harper & Row, 1956. An account of the ice ages, how we obtained knowledge of them, their effect on life, and a speculation about a possible future ice age. U

Zim, Herbert, and Elizabeth Cooper, *Minerals: Their Identification, Uses, and How to Collect Them*, Harcourt, 1943. A handbook. Includes locations for finding minerals. U

Zim, Herbert, *What's Inside the Earth?*, Morrow, 1953. Answers common questions about mines, caves, wells, earthquakes, volcanoes, and mountains. Well illustrated. I

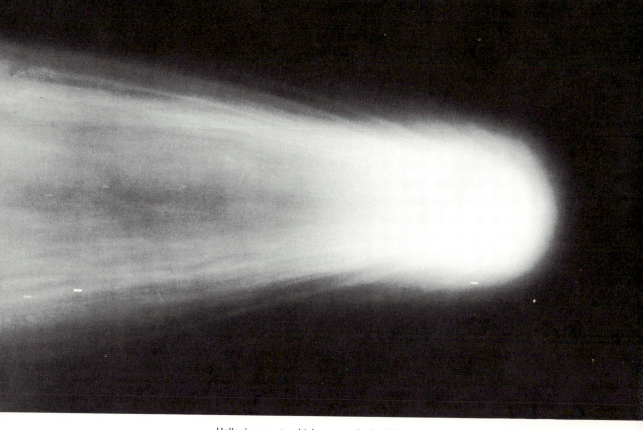

Halley's comet, which approached within about 50 million miles of the earth in 1910.

9 The Stars and Planets

Simple classroom experiences can help children to develop concepts underlying the behavior of bodies in space and to separate fact from fantasy in the pseudo-science to which many are exposed.

THE SOLAR SYSTEM

The sun, its nine planets and their satellites, and the planetoids, comets, and meteorites make up the solar system. The name—solar system—derives from the dominance of the sun in size and mass as compared to lesser members of the system.

Earth: Rotation and Revolution

Ptolemy (c. 150 A.D.), the Alexandrian astronomer, believed that the earth was stationary and the center of the universe around which the sun, moon, and planets revolved (Fig. 9-1a). Without benefit of telescope or other instruments of modern science, what might be one's notion of the universe? Such a question may provoke interest and discussion among children, as well as respect for and recognition of Ptolemy's contribution. Present-day knowledge may appear a little quaint tomorrow.

Almost 1500 years after Ptolemy, the Polish astronomer Nicolaus Copernicus (1473–1543)

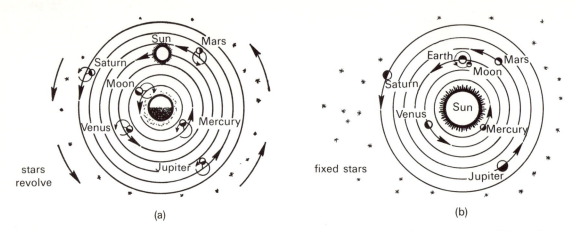

stars revolve

fixed stars

(a)

(b)

FIGURE **9-1** Two versions of the solar system: (a) the Ptolemaic, with the earth as the center of the universe; (b) the Copernican system.

revived a theory suggested by the Greeks but abandoned under the tremendous influence of Ptolemaic thought. Copernicus claimed that the sun—rather than the earth—was the center of the universe and that the earth *rotated* once daily in its annual *revolution* about the sun (Fig. 9-1b). It remained for Johannes Kepler (1571–1630) and Galileo Galilei (1564–1642) to establish direct experimental evidence of the truth of Copernican theory. Galileo's evidence was his observation that Jupiter's moons changed position each successive night, from which he concluded that they were revolving around the planet. By analogy, Galileo postulated, Earth and Jupiter and the other planets could revolve around the sun. As is often the case with new ideas, his hypothesis was, for many years, violently rejected.

Sky study may be a child's first real opportunity to check the evidence of his senses against the accumulation of scientific knowledge. Young children can make observations of the sun's apparent daily motion or path across the sky. Point out the sun's position in the sky during the morning and again in the afternoon or, perhaps, to the fact that some schoolrooms have sunlight in the morning while others have it in the afternoon. Similar observations can be made at home. Children can also note their shadows on the playground, or mark the moving path of sunlight in

the classroom at 10-minute intervals. It may take several successive experiences before the majority of the class can point out the sun's path through the sky.

With young children, the concept of direction should be limited to those of east and west. Outdoors on a sunny morning, one can point out that the sun is in the east, making the shadows point west.

Once children believe that the sun moves in an east–west path, the idea that the earth is in motion relative to the sun may be explained— perhaps with the moving-vehicle analogy. (From a rotating merry-go-round, for example, stationary objects appear to be in motion.)

The phenomenon of night and day alternation can be demonstrated using a globe. With a lump of clay, mark on the globe the approximate location of the school. Set the globe on the window sill with the marker facing the sunlight. Rotate the globe a half turn so that the marker is in shadow. Some children will grasp quickly that this is how darkness comes to their part of the world. Move the globe in quarter turns (90°) to signify six-hour intervals and a corresponding difference in daylight.

Children may make a globe from plaster of Paris and newspaper with a solid metal curtain rod as the axis. Remove one side of a sturdy box and cut a semicircular opening (10–12 inches in radius) in another side, as shown in Fig. 9-2. Slip a solid metal curtain rod (round in cross-section) through two screw eyes (Fig. 9-2) so that the rod can be rotated in the eyes. With the rod in place in the box, shape newspaper around it to form a ball, using cord to hold the paper in place. Mix plaster of Paris to a thick paste and apply it by hand to the paper shape to form a rough ball. Allow to set for 20 minutes, then gradually build a smooth sphere by rotating the ball so that excess plaster is scraped off by the semicircular edge. Allow the ball to set for several days, then insert one end of the rod in a wood base so that it makes an angle of $23\frac{1}{2}°$ with it. Paint the land and water features onto the surface.

Children can take in the concept of rotation by outdoor observation and by various other means: by twirling themselves (outdoors) for example, and by pretending to be the earth, turning slowly before a lamp (the sun) so that the face is fully illuminated ("noon"), then slantingly lit (early morning or late afternoon), and finally, with the back to the light, in shadow ("night").

Revolution (movement of the earth around the sun) can be illustrated by having one child (in

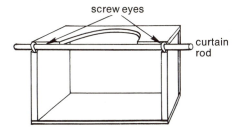

FIGURE **9-2**   Form for making globes.

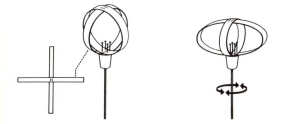

FIGURE **9-3**   Effect of the earth's rotation on its shape.

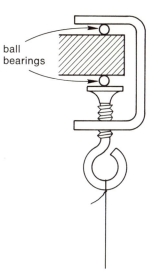

FIGURE **9-4**   C-clamp arrangement for free-swinging weight.

a darkened room) carry a globe in a circular path around another child who holds a light.

One consequence of the earth's rotation is a slight flattening at the poles and a slight bulge at the equator. IGY (International Geophysical Year) measurements show that the earth tends to bulge just below the equator. (In fact it is very slightly pear-shaped, being 23 minutes wider just below the equator.) To illustrate the reason for this, the children prepare two loops (Fig. 9-3) made of paper strips glued together at the ends. Attach one loop at right angles to the other, again gluing their points of contact. Pin, as shown, to a cork into which a large nail or rod has been pushed to form a kind of spindle. When the cork is twirled, the loops will flatten top and bottom and bulge at the middle (Fig. 9-3).

A little more than a century ago, the French physicist, J. B. L. Foucault, proved that the earth really turns, by the simple expedient of hanging a long free-swiveling pendulum from the dome of the Pantheon in Paris and noting the path of the pendulum's swing. That path was an arc, not a straight line, indicating that the earth rotated under it. One can observe the same phenomenon in many high-ceilinged public buildings where heavy lamp fixtures are suspended by a long wire

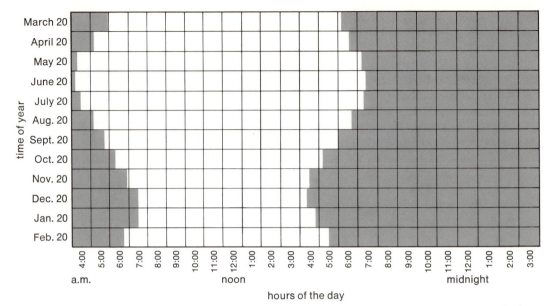

FIGURE **9-5** Typical annual span of daylight in a region in the middle latitudes of the northern hemisphere—in this case, northeast United States (New York State).

from the ceiling. A free-swiveling device for such an experiment can be made of a C-clamp (used in woodworking) with two ball bearings placed as shown in Fig. 9-4. (A fisherman's swivel attachment may also be used.) Tighten *lightly* and attach a long cord to support a small "plumb-bob" weight. Mark the direction of the swing at the start and note the change of course that has occurred after a few hours.

Earth's annual revolution about the sun is not directly perceived by our senses, nor does one notice the tremendous speed with which the earth travels in orbit—over 500 million miles per year or 66,600 miles per hour. Rotation, too, occurs at great speeds: a person living at the equator travels 24,000 miles (Earth's circumference) per day. (As an exercise in simple division, children can calculate that the speed of rotation is about 1000 miles per hour.) The northern latitudes common in the United States rotate at a speed of about 800 miles per hour.

Children may notice that one can see, over a period of days, a shift in the position of the shadows of fixed objects. To verify this shift or to focus attention on it, make a hole the diameter of a pencil in a piece of cardboard. Tape the cardboard to a sunny window and place a sheet of paper where the sunlight coming through the hole will fall on it. Trace the outline of the spot of light and record the time and date within the outline. Repeat this daily at the same time of day and note the shift in the outline. Point out the connection between the movement of the spot of light and the revolution of the earth around the sun.

Newspapers and almanacs provide evidence (in their records of sunset and sunrise) of changing hours of daylight and dark. Fig. 9-5 shows a typical record of the night-day relationship in the middle latitudes of the northern hemisphere. Charting these changes is a useful demonstration and particularly graphic in the northern latitudes at a season when the sun describes a low arc in the sky. (Using symbols to represent the earth and a light source to represent the sun sometimes confuses elementary-grade children. When children do not make the connection between the models and the actual phenomena they give evidence of need for such "primary reading" or direct experience as is described above.)

The seasons are a product of Earth's revolution about the sun and of the $23\frac{1}{2}$-degree tilt (in relation to the plane of its orbit) in the earth's axis. To demonstrate this, mark the "north pole" of each of four styrofoam or old tennis balls (whiten the latter with water paint or tempera) with a knitting needle, and, perhaps, roughly sketch in the continents. Set each ball at the earth's approximate tilt (Fig. 9-6) in the open end of a soup can or milk bottle to keep the ball from rolling. Place the cans with the balls, regularly spaced, around an unshaded light, which simulates the sun shining in all directions.

Because Earth's axis is tilted, the sun's rays strike different parts of the earth at different angles. To illustrate how the angle of tilt determines the intensity of the sun's rays, point a large flashlight through a mailing tube directly at a blackboard or floor in a darkened room; then point the tube at an angle to the surface. The oblique rays cover a larger area but are not as bright as the direct rays. (A photographic light meter may be used to show the differences in intensity.) Thus a portion of the earth's surface that receives relatively direct rays is experiencing summer—for example, the upper portion (northern hemisphere) of the ball at the left in Fig. 9-6, and the lower portion (southern hemisphere) of the ball at the right. The point may be made that it is winter in the southern hemisphere when it is summer in the northern, and vice versa. If Earth turned, like a top, on a horizontal plane (relative to the sun), there would be no alternation of seasons as we know it, though the earth is 3 million miles nearer the sun in winter.

The distance to bodies far out in space is determined by a method based on the apparent annual (caused by Earth's revolution) back-and-forth shift of stellar bodies. This phenomenon is called parallax, and the method based on it was first suggested by a Greek mathematician, Aristarchus (c. 250 B.C.), when he tried to measure solar parallax directly by geometrical means.

To illustrate Aristarchus' brilliant concept, have children look with one eye at the vertical lines of a nearby window frame against the light,

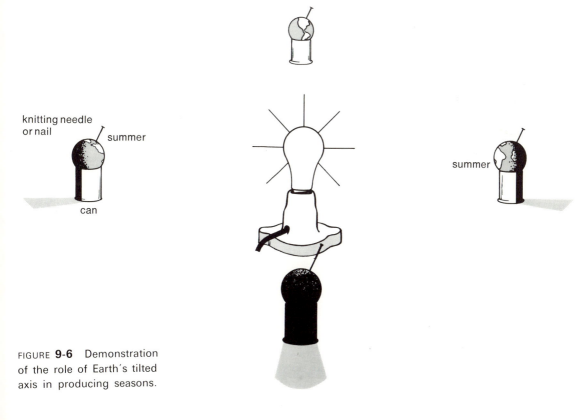

knitting needle or nail

summer

can

summer

FIGURE **9-6** Demonstration of the role of Earth's tilted axis in producing seasons.

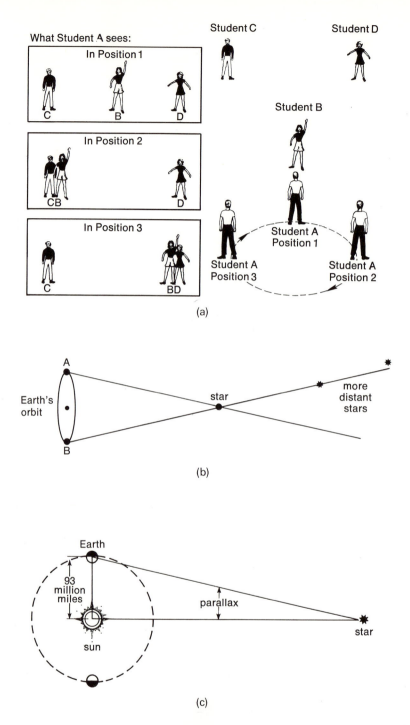

FIGURE **9-7** Parallax effects: (a) When Student A changes position, he notes an apparent change in the position of Student B in relation to Students C and D; (b) a star viewed from Earth at Point A in its orbit seems to have shifted to the left (in relation to more distant stars) when viewed from Point B; (c) parallax determined using the distance from the sun to the star as one leg of the triangle.

and then, simultaneously, close the eye and open the other. The lines of the frame will appear to have shifted in relation to the background. Of course, they have not; what has changed is the angle of observation. To demonstrate this another way, position four children as shown in Fig. 9-7a. When Student A changes position, Student B will seem (to Student A) to shift in relation to Students C and D. In much the same way, as the earth revolves about the sun, and the angle of observation of the stars changes, certain stars seem to shift in relation to the stars near them (Fig. 9-7b). The two lines of sight to the star and a line connecting the two points from which the sightings are made form a triangle whose base and two base angles are known. With this information, the distance to the star can be calculated trigonometrically. This can also be done as shown in Fig. 9-7c, where the base of the triangle is the distance from Earth to the sun, and the line from sun to star makes a right angle with the base.

In actual practice, distances to the stars are determined as follows: a star and some stars near it are photographed and studied under magnification. Six months later, when the earth is on the opposite side of the sun, the star (and "background" stars) are again photographed and studied. Extremely fine measurements of the star's apparent movement in relation to the stars near it will give what is in effect the angles of observation. With the length of the baseline (186,000,000 miles, the diameter of Earth's orbit) known, the computation can then be made.

The Sun

The kindergartener who avers that the sun moves is not really in error. As the earth revolves around the sun at about 66,600 miles per hour, the solar system is moving at about 43,000 miles per hour. While the earth rotates once a day (at about $18\frac{1}{2}$ miles per second), the sun rotates once in 25 days (at about 13 miles per second) as, with its entourage of planets, it orbits through the Milky Way galaxy (see below).

The sun is big enough to hold a million Earths. The sun, on the same scale as a $\frac{1}{4}$-inch Earth,

would be 27 inches in diameter. The temperature of the sun is believed to be 11,000°F at the surface and 100,000,000°F or more in the interior; steel would boil easily, even on its surface. Looking at it directly can damage the retina. Very young children should understand that the sun heats the whole earth, and that it never ceases to shine—day or night, gray day, or clear. In this respect, one can point out that an airplane flying above the clouds is in sunshine, and that, when it is night in our side of the world, the sun is shining on the other side. For a discussion of the sun's light and the colors of the spectrum see Chapter 15.

To illustrate the different amounts of radiation the planets receive from the sun, put an unshaded 75- to 100-watt light bulb (representing the sun) at one end of a room and a pinhead at the other (Earth). In this arrangement, the amount of light falling on the pinhead is roughly proportional (in terms of surface presented) to the amount of sunlight falling on the earth. Hold a thermometer about 2 feet away from the unshaded light bulb for two minutes. Check the temperature and repeat, holding the thermometer 1 foot and then 2 inches away from the bulb. The readings represent relative temperatures at proportional distances for Pluto, Earth, and Mercury, respectively.

Although the sun is our nearest star, it is 93 million miles away. Traveling at 50 miles per hour it would take nearly 200 years to reach the sun; about 12,000 Earths in a row would be needed to cover the distance (about 3700 times the distance around our equator). Light from the sun reaches us in about eight minutes. Our next nearest star is more than 24 trillion miles away. So many stars are so much farther out in space that astronomers save time and trouble by using as a measure of distance the *light year*—the distance light will travel in a year; at 186,000 miles per second this is about 6,000,000,000,000 miles. Thus astronomers find it more convenient to say that our next nearest star, Alpha Centauri, is four light years (rather than 24,000,000,000,000 miles) away.

The *parsec*, a still larger unit of measure for

astronomical distance, is approximately 3.3 light years. As an exercise in the use of large numbers, children may enjoy converting to miles, or other terrestrial linear units, the distances (in light years) of the following stars: Vega, 37; Pollux, 33; Arcturus, 40; Castor, 45; and Regulus, 77.

To measure the distance to the sun or moon, which are not outside the solar system and, hence, not subject to the same parallax effect as bodies far out in space, observatories across the world measure simultaneously the angles of their lines of sight to the center of the sun's or moon's disk. These, together with the known straight-line distance between them, supply the necessary data for the computation.

Solar eclipses   A few times during one's lifetime one may see an eclipse of the sun. A total eclipse lasts only seven minutes and, during it, birds and animals act just as though it were night, preparing to sleep or to wake, depending on whether they are nocturnal or not. Eclipses give astronomers a chance to study the corona (the circle of light around the sun that is visible above the rim of the eclipsing moon) and the gaseous eruptions, or flares, from the face of the sun, which are sometimes 3000 or 4000 miles high. The colors of the incandescent gases in these solar prominences help scientists identify the elements in the sun, somewhat as one identifies elements with flame tests (Chapter 10). Because many of the elements in the sun are also found on Earth, scientists think that the earth was once part of the same material that made up the sun. One theory postulates that the solar system was a huge

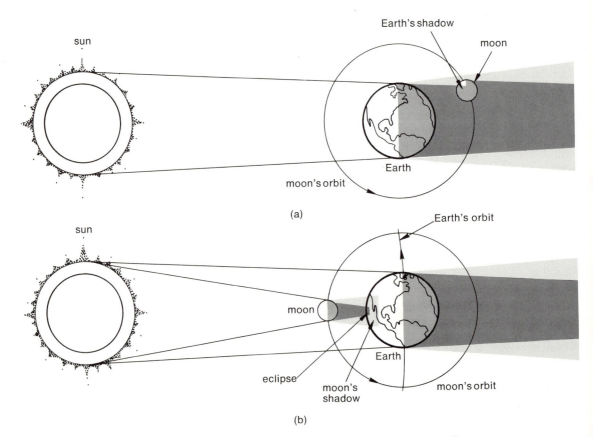

FIGURE **9-8**   Positions of Earth, sun, and moon during (a) lunar eclipse; (b) solar eclipse.

gas and dust cloud that under gravitational stresses gradually condensed to form the planets and the sun.

A solar eclipse occurs when the moon comes between the earth and the sun—at least twice a year. The shadow of the moon, round like that of the earth, but smaller, has two regions, that of deep shadow—the umbra—and that of partial shadow—the penumbra. The umbra is about 240,000 miles long (from the moon to Earth) and shaped like a slightly truncated cone, the small end of which (at Earth's surface) is never more than 160 miles in diameter (Fig. 9-8b)—one reason why we see a total eclipse so infrequently.

A simple way to show the mechanism of solar eclipse is to hold a small disk or coin a few inches in front of one eye in the line of sight between the eye and a ceiling light so that the coin completely hides the light. The coin represents the moon and the ceiling light the sun. Children observing this will note that the coin casts a shadow on the eye of the viewer.

Using an unshaded light (to represent the sun), a styrofoam ball (the moon), and a small globe, children can work out relative positions of these three objects in both solar and lunar eclipses (Fig. 9-8). Because solar eclipses are rare, astronomers will travel thousands of miles to see one in the hope that weather conditions will allow them to study the corona. Most almanacs give dates and areas where eclipses may be observed: for example, two visible in the United States will take place on: February 26, 1979 (Idaho and Montana), and August 21, 2017 (entire continental United States). Even during an eclipse one should not look at the sun with the naked eye, but through black film negative or protective dark glasses. Near the edge of the moon's shadow, one may see a reddish ring, the chromosphere, a luminous layer of gas overlying the surface of the sun.

Sunspots (Fig. 9-9), which appear on the surface of the sun can be viewed as follows. Point field glasses (binoculars) or a simple telescope at the sun and focus it so that a bright, clear image of the sun appears on a white paper placed a

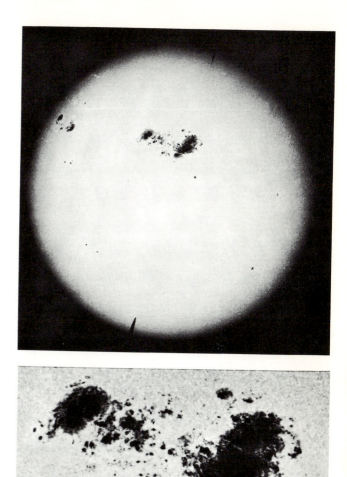

FIGURE **9-9** At top, the entire solar disk, showing sunspots and, below, an enlargement of the great spot group of April 7, 1947, taken at Mt. Wilson Observatory.

short distance beyond the eyepiece (Fig. 9-10). (*Never* look at the sun directly through a telescope.) If there is sunspot activity at the time, the sunspots may be seen as small dark blobs on the paper. Sunspots come and go on the sun's surface and are related to electromagnetic activity such as that which blocks certain kinds of radio transmission on earth.

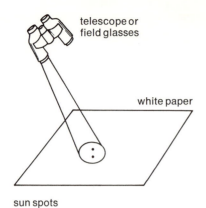

telescope or field glasses

white paper

sun spots

FIGURE **9-10** Sunspots projected through telescope or field glasses.

The Moon

Children too young to have seen the moon at night can see it in the daytime under certain conditions. Their observations concerning the moon can be sharpened by asking if it has the same shape and size as the sun, and if it is brighter or dimmer. For very young children, one might point out the effect of distance on apparent size; good examples are a penny held close to the eye and then at arm's length, a bird flying low overhead looking bigger than an airplane in the distance. Children can also compare, in a darkened room, the light from different-sized sources—a large and a small flashlight. Sunlight is always bright enough for reading, moonlight ("second-hand," reflected light), rarely. In a darkened room, have children look at a picture or book by lamplight, then by light reflected from a chalk-smeared mirror.

About 50 moons could fit inside the earth. The moon's diameter is $\frac{1}{4}$ that of Earth (2000 and 8000 miles, respectively). It is our nearest neighbor in space, being about 240,000 miles away—ten times the earth's circumference. The sun is nearly 400 times farther from Earth. If the sun were about 400 miles away, the moon, relatively speaking, would be about a mile distant.

Moon phases Children will notice that the moon changes shape. Have them draw or cut out the shape as they see it, or prepare a set of cutouts, ranging from a thin crescent through quarter and half up to a full moon, and have children pick out the shape they saw. Once they can arrange the cutouts in order, they will have begun to gain a concept of the waxing and waning moon. Also useful is a picture record of the moon's phases on different dates; these can be placed against cutouts of the local skyline to help children relate them to their environment.

Children may profit by demonstrating the phases of the moon with white styrofoam balls or papier-mâché models; a playground ball scrubbed clean or painted with a light-colored water paint works well.

Holding the ball (the "moon") aloft on a knitting needle or stiff wire pushed through its center, a child (the "moon") rotating slowly eastward (Earth's motion) before the "sun" (a strong light source such as a projector lamp) he will see the shapes of the phases of the moon as the area of the ball that is illuminated changes. One can also impale a small fruit or ball on the point of a pencil-box compass and revolve it about themselves in relation to a light source to get the same effect. A more elaborate method (Fig. 9-11) involves setting a globe ("Earth") on a box in front of a light (the "sun") and having one child move a small ball (the "moon")—suspended by a string from the end of a yardstick or dowel—around the globe. Children sitting on the floor around the box can watch the "moon" from the direction of "Earth." (This method can also be used to demonstrate the nature of eclipses—lunar and solar.) Another variation is simply to have one child carry a ball around the others, seated (facing out) in a circle on the floor, while another child holds and directs a strong flashlight at the ball. In this manner the seated children get an "Earth's-eye" view of the "moon" moving about them.

Demonstrations should never take the place of actual observations of the moon. Since the moon rises in the east and sets in the west, the children will judge from such observation that the moon moves like the sun. Noting the position of the moon with respect to the nearest bright star and watching its relation to that star over a period of days will show that the moon really moves eastward; it is the earth's rotation that makes it appear to move in the opposite direction.

Since the moon's speed of rotation and revolution are the same (28 days), it always presents the same side to Earth. This slow rotation means long days and nights on the moon—each about fifteen Earth days long. To illustrate how the moon makes just one turn (rotation) as it travels around the earth one needs a "dolly" (used by school custodians for moving heavy objects) or a child's wagon. Have one child pull another (the "moon") in a circle around the room. The child riding should be facing in, toward the center of the circle ("Earth"). Circling the room, he has turned around (rotated) once.

Looking at the moon through a telescope, or even binoculars, will show that parts of its surface are very rough. The apparent face (the "Man in the Moon") is caused largely by shadows cast by the moon's mountains and craters. Children can roll clay balls and make deep indentations in their surface. Shining a strong light across the balls will demonstrate how the irregularities of the surface produce shadows. Before the recent close approaches and landing, astronomers obtained information about the height of mountains on the moon largely by measuring the shadows cast by them. Until 1959, when the Soviet Union photographed it from an orbiting television camera, it was thought that man would never see the other side of the moon. (See discussion above of moon's rotation.)

Lunar astronauts must bring their oxygen because there is none on the moon; they also need special equipment to protect them from the extreme heat and cold of the moon's bare surface. Since the smaller moon has one sixth Earth's gravitational pull, astronauts also need special training for moving under conditions of low gravity. On the moon, a 72-pound boy would weigh about 12 pounds and could easily jump to a height of 24 feet. (Acting out conditions on the moon can provide excellent motivation for research reading and listening.)

The moon, like the sun, usually looks bigger when it is near the horizon. This is an optical illusion (see Chapter 15)—it *looks* bigger when it is seen in relation to objects on the skyline, and smaller when isolated in the great expanse of the sky. Children can check this by sighting the moon through a paper clip fitted over the edge of a yardstick (Fig. 9-12). Hold the stick beneath the eye, and slide the clip until the moon just occupies the space between the prongs. Compare two such sightings—one made when the moon rises and one later. If the moon were *actually* larger on the horizon, then the setting of the clip on the yardstick would differ (closer to the eye) from the setting for the other sighting.

Again, the moon and sun look redder when close to the horizon. This is also an optical effect,

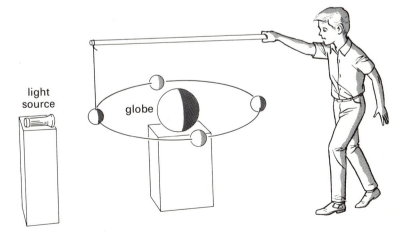

FIGURE **9-11** Method of demonstrating phases of the moon.

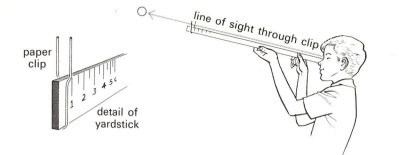

paper clip

detail of yardstick

line of sight through clip

FIGURE **9-12** Sighting the moon to verify illusionistic character of apparent changes in size. Detail of paper-clip sight is at left.

related to the fact that dust particles in the air tend to absorb most of the colors that make up light, allowing through only the colors at the red end of the visible spectrum. The more dust the greater the effect. When close to the horizon, the moon or sun are being seen through more dust than when they are overhead (Fig. 9-13).

As indicated above (in Fig. 9-8 and in the description of solar eclipses), lunar eclipses are the result of the intervention of Earth between the sun and moon. From manipulation of models duplicating the arrangement in Fig. 9-8a, children may be able to demonstrate why lunar eclipses are more common than solar and occur only during a full moon, why a solar eclipse must fall at the dark of the moon, and why solar and lunar eclipses do *not* occur once a month. From the start, one should make clear that models do not present a wholly true picture. For example, the relative sizes and distances of sun, moon, and Earth would be hard to represent correctly, so

that the shadows cast are much larger, relative to the size of the models, than they are in actuality; for example, as mentioned above, during a solar eclipse the moon's shadow never covers an area more than 160 miles in diameter.

If it were not for the difference between the plane of the earth's orbit and that of the moon, lunar eclipses would be more frequent. The plane of the moon's orbit is inclined 5° to that of the earth. Thus, the moon passes through the earth's shadow only occasionally. This and other aspects of lunar eclipse can be demonstrated with balls of clay held in the beam of a flashlight so as to duplicate the relationships of Earth and the moon as shown in Fig. 9-11.

The Planets

Sky watchers in ancient times noticed that certain celestial bodies remained in approximately the same part of the sky night after night, while others kept changing position. Sometimes these latter appeared to reverse direction, and were therefore called *planets* (wanderers). The stationary points of light are stars. Both planets and stars appear through binoculars or telescopes as shining disks. However, astronomers consider stars as incandescent gaseous matter like our sun. Planets are smaller bodies, no longer gaseous. Like the moon, they glow in the reflected light of the sun. Even without the aid of telescopes, the ancient astronomers were able to observe and record the motions of the five planets nearest the sun—Mercury, Venus, Mars, Jupiter, Saturn; Mercury, being nearest the sun and smallest, is hard to see. The three outermost planets—

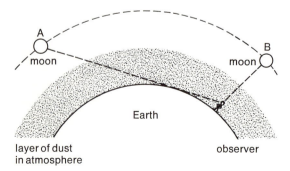

A
moon

B
moon

Earth

layer of dust in atmosphere

observer

FIGURE **9-13** Line of sight (dashed line) to moon on horizon (A) travels farther through the dusty zone in the atmosphere than line of sight to moon overhead (B).

Uranus, Neptune, and Pluto—can be observed only through telescopes. Pluto was not discovered until 1930, when it was located by the American astronomer, Percival Lowell, whose observations of the motions of Uranus and Neptune indicated the existence of a gravitational force, which led him to suspect the presence of the then unknown planet.

There is a family resemblance among the planets: all are spheres spinning on their own axes, all travel in elliptical orbits around the sun, all are composed of the same elements, and all follow a definite pattern of spacing in their distance from the sun—with the exception of the space between Mars and Jupiter. A German astronomer, Bode, noticed the gap in this pattern and concluded that a planet was missing. In 1801, in the search for the "lost planet," an Italian astronomer discovered Ceres—a tiny "planetoid" less than 500 miles across. Since then, more than 1500 planetoids (also called asteroids) have been found in this region.

The nine planets move in orbits on approximately one plane. A plane of orbit can be readily illustrated by swinging a weight at the end of a string. Useful for young children is a representation of the Copernican system (Fig. 9-1b) drawn in chalk on the classroom floor. A larger representation of the system, which will help convey the immense dimensions involved, can be set up outdoors, as follows. Needed are a few balls of kite string, eight cardboard cartons, and an open space—such as a playground—large enough to accommodate a 500-foot line. Using a scale of one foot to one million miles, have pairs of children measure off pieces of string representing the distances of the various planets from the sun. Begin with Mercury (36 feet), then add another piece of 31 feet, giving a total of 67 feet for Venus' distance from the sun. Another team can then add 26 feet to give a total of 93 feet for Earth's proportionate distance from the sun. Forty-eight feet more brings the total to 141, the relative distance to Mars. Four pairs of children may be involved in measuring the 342 feet needed to bring the total to 483 feet—Jupiter's distance from the sun. (Fifty- or one hundred-foot

surveyors' tapes may be used if children exhibit sufficient care and knowledge to handle these expensive tools.) Then, beginning at some prominent point (the "sun"), such as a backstop in a playground, have the children lay out in a straight line, end to end, the pieces of string. As each string is laid down, have a child mark its end with an appropriately-labeled carton—for example, a carton marked, in large letters, ME (for Mercury) at the end of the first string, then one marked V(enus) at the end of the next string, and so on. As this is done, have the class look back periodically to note the diminishing size of each marker as the distance lengthens. Looking back toward the "sun" from the J(upiter) marker should immediately impress the children with the enormousness of the distances involved, even on the reduced scale employed. The great gap between Mars and Jupiter should also be noted. (Most representations of the solar system showing the planets in concentric rings fail to reveal this gap.) Children may enlist a parent's after-school cooperation in completing the system by plotting the positions of the three other outer planets to the same scale; this should go well beyond the school ground, with Pluto more than one hundred times (3670 feet) further from the "sun" than Mercury. (Table 9-1 gives these distances for all the planets, as well as other data on the solar system.)

Children may also wish to prepare scale models of the five planets to be combined with the linear model just described. The models can be made of cardboard cut to a scale of one inch to one thousand miles. While this scale is not the same as that of the linear model, using the same scale would yield measurements too small to be visually useful. The disks should have the following diameters: Mercury, 3 inches; Venus, $7\frac{1}{2}$ inches; Earth, 8 inches; Mars, 4 inches; and Jupiter, 88 inches (or an arc of an 88-inch circle). Glue or tape each disk except Jupiter's to a drinking straw, and tack the straw to the respective carton markers; this gives the disk better visibility. A 2-inch disk, representing the moon, should be mounted 3 inches from the Earth disk. (On the linear scale, 3 inches represents one quarter mil-

Table 9-1   PLANETARY DATA

Planet	Diameter[a] (miles)	Distance from sun (millions of miles)	Revolution in orbit (years)	Number of moons
Mercury	3000	36	$\frac{1}{4}$	0
Venus	7575	67	$\frac{2}{3}$	0
Earth	8000	93	1	1
Mars	4215	141	2	2
Jupiter	88,000	483	12	11
Saturn	75,000	886	29	9
Uranus	31,000	1786	84	4
Neptune	33,000	2792	165	1
Pluto	3000	3680	249	0

[a]The sun has a diameter of 864,100 miles; the moon, 2160 miles.

lion miles, the approximate distance of the moon from Earth.)

Planetary orbits are not circular but slightly elliptical. As a class activity, ellipses may be drawn with the aid of a loop of string and two pins (Fig. 9-14).

To emphasize the idea of orbits as invisible paths, one can point out to children that though they move in and out of the classroom every day, they leave no visible path on the floor. In a play exercise that can be gradually expanded in complexity, children can act out the movements and positions of the members of the solar system. With one child, representing the sun, standing or sitting at the center of the room, other roles can then be added on: the earth, another child walking around the "sun," a "moon" walking around the "earth," and so on. Developing the concepts of orbit and motion can be related by discussion and outdoor observation to the earth's revolution in orbit and the change of season.

Mercury, Venus, Mars, Jupiter, and Saturn are visible to the naked eye. Most almanacs will tell when and where as well as offering much additional information of interest and use in any aspect of astronomy and space.

Mercury has no atmosphere. The distant planets are too cold and too small to exert the

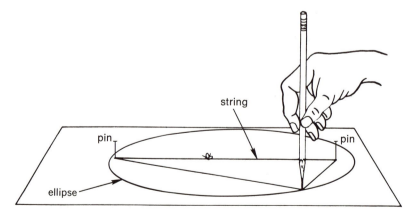

string

pin

pin

ellipse

FIGURE **9-14**   Drawing an ellipse with the aid of two pins and string.

gravitational pull necessary to hold an atmosphere. There is no evidence of oxygen on Venus. Mars's atmosphere contains carbon dioxide and traces of oxygen; it should be able to support plant life. Jupiter's atmosphere includes ammonia and methane, gases poisonous to humans. There has been much speculation about life on Mars but, even with the recent close approaches by space "probes," no one knows for sure. The possibility of life as it exists on Earth occurring elsewhere in the solar system is doubtful, although the likelihood is great that it exists in some of the myriad other "solar systems" in space.

Comets and Meteors

Comets and meteors also travel around the sun. The name "comet" means "long haired" in Greek and is related to the long luminous "tail" that is visible (and longest) when the comet is nearest the sun. The tail results from the pressure exerted by the sun's light, which pushes gases out of the comet's head, much like wind blowing flame away from a fire.

For the same reason, the tail is always pointed away from the sun, whether the comet is approaching or moving away from it. Most comets are small, but some have heads thousands of miles across and tails millions of miles long. Like the tail, the head of a comet is made of particles of dust and gases. The gas composing the tails is so thin that Earth and other planets have passed through them without effect. The heavier the particles of gas, the more curved the tail.

Over a thousand comets have been seen—some regularly, but most are visible only through a telescope. The most famous is Halley's comet; the English astronomer for whom it is named studied this comet so thoroughly in 1682 that he was able to predict its orbit and return—once every 75–76 years. From the date of its most recent appearance (1910), children can calculate the date of its next possible sighting.

Meteors, the smallest members of the sun's circus, are tiny mineral fragments burning from the friction of the earth's atmosphere as they plunge through it toward Earth. A meteor makes a sudden thin streak of light across the sky; a comet shows as a steady streak of light during the nights it is visible. The common "shooting star" is really a meteor, not a star. Meteors are much more common than comets; as many as five to ten meteors per hour may be visible of a night to the naked eye.

While remnants of meteors may fall to Earth as dust, some larger pieces—called meteorites—also reach Earth's surface. These odd-shaped lumps often resemble cinders or furnace clinkers, although some are much heavier than coal, consisting mainly of nickel, iron, and cobalt; others, of lighter materials, are called *stone* meteorites. The Museum of Natural History in New York City has on exhibit a 14-ton meteorite, which fell near Willamette, Oregon, and a 36-ton meteorite found in Greenland by Admiral Peary. The Eskimos there had used fragments of it to make metal arrow points and tools.

Craters made by meteorites look exactly like those on the moon. In Arizona, a crater about $\frac{3}{4}$ of a mile across is believed to have been made by a giant meteorite that buried itself so far below the surface that it has not yet been found. Cedars growing around the rim of the crater are over 700 years old.

The Chubb meteorite crater in Canada is $2\frac{1}{2}$ miles in diameter and contains a lake 2 miles across. A meteor that landed in Siberia in 1908 burned the forests for 25 miles around. Earth and moon craters made by meteorites may be reproduced in classroom miniature. To do so, line a shoe box with foil or plastic and cover the bottom with soft clay or plaster of Paris. Drop greased balls of clay, marbles, billard balls and the like from directly above or at an angle (tip the box). Remove the balls before the surrounding area hardens.

To make graphic the role of friction in turning the bright and shining material of a meteorite into a charred black lump, have children rub their hands together slowly, then fast, noting which way generates the most heat. Airplanes that travel at very high speeds have refrigerated cockpits to counteract the high heat of friction produced by moving through the air quickly. The heat shield on space capsules has a similar function. The thousands of tiny rocks pulled by the sun's gravity meet Earth's atmosphere while moving at 20–40 miles per second. They begin to burn or glow about 100 miles up above Earth's surface.

OUTSIDE THE SOLAR SYSTEM

Earth, the other eight planets, the sun, and the planetoids make up the solar system, which wheels slowly in space. But the solar system, large as it is, occupies but one small region toward the edge of the huge Milky Way galaxy—a whirling mass of hot gases, billions of stars, and interstellar dust (Fig. 9-15). The Milky Way, in turn, is only one of many galaxies sighted and studied by astronomers. It is off-center from the universe of galaxies so far discovered. Thus far astronomers have determined the distance of about 100 galaxies.

The Stars

Most of the stars one sees with the naked eye are in the Milky Way galaxy, which is shaped somewhat like a fried egg or a pair of cymbals. Looking from Earth, inside the galaxy, the stars appear closer together toward the rim. Children observing the night sky will note that stars are of unequal brightness. This brightness is described in terms of "magnitude"; sixth-magnitude stars are the faintest visible without optic aids, and first-magnitude stars are $2\frac{1}{2}$ times brighter than second-magnitude stars and 100 times brighter than sixth-magnitude stars. Using different-sized light bulbs, they can recognize the basis for differences in the brightness of the stars. Looking at a flashlight at close range and at a distance can help clarify the concept too, and comparing the light from a flashlight in a darkened and in a light room will help explain why stars are more visible at night.

About 200,000 stars have been seen and catalogued with the aid of telescopes. Of these, 2500–3000 can be seen with the naked eye. The larger stars have been known and observed since ancient times. Most have Arabic names, and several begin with the Arabic prefix *al* meaning "the"; for example, Algol, the demon, in the constellation of Perseus; Altair, the flier, in Aquila, the Eagle; Aldebaran, the follower (because it follows the Pleiades, the "eye" of the constellation Taurus, the bull). Arcturus means

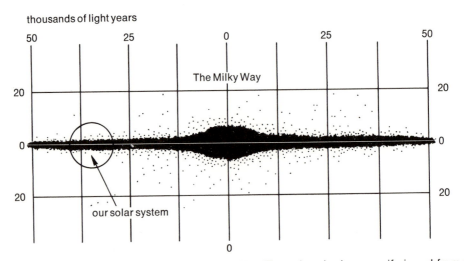

thousands of light years

The Milky Way

our solar system

FIGURE **9-15** Relation of the solar system to the Milky Way. The galaxy is shown as if viewed from the edge of its disk-like mass.

Table 9-2

RELATION OF STAR COLOR AND TEMPERATURE

Color	Approximate surface temperature (°F)	Typical star
blue-white	above 36,000	Rigel
yellow-white	13,500	Procyon
yellow	11,000	Sun
orange	7500	Arcturus
red	5500	Antares

"the star of the shepherds of the heavenly herds." Planes and ships navigate with respect to the positions of these and other brighter or first-magnitude stars. Some of the other great stars are listed in Table 9-3.

To illustrate the relationship between star color and temperature (Table 9-2), heat a piece of iron wire (such as picture wire) until it glows red.

Hold the wire with pliers or kitchen tongs and, as an added precaution, have pot holders and a sheet of asbestos ready. Continue to heat the wire, which, as it grows hotter, will glow orange, then yellow. With a blow torch or propane burner, the temperature may be raised to the point where the tip turns white. The hottest stars have a blue-white color. Earth's nearest star, the sun, is medium hot (and yellow). Rigel, 14,000 times brighter than our sun, is blue-white. Betelgeuse is a red giant, one of the biggest stars known. Capella is yellow, like our sun. Aldebaran, orange, is cooler than our sun.

Constellations

There are about 90 named star groups called constellations. Children will enjoy becoming familiar with the major circumpolar constellations and with those of interest because they contain some prominent star or object of astronomical significance such as double stars, clusters, and

Table 9-3   SOME CONSTELLATIONS VISIBLE IN NORTHERN LATITUDES[a]

Spring	Summer	Fall	Winter
Leo, the Lion (Regulus)	Lyra, the Lyre (Vega)	Andromeda, the Maiden	Orion, the Hunter (Rigel, Betelgeuse)
Auriga, the Charioteer (Capella)	Cygnus, the Swan (Deneb)	Pegasus, the Horse (Algol)	Canis Major, Big Dog (Sirius)
Gemini, the Twins (Pollux)	Scorpio, the Scorpion (Antares)	Perseus the Knight	Canis Minor, Little Dog
Cancer, the Crab	Aquila, the Eagle	Hercules, the Hunter	Taurus, the Bull
	Boötes, the Herdsman (Arcturus)		The Pleiades, Seven Sisters
	Delphinus, the Dolphin		Aries, the Ram
	Northern Crown, the Corona Borealis		Cepheus, Andromeda's Father
	Draco, the Dragon		Cassiopeia, Andromeda's Mother
	Serpens, the Snake		

[a] Names in parentheses are of major stars associated with the various constellations. At times, some constellations will be below the horizon and, hence, not visible.

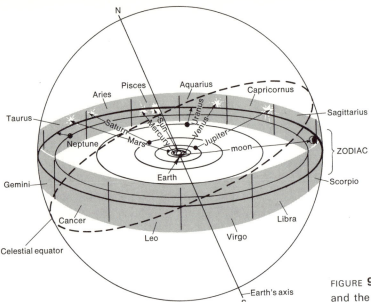

FIGURE **9-16** The zodiac in relation to Earth and the other planets.

nebulae (interstellar cloudlike masses). The stars composing constellations differ from other visible stars in that they move or drift slowly as a group. Table 9-3 lists constellations visible in the northern hemisphere according to season.

The Zodiac

Children can observe that the sun, the moon, and the planets follow roughly the same path in the sky. At our latitude this broad band—the zodiac—arches high across the southern sky (Fig. 9-16). Most of the constellations parade along an imaginary equatorial line called the *ecliptic*. The zodiac extends 8° on each side of the ecliptic, to make an imaginary belt 16° wide. This is divided into twelve sections of 30°, each of which includes a constellation, called a *sign* of the zodiac (Fig. 9-17).

The signs of the zodiac are: Aries, Taurus, Gemini, Cancer, Leo, Virgo, Libra, Scorpio, Sagittarius, Capricorn, Aquarius, and Pisces. To help children understand why at different seasons one sees different constellations, have them copy the twelve signs of the zodiac on large cards or white paper. Lay the cards in a circle on the floor around an unshaded lamp and move a globe around the light as shown in Fig. 9-17. With Earth in the orbital position shown in the figure, an Earthly observer would see the constellations Virgo, Libra, Scorpio, and Sagittarius, and the sun would be said to be in Taurus (a line of sight from Earth toward the sun, if extended, would point toward Taurus). Since the planets move in nearly the same plane, each one will seem at different times to be among the stars of the various constellations. For example, in Fig. 9-16, Jupiter would seem from the earth to be in the constellation Capricornus, and Saturn in Aries. With binoculars one can see the beautiful autumn constellation of Andromeda. To do this locate, with the naked eye, the approximate position of the nebula within the constellation, as shown in Fig. 9-18. Then, without shifting, raise the glasses to the eyes. Through the glasses, the nebula is a hazy patch, like light shining through tissue paper. One of the closest constellations outside our galaxy, Andromeda is a mere 2,800,000 light years away. With binoculars, one can also see the nebula in Orion (Fig. 9-18), a fall and winter constellation within our own galaxy. The Orion nebula, like that in Andromeda, is also visible as a fuzzy patch rather than the twinkling pinpoint of light it would be as a single star. Small as it appears, it takes fifteen years for light to cross it.

Children enjoy the myths connected with names of the constellations, including some of the

American Indian legends—for instance, the one that designates the stars in the handle of the Big Dipper as the Robin, the Bluejay, and the Chickadee. The story has it that the double star in the middle is the Chickadee, who is carrying a pot in which the three birds hoped to cook their quarry, the Great Bear. The Robin, because he is the star nearest the Bear, was splattered with blood when they killed the Bear with their arrows, which is why the Robin's breast has been red ever since.

With binoculars, one can also see the star clusters associated with our galaxy. One such, the Beehive, is in the summer constellation Cancer, the Crab (Fig. 9-16), a faint group of stars, usually low in the southeastern skies in northern latitudes. The Beehive is so named because of its fancied resemblance to a swarm of bees. In the winter, constellation Hercules (Fig. 9-18) is a star cluster that looks like a single star to the naked eye; telescopic photographs have revealed it to be composed of over 30,000 stars which, despite

their seeming closeness, are separated by billions of miles.

The Big Dipper appears to be pouring into the Little Dipper, the end of the "handle" of which is Polaris, the Pole or North Star. The Big Dipper has been called the Clock in the Sky. The position of the Dipper handle changes not only with the hour of the night but also with the seasons. For example, on a winter night, the handle of the Dipper generally hangs low; in summer, about the same time of evening, the handle is high. But in any position, the two end stars in the bowl always point to the North Star (see arrow Fig. 9-18). (Children can find north by remembering that it will be to the right of sunset.) The North Star does not rise or set and, although it is brighter than our sun, appears insignificant because it is 470 light years away. The North Star is the pivot (see Fig. 9-18) for five circumpolar constellations: the two Dippers; Cassiopeia, the Queen; Cepheus, the King; and Draco, the Dragon. Once the two Dippers have become

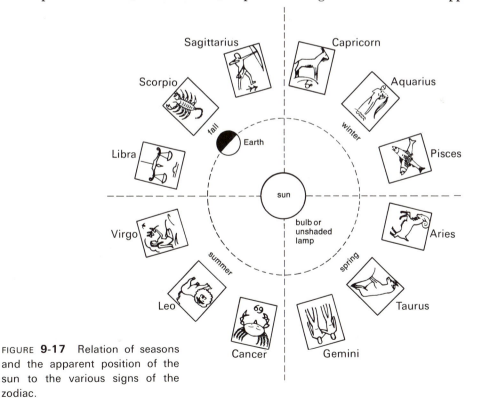

FIGURE **9-17** Relation of seasons and the apparent position of the sun to the various signs of the zodiac.

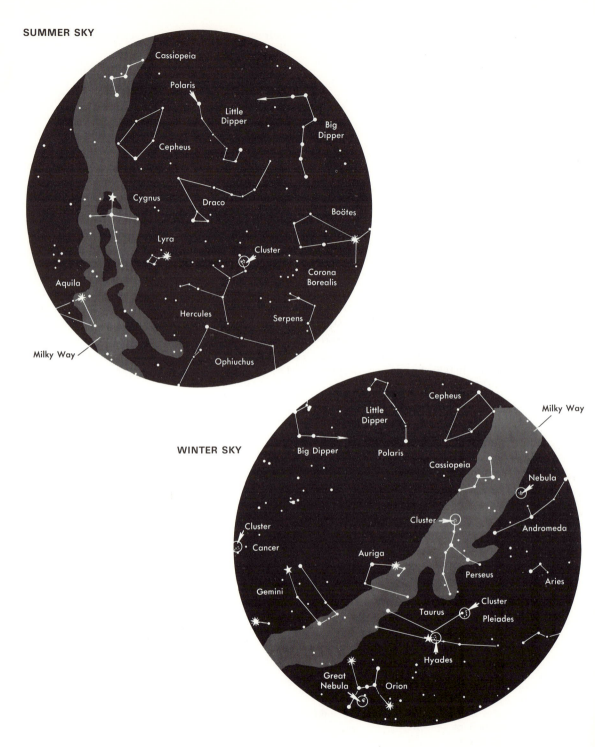

FIGURE **9-18** Star charts of the summer and winter skies (northern hemisphere), showing the constellations as they appear in May and in January–February, respectively.

familiar, children should have no trouble finding Cassiopeia, which looks like a battered M or W, and faces the Big Dipper on the other side of the North Star. (Although the North Star has been a guide to navigation for centuries, astronomers have evidence that it is drifting through space together with the other stars. The patterns of constellations are also gradually changing.)

The motions of the circumpolar constellations can be demonstrated with an umbrella. With the place where the ribs converge representing the North Star (and the end of the handle of the Little Dipper), outline the Little Dipper with chalk or adhesive disks inside the open umbrella. Mark the Big Dipper stars and add Cepheus, Cassiopeia, and Draco in their appropriate positions (see Fig. 9-18). When the umbrella is twirled overhead, the star groups should move much as they do outdoors. In the same way, children can observe and reproduce the position of any circumpolar constellation at any time. To make the relationship between the constellations and the rotating earth more graphic, make holes at the North and South poles of an old globe and slip it over the rod of the umbrella. (The umbrella handle must be removed.) The globe can then be turned. With a bit of modeling clay marking one's location on the globe, children can imagine themselves on Earth looking up at the sky—that is, at the inside of the open umbrella—and watching the constellations appear to wheel about Polaris.

Place a misaligned row of dots on the blackboard, and ask for volunteers to rearrange the dots in the form of the Big Dipper. After doing this, children should be ready to make a milk carton constellation finder (Fig. 9-19). After rinsing the carton, cut off the bottom and cut slits on two opposite sides large enough to admit a 3 × 5 card, black or blue construction paper cut to the same size, or similar material. With a pin, prick out a pattern of a constellation in the center of the card. The constellation pattern can then be seen by holding up the card-end (bottom) of the carton to the light while viewing the card through the spout end (top).

To study the constellations at first hand, divide children into teams and have the members of each familiarize themselves with the outline of a particular constellation and its neighbors. Each team should be accompanied by a parent or other adult and should have a strong flashlight, extra dry cells and bulbs, a chart of their constellation and its neighbors, and a star map for the sky at that season. Such maps are often published monthly by newspapers or science magazines. Select maps which are relatively simple; many star maps are inappropriate for young children because they show too much. The flashlight is useful in pointing out the general direction of the constellation being studied. The constellations will be seen more readily if the flashlight lens is covered with red cellophane, since red light does not interfere with the eye's adaptation to the dark.

If the Big Dipper can be seen, have children imagine a line through the top two stars of its handle. If it is winter, the line, taking a kind of "great circle" course, will run through Auriga, the Charioteer, and extended, close to Taurus, the constellation that encompasses the Pleiades (off to one side) and Hyades, a V-shaped cluster of stars in the middle of the constellation. Extended further, the line comes upon Orion, a prominent and easily identified winter constellation with a bright line of stars (Orion's belt).

A line through the two end stars (see the arrow, Fig. 9-18) of the Big Dipper point to Polaris. Extended the line leads to Cepheus (Andromeda's Father), shaped like a child's drawing of a house. Clockwise from Cepheus about Polaris is Cassiopeia (shaped like a crude M or W), beyond which is Andromeda, the legendary maiden chained to

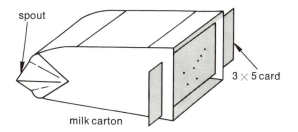

FIGURE **9-19** Milk-carton constellation finder.

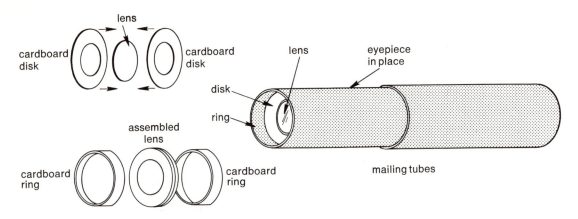

FIGURE **9-20**   Assembling a refracting telescope.

a rock. Associated with Andromeda is Perseus, named for the mythical hero who freed the captive Andromeda.

Children may make up other guide lines or interrelationships among the constellations. Eventually they can become so familiar that it is necessary to see only a portion of the sky to know in what direction Polaris lies. In the long run, the best way to study the geography of the heavens is at first hand, outdoors, at night, and looking upward with a star guide in hand and a flashlight whose lens has been covered with red cellophane. It is surprising how quickly it all becomes like one's own backyard, which, in a sense, it really is.

TELESCOPES

Astronomical telescopes, one of the principal instruments for exploring the universe, are of three general types—refracting, reflecting, and radio, the latter in actuality a radio receiver, not an optical device.

Refracting Telescope

A simple refracting telescope (Fig. 9-20) can be made using two lenses fixed in tubes in such a way that the distance between the lenses is adjustable.

The better the lenses, the better the telescope. A stamp magnifier (focal length about 1 inch) makes a good eyepiece, and a high school laboratory or an optician's lens (with a focal length of about 8 inches) makes a good objective. (Both lenses are convex, like a hand-glass lens, which children can feel and see.) Lenses of this kind will produce a better instrument than that with which Galileo discovered the moons of Jupiter.

To determine the focal length of a lens, stand beside a wall 30 feet or more away from a window and move the lens until it focuses the smallest *sharp* image of the window on the wall. The distance from the center of the lens to the wall is the focal length.

Use two mailing tubes (one just small enough to slide inside the other) to hold the lenses, which should be mounted as follows. Cut four disks of cardboard—one pair the inside diameter of the larger and one pair the diameter of the smaller tube. Out of the center of each disk, cut another with a diameter just under that of the lens. Center a disk on each side of a lens and glue them to the lens edge and to each other. By gluing a cardboard ring on each side of it, anchor a lens assembly in one end of each tube—the smaller (eyepiece) lens in the smaller tube. The cardboard rings (see figure) can be $\frac{1}{2}$-inch sections of mailing tubes—those for the larger lens cut from the smaller tube, and those for the smaller lens cut from an even smaller one or from the same tube, with the diameter of the ring reduced by cutting out a piece and taping the ends together.

Reflecting Telescope

A reflecting telescope (Fig. 9-21) consists of a concave mirror, an eyepiece lens a little beyond the focal point of the mirror, and, usually, a flat mirror set at an angle of 45° to the concave mirror and used to reflect the light focused by the latter into the eyepiece. The reflecting telescope at Palomar Observatory uses a 200-inch mirror.

To find the focal length of a concave mirror, place it so that sunlight falls on it, and make a cloud of chalk dust over it. Light reflected from the dust particles will make visible the cone of focused rays.

Reflecting telescopes can be larger than the

FIGURE **9-22** Radio telescope antenna at Jodrell Bank.

typical refracting telescope through which observatory visitors look. Most astronomical observation today is done by photography (long exposure), a method much more exact and sensitive than the impressions received by the human eye; it also provides a permanent record.

The bigger our telescopes, the farther the universe seems to stretch before us. Visible light waves are but a small fraction of the electromagnetic waves that bathe the universe, so that astronomy based on optical telescopes has been like seeing the universe through a keyhole.

Radio Telescope

Thus while optical telescopes collect the visible part of the electromagnetic spectrum, radio telescopes (Fig. 9-22) gather the invisible radio waves radiated by stars so distant or indistinct that their light cannot be seen. They do this by focusing radio waves by means of great parabolic reflectors. While most of these "big dishes" are upright, the world's largest lies in a naturally eroded bowl in the limestone hill country of Puerto Rico.

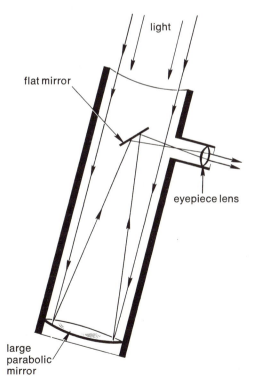

FIGURE **9-21** Cross-section of a reflecting telescope.

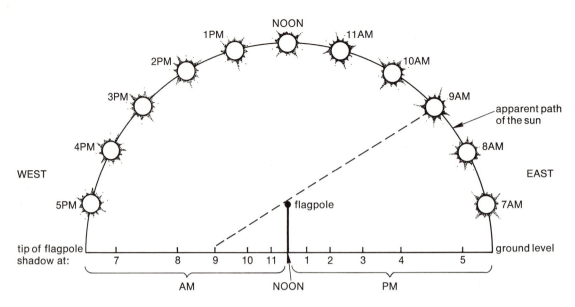

FIGURE **9-23** Direction of shadows cast by flagpole in relation to time of day or apparent position of sun.

Children can observe similar reflection of sound waves from any parabolic surface such as a wall heater or metal bowls.

ASTRONOMICAL TIMEKEEPING AND NAVIGATION

The first timekeeping was done by means of shadow sticks and stones and other kinds of crude markers. From such activities evolved the sundial, still in use, though largely ornamental. It is believed that Egyptian obelisks, such as "Cleopatra's Needle," were the shadow sticks, or gnomons, of giant sundials.

Constructing a sundial can help emphasize the

relationship between the sun and earth. A school flagpole, if it stands free, can make a giant sundial: In northern latitudes its shadow in the morning will point west, at noon, north, and in the afternoon, east (Fig. 9-23). Number twelve flat sticks of the same size one through twelve. Every hour on the hour drive the appropriately numbered stick into the ground at the point where the shadow is cast by the pole. Use a length of rope tied to the pole as a guide so that all sticks will be the same distance from the pole. By sundown the sticks should form a pattern similar to the face of a sundial (Fig. 9-24).

A similar sundial may be made by marking a spot on a paved area in the sun. Every hour have a child stand on the spot, and mark the direction

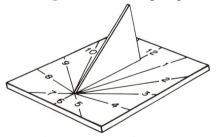

FIGURE **9-24** Sundial using a right triangle as a gnomon.

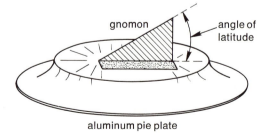

FIGURE **9-25** Pie-plate sundial showing gnomon mounted at angle of latitude.

168 The Stars and Planets

of his shadow with a line drawn along its axis.

Sundials can be made of aluminum pie plates. Using a protractor, mark off the face of the plate into 15° sections (one for each hour). For a gnomon or pointer glue a wedge-shaped piece of cardboard to the plate, its edge making an angle with the plate (Fig. 9-25) corresponding to the latitude at which the sundial will be used. Orient the plate so that the gnomon points toward the North Pole. The shadow of the pointer will fall on the horizontal surface beneath. Note that the shadow is shorter closer to noon.

Because sundials are no use at night and in cloudy weather, men invented other timekeepers, such as the water clock (clepsydra) and (in the eighth century) the hourglass—in shape and principle like an egg timer. The hourglass, usable aboard ship where the sundial and water clock were not, was an important aid to early navigation. It is said that the modern pendulum clock is a result of the fact that Galileo's mind wandered in church one day. Noticing the swinging of a lamp suspended from the ceiling by long chains, he timed it by his pulse and discovered that the swings were regular. After Galileo's keen observations and experiments, watchmakers added a swinging weight (pendulum) to the large, heavy egg-shaped timepieces carried on their rounds by watchmen. A weight suspended (from a door frame, perhaps, or chart rack) on a string about 39 inches (one meter) long should complete its swing about once every second. Children can discover that shortening the string quickens the swing, and vice versa. (See p. 147.)

One of the important contributions of astronomy is correct, or sidereal (star), time. When the earth rotates once on its axis, the stars appear to move once across the sky, or in the case of circumpolar stars (see p. 163), circle around the North Star once (Fig. 9-26). A star day or sidereal day is the amount of time it takes for the earth to make one full turn. A star will seem to travel 360° or 24 star hours in a star day. A star, observed at the highest point of its circle in the sky, will travel west 15° every hour (360 divided by 24). If, at 7 P.M., a star first sighted at 6 P.M. seems to have moved, say 16°, the clocks by which the movement is timed are fast; if it has moved *less* than 15° the clocks are slow.

The amount of time from sunrise to sunrise is called a solar day. Clocks and watches are adjusted to keep solar time, but are checked by sidereal time against star signposts in the sky.

Finding one's way at sea or in the air is quite a different matter from finding one's way on land, where one has "landmarks" and where measuring distance traveled is relatively simple. For fliers and sailors alike, time is inseparable from distance, and the most serious handicap to early navigation was the lack of accurate time-keeping devices. The great voyages of exploration during the fifteenth century were undertaken by men better equipped with courage than with instruments of navigation. During the sixteenth century the making of maps—prime aids to navigation—became a real art; map projections still used today (such as the *mercator*) were invented.

FIGURE **9-26** Star trails around the North Star, a result of keeping the camera aperture open for a relatively long period while the stars "move," leaving a "trail" on the film.

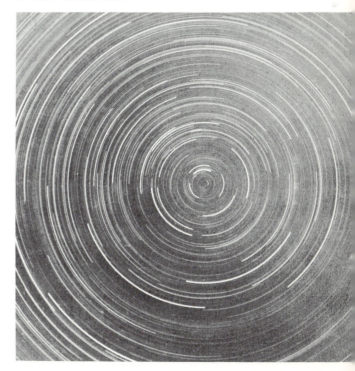

Early cartographers marked off the globe with equally spaced east–west (latitude) and north–south (longitude) lines.

These lines may be seen on most globes—the lines of latitude parallel to each other (and called *parallels*) and the lines of longitude converging at the poles (and called *meridians*). Each line of latitude or longitude is a degree of a circle (since the earth is roughly spherical); thus, every line (or degree) of latitude or of longitude marks off about 70 miles (360° times 70 equals, roughly, 25,000 miles, the circumference of the earth). Each degree is divided into minutes, of which each equals about 6000 feet (1 nautical mile), and seconds (about 100 feet). Since it takes the earth 24 hours to turn full circle, or 360°, early cartographers divided 360 by 24 and drew a meridian line every 15°. (Thus 1 hour equals 15° of longitude, east or west.) In 1884, by international agreement, *prime meridian* (0°) was designated as the line that passed through the Royal Observatory in Greenwich, England. Starting at the prime meridian, the meridian lines go east and west up to 180°. Thus the 180th meridian is directly opposite the prime meridian (through the earth) and is the same for both east and west. This can readily be illustrated with the peel of an orange or grapefruit. An analogy can be made between these lines of latitude and longitude and the grid patterns of cities where avenues run north–south and streets east–west.

Early sailors found their latitude with the help of an astrolabe, a crude instrument for measuring the height (altitude) of the sun and stars. More accurate calculation of latitude was made possible when the sextant, a more refined version of the astrolabe, was invented.

To make a simple astrolabe (Fig. 9-27), tie a piece of string to the midpoint of the flat edge of a protractor and tie the other end to a paper clip or other weight. Tape a drinking straw to the same edge and sight through it on the North Star. The string will mark off on the protractor the figure corresponding to the latitude of the observer.

One can estimate latitude simply by pointing with the outstretched arm to the North Star. The

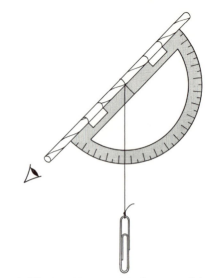

FIGURE **9-27** Working model of an astrolabe.

angle the arm makes with the earth's surface is the latitude. For example, if one were standing at the North Pole, the arm would point straight overhead (latitude 90°); at the equator, the arm would point straight out (latitude 0°). Two rulers hinged together with adhesive tape can be used essentially the same way. Point the end of one ruler to the North Star, the other to the center of the globe (that is, at right angles to the globe surface as if the ruler were someone standing on the earth's surface). The angle enclosed by the rulers gives the latitude.

To find longitude, one needs to know the time at a given meridian, generally the prime meridian at Greenwich. (Every ship has an accurate clock (chronometer) set at Greenwich time for this purpose.) Then, with a sextant, one determines when it is noon, sun time—that is, when the sun is at its highest point in the sky. Thus, since the earth turns from west to east, if it is 3 P.M. Greenwich time where it is noon sun time, one is 3 hours (or 45°—see above) west of the prime meridian, or at 45° west longitude. Children can get a clearer understanding of the mechanism using "ship" cutouts on a sheet of paper ruled with grid lines. Assume it is noon aboard each ship; then, given different Greenwich readings from the ships' chronometers, children can compute the ships' longitude by simple arithmetic.

SUGGESTED PROJECTS

1. One resolution of the problems of early navigation is integral to the story of Harrison's chronometer, or the man who worked 50 years to win a prize. Children may wish to dramatize the story.

2. Locate and compare pictures or diagrams of the solar system, many of which show the planetary orbits as concentric rings spaced at regular intervals. From their experience in laying out a playground planetarium, children can make corrected drawings showing elliptical orbits and the wide gap between the four inner and the five outer planets.

3. Over a dozen star clusters, variables, and nebulae can be seen through binoculars. Children and their parents can find help in finding them and other features of interest in such works as *Astronomy with an*

Opera Glass, by Garret Serviss, *A Field Book of Stars*, by W. T. Olcott, and *Discover the Stars*, by Gaylord Johnson and Irving Adler (available in an inexpensive paperback edition).

4. Observe and map the position of one constellation over a period of several weeks, preferably at regular intervals. Record the time and date of each observation.

5. To make latitude and longitude lines more readily comprehended attach a grid of strings to the classroom ceiling in correct north–south orientation.

6. Children may enjoy choosing one of the planets for special study. They can work in teams to do the necessary reading and writing, art, and construction on their planet.

BIBLIOGRAPHY

(**P** indicates recommended for primary grades, **I** for intermediate grades, **U** for upper grades.)

Ames, Gerald, *Planet Earth*, Golden Pr., 1963. Earth and its relationship to the other planets from the viewpoint of the space age. Considers geological and meteorological discoveries. An oversize book, excellent drawings, diagrams, charts, and maps. **U**

Asimov, Isaac, *Mars*, Follett, 1967. Mars in relation to the other planets, its physical aspects and moons compared with Earth's. **I**

Baker, Robert H., *Introducing the Constellations*, rev. ed., Viking, 1957. Revised, expanded edition of an old favorite, with a new chapter on telescope-making and amateur astronomy. **U**

Bell, Thelma, *Riddle of Time*, Viking, 1963. Aspects of man's awareness of time—the history of the calendar, the development of timepieces, the standardization of public time, cycles and rhythms of biological time, the geologic calendar, the time dimension in stellar distances, and Einstein's laws of relativity. **U**

Bendick, Jeanne, *The First book of Time*, Watts, 1963. Concepts of and ways of measuring time; drawings and diagrams. **U**

———, *Space and Time*, Watts, 1968. Concepts about the nature of space and time, each illustrated. The use of the discovery method and simple experiments. **U**

Bischof, George and Eunice, *Sun, Earth and Man*, Harcourt, 1957. Interrelations and adaptation of men to their planet and the sun. **U**

Boeke, Kees, *Cosmic View: The Universe in 40 Jumps*, Day, 1957. Develops concept of immensity of universe by showing 40 views of an object, each ten times farther away. **U**

Branley, Franklyn M., *The Big Dipper*, Crowell, 1962. Elementary explanation of how to locate the Big Dipper. Retells some of the legends about it. Colorful, graphic illustrations. **P**

———, *A Book of Mars For You*, Crowell, 1968. A Mariner IV trip gains new knowledge about Mars composition, craters, canals, and possibility of life. **I**

———, *A Book of Stars For You*, Crowell, 1967. Important concepts, simply explained including how stars are made and how they produce energy. **U**

———, *A Book of the Milky Way Galaxy for You*, Crowell, 1965. Concentrates on the Milky Way galaxy and its relationship to other galaxies and constellations. Describes the work of astronomers, defines the light year, and demonstrates its use. **I**

———, *Mars, Planet Number Four*, rev. ed., Crowell, 1962. Concise description of Mars; compares its known physical aspects with those of Earth; speculates on "canals"; the possibilities of life on Mars and of man's landing on it. Charts of planetary data, a bibliography, and an index. **U**

———, *What the Moon is Like*, Crowell, 1963. Simple concise presentation of some facts about the moon. Bold, uncluttered drawings. **P**

Bulla, Clyde Robert, *What Makes A Shadow?* Crowell, 1962. An introduction for the young child. Well illustrated. **P**

Chamberlain, Joseph M., *Planets, Stars, and Space,* Creative Educational Society in Cooperation with the American Museum of Natural History, rev. ed., 1962. An attractive introduction. **U**

Chester, Michael, *The Moon: Target For Apollo*, Putnam, 1963. A history of the studies of the moon. Also covers mapping the moon's surface, lunar eclipses, the moon's influences on life on Earth, and preparations for Project Apollo. Many diagrams and charts. **U**

Freeman, Mae, *Fun With Astronomy*, Random, 1953. Observations and activities, instructive descriptions. **I**

Gallant, Roy A., *The ABC's of Astronomy*, Doubleday, 1962. Definitions for 500 terms for the amateur astronomer. Diagrams, charts, photographs, and statistical tables. **U**

———, *Exploring the Planets*, rev. ed., Doubleday, 1967. Review of the basis of astronomy and theories concerning the origin of the Solar System. One chapter for each planet. Dramatic and colorful new illustrations from NASA. **U**

Hellman, Hal, *Navigation*, Prentice-Hall, 1966. Development of techniques of navigation. Navigational problems of sea and air travel, and the use of wind, water, and especially the stars. Informative illustrations. **U**

Knight, David, *The First Book of Mars*, Watts, 1966. Information on Mariner IV's flight to Mars includes a summary of the information obtained, description of the journey, and explanation of how the equipment worked. One chapter about past beliefs about the planet. **U**

Lewellen, John, *True Book of Moon, Sun, Stars*, Children's Pr., 1954. In large type for young readers. **P**

Meyer, Jerome S., *Picture Book of Astronomy,* Lothrop, 1945. Clear, satisfying explanations of typical questions raised by young children. **I**

Moore, Patrick, *Telescopes and Observatories*, Day, 1962. How lenses and telescopes work, a brief history, and the importance of the work of observatories. Directions for making a simple telescope, numerous color illustrations, and a list of the world's largest telescopes. **I**

Neal, Harry Edward, *The Mystery of Time*, Messner, 1966. Comprehensive account of man's unraveling of the mystery of time, which led to the invention of the calendar and time-keeping devices. **U**

Orr, Clyde, Jr., *Between Earth and Space*, Macmillan, 1959. Weather, climate, and other aspects of the atmosphere. **U**

Piper, Roger, *The Big Dish*, Harcourt, 1963. The new science of radio astronomy and the use of the radio telescope introduced through a description of the work at England's Nuffield Radio Astronomy Observatory. **U**

Polgreen, John and Cathleen, *The Earth in Space*, Random, 1963. Earth's place in the solar system, galaxy, and universe. **I**

Ravielli, Anthony, *The World is Round*, Viking, 1963. An attractively illustrated, clear explanation of why the earth seems flat and the ways man has uncovered evidence that it is round. **I**

Rey, H. A., *Find the Constellations*, Houghton-Mifflin, 1954. Clear, accurate, intriguing illustrations. **I**

Ronan, Colin A., *The Stars*, McGraw-Hill, 1966. Brief information about the sun, the moon, and familiar stars. Descriptions of optical and radio telescopes. Lists major planetaria and observatories in the United States open to visitors. **U**

Schealer, John, *This Way to the Stars*, Dutton, 1957. Lively description of our solar system. **I**

Schloat, G. Warren, Jr., *Andy's Wonderful Telescope*, Scribners, 1958. Observable phenomena of optics of telescopes. **I**

Schneider, Herman and Nina, *You Among the Stars*, W. R. Scott, 1951. Excellent beginning method of learning about the sky. **I**

Wolfe, Louis, *Let's Go to a Planetarium*, Putnam, 1958. Typical planetarium show and building. **I**

Zim, Herbert, *Shooting Stars*, Morrow, 1958. History and study of meteors. **I**

Zim, Herbert, and Robert Baker, *The Sun*, Morrow, 1953. Excellent information on sun's spectroscope, solar energy, tides, sunspots, and eclipses. Some experiments. **I**

Performing a chemical experiment in the classroom.

10 Chemistry for Children

Everything in the world is composed of chemicals. Generally, a chemical is matter whose nature and elemental substance (or substances) are known. A chemical is identified by what it does, by its properties. Everyday one uses common chemicals—water, sugar, and salt, for example.

ELEMENTS, COMPOUNDS, AND MIXTURES

Chemicals such as copper, silver, and gold are composed of only one substance. Any chemical made of only one substance is called an "element," of which there are at least 103; some are very rare and some have been produced only in a laboratory. Compounds are substances that have a fixed composition of two or more elements combined to form another substance; mixtures have no fixed composition.

Compounds are formed by the exchange and/or joining of the atoms of which elements are composed. This chemical behavior of atoms is determined largely by the number and distribution of electrons in their shells (Fig. 10-1). The negative electrical charges of the electrons of an atom are balanced by the positive charges in its nucleus. When atoms lose their electrical balance, they become ions, which are either positively or negatively charged, depending on whether they gain or lose electrons in the process.

Atoms tend to be one of two types—electron-losing or electron-gaining—those of one type tending to combine with those of the other. Metals tend to be electron-losers and the non-metallic elements—like oxygen, chlorine, sulfur,

bromine, phosphorus, and iodine—tend to be electron-gainers. Hence, the widespread occurrence of common compounds such as rust (iron plus oxygen = iron oxide), silver tarnish (silver plus sulfur = silver sulphide), and salt (sodium plus chlorine = sodium chloride).

Most of the things we use are compounds or mixtures (of elements and/or compounds). Children can make a pegboard exhibit of chemicals such as the following, categorized as shown:

elements	compounds	mixtures
lead	salt	baking powder
iron	sugar	paper
aluminum	water	soil
mercury	glass	cement
sulfur	coal gas	cake

The difference between compounds and mixtures can be clarified by mixing dry sand and sugar and showing children that the mixture is composed of two kinds of grains. With patience, one can be separated from the other because they are different substances. Sugar and salt dissolved in water will not be visually distinguishable, but can be recovered separately by evaporation. Asking children to separate the sodium and chlorine of some salt can emphasize the fact that these two elements have combined to make one substance.

The Elements Composing Water

Water, a most important chemical, is a compound, and thus can be decomposed into its elements—hydrogen and oxygen—by application of a small amount of electrical energy (electrolysis), as shown in Fig. 10-2. Needed are a glass beaker or wide-mouthed jar, two battery clips (available at hardware or automobile supply stores), bell wire, three $1\frac{1}{2}$-volt dry cells, two test tubes, a square of cardboard (large enough to span the mouth of the jar), sodium sulfate (safer than the sulfuric acid usually recommended), and two platinum electrodes. (These are inexpensive and better than the carbon rods from discarded flashlight cells, stainless-steel knife blades, or gold nibs from old pens that may also be used. If

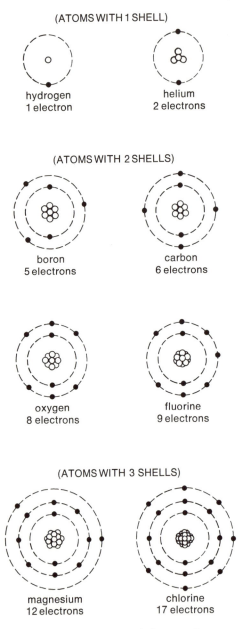

(ATOMS WITH 1 SHELL)

hydrogen
1 electron

helium
2 electrons

(ATOMS WITH 2 SHELLS)

boron
5 electrons

carbon
6 electrons

oxygen
8 electrons

fluorine
9 electrons

(ATOMS WITH 3 SHELLS)

magnesium
12 electrons

chlorine
17 electrons

FIGURE **10-1** Arrangement of electrons in atoms of some typical elements.

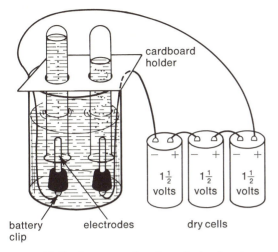

FIGURE **10-2** Apparatus for electrolysis of water or brine.

carbon rods are used, it is necessary to drive out residual wax by holding the rods with tongs or pliers over an open gas flame of a stove until the rods are dull red; do not attach clips and wire to the battery until cool.) Cut holes in the cardboard so that the tubes are held snugly, dissolve as much sodium sulfate as possible in a glass of cold water, fill the tubes with the solution and put the remainder in the jar, invert the tubes over the electrodes, and connect the batteries to the electrodes. With current flowing, gas in the tube connected to the negative (battery case) terminal bubbles up from the electrode twice as fast as in the tube connected to the positive (center post) terminal. Hydrogen gas is generated at the negative electrode, oxygen at the positive. (The sodium sulfate does not decompose and is used only to enhance conduction of electricity by the water.) To test for oxygen, light one end of a slender wooden stick or swab stick; then blow out the flame and immediately insert the glowing tip into the oxygen generator tube. Oxygen will make a glowing tip burst into flame (Fig. 10-3).

To test for hydrogen, plug the mouth of the other tube under water with the thumb and then remove the tube from the water. Hold a lighted match near the tube mouth and remove the thumb; the small pop that results is the typical hydrogen explosion. (There is no hazard involved.) Many children are already familiar with the chemical symbol or formula for water—H_2O—and may wish to observe hydrogen collecting twice as fast as oxygen during the electrolysis experiment.

The Elements Composing Salt

Common table salt is a compound composed of the elements sodium, a metallic solid, and chlorine, a greenish gas. To separate the compound into its elements, set up equipment as for the electrolysis of water (Fig. 10-2), substituting a saturated salt solution for the sodium sulfate solution.

Chlorine gas will form in the tube inverted over the positive electrode (connected to the center pole of the battery). The small amount formed is harmless. Hydrogen will collect at the negative electrode; the sodium combines with the water to form a weak solution of sodium hydroxide (household lye). A few drops of phenolphthalein (obtainable at a drugstore or chemical supply store or from laxative tablets such as Feen-o-lax, which have it as a principal ingredient) will turn the solution pink if sodium hydroxide is present—evidence that the electrolysis of the brine has produced a recombination of elements into new substances.

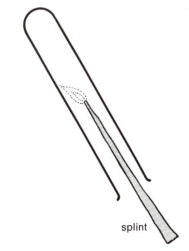

FIGURE **10-3** Test for oxygen.

THE FORMS OF MATTER

Solids, Liquids, and Gases

Water, the familiar liquid, can turn into gas (steam) or solid (ice). Children can watch the transformation by observing ice melt or a kettle boil, although steam is really invisible: What one sees is water vapor condensing from the steam, which actually occupies the "empty" space between the spout and the cloud of what is commonly called steam.

Dry ice, used to refrigerate perishables such as ice cream (in vendor's boxes) and vegetables (in railroad refrigerator cars), is carbon dioxide in solid form. Vaporization of the solid carbon dioxide occurs spontaneously at room temperature. To demonstrate the presence of the gaseous carbon dioxide, put a few lumps of the solid form into a loosely covered jar or, for a more dramatic effect, into a jar with an inch or two of water in the bottom. (Always use kitchen tongs to handle dry ice.) Lower a lighted candle (suspended from a pipe cleaner twisted around it) into the jar immediately upon removing the cover. The carbon dioxide gas will put out the candle. Another way of generating gaseous carbon dioxide is described in Chapter 16. See also under *Chemical Tests*, below, for a means of identifying carbon dioxide.

The interaction of two gases can form a solid. To show this, fasten small wads of cotton or paper toweling to one end of each of two pipe cleaners. Dip one wad in dilute hydrochloric acid, another wad in ammonia (ammonium hydroxide). Bend the free end of the pipe cleaners into a hook and hang them opposite each other on the inside of a glass. A white cloud of ammonium chloride particles forms, which eventually deposits as a visible salt on the surface of the glass.

The interaction of two fluids can also produce a solid. One can show this with solutions of kitchen washing soda and calcium chloride, available at hardware stores. (Calcium chloride is used to melt snow and ice on sidewalks, to settle dust on gravel roads, or to dry out damp cellars and closets.) Using about an ounce of each in a tumbler of water, make solutions of calcium chloride and of washing soda. Pour the solutions, one after the other, into a quart jar. The heavy white solid is precipitated (separated out of solution and settled) chalk, which is mainly calcium carbonate ($CaCO_3$). This common chemical is a basic component of bone, milk, and limestone, as well as of many commercial products.

The hardening of cement and of plaster of Paris are other examples of chemical reactions that end with the formation of a solid. As in many other chemical reactions, the component materials must be in solution (usually in water) for the reaction to occur, and the reaction is accompanied by the release of heat.

Emulsions and Colloids

Many common chemicals such as liquid soap, paint, mayonnaise, and the like are, strictly speaking, neither liquid nor solid, but are emulsions or colloids, mixtures (usually of liquids) in which one is dispersed in the other in particles so small that they do not settle out on standing. Soap (as distinct from detergents, which do not work by emulsification) acts by dissolving water-soluble dirt, by emulsifying grease and oil, and by *ad*sorption of dirt particles on the surface of the tiny bubbles composing suds or lather.

Making soap in the classroom can reinforce children's concepts of chemical interaction. An important activity of pioneer days, soap-making begins with the collection of bacon grease and other fats. Needed are about 6 pounds of grease or a similar amount, as stated in the recipe on a can of household lye. (*Caution:* Lye on the skin can cause severe burns; spattered in the eyes it can produce instantaneous blinding. See instructions on can label for treatment.)

To purify the grease, melt and strain it (through a piece of cheesecloth) into a kettle holding 2–3 quarts of water. Bring to a boil, stirring frequently. Cool until the fat can be lifted. Repeat the boiling step once or twice to remove salt and other sediment.

Place a vessel holding 2 pints of *cold* water on the ground outdoors. (Use only enamel ware, crockery, or iron vessels of about 2 gallons capacity and a wooden or stainless steel tablespoon or stick for stirring.) Using rubber gloves and apron, and with children watching from a standing position (to reduce risk of being spattered), *very slowly* pour the contents of a lye can into the water. For extra safety, stir until all the lye is dissolved. The solution becomes very hot as the lye and water mix with a release of energy. Children should be prepared for this part of the process by reading a chart of directions from the lye can. (This use of the directions as an exercise in reading can be continued with a discussion of home safety.)

When the lye and water solution feels lukewarm through the bottom of the container, slowly add melted *lukewarm* grease, stirring constantly until the mixture becomes as stiff as honey. Add perfume if desired and stir until the soap becomes the consistency and color of divinity fudge (about 20–30 minutes).

Pour into a mold such as a large flat Pyrex dish or a box lined with waxed paper. Leave until hard enough to cut into pieces about 3 inches square. Turn the pieces out onto a clean surface to dry in sunshine. Turn daily and allow to harden for about three weeks before using. (When the soap is partially hardened, each child may take a piece home.)

As stated above, the function of soap in laundering is to emulsify greasy or oily dirt by breaking it into tiny particles, which are surrounded by a film of soap molecules, so that they become dispersed in the water. Detergents, as distinguished from soaps, clean by speeding the wetting process; this is done by reducing the surface tension of the water (see Chapter 6). To observe the difference, drop pieces of white cotton string into two tumblers of water—one with a teaspoon of liquid detergent added and one with soap powder added. The string in the soap solution will float on the surface; that in the detergent will rapidly become water-soaked and sink.

Common mayonnaise is a colloid or emulsion made of oil, vinegar or lemon juice, and egg yolk, the latter stabilizing the particles of oil (much as soap does particles of oily dirt) so that they do not coalesce and do remain suspended in the surrounding fluid. To demonstrate, shake vigorously in a tall thin container (such as an olive jar) three parts salad oil and one part vinegar, and let stand. Very shortly the oil and vinegar will separate. Add the egg yolk and shake again. This time the mixture remains in suspension.

Ordinary oil paint is another example of emulsion. To prepare some, grind (in a mortar or similar vessel) a very small amount of pigment, such as ferric oxide, available from a paint or hardware store, and a few tablespoons of linseed oil. Add a little turpentine to make the paint spread. When the mixture is thoroughly ground and emulsified, apply where needed.

A *nicotine spray* for indoor plants infested with pests such as aphids (see Chapter 2), red spiders, and mites is also an emulsion; it can be made as follows. Boil tobacco from a cigarette in a can for 5–10 minutes, using about 2 tablespoons of water. Then filter out the tobacco and add a few drops of liquid soap to the remaining fluid; dilute with water up to about a cupful. The colloidal properties of the soap solution help spread the spray and clog the spiracles of sucking insects such as aphids. Apply the emulsion with an old spray gun or aspirator and observe the effect on aphids.

VOLATILE SUBSTANCES

Volatile substances—liquid or solid—are those that have a very high rate of evaporation at ordinary temperatures.

Draw a pair of identical circles or squares on a blackboard and moisten the area of one with water and the other with cleaning fluid or alcohol, which is safer and available from a school nurse. (*Caution:* Do not open in the classroom vessels containing cleaning fluids—such as Carbona— that are composed in whole or part of carbon tetrachloride, which is extremely volatile and toxic.) The alcohol or cleaning fluid, far more volatile than water, dry faster.

With a medicine dropper, place a few drops (the same number of each) of such solvents as kerosene, turpentine, nail polish remover, alcohol, and white gas in the center of a piece of blotting paper (a separate piece for each substance). Compare the speeds of evaporation of the various chemicals. (The risk of combustion increases with the speed of evaporation, since a substance in its gaseous or vaporized form presents more surface at which the oxidation reaction—combustion—can take place. For safety, keep windows wide open and see that there is no open flame in the room.)

To illustrate the differences in dangerous flammability of cleaning solvents, place a teaspoon of perchloroethylene cleaner in a metal jar top or painting dish. Try to ignite it with a match. Taking precautions, repeat using *only a drop or two* of a flammable naphtha-type cleaner. Such investigations may motivate careful reading and comparison of labels of many household chemicals. Have children check insecticides, for example, which, because of their flammable vehicle, should not be sprayed near open fires or hot surfaces.

Naphtha crystals, mothballs, and moth flakes—volatile solids—placed in an open dish or box will show a noticeable reduction in size within a few days. To demonstrate sublimation, the conversion of a solid to a gas and the reversion of the latter to a solid, heat a very few naphtha crystals in a pyrex tube over a Sterno or candle flame (melted crystals are *flammable*.), rotating the tube slowly to avoid fracturing caused by unequal heating. The large, shining, fern-like crystals deposited on the cooler parts of the tube are sublimated naphtha crystals. (*Caution: These materials are flammable.*)

ACIDS AND ALKALIS

Another way of grouping or identifying chemicals is according to whether they are acid, alkaline (base), or neutral. Acids and bases, if united, neutralize each other, forming new, relatively inactive (neutral), compounds—that is, compounds less likely to combine with other substances. The weak acid of insect bites or bee

stings is similarly neutralized by dabbing them with ammonia water, a base.

Children will be interested to observe (and certainly to sample) the results of neutralizing the tomatoes (acid) in cream of tomato soup with soda (base). Experienced cooks add a pinch of soda to keep the tomatoes from curdling the milk or cream. A sour-milk chocolate cake can be made in a school oven or portable classroom oven. Sour the milk (evaporated and diluted with water, one to one) by adding vinegar (acid) to it in the proportion of 1 tablespoon to a cup of milk.

A class discussion with a school dental hygienist can point up the acid reaction produced in the mouth by many foods with high sugar content. (Yeast cells working in a sugar solution, as in bread-making, give an acid reaction to litmus.)

To show how acid can erode bone, soak clean chicken bones in concentrated vinegar (acid). After several days the bones are as pliable as rubber because of the removal of bone calcium by the vinegar. Although teeth have an enamel layer, which is resistant to vinegar, a tooth left in a glass of cola drink may dissolve very quickly because of the drink's acid content.

OXIDATION

In oxidation, an important process that is the basis of many chemical reactions, the element oxygen combines with other elements to form compounds called oxides.

Common 3% drugstore hydrogen peroxide is a safe and convenient source of oxygen. The chemical formula for hydrogen peroxide, H_2O_2, indicates that each molecule contains one more atom of oxygen than does a molecule of water, H_2O. To free this extra oxygen, drop iron oxide (rust) into a test tube or pill bottle holding hydrogen peroxide. Lower the container into hot water and watch for oxygen bubbles; then test for oxygen (Fig. 10-3). One can also pour peroxide on a cookie sheet or other metal sheet and observe the formation of oxygen bubbles, or the peroxide can simply be warmed in a tube. Test

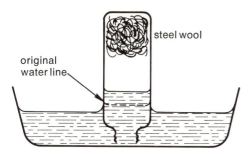

FIGURE **10-4** Consumption of oxygen in oxidation of steel wool permits rise of water in vessel.

again for oxygen as described above, using a glowing match or splint.

To demonstrate oxidation, pack moist steel wool, washed in detergent and thoroughly rinsed, firmly into the bottom of a test tube or a long, narrow olive jar so that it will remain in place when the jar is inverted. Place the jar or tube mouth down in a shallow pan of water (Fig. 10-4). Mark the water level inside the test tube with a rubber band or crayon line. Rusting or oxidation of the iron in the steel wool will use up oxygen in the container. As a result (if there was enough steel wool to combine with all the oxygen present), within a day or two the water level should have risen about one-fifth the height of the tube (since air is about 20% oxygen). Stopper the tube with your thumb and remove from the water bath. To check whether oxygen has been used up, test as before with a glowing splint. Note that the steel wool has become brown with rust, or iron oxide.

Fire (see Chapter 16), or combustion, is a rapid form of oxidation in which the reaction between the oxygen and the thing oxidized is accompanied by considerable heat and flame. A candle in a closed jar will burn for only a short time—until it has consumed most of the oxygen in the jar. The remaining gas is mostly nitrogen with some carbon dioxide, residual oxygen, water vapor, and inert gases. (See below, under *Combustion and Heating,* and Chapter 5.)

"Magic writing," a simple application of oxidation, may interest children. With the end of a used match or a nurse's swab stick, write in milk or lemon juice on squares of bond paper.

When the writing dries, it becomes invisible. Held over a heat source such as a hot plate or light bulb, the writing will slowly reappear, brown.

CHEMICAL TESTS

Certain chemicals provide telltale clues to their identity or presence by reacting in certain ways. Some tests based on these reactions are as follows.

Iodine and Starch Color Reaction

Before the test, prepare a glass jar of cornstarch or laundry starch and hot water. Use relatively little starch so that the solution will appear clear. Set out in plain view on a desk or table next to another vessel containing plain water. Drop into the starch solution a little tincture of iodine (such as is used as an antiseptic) and stir. This "water" turns blue. The children's curiosity will (with your guidance) lead to treating the contents of the other jar in the same way, with a few drops of iodine solution. The brown tinge that results when iodine is dropped into "plain" water is very different from the characteristic blue color produced when iodine combines with starch.

Flame Colors of Elements

Chemists often identify substances by "flame testing" the material. For instance, substances containing the element *sodium* vaporize with a bright yellow flame. To demonstrate, dip the end of a wooden swab stick in water and then in salt (*sodium* chloride). Hold over a flame and note the yellow color when the salty tip kindles. Boric acid produces a green flame, while that of powdered copper nitrate is blue-green. Nitrates of strontium give off a red color, and potassium kindles or vaporizes into reddish-purple flames (often masked by the presence of sodium or other elements).

Crystals of nitrates of copper, potassium, sodium, or strontium, added during candle-making while the wax is still warm, will result in candle flames of colors indicated above for the various substances. Straining the wax before pouring makes for clearer colored flame.

Children will enjoy making candles from cotton-cord wicking and old candle ends or paraffin melted and poured into double paper cups or half-pint milk cartons to cool. Use one kind of crystal per cup or container.

Litmus Paper

Most scientific supply houses and drugstores carry small strips of pink and blue paper that have been dipped in litmus solution. The blue paper turns a reddish color if dipped in acids such as vinegar and lemon juice. The pink paper turns a bluish color when dipped in such bases as ammonia and in solutions of borax, washing soda, and the like. To observe an alkali neutralize an acid, dip a strip of blue litmus paper in vinegar. The strip turns red. Then dip it into ammonia water, and it will revert to its original blue.

Most households include dry acids, such as cream of tartar, citric acid, or boric acid powder. Dissolve any of these in water and test with litmus. Test again, using only the dry acid to show that chemicals must be in solution for the reaction to occur.

Chemicals in certain salts are neither acidic nor basic. Litmus paper dipped in a solution of table salt, for example, will not change color. Tap water and soil samples stirred in water may also be tested with litmus paper.

Other Indicators

Youngsters troubled by chapped hands in cold weather may be interested in determining whether the family soap is too strong or caustic. Have each child who brings soap from home scrape some into a half glass of water. Dissolve the soap and add a half teaspoon of phenolphthalein (from a local pharmacy) to the solution. In the presence of strong soaps, the phenolphthalein indicator will turn the solution a very dark pink; the milder (less basic) the soap, the lighter the pink.

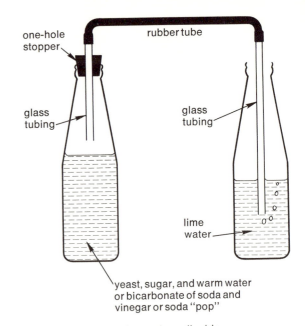

FIGURE **10-5** Test for carbon dioxide.

The juices of certain fruits and vegetables can be used as acid–alkali indicators. For example, shred red cabbage and heat in water until the water is a deep purple. Drain and save the liquid, add more water to the cabbage, and heat again. Draw off the colored liquid again and add to the first batch of solution. Saturate paper toweling or filter paper with the solution and let dry. Repeat until the paper is well impregnated, then cut into small strips for use in the same way as litmus paper. The red cabbage may be treated in rubbing alcohol. When the alcohol turns purple, add vinegar. The solution should become deep red, as with litmus paper exposed to acid. Pinches of baking soda or ammonia (basic) turn the solution green. Vinegar will bring back the red color.

Limewater Test for Carbon Dioxide

Carbon dioxide is a colorless gas that can be very quickly and easily identified. Limewater through which carbon dioxide is bubbled becomes milky. Limewater can be purchased very inexpensively at a drugstore or made by dissolving some calcium oxide in water.

Left exposed to the air in a shallow dish for an hour or so, limewater will develop a thin, milky crust as the carbon dioxide in the air combines with it. Fig. 10-5 shows an arrangement for testing for carbon dioxide with limewater; the generating bottle can contain soda "pop," yeast, and sugar in warm water, or vinegar and bicarbonate of (baking) soda (see soda–acid fire extinguishers, below, and Chapter 16). One can also blow through the delivery tube, sending exhaled carbon dioxide through the limewater.

CHEMICAL REACTIONS IN DAILY LIFE

Many daily activities in home and classroom are made possible by the interaction of chemicals. Ninety per cent of the earth's crust is composed of four elements (oxygen, 50 %, silicon, 25 %, aluminum and iron, 15 %). With aluminum, potassium, magnesium, and sodium, you can represent the major chemical components of the rocks. An important dozen of elements or about $\frac{1}{8}$ of all elements are building blocks of living things. You may wish to use the fractional representations to illustrate mathematical units.

To familiarize children with elements in everyday life, assemble real or symbolic examples of nine chemical elements—carbon, sulfur, iron, copper, silver, tin, gold, mercury, and lead—known and used by the time of Christ. For use with an overhead projector, you may wish to develop a series of transparencies illustrating the evolution of the periodic table as new elements were discovered. In the periodic table (Fig. 10-6) adjacent elements often have similar properties. The complete periodic table of elements represents, in organized, compact form, the discoveries made by hundreds of scientists over hundreds of years.

Action of Carbon Dioxide

A diverting demonstration employing the action of carbon dioxide is as follows. Drop 1 cup of mothballs into a gallon jar holding about 3 quarts of water to which $\frac{3}{4}$ cup baking soda and 1 cup of vinegar have been added. Sinking to the bottom, the mothballs become coated with a layer of carbon dioxide bubbles, which, being lighter, make the mothballs rise. When the balls reach the surface, the bubbles break and the mothballs descend. This rising and falling continues until the soda–acid reaction is completed.

Bread-making A chemical reaction is necessary to produce a substance important in every country of the world—bread. Bread-making depends on the release of gaseous carbon dioxide. Crumble a yeast cake in a glass jar. Add 1 tablespoon of sugar and $\frac{1}{3}$ cup of warm water. Stir until smooth. Within an hour, a spongy mass full of bubbles will form. The smell of fermentation is due to the conversion of sugar to alcohol by yeast cells (see Chapter 3). The bubbles are carbon dioxide, which can be identified as described under *Chemical Tests*, p. 180.

Baking powder, which contains bicarbonate of soda (with acid substances in dry form), will also release carbon dioxide, and thus may be used in place of yeast to make bread rise. Mix dry 1 tablespoon of flour and $\frac{1}{2}$ teaspoon of baking powder. Add water and stir to make dough. Using a cooking spoon with a long wooden handle, hold a spoonful of dough over heat until the dough doubles in size. Cut or pull off the top layer and examine the soft, spongy texture created by the carbon dioxide bubbles trapped throughout the mass. To make baking powder, mix dry 1 teaspoon of bicarbonate of soda, 2 teaspoons of tartaric acid, and 1 teaspoon of cornstarch. Test with a lighted match; if carbon dioxide gas is being given off, the flame will be extinguished. The sour-milk chocolate cake described above under *Acids and Alkalis* used baking soda (sodium bicarbonate) rather than baking *powder* because the acid properties of the sour milk performed the carbon dioxide-releasing function of the acid substances in the baking powder.

Carbon dioxide gas is also formed by the reaction between vinegar and baking soda. Needed to demonstrate the pressure of the gas generated are a bottle, a cork to fit, and a funnel. Through the funnel pour first a handful of baking soda and then half a cup of vinegar into the bottle. Cork the bottle quickly but not tightly, shake it once or twice, and then set it inside a can that encloses the whole bottle to prevent tipping and as a safety measure should the bottle burst. Stand back and await results. Very shortly the pressure of the carbon dioxide released by the combination of the vinegar and the soda makes the cork fly out with a sharp report. (Use open floor space for this demonstration.)

Carbon dioxide may be collected by the displacement of water (Fig. 11-5) from any of the reactions described above.

In fire-fighting Carbon dioxide is also an essential element in certain kinds of fire extinguishers, such as the wall type, which operates by a reaction between an acid and sodium bicarbonate (Chapter 16). The capacity of carbon dioxide to smother a flame can be illustrated as follows.

1 1.008 **H** Hydrogen			

KEY:

Atomic Number ———— **20** 40.08 ———— Atomic Weight

Symbol ———— **Ca**

Calcium

3 6.941 **Li** Lithium	**4** 9.012 **Be** Beryllium
11 22.99 **Na** Sodium	**12** 24.31 **Mg** Magnesium

19 39.10 **K** Potassium	**20** 40.08 **Ca** Calcium	**21** 44.96 **Sc** Scandium	**22** 47.90 **Ti** Titanium	**23** 50.94 **V** Vanadium	**24** 51.99 **Cr** Chromium	**25** 54.94 **Mn** Manganese	**26** 55.85 **Fe** Iron	**27** 58.93 **Co** Cobalt
37 85.47 **Rb** Rubidium	**38** 87.62 **Sr** Strontium	**39** 88.91 **Y** Yttrium	**40** 91.22 **Zr** Zirconium	**41** 92.91 **Nb** Niobium	**42** 95.94 **Mo** Molybdenum	**43** 98.91 **Te** Technetium	**44** 101.1 **Ru** Ruthenium	**45** 102.9 **Rh** Rhodium
55 132.9 **Cs** Cesium	**56** 137.3 **Ba** Barium	**57** 138.9 **La** Lanthanum	**72** 178.5 **Hf** Hafnium	**73** 180.9 **Ta** Tantalum	**74** 183.9 **W** Tungsten	**75** 186.2 **Re** Rhenium	**76** 190.2 **Os** Osmium	**77** 192.2 **Ir** Iridium
87 223 **Fr** Francium	**88** 226.0 **Ra** Radium	**89** 227 **Ac** Actinium						

58 140.12 **Ce** Cerium	**59** 140.91 **Pr** Praseodymium	**60** 144.2 **Nd** Neodymium	**61** 147 **Pm** Promethium	**62** 150.4 **Sm** Samarium
90 232.0 **Th** Thorium	**91** 231.0 **Pa** Protactinium	**92** 238.0 **U** Uranium	**93** 237.0 **Np** Neptunium	**94** 242 **Pu** Plutonium

FIGURE **10-6** Simplified periodic chart.

NOTE: Atomic weights shown in Table 21-1 have been rounded off to whole numbers and so differ slightly from weights shown here.

Drip some candle wax into the bottom center of a coffee can and anchor the butt of the candle in it as it hardens. Relight the candle and pour a glass of saturated solution of bicarbonate of soda into the can. Slowly add vinegar. If the candle flame is near the solution level, the flame will be smothered by carbon dioxide. To be sure that the invisible carbon dioxide gas is responsible, repeat using only vinegar or only bicarbonate of soda.

Cleaning, Bleaching, and Stain-removing

Like most alkalis, household ammonia acts to produce an emulsifying—and, hence, a cleansing—effect. (Most cleaning agents contain chemical bases such as ammonia water as emulsifying agents.) Children may clean classroom windows with ammonia solution and plain and soapy water, noting which leaves the least residue.

						2 4.003 He Helium
	5 10.81 B Boron	6 12.01 C Carbon	7 14.01 N Nitrogen	8 15.99 O Oxygen	9 18.99 F Fluorine	10 20.18 Ne Neon
	13 26.98 Al Aluminum	14 28.09 Si Silicon	15 30.97 P Phosphorus	16 32.06 S Sulfur	17 35.45 Cl Chlorine	18 39.95 Ar Argon
28 58.71 Ni Nickel	29 63.55 Cu Copper	30 65.37 Zn Zinc	31 69.72 Ga Gallium	32 72.59 Ge Germanium	33 74.92 As Arsenic	34 78.96 Se Selenium	35 79.90 Br Bromine	36 83.80 Kr Krypton
46 106.4 Pd Palladium	47 107.9 Ag Silver	48 112.4 Cd Cadmium	49 114.8 In Indium	50 118.7 Sn Tin	51 121.8 Sb Antimony	52 127.6 Te Tellurium	53 126.9 I Iodine	54 131.3 Xe Xenon
78 195.1 Pt Platinum	79 196.9 Au Gold	90 200.6 Hg Mercury	81 204.4 Tl Thallium	82 207.2 Pb Lead	83 208.9 Bi Bismuth	84 210 Po Polonium	85 210 At Astatine	86 222 Rn Radon

63 151.9 Eu Europium	64 157.3 Gd Gadollnium	65 158.9 Tb Terbium	66 162.5 Dy Dysprosium	67 164.9 Ho Holmium	68 167.3 Er Erbium	69 168.93 Tm Thulium	70 173.0 Yb Ytterbium	71 174.9 Lu Lutetium
95 243 Am Americium	96 247 Cm Curium	97 247 Bk Berkelium	98 251 Cf Californium	99 254 Es Einsteinium	100 253 Fm Fermium	101 256 Md Mendelevium	102 254 No Nobelium	103 257 Lr Lawrencium

One can demonstrate the results of the emulsifying effect of ammonia water with two pocket combs, each having some natural hair oil and dust particles in them. Set one in a pan of water to which a teaspoon or two of household ammonia has been added. After 20 minutes, remove and rinse in clear water. Wash another comb in plain or soapy water. (One may point out that warm water is more effective than cold in all cleaning operations because heat speeds molecular movement, an important factor in producing chemical reactions.)

Stain-removing and Bleaching

Bleaching agents work by changing the original matter into a colorless compound, usually by oxidation (see above) or reduction (removing oxygen from a compound). Lemon juice, for example, is one such agent, and will lighten the color of tea. Lemon juice is, thus, a frequently used remedy for household stains. Try removing ink writing on paper and cloth with lemon, vinegar, milk, onion, or household bleach. (Use care with bleach; apply with an old paint brush and avoid splashing.) Or add food coloring to a jar of water, then add a few drops of chlorine bleach and observe color changes.

Make a solution of 1 cup 3 % hydrogen peroxide and $\frac{1}{2}$ cup water. Add a few borax crystals to make the solution basic (test with litmus). Boil some brightly colored wool in the solution for about ten minutes and compare the resulting color with that of samples of wet but unbleached wool and wool soaked in household bleach. (Review safety measures in handling household bleach.)

Investigation of stain removal may lead to consideration of chemical reactions between metals and certain foods. Children may have noticed, for example, that aluminum pans look almost new after rhubarb or tomatoes have been stewed in them or after water with a little vinegar added has been heated in them. The acid in these foods removes the thin film of stain on the metal by forming a new compound made up of elements from the acid and from the compound that is the stain.

To investigate why egg stains silver, rub a clean piece of silver first with the white, then with the yolk, of a hard-boiled egg. The sulfur in the yolk causes the silver to tarnish (form a sulfide film), as can be verified by bringing some powdered sulfur into contact with the silver. Rubber bands left in contact with silver will also tarnish it because of the residue of the sulfur used in vulcanizing the rubber in the bands.

To clean silver coins, dissolve a teaspoon each of salt and bicarbonate of soda in enough water to cover the silver. (Use an aluminum pan or an enameled or glass pan with some pieces of aluminum foil in it.) Bring to a boil, let stand, then rinse and dry. The mechanism here is similar to that operating in the case of the aluminum pan described above.

Brass and copper cleaners act by a chemical reaction that transfers metals from one material to another (in effect, metal plating). Needed to investigate copper plating are 1 ounce of copper sulfate (available from a druggist) and 3 drops of sulfuric acid dissolved in 9 parts of water by weight. Copper sulfate dissolves slowly; if crystals are large, use a milk bottle or rolling pin to pulverize them. (Small crystals dissolve more readily than large ones (see Chapter 6, p. 108). Suspend a well cleaned iron or steel key or old knife blade in the solution; in about 10 minutes the metal will be coated with a thin layer of copper. Electricity (the flow of electrons) carries the copper, atom by atom, through the solution and deposits it on the key or knife blade. This process of electroplating is the basis of many industrial processes.

Cooking

Many chemical changes take place during cooking because of the application of heat, which speeds the movement of the molecules involved—as mentioned above. Breakfast toast is a good illustration of such change. To demonstrate, dip a slice of toast (cut into strips) into a dish of iodine water (see p. 179). The inner portion will turn blue in the typical starch reaction, while the surface layer (of dextrin) remains brown. If simple sugars such as dextrin are digested more easily than starches, which is better for invalids—toast or bread?

Combustion and Heating

Burning solid fuel produces heat, smoke, ashes—all different from the original substance. A few wood chips burned in a metal plate will demonstrate this adequately. Gas, another product of combustion, may be generated on a safe scale in the classroom as follows. Punch a nail hole in the center of a metal coffee can cover. Put thin pine chips into the can and close the lid securely. Set the can on an electric hot plate. After a few minutes, try periodically to ignite the smoke or gas escaping through the hole; it should eventually ignite and burn. When the flame goes out, open the can (after it has cooled); the substance remaining in the can is charcoal (carbon) plus some minerals that may not have been driven off by the heating.

As children may recall from the discussion of flame testing (p. 179), heat energy can help chemists identify the chemical building blocks of substances. To test for elements in a common compound, heat half a cup of sugar over low heat. (Use a disposable, shallow, metal container.) The sugar will melt, bubble, and eventually turn black. Have children compare the black residue with the charcoal made from heating wood chips in a closed container (above). Charcoal and the burnt sugar can be used for drawings. Cornstarch heated in the same way as sugar produces the same black residue. Many common chemicals contain carbon.

Heating can also help identify some other substances common to sugar, starch, and wood. Heat a teaspoon of sugar in a small metal can with a glass inverted in it. Moisture condenses on the cool surface, indicating the presence of water in the sugar (not as part of the sugar molecule, but as water trapped in the crystalline structure of the sugar). Water can be collected similarly by burning a candle or by heating cornstarch or wood chips. Heat flour (95 % starch), or a slice of bread, in an open vessel until scorched and hold the vessel close to a cool mirror or a blackboard; the condensation that appears on these surfaces shows that elements of water were present in the starch. Similarly, moisture will condense on a piece of cold metal held above a burning candle. Analogies may be made with the clouds that often form over forest fires. (In the case of the candle, the water is a product of the recombination of elements that takes place during combustion; in the case of the starch and wood, the water is a product of distillation.)

Substances that char and produce moisture (as a result of the breakdown of their compounds and the recombination of elements) give evidence of containing the elements carbon, hydrogen, and oxygen. Such substances form a category called *carbohydrates*, which includes many foods (see Chapter 11). Organic (carbon-containing) compounds, known as hydrocarbons, contain only hydrogen and carbon; illuminating gas and petroleum products such as candles are examples.

Copying Processes

Blueprinting and other copying processes also illustrate chemical change. Blueprint paper is made by coating white paper with light-sensitive chemicals. Just as electricity energizes the reaction in electroplating, sunlight energizes the reaction here. Children, working in teams of three, preferably, can make blueprints of leaves or other flat objects as follows. Blueprint and Ozalid paper are available from science supply houses and blueprinting or drafting firms. If the paper comes in wide rolls, the supplier may cut it to the same size as small standard windowpanes. Hinge a piece of window glass (beveled with steel wool or emery paper or edge bound with tape) and cardboard together along one edge with adhesive tape. Lay the blueprint paper (sensitive or emulsion side up) on the cardboard with the leaf or other material on the paper. Close the glass cover and set the whole "sandwich" in the sun until the paper turns blue. Remove the paper and wash it thoroughly in cold water. The print will last longer if dipped in photographic fixative solution (one pinch of potassium dichromate crystals to a glass of water) before rinsing. Hang up the print and allow it to dry.

Interesting brown prints can be made on Ozalid paper in much the same way, the only difference being that the paper is developed by rinsing in weak ammonia water rather than in plain water.

SUGGESTED PROJECTS

1. Children, individually or in teams, can make a wall-size table of the elements (with models of simpler elements attached) as well as a display of common elements such as iron, copper, and aluminum attached with colored yarn to a descriptive chart.

2. To make individual "crystal gardens," pour about 4 tablespoons each of salt (noniodized), water, liquid bluing, and household ammonia slowly over lumps of brick, coal, clinker, coke, charcoal briquet, or other porous matter standing in a 6-inch saucer. Add food coloring, mercurochrome, or red ink for color. Let stand undisturbed. The following chemicals coming out of solution will also form colored crystals: nickel nitrate or cobalt nitrate, ferric chloride, mercurous nitrate, and ferrous sulfate.

3. Flame tests of the following compounds make a colorful and attention-holding display: sodium chloride, calcium chloride, strontium chloride, and copper sulfate.

4. Encourage "science-prone" children to read Michael Faraday's *Chemical History of a Candle* and to demonstrate some of the ideas and experiments described.

5. Children interested in chemistry or electricity can report on and demonstrate the transformation (as in batteries) of chemical energy into electrical energy.

6. Alone or in teams, children interested in photography can report on the chemistry involved in developing and printing photographs.

7. Use strong tea or dissolve $\frac{1}{4}$ teaspoon tannic acid in 1 teaspoon water. Dissolve $\frac{1}{4}$ teaspoon iron (ferrous, not ferric) sulfate in a like quantity of water. Note the color of each solution; then observe when you pour the two together. The new substance is old-fashioned ink. Test some writing with ink stain removers. If iron sulfate is not easily available, use any water-soluble iron compound. The sulfate is the compound that contains both sulfur and oxygen.

BIBLIOGRAPHY

(**P** indicates recommended for primary grades, **I** for intermediate grades, **U** for upper grades.)

Asimov, Isaac, *Building Blocks of the Universe,* Abelard-Schuman, 1957. Origins, properties, and uses of elements. **U**

Beeler, Nelson, and Franklyn M. Branley, *Experiments in Chemistry,* Crowell, 1952. Chemistry of everyday objects by observation and experiment. **I**

Blackwood, Paul, *Push and Pull: The Story of Energy,* McGraw-Hill, rev. ed., 1966. Sources and uses of energy in various forms. Simple experiments. **U**

Carona, Philip B., *The True Book of Chemistry,* Children's Pr., 1962. Brief introduction to the elements, chemical symbols, and formulas. **U**

Carrier, Elba, *Humphrey Davy and Chemical Discovery,* Watts, 1965. Research, inventions, discoveries of Sir Humphrey Davy. **U**

Cooper, Elizabeth, *Discovering Chemistry,* Harcourt, 1959. Clear, simple explanations of the elements, structure and symbols, and how formulas are derived. Gives instructions for setting up a home laboratory. **U**

Freeman, Mae and Ira, *Fun With Chemistry*, Random, 1954. Simple chemistry experiments. **U**

———, *The Story of Chemistry*, Random, 1962. Simple explanation of chemical principles in relation to everyday life. A few simple experiments, numerous diagrams, and glossary. **I**

Gallant, Roy A., *Exploring Chemistry*, Garden City, 1958. Historical development, practical applications, and future problems. **U**

Goldin, Augusta, *Salt*, Crowell, 1965. Brief, simple introduction to salt—its chemical makeup, sources, and use in food and as a preservative. **I**

Irwin, Keith G., *Chemistry First S-T-E-P-S*, Watts, 1963. Freeman's *Fun With Chemistry* with additional information on metals. Briefly summarizes the importance of chemistry to modern life. **U**

Morgan, Alfred, *First Chemistry Book for Boys and Girls*, Scribners, 1950. Sixty-four activities using household equipment. **U**

Newcomb, Ellsworth, and Hugh Kenny, *Miracle Fabrics*, Putnam, 1957. Research on and development of synthetic materials. **U**

Schloat, G. Warren, Jr., *The Magic of Water*, Scribners, 1955. A general description of the composition, use, and value of water. Several simple experiments; photographs and diagrams. **I**

Schwartz, Julius, *It's Fun to Know Why: Experiments With Things Around Us*, McGraw-Hill, 1952. Safe and easy experiments illustrating the properties and uses of familiar materials. Illustrated and indexed. **U**

Stone, A. Harris, *Take a Balloon*, Prentice-Hall, 1967. Fundamental ideas in physics and chemistry, simply written and charmingly illustrated. Open-ended approach. **U**

Swezey, Kenneth, *Chemistry Magic*, McGraw-Hill, 1956. Presents activities and common tests. Various laboratory techniques are explained and apparatus described. **U**

Vries, Leonard de, *The Second Book of Experiments*, Macmillan, 1964. Seventy-two easy-to-perform experiments requiring only readily obtainable materials. Divided into five groups: force, sound, gases, liquids, and heat. Lists the needed materials, gives a clear explanation, and presents the underlying scientific principle. **U**

White, Anne Terry, *Rocks All Around Us*, Random, 1959. Nontechnical account of the formation of various kinds of rock and the geological background of each. **I**

Zim, Herbert and Elizabeth Cooper, *Minerals: Their Identification, Uses, and How to Collect Them*. Harcourt, 1943. A useful handbook. Includes locations for mineral-hunting. **U**

Drying cakes of high-protein blue alga for food in the Republic of Chad, Africa.

11 Life Processes

HUMAN NUTRITION

The energy we need to function—seemingly boundless in children—requires fuel. Fuel implies burning or oxidation, and fuel for all living things—both plants and animals—is food. With every green leaf a solar energy trap, plants are the great producers—and animals the consumers—of energy.

Major Food Categories

For man there are three main categories of food—the proteins, carbohydrates (sugars and starches), and fats or oils—all of which are essential to human nutrition. The various foods also contain minerals and vitamins. Proteins are essentially for growth and repair of body tissue, though proteins in excess of growth needs can be used by the body for energy. Sugars, starches, and fats provide energy. Minerals build bones and have specific roles in the chemical reactions that are part of the functioning of the body. Vitamins also have different functions in health and growth.

Proteins The body is made up mainly of proteins, complex compounds of nitrogen, with carbon, oxygen, and hydrogen, and often other components. Animals are the principal source of proteins (as well as fats and some minerals—see below).

The characteristic odor of burnt hair or burnt

feathers in foods subjected to charring or burning is a fairly reliable indicator of the presence of protein. A few drops of 3 % copper sulfate solution and of household ammonia added to milk should react with the protein in the milk by turning it violet. Solid protein foods can be tested with the same solution if they are liquefied before the copper sulfate and ammonia solution is added. (Cooked foods react more readily than raw.) The presence of gluten, a protein component of flour, can be established with the same solution, but only after the starch component has been removed as follows: Stir a cup of flour with water until it forms a stiff paste. Knead for about ten minutes and put into an old sugar bag or piece of cheesecloth. Continue kneading under water, rinsing until little milkiness appears in the water. Test the residue in the bag. That lean meat (muscle) is mainly protein can also be proved with the copper sulfate-ammonia solution.

To separate the protein and other components of milk, let some raw or nonhomogenized milk stand in a refrigerator until all the cream (the fat in the milk) has come to the top. Remove this carefully, heat the remainder until lukewarm, and add white vinegar, a few drops at a time, stirring until the milk curdles. Remove the solid part (curds) from the liquid (whey) by filtering through paper toweling fitted inside a funnel. The curds, or casein, may be tested for protein. Light curds, or milk albumin, should appear when the whey is brought to a boil. Filter these off and test for protein. If the filtrate from the milk albumin is evaporated (using an uncovered double boiler), milk sugar (see below) will remain.

Carbohydrates (sugars and starches) Carbohydrates are compounds of carbon, hydrogen, and oxygen; plants are their main source. Sugar may be tested for with prepared indicators such as Clinitest tablets or matchlike Clinistiks, both (together with color charts) available from druggists. The tablets make a blue solution. In the presence of a 2 % (or greater) concentration of simple (glucose) sugars, the solution turns brick red; 1 %, yellow, and $\frac{1}{4}$ %, green. No heating is necessary. Tips of the matchlike devices turn color correspondingly.

Sugar is used by the body solely for quick energy. To demonstrate why, dissolve sugar, cornstarch, and other soluble dry foods each in a test tube or tumbler of water. Because sugar is the first to dissolve (or slip between the water molecules), it is the substance that can move most quickly into the blood stream and, thus, to cells needing energy.

Energy foods, such as sugar and starch, release heat. (Lay the paper across the open top of a tin can; do the experiment near a sink.) Ignite a piece of paper on which a teaspoon of sugar or starch has been placed. The sugar will seem to boil, then produce a blue flame and accompanying heat. Or coat a sugar lump with fine ash (as from a cigarette) and hold with kitchen tongs over heat (candle, Sterno, alcohol lamp). The sugar will melt and then ignite.

All carbohydrates produce water vapor when they burn; the vapor will condense on a cool mirror held above the flame. Burning a piece of bread will give the same result. The moisture in one's breath is a product of the slow "burning" of energy foods in our bodies.

In the body, complex sugars are reduced by saliva in the mouth and by intestinal enzymes. Apply saliva to a sugar lump. After an interval, test for sugar as described above. Lemon juice tested for sugar shows as much color reaction as a sweet orange; lemons, nevertheless, taste sour, because their sugar content is screened by their high citric acid (which is sour) content.

One of the most common starch tests is that using iodine (Chapter 10). A drop of household iodine touched to a cracker immediately turns from brown to blue, as it will on a slice of raw potato. In many fruits, starch changes to sugar as the fruit ripens. Thus, the iodine test applied to apples in different stages of ripening will show a graduated reaction, the apples that are still green showing the greatest starch content.

To determine the relative solubility of starch and sugar, add a teaspoon of each to separate tumblers of water. Stir well and let stand. Filter some of each solution into tumblers. Test for sweetness of the sugar solution and test the filtrate from the starch solution with iodine.

Children can make starch from raw potatoes. Grate several and make a bag around the pulp with a piece of old sheet or sugar bag. Dip the bag several times in a little water and filter the milky liquid that results. The substance that will be retained by the filter is starch; spread it to dry in a flat pan near heat.

Fats Fats, like carbohydrates, are generally composed of carbon, oxygen, and hydrogen, but with the components arranged and combined in a different way. As with carbohydrates (see below), fats are primarily sources of energy. That fats can produce heat may be readily demonstrated by making fat "candles" or, in effect, oil lamps: Fill metal bottle caps with a variety of fats and oils and use soft cotton string for wicks. The body as a whole releases energy at about the same rate as a 100-watt bulb.

A simple test for fats and oils consists in placing a dab of the specimen on paper, which fat or oil will make translucent—the more so, the more the paper is warmed. In general, oils come from plants, and solid or semisolid fats come from animals, although some commercial fats are made from plant oils.

Fats or oils can be extracted as follows. Working outdoors, immerse pulverized nut meats in cleaning fluid containing carbon tetrachloride. (*Do not inhale fumes.*) Leave several hours or overnight in a closed container, then filter and pour the filtrate into a shallow dish. The residue after evaporation of the solvent will be oil or fat. An oil film will appear in a tumbler of water into which crushed nut meats have been put.

If Brazil nuts, butternuts, walnuts, or whole peanuts—each on a needle imbedded in a cork on a metal pan or asbestos pad—are ignited, the Brazil nut, with its high fat content, will have the largest and longest burning flame.

Examined with a microscope, a drop of milk diluted with water will show small, ball-like droplets of fat, which give milk its characteristic color.

Vitamins Vitamins, a variety of complex chemical compounds, may be regarded as activators. The B-complex vitamins and Vitamin C, as part of food enzymes, activate the release of energy and synthesis of body compounds within cells. Both plant and animal tissues are sources of vitamins. Because many vitamins are water-soluble and some are easily destroyed by heat, one should cook with minimal heat and water. Others are decomposed by sunlight, and foods containing them should be stored in a cool, dark place.

To test for Vitamin C, dilute 1 drop of 10% ascorbic acid (Vitamin C, available from a druggist) in 20 drops of water. Add iodine and dilute in 100 parts of water. The brown color of the iodine disappears completely, leaving the liquid clear. The more Vitamin C, the quicker the iodine color will disappear. Or mix 10 drops of boiled starch and 1 drop of iodine in a half glass of water. As described for the starch test above, the mixture will turn blue. Addition of citrus foods, such as lemon juice, will make the blue color disappear. Children may test foods not likely to contain Vitamin C—proteins or fats, for example.

Testing for Vitamin A may be done (only by the teacher) as follows. Dissolve a Vitamin A capsule or one containing Vitamin A in $\frac{1}{4}$ ounce of carbon tetrachloride. (*Do not inhale fumes; work outdoors.*) Using tweezers, add one crystal of antimony trichloride, obtainable from a high school science laboratory or a chemistry set. (*Handle crystals with tweezers only.*) The white crystal will turn blue, the strength of the color depending directly on the amount of Vitamin A present.

Children can cut out pictures to depict meals containing the chief vitamins—A, B_1, B_2, C, D, and G. No one food contains all the vitamins. The vitamin content of packaged goods such as cereals is often listed on the wrappers, and children may enjoy comparing the various ones as well as the vitamin percentages of different vitamin pills (also shown on the label). The latter may differ considerably.

Minerals Most foods contain minerals that are important to the body. The ash of a burned piece of bread is light gray, rather than the black of pure carbon, indicating the presence of minerals in the bread. Plants extract such minerals as calcium and iron from the soil.

Iodine is needed for proper functioning of the thyroid gland; without it, a deficiency disease called goiter can develop. To make up the deficiency of iodine in the water and soil in certain regions, salt processors add iodine, to make "iodized salt." To test for iodine in salt, fill a test tube one quarter full of dry cornstarch; add the same amount of salt. Wet the salt by adding a little household bleach. If the salt is iodized, a dark blue-black dividing line (the starch test above) will form between the salt and the starch.

Calcium is essential to normal blood clotting, muscle contraction, and nerve functioning. Calcium and phosphorus are necessary for bone growth. To demonstrate the high calcium content of bone, boil some chicken bones and scrape clean of any adhering muscle tissue or ligaments. Place in a covered jar of concentrated vinegar. After several days, the bones should be rubbery enough to tie into knots because the vinegar (dilute acetic acid) has dissolved out the bone calcium. That bone is living or growing tissue can be shown with a marrow bone cut across so that blood vessels can be seen. All animals with bony skeletons need foods containing calcium; invertebrates do not. Point out why the first food of young mammals is the mother's milk.

Iron is used by the body to form hemoglobin, the red blood pigment that carries oxygen from lungs to cells (see p. 199).

Potassium, sodium, and chlorine are involved with maintaining water balance in the body. Potassium is abundant in animal and plant foods, and sodium and chlorine are present in foods and table salt.

Copper, cobalt, magnesium, manganese, molybdenum, and zinc take part in various chemical reactions in the body.

Fluorine, although it may not be essential, gives developing teeth substantial protection against decay. It occurs in many foods and natural water supplies and in some places is added to water supplies.

Digestion

Food substances must be changed chemically if the body is to use them, and to change them chemically they must first be liquefied. Food is liquefied with saliva as one chews, and juices in the body keep food moist as it dissolves. Saliva, which is partly water, is just one of these juices. The body in fact is 90 % water. When food reaches the stomach, the substances of which it is composed could not get to the other parts if they were not carried through the blood, which is 66 % water. One can live for a month without food, but not more than three or four days without water.

No one has ever been able to build a machine that duplicates all the complex processes of digestion in the body. In the nineteenth century, a doctor was able to observe what happened inside the stomach of a patient who had been injured in a hunting accident. Among other things, he discovered that emotions had a great deal to do with digestion. If the patient was angry or upset, his stomach reacted in such a way that food might be only partly processed or not at all, causing indigestion.

All grinding of food is done by the teeth; the stomach can only churn the ground and dissolved particles by lengthwise and crosswise muscle action of the organ. Children can try grinding some food between two flat stones, Indian-fashion. (Taste is largely a function of the taste buds in the tongue. The taste buds are not uniformly distributed over the tongue and this may be demonstrated by touching a toothpick dipped in sugar water to various parts of the tongue. The most taste-sensitive can be located with the aid of a mirror.)

The stomach's temperature, normally about 100°F., rises during exercise and falls during sleep or rest. This temperature-activity relation may make understandable how very hot or very cold foods may interfere with the functioning of the stomach. The concept of the digestive tract as a *system* of organs (Fig. 11-1) may be presented in terms of an analogy with a mechanical apparatus—the mouth a hopper, the teeth grinders, the tongue a mixer (mixing food with saliva), and the muscles of the esophagus a conveyor belt pushing food into the stomach.

Not all parts of food can be digested. Some food leaves the body in solid form, some in liquid. The chemical changes in food are produced by various substances secreted by the body; saliva is one of these. As one chews a soda cracker slowly and thoroughly, it begins to taste sweet as the enzymes in the saliva begin to change the starches in the cracker into the more digestible sugars.

In addition to the enzyme, *ptyalin*, in saliva, there are other enzymes in the small intestine and stomach that continue the process of changing starches to sugars. To demonstrate the change induced by saliva, make paste of a tablespoon of cornstarch and a cup of water. Heat to boiling, and cook for ten minutes, stirring constantly to prevent burning. Put a tablespoon of the very thin paste in each of two jars, adding saliva to one jar and a teaspoon of water to the other. Set in a warm place. In an hour the saliva will change the starch to sugar and the paste will have dissolved. The paste with plain water will be unchanged.

Starch stored in roots must be changed into sugar before plants can use it. For example, parsnips dug in the fall are rather tasteless; by spring they are sweet and tasty. During the summer, parsnips store starch in their fleshy roots. Toward the end of winter, this starch begins to change to sugar. By spring the plant sugar is carried up into the stems and leaves, where it is used to provide the energy necessary to make flowers and seeds. (Parsnips are biennials, plants that make enough food during the first year to carry them into bloom during their second and final season.)

Within the stomach, proteins begin to change chemically. To observe such chemical change, place protein food samples in dilute hydrochloric acid and pepsin (two of the digestive chemicals found in the stomach). After 24 hours, the protein will be broken down—changed in appearance and partly liquefied. The same effect can be

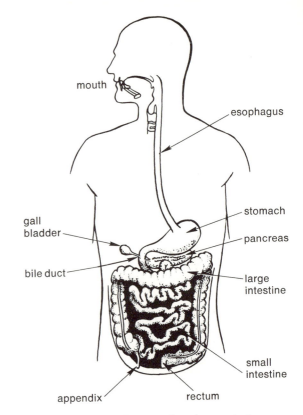

FIGURE **11-1** The human digestive tract. Arrangement of organs permits lateral and horizontal churning of food.

obtained with a water solution of tablets containing pepsin and another enzyme, papain, or a meat tenderizer containing papain. Ground beef left in the solution will be nearly liquefied in 24 hours.

Bile, secreted by the liver, helps in digestion by emulsifying fats and oils in the intestines.

Oxidation of food The "slow smokeless burning of decay" in Robert Frost's woodpile is a poet's way of describing slow oxidation. Slow oxidation (as rusting) may be observed in the experiment with steel wool (described on p. 179, Chapter 10). In another example of the effect of slow oxidation, a bushel or so of fresh grass clippings, fresh-cut hay, or fallen leaves, stored in a warm, dark place for a day or two, will usually have an interior temperature higher than the outer air. This can be verified with a thermometer and may be rechecked in about a week. On cool mornings, have children watch for water vapor ("steam") rising from a pile of leaves or grass cuttings. Slow oxidation will also release heat energy inside a pile of fresh manure. Green hay stored without curing can generate sufficient heat to cause spontaneous combustion.

The body is unusual in its ability to oxidize or use fuel at relatively low temperatures. (The slow oxidation of sugar produces a temperature higher than normal in the body, but evaporation of moisture through the sweat glands and heat radiation from the skin keep the body temperature near 98.6°F.—usually higher in children.)

To investigate slow oxidation of food at low temperatures, shake down two laboratory or kitchen thermometers to the same low reading. Insert in one-hole stoppers that fit two small Thermos (vacuum) bottles, one holding $\frac{1}{2}$ cup of dried vegetable seeds (peas, beans, squash, radish), the other the same amount of soaked seeds. The thermometers should not touch the seeds, which should occupy about one fourth of each bottle. (Do not stopper tightly, as germinating seeds expand.) Take temperature readings at the start and again at intervals of a few hours, for 24–48 hours. The temperature reading for the bottle of soaked seeds should be higher because of the oxidation started by soaking them.

Calories

Calories are a measure of the energy value of foods as inches measure length and width or pounds measure weight. A calorie is defined by physicists as the amount of heat needed to raise the temperature of 1 gram (1 cubic centimeter or 15 drops) of water 1 Celsius or Centigrade degree. (One Celsius degree equals 1.8 Fahrenheit degrees; see table in Appendix.) The nutritionist's calorie is a "giant" unit equal to 1000 of the scientist's calories—thus, the amount of heat needed to raise the temperature of a quart of water (approximately 1000 grams) one Celsius or Centigrade degree.

Children may frequently hear about calories at home, and many upper-grade girls are calorie-conscious; they may want to investigate such matters as the calorie requirements of growing children as compared to adults of different sexes and age groups. The calorie count of every food depends on how much protein, fat, and carbohydrates are present. To establish that "calories should be chosen for the company they keep"—that is, to emphasize the greater importance of balance in diet, rather than simply total intake—tabulate calorie counts for foods listed in the daily menus that children record. From the data children might construct arithmetic word problems.

Sixth-graders are estimated to need 1 calorie per hour per pound of body weight. With this as a basis, children can calculate their daily (24-hour) caloric need; for example, a 100-pound child would need $24 \times 100 = 2400$ food calories. From tables showing the number of calories in different foods, children can also calculate the total daily food calorie intake. School health personnel can act as valuable resources for calculating individual variations.

Diet and Maintenance of the Body

The human organism does many different things in one day; it may *hear* the alarm clock in the morning, *open* one eye, *look* at the clock, *lift* off the covers, *slide* out one foot after another, *step* into slippers, and so on.

While the human body is like a machine[1] in some ways, it is more unlike than like and can do many things a machine cannot. It can guide itself, think, and repair itself. Although both require air to burn fuel and both give off wastes, body fuel is burned at a fairly low rather than high temperature; it is burned in cells all over the body, not in one place; and bodies can grow.

The body is always at work. For example, even during sleep, the heart keeps pumping, the dia-

[1]One may engage children's interest with riddles such as the following: "I am the best machine in the world. I can lift things. I can remember things I do. I can change a glass of milk into part of me. I need something to make me go, and I can get it myself. I can repair myself. I can think and figure. There are millions like me. What am I?"

phragm and chest muscles keep us breathing, and digestion continues. Even for a machine age, the amount of work the body does in a day is surprising. One aspect of maintenance of a healthy body is correct nutrition. To foster healthful attitudes concerning food, one may point out that nutrients are, in effect, chemicals necessary to the functioning of cells (Fig. 4-12). Evidence indicates that for adequate nutrition children must have, daily, at least three glasses of milk, two servings of meat (or fish or poultry), four servings of vegetables and/or fruit, and four servings of bread and/or cereals.

Many food processors offer illustrated charts describing the major food groups (available, for example, from the Florida Citrus Commission, Lakeland, Florida, and the National Dairy Coun-

cil, Chicago, Illinois) and nutrition guide sheets, the latter available in several languages. ("Always Breakfast Time Somewhere," a comparison of children's breakfast around the world, available from the National Dairy Council and intended to improve nutrition habits, can also seed concepts of time zones.)

A model menu, offering a balanced diet that provides all minimum daily requirements might consist as follows: for breakfast—fruit, cereal or egg or both, toast or roll and butter, and milk; for dinner—a main protein dish, vegetable, potato, bread or roll and butter, milk, and dessert; and for lunch or supper—a main protein dish, vegetable, bread and butter, milk, and fruit.

Using the following equivalencies (in terms of protein, vitamin, and mineral content) can pro-

Table 11-1 VITAMIN SOURCES AND FUNCTIONS

Vitamin	Uses	Sources
A	Promotes smooth, soft, healthy skin, healthy eyes, good night vision; increases resistance to infection.	Milk and milk products, egg yolk, liver, tomatoes, deep yellow fruits and vegetables, dark green and leafy vegetables.
B_1 (thiamine)	Promotes healthy nerves, good appetite and digestion; helps cells use food for energy; prevents beriberi.	Liver, other meats, fish, poultry, dried beans and peas, eggs, enriched and whole-grain breads and cereals, milk, white potatoes.
B_2 (riboflavin)	Helps keep mouth and eyes healthy; helps cells use oxygen.	Milk and milk products, meats, fish, poultry, eggs.
C (ascorbic acid)	Helps keep gums, skin, muscles, and blood vessels healthy; increases resistance to infection; prevents scurvy.	Citrus fruits, strawberries, cantaloupe, tomato, green pepper, broccoli, raw greens, raw cabbage, potatoes.
Niacin	Helps keep skin, nerves, and intestines healthy; prevents pellagra.	Liver, other meats, fish, poultry, milk, enriched and whole-grain bread and cereals, potatoes.
D	Helps build strong bones and teeth; prevents rickets.	Irradiated milk, fish-liver oils, sunshine.

SOURCE: A. Piltz, *How Your Body Uses Food* (Natl. Dairy Council, 1960).

vide children with opportunities to deal with standard units of measure.

1 glass milk = 8 ounces or $\frac{1}{4}$ quart
1 slice American cheese (1 oz.) = $\frac{3}{4}$ glass milk
$\frac{1}{2}$ cup creamed cottage cheese = $\frac{1}{3}$ glass milk
$\frac{1}{2}$ cup ($\frac{1}{4}$ pint) ice cream = $\frac{1}{4}$ glass milk

(Cups, spoons, ounce glasses, and household scales should be kept available.) An ounce of cooked lean meat, poultry, or fish provides the same amount of protein as one egg, one slice of cheese (American or Swiss—1 ounce), two tablespoons of creamed cottage cheese (1 ounce), two tablespoons of peanut butter (1 ounce), or half a cup of cooked dried beans or peas.

As stated above, vitamins and minerals are also essential to health; Table 11-1 shows some of the sources and functions of the six most important vitamins.

Muscles get tired because a waste product, lactic acid, accumulates as the muscles are used. Rest permits the wastes to be carried away, broken down, or absorbed. Because muscle is rebuilt with protein, minerals, and water, diet for athletes in training is often rich in such protein foods as meat, eggs, cheese, fish, yogurt, and milk. The considerable growth undergone by elementary-grade children requires abundant protein.

Using tests described on pp. 188–191 children can see that milk contains fats, proteins, and carbohydrates in about the proportion needed for proper nutrition. Milk lacks only iron and Vitamin C, making it the most nearly perfect food known.

RESPIRATION

Plants and animals convert their fuel—food—into energy by burning. Burning requires air—specifically, the fraction of air that is the element called oxygen (Chapter 10). (In the human body this slow burning, or oxidation, of food takes place at about 98.6°F.; in cold-blooded animals such as frogs and toads, body sugars may be oxidized into glucose at body temperatures even below 50°F.)

FIGURE **11-2** Mosquito wrigglers (larvae of Culex mosquitoes) breathing through tubes at the surface of the water.

In Animals

In the higher animals, oxygen is obtained by *inspiration* (breathing in), and the gaseous products of oxidation are discharged by *expiration* (breathing out). Respiration (the whole process) occurs in the respiratory organs, but the oxygen thus obtained is distributed (via the blood) to all the cells and tissues of the organism.

In simpler animals, such as the earthworm, there is considerable diffusion of gases (inflow and outflow) through the moist skin membrane. Because gases will not diffuse through the dry membrane, earthworms left in open air (where they dry off) will literally suffocate. While the earthworm circulatory system carries gases to and from interior cells, dry-land insects depend on a system of tracheal tubes, which open to the air at spiracles, paired openings in the body wall (Fig. 2-12). Water insects with spiracle openings would drown if their trachea did not branch into anterior sacklike gill appendages.

Insects such as the mosquito larva or wriggler

have a breather tube (Fig. 11-2), which they extend above the water surface when they are drawing air in. This necessity makes the wriggler susceptible to control by a film of kerosene spread on the water where it breeds.

Although tadpoles breathe through gills, frogs have lungs. Because they cannot draw air into their lungs as we do, frogs spend their lives literally swallowing air. In this process, they draw in air through the nostrils by lowering the floor of the mouth. The nostril flaps then close, the floor of the mouth rises, and the air trapped in the mouth is forced into the lungs.

Fish "breathe" by extracting dissolved oxygen from the water; the extraction is carried out by the gills, which have a highly absorptive surface. Fish gills are bright red because the blood vessels into which the oxygen moves are covered with only a thin membrane of tissue.

To emphasize the oxygen content of water, have children count and time the bubbles that collect in a glass of cold tap water when it stands. These bubbles form from air dissolved in the water.

In Plants

Plants and many animals (see above) do not breathe in the sense that humans do. However, plant cells do interchange gases necessary for cellular functioning. Animals need much energy in order to move about as well as to maintain body processes. Plants need less energy because they are stationary. Like animals, plants need oxygen to convert their stored food into energy. To establish that plants must have air, soak in water overnight peas, beans, bird or grass seed. Put the seeds into two bottles half full of cotton or soil so that they can be seen through the glass. Add a little water, tightly cork one bottle and seal with candle wax or paraffin, leaving the other bottle open. Put both bottles in a warm, dark place for two or three days. Check daily and replace water evaporated from the open bottle. Note in which bottle seed germination occurs *first,* in which germination is *best,* and how soon

FIGURE **11-3** Lamp-chimney model of human breathing apparatus.

seedlings in the corked bottle show lack of oxygen.

Stomata (Chapter 3), the specialized cells that are air gateways for leaf cells, are most numerous on the underside of leaves from common succulents such as Bryophyllum, Echeveria, Kalanchoe, Pepperomia, or Sempervivum. They may also be seen readily in fern, lettuce, or Tradescantia (spider lily). To observe them under a microscope, tear the leaf toward the main vein. With tweezers, strip bits of thin lower epidermis and place in a drop of water on a slide.

In Man

In man, air is drawn in by the bellows-like action of the chest cavity and lungs. Raising the ribs and depressing the diaphragm enlarges the cavity, creating a partial vacuum around the lungs and, thus, allowing air to penetrate to the lungs via the mouth, trachea, and bronchi. A model of the action of the chest cavity, lungs, and diaphragm can be made using a lamp chimney, a two-hole stopper, two pieces of plastic feeding tubing, two rubber balloons, rubber sheeting or plastic film, and some elastic bands. As shown in Fig. 11-3, attach a balloon (with rubber bands)

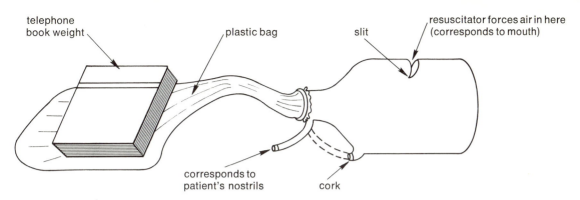

FIGURE **11-4** Device for demonstrating mouth-to-mouth resuscitation.

to each tube. Insert the tubes into the stopper and the stopper into the top of the chimney. Stretch the rubber sheeting or plastic film across the base of the chimney and attach with rubber bands. A cork may be used instead of a rubber stopper. Tubing will slip into the stopper hole more easily if moistened with water. Stopper holes that are too small can be reamed out with a small triangular metal file or a rat-tail file.

To illustrate inhalation pull on the rubber sheeting (representing the diaphragm). The balloons (lungs) will inflate as air enters them because of the differential in air pressure created when the sheeting is drawn down and the volume of the lamp chimney (chest cavity) is, in effect, increased.

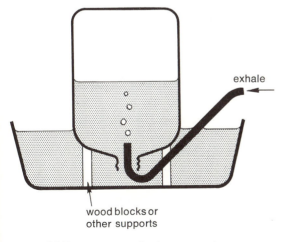

FIGURE **11-5** Apparatus for lung capacity test.

If a vessel larger than the lamp chimney is used, a Y-tube (more realistically representing the structure of the trachea and bronchia) may be substituted for the two straight pieces of tubing.

Mouth-to-mouth resuscitation may also illustrate the breathing mechanism. Children can practice it using a plastic bleach bottle and plastic bag (Fig. 11-4) arranged on a slanted surface to simulate the chin-back position necessary for an unobstructed windpipe.

The neck of the bottle represents the windpipe, the cut handle the nostrils, the plastic bottle the head, the plastic bag the lungs, and the book the rib cage. Cover the slit in the bottle with a fresh strip of acetate as each child takes a turn. Blowing into the bottle (mouth) and, thus, forcing air into the bag (lungs) raises the telephone book or other weight (rib cage).

Children can determine their lung capacities using the simple device shown in Fig. 11-5. Invert a gallon jug of water in a half-filled dish pan and insert the rubber tubing as shown. (Keep the jug as full as possible; insert straws in the tube as disposable mouth pieces.) After marking the water level in the jug with a grease pencil, have the subject exhale as deeply as possible through the tube. The water displaced by the exhaled air is a rough measure of lung capacity. As different children measure their lung capacity, they may discover that body size and lung capacity do not necessarily correspond. To discover how exercise affects breathing, repeat the test after strenuous exercise by the subjects.

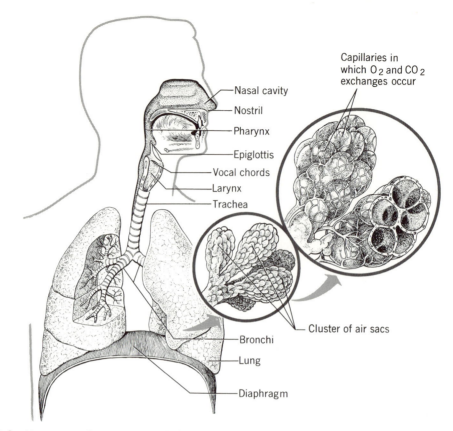

Capillaries in which O_2 and CO_2 exchanges occur

Nasal cavity

Nostril

Pharynx

Epiglottis

Vocal chords

Larynx

Trachea

Cluster of air sacs

Bronchi

Lung

Diaphragm

FIGURE **11-6**   Human respiratory tract and detail of air sacs.

To estimate the amount of air (in gallons) inhaled per minute, divide the number of exhalations per minute in normal breathing (14–20) by the number of normal exhalations necessary to empty the gallon jug of water.

The lamp chimney model is a correct one in all but one respect—the chest cavity in man is flexible. Children can check this by measuring upper chest dimensions with a tape after an inhalation and after an exhalation. One can also check lung space changes by placing a hand against the ribs while breathing. Pressing the hands hard against the diaphragm will make it impossible to inhale.

Children can check on the composition of exhaled air by inserting a lighted candle (see the carbon dioxide test, p. 182) into the jar (Fig. 11-5) used in the lung capacity test above.

AIR PRESSURE

That a slight lowering of the diaphragm draws air into your lungs is explainable by the fact that air is everywhere, about 15 pounds of it pressing on every square inch of your body (see Chapter 5). The pressure is not noticeable because it is exerted equally on the inside and outside of the body. Thus, the body does not collapse from the weight of air because it has many inner air spaces (as well as a skeleton) to support it. Note, for example, that beef or chicken lungs will float in water because of air trapped in the tiny lung alveoli (air sacs).

To understand the concept of air pressure, children need experiences with square inches and 15-pound weights. For example, one might display a square inch of colored paper pasted on the middle of a large white sheet of paper, or estimate 15-pound weights—say, of books—and check them on household scales. More striking, perhaps, is calculation of the amount of air pressure on the hand of an average-sized, middle-grade child (about 200 pounds). This can be made graphic by covering the hand with inch squares of paper (representing 15 pounds per square inch) and totaling the squares. Air pressure is equal in all directions—up, down, and sideways—and is balanced by pressure within the hand. We are accustomed to this weight of air, but recognize immediately an additional weight held in the hand, for it is not balanced by pressure within the hand and so must be sustained by an increase in muscular tension and the resistance of tissue.

How total air pressure on the body can be calculated is shown in Chapter 5, p. 84, and Fig. 5-3.

Oxygen-carbon dioxide interchange Respiration is the name not only for the physical act of breathing, but also for the exchange of oxygen and carbon dioxide by the blood cells that takes place as a result of breathing. (The heart and lungs lie close together in the chest cavity behind the tough flexible protection of the ribs. This protected proximity allows for quick exchange of blood between heart and lungs at minimum energy expenditure.)

As shown in Fig. 11-6, inhaled air passes through the trachea into the bronchial tubes, which branch and divide into fine channels called bronchioles (less than $\frac{1}{100}$ inch in diameter) which terminate in little clusters of air sacs. These alveoli are thin-walled structures bounded by an extremely thin layer of flattened cells. Pressed close against this membrane is a tangled mass of thin-walled capillary blood vessels. It is here, through the damp thin cell walls of the alveoli, that oxygen brought into the lungs by breathing diffuses into the blood (whence it is carried to the cells that compose body tissue) and the carbon dioxide, a waste product of body processes, diffuses out of the blood, to be exhaled.

Thus, the heart pumps oxygenated blood throughout the body and pumps carbon dioxide-laden blood into the lungs for aeration. The magnitude of the work done by the heart can be demonstrated as follows. Double up the fists to approximate the size of the heart. Mimic heart action by immersing the fist in water and, by squeezing, squirting water between the thumb and forefinger. Children can note how quickly, at the rate of 60–70 times per minute (80–90 times in children) the hand tires. Point out that the heart works night and day, and that its only rest is in the pause between pulses.

Making the heartbeat, or pulse, visible can be intriguing. To do so, have a child rest one arm on a flat surface. Tape a paperclip (bent as shown in Fig. 11-7) to the wrist. A soda straw slipped over the clip will twitch with each heartbeat when the clip is correctly positioned over the artery near the surface in the wrist. With each beat of the heart, blood is pumped into the arteries, which expand slightly under the pressure of the blood; this action moves the straw. The blood might be likened to a conveyor belt, carrying life-giving oxygen to all tissues and collecting waste, the carbon dioxide which is always an end product of burning. In the "slow burning" inside

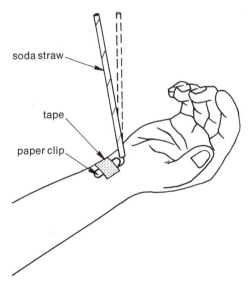

soda straw

tape

paper clip

FIGURE **11-7** Making the heartbeat visible.

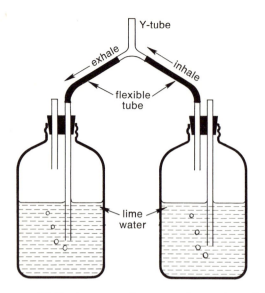

Y-tube

exhale

inhale

flexible tube

lime water

FIGURE **11-8** Apparatus for comparing carbon dioxide content of inhaled and exhaled air.

the body, some oxygen is combined with carbon from food to form carbon dioxide.

To demonstrate the presence of carbon dioxide in exhaled breath, have children blow through straws into $\frac{1}{3}$ tumbler of clear limewater. As described on p. 180, Chapter 10, limewater is an indicator for carbon dioxide, forming a cloudy precipitate when brought into contact with it. (The precipitate, calcium carbonate, is the same chemical compound that makes up most of the body skeleton.) One can also breathe into a clear plastic bag (about fifteen times) containing a glass saucer of limewater to produce the same effect. (Set up a "control" by enclosing another dish of limewater in another bag for ten minutes; compare the presence of precipitate in the dishes.)

One can compare exhaled and inhaled air with an apparatus (Fig. 11-8) made as follows: Insert one long and one short piece of glass or plastic tubing into each of two two-hole stoppers. Insert the stoppers into two flasks containing enough limewater so that the longer tubes extend down into the solution. Using two lengths of rubber tubing, connect one end of a Y-tube to the longer tube in one flask and one end to the shorter tube in the other flask. Squeezing the rubber tubes shut

alternately, inhale through the shorter tube and exhale through the longer. The limewater in the flask through which the exhaled breath has passed will show the presence of carbon dioxide (cloudiness); the liquid in the other bottle (inhaled air) will remain clear. (Instead of a Y-tube, one can use separate tubes, with the subject holding his breath as he moves back and forth.)

Point out that plants give off oxygen and use carbon dioxide during photosynthesis (Chapter 3), while animals do the opposite.

The absorption of oxygen is, of course, effected by its availability. Anyone who normally lives near sea level and travels into the mountains may notice slight symptoms related to lower air pressure and correspondingly lower oxygen content. At 18,000 feet, for example, there are only half as many oxygen molecules per volume as at sea level. At 25,000 feet, a candle flame will go out, and most humans without supplemental oxygen will have "blacked out." To satisfy normal oxygen requirements at 12,000 feet, the breathing rate must be twice what it is at sea level. At 12,000–15,000 feet, there is impairment of vision, hearing, capacity for movement, and ability to think clearly—all a result of lack of oxygen. At 63,000 feet, air pressure is so slight that the body fluids of mammals, if unprotected, would vaporize ("boil"). The resulting sudden distention of the tissues would cause instant death. (These are some of the physiological problems of space travel.)

Filtration Anyone who has watched particles floating in a beam of light is aware of some of the normally invisible burden of air. The non-living particles (soot and dust) are of less concern than the living particles—microbes and their spores. Bacterial counts differ greatly according to environment: an average inhalation of $\frac{1}{3}$ cubic foot of air per minute in high mountains would take in only one microbe about every 20 minutes. In a crowded theater, the average person would inhale about 60,000 microbes per breath. Samplings have shown an average of 50 million microorganisms (not all harmful) in a gram of dust from city streets. In the same amount of indoor dust, samplings yielded about four million bacteria.

Fortunately, the structure of the nasal passages provides a three-way air conditioning system. The nose, the chief filtering organ, does preliminary screening by means of fine inner hairs through which the air must pass. Furthermore, bony shelves divide the nose into a labyrinth of passages. These are lined with tissue full of glands constantly secreting a mucus to which particles passing the first screens adhere. Some special cells in the nasal membranes have fine whiplike projections, called cilia, on their free surface. The continuous lashing of the cilia keep in motion the fluid secretion covering the cell. The trachea, or windpipe, is also covered with cilia and mucus for entrapping any particles that pass the nasal hairs and the sticky nasal passages. The whole nose and windpipe structure also warms and moistens the inhaled air.

Many thousands of times a day (especially in urban areas) one breathes air loaded with dust, soot, bacteria, spores, and other foreign matter. (Smog, which now characterizes many urban areas, is often produced by condensation of moisture in the air on dust particles. Most smog is smoke and hydrocarbons reacting in complex ways. To simulate smog, blow as much air as possible into a gallon jug. Note that there is little or no vapor in the jar, and let the air escape.

Invert the jug and thrust a lighted match into the jug. Again blow into the jar and release the air quickly. A miniature cloud of smog should result.)

Exhaled air contains about 16 % oxygen. Air with only 17 % oxygen can be breathed without a difference being noticed. Exhaled air mixes very quickly with the surrounding air and soon regains its normal 21% oxygen content. Indoors, enough fresh air seeps through the cracks around windows and doors to keep oxygen percentage close to normal, and even poorly ventilated rooms rarely show a drop of more than $\frac{1}{2}$ % in oxygen. It is the difference in the amount of water vapor and odors in indoor or outdoor air that makes one conscious of poor ventilation; a relative humidity of 50–60 % is best for health (see Table 7-1).

The air near the nose and next to the body is the part that affects health. Circulation of air keeps it from forming a layer that contains too little oxygen or too much carbon dioxide. More important, moving air prevents too high a temperature or too much moisture close to the body. The body maintains a constant temperature by evaporation of moisture through the skin; thus, too moist or too hot air interferes with the temperature-regulating function.

SUGGESTED PROJECTS

1. To determine how animals such as hens and earthworms (which lack teeth) pulverize food, have children examine a chicken gizzard.

2. Compare the grinding teeth of herbivores (plant-eaters) and the tearing teeth of carnivores (flesh-eaters) to see the relationship of tooth structure to food habits.

3. Demonstrate emulsification (such as that effected by bile) by shaking fat or oil together with soap solution. Observe how fat globules are surrounded and separated by the emulsifying agent—soap.

4. Although 24 ounces of sugar or 4 pounds of eggs would supply an average daily calorie need, neither

would make an adequate diet. Have children prepare an exhibit or demonstration to explain why.

5. Investigate differences in calorie needs determined by sex and/or occupation.

6. A library can supply the facts for children to dramatize Dr. Lind's discovery of the cure for shipboard scurvy and why British sailors became known as "limeys."

7. Children may report on the need for supplementary vitamins.

8. Show right and wrong ways to cook in order to preserve vitamins.

9. Clarify differences between vitamins and minerals in food by an exhibit of minerals necessary for health—for example, iron, calcium, sodium, potassium, sulfur, magnesium, iodine, and fluorine.

10. To show the importance of soil minerals for *growing* food plants, plant bean or tomato seedlings in soil that has been washed five or six times in hot water to leach out the minerals. Use seedlings in an equal amount of unwashed soil as a control.

11. A school nurse may be willing to talk to a class on various aspects of nutrition.

12. Arrange for a committee of children to visit the school dietitian to inquire into the planning of school lunches.

13. Record some television food commercials and have children evaluate them on the basis of their information on the investigations into the elements of good nutrition.

14. Integrate lessons in science and in decimals and percentages by having children examine labels of vitamin bottles listing contents.

15. Have Red Cross representatives, firemen, policemen, or lifeguards demonstrate new methods of artificial respiration.

16. Children may make an exhibit of underwater breathing apparatus used by skin divers.

17. Planning and collecting articles and pictures on problems of breathing in high-altitude flying or space travel can be useful. An airline may be willing to lend an oxygen mask such as those kept on hand in commercial jet planes.

18. Children may wish to bring in illustrative materials and set up experiments on the principles of air conditioning, especially those aspects related to the cleaning and filtration of air for use in emergencies, when cabin pressure drops.

BIBLIOGRAPHY

(**P** indicates recommended for primary grades, **I** for intermediate grades, **U** for upper grades.)

Banks, Marjorie A., *How We Get Our Dairy Foods,* Benefic, 1963. A simple, factual introduction, well-illustrated with photographs. **P**

Brooks, Anita, *The Picture Book of Salt,* Day, 1964. What salt is, where it is found, how it is mined, and its importance to men and animals; informative photographs. **U**

Callahan, Dorothy, and Alma S. Payne, *The Great Nutrition Puzzle,* Scribners, 1956. Techniques and experiments for discovering facts about food and nutrition. **U**

Carlson, A. J., and V. E. Johnson, *Machinery of the Body,* University of Chicago, 1953. Most complete reference for teacher with some science background.

Cosgrove, Margaret, *The Wonders Inside You,* Dodd, Mead, 1955. Excellent presentation of human anatomy. Very useful index. **I**

Elgin, Kathleen, *Read About the Hand,* Watts, 1968. Description of bones, muscles, nerves, and blood vessels working together to enable the hand to function. **I**

Epstein, Samuel and Beryl, *The First Book of the World Health Organization,* Watts, 1964. Brief explanations of providing mass medical attention for large populations in backward countries, and how people are taught principles of sanitation and nutrition. **U**

Fenton, Carroll, and E. T. Turner, *Inside You and Me,* Day, 1961. Introduction to the human body. **I**

Georgiou, Constantine, *Whitey and Whiskers and Food,* Harvey, 1964. Presents an experiment to study the effect of diet on two white mice. Step-by-step description of how to build cages, make charts and graphs, and record results. **I**

Glemser, Bernard, *All About the Human Body,* Random, 1958. Meaningful descriptions of body structure and function. **I**

Goldin, Augusta, *Salt,* Crowell, 1965. Introduction to salt—description of chemical makeup, sources, use in food and as a preservative. **I**

Hammond, Winifred, *Plants, Food, and People,* Coward, 1964. Covers the hunter-gatherer people, the four main plant foods of the world—rice, wheat, corn, and cassava—and future uses of plants in space travel; photographs and thorough index. **U**

Hinshaw, Alice, *The True book of Your Body and You*, Children's Pr., 1959. Beginning biology; discussions of bones, muscles, brains, nerves, skin, eyes, ears, noses, the digestive system, blood, heart, and lungs. **I**

Lewis, Alfred, *The New World of Food*, Dodd, Mead, 1968. Food production and processing, with emphasis on the need for developing more and better sources; good photographs. **U**

Novikoff, Alex, *From Head to Foot*, International, 1946. First-rate presentation of functional physiology. Vivid diagrams. **U**

Parish, Peggy, *The Story of Grains: Wheat, Corn, Rice*, Merrill, 1965. Brief introduction to grain from its early use to its present importance. **I**

Ravielli, Anthony, *Wonders of the Human Body*, Viking, 1954. Simple, clear anatomy book. **I**

Schneider, Herman and Nina, *How Your Body Works*, W. R. Scott, 1949. Imparts a sense of wonder for our amazing body machinery. **U**

Schneider, Leo, *Lifeline: The Story of Your Circulatory System*, Harcourt, 1958. Story of blood function and circulation. **I**

Selsam, Millicent, *How Animals Eat*, W. R. Scott, 1955. Simple explanation of food chains in nature. **I**

Showers, Paul, *Follow Your Nose*, Crowell, 1963. The process of smelling and other functions of the nose. Amusing, instructive illustrations. **P**

———, *Hear Your Heart*, Crowell, 1968. Describes shape and size of heart, heart beats of persons of different ages, function and operation of veins and arteries.

Uhl, John Melvin, *About Grasses, Grains and Canes*, Melmont, 1964. Description of the grass family and food plants, their economic value and geographical distribution. **I**

Weart, Edith, *The Story of Your Respiratory System*, Coward-McCann, 1964. The nature and function of the respiratory system, especially the lungs and the nose. Clear illustrations and diagrams. **U**

White, Anne Terry, *Windows on the World*, Garrard, 1965. Describes man's five senses and shows how they are able to interpret stimuli, and how the use of communication media helps to extend them; drawings and charts, most in color. **U**

Zim, Herbert, *Our Senses and How They Work*, Morrow, 1956. Clear text and illustrations explain senses and sense perception, and combinations of senses. **U**

———, *Your Food and You*, Morrow, 1957. Function of food and digestion. **I**

12 Fibers and Cloth

Most cloth is made of fibers woven or intertwined in some way. The kind of fiber and the way in which it is intertwined determine the character of the resulting cloth.

KINDS OF FIBERS

Children can help collect a wide variety of fabrics, including swatches and thread. Individual threads for comparison can also be obtained by separating them from the various swatches.

Classify the fabrics into three main categories: those made from plant fibers, from animal fibers, and from synthetic fibers. It may be useful to have children learn where the fibers come from and how they are woven into cloth.

Plant Fibers

Cotton is the most widely used plant fiber. Cotton fibers are the hairs found on the seeds of the cotton plant. If possible, obtain a cotton boll on its stem. Examined under a microscope, the cotton fibers (use a few strands of absorbent cotton) will look like a flattened, irregular, twisted ribbon (Fig. 12-1). Many high school chemistry and physical science textbooks (and books on identifying textiles) have excellent pictures of fibers as seen through a microscope.

Cloths made from cotton are cheesecloth, organdy, chintz, gingham, crinoline, muslin, percale, calico, velveteen, seersucker, some poplin, sailcloth, and canvas. Most cotton thread has been treated to make it smooth and lustrous; this is done by stretching the cotton and immersing it in a concentrated solution of cold sodium hydroxide (lye). Cotton treated in this manner is said to be mercerized.

Another common plant fiber is linen, which comes from the flax plant. This fiber is long, lustrous, and smooth. Under the microscope it looks like bamboo cane, with jointed cells and split, tapered ends (Fig. 12-1). Point out that linen is often used to make handkerchiefs, tablecloths, napkins, summer clothing, and blouses.

Jute and hemp, other plant fibers (Fig. 12-1), are not as fine as cotton and linen, and are used to make carpet backing, rope, twine, and sacks.

Animal Fibers

Wool is the most commonly used animal fiber. The fiber is obtained from the soft, hairy covering of sheep and sometimes goats. Under the microscope, the wool fiber looks like a long cylinder with scales on it (Fig. 12-1). The fiber is very curly and springy. Cloth made from wool includes cashmere, camel's hair, alpaca, covert cloth, flannel, gabardine, mohair, serge, tweed, and worsted.

Silk, another common animal fiber, was once quite popular, but has been replaced to a great extent by such synthetic fibers as Nylon, Orlon, and Dacron. Silk is made by the mulberry silkworm when spinning its cocoon. Under the microscope the silk fiber appears as a thin, long, smooth, and lustrous cylinder (Fig. 12-1). Cloths made from silk include brocade, brocatelle, chiffon, crepe, velvet, crepe de Chine, foulard, lamé, moiré, satin, taffeta, tulle, and faille.

Synthetic and Other Fibers

Rayon is one of the first successful artificial fibers. It is made from cellulose. When manufactured, the rayon fibers resemble silk. Under the microscope, the rayon fiber looks like a smooth, lustrous cylinder (Fig. 12-1). Rayon can be made into cloth that is hard to distinguish from silk, cotton, linen, or wool. Celanese is one form of rayon.

Today there is a wide variety of synthetic fibers; all have trade names such as Nylon, Orlon,

Dacron, Vinyon, Aralac, Acrilan, Velon, Dynel, Banlon, and Lycra. Like rayon, these fibers resemble silk, and under the microscope look like smooth, lustrous cylinders. Synthetic fibers are easily identified because of their uniform thickness. (The thickness of natural fibers varies.) Synthetic fibers are made into fabrics that have special properties, taken up later in the chapter.

Glass and asbestos can also be spun into thread and woven into fabrics. Glass fibers are made by stretching melted glass into fine filaments, which are spun into thread for weaving into cloth. Lightweight glass fibers are used to make long-lasting window curtains, drapes, and lamp shades. Heavier glass fabrics are used to make fireproof theater and school curtains.

Asbestos, which is a rock that is fibrous in structure, is shredded to make asbestos fibers. These fibers can then be spun and woven to make asbestos cloth. Asbestos cloth is used in fireproof theater curtains and protective suits for use by fire fighters.

IDENTIFYING FIBERS

Not long ago, most fabrics were made of wool, cotton, linen, or silk. It was easy to identify them just by feeling and looking. Today a wide variety of synthetic fibers has appeared on the market, and manufacturers have learned how to combine many fibers in making a single fabric, making it difficult to analyze completely or identify all fabrics. However, there are some simple tests which help greatly in distinguishing fabrics, the most common being the burning test and chemical tests.

The Burning Test

For the burning test, use both a strip of fabric (about 2 inches wide) and individual threads long enough so that one end can be touched to a match flame while the other may be held comfortably without burning one's fingers. (Obtain individual threads by pulling both from the warp—the lengthwise threads—and from the filling—or woof—of the fabric.)

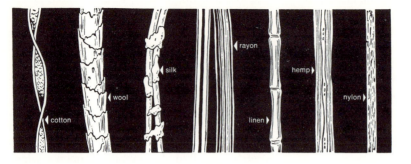

FIGURE **12-1** Fibers greatly magnified.

Apply a match flame to each sample of fabric and carefully note the appearance of the burning, the odor given off, and the size and nature of the ash. It may be helpful to test the thread first and then confirm the test with the strip of cloth. The individual threads may give some idea of the mixtures of fibers used.

Cotton and linen Pure, untreated cotton or linen burns with a large flame and leaves almost no ash. The odor, if any, is quite similar to that of burning paper. After the flame goes out, a glowing spark may continue to travel through the unburnt material.

Cottons treated to give them a special finish will burn with a much smaller flame, seeming to char rather than burn completely. The ash retains the shape of the original material.

Wool Wool will either smoulder or burn with a very tiny flame. However, the odor of burnt hair or feathers is unmistakable. A gummy, beady, coke-like ash accumulates and forms balls along the edge of the burning portion. Wool leaves much more ash than cotton or linen.

Silk Pure, untreated silk also burns slowly and with a tiny flame. Its characteristic odor is also of burnt hair or feathers. The ash is black and shiny and, along the edge of the fabric, forms into tiny brittle balls that crush easily when pressed between thumb and forefinger.

Often silk is weighted (stiffened) by soaking in a solution of mineral (metallic) salt, usually a tin compound. Weighting the silk gives the pure silk more "body" and also makes it easier to dye. Weighted silk will char, not burn, and leave a black ash that has the same shape as the original cloth.

Synthetics All types of rayon are made from cellulose and, like cotton and linen, will burn with a large flame. However, the ash will vary, depending on the kind of rayon. Viscose rayon and cuprammonium rayon, if unweighted, will burn, like cotton, with a large flame and leave little or no ash. Acetate rayon burns with a large flame and gives off an odor like burning punk. It melts as it burns and leaves an ash very much like silk—black and shiny and forming tiny balls. However, these balls of ash become quite hard when cool and cannot be crushed easily between the thumb and forefinger.

Although Nylon and other synthetic fibers do not burn, some of the dyes and finishes used may. Usually Nylon fibers melt, leaving a brown mass at the edge of the material. In some cases, there is a characteristic odor unlike that of any other fiber. Since all synthetic fibers react the same way to flame, the burning test can serve to identify them only as a group, not individually.

Chemical Tests

When identifying fibers by chemical tests, use very small pieces of fabric. Necessary chemicals may be available from high school chemistry teachers (who can also help with the solutions) or from scientific supply houses or druggists. When working with chemicals, especially acids and bases, *take care not to spill them on your person or clothes. Should this happen, quickly wash with plenty of water.*

With sodium hydroxide Using a Pyrex container, make a dilute solution of sodium hydroxide by dissolving 2 teaspoons of lye in a pint of cold water. (*Caution: Use care in adding lye to water.*) Boil the solution *gently,* using a gas stove, electric stove, or a hot plate. With forceps, drop a cloth sample into the boiling solution and boil gently for about ten minutes. Animal fibers, such as wool and silk, will dissolve; all other fibers will not. With cloth that is a mixture of wool and cotton, the wool will dissolve, leaving the undissolved cotton behind. Thus this is also a test to determine whether material is pure wool. One may also weigh the cloth sample before putting it into the lye solution. After ten minutes remove what is left, using a forceps, wash the remnant in running water, and put it on a blotter or other absorbent material. Let the remnant dry completely, and then weigh it. From the difference between the two weights it is possible to calculate the percentage of wool and other material in the fabric.

With hydrochloric acid Using caution, pour cold concentrated hydrochloric acid into a small beaker or glass tumbler. (*Never never pour water into acid; always pour the acid into water.*) Put very small pieces of fabric, or just fibers, into the acid. Use a glass rod or swizzle stick to stir the fabric or fibers in the acid. Silk will dissolve in the hydrochloric acid. Rayon will also dissolve, but very, very slowly. Wool fibers will swell, but will not be destroyed. Cotton and linen are unaffected by the acid. Nylon is weakened and becomes brittle, but Orlon is not affected.

(To dispose of the acid, slowly pour it into a large container of water. Then pour the mixture down the sink or drain, letting the water run for some time to protect the plumbing from the corrosive action of the acid.)

With sulfuric acid Pour some of a 2 % solution of sulfuric acid into a small beaker or glass tumbler. Stir the solution with a glass rod or swizzle stick. Put a drop or two of the solution on the pieces of fabric to be tested. Animal fibers will be unaffected, plant fibers will char, Nylon will become slightly brittle, and Orlon will be unaffected.

To test if a sample of fabric is a mixture of wool and cotton, put two drops of the sulfuric acid solution on the sample. Allow the acid to penetrate, then place the fabric between two sheets of paper and press with a hot iron. If the material contains cotton, a charred spot will appear where the acid was dropped. Rub the charred spot gently between thumb and forefinger; it will fall away, leaving the unaffected wool behind.

With indicator paper Place a small piece of a fabric in two test tubes. Push the fabric to the bottom of the test tube with a glass rod, swizzle stick, or pencil. Place a piece of moistened red litmus paper across the top of one test tube. Across the top of the second test tube place a piece of moistened lead acetate paper. (*Dry lead acetate is highly flammable by spontaneous combustion. It must always be kept in a water solution.*) If prepared lead acetate paper is not available, cut narrow strips of filter paper and dip them in lead acetate solution. Heat both test tubes. Cotton, linen, rayon, and synthetic fibers do not give off fumes that affect these papers. Wool or silk give off ammonia vapor, which turns the red litmus paper blue. In addition, wool gives off sulfide vapors which turn the colorless lead acetate paper black or brownish black.

With ink Linen, hard to distinguish from cotton, especially if the cotton has been treated, can be distinguished with ink. To do so, wash and thoroughly dry a piece of linen and a piece of cotton. Place a drop of ink on each sample. In the linen sample, the ink will be absorbed quickly in an even circle; in the cotton the ink will be absorbed irregularly and not so quickly.

With other substances A drop of olive oil or glycerin on fresh, dry, clean samples of linen and cotton will make a translucent spot on the linen; the cotton remains opaque.

Acetate rayon will dissolve in acetone, chloroform, and to some extent, in alcohol. No other rayons or other fibers will dissolve in these reagents.

Chlorine bleaches will destroy animal fibers but will not affect plant fibers. Bleaches that do not contain chlorine, such as hydrogen peroxide, must be used for animal fibers. Chlorine bleaches weaken Nylon, but do not affect Orlon.

PROPERTIES OF FIBERS

Wear Resistance

Wear resistance of fabrics may be tested with a small electric motor and an abrasive wheel, both available in hardware stores and hobby shops. A pupil may be able to provide a small motor from a motor-operated toy. If the motor is not equipped to accommodate the shaft of the abrasive (or grinding) wheel, drill a hole longitudinally in a wood dowel or length of broomstick about 1 inch long. The diameter of the hole should be slightly smaller than the diameter of the shaft on the motor. Force the motor shaft firmly into the hole in the dowel (Fig. 12-2). Cement a strip of fine sandpaper or crocus cloth (No. 400 or 600 available at hardware stores) around the dowel. The crocus cloth contains very finely powdered emery, which is an excellent abrasive.

Sew a very small hem at the top and bottom of strips of different fabrics—each about 7 × 2 inches and of about the same thickness. Clamp a pine board about 24 × 6 × $\frac{3}{4}$ inches to the edge of a table, or rest the board on the backs of two

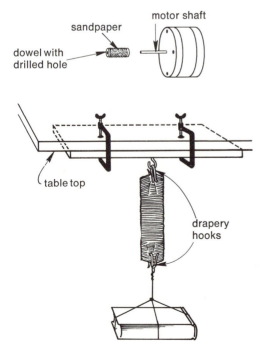

FIGURE **12-2** Testing fabrics for resistance to wear.

chairs placed back-to-back a few feet apart. Screw a cup hook into the underside of the board. Slide one of two large drapery hooks in at the top of one length of fabric and suspend it from the cup hook. Slide the other hook in at the bottom of the length of fabric and suspend one or two books from it on a string.

With the motor running, hold the sandpaper wheel against the taut cloth. Note how long it takes to wear a hole in the cloth. Repeat the experiment with the other cloth samples and note how long it takes for each to wear out. Make a list of the fabrics in the order of their resistance to wear.

Dry and Wet Strength

Sew small hems at the top and bottom of samples of fabrics about 7 × 3 inches and of about the same thickness. Clamp a piece of pine board about 24 × 6 × $\frac{3}{4}$ inches to the edge of a table, or rest the board on the backs of two chairs. Attach the top hem of the cloth to the underside of the board by means of a row of tacks (Fig. 12-3). Push a drapery hook through the cloth just above the bottom hem, and slip the handle of a small bucket or pail over the other end of the drapery hook. Then add weights to the bucket until the fabric rips. The weight of the bucket plus the sum of the weights inside the bucket will indicate the strength of the dry fabric. Repeat the experiment with the other cloth samples.

Synthetic fabrics like Nylon, Orlon, and Dacron are the strongest. Cotton and silk are next, followed by the rayons and finally wool.

When the dry strength of the fabrics is known, repeat the experiment using the same materials when wet. Cotton is the only material that becomes stronger when wet. Saran loses no strength, silk, wool, Nylon, Orlon, and Dacron lose strength slightly, and all the rayons become much weaker.

Water-absorption

Cut samples of fabrics of equal size (about 6 inches square) and of about the same thickness.

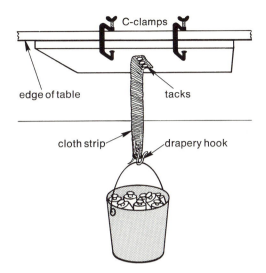

FIGURE **12-3** Testing fabrics for wet and dry strength.

Fill a number of identical glass tumblers with water to the same level. Iron each sample flat, then, with forceps or tweezers, dip each into a tumbler of water for at least a minute. Then lift the cloth from the glass, let any excess water drip back into the tumbler, and hang each cloth to dry on a cord or clothesline. Note how much water each cloth sample soaks up and how long each sample takes to dry.

Wool will absorb the most moisture. Pure rayon, silk, acetate rayon, linen, and cotton are next. (All absorb about the same amount.) Nylon will absorb little water, and Orlon even less. Dacron will absorb almost none.

Note the smoothness of each sample after it has dried. Have children note that some materials shrink. Wet them again and try stretching them, this time while they are wet. Some materials will stretch under these circumstances.

CLOTH

Children can understand that since clothing helps our bodies adjust to changes in the weather and climate and protects us in inclement weather, the kind and amount of clothing we wear depend, to a large extent, on the seasons and on the climate in which we live. The ability of clothing to mitigate extremes of temperature is determined by many factors involving the cloth of which it is made.

The Fibers and Weave

Cloth made of wool is one of the best for cold weather. Examine some wool fibers again (with a microscope) as well as a woolen sweater. Children can note the air spaces between the wool fibers, called "dead" air spaces because air trapped in them cannot circulate. This lack of circulation gives good heat protection by preventing body heat from escaping to the surrounding air. The fur lining of a glove displays similar air spaces between the hairs. Rock wool (Chapter 13) is an excellent insulating material in buildings because it is fluffy and has many air spaces.

The nature of the weave of the fabric is another important factor. In the summer, loose open weaves are desirable since comfort depends on air circulating freely through the garment, which allows perspiration to evaporate faster. The quicker the perspiration evaporates, the cooler one feels.

Chapter 6 includes many demonstrations of evaporation and its effects; a few of those more readily performed are as follows. Let two identical bottles of alcohol and of water stand overnight so that they both reach the same temperature. Put a drop of water from the bottle on the back of a child's hand. The drop will evaporate and the hand will feel cooler. Then simultaneously put one drop of water on the back of one hand and one drop of alcohol on the back of the other. The alcohol will evaporate more quickly than the water, and the hand with alcohol will feel cooler. Point out that heat is needed to do the work of evaporation. This heat comes from the surface from which the liquid is evaporated, and that is why the hands felt cooler. Because alcohol evaporates faster, it takes heat from the surface of the hand faster, thereby producing a greater cooling effect.

Children may recall that when swimming they

feel cool or even cold (especially on a windy day) when they come out of the water: The evaporation of the droplets of water on the skin results in rapid cooling. Therefore, the more open the weave of a fabric, the better the circulation and the better the opportunity for fast evaporation of perspiration.

Children may recall the warmth of leather garments and gloves. Leather has tiny pores, so tiny that the spaces even in very tightly woven material seem like huge holes by comparison. Thus air can penetrate leather only very little. A combination of leather (on the outside) and wool or fur is about the warmest combination possible. Eskimo clothing reflects this fact.

The fit of a garment is also, of course, a factor in keeping comfortable. In the summer, loose clothes allow free air circulation to evaporate perspiration. In the winter, a tighter (but not too tight) fit is more desirable. Actually the tightest fit should be around the neck and extremities to prevent heat from escaping. A small layer of still air trapped between the skin and clothing, helps conserve body heat.

Weight

Another factor is the weight of the fabric. The heavier the fabric, the more layers of fiber and thus the greater the amount of dead-air spaces to prevent body heat from escaping. Thus, we wear heavy clothes in cold, and light clothes in warm, weather.

Color

The color of cloth (as of any material) makes a difference too. Many experiments (Chapter 13) can show that the darker the material, the more radiated or radiant heat it absorbs, and the hotter the material becomes. Point out that the sun radiates heat, too. Identical thermometers, the bulb of one wrapped in black cloth, and the other in white cloth (both of the same material) will show different readings if placed in the direct sunlight and read at 10-minute intervals for a half hour. The thermometer under the black cloth will show a greater rise in temperature; thus, light clothes are preferred in the summer.

SUGGESTED PROJECTS

1. Have children try to identify different samples of cloth as well as the material in their garments. Lead into the study of different kinds of fibers.

2. Children can make a list of articles in the home that are made of synthetic fibers. Lead into the study of the various fibers, natural and synthetic, and their different properties.

3. Children may enjoy removing stains from various materials. The U.S. Department of Agriculture offers a simple yet comprehensive booklet on the subject:

Stain Removal from Fabrics, Home Methods, Farmers Bulletin No. 1474, 1942.

4. Make a list of clothing worn in the summer and winter. Include such things as open-toed shoes in the winter and furs in the summer. Discuss whether the selection is based on fashion or common sense.

5. Discuss the kinds of clothing worn in different seasons of the year. Compare the value of different materials for keeping comfortable in warm and cold weather.

BIBLIOGRAPHY

(**P** indicates recommended for primary grades, **I** for intermediate grades, **U** for upper grades.)

Adler, Irving, and Ruth, *Fibers*, Day, 1964. Concise account of natural and man-made fibers, with the sources and processing briefly described; drawings and simple diagrams. **I**

Ahrens, Maurice R., et al. *Living Chemistry*, Ginn, 2nd rev. ed., 1961. Excellent chapter for teacher reference on fibers and clothing. Includes tests for identification of fibers. **U**

Allen, Agnes, *The Story of Clothes*, Roy, 1958.

Buehr, Walter, *Cloth: From Fiber to Fabric*, Morrow, 1965. The history of cloth from the earliest crude loom to a modern fabric mill with all the processes and machinery involved. The part cloth has played in economy and politics is told. **U**

Cavanna, Betty, and G. R. Harrison, *The First Book of Wool*, Watts, 1966. The history and uses of wool, and the processes of growing, spinning, and weaving it. Photographs on each page. **U**

Cooper, Elizabeth, *Silkworms and Science, the Story of Silk*, Harcourt, 1961. A history of silk production, a description of the life of the silkworm, information about mulberry trees, and complete directions for growing the worms and obtaining silk. **U**

Lazarus, Harry, *Let's Go To a Clothing Factory*, Putnam, 1961. Clear, accurate description of a boys'-shirt factory. Well-illustrated. **I**

Nighbert, Esther, *The True Book of Cloth*, Children's Pr., 1955. The sources and manufacture of wool, cotton, linen, silk, and the new synthetic fabrics simply described. **P**

Petersham, Maud and Miska, *Let's Learn About Silk*, Harvey, 1967. A brief description of the making of silk, with a history of the silk industry. Maps and diagrams. **I**

Shannon, Terry, *About Ready-to-Wear Clothes*, Melmont, 1961. History of and current methods used in the garment trades. Discussions of designing, pattern-making, cutting, stitching, and finishing are included. **I**

Wormser, Sophie, *About Silkworms and Silk*, Melmont, 1961. A classroom situation is used to describe how to hatch and raise silkworms. Also covers the manufacture of silk and the silk industry. An artificial situation well handled. **I**

Carpenter at work on the roof and roof supports of a frame building.

13 *Housing*

The kind of shelter common to a region is generally related to its climate, and, even with the tendency toward standardization in the world today, the relationship may still be seen.

VARIETIES OF SHELTER

In Hot, Dry Climates

In the desert, nomads, who must carry their homes with them, use lightweight tents made of cloth or material woven from goat and camel hair. These tents provide shelter from the hot sun and from sandstorms. Because of the heat of the desert, one side of the tent is kept open to provide circulation of air; there may also be a top open-

ing. In other arid lands (such as Mexico) adobe houses are used. Adobe blocks are made of clay mixed with straw to hold the clay together, baked dry in the sun. The thick adobe walls help keep out the sun's heat. In the Congo, grass huts are used. These huts look like inverted bowls and are covered from top to bottom with long grass or fibers obtained from the bamboo plant, coconut palm, and so on. A grass hut is the coolest kind of home, providing protection from the sun's rays and excellent circulation of air.

In Hot, Wet Climates

In hot, wet lands grass huts are also used, but are placed on long poles and stilts or are built in trees. This type of home not only provides a suitable and cool shelter but also protects the occupants from damp or muddy ground, floods, and predatory animals.

In Cold Climates

Two types of homes are generally used in cold lands. In the very far north, the Eskimos build snow houses, called igloos, for shelter during the winter. The igloo is a round hut with an entrance tunnel made of blocks of snow. The tunnel limits the cold wind entering the igloo. In the summer, Eskimos use tents made of animal skins. Farther south, Eskimos and Indians live in houses made of earth, which are built half under and half above the ground. A house is generally warmer if part of it is underground.

In Temperate Climates

Houses in the United States are more or less representative of those in most regions that have a temperate climate. Those in farm areas are usually one- and two-story wood frame houses, with brick or stone chimneys. A wood barn, much larger than the house, stands nearby.

In the cities and suburbs, there may be single buildings containing one and two stories or apartment buildings containing many stories. The houses may be made of stone, brick, wood, or combinations of these three. Many different materials are used in building these homes, including concrete, stucco, tile, marble, glass, metal, plastics, etc.

THE PARTS OF A HOUSE

If a house or other building is being constructed nearby, have the class observe the process. Revisit the site at each important phase of construction. A local building contractor can also be quite helpful if he is willing to visit the class and describe the building of a house. He may also be able to provide samples of material, pictures, and booklets on the subject. Children may be able to report to the class about new houses being erected in their neighborhoods.

The Foundation

Most children will know that a building begins with the foundation. A firm foundation is necessary to support the heavy load of a house and its contents. For most conventional buildings, a deep hole is dug which will serve as a future basement. The floor and walls of the basement are lined with any one of many materials, concrete being the most commonly used because it is sturdy and economical. Concrete is made by mixing cement, sand, gravel, and water. The cement, which binds the other ingredients together, is itself a mixture of limestone and clay, baked until it forms a hard mass. This mass is ground into a fine powder. Children will note how workmen mix the concrete and then pour it into wooden forms in which it hardens. After it has hardened, the forms are removed.

A heavy wood sill usually completes the foundation. This sill is placed in soft mortar on top of the concrete basement walls and then bolted to them so that it cannot shift. It must be set absolutely level because it is the basis for the entire framework of the house.

Another material used for foundations is concrete blocks. These usually have spaces that reduce the weight and the amount of concrete needed. (These spaces also somewhat reduce the supporting strength of the blocks.) Other materials for basement walls are natural stone, hollow tile blocks, and bricks. Bricks and tile are made of baked clay. Where the foundation must support a very large framework, steel beams are used for additional support. These beams are usually called I-beams because of the shape of their cross sections.

When the basement of a house is to be used for living, asphalt, vinyl, or rubber tile is usually laid over the concrete base. A hardware or department store or a contractor may have samples of tile used for this purpose.

Many houses are built with a slab foundation instead of a basement. To do this, the earth is leveled, the outline of the slab is laid out with boards or other kinds of formwork to retain the concrete, which is poured directly onto the ground. Since there is no basement, the furnace, hot-water heater, and laundry equipment are put into a utility room, usually located next to the kitchen.

Framework and Walls

Once the foundation is in, a skeleton, or "framework," is put up. This consists of long pieces of wood "two by fours," so called because they measure roughly 2 inches by 4 inches. For large buildings, steel beams or girders are used as framework.

When the framework is up, it is covered with an outer and an inner wall. In wooden buildings, this consists of first a layer of boards—sheathing—nailed to the two by fours. (Sometimes the sheathing is made of synthetic materials.) A layer of heavy building paper is laid over the sheathing to prevent the air from passing between the boards or through any knotholes. The third layer is the one visible on the outside of the completed building and is called "siding." It usually consists of long, narrow boards laid so they overlap. This overlapping helps make the house weathertight. Sometimes wood or aluminum siding or asbestos shingles are used as an outer layer. Brick is also quite popular. The bricks are held together by mortar, a mixture of lime, cement, sand, and water. The mortar also helps make the brick wall weathertight and water-resistant. Natural and artificial stones are often used too. In many cities, especially in warm climates, stucco is used as an outside wall. Some stucco is made of cement and sand, while other kinds are made of lime and sand. Made up into a thick paste with water, the stucco is daubed onto a wire mesh fastened to the framework of the house, where it dries to form a hard, thick layer. Stucco can be any color. Terra cotta, an ornamental wall material, is made of baked clay. Also used in wall-building are translucent-glass bricks, each made from two glass boxes sealed together to form a hollow block. Some of the air is withdrawn from the enclosed space to augment the insulating qualities of the block.

The most common type of inside wall is made of plaster applied to stiff wire mesh nailed to the two by fours: first a rough coat (lime, sand, a little cement, and water), than a final coat (chiefly plaster of Paris and water, with a little lime). The finished plaster is painted or papered.

Plasterboard, a sandwich of cardboard with a plaster filling, is often used for interior walls. Plywood, used for both floors and walls, is made of thin sheets of wood fused with resins under extreme pressure and heat. The layers of wood are called plies. Collect samples of plywood and have children count the number of plies. The most common number is three, but plywood with five and seven plies is readily available.

In some homes, panels and veneers of costlier wood (mahogany, for example) are used as inside walls. Glass blocks may serve as an inside wall too.

Floors

The best floors are made of two layers: a poor-grade lumber and a top-grade hardwood lumber placed over that. The latter is "tongue and groove" (a ridge on one piece fits into a groove in the next) to make a tight joint. Usually long lengths of oak are used, but less costly pine is also popular. In some homes, the top layer consists of small pieces of wood set in a mosaic pattern, called parquet. Some homes have marble floors.

Quite common in kitchens and bathrooms are floors covered with asphalt, rubber, composition, or ceramic tile.

The Roof

The framework for roofs is usually made of two by sixes. On top of these go a sheathing similar to that used for the outside walls of the house, then the water-resistant part of the roof. High-cost roofing materials include slate, clay tile, and such metals as aluminum, copper, and lead. These last indefinitely and need little or no repair. Me-

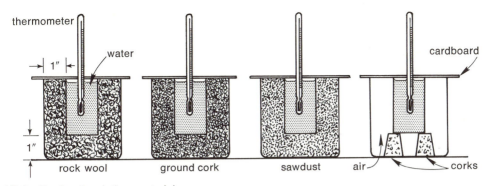

FIGURE **13-1**   Testing insulating materials.

dium-cost materials include asbestos shingles, cement tile, and metal tile. These need occasional repair. Low-priced materials include wood shingles, asphalt shingles, galvanized iron (iron coated with zinc), and tar paper. These need frequent replacement, repair, and/or painting.

Fixtures

Steel is used for nails, bolts, hinges, screws, and locks. Gutters and rain spouts are made of aluminum, copper, or galvanized iron. Bronze, an alloy of copper and tin, is often used for special door knobs, locks, and hinges. Cast iron, lead, copper, and brass are used in plumbing. Heating systems are usually made of cast iron, steel, or sheet metal. Plumbing fixtures may be chromium-plated, nickel-plated, or iron.

CONTROLLING INTERIOR ENVIRONMENT

Insulation

For home comfort and economy, it is quite important to prevent heat from escaping in the winter and to keep it out in the summer. There is heat loss around doors and windows of homes. Children can feel cold air coming in by placing their hands near the bottoms of exterior doors. This loss can be overcome by filling cracks around the frames of windows and doors with a putty-like material such as calking compound. Cracks between the frames and door or window sashes

can be closed by using weather stripping made of felt or thin springy metal. In cold climates, storm windows help reduce the loss of heat because the air space between them and the regular window is a poor heat conductor—that is, a good insulator. Storm doors work the same way.

The chief heat passage is through the walls and roof. Therefore, it is both wise and economical to insulate a newly built house. "Rock wool" is an excellent insulator. Being fluffy, it forms many small air spaces in which the air cannot move ("dead air"), thus limiting the conduction of heat. Rock wool, a mixture of stone and slag, is made into large, thick mats or "batts" that are laid over an attic floor and fastened into exterior walls when the house is being built. For older houses built without insulation, rock wool can be blown into hollow spaces between the outer and inner surfaces of exterior walls. Other materials used for insulation are mica, cork pellets, and rock wool pellets. Sometimes wallboard or mortarboard is used as an insulator.

Needed to demonstrate the different insulating capacities of various materials are four large tin cans of the same size and four smaller tin cans of the same size. The smaller cans should fit inside the larger with at least 1 inch of space at the bottom and around the sides. Obtain rock wool and sawdust from a hardware store or lumber yard, and ground cork from food stores (grapes and other fragile fruit usually come packed in ground cork).

As shown in Fig. 13-1, place the four smaller cans inside the larger, packing the rock wool around and under one, and the ground cork and sawdust in the same manner around each of two other cans. For the fourth can, place two corks about 1 inch high on the bottom of the larger can and rest the smaller on them. (This will provide an air space around and under the small can.)

In the center of each of four squares of heavy cardboard large enough to cover the larger tin cans, make a hole just large enough to accommodate a thermometer. Pour boiling water into each inner can until each is almost full, making sure all the cans are filled to the same height. Cover each can with a cardboard cover containing a thermometer. Have children note the temperature of the water in each can every few minutes. List the cans according to their rate of cooling, putting the slowest to cool on top and the quickest at the bottom. Children should realize that the material in which the water cooled slowest is the best insulator—a substance that is a poor conductor of heat.

Insulation has one major disadvantage. Moist air—that is, air containing water vapor—gets into the insulating material and, when temperature changes occur, the water vapor condenses into water, which causes decay in the walls and spoils plaster, wall paper, and paint.

Thin sheets of bright metal (foil) such as aluminum are also used as insulation. This thin sheet

of metal is put on the surface of some fiberboard or wallboard material, or even on paper. The bright metal surface reflects the radiant heat waves and thus prevents them from passing through the walls, ceilings, or roof.

A simple experiment will demonstrate this graphically. Cut two small holes at diagonally opposite corners of a heavy rectangular cardboard box (Fig. 13-2) large enough to accommodate a 60-watt bulb and leave about 2 inches on each side. Cut a window in two opposite sides of the box. Obtain two small panes of glass, slightly larger than the windows. Cut a piece of aluminum foil to the same size as a glass pane and glue it to one pane at the edges. Make sure the aluminum is pressed close to the pane and is quite smooth. Attach both panes of glass to the windows, using glue, cellophane tape, or rubber bands. The pane covered with the aluminum should have the aluminum on the outside, away from the bulb.

Using the hot paraffin from a burning candle, attach a long tack to the outside surface of each pane. Place the box over a 60-watt bulb (cut out one side if necessary), turn on the current, and note which tack falls off first. Also touch each outside surface to see which is hotter. The pane with the aluminum foil reflects the radiated heat of the bulb and is therefore cooler. As a variation, prepare two panes of glass as before, attach the tacks, and place the panes of glass equidistant from and on either side of a candle or light bulb. The tacks should be pointing away from the heat source. The panes of glass can be held upright by inserting them between books lying flat on a table.

Color

The different reflectivity of different colors can play a part in controlling the temperature in a building. To demonstrate how, blacken with flat paint one half of a can inside and out; leave the other half shiny. With the paraffin from a burning candle, fasten two long tacks to the outside of the can, one in the center of the blackened portion, the other directly opposite in the center of

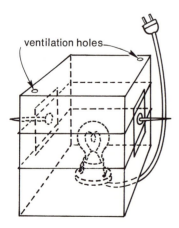

FIGURE **13-2** Apparatus to demonstrate that bright, shiny metal is a good insulator.

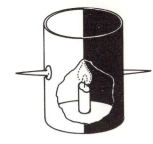

FIGURE **13-3** Demonstrating that dark, dull surfaces absorb heat better than shiny, smooth surfaces.

the shiny portion (Fig. 13-3). Put a lighted candle inside the can at the center of the base of the can. Have children note which tack falls off first. By touching with your finger tips, also test which surface—the shiny or the black—becomes hotter. The phenomenon can be shown, too, with the tops of two tin cans of equal size. Blacken both sides of one of the tops with flat paint and leave the other shiny. Using spring-type clothespins as holders or forceps, hold both tops equally close to a 100-watt lighted bulb or directly in the bright sun's rays. After a while, note which top is hotter by touching the tops with the finger tips.

Or darken the outside of one of two large tin cans by smoking it thoroughly with a candle flame. Pour the same amount of cold water into each can. Take the temperature of the water in each can and record the readings. Place both side by side on a table in bright sunshine. After at least a half hour, take the temperature of the water in each can and record the readings (Fig. 13-4). The water in the darkened can will be warmer.

Children should realize that objects with dull, dark surfaces absorb and radiate heat better than objects with smooth, shiny surfaces. Objects with smooth, shiny surfaces reflect heat very well but are not good absorbers or radiators of radiant heat.

Help them understand that black or dark-colored roofs absorb more of the sun's rays in the summer and make houses warmer; light-colored roofs reflect more of the sun's rays and thus help keep houses cooler. While dark-colored roofs are a help in the winter, insulation already

helps keep houses warm, and the additional heat from a dark-colored roof in the winter is more than offset by the discomfort produced in the summer.

Point out also that dark-colored radiators in the home would emit more radiant heat than radiators that are silvered or painted white. However, most people forego this advantage because light-colored radiators seem more attractive.

To show the effect of radiant heat on different colors, paint (with tempera) the bottom and round portion of each of three Florence flasks with a different color. Paint the fourth flask silver or aluminum. Insert a one-hole rubber stopper in each flask and a 12-inch piece of glass tubing in each stopper. (Use a twisting motion when inserting the glass tubing to prevent it from breaking.) One end of the tubing should be flush with the bottom of the stopper.

Invert each flask on a burette clamp attached to a ring stand. Fill four beakers almost full of cold water colored with red or blue ink and adjust the burette clamp so that the glass tubing projects well into the beaker (Fig. 13-5).

Have children warm the flasks with both hands until bubbles stop coming out of the glass tubing into the colored water. In a short while the col-

FIGURE **13-4** Water in a darkened can becomes warmer more rapidly in the sunlight than that in a light, shiny can.

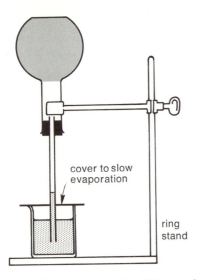

cover to slow evaporation

ring stand

FIGURE **13-5** Demonstrating the different effect of radiant heat on different colors.

ored water will rise in each tube. Mark the level of the water in each tube with a crayon, or tape or wire around the tubing. Then move all four ring stands with the flasks to bright sunshine. After at least a half hour, note which colored water level fell the most. Children will realize that the darker the paint, the more heat is absorbed. The hotter the flask becomes, the hotter the air inside it and the further down this hot air pushes the colored water in the tubing.

Circulation

The circulation of air in a room is a very important aspect of proper ventilation. A ventilation box, which will show this quite clearly, can be made of a wooden or heavy cardboard box about 20 × 15 × 5 inches. Bore three holes about 1 inch in diameter as follows: two in one end of the box and one hole in the top of the box to one side (Fig. 13-6). Insert corks or stoppers into the holes. Paint the inside of the box a dull black. Cover the open end of the box with a pane of glass (available from a hardware dealer or glazier). Hold the glass on with long thin nails hammered part way into each end of the box (top and bottom) and then bent around to the front

of the box. Tape the pane (at its ends) to the box so that it fits snugly.

Place a small burning candle in the center of the box. Remove the bottom end cork for a moment, introduce some smoke, and replace the cork. (Make smoke with a cigarette, punk, joss stick, or smoldering facial tissue or paper towel. If the tissue or paper towel is used, roll a piece tightly, light it, then blow out the flame.) Observe the two currents in which the smoke moves (Fig. 13-6a), rising and falling. These are called convection currents (Chapter 17). Point out that the air next to the flame is heated, expands, and thereby becomes lighter. This lighter air floats to the top and is replaced by colder air, which flows down to take its place. This colder air soon becomes heated, expands and rises, is replaced by colder air flowing down, and so on. In this way, a convection current is set up; the smoke makes its path and direction visible.

Move the candle to the end of the box that is opposite the holes. Allow smoke to enter from the bottom end hole for a few moments; then replace the cork. Again observe the convection current that has been set up. Compare the action of this current with that set up by a radiator in a room.

Then blow quite a bit of smoke in at the bottom end hole. When the box is thoroughly filled with smoke, remove both end corks (Fig. 13-6b). This will give the same effect as opening a window at the top and bottom in a heated room. A convection current of air is set up that covers every part of the room, producing a proper circulation of air. It is helpful to provide a continuous supply of smoke at the bottom end hole.

Call attention to the fact that, wherever possible, radiators are placed under windows. In this way, the cold air which drops down from windows passes immediately over the hot radiator. The radiator then heats this air and sets up a convection current. Thus, all parts of the room become heated, while there is a constant supply of fresh air.

To detect and trace convection currents in the classroom, attach long, narrow strips of very thin paper to a stick or yardstick. (Thumb tacks will hold the strips in place.) Now place the paper strips over a hot radiator and notice the direction that the strips assume. Repeat the process in different parts of the room and at different heights. Use a chair, table, or step ladder to reach near the ceiling.

To reproduce the action of a draft in a fireplace or in a stove or furnace with a chimney, fill the ventilation box thoroughly with smoke. Then

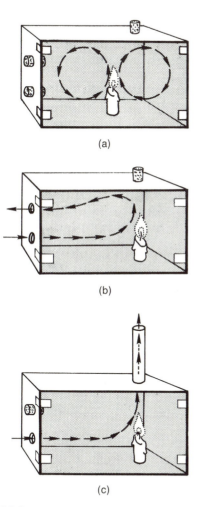

(a)

(b)

(c)

FIGURE **13-6** A ventilation box, showing (a) convection currents; (b) the effect of opening a window at the top and bottom in a heated room; (c) the action of a draft in a fireplace or furnace with a chimney. Arrows indicate the course of the current (smoke) in the box.

remove the corks at the bottom end hole and at the top (Fig. 13-6c). Place a glass chimney over the hole at the top of the box, or use 6-inch pieces of a mailing tube or the tube from a paper towel roll. Continue supplying smoke at the bottom end hole. Children will note that the cold air flows in at the bottom while the hot air (and/or waste gases) go up the chimney.

Proper window ventilation may also be illustrated by a convection box made from a cigar box. Cut holes in the side to accommodate small chimneys or glass cylinders. Replace the cover with a pane of glass hinged with adhesive. Use canned cooking fuel, such as Sterno (small size), for the heat source. Trace convection currents by introducing smoke first at the upper hole and then at the lower hole.

Waterproofing

Preventing water from penetrating basement walls is often a difficult problem; cement blocks, tile, and mortar are all porous. The best way to make basements waterproof is to apply heavy coatings of asphalt to the outside walls. Silicones and other plastic resins are also good, but they are more expensive than asphalt. When these protective materials are applied to the outside walls, the water runs off the walls smoothly and quickly. But when these materials are applied to the inside walls, the water pushes them out of the pores of the concrete.

Sometimes exterior walls are waterproofed with wax or oil dissolved in naphtha, kerosene, or benzene. The waterproofing material is then applied as paint. Ordinary house paints are also used to protect the wood from the elements—chiefly water.

Children may like to test some waterproofing materials. To do so, coat some wood shingles (from a lumber yard) with asphalt paint or other waterproof paint. Compare the effects of water on waterproofed and nonwaterproofed shingles. Melt about a quarter of a pound of paraffin (clear candles will serve the purpose) in an old pan over a hot plate on low heat. (*Caution: It is flammable.*) In another pan, heat a pint of water nearly to boiling. Then, stirring vigorously, slowly add the melted paraffin to the hot water. Remove the pan containing the mixture from the hot plate and continue stirring while the mixture is cooling.

With a brush, coat a piece of paper, cardboard, or fiberboard on the side which is to be in contact with water. Place this paper in the oven set at a temperature of 125°F (the melting point of paraffin). Keep the paper in the oven for a very short time, just long enough for the wax to coalesce into a continuous film. No matter how long you expose this surface to water, the material will remain waterproof.

Fireproofing

Fire is a constant hazard, especially in homes. Collect various building and roofing materials and test them with a flame for their ability to burn. Let children decide which are fireproof and which flammable. Point out how fireproof materials are made of stone, brick, tile, slate, clay, plaster, and metal. Note the fire-resistant qualities of asphalt, mica, rock wool, and porcelain.

Fireproof paints usually contain water glass (sodium silicate), which may be obtained from a hardward store, paint store, or chemical supply house. Paint a strip of wood with at least three coats of water-glass solution. (Allow each coat to dry before the next is applied.) When the last coat has been applied and is dry, hold the wood over the flame of a Bunsen burner or a gas range. The coating will swell and a froth will form, but the wood will not burn. (Methods of fireproofing paper and cloth are also described in Chapter 16.)

SUGGESTED PROJECTS

1. Have children make a list of the materials used to build a house. Lead into a study of different kinds of houses and the materials used to build them.

2. Have children discuss the advantages and disadvantages of homes with and without basements.

3. Make a list of the different provisions made when building a house to prevent heat loss and relate this to the study of insulation and the properties of insulating materials.

4. Examine specimens of different insulating material through a magnifying glass.

5. Have the children describe those conditions which they think make for ideal weather. They should include a temperature a little over 70°F, air that is neither very moist nor very dry, good air circulation, and air free of dust. Point out how home design tries to duplicate these conditions. Have children name and study the different parts of the home that help maintain comfortable weather conditions indoors.

6. Have a member of the fire department speak to the class on home fire hazards and how to prevent them. Lead into a discussion of fireproofing materials for the home.

BIBLIOGRAPHY

(**P** indicates recommended for primary grades, **I** for intermediate grades, **U** for upper grades.)

Ahrens, Maurice R., et al., *Living Chemistry*, Ginn, 2nd rev. ed., 1961. Contains a chapter on housing material and kinds of homes. Good teacher reference. **U**

Barr, George, *Young Scientist Looks at Skyscrapers*, McGraw-Hill, 1963. Latest techniques in building construction from the preliminary testing of the subsoil to the finishing touches on a skyscraper. **U**

Buehr, Walter, *Rubber: Natural and Synthetic*, Morrow, 1964. History and development of the rubber industry from its primitive form in the Amazon jungles to highly mechanized synthetics factories. **I**

Carter, Katherine, *The True Book of Houses*, Children's Pr., 1957. Very simple treatment of homes and building materials. **P**

Colby, Jean, *Tear Down to Build Up*, Hastings, 1960. Describes the tools and machinery used, the operators of the machines and other workers, how they wreck buildings, and why it is necessary. **U**

Devlin, Harry, *To Grandfather's House We Go*, Parents' Magazine Pr., 1967. A pictorial history of American domestic architecture—a full page color picture of a type of house, with text and detail drawings on the facing page. **U**

Goodspeed, J. M., *Let's Go Watch a Building Go Up*, Putnam, 1956. Simple description of how a house is built and the materials used in building it. **I**

Hoag, Edwin, *American Houses: Colonial, Classic, and Contemporary*, Lippincott, 1964. Story of American houses from log cabin to skyscraper, emphasizing the influence on architecture of the manners and customs of the people who do the building. **U**

Iger, Martin, and Eve Marie, *Building a Skyscraper*, Young, Scott Books, 1967. The book follows in text and photographs the building of one skyscraper through all the building stages. **U**

Meyer, Jerome S., *Iron & Steel*, World, 1966. Well-organized, lucid presentation highlighting the history, production methods, and uses of iron and steel. Pleasing format, large print and clear-captioned photographs. **U**

Newcomb, Ellsworth, and Hugh Kenny, *Miracle Plastics*, Putnam, 1964. History, scientific background, and products of an essential industry. Included are brief biographical sketches of the people who brought plastics to their present state, and a list of different kinds of plastics and their properties. **U**

Pearl, Richard, *The Wonder World of Metals*, Harper & Row, 1966. Useful book on metals—how discovered, how mined today, and how used. An index and good black and white photographs. **I**

Rockwell, Anne, *Fillipo's Dome*, Atheneum, 1967. The building of the dome for the Cathedral of Florence in the fifteenth century. **U**

Stockard, Jimmy, *Experiments for Young Scientists*, Little, Brown, 1964. Simple experiments (with safety rules and illustrations) demonstrate scientific principles and facts concerning air, water, light, sound, simple machines, and electricity. **I**

Woodward, Hildegard, *Time Was*, Scribners, rev. ed., 1962. Changes in family living brought about by some modern inventions; illustrated. **U**

Listening to sounds reverberating from the hard walls of a sea shell.

14 Sound

Sound is produced by vibration. This can be shown in many ways. Pluck a rubber band stretched between the fingers or around an open cigar or chalk box, pointing out how the band moves back and forth, or vibrates, rapidly. These rapid vibrations produce the twanging sound. Have children hold a finger to the larynx while they hum, speak, or sing so that they can feel the vibrations of their vocal cords.

Many familiar objects can be used to show that vibrating bodies produce sound: Hold a blade of grass (or a thin strip of plastic material of the same thickness) between the thumbs and the balls of the hand and blow through the gap between them. The stream of air will make the grass blade vibrate enough to produce a shrill sound. Fold in half a 2 × 5-inch strip of paper and tear a small semicircle from the center of the fold (Fig. 14-1). Holding the folded paper between forefinger and middle finger (do not cover the hole), press the lips between the open ends of the paper and blow hard. The strips of paper will be parted slightly by the air, which will then escape through the hole at the end, allowing the strips to collapse together again. This alternate bellying out and collapsing will occur very rapidly, causing a vibration that will produce a squeal. With a strong string tied through a hole in one end, swing a 12-inch ruler (or similar piece of wood) in a circle. The ruler will vibrate, producing a "groan." The vibration in this case is caused by the alternate rapid parting of the air (at the leading edge of the ruler) and its coming together (at the trailing edge).

Or make a tom-tom out of a large tin can and a sheet of thick rubber (from a heavy toy balloon or old inner tube) stretched across its mouth and fastened with a rubber band or string tightly tied around the edge. When the tom-tom is struck, children can feel the vibrations in the drumhead or see their effect on small pieces of cork dropped onto the sounding drum.

An object producing sound is usually vibrating so rapidly that the vibrations cannot be seen or can be seen only as a faint blur. Strike a tuning fork (available from a music or science teacher, or a piano tuner) sharply against the kneecap or the rubber heel of a shoe. When sound is produced, the motion of the prongs of the tuning fork will, at best, be a blur. The fork's vibrations can be demonstrated, however, by dipping the prongs into a full glass of water immediately after striking. The vibrations will cause the water to spray. Or observe how the prongs rattle a sheet of paper to which they are touched. (If using a dinner fork, strike it as hard as possible and perform the experiment as quickly as possible; plucking two of the tines, then quickly bringing the tines to your ear, may be even better.)

An object must vibrate at least 16 times a second and not more than 20,000 times a second to produce sounds audible to the human ear. Vibrations beyond the range of our hearing are called *ultrasonic.*

SOUND WAVES

Vibrating objects produce sound *waves,* each vibration producing *one sound wave.* Sound waves are propagated as follows. When an object vibrates, it moves back and forth rapidly. As it moves one way, it presses the particles or molecules of the gases in the air (or whatever the medium) closer together, producing a *compression;* as it moves back, the molecules spring back,

then spread farther apart, producing a *rarefaction.* Molecules doing this push against neighboring molecules just as the object pressed against them. Thus the compressions and rarefactions are passed along through the material of the medium, producing sound "waves." Although these waves have been transmitted by the molecules in the air, the molecules themselves have traveled back and forth only a very short distance. The sound waves move away from the vibrating body just as ripples or water waves spread out from the spot where a stone has been thrown into water. However, sound waves differ from water waves because they travel not just on a surface, but in all directions from their point of origin, and are invisible. Refresh children's memory of water waves by dipping a finger in and out of the water in a tub or basin. Point out how the waves spread out rapidly in expanding circles.

Sound waves can, in a sense, be made visible with the device shown in Fig. 14-2. Attach the hacksaw blade (available from a hardware store) to the block as shown, and tape or cement a small, firm piece of broom straw to the free end of the blade. Smoke a small sheet of glass by moving a candle flame around slowly on its underside. Place the hacksaw blade so that the broom straw just touches the layer of soot on the glass. Set the hacksaw blade vibrating, and as it vibrates, pull the smoked glass slowly under the broom straw. A wavy track of the sound waves will be left under the soot. This wavy track is

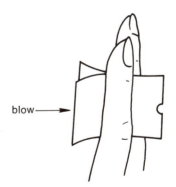

blow——⟶

FIGURE **14-1**   Producing sound with a vibrating piece of paper.

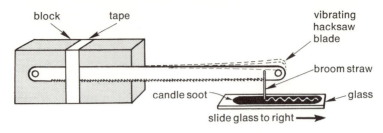

FIGURE **14-2**   Making a wave pattern with a vibrating hacksaw blade.

not the actual form of sound "waves," which are really compressions and rarefactions of the air (see above), but a kind of reflection or translation of them into a visible form. If the hacksaw blade is vibrated more strongly (in effect, a louder sound), the waves produced will be larger. The same experiment can be performed by attaching the broom straw to one tip of the tuning fork. Varying the length of the vibrating part of a hacksaw blade or using tuning forks of different frequencies will produce waves of different sizes.

To help children understand how sound travels, one can show how waves move in a coiled spring (Fig. 14-3). Use a spring such as the one from the roller of a window shade or a "walking spring" type of toy. Fasten one end of the spring to a cup hook screwed into the top of a door frame. Tape a piece of paper to every fifth coil. Attach a block of wood to the bottom of the

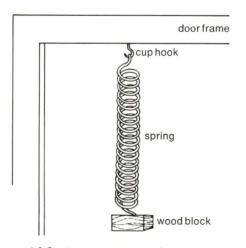

FIGURE **14-3**   Arrangement to demonstrate compression and rarefaction.

spring and then press together several coils of the spring near the bottom end, then, quickly release the coils. The coils expand, and, in so doing, cause the neighboring coils to compress and then expand. Thus, the impulse travels from coil to coil with a back-and-forth motion—that is, by a series of alternate compressions and rarefactions.

Another demonstration involves spreading the spring or coil across the room, with each end held by a child. Have one child strike the coil with a pencil at a point just beyond the fingers holding the coil. Note how the impulse travels along the coil and back, in a series of compressions and rarefactions.

Transmission of compression can be shown using six checkers (Fig. 14-4). With the fingers of the left hand, press down firmly on four checkers placed side by side and touching. Place a fifth to the left of but touching the end checker of the four. Make sure all five checkers are touching. Place a sixth checker a few inches to the right of the five checkers. With the right hand, snap the free checker against the end of the row. The end checker on the left quickly moves away because the checker first struck was compressed slightly. This compression was passed on, or transmitted, to the other checkers until it reached the last checker, which was free to move. Point out that sound vibrations travel through air in much the same way.

Sound waves travel in all directions, the molecules in the air transmitting the impulses to their neighboring molecules. With a child facing the wall in each corner of the classroom, have a fifth child stand in the center of the room and make a sound. Have the children in the corners raise

FIGURE **14-4**   Compression transmitted through a series of checkers.

their hands as soon as they hear the sound. Then, have a child, standing halfway between one child at the top of a stairway and another at the foot, make a sound. The class will readily conclude that sound travels in all directions.

Arrange four rows of dominoes in the shape of a cross. Leave a space in the center of the cross slightly smaller than the diameter of a rubber ball. Now push a rubber ball into the center of the cross, causing the four nearest dominoes to tip over (Fig. 14-5). Each domino, in falling, will cause its neighbor to tip over. These, in turn, will strike their neighbors. This toppling travels down all four lines until the last domino falls. If the rows of dominoes extended the length of the room, the disturbance would travel that distance.

Sound waves are transmitted through liquids and solids as well as gases. Since children will have been hearing the sounds produced in class, they will have inferred that sound waves travel through air (which is a gas) to their ears. Show this phenomenon once more by having two children speak to each other through a long garden hose, open at both ends, very much as through a telephone. Now show that sound waves travel through liquids. (The sound of a dripping water faucet can be heard very clearly when the ears are submerged in the water into which the drops are falling.) While one child notes the sound produced, have a child first strike together two rocks in air, then again under the water in a large battery jar. If the listener puts his ear against the side of the jar, he will note that the sound through

the water is louder than it was in air. Water carries sound better than air.

Have a child place his ear against one edge of a table top while another scratches the opposite edge lightly, or place the base of a vibrating tuning fork against one end of a yardstick while a child puts his ear to the other end. The transmission of sound through solids can also be shown with a tin-can telephone. Use two juice cans, each with one end removed. Punch a hole in the remaining ends and run a string (waxed with paraffin or candle wax) at least 25 feet long from one to the other. Tie a large knot at each end of the string inside the can, or tie a nail or button to the string ends. The "phones" must be held far enough apart so that the string is taut. One child talks into one can while the other listens at the other can. Thin wire instead of string will produce a louder and clearer sound since metals carry sound better than string. Children may discover that the sound will be muffled if they hold the can anywhere but by its rim. Children can experience beautiful chime-like sounds by use

FIGURE **14-5**   Demonstrating that sound waves travel in all directions.

of a 3- to 4-foot piece of string and a tablespoon. Tie the spoon at the midpoint of the string, loop the ends of the string once or twice around the forefingers, place a forefinger in each ear, and swing the spoon so that it strikes a table edge or other hard surface. Sounds can be varied by using different spoons and forks and pairs of spoons or forks. Fine wire instead of string will produce a better sound.

The superiority of metal in the transmission of sound is evident if one substitutes a curtain rod for the yardstick in the experiment described earlier. A loud-ticking wristwatch or an alarm clock may be used, as well as the vibrating tuning fork.

Children enjoy devising a code and sending messages to another classroom by tapping on a radiator. If the radiator is hot, the child who is listening can press a metal rod against the radiator and put his ear to the rod instead of the radiator. Messages can be sent back and forth this way. Children can also place their ears against their desk tops while the teacher taps on her desk gently with a pencil; the sound will be carried from the desk through the floor to the desk top. Or strike the prongs of a tuning fork or dinner fork, and then touch the handle of the fork to the bone just behind the ear; a distinct sound will be heard. Repeat the procedure touching the fork to other bones of the head. The loudness of the sound heard will depend on the amount of flesh between the handle of the fork and the bone. (The more flesh, the greater the amount of insulation and the softer the sound.) Then set the prongs of the fork vibrating and place the handle firmly between the teeth; the sound will be most distinct.

Sound waves, then, must have a solid, liquid, or gaseous medium by which they can travel. The loud ticking of an alarm clock, heard even when placed under a large glass bell jar, would soon fade out if the air were pumped out of the jar.

Sympathetic Vibrations

Push the handles of two tuning forks that have the same frequency of vibration (or pitch) into one-hole stoppers—one handle to each. Knock out one end of each of two cigar boxes. In the center of each box, make a hole slightly smaller than each stopper and insert the stoppers into the holes so that the tuning forks are firmly erect. Place the boxes with open ends facing each other, and adjust the position of the tuning forks so that they are in direct line with each other (Fig. 14-6). Strike one tuning fork with a rubber hammer made by inserting a sharpened stick or pencil into an eraser.

When the first fork was made to vibrate, it caused the molecules of air around it to vibrate, producing sound waves with a definite frequency of vibration. The molecules of air pushing against the prongs of the second tuning fork (tuned to the same pitch as the first) were able to cause the second fork to vibrate in unison with the first, so that the second fork then produced sound too.

The same phenomenon can be obtained with two milk bottles or soda bottles of the same size. While he is holding the mouth of one bottle close to his ear, have a child blow across the mouth of the other bottle until he produces a strong, clear note. When blowing a note with one bottle, the child will hear a similar, but weaker, note in the second bottle. Because the bottles are the same size and shape, their air columns, which vibrate to produce the sound, will do so at the same frequency. Consequently a noise produced

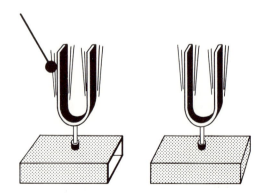

FIGURE **14-6** One tuning fork producing sympathetic vibrations in another.

by one bottle will set up sympathetic vibrations in the second bottle.

Often, when music is being played in a room, some object will begin to vibrate. The reason is the same: The natural frequency of vibration of the object is the same as the frequency of vibration of the musical tone.

Children can recall how, when pushing someone on a swing, it is necessary to time the push to coincide with the natural vibration rate of the swing.

Music

The number of sound waves produced per second by a vibrating body determines the pitch of the sound produced. Thus, the more vibrations per second, the higher the tone, and the fewer vibrations, the lower the tone. The number of vibrations per second is the *frequency,* and the "highness" and "lowness" of a sound its *pitch.*

Rubbing one's fingernail lightly across the cover of a cloth book produces a sound as the fingernail vibrates when it moves across the threads of the book. Moving the fingernail more quickly produces a higher tone—an increased number of vibrations per second. The same effect can be produced by rubbing the fingernail across the teeth of a comb.

The tones produced by string instruments are determined primarily by the thickness and tension of the "strings," which determine how rapidly they will vibrate. One can show this with a two-string guitar (sonometer), made as follows (Fig. 14-7). Drive two nails (near one end and about 3 inches apart) into a board or piece of plywood about $36 \times 6 \times \frac{3}{4}$ inches. Loop a thin steel wire about 4 feet long firmly around one nail and loop a similar length of thicker wire around the other nail. Lead the wires across the board, as shown, and attach each to the handle of a pail half full of water or stones or bricks. Slip one spring-type clothespin or small wedge under each wire near the nail and another two thirds of the way across the board. The wedges isolate one portion of a string by preventing vibrations from passing beyond them.

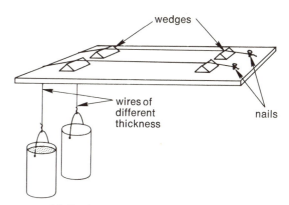

FIGURE **14-7** A sonometer.

Pluck each section of wire between the wedges and note the musical sounds produced: the thinner (lighter weight) the wire, the faster it will vibrate and the higher the tone will be. If one shortens the section of string that vibrates by moving the wedges closer together, the string will vibrate faster, and the note produced by the vibrating string will be higher. Children can reproduce the musical scale this way, bringing the wedges a little closer together to produce each successively higher note.

With the wedges in their original positions, add more water or stones to the pails and pluck the strings with each addition. The greater the pull on the string, the faster it will vibrate, and the higher the musical note will be. The rubber band described in the opening paragraph of this chapter can also show the effect of thickness and tension. A thinner band, even though the same length, will produce higher tones. Increasing the tension on each rubber band by stretching it will make the tones higher.

Although all string instruments depend on these properties of vibrating strings to produce their musical sounds, the vibration is not always produced in the same way; in the violin, for example, it is usually produced much as the fingernail drawn across the book cover produces sound (by friction), but in the piano it is produced by percussion (the string is hit with a hammer). A demonstration with the school piano helps show these properties clearly. Children may be interested in classifying the organ and harpsi-

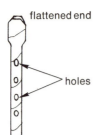

flattened end

holes

FIGURE **14-8** A soda straw saxophone.

chord. Point out that the harder one plucks or bows a string, the more strongly it vibrates and, hence, the louder the sound.

Wind instruments such as the flute, organ, trombone, and French horn depend on vibrating columns of air for their musical tones. To illustrate, put a glass or metal tube about 12 inches long and $\frac{1}{2}$ inch in diameter into a bottle nearly full of water. Blow across the top of the tube, holding it still while moving the bottle of water up and down. As the length of the column of air in the tube changes (because the bottle is being raised and lowered), different notes will be produced. Point out that the shorter the air column, the more rapid the vibration and the higher the note produced.

The relation between the length of the air column and the musical tone can be shown in many ways. Blowing across the tops of different size bottles (all having the same size neck) is one way. With a little practice, children can reproduce the musical scale using eight soda bottles (of the same size) filled with water to different levels. (A medicine dropper is helpful in adjusting the exact amount of water necessary to produce each note.) Blowing across the tops of the bottles will set the air columns inside (each a different length) vibrating.

A popular musical toy employing a vibrating column of air is the soda straw saxophone. To make one, flatten about $\frac{1}{2}$ inch of one end of a soda straw. (A plain white soda straw works best.) Cut off both corners of this flat end (Fig. 14-8). Holding the flattened end (in effect, a reed) in the mouth, blow very hard. To produce sound it may be necessary to moisten the flattened end with saliva. If it becomes too moist

and sticks together, cut off the end and start over. Once the sound is produced, quickly shorten the straw with a pair of scissors, cutting off about an inch at each time. The ever shorter vibrating air columns will produce the tones of a musical scale. One can also cut small holes in the straw about 1 inch apart. Cover the holes with the fingers, blow into the straw to produce a musical note, and then release various fingers. The nearest open hole determines the length of the vibrating air column and, consequently, the musical tone produced.

Blowing hard into a wind instrument will make the sound louder. (The air inside the instrument vibrates more strongly.) Point out that blowing harder into a wind instrument will sometimes make the sound higher as well.

Percussion instruments are of two kinds—solid, such as the xylophone and chimes, and hollow, with a skin or membrane of some kind stretched over them, such as the drum. When the materials are made to vibrate, the air inside these hollow containers vibrates also.

Use a xylophone to show that the shorter the bar, the higher the sound produced; the longer the bar, the lower the sound. Place a sheet of rubber (a rubber dam, available from a scientific supply house, or a piece of a rubber balloon) over the mouth of a glass jar and, grasping the sheet with both hands, pull downward while a child strikes it with the eraser end of a pencil. Children will note that the tighter the rubber drum head, the higher the sound produced. With a wider-mouth jar, the sound will be lower.

Using a piece of an old inner tube (thicker than the balloon or rubber dam) will show that the thicker the rubber, the lower the sound. Children should also conclude at the same time that the harder the membrane is struck, the more strongly the material vibrates, and the louder the sound.

Speech

Speech is sound produced by the vocal cords (Fig. 14-9) and shaped by the parts of the mouth. The passage of air (from the lungs) across the cords makes them vibrate and produce sound. To illustrate, stretch a rubber band between the fingers and blow hard across it. The vibration produced can be felt in the fingers; if the stream of air is strong enough, sound will be produced. Increasing tension in the band raises the pitch of the sound. Artificial "vocal cords" can be made by stretching rubber strips across the top of a tube and taping them in place. Blow air through the tube to produce sound.

The vocal cords are two flat bands of tissue (Fig. 14-9); tiny muscles on each side control the tension of the cords, which determines the pitch of the sound they produce.

Children may note the sound vibrations produced by the vocal cords by pressing a thumb and forefinger against the larynx while singing or speaking. They can also sing the musical scale while observing the different vibrations and the changes in tension. Point out that men have longer and thicker vocal cords than women, which largely explains why their voices are lower than those of women.

In another demonstration of the operation of vocal cords, grasp each side of the neck of an inflated balloon with the thumb and forefinger of each hand just below the balloon's opening. As the air escapes from the balloon, pull slightly to stretch the rubber. The vocal cords produce sound in much the same way. Increasing the pull on each side of the balloon increases the tension of the rubber membranes, making the sound higher.

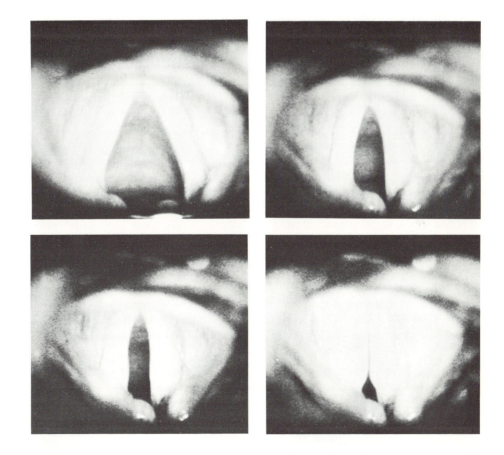

FIGURE **14-9** Change in position of vocal cords from breathing (upper left) to voicing. Pictures were taken with a laryngoscope fitted with a camera.

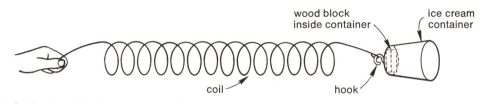

FIGURE **14-10** Amplification of sound when original sound sets a larger surface vibrating.

SOUND AMPLIFICATION

The larger the amount of air that is set vibrating, the louder the sound produced. Strike a tuning fork and hold it in the air for the class to hear. Then strike it again, but this time put the base of the tuning fork against a table top or a chalk board. The second sound is much louder because the tuning fork makes the table top or chalk board vibrate also. This larger vibrating surface or area sets a greater amount of air vibrating. The table top or chalk board thus acts as a sounding board or *amplifier*.

Screw a cup hook through the sealed end of a quart ice-cream container and into a small block of wood inside the cup (Fig. 14-10). Slip the cup hook over one end of a wire coil such as was used in Fig. 14-3. When the wire is tapped with a pencil, a loud whine comes from the container. This happens because the end of the container sets a large amount of air vibrating, and the sound is thereby amplified.

Another way of illustrating amplification employs a needle or rounded toothpick and a 3 × 5-inch card. Put the point of the needle into the groove of a revolving phonograph record. The sound will be quite faint. Then put the needle through one end of the card (Fig. 14-11) and repeat the procedure. The sound will be louder

because the card also vibrates, causing a much larger volume of air to vibrate. Or make a cone of heavy wrapping paper, fold the small end, and force the needle through the entire thickness of the paper (Fig. 14-12). Put the needle into the groove of the revolving record; the sound will be heard all over the room.

SOUND CONTROL

When sound waves hit solid objects such as a wall, ceiling, or cliff, they bounce back. These rebounding sound waves (or *echoes*) can be stopped in a large room or auditorium, by sound-absorbing material hung on walls and window frames. Carpets also help absorb some of the sound waves, as do the clothing and bodies of persons in the room.

To show how sound waves can be absorbed, place an alarm clock in a cardboard box with the open side facing a child. Have the child walk away from the box in a straight line until the ticking is barely audible. Note the distance. Fill the space in back of the alarm clock with cotton and have the child move back to the box until the ticking is audible again. Note the change in distance.

FIGURE **14-11** Mechanical amplification of sound.

FIGURE **14-12** Sound amplification with a phonograph "megaphone."

SUGGESTED PROJECTS

1. Obtain a model of the ear or enlarge to chart size a drawing of one in a textbook. Study the different parts and their functions, and trace the path of a sound wave from the outer ear through the middle and inner parts to the brain.

2. Investigate the vocal cords in the same way. Show the position of the vocal cords during breathing and when sound is being produced.

3. Have children try to recognize objects on the basis of their sound only. Conceal the object or have the class face away from it.

4. Show how the sounds are produced by musical instruments brought to class by children. Include such humming instruments as the kazoo and the paper and comb. Develop the concept that sounds produced by the same number of vibrations per second also have the same pitch.

5. Show how a dog whistle differs from regular whistles, and use to develop understanding of the wide range of frequency in nature and the variations in limits of audibility.

6. Place a 6-inch flexible plastic ruler on a table, with 2 inches of the ruler extending beyond the table's edge. Holding the ruler firmly with one hand, start the extended portion vibrating. Repeat, using lengths of 3 and 4 inches. Develop the idea that the greater the frequency of vibration, the higher the pitch.

7. Have children identify what is vibrating in the case of the sound of a door slamming, raindrops on the window, the rustling of cloth, a child whistling, a book falling onto a table, a child scratching his arm, the screech of automobile brakes, and wind blowing. (Wind through telephone wires will often make them hum.)

8. Have children listen to the pitch change as a bottle is filled with water and as water from the "hot" faucet begins to run warmer.

BIBLIOGRAPHY

(**P** indicates recommended for primary grades, **I** for intermediate grades, **U** for upper grades.)

Adler, Irving and Ruth, *Your Ears*, Day, 1963. Simplified explanation of anatomy and function of human ears. Includes a brief discussion of deafness and what can be done about it. **U**

Anderson, Dorothy, *Junior Science Book of Sound*, Garrard, 1962. Discussion on an easy level of all the properties of sound. **I**

Baer, Marian E., *Sound*, Holiday, 1952. Experiments showing the properties of sound. **U**

Barr, George, *Research Adventures for Young Scientists*, McGraw-Hill, 1964. Various science concepts arranged in ten categories with specific suggestions for experiments. **U**

Beeler, Nelson, *Experiments in Sound*, Crowell, 1961. Practical experiments about sound. **U**

Bennett, Marilyn and Sylvia Saunders, *How We Talk: The Story of Speech*, Lerner, 1966. An account of various aspects of speech: anatomical structures, regional accents, speech problems, and difficulties involved in using a foreign language. **U**

Brandwein, P., et al., *You and Science*, Harcourt, 1960. A junior high-school survey of science, with many simple demonstrations suggested. **U**

Branley, Franklyn M., *High Sounds, Low Sounds*, Crowell, 1967. Explanation of how vibrations are made, how they are carried to the ear and how they produce sounds. Several simple experiments are included which use items found in a home or classroom. **I**

Brinckerhoff, R. F., et al., *Exploring Physics*, Harcourt, 1959. Principles of physics on the high-school level. **U**

Brinckerhoff, R. F., et al., *The Physical World*, Harcourt, 1958. General survey of physical sciences on the high-school level. **U**

Freeman, Ira, *All About Sound and Ultrasonics*, Random, 1961. About the nature, behavior, and practical applications of sound. Suggested experiments; glossary and illustrations. **U**

Geralton, James, *The Story of Sound*, Harcourt, 1948.

Information on sound at children's level. **U**

Irving, Robert, *Sound and Ultrasonics*, Knopf, 1959. The nature of sound, different kinds of sound, recording and transmitting sound, and sounds we cannot hear. **U**

Kettelkamp, Larry, *The Magic of Sound*, Morrow, 1956. Experiments on the nature of sound. **U**

———, *Singing Strings*, Morrow, 1958. Discusses stringed instruments and gives clear instructions on how to make simplified versions of the harp, piano, violin, and guitar. **U**

Knight, David, *The First Book of Sound*, Watts, 1960. A basic introduction to the nature of sound and its properties. **U**

Lynde, Carleton J., and F. Leib, *Science Experiences With Ten-Cent Store Equipment*, Van Nostrand, 3rd rev. ed., 1960. Experiments on sound and music. **U**

Meyer, Jerome S., *Sound and its Reproduction*, World, 1964. The nature of sound: sound-wave motion, the speed of sound, musical tones, resonance and amplification, and methods of recording and reproducing sound. One chapter deals with ultrasonics in medicine and industry. **U**

Miller, Lisa, *Sound*, Coward-McCann, 1965. Simple explanation of the basic fundamentals of sound— pitch, frequency, amplitude, and wavelength. **I**

Olney, Ross, *Sound All Around: How Hi-Fi and Stereo Work*, Prentice-Hall, 1967. The how and why of sound presented in text and pictures. Hi-fi, amplifiers, tuners, and record-players are covered. Includes a glossary of hi-fi terms and a guide for making items mentioned. **I**

Parker, Bertha, *Sound*, Harper & Row, 1957. The nature of sound and music; includes experiments. **U**

Pine, Tillie S., and Joseph Levine, *Sounds All Around.*, McGraw-Hill, 1959. Simple explanation of the principles of sound, including experiments using materials in the home. **P**

Podendorf, Illa, *True Book of Sounds We Hear*, Children's Pr., 1955. Easy-to-read introduction, clear illustrations. **I**

Posell, Elsa, *This Is an Orchestra*, Houghton-Mifflin, 1950. Orchestral instruments pictured and explained. **U**

Showers, Paul, *How You Talk*, Crowell, 1966. In simple language, how the lips, tongue, teeth, and larynx help produce sounds: color illustrations **I**

———, *The Listening Walk*, Crowell, 1961. Appealing story to develop the art of listening. **P**

Stockard, Jimmy, *Experiments for Young Scientists*, Little, Brown, 1964. Simple experiments (with safety rules and illustrations) demonstrate aspects of air, water, light, sound, simple machines, and electricity. **I**

Stone, A. Harris, *Take a Balloon*, Prentice-Hall, 1967. Fundamental ideas in physics and chemistry, including information on sound and pitch. Openended approach. **U**

UNESCO, *UNESCO Source Book for Science Teachers*, UNESCO Publication Center, 2nd. rev. ed., 1966. A sourcebook of experiments for the classroom teacher.

Vries, Leonard de, *The Second Book of Experiments*, Macmillan, 1964. Seventy-two easy-to-perform experiments requiring only readily obtainable materials and divided into five groups: force, sound, gases, liquids, and heat. Lists the needed materials, gives a clear explanation, and presents the underlying scientific principle. **U**

Windle, Eric, *Sounds You Cannot Hear*, Prentice-Hall, 1963. Elementary explanation of ultrasonics from manifestations in bats to uses in medical research. Well-organized; clear drawings. **U**

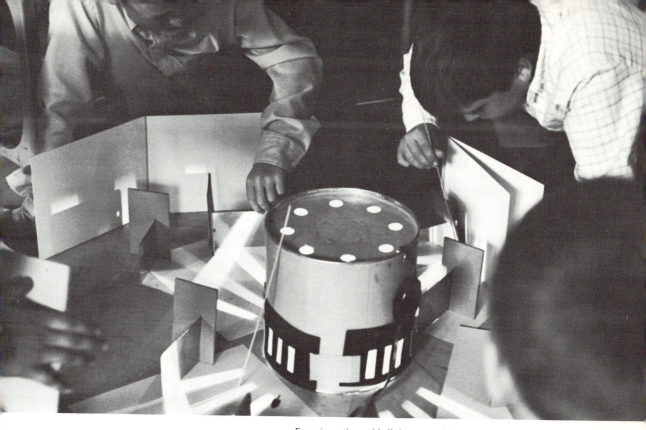

Experimenting with light transmission and reflection in the classroom.

15 Light and Color

Light is a phenomenon of the physical world that is usually taken for granted, but without which life would be very different. Without light there would be no color. Without light there would be no plants and, therefore, no animal life on earth. Our lives are conditioned to a large extent by light. People who move to extreme latitudes, as in Alaska, find it difficult to get used to the long nights; children find it strange going to and from school in darkness and having no outdoor recess during the long night. Not only recreation but also entire industries such as photography and motion pictures depend on the controlled use of light. The same holds true for modern scientific instruments such as microscopes and telescopes. The bending of light rays in mod-

ern medical diagnostic tools is another illustration of the importance of light and the utilization of its properties.

A device that is excellent for studying light and light rays is a smoke box. To construct one, replace the top and front side of a wooden box (about $2 \times 1 \times 1$ feet) with window glass, cellophane, or clear plastic. Tape the glass, cellulose, or plastic firmly in place with black cloth tape. Replace the rear end of the box with a black cloth, taping it to the box at the top and tacking it at the sides. Best is an arrangement with two pieces of black cloth that overlap about 4 inches at the middle (Fig. 15-1), which will allow easy access to the box to move objects about.

Paint the inside of the wooden parts of the box

with flat black poster paint. About halfway down one end of the box and about 3 inches from the front end, cut a hole about 3 inches long and 2 inches wide. Tack a piece of black paper or cardboard over the hole, first cutting slits in it to provide the kind of light rays desired.

A 5 × 8-inch index card tacked on the inside of the opposite end of the box acts as a screen. (This will display projected images beautifully when working with lenses.) For a light source, rest a three-cell focusing flashlight on a block of wood about 2–3 inches from the hole covered with black cardboard. A slide projector with the front lens (objective) removed is even better. If using a flashlight, focus it so as to produce a parallel beam. If it is too near the hole in the box, and the light rays are scattered or not clearly defined, move the flashlight back and forth until well-defined parallel rays of light are obtained. This can also be done by covering the flashlight lens with black masking tape and cutting a very small hole in the tape.

Smoke can be made from many things—punk, incense candles, cigarettes, etc. "Touch" paper can be bought (from a scientific supply house) or made as follows. Dissolve as much potassium nitrate as possible (from a drugstore or high

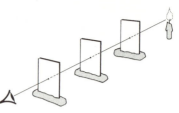

FIGURE **15-2** Demonstrating that light travels in a straight line.

school chemistry teacher) in a small, deep saucer of water, stirring with a spoon. Dip strips of paper in the solution and let them dry. Lighted with a match, the strips will smolder and give off much smoke.

CHARACTERISTICS OF LIGHT

Some of the behavior of light is explainable by a theory of light as waves, some by the corpuscular theory (light as particles), and some by both. Light travels at 186,000 miles per second in a straight line; the latter characteristic can be illustrated with three 3 × 5-inch index cards. With a paper punch or a pencil point, make a hole at the center of each card—the point of intersection of two diagonals. Tack each card to a small wooden block so it will stand upright. Place a lighted candle on a table and have a child align the cards so that he can look through all three holes and see the candle flame (Fig. 15-2). (Be sure the candle is at the right level so that the center of its flame will be level with the holes.) After calling attention to the fact that the holes are all in a straight line, move any of the cards a little and have children try to see the candle flame. Point out that the candle flame is seen only when the cards are aligned so that light can pass through the holes in a straight line. Students can also do this individually at their desks, sighting at a lamp on the teacher's desk. It may be useful to compare light's straight path with the way sound is transmitted (Chapter 14). Looking at a candle flame or a lighted electric bulb through a soda straw can convey the same idea. Bending the straw a bit makes it impossible

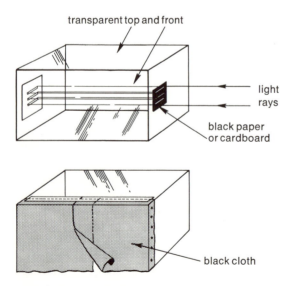

transparent top and front

light rays

black paper or cardboard

black cloth

FIGURE **15-1** A smoke box for studying light and light rays.

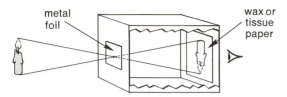

FIGURE **15-3** A pinhole camera.

to see the light, because it cannot pass around the curve.

A striking example of light traveling in straight lines is the pinhole camera. In the center of one end of a small cardboard box, cut an opening about 2 inches square. Tape or glue a piece of aluminum or tin foil over the opening. With a fine needle, make a tiny hole in the center of the foil. In the center of the opposite end of the box, cut an opening at least 3 inches square, and tape or glue a piece of waxed paper or tissue paper over it. Blacken the inside of the box with flat black paint or ink.

Darken the room and point the pinhole end of the camera at a burning candle about 6 inches away (Fig. 15-3). Move the camera back and forth until the image that appears on the paper becomes sharp and clear.

Call the children's attention to the fact that the image is inverted and that this could happen only if light travels in straight lines. As shown in the figure, the rays of light from the top part of the candle pass through the pinhole and fall on the bottom of the wax or tissue paper, while the light from the bottom part of the candle passes through the pinhole to the top of the paper. Showing this on the blackboard as it is

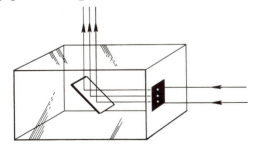

FIGURE **15-4** Mirror reflecting light rays entering and leaving a smoke box.

shown in Fig. 15-3 (straight lines drawn from the top and bottom of the candle through the pinhole and so on) can help clarify the concept for children. Such a diagram can also help explain the effect on the image of moving the pinhole camera closer to the candle. Have the children note what happens to the size of the image.

Transmission

The extent to which light can pass through substances varies: *transparent* materials allow all or nearly all light to pass; *translucent* objects scatter, or diffuse, some of the light; and *opaque* substances, of course, allow no penetration. Common transparent materials are glass, cellophane, clear water, and air. Children may read a page through a pane of clear glass, noting how clearly the printed material on the page can be seen. Or have children look briefly at the filament of a lighted clear-glass electric bulb.

Repeat the experiment with the printed page, using a pane of frosted or ground glass and a frosted glass electric bulb. Frosted glass windows show nicely how not enough light passes through to permit objects to be seen clearly. Common translucent materials are frosted glass, tissue and waxed paper, thin silk, parchment, paraffin, clouds, and milky liquids.

Heavy black paper taped onto a window pane or around a 15-watt lighted electric bulb will illustrate opacity. (Do not keep the paper on the hot bulb long.) Wood, metal, and heavy cloth are other common opaque substances.

A focused beam from a flashlight aimed, in a darkened classroom, at a pane of clear glass, a pane of frosted glass, and a square of wood will illustrate all three properties at once. A smoke box is ideal for this experiment.

Reflection

The smoother the surface, the more light it reflects. One can demonstrate this with the smoke box described above. Each slit in the black paper should be about $\frac{1}{4}$ inch in width. Fill the smoke box with smoke, focus a flashlight down to a

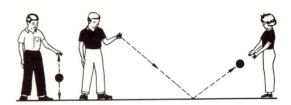

FIGURE **15-6**   Reflection of a rubber ball.

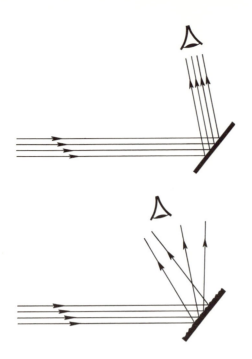

FIGURE **15-5**   Regular (above) and diffuse reflection.

parallel beam, and aim it at the slits in the black paper. (Be sure the flashlight is far enough away so that the light rays are parallel.) Children can see that the three rays of light in the box are parallel. Then hold a plane mirror at a 45° angle in the box (Fig. 15-4) and observe how the light beams are reflected at the same angle as the incoming beams and how clearly defined they are. Place one eye directly in the path of the reflected rays leaving the top of the smoke box. Point out that the glare is almost as great as if one had looked directly into the flashlight.

The phenomenon can also be illustrated simply by directing the focused beam of a flashlight at a slant onto a mirror in a darkened room. Clap blackboard erasers repeatedly over the mirror to produce a dust. Reflection of light from the dust particles will make the light rays visible.

Most of the things we see do not have smooth surfaces. When light falls on a rough surface, the rays are diffused, scattered, in all directions. When these diffused reflections reach the eye, one sees the object.

This kind of reflection can be shown in a smoke box as follows. Roughen a piece of clear plastic by scouring it in a circular motion with some steel wool until the surface is uniformly dull. Attach the plastic to the mirror with tape or rubber bands. (Wax paper can be used instead of the roughened plastic.) Repeat the experiment with the smoke box or in the darkened room. Children will observe how the rays of light are not reflected in regular beams but are scattered. Place the eye again in the reflected rays and notice the difference in brightness (Fig. 15-5).

Children may draw the conclusion that in order to see a nonluminous object: (1) there must be a source of light, (2) the light must strike the object; and (3) the light must be reflected from the object to the eye.

Light-colored objects reflect more light than dark-colored objects. Have children note which objects are more easily visible after the eyes are adapted to the semidarkness of a darkened room—the light-colored objects or the dark—and which rooms are brighter, those with light-colored or those with dark-colored walls.

Mirrors   To make it easier for children to understand how light behaves with mirrors, first study how a rubber ball is reflected by a surface (Fig. 15-6). Throw the ball straight down, and it will bounce straight back along the same path.

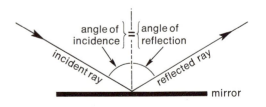

FIGURE **15-7**   The angles of incidence and reflection.

Let two children stand some distance apart and then bounce the ball back and forth to each other. Point out that the ball bounces up at an angle more or less the same as that at which it is thrown down, but in the opposite direction. Have the two children vary the distance between them and observe how the new angle at which the ball strikes the ground is reflected in the angle at which it bounces up.

Direct an approximately parallel beam from a strong focusing flashlight at a waist-high mirror in a darkened room. Have one of the children shine the light directly at the mirror. The ray will be reflected back along the same path. With the ray of light directed at a slant or angle, the rays will be reflected at the same slant or angle, but in the opposite direction; these angles are called the angle of incidence and the angle of reflection, respectively (Fig. 15-7).

These angles can be demonstrated more graphically as follows. Cut a $\frac{1}{4}$-inch wide slit along one end of a small shoe box a short distance from the top of the box (Fig. 15-8). Paint the inside of the box with flat black paint and place it so that bright sunlight penetrates the slit and falls

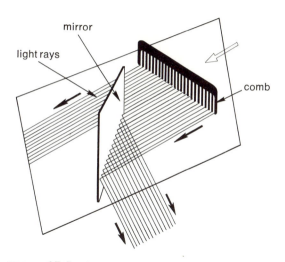

FIGURE **15-9** Angles of incidence and reflection demonstrated with comb and mirror.

on the bottom of the box. Place a mirror at that point. Note the reflected beam, and set another mirror in the path of the reflected beam, noting the second reflection. A diagram of the paths of the light rays, drawn on the blackboard, can be helpful. Draw a perpendicular line (as in Fig. 15-7) at the point where the light strikes the mirror and changes direction. Point out that the angle between the perpendicular and the ray that strikes the mirror (the angle of incidence) and the angle between the perpendicular and the ray that leaves the mirror (the angle of reflection) are equal.

In another way of showing this, hold a comb in the sun's rays so that the rays shine through the teeth and fall on a piece of white cardboard. By tilting the cardboard, make the rays of light on the cardboard several inches long. Place a mirror diagonally in the path of these rays (Fig. 15-9) and point out that the beams which strike the mirror are reflected at the same angle. Turn the mirror and note how the angles change.

The whole class can be used to demonstrate angles of incidence and reflection: With children seated in a series of equal parallel rows (Fig. 15-10), hang a large mirror from the blackboard so that it is in the center of the wall. Adjust the

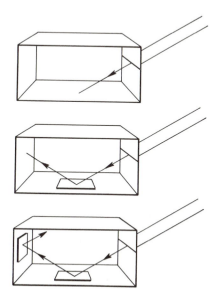

FIGURE **15-8** Showing angles of incidence and reflection.

height of the mirror so that the children can see each other in it. Draw a chalk line on the floor so that it is perpendicular to the front wall at a point directly under the mirror. Ask Pupil 1 to tell the class which of his fellow pupils he sees in the mirror. Most likely he will name Pupil 6, who will see Pupil 1, in turn. Draw chalk lines on the floor from Pupil 1 and Pupil 6 to the point where the perpendicular line meets the front wall. Compare the two angles. Repeat the process for Pupils 2 and 5, and so on.

One can plot and measure angles of incidence and reflection as follows. Tape a pocket mirror to a block of wood so that it stands upright (or hold the mirror upright by placing it between the pages of two books standing up and facing each other). Draw a straight line parallel to the upper edge of a piece of paper, and place the mirror so that its edge rests on the straight line. Stick a pin into the paper about 6 inches in front of the mirror and a little to the left of its center (Fig. 15-11). Sight along the edge of a 12-inch ruler with one eye, as shown in the figure. Move the ruler until its edge is in direct line with the mirror image of the pin. Hold the ruler in this position and draw a pencil line at its edge. Extend the line until it meets the mirror, pushing the mirror away if necessary. (The parallel line you

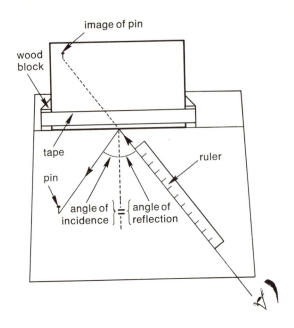

FIGURE **15-11** Constructing angles of incidence and reflection.

drew originally will show you where the mirror stood.) At this point, draw a line perpendicular to the line indicating the position of the mirror. Draw another line from this point to the pin. Use a protractor to measure the two angles, as shown in the figure.

If two children move about to various positions with relation to the mirror, they will find that one cannot see the eyes of the other in the mirror unless the second can see the eyes of the first. Rapid learners will probably be able to find why this is so.

Unsilvered glass—that is, not a mirror—may also act as one. Clean and polish a piece of window glass about 6 inches square. Have children try to see their reflections in the glass when it is lying on white paper and when it is lying on black paper.

When light strikes glass, most of it passes through, but some is reflected from the surface of the glass. When the glass is placed on white paper, the light passing through the glass is reflected back from the white paper. However, this light is diffusely reflected and interferes with (and thus makes it very difficult to see clearly) the

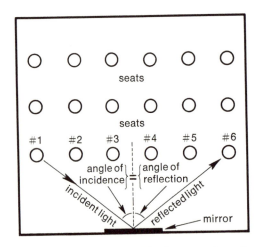

FIGURE **15-10** Arrangement in classroom (seen from above) to demonstrate angles of incidence and reflection.

reflection from the surface. When the glass is placed on black paper, the light passing through the glass is absorbed, allowing the light reflected from the surface of the glass to be seen clearly. Children may recognize that this is why a window is a fairly good mirror at night. Common glass reflects about 10% of the light and transmits about 90%.

In plane mirrors, the image is the same size as the object and seems just as far "behind" the mirror as the object is in front of it. This may be seen in the case of the image of the pin in Fig. 15-11 and may be made more graphic as follows.

Clean and polish a piece of window glass about 6 inches square. Set the glass upright by placing it inside the pages of a book standing on edge. (Be sure the glass is exactly vertical.) Darken the room and place a lighted candle in front of the glass (Fig. 15-12). Compare the size of the image with the size of the object.

Place a second candle, exactly the same size as the lighted candle, in back of the glass. Move it about until the image of the burning candle fits exactly with the unlighted candle (no matter from which angle it is viewed) so that the unlighted candle seems to be burning. Measure the distances of both candles from the glass and compare. One may also place a glass of water in back of the glass or one's hand, moving them about until the lighted candle seems to be burning in the water.

Water can also act as a mirror. To see this, place a pan almost full of water near a window so that sunlight falls on it. (*Warning: Do not let children look at a direct image of the sun.*) Look for a bright spot on the wall or ceiling. Strike the side of the pan with the hand just hard enough to cause the surface of the water to form ripples. The spot of light will dance about, but will be less bright and sharp.

A periscope is a surefire way of arousing interest in how light is reflected. To make one, tape two rectangular pocket mirrors at a 45° angle across both ends of a wooden cheese box or a shoe box (Fig. 15-13). (The mirrors may be glued to pieces of cardboard that fit into the box. A protractor or a square of paper folded along its diagonals to make two 45° angles can be used by the class to measure and check the angle.) Cut a window in the box wall opposite the midpoint of each mirror, as shown in the figure. The dimensions of each window should be slightly smaller than the dimensions of the mirrors. Replace the box cover.

Have one child look into the periscope while concealed behind some object, and describe to his classmates what he sees or what they are doing. Help children understand that light enters the top window and is reflected by the top mirror down to the bottom one, which then reflects the light into the observer's eye. Children may be able to explain why the mirrors must be placed at 45° angles.

A longer periscope can be made of a cardboard mailing tube about 2 inches in diameter. Use at least 2 feet of tube, fixing the mirrors in slits at the same 45° angle about 3 inches from each end

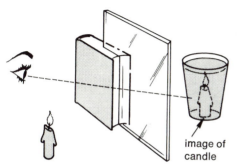

FIGURE **15-12** Making plane glass act like a mirror.

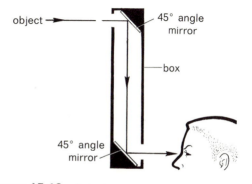

FIGURE **15-13** A periscope.

Characteristics of Light **239**

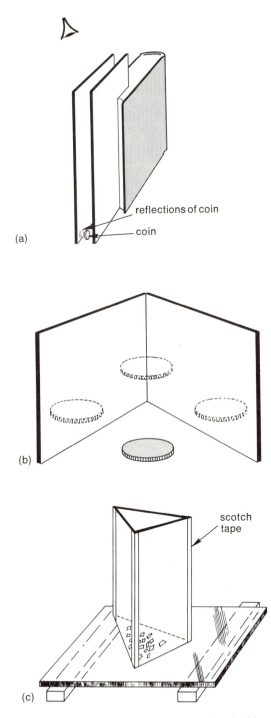

(a)

reflections of coin

coin

(b)

(c)

scotch tape

FIGURE **15-14** Multiple images produced with mirrors (a) parallel, (b) hinged at an angle to each other, and (c) in a triangular (kaleidoscope) arrangement.

of the tube and cutting windows opposite the mirrors as before.

Multiple images of one object can be obtained by standing two mirrors on edge, parallel to and facing each other. Keep the mirrors upright by placing them between the pages of a book (Fig. 15-14a). Place a coin between the mirrors and look over the edge of one mirror into the other. Repeat the process with a lighted candle. Point out that one sees many images because light from the coin or candle is reflected back and forth many times. Or hinge two mirrors together with tape and set them at right angles to each other (Fig. 15-14b). Place a coin or lighted candle between the mirrors and note the number of images formed. Bring the mirrors closer together, making the angle between them smaller. Children will note that as the angle decreases, the number of images increases. The mechanism involved may be demonstrated (Fig. 15-15) by using the rubber-ball analogy: The wider the angle embraced by two walls against which a ball is thrown, the fewer the number of times the ball will bounce (be reflected).

Beautiful multiple images can be obtained from a kaleidoscope. To make one, tape together three long rectangular mirrors, all of the same size, to form a triangle (Fig. 15-14c) with the reflecting surfaces on the inside. Metal camp mirrors, cut with tin shears or a hacksaw, can also be used. Sprinkle tiny pieces of colored paper on a pane of glass set on two blocks of wood. Set the kaleidoscope over the paper bits on the glass. Six-sided patterns will be seen. Tap the glass or turn the kaleidoscope to change the pattern shape and color combinations. Repeat the experiment, using colored beads, bits of colored glass, colored yarn, or tiny pieces of colored ribbon.

Images in a mirror are reversed. To illustrate, have children write their names on a piece of paper and hold the paper up to a mirror. Or write a name in ink very heavily, blot the paper with a fresh blotter, and then hold up the blotter with the reversed signature to the mirror.

A sheet of carbon paper placed with its carbon side up under a sheet of paper will produce a

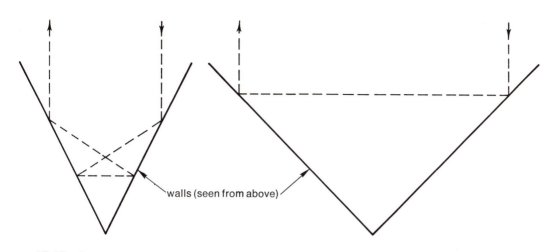

FIGURE **15-15** Demonstrating how angle of two reflecting surfaces determines number of reflections produced. Dashed line indicates path of ball thrown against a wall.

reversal of whatever is written on the paper. Held up to a mirror, the reversal will be reversed again and hence readable. With the reversal effect in mind, have children look into a mirror and raise a hand, noting that the mirror image seems to raise the opposite hand. Or have two children face each other and act out the action, one child taking the role of the mirror, so that when one raises his right hand, the child representing the mirror must raise his left. An object viewed in two mirrors hinged together at right angles will appear unreversed, as in the case of the alarm clock in Fig. 15-16. Here the light from half the clock face goes to the left mirror, is reflected to the right mirror, then back to the eye; the light from the other half of the face goes to the right

mirror, is reflected to the left mirror, then back to the eye. Thus, the image is reversed once at each mirror—twice altogether—so that the face is seen as it usually appears.

Curved mirrors produce effects determined by the direction (relative to the object reflected) in which they curve. A concave mirror (the center closer to the subject) forms a larger image of an object, while a convex mirror (the center farther from the subject) forms a smaller image of an object. A smooth, polished, pliable metal sheet from a tinsmith will act like a flat mirror. Bent so that the hollow side is away from the subject and held vertically, the sheet-metal mirror will give an image that is long and thin (Fig. 15-17). Bent the opposite way, it produces a short, fat image.

Children may see their images distorted in a highly polished metal coffeepot or teapot, which will usually offer both concave and convex surfaces. Good examples of curved mirrors are a shaving mirror (concave) and the rear-view mirror of a car (convex). Amusement-park mirrors that distort the shape of the body are good examples of concave and convex mirrors.

Refraction

Rays of light change direction when they pass at an angle from one transparent substance into

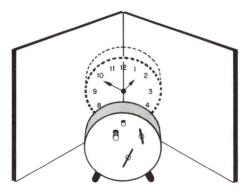

FIGURE **15-16** Reversing a reversed image.

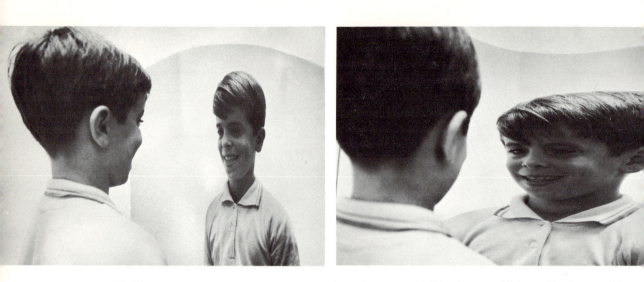

FIGURE **15-17** Distortions produced by convex (left) and concave (right) mirrors, which act like lenses of the same name—the convex mirror narrowing the image, the concave widening it.

another. This bending of light, called refraction, occurs because light travels faster through some substances than others so that it is bent slightly at the point where its speed changes. To show this, fill a rectangular fish tank with water to within about 2 inches of the top. Add just enough fluorescein (from a science supply house or pharmacist) to the water to make it yellow. Cover the top of the tank with cardboard with a $\frac{1}{8} \times$ 1-inch slit in it, as shown in Fig. 15-18. Fill the air above the water with smoke (use smoke paper, p. 234) or chalk dust.

Shine a ray of light straight down into the fish tank, pointing out that there is no change in direction of the ray when it passes from the air into the water. Then shine the ray of light into the water at a slant or angle and observe how the ray is bent.

The experiment may be done with a glass of water to which a few drops of milk have been added so that the ray can be seen distinctly as it bends.

Place a stick in a glass of water so that some of the stick remains above the surface of the water. Keep the eyes level with the surface of the water and look at the point where the stick meets the water. The stick will appear to be broken or bent because the rays of light that come from the part of the stick in the water are bent as they leave the water and enter the air. Another striking demonstration of refraction can be done as follows.

Place a coin on the bottom of a pan or coffee can near the edge of the pan. Have one child step close enough to the pan to see the coin clearly, then back to the point where the pan wall blocks his view of the coin. While the first child stays in this position, have another pour water into the pan—slowly so as not to move the coin. At some point as the water rises, it will reach a level where the coin will emerge into full view of the first child. With the water added, light from the coin is bent at the surface (where it passed from the water into the air), enabling the pupil to see the coin again (Fig. 15-19). The coin will seem to have changed position.

Remind children that water appears to be more shallow than it really is: What seems to be chest-deep in a swimming pool is often over one's head. A ruler lowered into a saucepan full of water seems to become shorter as it goes into the water.

The bottom of a glass of water seems to be closer than the table on which it rests. Placing a finger on the side of the glass where the bottom appears to be will show that the water seems to be about three fourths as deep as it really is. Point out that this discrepancy occurs because the light rays from the bottom of the glass are bent as they leave the water, just as with the coin in the pan.

Lenses

Lenses are transparent substances, such as glass, which have regularly curved surfaces. (See discussion of lenses used in microscopes in Chapter 4.) Just as there are two kinds of mirrors, concave and convex (see above), there are concave and convex lenses. Viewed in cross section, a convex lens is thicker in the middle than at the ends; a concave lens is thinner in the middle than at the ends. The convex lens brings, or focuses, rays of light together; the concave lens spreads out the rays (Fig. 15-20). A convenient mnemonic is the "cave" in concave, caves being "hollow."

A magnifying glass is a convex lens. To demonstrate the principal focus or focal point of the lens, place it against a piece of black paper held more or less at right angles to the sun's rays. Slowly lift the magnifying glass from the black paper until a position is reached where the rays

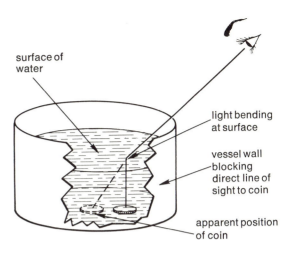

surface of water

light bending at surface

vessel wall blocking direct line of sight to coin

apparent position of coin

FIGURE **15-19** How a coin otherwise invisible is visible under water.

form a bright spot on the paper; this bright spot is the focal point—where the parallel rays of the sun are brought together. The distance between this point and the center of the lens is called the focal distance or focal length. The temperature at the focal point is high enough to ignite a match or even the paper itself, if it is held for some time at the one position.

The lenses of glasses used by nearsighted persons are concave and therefore will show only a broad, diffuse area of light (rather than a bright focal point) if placed in the sun's rays. The lenses of glasses used by farsighted persons are convex, and will focus an image as do ordinary magnifying lenses. Children may obtain lenses from

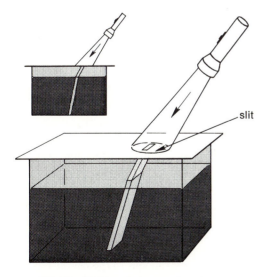

slit

FIGURE **15-18** Making light rays bend.

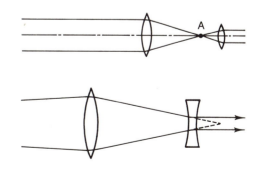

A

FIGURE **15-20** The action of convex and concave lenses on light rays.

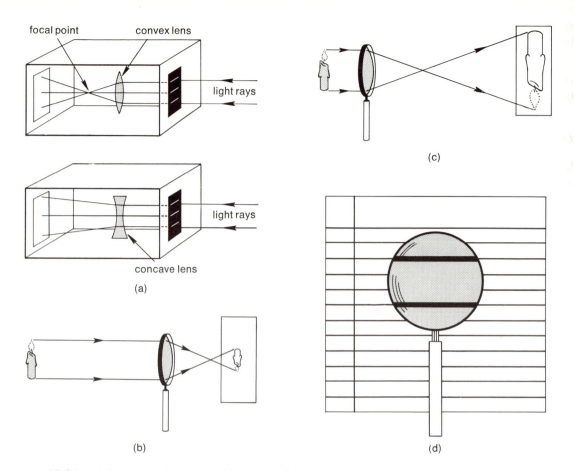

FIGURE **15-21** (a) Demonstrating effect of lenses on light rays in a smoke box; (b) how a convex lens forms an inverted image; (c) obtaining a larger inverted image; (d) finding the magnifying power of a lens.

discarded glasses or from an optometrist or optician.

A smoke box (p. 234) is ideal for showing what convex and concave lenses do to parallel rays of light (Fig. 15-21a).

To illustrate how the convergence (and then divergence) of light rays brought about by a convex lens produces an inverted image (Fig. 15-21b and c), darken the room except for one window. Have a child stand with his back to the window and hold an unlined 5 × 8-inch index card up to the light, while moving a magnifying glass back and forth before the card until a clear image of whatever is outside the window appears on the card. Note that the image is smaller and

inverted. Or darken the entire room, stand a lighted candle on a table, and have one child hold a large sheet of white cardboard about 3 feet away from the candle. Have another child hold a magnifying glass (convex lens) near the screen in the path of the candle's rays, then move the lens slowly toward the candle until a clear image (inverted) is seen on the screen. The image will be smaller than the object (Fig. 15-21b), but by changing the flame-to-lens or lens-to-screen distance (Fig. 15-21c), one can produce an enlarged image, even projecting it onto a distant wall.

Thus, the closer the lens to the candle or other object (up to a certain point), the larger the image will be. Brought very close to an object, a convex lens will magnify, and the image will not be inverted. A magnifying glass shows this to good effect.

To find the magnifying power of a lens, focus it over lined paper (Fig. 15-21d) and compare the number of spaces seen beyond the boundary of the lens with the number seen through the lens. The greater the curvature of the lens, the greater the magnification.

Many curved, clear objects will magnify—glass jars or tumblers, for example. Children can dip a finger or pencil into a glass of water and observe how it is enlarged when looked at from the side (through the glass). Or observe a fish in a round fish bowl (looking at it first from the top and then from the side) or various objects in an olive jar filled with water. A ruler or a lighted candle or other object viewed from behind the jar will also be magnified. Clear glass marbles will also magnify, as will a drop of water. (See p. 72, Chapter 4.)

An astronomical telescope can be made of two convex lenses, as described on p. 166, Chapter 9. The magnification in a two-lens telescope is the product of the larger focal length and the shorter: A 10-inch focal-length objective lens and a 1-inch focal-length eyepiece lens give a magnification of 10.

To use a telescope as a microscope, set the object to be magnified on a pane of clear glass resting on two blocks of wood or on two books

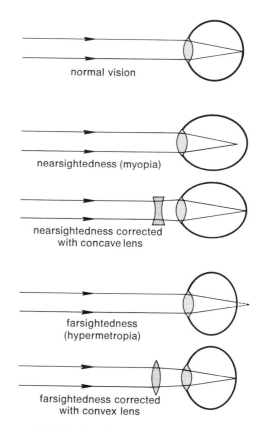

FIGURE **15-23** How lenses correct nearsightedness and farsightedness.

(Fig. 15-22). A plane mirror, as shown, underneath the glass will help concentrate the light, which should be bright. Use a small mirror on a stand, which can be tilted until light is reflected directly onto the object. Slide the telescope tube back and forth until a clear image is obtained. For a microscope, it is best to use an eyepiece lens of very short focal length, such as $\frac{1}{4}$ or $\frac{1}{2}$ inch.

How Eyeglasses Help Us See

Many people have eyeballs of just the right shape so that the eye lens focuses the light exactly on the retina. Nearsighted people, however, have eyeballs that are too long (relative to the focal length of the lens), so that light is focused in front of the retina and distant objects seem blurred.

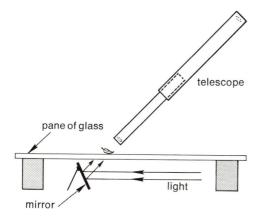

FIGURE **15-22** Using a telescope as a microscope.

The farsighted have eyeballs that are too short, so that the lens focuses the light behind the retina and near objects seem blurred. These eye defects can be corrected by using glasses with special lenses (Fig. 15-23). How this may be done is shown by the following experiment. Find the focal length or distance of a convex lens. Cut a cardboard circle with a diameter equal to the focal length of the lens. Place the lens at the edge of the circle, and shine a beam of light through the lens. If the point of focus of the lens does not fall exactly at a point on the edge of the cardboard circle farther from the lens, trim the circle until this effect is produced. (The beam of light may be obtained from a strong focusing flashlight or from a slide projector with the front lens removed.) Label this cardboard circle "normal eye."

Cut two other cardboard circles, one slightly larger and one slightly smaller than the first circle; these represent nearsighted and farsighted eyes and should be so labeled. Have children observe how the convex lens, held against the edge of these circles, focuses the light either before the edge or behind it.

To show how nearsightedness is corrected, shine a beam of light through the convex lens across the "nearsighted" cardboard eye. Using a pair of eyeglasses from a nearsighted person, move one of the lenses back or forth in the beam from the convex lens until the light is definitely focused at the edge of the part of the cardboard eye away from the convex lens. (The lenses in these glasses are concave.)

To show how farsightedness is corrected, shine

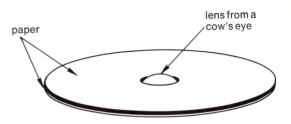

FIGURE **15-25**   The lens of a cow's eye mounted between sheets of heavy paper.

a beam of light from the convex lens across the "farsighted" cardboard eye. Interpose a second convex lens, or a convex lens from the eyeglasses of a farsighted person, and manipulate as described above.

Lenses of one kind or another are basic elements in the eyes of most animals and insects. The lens in the animal eye is much like the glass lenses discussed above. Basically, light passes through and is focused by the lens on the light-sensitive retina, where electrical impulses are generated by the light. These are carried by the optic nerve to the brain, where the inverted image formed by the lens is, in effect, reinverted. To demonstrate the parts of the eye, cut through the middle of a cow eye (available from a butcher) from front to back. The eye will collapse when the fluid in it escapes, but the parts, as shown in Fig. 15-24, should be recognizable.

To show that the lens operates like any mechanical lens, carefully dissect one from another cow eye, mount it between two sheets of heavy paper with a hole cut in the center (Fig. 15-25), and use it as in the experiments described above for convex lenses.

The eye and the camera are similar. Children may see the many points of correspondence by comparing a simple camera and the parts of the eye as shown in Fig. 15-24: The eyeball itself corresponds to the light-proof body of the camera; the iris to the diaphragm, which controls the size of the opening that allows light to enter; the retina to the film; and, of course, the lens corresponds to the same in the camera. Children may see the action of the iris in the human eye by observing the eye of a classmate as he emerges

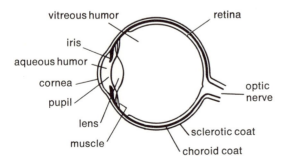

FIGURE **15-24**   Cross-section of an eye.

from a darkened room or corner and then after he has stepped close to the light at a window. The irises, widened after the stay in the dark (to allow maximum light into the eye), begin to close down on exposure to the light.

The point at which the optic nerve is attached to the retina (Fig. 15-24) is a "blind spot." To demonstrate this, make a cross and a circle 3 inches apart on a 3 × 5-inch index card. With the right eye closed, hold the card at arm's length, stare fixedly at the symbol on the right, and slowly move the card closer to the eyes. The left-hand symbol will disappear from view when the card reaches a point where that symbol is focused on the blind spot. The experiment may be repeated closing the left eye and focusing on the left-hand symbol.

Each eye produces a separate image (combined by the brain), giving binocular vision, which is important in perception of depth, or distance. Children can see this by holding two pencils at arm's length, erasers facing, and about 2 feet apart. Have them try to bring the erasers together, noting how difficult this is when keeping one eye closed. Or look through a paper or cardboard tube (about 1 inch in diameter) with one eye while looking at the palm of one hand (fairly close to the eye) with the other. The circular image seen through the tube will be superimposed on the image of the hand, giving the impression of a "hole" in the hand.

Motion pictures are made possible by an effect called "persistence of vision," in which the image of a subject remains with the eye for $\frac{1}{16}$ second after the object has been viewed. One can illustrate this easily by swinging a flashlight or any glowing object in a circle in a darkened room. The path of the light is seen as a briefly persisting circle because the image of the earlier positions of the light has not yet faded by the time the light reaches its final position. Children can achieve the effect of motion produced in animated films by drawing a stick figure (one each on about 20 index cards) in a progressively changing position—walking, running, raising its arms, and so on (Fig. 15-26). Holding the cards in a pack and flipping them rapidly with the thumb will produce the effect of movement as each slightly changed image of the figure succeeds another before the image of the preceding one has disappeared.

Persistence of vision can also "put the bird into its cage," as shown in Fig. 15-27. Draw a bird cage on a white card about 2 inches square. On the other side, draw a brightly colored bird. With a single-edge razor, slit the eraser of a pencil down the middle as far as it will go. Insert the card in the slit and hold the card firmly by pushing a short pin through the eraser and card. Roll the pencil back and forth quickly between the palms. The bird will seem to be inside the cage. The rapid turning of the card presents each picture to the eye before the other can fade; thus, the images seem simultaneous.

FIGURE **15-26** Figure drawn in a series with position of arms changing gradually from horizontal to vertical. Flipped through rapidly, figures give an impression of motion of the arms.

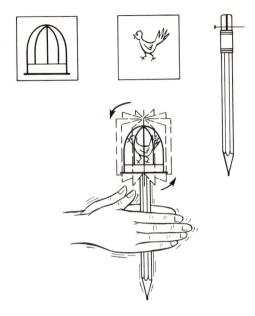

FIGURE **15-27** Putting a bird inside its cage.

DIVIDING LIGHT INTO ITS PARTS

The white light of the sun is composed of all the colors of the spectrum. This may be shown with a glass prism or, if a prism is not available, a three-sided crystal from a chandelier. Cut a narrow horizontal slit about $\frac{1}{8} \times 1$ inch in a piece of dark cardboard. Paste the cardboard to a window and darken other windows. Place a table near the window so that the sun's rays fall on the table. Set one edge of the prism in modeling clay or soft wax and place the prism on the table so that the beam of sunlight passing through the slit in the cardboard passes through it. If the prism is correctly positioned, a beautiful band of colors, or spectrum, will be formed on a white screen or cardboard mounted on the opposite wall (Fig. 15-28). Because each color passes through the prism at a different speed, they emerge from the opposite face of the prism at different angles and, hence, become separate. One can illustrate this by clapping blackboard erasers so that the chalk dust passes through the path of the beam of light between the prism and the wall. A magnifying glass placed between the prism and the screen will recombine the colors to form white light.

To make a prism, tape together at the edges three microscope slides or three 2 × 2-inch slide cover glasses, as in Fig. 15-29. Firmly imbed the ends in a flattened lump of modeling clay and fill the resulting triangular vessel with water.

A mirror submerged in a pan of water (Fig. 15-30) will also produce the spectrum. Let sunlight fall on the mirror from the slit in the cardboard, as described above. Stirring the water with the fingers will produce interesting effects.

Spectroscope

In addition to breaking up light (or producing a spectrum) by means of a prism, one may do

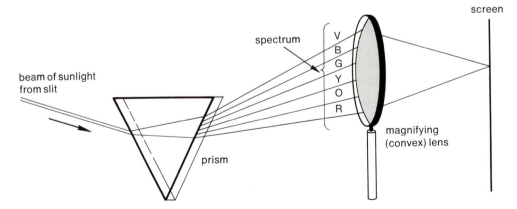

FIGURE **15-28** Obtaining a spectrum with a prism and recombining the colored rays with a convex lens.

so with a spectroscope, which can be made of a hollow cardboard mailing tube 14–18 inches long. Cover one end with aluminum foil, holding it firmly to the tube with a rubber band. With the corner of a razor blade, make a slit 1 inch long in the foil (Fig. 15-31).

Cut 1 square inch from a sheet of diffraction grating (available from scientific supply houses) and attach it to the other end of the mailing tube with four strips of black friction tape as shown in the figure. The lines of the grating should be parallel to the slit in the foil. Holding the slit in the aluminum foil parallel to the filament in the bulb, look through it and the diffraction grating at a lighted electric bulb that is *not frosted*.

For best results, stay at least 3 feet from the bulb; the farther away, the larger the spectrum produced. The spectrum should appear a bit to one side. Results are better if the room is darkened.

Two slits in the aluminum foil (as close together as possible) will produce even better results. Results almost as good may also be obtained by eliminating the tube. Have each child hold a 1-inch square of diffraction grating to an eye and look at the lighted, unfrosted bulb. An 8 × 10-inch sheet of diffraction grating will provide 1 × 1-inch squares for 80 children, so that each may do the experiment individually.

To perform the same experiment using sunlight

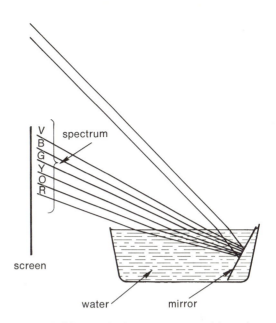

FIGURE **15-30** Producing a spectrum with a mirror under water.

instead of a lighted, unfrosted bulb, pull shades so that each is 6 inches from the window sill. Cover part of the exposed window pane with black construction paper with a vertical slit in it and observe the slit of sunlight either with the mailing tube spectroscope or by holding the square of diffraction grating to the eye.

If diffraction grating is not available, make some by stretching a piece of black plastic electrical tape *tightly* over the length of a microscope slide. Cut the tape vertically all the way through with a razor. The tape will separate slightly, producing a slit. Have children hold the microscope slide to the eye so that the slit is vertical and look through it at an unfrosted bulb. Al-

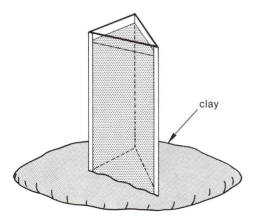

FIGURE **15-29** A homemade prism.

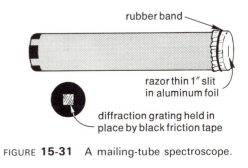

FIGURE **15-31** A mailing-tube spectroscope.

though the result will not be as sharp as with commercial diffraction grating, a spectrum will appear.

Rainbows

Rainbows are produced by droplets of water in the atmosphere that act as prisms and break up sunlight to form the beautiful arch of rainbow colors. One may produce one's own rainbow by spraying a fine mist from a hose against a dark background of trees. This should be done in early morning or late afternoon while standing with one's back to the sun. Or place a glass tumbler on a window sill when the sun is shining brightly. As in the exercise above with the glass prism or crystal, paste a piece of dark cardboard with a narrow slit in it to the window and darken the other windows. Adjust the tumbler so that it extends a little over the inside edge of the window sill, and fill it with water. A rainbow will be formed on a sheet of white paper placed on the floor (Fig. 15-32).

Rainbow colors seen on soap bubbles are caused by refraction of light by the different molecular layers in the soap bubble, which is several molecules thick. An oil film on water on the ground acts the same way. To see this, fill a shallow plate with a dark solution of water and

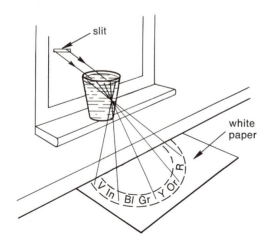

FIGURE **15-32**   A rainbow formed by light passing through a tumbler of water.

black ink. Put the plate where the light is very bright, but not in direct sunlight. While looking at the surface of the water, so that the light from the sky is reflected to the eye, place a drop of oil or gasoline in the water at the near edge. A brilliant flash of rainbow colors will move across the plate toward the far side of the plate. Or let one drop of Duco cement fall on the water in a large pan. The cement quickly spreads out into a thin sheet having beautiful rainbow colors. Carefully slip a piece of dark cardboard or paper under the sheet of cement and lift it out. Examine the permanent colors on the cardboard.

Reflected and Transmitted

A colored transparent substance will transmit only light of the same color as the substance. Show this by holding a clear sheet of glass or cellophane in the path of a ray of light in the smoke box. The light falling on the screen at the end of the box is white. Then hold a sheet of red glass or cellophane in the path of the ray so that the light falling on the screen is red. The red glass or cellophane transmitted the red part of the light and absorbed all the other colors of the white light. Repeat this, using different colored glass or cellophane. Point out that in the theater, colored spotlights are thrown on the stage in this way. (If the smoke box is not available, use a focusing flashlight in a darkened room. Cover the glass of the flashlight with black masking tape and make a tiny slit in the tape to produce a single ray of light.)

A colored opaque substance will reflect only light of the same color as the colored substance. All the other colors in white light are absorbed. A piece of red cloth looks red because it has absorbed all the colors of the spectrum except red, which it reflects. White cloth looks white because most of the light is reflected. Black cloth, on the other hand, looks black because most of the light has been absorbed, leaving almost none to be reflected.

Place a piece of red cellophane over the glass of a flashlight and shine the resulting red light on blue paper. The paper will appear black be-

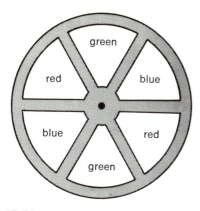

FIGURE **15-33** A color wheel.

cause, being blue, it can reflect only blue and not red. Shone on red paper, however, the red light will be seen as red. Children can shine the red light on objects of various colors and make a chart of the results. Repeat the experiment using different colored lights.

COMBINING THE PARTS OF LIGHT

Figure 15-28 indicated how the component colors of light could be recombined by a magnifying glass to form white light. This can be done in other ways as well: Cut a cardboard disk 3 inches in diameter and divide it into six pie-shaped sections (Fig. 15-33). With crayons, color each section and attach this "color wheel" to the shaft of a tiny electric motor such as is found in many battery-operated toys and which may also be obtained in hobby shops. Secure the disk by wrapping cellophane tape around the motor axle. With the motor on, all the colors of the turning disk will seem to blend, producing a creamy white. (If one color predominates, scrape some of it off.) The same effect can be produced with a similar but smaller color wheel thumbtacked to the flat surface of a top. Spin the top and the colors will blend. (Many toy shops sell tops of all sizes with color wheels painted on them.)

Cover the lenses of three flashlights of the same size and brightness with colored cellophane—red on one, dark blue on another, and green on the third. Add layers where necessary in order to obtain light of equal intensity from all three. Shine all three flashlights at the same spot on a piece of white cardboard (Fig. 15-34). The area where the three colors overlap will appear white. Combining red, green, and blue, the primary colors (in light), produces white, as it did with the color wheel. Combining red and green light will produce yellow; blue and green, blue-green; and red and blue, purple. These three primary colors are used to produce all the colors of color television.

When primary colored lights are combined, they have an additive effect. However, colored *pigments* in combination are subtractive. To demonstrate, mix yellow and blue paint. Yellow pigment has some green in it, as does blue. When the blue and yellow pigments are combined, the yellow and blue are absorbed, leaving only the green to be reflected. In the same way, red and yellow paint combined produce orange, and red and blue produce violet. The three primary colors of opaque objects are red, yellow, and blue; mixed together these three paints produce not white but black, since this combination absorbs all colors and reflects none.

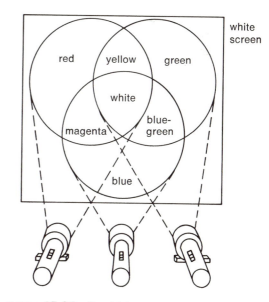

FIGURE **15-34** Combining primary-color light.

EFFECTS OF LIGHT

Light produces changes in certain substances. To illustrate this, fold a piece of dark construction paper in half and cut a design in the upper half. Refold so that the cut-out design rests against the other half and put it where the sun can shine on it for a few days. The design will appear on the lower half of the paper. The sunlight passing through the stencil-like design lightens the color of the construction paper.

A piece of dark construction paper left on a window sill for a few days will be lighter in color than a piece of the same paper left in a drawer for the same time.

The cloth under the lapel of a dark blue jacket that has been worn for at least a year will be quite different in color from the rest of the jacket, which has been constantly exposed to light.

Obtain a few crystals of silver nitrate (*Caution: This chemical is caustic and will stain fingers and clothes.*) from a high school chemistry teacher or pharmacist and dissolve them in a saucer containing about 2 tablespoons of water. With a brush dipped in the solution, paint the surface of a smooth sheet of writing paper. (Do this in a fairly dark corner of the room.) Then place a coin or button on the paper and lay the paper in bright sunlight. After a few minutes, remove the coin. The paper will have turned brown, except where the coin has covered it. Point out that camera film is coated with silver salts. Light affects the salts to produce an image on the film. Repeat the experiment, laying a photographic negative over the paper. A positive image, or picture, of the negative will appear. The light changes the silver nitrate chemically, releasing silver, which forms the black part of the image.

Place a leaf on fresh blueprint paper. Weight the leaf down with a sheet of clear glass, and expose the paper with the leaf on it to the sunlight for several seconds. Remove the leaf and wash the paper with cold water. The blueprint paper is covered with chemicals that are sensitive to light and soluble in water. When light strikes these chemicals, a new chemical is formed that is bright blue and insoluble in water. The coating on the blueprint paper under the leaf was not exposed to the light and so remained soluble. The cold water washed away these chemicals, leaving a silhouette of the leaf (in white) on a background of bright (insoluble) blue.

Shadows are the relative absence (or diminution) of light that occurs when an opaque body interrupts the passage of light. Those light rays create an outline for the shadow. To show this, suspend a white bed sheet, darken the classroom, and place a bright lamp about 5 feet behind the sheet. Have two children stand between the sheet and the lamp, one near the sheet, the other farther away. Point out that the shadow of the child near the sheet corresponds more or less to his real size; the shadow of the child farther from the sheet and nearer the lamp will look gigantic.

SUGGESTED PROJECTS

1. Discuss the difference between direct and indirect lighting and list the advantages and disadvantages of each.

2. Have a lighting expert evaluate school lighting and demonstrate use of a light meter, perhaps checking the amount of light in different parts of the room, the auditorium, the cafeteria.

3. Show how a person can see the back of his head using two mirrors. Lead into the study of the reflection of light and mirrors.

4. Have some children demonstrate use of an eye chart to lead into the study of nearsightedness and farsightedness. Discuss care of the eyes.

5. Have a pupil who develops his own pictures demonstrate the process.

6. Arrange for a high school photography club, a professional photographer, or a competent amateur to show how enlarging is done.

7. Have children examine the construction and operation of a slide projector or film strip projector, and continue with a study of lenses. Ask why the slides or film are inserted upside down. (Inversion of the image by convex lenses.)

8. Discuss how motion pictures are made and projected. Let a pupil who has a movie camera and projector demonstrate them. Show how persistence of vision creates the illusion of motion.

9. Study operation of a microscope, emphasizing the part lenses play in magnification.

10. From a book on interior decoration, have children find out which colors seem to produce the most pleasing combinations for walls, draperies, and so on.

11. Investigate how objects were camouflaged during the war and which animals have protective coloration.

BIBLIOGRAPHY

(**P** indicates recommended for primary grades, **I** for intermediate grades, **U** for upper grades.)

Adler, Irving, *Color in Your Life*, Day, 1962. Covers all aspects of color from a scientific point of view. **U**

———, *The Secret of Light*, International, 1952. Presents simple concepts of light and color, with theories about light and its properties. Includes sections on the relationship between light and atomic energy and on man's use of light to conquer nature. **U**

Adler, Irving, and Ruth, *Shadows*, Day, rev. ed., 1968. Covers the shadow cast by the moon, how to measure the height of a tree, how to tell time by a shadow, how to make shadow pictures. **I**

Beeler, Nelson, and Franklyn N. Branley, *Experiments With Light*, Crowell, 1958. Discusses the nature of light and its properties; includes lenses and their use in microscopes and telescopes. **U**

Bragdon, Lillian J., *Let There Be Light*, Lippincott, 1959. Describes man's use of fire, coal, gas, oil, and electricity to produce light. Explores future in lighting. **U**

Branley, Franklyn M., *North, South, East, and West*, Crowell, 1966. Helps children learn to tell directions by using their shadows. Beginning instructions on the use of the compass and beginning map reading included. **P**

Bulla, Clyde Robert, *What Makes A Shadow?*, Crowell, 1962. Answers the title question, also shows how to make simple shadow pictures with the hands. Well illustrated. **P**

Carona, Philip B., and Polly Balian, *Mirror on the Wall: How it Works*, Prentice-Hall, 1964. Simple explanations of light and how it shows an image in a mirror; clear illustrations. **P**

Feravolo, Rocco, *Junior Science Book of Light*, Garrard, 1961. Basic information about light. Simple experiments made more understandable by clear diagrams and illustrations. **I**

Freeman, Ira, *All About Light and Radiation*, Random, 1965. Lucid presentation of the principles of the science of light and radiation, Interesting discussion of the application's of X-rays, ultraviolet rays, and infrared rays; charts, diagrams, and photographs. **U**

Freeman, Mae, *Fun and Experiments With Light*, Random, 1963. Experiments for fifth and sixth graders using common materials, each with photographs and clear directions. **U**

Healey, Frederick, *Light and Color*, Day, 1962. Brief explanations and some home-style experiments invite the reader to make discoveries about light and color. A glossary of technical terms is helpful. **U**

Hellman, Hal, *The Art and Science of Color*, McGraw-Hill, 1967. From the physics of light and color, and some interesting effects, to practical applications. Simple experiments to carry out with readily available materials. Excellent bibliography. **U**

Kohn, Bernice, *Light You Cannot See*, Prentice-Hall, 1965. Various types of the invisible rays of the electromagnetic spectrum. Covers infrared rays, ultraviolet radiation, radio waves, microwaves, X rays, Gamma rays, cosmic rays, lasers, and lensless cameras. **U**

Mason, George F., *Animal Vision*, Morrow, 1968. Explains the animal and human eye and the functions of their parts. **U**

Meyer, Jerome S., *Prisms and Lenses*, World, 1959.

Explains the principles of light as they apply to prisms and lenses. **U**

Neal, Charles D., *Exploring Light and Color*, Children's Pr., 1964. Discussion of the properties of light and color as part of the science of optics. Many experiments using readily obtainable materials. Includes directions for constructing a kaleidoscope, a microscope, and a telescope. **U**

Paschel, Herbert P., *The First Book of Color*, Watts, 1959. The bases of light and color. **U**

Perry, John, *Our Wonderful Eyes*, McGraw-Hill, 1955. Structure, function, and proper care of the eyes. **U**

Pine, Tillie S., *Light All Around*, McGraw-Hill, 1961. From simple things that help us see at night, to the principle of the periscope. It could lead to further explorations of electricity, color, astronomy, and submarines. **I**

Polgreen, John, *Sunlight and Shadows*, Doubleday, 1967. The role of the sun, the reasons for the seasons, and how the earth spins. Several experiments and large, clear pictures and diagrams included. **I**

Ruchlis, Hy, *The Wonder of Light*. Harper, 1960. All aspects of light and its effects introduced and explored in clear, non-technical language and illustrated with diagrams and photographs. **U**

Sands, George, *Why Glasses? The Story of Vision*, Lerner, 1960. Simple explanation of how eyes function and why some people need glasses. Large, clear illustrations. **U**

Stockard, Jimmy, *Experiments for Young Scientists*, Little, Brown, 1964. Simple experiments (with safety rules and illustrations) demonstrating principles concerning air, water, light, sound, simple machines, and electricity. **I**

Using fire in one of its age-old roles—to clear a field before planting.

16 Fire

Fire is a constant fascination. Eyes are drawn to the glowing candles on a birthday cake and to the changing colors and shapes of the flames in a fireplace or campfire. The flare and glare of rockets and fireworks excite the imagination, and the raging flames of a burning building or forest fire invite awe and terror. Fire is a constant and pervasive part of one's environment.

THREE ESSENTIALS FOR FIRE

Fire—flame and heat—can occur only when some of the chemicals composing a fuel combine with the oxygen in the air. This chemical combination (see Chapter 10) takes place only if the temperature is high enough; how high depends on the fuel, for different fuels have different temperatures (kindling temperatures) at which they will combine with oxygen to produce flame and heat. Thus, the three elements needed to produce fire are a material that will "burn"—that is, fuel—enough heat to kindle the fuel, and air (or, rather, the oxygen in air).

Fuel

Natural fuels include wood, coal, crude oil, and natural gas. Derived or manufactured fuels include paper, wax, coke, charcoal, fuel oil, gasoline, kerosene, fuel gas, propane gas, and butane gas.

The surface area of a fuel plays an important part in getting the fuel to burn because the chemical combination of the fuel with oxygen (burning) takes place at the surface of the fuel. The greater the surface, the easier it will burn. To illustrate, first burn a sheet of paper crumpled into a tight ball, then burn a similar sheet spread out, and compare the rates of burning of both. One can do the same thing with two small pieces of absorbent cotton about the same size, one rolled into a tight little ball. Hold both with forceps or tongs while burning them.

Help children understand that with greater surface area a greater amount of oxygen can reach the fuel, and the rate of burning will therefore be increased. This is why powdered fuel burns so quickly. (See below under *Fire Hazards.*) Try setting fire to a lump of coal, then powder the coal and place it in a long-handled spoon. Holding the spoon as far away as possible, sprinkle some of the powdered coal into the flame of a Bunsen burner. The powder will burn quickly, giving off much heat.

Loosely fill a soda straw about one fourth full of lycopodium powder or fine, dry cornstarch. (Lycopodium is available at drugstores. The starch may be dried by placing it in an open dish on top of a hot radiator for a few hours.) Blow the powder or starch directly across the top of the flame of a Bunsen burner (Fig. 16-1), alcohol lamp, or Sterno flame. (Be sure to blow away from children.) A long flame results as all the powder burns instantly.

Also try to burn a solid piece of aluminum, then sprinkle aluminum powder onto a metal tray and put a gas flame to the powder. It will burst into flame. Or try to burn an iron nail, then carefully sprinkle iron filings into a gas flame; the iron particles will catch fire. (If a Bunsen burner is unavailable, use a portable gas tank torch sold in hardware stores.)

To show how one fuel—coke—is made, use a metal can with a tight-fitting cover, such as a coffee can. Punch a small hole in the center of the cover. Fill the can about one fourth full of soft coal that has been crushed or broken into small pieces. Heat the can and its contents on

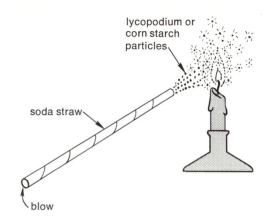

FIGURE **16-1**   Flash burning of small particles.

a hot plate or electric stove. A smoky gas will soon come through the nail hole. Wait a short while until all the air has been driven from the can; then try periodically to light the gas, which, with some smoke, is escaping from the hole. Heat the can until all the gas has burned. After the can has cooled, children may examine the contents. The solid black material is coke; the emitted gas was coal gas.

Repeat the experiment, using short pieces of wood. This time charcoal is formed. Or try using a crumpled sheet of newspaper or paper towel.

So that children can actually see what happens when the materials are heated in the absence of air, repeat the experiment using, instead of a tin can, a Pyrex test tube fitted with a one-hole cork stopper containing a short glass tube (Fig. 16-2). Place some crushed soft coal in the test tube, stopper tightly, and heat strongly over a Bunsen burner flame. Keep the burner moving to vary the point of heating. Light the gas that is given off and continue heating until no more gas is formed. Let the test tube cool, then break it and examine the coke that has been formed. As with the can, the experiment may be done using short pieces of wood.

To illustrate the burning of a liquid fuel, ignite some kerosene or alcohol in a small bottle cap. A Bunsen burner may be used to show gas combustion.

All fuels contain carbon; the products of the experiment above—coke and charcoal—are forms of carbon. A white china dish held above a candle flame will soon develop a black sooty spot, and flames from other fuels will have the same effect. This soot is unburned carbon, one of the components of most fuels. When the flame touches the dish, the porcelain cools the flame and the unburned carbon deposits on the dish.

As described in Chapter 10, one of the products of burning is carbon dioxide gas. Remind children that carbon dioxide (CO_2) is formed when the carbon (C) of the fuel combines with the oxygen (O_2) in the air. Use limewater (Chapter 10) to test for its presence as follows. Apply a lighted match to the bottom of a candle until the paraffin softens. Set the candle immediately in a tall drinking glass and hold the candle firmly until the paraffin hardens. Carefully pour limewater into the glass until it is one fourth full. Light the candle. Cover the glass with a saucer. When the candle goes out, shake the glass, keeping it well-covered with the saucer. The limewater becomes milky, showing the presence of carbon dioxide.

FIGURE 16-2 Making coal gas.

Or wrap a piece of copper wire around a candle. Light the candle and lower the candle into a tall bottle. When the flame goes out, remove the candle. Add some limewater to the jar, hold a hand over the mouth of the jar, and shake it. The limewater turns milky. Compare with some limewater shaken up in a jar of air only.

Another component of most fuels is hydrogen. Remind children that water is composed of two parts of hydrogen and one part of oxygen (H_2O). In the process of burning, the hydrogen of the fuel combines with the oxygen of the air to form water. This can be shown as follows. Chill a glass or beaker and hold it over a candle flame for a few seconds. A film of moisture forms on the glass. Repeat the experiment, using a chilled spoon. The spoon fogs up, and droplets of water may form. One of the products of burning, then, is water. Test other flames in this way to see if water is one of the products of burning.

Fuels usually contain carbon and hydrogen in complex forms. Benzene is C_6H_6. Good gasoline is C_8H_{18}. When fuels are burned, the heat breaks these complex substances into simpler substances which are gaseous. It is these gases that produce the flame.

Kindling Temperature

Usually fuels do not ignite by themselves, no matter how easily they burn; they must be heated until they are hot enough to burst into flame. The temperature at which the substance bursts into flame is called its *kindling temperature,* and each substance has a different kindling temperature.

To demonstrate differences in kindling temperature, bring a candle, celluloid film negative, twist of paper, twist of cotton cloth, thin stick of wood, and piece of coal to the flame of a Bunsen burner or alcohol lamp and note how long each takes to start burning. Hold the specimen in kitchen forceps, pliers, a long-handled spoon, or a long fork with a wooden handle. Have a pan or pail of water handy for safety. Try several other substances and have children list them in order of ease of burning.

To compare kindling temperatures, place a

sheet of iron or copper about 6 × 6 inches on a ring stand, tripod, or bricks (Fig. 16-3). A four-armed cross of metal cut from a tin can may be substituted for the sheet. Put the head of a match, a piece of sulfur, wood, and coal on the sheet or on each end of the arm. The materials must be approximately the same size and equidistant from the center of the sheet or cross. Place a Bunsen burner beneath the center of the sheet or cross, and light it. Note the order in which each material reaches its kindling temperature and bursts into flame. The coal may not burn. Actually, a fuel begins to burn only when enough of the fuel has vaporized. The kindling temperature involves vaporizing the material to the temperature at which the vapor bursts into flame. In a candle, for example, the wax must melt and then vaporize before a flame will be produced. This can be shown by inserting a long thin glass tube into the blue part of the candle flame and then igniting the gas or vapor that emerges from the other end of the tube (Fig. 16-4).

Air (Oxygen)

Halloween time provides an excellent opportunity to show children that air (or, rather, the oxygen component of air) is necessary to fire. If preparing a jack-o-lantern, first cut off the top of the pumpkin and scoop out the flesh and seeds. Before cutting out the nose and so on, place a candle inside the pumpkin, light it, and replace the top of the pumpkin. After a short while, lift

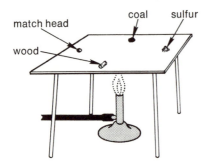

FIGURE **16-3** Comparing kindling temperatures of various substances.

up the pumpkin top and note that the flame has gone out. Now cut out the eyes, nose, and mouth, relight the candle, and put back the pumpkin top. The candle continues to burn brightly because it now has a constant supply of air through the holes made for the eyes, nose, and mouth. So that the process is visible, repeat, using a milk bottle inverted over a candle.

Stand at least six candles no more than 3 inches long on cardboard squares, index cards, or metal can covers (which are best). If necessary, cut new or used candles into the desired lengths and cut the paraffin away from one end until a wick remains that is at least $\frac{1}{4}$ inch long. Try to have all candles uniform in diameter and height. Fasten the candles to the cardboard or metal covers with 3 or 4 drops of hot wax.

Light one of the candles and set a glass jar or drinking glass over the candle. The flame will gradually go out. Light five candles in a row and, at the same time, cover four of them with different sizes of glass jars—preferably a half-pint, pint, quart, and gallon jar. This will help show that there is twice as much air in the pint jar as there is in the half-pint jar, and so on. The fifth candle, uncovered, is the "control." Using an electric clock or wristwatch with a sweep-second hand, have children note how long it takes for each covered candle to go out. The more air there is in the jar, the longer the candle will burn. The candle under the pint jar will burn about twice as long as the candle in the half-pint jar, and so on. Have children consider the relationship between the amount of air in the jars and the length of time the candles burn.

For another useful demonstration of the function of air in fire, cover two burning candles with glass chimneys (available from a hardware store) or two No. 2 cans with their tops removed and with a smaller opening cut in the bottom. Slip a flat stick or a pencil under one chimney. This candle will continue to burn because it has a ready supply of air entering from the bottom. The other candle goes out.

To show that it is only part of the air mixture—the oxygen—that supports burning, fasten

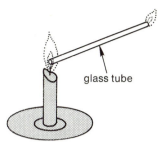

FIGURE **16-4** Demonstrating that a flame is a mass of burning gas.

a birthday-cake candle to the bottom of a small pan with a few drops of wax. Carefully pour about an inch of water into the pan and put a tall, clear drinking glass over the candle. The candle will soon go out and the water will rise somewhat in the glass. Children should understand that a part of the air (oxygen) has been used in the burning of the candle and that the water rises to take its place. Measure the height of the glass and the distance that the water rose in the glass. The water will have risen a distance corresponding to the amount of oxygen that has been used.

For upper-grade children who would like to measure precisely the amount of oxygen, set some red phosphorus on a flat cork or piece of plywood as a float. Red phosphorus can be obtained from a high school chemistry teacher or from a science supply house. (*Never use yellow [or white] phosphorus. More active than the red, it bursts into flame on contact with air.*) Place the cork in a basin of water and hold a large olive jar over the float. Touch the red phosphorus with a hot wire that has been heated in a candle flame. Then cover the float with the jar. At first a cloud of white phosphorus pentoxide forms, but this soon dissolves in the water. As it dissolves, water rises in the jar. Lift the jar to the point where its mouth is just below the water surface and measure the amount that the water rose.

The water will have risen about one fifth or 20% of the height of the jar, which roughly corresponds to the percentage of oxygen in the air. Actually a candle (unlike phosphorus) goes out

before all oxygen is removed, or when about less than 15% of oxygen is left.

Or wrap a piece of soft, thin wire around a candle, bending part of the wire to serve as a handle. Light the candle, lower it into a pint jar, then cover the jar with a sheet of glass or metal. The flame will soon go out. Remove the candle, keep the jar covered, relight the candle, and put it quickly into the jar. The flame will go out almost at once because so much of the oxygen in the jar has already been used that there is no longer enough to support combustion.

STRUCTURE OF A FLAME

A flame is a mass of burning gas; therefore, solid or liquid fuels must first be vaporized (by raising them to kindling temperature) if they are to burn. This was demonstrated above with a candle flame (Fig. 16-4) and a glass tube.

In another example of this, light a match and lower it to the wick of a candle. It will be necessary to actually touch the wick in order to light it. Let the candle burn for two or three minutes, and note the pool of melted paraffin around the base of the wick. Blow out the candle flame and immediately begin lowering a lighted match to the smoking wick. The wick will now light before the match touches it. Sometimes it is possible to light the candle this way when the match is an inch or more above the wick.

When the wick of a candle is first lighted, the heat of the burning wick melts the paraffin. The melted paraffin rises by capillary action (see Chapter 7) to the top of the wick, where the flame vaporizes it and it burns, becoming part of the flame. As long as the candle burns, paraffin will melt, rise up the wick, and then change to a gas, which burns. When the candle flame is extinguished, the warm wick continues to form gas for a short time. This gas, rising from the wick, is what ignites when the match has not yet touched the wick. Children can observe how the fuel rises in the lamp wicks of alcohol and kerosene lamps.

Have children carefully examine a candle flame and then draw what they see. Call attention to the two regions of the flame. The one next to the wick is dark, while the outside region is bright yellow. The gas of which the dark region is made cannot get as much air as the yellow outside region. Therefore, the gas in the dark region is not burning as completely and is not as hot. This can be shown by holding a round stick about 6 inches long in a candle flame almost touching the wick. Hold it there for a few seconds, then quickly lift it straight out of the flame. Note the dark ring which is formed, with the center uncharred. The uncharred part was in contact with the cooler inside region. The same effect can be shown by using a filing card. Hold it horizontally in the flame just above the wick. Remove the card as soon as it begins to scorch.

The Bunsen burner offers an excellent opportunity to observe how the supply of oxygen affects a flame. Adjust the opening at the base of the burner so that the flame is blue. Air (which contains oxygen) is able to come in through the opening and mix with the gas. The blue flame shows that the gas is being completely burned. Now close off the opening with the fingers, shutting off the supply of air. The flame changes from blue to yellow. The yellow color comes from hot but incompletely burned particles of carbon in the gas.

Hold a white china dish first against the yellow flame, then against the blue flame. The yellow flame will make the dish quite sooty, owing to the presence of the incompletely burned particles of carbon. The blue flame will form little or no soot, because the fuel is burning completely.

The yellow flame is not as hot as the blue. To show this, bring equal quantities of water to a boil with each flame, and note which causes boiling first.

Just as in the candle, the inner portion of the Bunsen flame is cooler than the outer because it does not get as much oxygen. Show this with a matchstick about 2 inches long. Push a pin through the match just below the head until the

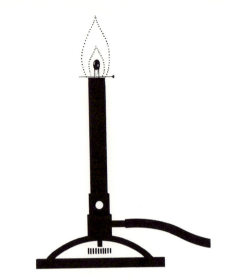

FIGURE **16-5** Demonstrating that the inner part of a flame is cooler than the outer.

pin extends about the same distance from each side of the match. Place the match, head up, into the barrel of an unlit burner, with the pin resting on the burner and supporting the match (Fig. 16-5). See that the match head is in the center of the tube. Adjust the opening at the base of the burner to allow as much air as possible to enter. Turn the gas on full and light the burner, igniting the gas from one side of the top of the barrel. Usually the gas will burn without setting the match on fire because the temperature of the inner portion of the flame is below the kindling temperature of the match head. Sometimes the match will burst into flame after the gas has been burning a while. If the school does not have a gas supply, use a simple portable gas burner and tank.

EXTINGUISHING AND PREVENTING FIRE

If any one of the three conditions necessary to have fire is missing, the fire will go out. If the fuel is removed, the fire cannot continue. A campfire can be put out be scattering the burning wood. In forest fires, the fire fighters clear a broad path or "fire break" around the burning area. A

When the fire reaches the path, it has no more fuel and goes out. In the case of fire in or near an oil tank, nearby tanks are emptied quickly. If a building is on fire, the gas supply is turned off and adjacent buildings are wet down with hoses.

Fire can be stopped by cooling the flammable material below its kindling temperature. To show this, turn on the gas full force in a Bunsen burner. Hold a sheet of iron, copper, or aluminum gauze about 2 inches above the barrel. Apply a lighted match to the gas above the gauze. A flame will appear above the gauze but not below it because the gauze conducts the heat of the flame away from the gas. This keeps the temperature of the gas underneath the gauze below the kindling temperature. Children may want to make a model of a miner's safety lamp, which uses this principle. Needed are two flat corks about 2 inches in diameter, a dozen thumbtacks, and a piece of fine copper or aluminum gauze or screen 2–8 inches wide. Set a lighted candle upright on one of the corks. Wrap the gauze around both corks (forming a tube) and fasten it securely with thumbtacks (Fig. 16-6). If the mesh is not fine enough, wrap it around two or three times. The heat from the candle flame is conducted to all parts of the gauze which absorbs the heat and thus lowers the temperature to a point below the kindling temperature of any flammable gas nearby. If the model of the miner's safety lamp is set inside a jar, flammable gas can safely be allowed to flow into the jar.

Water, the substance most often used to put out ordinary fires, does so principally in two ways. It is able to absorb much heat, which cools the burning material below its kindling temperature. It also coats the fuel, reducing its contact with oxygen. Hold most of a wooden match in water until it is quite wet. Children can note the time it takes to light the moist head of the match in a candle flame and the time required to light a dry match.

Water's fire-preventing properties may also be demonstrated as follows. Soak a handkerchief in a liquid made of 2 parts alcohol and 1 part water. Squeeze out excess liquid and hold the handkerchief with tongs over a metal basin, keeping it away from flammable materials. Apply a lighted match to the handkerchief; the alcohol will burn, but not the handkerchief, because the water keeps the temperature of the cloth below that at which it kindles. Or fill a very small, flat cardboard box half full of water. Place the box on a metal screen supported on a tripod, iron ring, or between two stacks of bricks. Heat the box with a Bunsen burner; the water will boil, but the cardboard will not burn.

Keeping air (oxygen) away from a fire will extinguish it. The smothering of fires is the principle behind sprinkling sand on campfires and wrapping a person whose clothes are burning in a blanket, rug, or woolen coat. In the latter case, it is important that the victim not run, because the breeze will fan the flames—that is, bring more oxygen in contact with the fire. If there is a fire in a room, opening the windows will have the same effect.

The most commonly used method of keeping air away from a fire is to replace the air with a heavy nonflammable gas such as carbon dioxide. To demonstrate this, put some dry ice (solid carbon dioxide) into a metal pitcher. (Handle the dry ice with gloves because it can cause frostbite.)

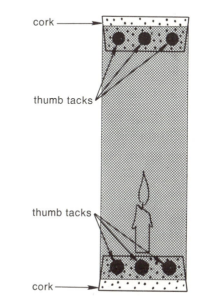

FIGURE 16-6 A model miner's safety lamp.

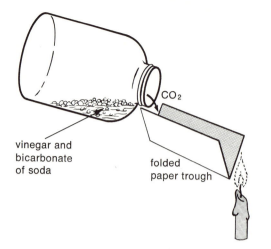

FIGURE **16-7** Carbon dioxide gas made with vinegar and bicarbonate of soda smothers a flame.

Let the pitcher stand while the dry ice sublimates (changes from solid directly to gas). Hasten this process by placing the bottom of the pitcher in hot water. (Carbon dioxide gas can be chemically prepared in the classroom. For details, see Chapter 10.) Wrap a thin wire around a lighted candle and lower the candle into the pitcher. The flame will go out. Another easy way to show the smothering quality of carbon dioxide is to tip a jar of vinegar and bicarbonate of soda so that only the gas formed flows down a paper trough (Fig. 16-7) aimed at a candle flame. Even more spectacular is the demonstration in which the carbon dioxide is poured down a trough containing many candles. Set five candles on a narrow piece of wood. Prepare a trough by tacking heavy paper or cardboard to the sides and ends of the wood. Tilt up one end of the piece of wood, light the candles, and pour the carbon dioxide gas down the trough. The candle flames will go out in succession.

In another demonstration, wrap a carbon dioxide cartridge (the kind that is used to make carbonated water at home) in a cloth and puncture it with a carbon dioxide cartridge gun. Aim the escaping gas at a candle flame. The cartridge gun may be obtained at a hobby shop, or the cartridge may be punctured with a sharp nail struck with a hammer. (It is necessary to act quickly, before all the carbon dioxide gas escapes.)

Fire Extinguishers

Ink-bottle extinguisher A simple fire extinguisher can be made as follows. With a hammer and nail punch a hole through the metal screw cap of an empty ink bottle that has a well on its side—such as the Skrip ink bottle. Insert a straw, glass tube, or straight medicine dropper through the hole (Fig. 16-8). Seal any openings around the hole with chewing gum or sealing wax. (To use a plastic tube or medicine dropper, punch a uniform hole slightly smaller than the diameter of the dropper and work the dropper in. The opening will be virtually airtight, making sealing wax unnecessary.) Fill the side pocket of the ink bottle with powdered bicarbonate of soda. Pour household vinegar into the bottle until it is about one fourth full. While pouring, be careful that the vinegar does not come in contact with the sodium bicarbonate. Screw the cap onto the ink bottle securely. The fire extinguisher is now ready. Crumple some paper in a shallow metal pan and set it afire. Tip the ink bottle upside down and aim the tube opening at the fire. It is not the carbon dioxide gas alone that puts out the fire, for the water helps as well.

Other soda-acid extinguishers The same experiment may be repeated on a large scale, using a milk or other wide-mouthed bottle (Figs. 16-9

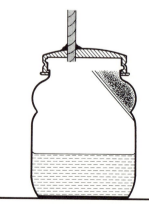

FIGURE **16-8** An ink-bottle fire extinguisher.

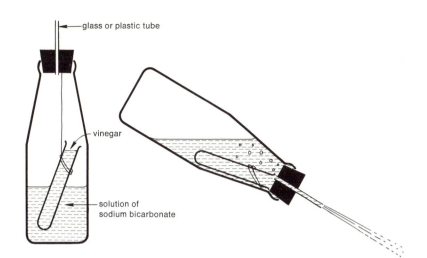

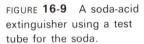

FIGURE **16-9** A soda-acid extinguisher using a test tube for the soda.

and 16-10). Insert a glass tube through a cork stopper that will fit the neck of such a bottle. Put the sealing wax or chewing gum around the point where the tube goes through the stopper. Fill the bottle half full of a solution of equal parts of vinegar and water. Fill a small test tube (Fig. 16-9) with powdered sodium bicarbonate and wrap some thin wire around the neck. Bend the other end of the wire into a hook and hang it from the lip of the bottle. Stopper the bottle tightly and invert it when ready to use. Figure 16-10 shows the same kind of extinguisher with the exception that the bicarbonate of soda is tied into a tissue paper bag instead of being held in a test tube.

In a commercial soda-acid fire extinguisher, the positions of the chemicals are reversed. The small vial contains sulfuric acid, which is a "stronger" acid than vinegar, and the rest of the container is filled with concentrated bicarbonate of soda solution.

Foam extinguisher Some fires, such as kerosene and oil fires, are difficult to put out with water or the usual type of fire extinguisher. To show this, pour $\frac{1}{4}$ ounce of kerosene into a small deep saucer. Light the kerosene and pour water onto it. Water, heavier than kerosene, sinks to the bottom, leaving the burning kerosene on top. Repeat this experiment, using the carbon dioxide extinguisher the rapid stream of which only stirs up the fire.

To combat kerosene and oil fires, a foam extinguisher must be used. To make one, dissolve as much baking soda as possible in a pint of water. Pour the resulting solution into a large jar. Put the white of an egg and some ground licorice root into the jar of baking soda solution and stir thoroughly. Then dissolve as much powdered alum as possible in another pint of water.

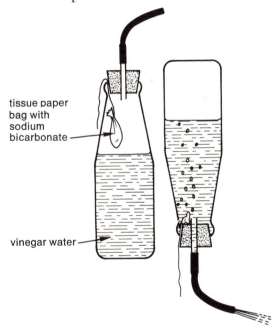

FIGURE **16-10** A soda-acid extinguisher using a tissue paper bag for the soda.

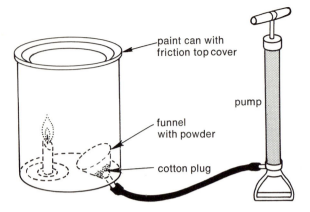

paint can with
friction top cover

pump

funnel
with powder

cotton plug

FIGURE **16-11** Demonstrating how fine powder can produce an explosion.

Pour the alum solution quickly into a large jar that contains the baking soda solution. A large quantity of white foamy bubbles of carbon dioxide gas are formed. These bubbles are slow to break because the egg white and alum of which they are made makes a tough film. The foamy bubbles cover kerosene and oil fires effectively, smothering them.

Fireproofing

Mix equal parts of borax, alum, and ammonium phosphate. Dissolve as much of the mixture as possible in a bowl two thirds full of warm water. When no more can dissolve, the powdered material will begin to accumulate in the bottom of the bowl. Dip pieces of cloth in this solution and allow to dry. Try to burn these pieces of cloth in a candle flame; compare with untreated pieces of cloth.

Another fireproofing solution for cloth may be made by using equal parts of borax and boric acid in enough warm water for both chemicals to dissolve completely. Treat the cloths, and test as described above.

Fireproof paints owe their fireproofing quality to the presence of water-glass (sodium silicate). To show this, paint a strip of wood with at least three coats of water-glass solution. Allow each coat to dry before applying the next coat. When the last coat has been applied and is dry, hold the stick over the flame of a Bunsen burner or gas range. The coating swells and a froth is formed, but the wood will not burn.

Paper may be fireproofed by dissolving 2 ounces of ammonium sulfate, $\frac{1}{2}$ ounce of borax, and $\frac{1}{2}$ ounce of boric acid in enough warm water to dissolve all three chemicals completely. Immerse the paper and allow it to dry.

FIRE HAZARDS

Fire is useful and essential for daily living. However, fire out of control is a dangerous and expensive hazard. There are many ways in which fire can be created accidentally, often with disastrous results.

Tiny particles of a flammable material create a hazard because the smaller the particles the more surface offered per unit of fuel. To demonstrate, partially fill a soda straw with lycopodium powder or fine, dry cornstarch. When the powder is blown across a flame (Fig. 16-1), a quick flash (rapid burning) results. This can be shown on a larger scale with a large metal can that has a tight-fitting, press-on cover. Punch a round hole at one end, put a funnel into the hole from the inside, attach a rubber tube to the small end of the funnel and set a candle inside the can opposite the funnel (Fig. 16-11). Tilt the funnel so that it is aimed at the candle wick. Place a small wad of cotton in the bottom of the funnel and then add a teaspoon of lycopodium powder. Light the candle and put the can cover on securely. With the mouth or with a pump attached to the rubber tube, blow a blast of air sharply into the can. The powder, now a cloud of dust, is kindled by the candle flame and burns explosively. The resultant sudden heating of the air and production of gases blow the cover up into the air. (*Caution: Do not perform the demonstration under a light fixture and be sure to have children stand back.*)

Kerosene sprayed from an atomizer across a candle flame will also burn with an explosive flash. The atomizer makes many tiny particles of the kerosene. (*Keep children back and exercise caution.*)

The same effect can be produced with a flammable gas. Punch a hole low on the side of a coffee can with a tight-fitting press-on cover. The hole should be large enough for a rubber tube to fit in snugly. Punch a smaller hole in the can cover, connect one end of the rubber tubing to a gas supply, and place the other end inside the hole at the side of the can (Fig. 16-12). Turn on the gas and let it enter the can until it has displaced *all* the air inside the can. Then light the gas escaping through the hole in the can cover. Turn off the gas and remove the tubing. The escaping gas burns quietly at first while fresh air is coming in the hole at the side of the can. Soon the combination of gas and air reaches the proportions of an explosive mixture—in which the particles of gas in the can, formerly surrounded only by other particles of gas, become surrounded by air. At this point there is an explosion and the cover blows off. (*Caution: The can should be shielded with fish net, screening, or wire gauze, and children should be kept well away.*)

The same effect takes place with gasoline, which, if allowed to, will evaporate quickly to form a gas. When mixed with air in the correct proportion (about 16 to 1), it forms an explosive mixture.

That a lighted cigarette can be a fire hazard can be shown with tinder. Tinder is very much like the decayed leaves and brush of a forest. One can make tinder by shredding dead bark and heating it in an oven. (A Boy Scout may be able to supply some.) Place the tinder in a metal pan and put the lighted cigarette on it. Blow gently

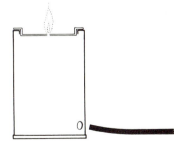

FIGURE **16-12** Gas can produce an explosion.

on the glowing tinder until the tinder bursts into flame. A flipped cigarette and a breeze make ideal conditions for a forest fire.

The sun's rays, when focused properly, can also cause fire. To show this, place a match in a metal pan, and, with a magnifying glass, focus sunlight on the match head. The match head will soon burst into flame. Focus the sunlight on a child's hand for a few seconds and have him note the heat produced. Or place a round goldfish bowl in the sunlight. Find where the sun's rays come together at a point, just as with the magnifying glass. Place the bulb of a thermometer near that point of focus. Note how the temperature rises. Discarded soda bottles acting as lenses can cause forest fires this way.

Have children rub a pencil eraser briskly on their desks and then place the eraser to their lips. The eraser will be quite warm. The heat, due to friction, is enough to start a fire. A knife placed against a grindstone produces enough heat to make sparks, which are burning particles of stone and iron that are rubbed off during the grinding. Persons working in flour mills wear rubber soles so as not to create sparks, which nails in leather soles might cause. Such sparks could set fire to the flour dust, causing the whole mill to explode into fire, just as the lycopodium powder did in the experiment above.

In the home, electrical wiring can be a hazard. The resistance of the wires to the flow of electric current produces heat. Sometimes the insulation surrounding the wires is worn away until the wires are exposed and touch. The heat of the wires when they short-circuit may set materials in the walls on fire.

Dismantle the electric cord from an old flatiron. The wire is wrapped in asbestos or mica rather than in the rubber usually found on ordinary electric wire. Hold the asbestos or mica in a candle flame to show that it does not burn. Place a piece of rubber from ordinary electric wire in a candle flame and show that it chars. Point out the necessity for special asbestos-insulated cords for appliances such as electric irons, toasters, heaters, and stoves, which get very hot when operating.

Another fire hazard is that of paper and fabric lamp shades which burn when they rest too near an electric light bulb. Show how a piece of paper wrapped around a 100-watt electric bulb that is lighted will scorch after a few minutes.

Christmas trees are very flammable, especially if not kept moist by standing in a bucket of water. Place in a large pan or basin a branch that has been allowed to dry in a warm room for several days. Note how much more easily it can be set afire than a freshly cut branch allowed to stand in water for a few days.

Oily rags are also a hazard because they can burst into flame by spontaneous combustion. When placed in a closet, the oil in the rag combines slowly with oxygen in the air, giving off heat, which cannot escape the closed closet. This added heat makes the oil combine more quickly with the oxygen, and correspondingly more heat is given off. This process continues until the oily rag becomes hot enough to reach its kindling point and burst into flame.

BUILDING A FIRE

The principles of building a campfire or a fire in a fireplace is based on the idea of arranging the materials so that one begins with easily kindled material, which in turn sets afire the next most easily kindled. A camper first piles up dry leaves, then small twigs, and finally heavier wood, always allowing plenty of air space. He uses a lighted match to heat the thin, quickly heated leaves to their kindling temperature. The heat of the leaves, in turn, heats the twigs to their kindling temperature. As the twigs burn, more air is able to reach up through the pile.

In a fireplace, the wood rests upon supports called andirons, which keep the fire off the bricks and thus permit a steady supply of fresh air underneath the fire. Paper, thin pieces of wood, and logs arranged in the same way as in the campfire progressively reach their kindling points. Coal takes a long time to reach kindling temperature.

Coloring Flames

Dry pine cones or small chips or blocks of dry wood soaked in various solutions and added to a campfire or fireplace will produce striking colors. One solution employs copper sulfate (obtain from a science supply house or drugstore) dissolved in water in the ratio of 1 pound of copper sulfate to 1 gallon of water. Stir thoroughly in wooden bucket or earthenware jar. Place cones in a mesh bag, like an onion or potato sack, and immerse them in the solution. Let them soak overnight, drain over the container for a few minutes, then spread the cones on a newspaper to dry overnight. In a fire they produce a beautiful emerald-green color. A Barium nitrate solution produces an apple-green flame; strontium nitrate, red; copper chloride, bluish-green; potassium chloride, purple. Potassium chloride and copper chloride are the least expensive. (Do not reuse the bucket or jar unless it is thoroughly cleaned. Do not pour remaining chemical solutions down sinks or drains unless the plumbing is made of lead. Even then the pipes should be flushed with water for some time after the solution has been disposed of. The solution may be poured directly into a sewer or into the ground in a waste plot or dump.)

Yule Logs

Yule logs, which produce rainbow colors, may be made as follows. Fold newspapers in half and roll them into logs about 3 × 16 inches. Tie the paper logs with twine. The following quantities of chemicals will make about eight logs: 5 pounds of copper sulfate (blue stone), 4 pounds of iron sulfate (green vitriol), and 3 pounds of rock salt—all dissolved in about 8 gallons of water. (Nurseries usually have these three chemicals.) Soak the rolled newspapers in this solution. Keep the container covered, and frequently turn the paper logs end over end. After 3 weeks remove the logs and let them dry thoroughly, preferably in the sun. One log will burn in a fireplace for several hours.

SUGGESTED PROJECTS

1. Make lists of fuels used in the community. Classify them as natural or manufactured, and note whether they are solid, liquid, or gas. Children may want to assemble a sample collection of fuels obtained from home or from fuel dealers. Discuss the advantages and disadvantages of each kind of fuel for various uses.

2. Examine the school heating system. Discuss what conditions are necessary to create fire and what products are formed by fire.

3. Investigate the cooking gas used in one's locality. Determine whether it is natural gas, bottled gas, or coal gas. Have children find out what it is, where it comes from, and how it is obtained.

4. Investigate the manufacture of the match. Have students report on its history. Demonstrate differences between friction matches and safety matches. Demonstrate the proper way to strike a match—away from, not toward one. Discuss the reasons for closing the cover of book matches before striking a match.

5. Make candles, using paraffin, candle wax, and odd pieces of candles. Heat them on a hot plate in the top of a double boiler. Add pieces of colored wax crayons to give the desired color. After the wax is melted, pour the wax into frozen juice cans or tin Jello molds. Put braided wicks in place and allow the wax to harden. The candles may be removed by soaking the cans or molds in hot water. Light the candles and study flames and the process of burning.

6. Study the construction and operation of cigarette lighters. Lead into a discussion of the conditions necessary for supporting fire and for extinguishing it.

7. Show why certain foods are called "fuel" foods by burning small amounts of butter or olive oil, bread, and nuts. Sugar, even though dipped first in ashes, will burn.

8. Find out how the fire extinguishers in your school work. Discuss the different methods for extinguishing fires.

9. Discuss fire hazards in the home. Make up safety rules.

10. Make two costumes of light net fabric. Treat one with fireproofing solution. Hang these costumes from a fence in the school yard. Have one child touch a lighted candle to each costume.

11. Have children examine a gas stove and compare it with a Bunsen burner.

BIBLIOGRAPHY

(**P** indicates recommended for primary grades, **I** for intermediate grades, **U** for upper grades.)

Adler, Irving, *Fire in Your Life,* Day, 1955. Historical and mythological background of fire, including the "phlogiston" theory. Explains what fire is and its use in industry. **U**

Barr, George, *Young Scientist and the Fire Department,* McGraw-Hill, 1966. Excellent material covering fire, how it was discovered, how to control and extinguish it. **I**

Brandwein, P., et al., *You and Science,* Harcourt, 1960. A survey of science with many simple demonstrations suggested. **U**

———, *You and Your World,* Harcourt, 1960. A survey of natural phenomena with many simple demonstrations suggested. **U**

Holden, Raymond, *All About Fire,* Random, 1964. Covers man's use of fire, and advances in fire-fighting techniques. **U**

Judge, Frances, *Forest Fire!,* Knopf, 1962. Modern methods of fighting forest fires, including the work and training of rangers, fire guards, lookouts, and fire-fighting crews. Well illustrated with photographs. **U**

Parker, Bertha M., *Fire,* Harper & Row, 1959. Discusses what fire is, how to produce it, and how to put it out. **I**

———, *Fire, Friend and Foe,* Harper & Row, 1941. Story of fire, with section on fire prevention. **U**

Torbert, Floyd, *Fire Fighters the World Over,* Hastings, 1967. History and development of fire-fighting techniques from ancient to modern times. **U**

Desert heat and the resultant differences in air density refract an image so that car and trees seem reflected in still water.

17 *Heat*

All substances are composed of molecules in motion. Heat is a direct manifestation of how rapidly these molecules are moving—the more rapid the movement, the higher the temperature.

Rubbing the hands together briskly produces heat, evidence of increased molecular motion. Bending a wire back and forth several times will make it get hot because the molecules have been made to move faster.

HEAT MAKES MATERIALS EXPAND

When heat is applied to a substance, the molecules move faster and are farther apart. When the substance is cooled, the molecules move more slowly and come closer together. In the solid state, the molecules are comparatively close together. In fact, scientists believe that in solids each molecule is fixed but vibrating. As the molecules vibrate more rapidly (in the solid state) or move farther apart (in the liquid state), the substance expands.

Solids

To illustrate how heat makes solids expand, remove the insulation from about 4 feet of bell wire (No. 18, available from a hardware store) and attach the wire to the backs of two chairs (back-to-back on a table) so that it is stretched tight. Using cotton thread or string, suspend a knife from the center of the wire so that the blade point just clears the table top. Then heat the wire by moving an alcohol lamp or Bunsen or propane[1] burner flame back and forth under it. In a few moments, the blade point will touch the table top. Point out that the wire, when heated, expands and thus becomes longer, causing the wire to sag. Have the children watch the knife after the flame is removed and the wire allowed to cool. As the wire contracts, the blade point rises until it again clears the table top.

Needed for another demonstration are two pieces of wood or dowels and a large screw and screw eye made of the same metal. The head of the screw should barely be able to pass through the screw eye. Screw each one into an end of the pieces of wood, leaving at least 1 inch of the metal exposed (Fig. 17-1). Heat the screw in a flame for a short while; then try to pass it through the screw eye. Because the screw expanded when it was heated, it will not be able to pass through. Now keep the screw hot in one flame and heat the screw eye in another flame. This time the screw will pass through the screw eye because both have expanded. Plunge the screw eye into cold water. Cooled by the water, the screw eye will contract and the heated screw will not be able to pass through. Cooling the screw in cold water will contract it and enable it once again to pass through the screw eye.

Figure 17-2 shows an arrangement for measuring the amount of expansion of a metal rod

[1] Small cylinders of propane gas—an excellent substitute for a Bunsen burner—are now available to the public. The cylinder, supported on a stand, has a valve which controls the amount of gas released.

FIGURE **17-1** A screw and screw eye prepared for demonstration of expansion of a solid by heat.

when heated. (Aluminum or copper is best, but brass or iron also works well. A flat strip is preferable, but a rod, such as a solid brass curtain rod, is satisfactory.) Glue or nail a 2×4-inch block of wood firmly to each end of a $\frac{1}{2}$-inch board about 3 feet long and 6 inches wide. With bent nails, securely fasten a 3-foot metal strip or rod to one wood block. Place a dowel or glass rod about $\frac{1}{4}$ inch in diameter on the second wooden block and rest the other end of the metal rod on the dowel or glass rod.

At its midpoint, glue or tack a cardboard arrow to the center of the dowel or rod. Cut out and mark a piece of cardboard as shown to make a dial. Tack the dial to the wooden block so that it is directly behind the arrow.

Heat the center of the metal rod with a candle. As the rod is heated, it expands, moving across the dowel or rod and causing it to rotate and

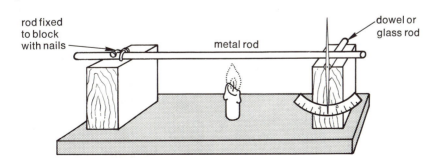

rod fixed to block with nails

metal rod

dowel or glass rod

FIGURE **17-2** Measuring the expansion of a metal rod.

the pointer to move along the dial. Heat the metal rod by moving the candle back and forth under it. Using three candles at one time, have children note how far the arrow moves (or how much the metal rod expands).

Children may have noticed the spaces between sidewalk slabs or between sections of railroad tracks. These allow the concrete or the track to expand in summer without buckling and to contract in the winter without forming cracks. Bridge construction also allows for expansion and contraction.

Note that telephone wires sag more in the summer heat than in winter cold. Iron rims are fitted onto wagon wheels while the rims are red-hot. When they cool, they contract and fit tightly on the wagon wheel. Steel rivets that hold steel girders together in buildings and bridges are put in red-hot. They contract when cold and hold the steel together.

When a metal cover on a glass jar is stuck tight, pouring hot water on the metal cover will cause it to expand so that it can be unscrewed more easily.

Rubber seems to be an exception to the rule that solids expand when heated. To illustrate, place a wooden board over two chairs placed back-to-back. Screw a cup hook into the underside of the board. Cut a rubber band in two and tie one end of it to the cup hook. Attach a teacup to the other end. Now pass a candle flame rapidly up and down the rubber band many times. (Do not hold the flame at any one spot too long, or the rubber will burn.) The teacup will be jerked upward as the rubber band contracts.

Rate of change Different solids expand and contract at different rates when heated or cooled. To demonstrate this, obtain a 12×2-inch strip of copper and of iron. If the iron strip is unavailable at hardware stores, cut one from a "tin" can, using tin snips. Brass can be used instead of copper. Trim the edges carefully so that they can be handled safely. Place the two strips together and punch holes in them at 2-inch intervals with a large nail (Fig. 17-3a). Bind the strips together with bolts passed through the holes. Make a handle of two pieces of wood placed one on each side of the strips and covering an end hole of those punched earlier. Bore a hole through the pieces of wood so that a bolt can be passed through them and the hole in the metal strips. Tighten a nut onto the bolt. The resulting compound bar (bimetallic strip) can also be purchased from a scientific supply company.

Place the compound bar in the flame of a Bunsen or propane burner or container of "canned heat." When the bar is heated, the copper expands more than the iron, so that the strip bends (Fig. 17-3b) away from the copper side of the strip; cooled, it bends the other way.

The compound bar can be used as a thermostat to show how the thermostat works as part of the

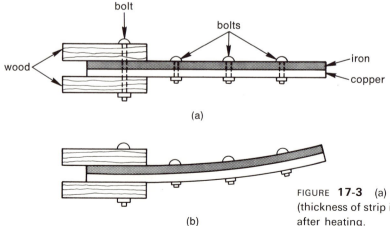

FIGURE **17-3** (a) Construction of compound bar (thickness of strip is exaggerated); (b) compound bar after heating.

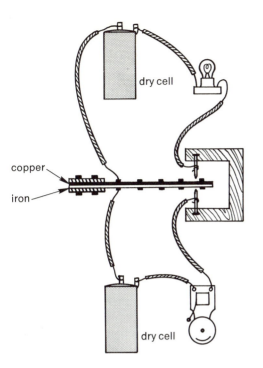

copper

iron

dry cell

dry cell

FIGURE **17-4**   A homemade thermostat.

heat control system in a room. Needed are two dry cells, bell wire, a bell, a miniature porcelain socket containing a one-cell electric bulb ($1\frac{1}{2}$ volts), and a U-shaped block of wood, as shown in Fig. 17-4. Punch nails into the top and bottom of the block of wood. Wire a dry cell and the bell to one nail and the compound bar. Connect a dry cell and the bulb to the other nail and the compound bar. Support the compound bar between two books, with the copper strip on top. The projection of the nails should be adjusted so that they are very close to but not touching the compound bar. Heat the compound bar. It will curve upward, touching the nail, and complete the bulb circuit, lighting the bulb. In a real thermostat, completing this circuit would shut off the furnace and thus reduce heat coming into the room. Remove the flame, let the bar cool, and then place small pieces of ice on it. The bar will bend down, touching the other nail, and complete the bell circuit. In a real thermostat, completing this circuit would ignite the furnace, sending heat into the room.

Liquids

To demonstrate the expansion of liquids when heated, fill a bottle to the top with water colored with red ink or vegetable dye. Insert a one-hole rubber stopper containing a glass or plastic tube about 12 inches long. (Use a twisting, rotary motion when pushing the tube into the stopper.) When the stopper is pressed into the bottle, the liquid will rise a short way up the tube. Mark the level with a rubber band around the tube. When the bottle is set in a jar or pan of hot water, the liquid will rise in the tube. If the bottle is then placed in a pan of very cold water, the level of the liquid in the tube will fall below the point marked by the rubber band.

Children should now realize that water will expand when heated and contract when cooled. Repeat the experiment with other liquids, such as alcohol or mercury, to show that the effect is the same. Or fill the bottle with very hot water. Stopper the bottle or cover the top and sides with plastic wrap to prevent the water from evaporating. When the water has cooled to room temperature, remove the stopper or covering. The bottle will no longer be filled to the top because when the water cooled it contracted, reducing its volume.

As stated above, when heat is applied to a liquid, the molecules of which it is composed move faster. This causes the molecules to move farther apart, and the liquid expands. When the molecules spread out, this increases the space between them so that the same amount of space is occupied by fewer molecules. This means that, when warm, liquids will weigh less per unit of volume. On the same basis, liquids weigh more when they are cold because the molecules are packed more closely together in the same amount of space. To prove this, fill a milk bottle with hot water that has been colored with red ink or vegetable dye. Fill an identical bottle with very cold, clear water. Hold a piece of cardboard firmly over the mouth of the bottle containing the cold water; invert the bottle and place it on the mouth of the bottle of hot water. Making sure that the mouths are exactly aligned, slowly pull out the cardboard. The colored (hot) water will immediately spurt up into the cold clear water. Point out that, even though both bottles have the same volume of water, the cold water weighs more than the hot water and immediately falls, pushing up the warmer, colored water.

Repeat the experiment but reverse the procedure, tinting the cold water and leaving the hot water clear. Invert the hot-water bottle and remove the card. Little happens because the colder, heavier (colored) water stays in the bottom bottle except for some minor diffusion.

The behavior of water when it approaches the freezing point is an exception to the rule that a substance contracts as it becomes colder. At ordinary temperatures, water expands when heated and contracts when cooled, like other liquids. However, water ceases to contract at a temperature of 39°F (4°C) and, if cooled still more, begins to expand and continues to expand until it freezes at 32°F (0°C). When it freezes and forms ice, it expands even more. This makes ice lighter than water, which explains why ice floats in water.

Since water at 39°F has contracted more than water at 32°F (the freezing point), the water at 39°F is heavier and sinks. This keeps the coldest water at the top and is why rivers, ponds, lakes, and oceans freeze first at the top. Thus, if water did not behave in this unusual manner but kept getting heavier as it got colder, then the coldest water would always be at the bottom, ice would form from the bottom up, and ponds and lakes might freeze solid, killing all living things in them.

To demonstrate the expansion of water as its temperature goes below 39°F, crack ice into small pieces by wrapping it in an old towel or cloth and hitting it with the broad side of a hammer. Fill a small bottle (with a screw cap) with water, leaving no air space. Screw the cap on, wrap the bottle in a piece of cloth, place it in a metal box or can, and pack the cracked ice around it, alternating layers of ice with layers of salt. (Pack the ice and salt compactly.) After a half hour remove the ice and salt and carefully unwrap the cloth. Point out that, when the water

began to freeze, it expanded and caused the bottle to burst. Repeat the experiment, using a small can with a screw top. The can may not burst, but it will swell under the pressure of the expanding water.

Should children wonder why a mixture of ice and salt was used, point out that salt lowers the freezing point of water. Show this by putting a thermometer into a mixture of finely cracked ice, a little cold water, and salt for five minutes. The temperature of the mixture will read well below 32°F (freezing point). Compare the temperature of a mixture of ice and water.

Gases

Gases also expand when they are heated and contract when they are cooled. Insert a 12-inch glass or plastic tube into a one-hole rubber stopper, and put the stopper into a soda bottle. Fill a bowl or jar with water colored with red ink or vegetable dye. Place the end of the tube in the bowl of colored water and heat the bottle by clasping it tightly with the palms of the hands or by wrapping a rag soaked in hot water around the bottle. Bubbles of air will come from the end of the tube as the air in the bottle is heated, expands, and pushes out of the tube.

Remove the hands or the hot cloth and hold the bottle upright by the neck with the fingers. After a while the colored water will rise into the tube. Point out that when the heated air cools it contracts, leaving a partial vacuum (Chapter 5, p. 86), which the colored water, entering the tube, fills. If the bottle is heated again, the water in the tube will move down.

In another demonstration of the expansion of gas, snap a small balloon over the neck of a soda bottle. (Stretch the balloon first to be sure it will inflate easily.) Place the bottle on a hot radiator or in a bowl of very hot water. The balloon will inflate as the air inside the bottle becomes heated and expands. Place the bottle in a bowl of ice or very cold water, noting how the balloon deflates as the heated air cools and contracts.

As with liquids, gases weigh less when heated. To show this, suspend two containers (cut from milk cartons) upside down from a ruler or stick (Fig. 17-5). The containers should be as nearly the same size as possible. Adjust the center loop and (if necessary) the end loops until the two containers are balanced. Hold an electric lamp under the open bottom of one container. As air in the container is warmed, the other container (unheated air) moves downward, showing that it is heavier. The molecules of air in the warmed container move faster and expand, and some of them leave the container. The molecules of cold air, less active, remain closer together; thus, the container of cold air holds more air molecules, and is heavier.

TEMPERATURE MEASUREMENT

The measurement of temperature fascinates children. They know from experience that some things are warmer or colder than other things. Because most children distinguish between hot and cold by using their sense of touch, point out that the sense of touch may not be accurate, and is sometimes deceptive. To illustrate, arrange, side by side, three pans of water—hot (as hot as children can stand without discomfort), lukewarm (about room temperature), and very cold. Have children put one hand in the pan of hot water and the other in the pan of cold water for about a minute. Then have them place both hands in the lukewarm water. They will note that the lukewarm water feels hot to the hand that was in the cold water, while the same water feels cold to the hand that was in the hot water.

Thermometers

It may be useful to remind children that temperature is actually a form of measurement, like the inch, foot, or yard, and that the thermometer stands in relation to temperature as the ruler does to distance.

Mercury thermometer Have the children examine a mercury thermometer and the markings on it. Note the bulb at the bottom, which contains the mercury, and the slender channel in the glass

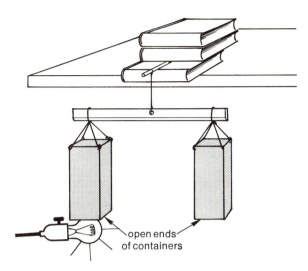

FIGURE **17-5** Demonstrating that heated air weighs less, per unit of volume.

tube, in which the mercury travels. Place the thermometer in a glass of warm water and observe the column of mercury rise in the tube; then place it in a glass of cold water and watch the mercury column fall.

Point out that when the thermometer comes in contact with warm objects, the mercury inside becomes warm, expands, and rises up the tube. The amount it will rise depends on how warm the mercury becomes. When the mercury comes in contact with cold objects, it cools and contracts, and the level in the tube falls.

Children should understand that the markings on the thermometer are manmade. To show how these markings are derived, stand a thermometer in a glass jar containing a mixture of ice and water for 20 minutes. This will reduce the temperature to the freezing point of water, which, on the Fahrenheit scale of temperature measurement, is 32°. Then boil water and place the thermometer in it for five minutes. This will increase the temperature to the boiling point of water, which, on the Fahrenheit scale, is 212°. (If this is done at a high altitude, the boiling point may register slightly lower than 212° because of the reduced air pressure.)

Point out that on the Fahrenheit scale the difference between the boiling point (212°) and the freezing point (32°) is 180°, and the distance between the two is divided into 180 equal spaces or, degrees Fahrenheit. On the centigrade or Celsius (metric or scientific) system, freezing point is designated 0° and boiling point 100°, so that the space between these two points on the thermometer is divided into 100 equal divisions, each of which is a degree Celsius. Thus, 32° Fahrenheit, or freezing point, equals 0° Celsius; 212° Fahrenheit, or boiling point, equals 100° Celsius.

It is not necessary to explain the Celsius grade scale in the lower grades unless children raise the question. Point out that in the United States the Fahrenheit scale is used for everyday nonscientific temperature measurements. The Celsius scale is used in the laboratory for scientific measurements.

Water thermometer   The oldest of the temperature-measuring devices is the water thermometer. To make a water thermometer (Fig. 17-6), fill a bottle with water colored with ink or vegetable dye. (If the thermometer will be kept outdoors in winter, replace a quarter of the water with rubbing alcohol to prevent freezing.) Insert a long glass or clear plastic tube into a one-hole rubber stopper and fit the stopper into the bottle. With a medicine dropper, add more colored water through the open end of the tube until the water is halfway up the tube. Fasten a white index card behind the tube with strips of cellophane tape.

Place the thermometer on the window sill and have the children mark the card at the level of the liquid. Also read the actual temperature on a standard commercial thermometer and have the children mark the temperature on the index card each day. In about a month, the water thermometer will be calibrated, and the children can read the temperature directly from the index card.

If space is available, each pupil can make his own thermometer. Half-pint cream or milk bottles can be used to conserve space.

Gas thermometer   Although a gas thermometer is the simplest of all thermometers, it is the most sensitive and accurate. Scientists use gas thermometers that usually contain hydrogen; for elementary school use, air will serve. Use a thin-walled, flat-sided medicine bottle that has a metal screw cap (preferred) or a cork. Fit a clear plastic drinking straw through a hole in the center of the cap or cork and put the cap on the bottle. Seal the straw in the hole with candle or sealing wax.

With wire or string fastened with nails, attach the inverted bottle to a thick flat board (Fig. 17-7). Place the end of the straw in a small glass or bottle of colored ink or vegetable dye.

Warm the bottle with the hands until many air bubbles move out of the end of the straw into the liquid below. Then remove the hands and wait at least fifteen minutes. A small column of colored liquid will rise in the tube to take the place of the warmed air that escaped (bubbles).

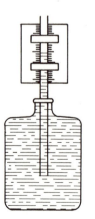

FIGURE **17-6**   A water thermometer.

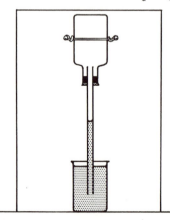

FIGURE **17-7**   An air (or gas) thermometer.

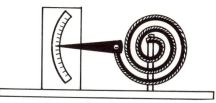

FIGURE **17-8** A metal thermometer.

Now place the hand against the bottle. As before, the air in the bottle becomes warm, expands, and forces down the liquid in the straw. Place a sponge soaked in very cold water on the bottle. The air thus cooled contracts and the liquid rises in the straw quite rapidly. On this thermometer, a difference of one degree may produce a difference of one or more inches in the level of the fluid in the tube.

Metal thermometer When temperatures are very high, a liquid thermometer cannot be used because the liquid would boil and break the bulb. Consequently, a solid (usually a metal) is used.

Remind children of or repeat the above-mentioned experiment illustrating how heat makes solids expand (Fig. 17-2). Point out again that, as the rod is heated, it expands and rubs against the wooden dowel, causing it to turn.

Remove the coiled spiral spring from an inexpensive or discarded oven thermometer. This spring is actually a coiled compound bar made of brass and iron welded together. When the coil is heated (or cooled), the metals expand (or contract), and cause the coil to turn, and, thus, move an attached pointer along a dial, indicating changes in temperature.

Straighten the coil and punch a hole in each end. Rewind the coil into a loose spiral about 2 inches in diameter, making sure that the brass side is on the outside. Nail or screw a $6 \times 3 \times \frac{1}{2}$-inch piece of wood to a larger piece of wood (Fig. 17-8). Draw a dial face on a white index card and glue or tack it to the side of the erect piece of wood. Nail a wooden dowel or narrow piece of wood (about 3 inches long) to the base, a few inches away from the dial. Tack the inside end of the coil to the top of the dowel. Cut a thin pointer from a tin can; using tin snips, punch

a hole into the broad end of the pointer, and tack or screw it to the outer end of the spiral. Bend the outer end of the spring until the pointer is at the midpoint of the dial.

Pass a lighted candle across the spring and have children note how the pointer rises. An electric bulb brought near will produce the same effect. Place the thermometer in the refrigerator or outside on a cold day, and note how the pointer falls. Put it on or near a radiator and the pointer will rise again.

Clinical thermometer A clinical thermometer may be bought in a drugstore or borrowed from a school nurse. Take the temperature of several of the children. Always sterilize the thermometer after each reading by dipping it into alcohol or an antiseptic solution and then rinsing in cold water. Let the children see how one shakes down the mercury column after each reading. Point out that the body temperature of most people is $98\frac{6}{10}$ (98.6)°F. Fever is an elevation of that temperature. Because body temperature is so important in detecting illness, the clinical thermometer is constructed so as to be very sensitive to changes in temperature. It is marked off in tenths of a degree, rather than in degrees, as in room thermometers.

In an ordinary thermometer, the level of the mercury begins to fall as soon as the thermometer is allowed to cool. This would occur as soon as the thermometer was taken out of the mouth, making it impossible to obtain an accurate reading of a person's temperature. To prevent this, in the clinical thermometer there is a constriction in the tube just above the mercury-filled bulb. When the thermometer is placed in the mouth, the mercury expands and forces its way past this constriction, but when the thermometer cools, the mercury cannot fall back past the constriction. The only way the level of the mercury can be brought down is by shaking the thermometer to force the mercury past the constriction and into the bulb.

A maximum-minimum thermometer While studying weather (Chapter 7), the class may want to keep a record of the maximum and minimum temperatures during a fixed period—perhaps 24 hours, or over a weekend. This can be done by adapting an inexpensive metal dial thermometer (like the one shown in Fig. 17-9) as follows. Remove the glass front. Bend the pointer end of the needle down to a position in which it barely touches the dial, and deposit a coating of soot on the dial with a candle flame. As temperature changes, the bent pointer of the needle will move through the soot and leave a white track. The left end of the track will indicate the lowest, or minimum, temperature, the right end the maximum temperature for any given period.

If the maximum-minimum thermometer is used to record outdoor temperatures, it should be placed under a shelter to protect it from rain or snow. After a reading is taken, the dial can be resmoked. Commercial maximum-minimum thermometers are U-shaped tubes containing mercury, which pushes against two little steel cylinders (called riders) positioned one in each arm of the "U." They are moved into contact with the mercury by drawing a magnet along the tubes.

Electrical thermometer Extremely sensitive electric thermometers are used to measure the temperature inside engines and other inaccessible places. The basis of these thermometers is the fact that two wires of different materials twisted together and heated will produce a small electric current. The hotter the metals become, the more electric current is produced.

To demonstrate, clean with steel wool a piece of No. 18 copper (bell) wire and a piece of iron wire the same length (about 15 inches) and thickness. Then twist the wires together at one end; if necessary, use pliers. (A piece of wire coat hanger may be used for the iron wire; scrape off all paint with sandpaper.)

Make a compass galvanometer (Chapter 19) by wrapping at least 50 turns of No. 26 or 28 copper wire around a compass over its north–south axis (Fig. 17-10). Connect the free ends of the copper and iron wires to the wires of the compass galvanometer. Heat the twisted ends of the wires in a candle or Bunsen burner flame. The compass needle will deflect, showing the presence of an

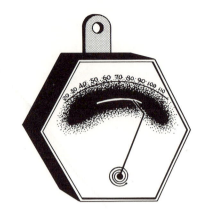

FIGURE **17-9** A maximum-minimum temperature thermometer.

electric current. Point out that if a dial face were placed underneath the compass needle, the needle would register changes in temperature: The hotter the twisted ends, the more the needle would deflect.

CHANGES OF STATE WITH CHANGES OF TEMPERATURE

To demonstrate the different effects of heat on different materials, place one of the following—an ice cube, a lump of butter, some lard or animal fat, a piece of solder, copper wire, and some iron or steel wire—in one of six small empty cans. (Roll the pieces of solder, copper, and iron into balls.) All six solids should be approximately the same size. Then heat each can over an electric hot plate. Note which solids melt and, if possible, the time it takes for each to melt. The ice, butter, and fat melt very easily. The solder takes longer to melt, and the copper and iron do not melt. Point out that the copper and iron will melt if heated to a higher temperature. (The experiment is more graphic if conducted with Pyrex test tubes and Bunsen burners, and when all six tubes are heated at the same time.)

Let the cans cool and have children observe that the melted substances become solids again. Most substances melt and solidify at the same temperature; butter is one of the exceptions, melting at one temperature and solidifying at a slightly lower temperature.

When the solid is heated, the molecules vibrate faster and faster. At a certain temperature, called the melting point, the molecules break loose and move around freely. This may account for the fact that solids have a definite size and shape, while liquids have a definite volume but no shape. When a liquid is cooled, the molecules come closer together. At a certain temperature, called the freezing point, the molecules stop moving freely and only vibrate; the liquid has become a solid again.

Pour some cold water into a Pyrex pot and heat the pot over a hot plate. Observe the water as it is heated to boiling. At first, small bubbles of gas form, some of which cling to the walls of the container; this is dissolved air, which is being driven out of the water. After a while, large bubbles of gas form, but they quickly collapse as they rise to meet the colder water above them. The hot water now begins to "hum" and "sing." When the water is hot enough, bubbles of gas will form continuously and rise to the surface. This is called the boiling point, and it is at this temperature that there is a steady conversion of liquid to gas or vapor.

Children should understand that when heat is applied to a liquid, the molecules move faster and spread farther apart. This continues until the boiling point is reached, when the molecules begin to move very rapidly, spreading very far apart and moving very freely in space. This is

why gases have neither definite volume nor definite shape.

In a demonstration of conversion of a gas to a liquid, hold a cold glass tumbler over the water vapor escaping from the spout of a teakettle. The vapor condenses when it strikes the cold glass because the cooled molecules move more slowly, reverting to the liquid state. This phenomenon of condensation does not take place only when water is boiling. The air contains water vapor ("humidity," see Chapter 7) in varying amounts; there is a limit to the amount of water vapor a volume of air can hold. When air containing water vapor is cooled, the air contracts (see above, p. 272). Since it now has a smaller volume, the air cannot hold as much water vapor as it did before. If the air has much water vapor in it (a high humidity), some of the water vapor will condense out as droplets of water. Experiments demonstrating this are shown in Chapter 7 ("Weather").

As other examples of the phenomenon, have the children recall how their breaths will cloud a mirror or "steam" on a very cold day. Point out that this "steam" is actually droplets of water condensing out, as are seen on cold bottles, pitchers of ice water, glasses of soda or lemonade, eyeglasses, and kitchen windows.

There are other interesting phenomena of state associated with water. Children may be interested to see that pressure causes ice to melt by raising the temperature above the freezing point at the focus of pressure. Place the broad end of an ice cube on top of a soda bottle. Wrap the

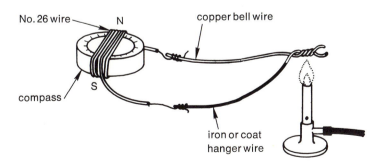

FIGURE **17-10** Heat produces an electric current (detected by a compass galvanometer).

Changes of State with Changes of Temperature **277**

ends of a piece of thin copper wire (No. 24 or 26) around the middles of two wooden dowels or pencils. Place the middle portion of the wire across the ice cube and push down hard on the dowels. The wire will slowly pass through the ice cube, but will leave the cube in one piece. Children should understand that, as the wire presses on the ice cube, the ice directly underneath the wire melts. This melting requires heat, which is taken from the rest of the ice. After the wire passes on, the colder ice refreezes the water. Or press two ice cubes together with a great deal of force for about half a minute. The pressure melts the two ends of the ice cubes, which then refreeze when the pressure is released. The making of snowballs depends on this same principle: Packing the snow together causes the outer parts of the snow crystals to melt, and the water thus formed refreezes when the pressure is released. The snow crystals making up the snowball are then held together by a network of ice. Point out too that, in ice skating, the pressure of the blade melts the ice and forms a thin film of water on which the skater moves. This also explains why one slips on ice or why automobiles skid on ice. If the ice is very cold, then the pressure may not be great enough to melt the ice and the skater's blade will tend to stick.

Boiling Point in Relation to Pressure

The boiling point of a substance is influenced by the air pressure on its surface. To show this, pour about an inch of water into a Pyrex baby bottle or a Pyrex flask with a tight-fitting cork stopper. Heat the bottle on a hot plate until the water boils vigorously. Wrap a cloth around the bottle, remove it from the hot plate, and place it on a cake tin or baking pan. Stopper the bottle tightly with the cork, invert it, and pour cold water, a little at a time, over it. The water in the bottle will boil vigorously each time the cold water is poured over the bottle, even though it is becoming cooler and cooler. Point out that, when the cold water is poured over the bottle, some of the vapor inside cools and condenses. This lowers the pressure on the water, enabling

it to boil at a lower temperature. Thus, when the pressure is reduced, the boiling point is reduced. If the pressure is increased, as with a pressure cooker, the boiling point is raised. This explains why one can obtain temperatures higher than the boiling point of water inside the pressure cooker and thus cook more quickly.

Review with children the phenomenon of evaporation (Chapter 6), which is a change from the liquid state to the vapor state. Spilled water, rain on the sidewalk, puddles, wet clothes placed on the clothesline, even ponds in hot weather—all dry up because water evaporates.

When liquids evaporate, they create a cooling effect because the process of evaporation requires heat. The liquid usually takes this heat from its immediate surroundings. Have children blow on a dry finger, then on a finger that has been dipped into water. (Blowing on the finger increases the rate of evaporation.) The moistened finger will feel cooler. Point out that for the water to evaporate it needs heat, and it takes this heat from its immediate surroundings, namely, the fingers. The quicker the liquid evaporates, the more quickly it takes up heat, and the cooler the finger becomes. Thus, liquids that evaporate very quickly have a greater cooling effect because they take up heat more rapidly. Drops of duplicator fluid, a volatile (easily evaporated) liquid, placed on the back of a hand, will evaporate more quickly than a similar amount of water on the other, making the former feel cooler.

One may also show this phenomenon using three thermometers and three pieces of cotton gauze. Soak one piece of gauze in water, the second in rubbing alcohol, and the third in duplicator fluid. Wrap the bulb of each thermometer quite well with one piece of the wet gauze. Fan the pieces of gauze with a cardboard or an electric fan. The thermometer wrapped with gauze soaked with the most volatile fluid will show the lowest reading.

The loose open-weave garments worn in the summer (Chapter 12) are cooler because they permit free circulation of air and, hence, produce more rapid evaporation of perspiration. Evaporation of perspiration keeps our bodies cool; the more rapid the evaporation, the quicker the heat is taken from the body and the cooler one feels. Have children recall the cooling effect of a breeze on a hot day. Fanning creates the same effect. Water evaporating rapidly from a wet bathing suit can cool one enough to produce a chill.

Point out that in hot, dry climates, water is often kept cool by evaporation. This is done by keeping the water in earthen jars or pots that are porous and so allow some of the water to seep through the jar wall. Thus, there is always a small amount of moisture on the outside of the vessel; as this moisture evaporates, it absorbs heat from the jar and its contents, thereby making them cooler. Using the same mechanism, mothers often keep milk bottles cool by wrapping a wet towel around them. This effect can best be produced when the climate is dry and there is little water vapor in the air. In moist climates or when the humidity is high, there is so much water vapor in the air that the rate of evaporation is slow. Thus, the amount of heat absorbed is quite small, and the cooling effect is reduced.

In Extreme Cold

Effects of extremely low temperatures may interest children. Needed to demonstrate these are some dry ice, acetone, and a No. 2 fruit or vegetable can. Dry ice may be available, on order, from stores that sell only ice cream or, perhaps, from truckmen delivering ice cream to school lunchrooms, or from colleges. Acetone can be purchased at a pharmacy or from scientific supply houses, or obtained from a high school chemistry teacher.

Wrap the dry ice in a towel or cloth and, by hitting it with a mallet (through the cloth), break it into small pieces. The temperature of dry ice is approximately 103° below 0°F. (*Be very careful, therefore, in handling it. Wear gloves and use tongs or a spoon to pick it up.*)

Place about 2 inches of acetone in the can and add dry ice to it a little at a time. There will be a violent bubbling at first, and a fog will form. This will settle down as the acetone is cooled.

When the bubbling stops, add dry ice until some pieces remain at the bottom of the can. (*Do not place fingers in the mixture.*)

Place a frankfurter (first showing that it is soft and pliable) in the acetone-dry ice combination. After a while, remove it with tongs and tap the chalk board with it to show that it is rock-hard.

Place a flower in the mixture also; it will freeze immediately. Upon removal, it will be beautiful, but very brittle. If it is squeezed lightly, it will disintegrate into tiny pieces.

A celery stalk treated in the same way will be hard as a brick when removed. Rubber bands will become brittle and break as will a grape or an orange segment lowered into the mixture at the end of a length of wire. (*Wear gloves when holding the wire.*)

Liquid mercury (in a Pyrex test tube) lowered into the mixture will quickly become a solid. (Mercury freezes at about 38° below 0°F.) Water in a small can will freeze solid in minutes. Moisture condensing on the outside of the can will be seen as frost or ice crystals.

The experiment with the mercury will show that mercury thermometers are useless in very cold parts of the Arctic and Antarctic. To show why alcohol is useful for low-temperature thermometers, place a Pyrex test tube of rubbing alcohol in the mixture; it will not freeze. However, alcohol is useless for high temperatures, because it boils away at about 178°F, a boiling point even lower than that of water (212°F). Mercury, however, is good for higher temperatures, because it boils at about 480°F.

To keep the dry ice-acetone mixture for a few hours, pour it into a wide-mouthed vacuum bottle. (*Use gloves while handling and take special care when pouring.*) Before discarding the mixture, let it stand in the can overnight. The surrounding air in the room will gradually bring the mixture to room temperature.

MOVEMENT OF HEAT

Heat travels by conduction, by convection (largely in liquids and gases), and by radiation.

By Conduction

In conduction, when heat causes the molecules in one part of some matter to move faster, these faster-moving molecules collide with their slower-moving neighbors. The neighboring molecules, receiving these harder collisions, begin to move faster also and, in turn, collide with nearby molecules. In this way all the molecules in the matter are soon moving faster. When molecules in a substance are moving faster, the substance is warmer. Thus, the heat is conducted molecule by molecule.

To illustrate conduction, place a silver spoon in a glass of very hot water; wait a few minutes, then touch the handle of the spoon. It will be very hot. Point out that the metal of the spoon bowl carried the heat of the water to the handle by conduction. Or roll a strip of paper about 12 × 3 inches around one end of a round brass curtain rod 12–15 inches long. Keep the paper wrapped tightly by slipping two rubber bands over it. Now obtain some long tacks or small nails. Using paraffin from a burning candle, attach tacks (Fig. 17-11) to the brass rod at 1-inch intervals. Hold the unwrapped end of the rod in a flame. Call children's attention to the fact that as the heat travels along the rod by conduction, the paraffin melts and the tacks fall off one by one. The toppling of a row of dominoes when the first is pushed over is another simple way of illustrating conduction. Each domino transmits its motion to its neighbor, just as each molecule in a heated body transmits its faster movement to its neighbor.

Solids differ in the rate at which they transmit heat by conduction. Needed to show this are a narrow wood block and four 12-inch rods of different materials—copper, brass, iron, and glass will do. Nail the rods to the wood block at different angles so that the four ends meet (Fig. 17-12). At the other end of each rod, attach long tacks or small nails with paraffin. At the point where the four ends meet, apply a flame. Note the order in which the tacks fall off; the better the conductor, the sooner the heat reaches the paraffin and melts it.

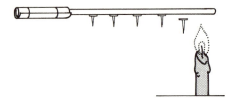

FIGURE **17-11** Tacks attached to a bar with wax fall off as heat travels through the bar by conduction.

Good conductors Metals are good conductors of heat even though they differ somewhat in the rate of conduction. Nonmetals, such as wood, glass, paper, and cloth, are poor conductors of heat. The molecules of which they are composed do not transmit motion very well to neighboring molecules.

Many experiments show that metals are good conductors of heat: Hold a wooden match at one end of a bare piece of wire while holding the other end in the hand. Be prepared to drop the wire because it heats up rapidly.

Wrap a handkerchief very firmly around a silver quarter and place the lighted end of a cigarette against the handkerchief. Although there will be a slight tobacco stain, the handkerchief will not char or burn because silver is an excellent conductor of heat and conducts the heat away before it can damage the cloth. If the coin is removed, the handkerchief or cloth will scorch immediately. This same effect can be achieved by wrapping a piece of white paper tightly around a wooden pencil that has a metal band to hold the eraser. Cover both the metal band and the wood. Heat the pencil over a candle flame at the point where the metal band is located. When the paper begins to char, remove the pencil and unroll the paper. The part of the paper covering the wood will be charred. The part of the paper covering the metal band will be untouched or only slightly charred because the metal band conducted the heat away.

Or pour hot water into an aluminum or other metal tumbler and a plastic tumbler. The metal tumbler will feel warmer because it is a good heat conductor. If cold water is used, the metal tumbler will feel colder because it conducts the heat away from the hands more quickly. A moistened finger applied to a metal rod on a very cold day will often freeze to the rod because the metal carried the heat away from the finger so quickly.

If one holds a piece of aluminum or copper window screening (about 6 inches square) in a candle flame, the flame will burn below the screen, but not above it. The flame is made up of burning gases and, because the heat is conducted away from the flame by the wires in the screen, the gases above the screen never reach the kindling point (the temperature at which they begin to burn).

This can also be shown with a Bunsen burner and tripod. Place the screen on the tripod and turn on the gas. Light the gas above the screen; it will burn above the screen because the heat is conducted away by the screen and thereby prevents the gas below the screen from reaching its kindling temperature.

Remind children of the project of making a model of a miner's safety lamp, as discussed in Chapter 16. Point out that the principle of the lamp is the same as that illustrated by the screen and Bunsen burner just described. The wire mesh conducts the heat of the miner's lamp away, thereby preventing any inflammable gas that might be in the air from reaching kindling temperature.

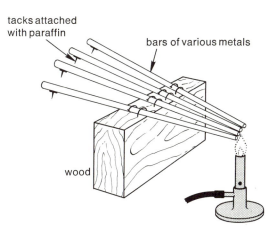

tacks attached with paraffin

bars of various metals

wood

FIGURE **17-12** Demonstrating that different metals conduct heat at different rates.

Poor conductors Glass is a poor conductor of heat. Point out that this is why a cold glass will often break if hot water is poured into it. The hot water makes the inner surface expand but, because glass is a poor heat conductor, the outer surface is slow to expand. The strain produced may crack the glass. Similarly, when cold water is placed in hot glass, the inner surface contracts quickly, but not the outer, again setting up a strain that may crack the glass.

This does not usually happen with thin-walled glasses, because in them the heat is transmitted to the outer surface more quickly. Pyrex glass can withstand most such changes in temperature because it has boron in it, which reduces the amount of expansion and contraction and thereby eliminates most strain.

Fold a piece of paper about 5 × 4 inches so that there are four thicknesses about 1 inch wide. Wrap this strip around the upper end of a test tube one third full of water. Hold the strip tightly together so that it holds firmly, and heat the test tube in a flame until the water boils. Because the paper is a poor conductor of heat, one can hold the heated test tube without discomfort.

As in the case of good conductors, there are variations in the rate of heat conduction among various poor conductors. The tiled bathroom floor feels colder to the bare feet than does the wooden floor. Both floors are probably at the same temperature, but tile, because it is a better conductor of heat than wood, carries body heat away more quickly and so feels colder. A carpet is a very poor conductor of heat, and so feels warmer than the wooden floor. A traffic officer will often keep his feet warm on a cold day by standing on newspaper or wood, because these carry heat away more slowly than pavement.

That liquids are generally poor conductors of heat may be shown with a test tube three quarters full of water. Place a piece of ice in the test tube, keeping it at the bottom of the test tube by means of a spring or small weight. Apply a flame to the upper part of the test tube. The water will boil away after a few minutes, but the ice will remain almost intact, because the heat is not carried down through the water to the ice.

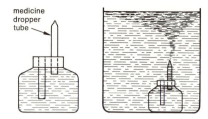

medicine
dropper
tube

FIGURE **17-13** Demonstrating that hot water is lighter than cold.

Gases are extremely poor conductors of heat. Recall or repeat the experiment with the tin cans and insulating materials under *Insulation,* in Chapter 13. Point out that air or gases are probably the poorest heat conductors. One reason why asbestos, rock wool, hair, fur, wool, and feathers are such poor conductors of heat is that they are porous or fibrous in structure, containing many dead air spaces—that is, spaces that are sealed off, so that the air in them cannot circulate. Such materials make good insulating materials because they are not only poor conductors but possess dead air spaces which can neither circulate nor conduct heat.

By Convection

Repeat experiments demonstrating how heat makes liquids expand and remind children that warm water is lighter and weighs less per unit of volume than cold water.

Fit an ink bottle or other small bottle with a two-hole rubber stopper. Push a small piece of glass tubing and the glass portion of a medicine dropper into the stopper, as shown in Fig. 17-13. The glass tubing should be level with the stopper and extend almost to the bottom of the bottle.

Fill the ink bottle with very hot water that has been deeply colored with blue or red ink or vegetable dye. Then fill a large wide-mouthed jar or empty aquarium with very cold water. Fit the stopper into the ink bottle and wipe off any colored water that overflows. Lower the ink bottle into the jar of very cold water quickly, but carefully, so as to keep the amount of disturbance of the water to a minimum. Have children note how the colored water leaves the medicine

dropper like smoke from a chimney, rising to the top. Also point out that the bottle remains full because the hot water, rising to the top and escaping because it is lighter, is replaced by the colder (heavier) water. (Observe the color of the water in the bottom of the small bottle.)

Convection in water To demonstrate convection in water, fill a Pyrex coffee pot with cold water. Stir some shredded blotting paper or sawdust into the water until they become thoroughly soaked and settle to the bottom of the pot. (Shred by rubbing the blotting paper against the fine part of a food grater.) Set the pot on an electric hot plate and heat the water. As the water gets hot, note how the particles move upward at the center and downward at the sides of the pot. Point out that the particles are being carried along by the movement of the water as it is heated. The hotter water rises to the top while the cooler water falls to the bottom. In this way the heat is carried from one place to another by currents in the water. This method of heat travel is called convection.

Repeat the experiment, placing the pot to one side of the hot plate so that only one side will be heated. The particles of blotting paper will go around and around the pot, as the water rises up one side of the pot.

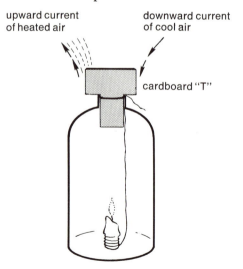

upward current
of heated air

downward current
of cool air

cardboard "T"

FIGURE **17-14** Convection currents keep a candle lighted.

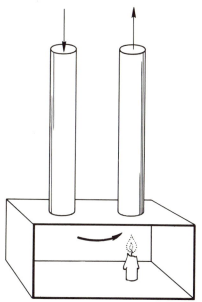

box side omitted to show position of candle

FIGURE **17-15**   Tracing convection currents.

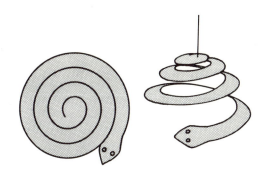

FIGURE **17-16**   A paper serpent sensitive to hot-air currents.

Convection in air   Heat can also travel in gases by convection. To illustrate this, set a lighted candle in a spot where it will be protected from stray air currents. Hold a lighted cigarette or a piece of smoking rope a short distance above the flame. The smoke will travel straight up into the air. Repeat the experiment over a radiator or electric hot plate instead of a candle. The rising air current will also cause a pinwheel to turn.

Or wrap a piece of wire around a candle, light the candle, and lower it into a bottle. The candle will go out very quickly because the air heated by it rises, preventing fresh air (containing oxygen) from entering the bottle in time to keep the candle lighted. Cut a piece of cardboard in the shape of a "T," the stem of which should just fit the neck of the bottle. Invert the bottle and swing it quickly a few times to fill it with fresh air. Lower the lighted candle into the bottle again by means of the wire. Immediately place the cardboard T into the neck of the bottle (Fig. 17-14). This time the candle will remain lighted.

Point out that the cardboard permits separation of the warm and cold air currents. To demonstrate, place a lighted cigarette or piece of smoking rope on each side of the cardboard. On one side the smoke will go down into the bottle, showing the presence of a current of cool air. On the other side, the smoke will rise, showing the presence of a current of heated air.

Movement of convection currents can be made graphic with a shoe box and two small mailing tubes or a cardboard paper towel tube cut into two equal lengths. In the bottom of the shoe box cut two holes slightly smaller than the openings of the cardboard tubes. Light a candle and secure the bottom firmly to the table with melted paraffin. Place the shoe box over the candle so that the candle is directly under one of the holes. Then set the two tubes over the holes (Fig. 17-15). Hold a smoking rope or paper over the tube without the candle under it. The smoke will go into the tube, showing that cool air is entering. Smoke will be seen leaving the tube with the candle under it, showing that the heated and therefore lighter air is leaving. Have the children trace the convection currents formed.

Children can make a paper "serpent" that responds to hot air currents. This is done by drawing a spiral on a sheet of heavy white paper. Finish the end of the spiral by drawing the head of a snake (Fig. 17-16). Cut along the spiral and suspend the serpent over a candle flame, hot plate, or radiator by a knotted thread passed through the center of the spiral. The rising heated air will make the serpent spin around and around. (If the spiral does not spread out evenly, the lines have been drawn too close together or too far apart.)

Recall or repeat the experiments with the ventilation box in Chapter 13. Children should be reminded that our homes are heated by air convection currents. (Review the proper method of keeping windows open for good ventilation and circulation of air in a room.) Long, narrow strips of very thin tissue paper attached to a stick or ruler can be used to detect the directions of convection currents in various parts of the room. Smoke can also be used to detect convection currents in the room and near windows opened at the top and bottom.

Have the children look at a heated radiator or hot plate that is in the sunlight. The heated air appears to waver and dance about as it rises. The same effect can be noticed outdoors on hot pavements and roads. Actually, the heated air, rising, creates some turbulence as it mixes with cooler air. The wavering is caused by the bending of the light rays as they pass through the irregular densities of the rising air.

Point out that in refrigerators the cooling unit is generally located at the top, so that the cold (heavier) air from the cooling unit falls to the bottom while the warmer (lighter) air rises to the top where it is cooled again. In this way a convection current is set up which helps keep all the food cold.

Winds are air convection currents on a large scale. They are caused, for the most part, by the unequal heating of the earth's surface at certain points. The air over some heated area becomes warm, expands, and rises. Colder air rushes in to take its place, and soon a convection current is started. In land areas near the equator, there is a continuous rise of heated air. There is a corresponding fall of cold air near the North and South Poles. The rotation of the earth helps swerve the direction of these large air currents. (See Chapter 5.)

By Radiation

Any one of three things may happen to radiant energy (heat rays) when they strike a substance. If the substance is transparent, the heat waves will pass through it, and the substance will remain cool; if the substance is smooth and shiny, the heat waves will be reflected and the substance will again remain cool; if the substance is dark and/or rough, the heat rays will be absorbed and the substance will become warm.

To demonstrate transmission of heat by radiation, have a child hold his palm under an unlighted electric light bulb. (A bent goose-neck lamp with the shade removed will serve the purpose.) When the bulb is turned on, the child will feel the heat on his palm almost immediately. Point out that the heat could not reach the hand so quickly by conduction (because air is a very poor conductor of heat) nor could it reach the hand (*below* the bulb) by a rising convection current. Children should understand that the glowing filament in a bulb gives off a *radiant* energy which is absorbed by the hand and converted to heat. For children in the lower grades, it is sufficient to say that the bulb sends out heat rays that make the hand hot.

To reinforce the concept, place a pane of glass between the bulb and the child's palm. He will still feel the heat although the glass will be cool. Children should realize that this radiant heat energy does not heat transparent objects; the rays pass through them, and it is only when the rays are stopped and absorbed by an object (like the child's hand) that they are converted to heat.

Children can also stand near a window and note that their faces feel warm where the sunlight falls on them, but the window panes remain cool. This establishes that the sun also gives off heat rays.

As with light (Chapter 15), radiant heat rays can be focused. To do so, use a magnifying or reading glass. Focus the sun's rays to a point on the hand or on a crumpled wad of tissue paper; the hand will soon feel uncomfortably hot, and the paper will ignite.

To show that radiant heat can also be reflected, have a child place a tilted mirror halfway between the lens and the point of focus (the spot where the sun's rays come to a point). Another child can move his hand about until he finds the new point of focus of the heat rays.

Recall or repeat the experiments on pages 218

and 219 in Chapter 13. Remind the children that bright, shiny, or smooth objects reflect heat rays, while dark, rough objects absorb heat rays. Recall the experiment on the effect of the sun's rays on light and dark clothing in Chapter 12.

Needed to show the absorption of heat are two balloons, two narrow-necked bottles of the same size, and some black water color or tempera paint. (Stretch the balloons and test to see that they inflate easily.) Paint one bottle black, pull a balloon over the neck of each bottle, and place both bottles in the sun. The black bottle will absorb the sun's rays more quickly, and its balloon will inflate first. Point out that on a hot day the black fender of an auto is hotter than the silvery, shiny chromium parts.

Or cut two circles of cardboard to cover the open ends of two cans of the same size. In the center of each cardboard disk, punch a hole large enough to admit a thermometer. Paint the outside of one can with flat black paint. Place the cardboard covers on the cans and insert the thermometers. Work in the shade and keep the cans in the shade until both thermometers show the same readings. Then place both cans in direct sunlight. Read the temperature of each thermometer after about 20 minutes. The black can will show a greater heat rise.

Repeat the experiment with equal amounts of cold water in the cans, but wait a half hour before reading the thermometers. The black can will again show a greater heat rise. Repeat the experiment, using equal amounts of hot water and placing the cans in a cool spot out of the sun. The thermometer in the black can will show a lower reading than the one in the shiny can. Point out that the black can radiated heat faster than the shiny can. As a result, the water in the black can cooled more rapidly than the water in the shiny can.

A vacuum bottle tends to maintain the temperature of its contents by blocking the effects of conduction. Unscrew the upper part of the metal case of the bottle and show children the silvered glass bottle inside. Using a diagram of the bottle on the chalk board, show the double walls in the bottle, pointing out that most of the air has been removed from the space between them in order to form a vacuum. With most of the air removed, there are very few air molecules to conduct heat away from or into the contents of the bottle. Furthermore, whatever molecules of air are present in the space are very poor conductors.

Call attention to the fact that both inner walls of the bottle are silvered. Thus, heat being radiated from hot liquids tends to be reflected by the silvered wall back into the liquid, while the outer silvered wall tends to reflect external radiant heat, keeping it from entering the thermos and warming cold liquids.

APPLICATIONS OF HEAT IN THE HOME

Children naming the kinds of heating systems in their homes may confuse the type of heating system with the kind of fuel used. The three most commonly used home heating systems are hot-air, hot-water, and steam. Radiant heating in the floor is obtained with circulating hot water, and some wall radiant heaters use electrical heating elements.

Hot-air Heating

A model of a hot-air heating unit may be made from two cans, one very much larger than the other. Cut the top and bottom off the larger can and punch three holes in it as shown in Fig. 17-17. Punch two holes in the smaller can (also as shown in the figure) and cut off one end.

Pass plastic tubing through the two pairs of adjacent holes in the large and small cans. The tube through the lower holes supplies fresh air for the burning fuel (candle), and the tube through the upper holes acts as a chimney to carry off waste gases from the burning fuel. The hole on the other side of the large can supplies the air to be heated which, in an actual heating system, would then pass through ducts to the various rooms of the building.

Firmly fasten a lighted candle to a table with

melted paraffin, and invert the cans over it. Hot air rising from the top of the larger can can be shown with a pinwheel, smoke, or narrow strips of very thin tissue paper attached to a stick or ruler.

Point out that in hot-air heating systems, the heated air rises by convection currents and travels to the rooms by means of large pipes called ducts. The air enters the rooms through grills called registers, which may be located in the floor, baseboard, or wall. The hot air heats the room by convection. When the air cools, it returns to the furnace through grills at the floor level and ducts. In modern hot-air systems, a blower helps move the hot air.

Hot-water Heating

How a hot-water heating system works can be shown as follows. Replace with one-hole rubber stoppers the metal screw caps of two rectangular cans, one quart-size and the other pint-size. Punch holes large enough to admit a one-hole rubber stopper in the lower end of one side of the large can and in the upper end of one side

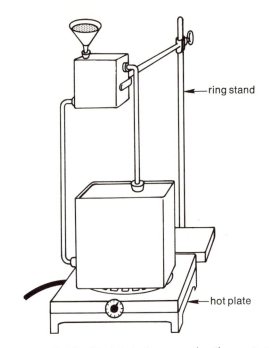

FIGURE **17-18**   Model of a hot-water heating system.

and the lower end of the opposite side of the small can (Fig. 17-18).

Insert plastic tubing as shown (or glass with rubber tubing to turn corners) and seal around the stoppers with plumber's sealing compound or sealing wax. Insert a large glass or plastic funnel in the stopper at the top of the smaller can. Use a ring stand and clamps to hold the small can in place.

Remove the stopper and funnel and add water until both cans are full. Then replace the funnel and add more water until the funnel is half full. Heat the large can on an electric hot plate.

Point out that the large can acts as the boiler. When the furnace heats the water in the boiler, the water expands and rises. Cold water flows down to take its place. As the heating continues, the warm water reaches the small can, which corresponds to the radiator in a building. Soon a convection current is established, and the water becomes warmer and warmer with continued passage through the boiler. The heat of the water in the radiator is transmitted by conduction

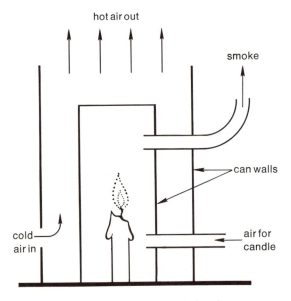

FIGURE **17-17**   Model of a hot-air heating system.

through the walls of the radiator where it heats the air in the room. The heated air sets up a convection current which distributes it in the room. The radiator also heats by radiation some of the objects in the room.

The funnel represents an expansion tank necessary to accommodate the increased volume of the water as it expands when heated. Without it the boiler, pipes, or radiator would burst.

Steam Heating

Needed to show how a steam-heating system works are a large flask and a one-hole stopper to fit, a pint-size rectangular can and a one-hole stopper to fit its mouth, an 8-inch and a 3-inch length of plastic or glass tubing, and another one-hole stopper to fit into a hole punched in the lower end of one side of the can.

Assemble the apparatus as shown in Fig. 17-19. A ring stand and clamps will help hold the can in place. Fill the flask one third full of water, and then heat it on an electric hot plate.

The flask acts as the boiler. The furnace heats the water in the boiler until it boils. The steam that is formed rises and enters the metal can, which corresponds to the radiator. Beyond this point, heating takes place as in the hot-water system.

When the steam in the radiator gives up its heat to the air in the room, the steam cools and condenses. This condensed water drains back to the boiler through the same pipe used for carrying the steam. The furnace then reheats the condensed water until it becomes steam again.

The radiator air valve in a steam-heat system serves to allow air that may be trapped in the radiator or pipe line to escape. While it opens to let air out, it closes upon contact with the steam. It also acts as a safety valve, opening when the pressure goes beyond the safety point.

Radiant Heating

In radiant heating, a relatively new method, a network of pipes is installed in floors, ceilings, or walls. Hot water circulates through the pipes, heating them by conduction; the pipes, in turn, radiate heat into the room. Because of the large surfaces involved, there is good radiation to all parts of the room.

Solar Heating and the Heat Pump

Solar heating is—at least in terms of the source of heat—a form of radiant heating. In it the sun's heat is gathered by means of special heat collectors, which usually consist of black metal plates or panels behind double panels of glass. The collectors are situated so that they face the sun, the rays of which pass through the double panels of glass and are absorbed by the black metal panels, which become hot. Water or air is used to transfer the heat from the collectors to the storage area, which contains chemicals that can store heat. When the heat is needed, it is released from the storage area and passes through the house. Usually the stored heat is converted into warm air and then circulated through the rooms by fans.

Solar heat is also used to supplement the more

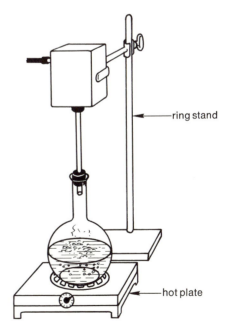

FIGURE **17-19** Model of a steam-heating system.

conventional heating systems. In this case, the walls of the building on the sides toward the south consist mostly of large windows. Radiant energy from the sun passes directly into the rooms, where the energy is absorbed and converted into heat.

In the heat pump, a network of pipes is buried in the earth. A pump run by an electric motor causes water to flow through the pipes. The circulating water takes heat from the earth. The heat is then taken from the water and concentrated for heating the home. Either a hot-water or hot-air heating system can be used to distribute the heat. The chilled water is returned to the earth. In the summer, the entire process can be reversed and the unit can be used to cool the home.

Air conditioners filter dust from the air, reduce the humidity, and cool. This last and chief function is achieved by a refrigerant, which passes through tubes or coils. The refrigerant, a liquid under pressure, is allowed to expand and changes into a gas. The liquid refrigerant needs heat energy to change into a gas, and takes this energy from its immediate surroundings. This makes the tubes or coils cold. Warm air blown across these cold tubes or coils is cooled. The refrigerant is compressed by a pump and changed to a liquid again. Heat is produced because of the work done to liquefy the refrigerant, and the air around the pump becomes hot. This unwanted hot air is passed outdoors. Cooling the air also lowers the humidity because some of the water vapor condenses out of the air.

SUGGESTED PROJECTS

1. Obtain a glass jar with a metal cover that is stuck tight. (One can create such a condition by placing a cover in hot water, screwing it on while it is still hot, and letting it cool.) Pour hot water on the metal cover until it unscrews quite easily. Lead into the study of expansion and contraction.

2. Have children examine a thermostat in the classroom or, where not available, the master thermostat. (The school custodian can show its location and explain its operation.) Lead into the study of expansion and contraction and also of the unequal expansion of metals.

3. Observe the construction of a Fahrenheit thermometer and note the markings on it. Find the temperature of the air in the room and outdoors. Lead into the study of thermometers and the measurement of temperature. Then compare a Celsius and a Fahrenheit thermometer. Lead into the study of how systems of temperature measurement are devised. (Some thermometers are marked with both scales.)

4. Observe how a medical (clinical) thermometer differs from other thermometers in construction and operation.

5. Have the children make water thermometers, using small milk or cream bottles, plastic tubing, and col-

ored water. Lead into the study of the thermometer and the measuring of temperature.

6. Have the class list the various uses of thermometers. Lead into a study of expansion and contraction, thermometers, and temperature measurement.

7. Soak a piece of cloth in water and suspend it from a string. Ask children for suggestions regarding how to dry the cloth as quickly as possible. Lead into the study of evaporation and factors affecting the rate of evaporation.

8. Observe the droplets of water that form on the outside of a pitcher of ice water that has been in a refrigerator for some time. Lead into the study of condensation.

9. Fill a glass with very hot water; then put a silver spoon in the glass. Fill an aluminum tumbler with hot water. Note how hot the metal becomes in each case. Lead into the study of heat travel by conduction.

10. Devise an experiment to determine the heat conductivity of various substances. Lead into the study of conduction and the molecular theory of heat.

11. Have children hold their palms near a lighted electric bulb or a heated radiator. Lead into the study of radiation.

12. Attach very thin tissue paper strips, about 6 inches long, to a ruler or stick. Use this device to detect and determine the direction of air currents in the room. Lead into the study of heat travel by convection.

13. Have the class collect information about the various types of heating systems by contacting community dealers or manufacturers. Discuss methods of heat travel used in these systems and compare their methods of operation and advantages and disadvantages.

14. Have the class visit an air-conditioned building and arrange for a demonstration of the parts of the air conditioner and how each functions.

BIBLIOGRAPHY

(**P** indicates recommended for primary grades, **I** for intermediate grades, **U** for upper grades.)

Adler, Irving, and Ruth, *Heat*, Day, 1964. Simple descriptions of the properties of heat and its uses in industry and daily life. **U**

Adler, Irving, *Hot and Cold*, Day, 1959. Explains heat and how to measure it, convection currents, how electricity produces heat, and how man uses heat. **U**

Feravolo, Rocco, *Easy Physics Projects: Air, Water and Heat*, Prentice-Hall, 1966. Forty-eight experiments—16 on air, 19 on water, 13 on heat. Lists materials easily obtainable and provides simple directions with clear explanations of concepts involved. Clearly illustrated with line drawings and black and white illustrations. **I**

———, *Junior Science Book of Heat*, Garrard, 1964. Discusses what heat is, where it comes from, how it is measured, and some of its uses. **I**

Lieberg, Owen S., *Wonders of Heat and Light*, Dodd, Mead, 1966. Solar energy, laser heat, heat measurement, light rays, and the uses of heat. **U**

Munch, Theodore, *What is Heat?*, Benefic, 1960. What it is, why it is important, and where we get it. **I**

Parker, Bertha M., *Thermometers, Heat and Cold*, Harper & Row, 1959. Good discussion of the phenomenon of temperature and of the devices used in its measurement. **U**

Ruchlis, Hyman, *The Wonder of Heat Energy: a Picture Story of the Part Heat Plays in Our World*, Harper & Row, 1961. About the importance and uses of heat. **U**

Scharff, Robert, *Rays and Radiation*, Putnam, 1960. Clear, simple text and drawings introduce a highly technical subject. Scientific terms are well defined, and there is a careful progression from visible to invisible radiation and from radiation that carries sound and pictures to radiation from the atom and from outer space. **U**

Vries, Leonard de, *The Second Book of Experiments*, Macmillan, 1964. Seventy-two easy experiments requiring only readily obtainable materials. Divided into five groups: force, sound, gases, liquids, and heat. Lists the needed materials, gives a clear explanation, and presents the underlying scientific principle. **U**

A crane lifting steel scrap by means of a huge electromagnet—the disk-shaped object at the center of the picture.

18 Magnets and Magnetism

Any object that attracts iron is a magnet. Natural magnets are found in many parts of the world and may be purchased at scientific supply houses. The natural magnet resembles a dark-colored rock and contains magnetic iron ore. It is usually called "lodestone" or "magnetite," and is said to have been named by shepherds in a part of Asia Minor called Magnesia.

Artificial magnets are usually made of hard steel (iron and carbon). Bar magnets can be rectangular or cylindrical; others are horseshoe- and U-shaped. Alnico magnets, the most powerful, contain not only steel but also quantities of aluminum, nickel, and cobalt as well. (The word "alnico" is made up of the first two letters of the three metals other than steel.) Alnico magnets are made not only in all the forms described above but also in a disk. Another variety of "artificial" magnet is the electromagnet, which consists of a coil of wire wound around an iron core. When an electric current flows through the coil, the electromagnet displays the characteristics of a bar magnet. (See below under *Magnetic Field* and under *Making Magnets.*)

Magnets can be obtained from old radio speakers, telephone receivers, and automobile speedometers. Hardware and variety stores offer a variety of sizes and shapes.

MAGNETIC ATTRACTION

Have children use magnets to try to pick up such things as iron filings, steel wool, iron or steel tacks, and paper clips. Have them note the force that holds the objects to the magnet, and how hard it is to pull them from the magnet. The force which holds objects to the magnet is called *magnetic attraction*. To show that magnetic force is a *mutual* attraction, use an iron nail to pick up a magnet.

To demonstrate what magnets attract, collect and test with a horseshoe magnet a wide variety of materials. A likely group would include thumbtacks, needles, pins, paper clips, toothpicks, a penny, a dime, a gold ring, brass paper fasteners, rubber bands, sand, bits of glass, leather, cloth, paper, aluminum, and tin foil. Children can list in two columns objects that the magnet picks up and those that it does not. Point out that all objects picked up were made of metal but that not all metal objects were picked up—not the copper penny, the silver dime, the gold ring, the brass paper fasteners, and any of the other objects made of nonferrous metals.

Examination of the list of objects picked up should show children that all have one thing in common: iron or (iron-containing) steel. They may then arrive at the conclusions that (1) magnets will not attract nonmetals, and (2) magnets will attract only certain metals, such as iron or steel. (Magnets will also attract nickel or cobalt: A Canadian "nickel" will be picked up by a magnet because it is nearly pure nickel, but an American nickel will not because it is mostly copper. A "tin" can, which is really made of sheet steel with a coating of tin, will also be attracted by a magnet.)

The power of attraction of magnets acts through nonmagnetic materials. To illustrate this, gradually bring a magnet closer to iron filings[1]

or thumbtacks. Note that the filings or tacks jump through the air (nonmagnetic material) to the magnet and that it is not necessary actually to touch the magnet to them. This attraction through nonmagnetic materials can be shown in other ways: Suspend a horseshoe magnet by cotton thread from the top of a magnet stand.[2] Loop a piece of thread around the point of a thumbtack and press it into the base of the magnet stand directly underneath the magnet. Tie a paper clip to the other end of the thread so that the clip is about $\frac{1}{4}$ inch from the magnet. The paper clip will be suspended in air and seem to defy gravity. The magnetic attraction passes through the air and overcomes the force of gravity.

Place some iron filings or thumbtacks on a pane of glass supported by two piles of books. Move a magnet about against the underside of the glass. The filings or tacks will move around with the magnet. Repeat the experiment using thin sheets of cardboard, wood, cloth, and aluminum foil. Or tape an iron nail to the underside of a very small plastic automobile that has wheels that turn. Place the automobile on the sheet of glass or cardboard. Hold the magnet underneath the glass and make the automobile move. (A drop of oil between the wheels and axle will help it move more easily.)

A thumbtack attached to the underside of a cork floated in an aluminum pan or Pyrex dish can be made to move in the same way, by moving a magnet underneath the pan or dish.

Iron filings or thumbtacks placed on a thin sheet of iron will not be moved by a magnet underneath the iron sheet. This is because the magnetic force of the magnet travels into the

---

[1] Iron filings, excellent for investigating the properties of magnets, may be purchased from scientific supply houses in a convenient shaker-type container or may be made from soft iron (not steel) obtainable from a machine shop or scrap-metal dealer. Clamp the iron firmly in a vise and file it with a medium-coarse file. (The finer the filings, the better they behave in the presence of magnets.) A grinding wheel produces the best filings and does the job very quickly. Filings can also be made by cutting oil-free steel wool into fine bits with a scissors. Machine shops may be willing to provide the actual filings, of which they have

an abundance. (Aluminum filings, of course, are useless.) Make sure filings are free of oil and grease; if necessary, wash them in detergent and dry by heating in a pan. Put the dried filings in a salt shaker whose cap has good-sized holes.

[2] A magnet stand (Fig. 18-1) may be made as follows. Screw together two pieces of wood—one about $7 \times 2 \times \frac{1}{2}$ inches, the other about $14 \times 2 \times \frac{1}{2}$ inches. Attach the resulting "L" to a piece of wood $12 \times 12 \times \frac{3}{4}$ inches, as shown. A temporary stand may be made from a ruler held in place by a stack of books above and below it.

are connected in series (Fig. 18-6a). Run the wire through the hole in the cardboard, shape it so that part of it is vertical, and adjust so that the bare portion is located just at the hole in the cardboard. Place four small compasses on the circle drawn on the cardboard in a north, east, south, and west position as shown. Touch the unattached end of the wire to the dry cell terminal to complete the circuit for two or three seconds. While the current is flowing, have children note that, in their new positions, the four compass needles follow the outline of the circle. Remove the compasses and sprinkle some iron filings on the cardboard. Again connect the dry cells for two or three seconds and tap the cardboard gently (Fig. 18-6b). The iron filings form a circular pattern around the wire.

MAKING MAGNETS

Temporary

Place some tacks (or paper clips, pins, nails, etc.) on a table and touch one of the tacks with a horseshoe magnet. Bring this tack to a second tack, which will be attracted to the first. After stringing together several tacks in this fashion, remove the horseshoe magnet. All the tacks fall off and separate because the tacks act as magnets only so long as the horseshoe magnet holds the first tack. The tacks are said to be magnetized by induction, and objects so magnetized are called temporary magnets. Or hold a large soft-iron nail about $\frac{1}{2}$ inch from the bottom of one leg of a strong U-shaped magnet. While holding the nail in this position, let its tip touch a pile of tacks. Some of the tacks will cling to the tip of the nail because the latter is temporarily magnetized by induction. With the horseshoe magnet removed, the nail loses its temporary magnetism, and the tacks fall off. (Some steel nails may remain slightly magnetized.)

Permanent

Test a large, soft iron nail and a steel knitting needle to see if they pick up iron tacks. Then stroke first the nail and then the knitting needle with one end of a bar magnet. Stroke each 40 times, being careful to stroke in only one direction and to lift the hand between strokes. Again test to see if they pick up the tacks. Both will behave as magnets. Record how many tacks each picks up, then test them again the next day. Although iron is easily magnetized, it loses its magnetism just as easily. Steel, more difficult to magnetize, retains its magnetism permanently. Have children try magnetizing the blade of a pocket knife, a file, or a pair of scissors in this way.

Again, stroke a steel knitting needle or hacksaw blade with the north pole of a bar magnet, this time slightly changing the procedure by stroking from the center of the blade or needle to one end. Do this 40 times, being careful to lift the

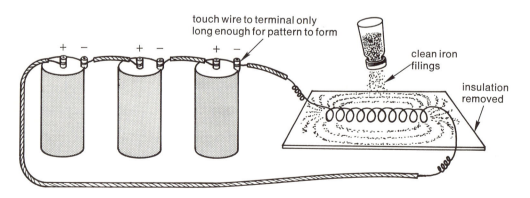

FIGURE **18-7** Demonstrating that a coil of wire carrying an electric current acts like a bar magnet.

hand between strokes. Mark with chalk the half of the blade or needle that was stroked by the north pole of the magnet. Then, with the south pole of the magnet, stroke from the center to the other end of the blade or needle 40 times and mark with chalk the half of the blade or needle so stroked. Suspend the blade or needle from a magnet stand and bring the north pole of a magnet first to one end of the blade or needle, then to the other end. The end of the blade or needle which is attracted to the north pole of the magnet is the south pole of a newly formed magnet. Be sure children see that the end of the blade or needle that was stroked by the north pole of the magnet has become a south pole. Similarly, the end stroked by the south pole of the magnet has become a north pole. Test the hacksaw blade or knitting needle with tacks or paper clips for magnetism.

Magnetize three steel sewing needles as described above so that each needle point is a north pole and each eye a south pole. Push the needles through disks sliced from a cork stopper. Place them in a large glass or plastic dish of water having sloping sides. Float all three with the points up. The corks will all repel each other. Now reverse one needle so that it floats with its point down. It will be attracted to the other needles because of the relationship of like and unlike poles.

Objects can be magnetized permanently by electricity. To do so, wind insulated copper wire (about 100 closely wound turns) of any kind about a narrow cardboard tube such as a mailing tube or one from a roll of paper towels. Connect the end of one wire to a terminal of a dry cell, and place the steel object to be magnetized inside the tube. (Try to keep the object in the part of the tube covered by the turns of wire.) Touch the end of the other wire to the other terminal of the dry cell for no more than about 5 seconds. Test the (magnetized) object for magnetic attraction on some iron or steel tacks.

If the object magnetized is made of hard steel, it will remain a (permanent) magnet; if made of soft iron, it will gradually lose its magnetism.

Electromagnets

A wire formed into a coil will (when the current is flowing) have a magnetic field like that of a bar magnet. To show this, wind about 2 inches of bell wire around a pencil to make a coil. Remove the pencil and attach one end of the wire to a dry cell. Touch the other end of the wire to the dry cell and bring a compass close to one end of the coil. Note that the coil has become a magnet. Move the compass to the ends of the coil and determine which are its north and south poles. Try picking up iron filings or tacks with one end of the coil. Children should soon conclude that a coil of wire carrying an electric current acts as a magnet with north and south poles. Reverse the connections of the wires to the terminals of the dry cell and, with a compass, check the poles of the coil again. Reversing the direction in which the current flows reverses the poles in the coil.

Then place the coil on a piece of white cardboard, and sprinkle iron filings about it (Fig. 18-7). Connect the ends of the wire to the dry cells and tap the cardboard gently. The filings will arrange themselves in the same pattern as that produced with the bar magnet.

Inserting an iron core into the coil will increase its magnetic strength; the resulting device is an electromagnet. To demonstrate this, wind a number of turns of bell wire around a large iron nail. Remove the nail, connect the ends of the wire to a dry cell, and see how many tacks or paper clips can be picked up with the coil. Put the iron nail back into the coil and repeat the experiment. Note how many more tacks or clips have been picked up.

Disconnect the dry cell and try to pick up tacks or clips with the electromagnet. Children will soon realize that this type of magnetism is temporary, existing only when an electric current is flowing through the wire.

That electromagnet strength is directly related to the number of turns of wire of the coil and to the strength of the current can be shown as follows. Wrap 25 turns of bell wire around a large iron nail, connect the ends of the wire to a dry cell, and count the number of iron or steel tacks that can be picked up with this electromagnet. Next attach two dry cells in series to the electromagnet. Note the greater number of tacks that can be picked up.

Then wrap 50 turns of bell wire around the iron nail and connect the ends of the wire to the terminals of one dry cell. Again count the number of tacks picked up. Finally, attach this nail with 50 turns to two dry cells in series and again count the number of tacks picked up.

Demagnetizing

Note how many tacks a magnetized steel knitting needle will pick up. Holding the needle with a pair of pliers, heat it in a flame until it is red hot and then continue to heat it for quite some time. Let it cool and test it again to see how many tacks it will pick up. Some of the magnetism has been lost because of the heating. If the needle were made hot enough and heated long enough, it would lose all its magnetism. Again, test another magnetized knitting needle by seeing how many tacks it will pick up. After pounding the needle with a hammer or striking the needle repeatedly against a solid object, again see how many tacks it will pick up. Jarring the needle caused it to lose some of its magnetism. Heating or striking the needles lessened their magnetism by rearranging their atomic domains so that fewer were aligned in the same north–south direction. (See Fig. 18-2.)

Whatever causes atomic domains of a magnet to lose their uniform orientation will tend to lessen the magnet's power. Hence, magnets should not be struck or heated or exposed to other magnetic influences for long. To keep a horseshoe or U-shaped magnet strong, a small flat piece of iron, called a keeper, is placed across its poles. An iron nail will also serve as a keeper. Usually bar magnets come in pairs. When they are put away, to avoid their demagnetizing each other, they should be placed side by side with the north pole of one magnet next to the south pole of the other.

EARTH AS A MAGNET

The earth behaves just as if there were a huge magnet inside it running north and south. As a result, the earth is able to magnetize objects. To show this, find out with a compass which direction is north. Hold an iron rod (a curtain rod of solid iron or steel will do; test for iron with a small magnet) about 2 feet long in a magnetic north–south position—that is, parallel to the direction of the compass needle. Tilt the rod at the angle of magnetic dip (see below) for your area. (A tilt of 65° is a rough approximation which will serve for many areas in the United States.) Then strike the end of the rod sharply a few times with a hammer. The rod will be magnetized slightly. This can be tested with a compass: the upper end of the rod will be a south pole and attract the north-seeking end of the compass needle; the lower end, a north pole, attracting the south-seeking end of the needle.

The poles can be reversed by turning the rod around and tapping it again. To demagnetize the rod, simply hold it in an east-west position and strike it sharply a few times with the hammer.

Many iron and steel objects which stand vertically may be magnetized by the earth's magnetism. Children can test for this by holding a compass near such things as steel pipes, lamp stands, fence posts or rails, and bridges, to see if they are magnetized. (Test at both ends, where possible, to check their magnetic poles.)

Recall the experiment where you showed that magnetic force would not pass through magnetic materials like iron and steel. The children should then be able to explain why a compass case is usually made on a nonmagnetic material like brass. The earth's magnetic force would never reach the compass needle if the case were made of iron or steel.

To make a model earth magnetic globe, insert a bar magnet into a small (6-inch diameter) cardboard or plastic globe. Orient the magnet so that the top (south pole of the magnet) emerges near the upper end of Hudson's Bay (approximately 73°35′ N. latitude, 92°20′ W. longitude), and the bottom (north pole of the magnet) emerges near the Antarctic at 70° S. latitude, 148° E. longitude. Place compasses at different positions on the globe and note how the compass needles align with the lines of force of the magnet. It may be necessary to tilt the globe at times. The magnet is placed with its pole near Hudson's Bay (in Canada) because that is the location of *magnetic* north, as opposed to *true* north, the point where the lines of longitude meet.

USING MAGNETISM

The Compass

A compass may be obtained from a local army surplus or variety store or, perhaps, from a pupil who is a Boy Scout or from a high school physics teacher. The case is usually made of brass rather than iron or steel in order to avoid the magnetic influence the latter might have on the needle. The card has letters on it standing for the directions, North, South, East, West. The compass needle is usually diamond-shaped, the half that points north is usually colored so that it can be identified easily and quickly.

To use the compass, hold it flat in the palm of the hand, keeping it level. In order to locate directions other than north, turn the case of the compass until the letter N is directly under the colored end of the needle. The other directions can then be read from the compass card.

A compass needle is, in effect, a bar magnet that is free to turn and, therefore, free to align itself with the lines of force of the earth's magnetic field. In doing so, it indicates magnetic north (and all other directions by inference) and so is useful in navigation. That a compass needle is magnetized can be proved by bringing a bar magnet near the compass (do not touch the compass case with the magnet): The north pole of the magnet will repel the north pole of the compass needle and attract its south pole.

That the north pole of a suspended bar magnet (or a compass needle) points to the north magnetic pole (despite the fact that like poles repel) is the result of a historical error. When men first recognized magnets and their poles, they called

the pole that *pointed north* the North Pole. This was before they realized that the earth behaved as a huge magnet and that, therefore, the pole of a magnet or compass needle that points to the north magnetic pole must really be a south pole (attraction of opposites). Because it would create much confusion now to change the names of the poles of magnets, we compromise by calling a north pole of a magnet a "north-seeking" pole, and the south pole of a magnet a "south-seeking" pole.

To demonstrate how a compass needle in a magnetic field aligns itself with the lines of force in the magnetic field, move a compass around a bar magnet on a table. Note how the direction of the needle changes as the compass is moved. As long as the needle is in the magnetic field of the bar magnet, it will point toward the nearer pole of the magnet. Have children compare the positions of the compass needle as it moves around the magnet with the positions the iron filings assumed around a magnet (Fig. 18-4).

A compass needle points to magnetic north. In order to tell where true north is, it is necessary to know the magnetic declination for one's area—the angle between true north and the direction in which a compass needle points. This angle varies at different parts of the earth; it can be zero (where the observer, true north, and magnetic north are in a straight line).

Children can estimate the angle of declination for their area by drawing two lines on a globe: one from their area to the true North Pole, and one to the magnetic north pole. The angle formed is the angle of declination.

A compass needle can be used to determine the unmarked poles of a magnet. To do so, simply bring the magnet near the compass and observe which end repels and/or which end attracts the needle.

Making a compass Children can make a simple compass by suspending a steel knitting needle or hacksaw blade (magnetized, as described above, by stroking with a bar magnet or by use of an electromagnetic coil) from a magnet stand. The magnetized needle or blade will soon come to rest in a north–south position. Have the chil-

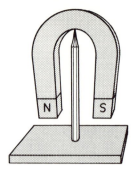

FIGURE **18-8** A horseshoe magnet used as a compass.

dren check this position with a commercial compass. (Be sure not to bring the compass too near the magnetized needle or blade.)

A horseshoe or U-shaped magnet can also be made to act as a compass: Glue a well-sharpened pencil upright in a hole in a block of wood 4 inches square and $\frac{1}{2}$–1 inch thick. Or hammer a long thin nail through the center of the block and file a fine point on the nail. The pencil makes a better support since the graphite of the point acts as a lubricant. Place the horseshoe or U-shaped magnet on the point of the nail or pencil so that it balances (Fig. 18-8). The magnet will slowly turn until it is in a north-south position. It should now be quite clear to children that a compass is no more than a small magnet.

Columbus used a simple floating compass when he discovered America. To make one, magnetize a large sewing needle as described above. Cut a flat circular disk from a cork stopper, push the needle through the cork so that it is perfectly horizontal (Fig. 18-9), and place the cork on the surface of the water in a glass or aluminum dish with sloping sides. Be sure to keep the cork and needle away from the sides of the dish. (Adding a teaspoon of detergent will lower the surface tension of the water and prevent the cork from moving to one side of the dish and staying there.) The needle will point north and south. As a variation, float the needle inside a milk straw (Fig. 18-9). It may also be floated without using the stopper or a straw; simply grease the magnetized sewing needle slightly with shortening, petroleum jelly, etc.; then, holding the needle

horizontally 2–3 inches above the surface of the water, lower it carefully and gently onto the water. The surface tension of the water will keep the needle afloat.

Children can also make a compass without using water by inserting a magnetized needle into a piece of very thin cardboard folded to make an inverted V (Fig. 18-10). Suspend the cardboard from a fine thread attached to a milk bottle cap or as shown in the figure.

A compass needle at the equator allowed to swing freely would be completely horizontal. The closer it approached the north magnetic pole, the more it would dip. At the pole it would be absolutely vertical, with the north-seeking (south) pole of the compass down. This happens because the compass needle tends to take a direction parallel to the direction of the lines of magnetic force.

Children can find out how much a compass needle will dip in their latitude and longitude, as follows. Push a knitting needle through the center of a cork stopper. Then push a sewing needle through the center but perpendicular to the knitting needle (Fig. 18-11). Support the ends of the sewing needle on the edges of two glasses, and adjust the knitting needle until it balances evenly. Next, using a compass, point the knitting needle (by shifting the glasses) toward the north magnetic pole. Then strongly magnetize the knitting needle and return it to the glasses. The knitting needle will dip to an angle at which the needle is parallel to the lines of force of the earth's magnetic field in that location. The amount of dips can be measured with a protractor. This angle of dip varies from locality to locality.

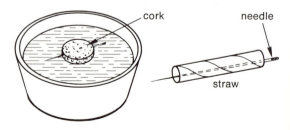

FIGURE **18-9** Floating compass.

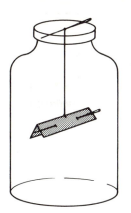

FIGURE **18-10**   A cardboard compass.

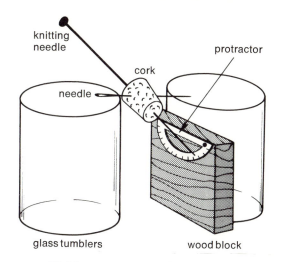

FIGURE **18-11**   A dipping needle.

Electric Motors and Buzzers

Essentially, electric motors are electromagnets rotating within the field of a permanent magnet. Details of how such motors operate and of how to construct models of them are given on pages 321–324 in Chapter 19. Buzzers, which operate by the rapid, alternate making and breaking of an electric circuit through an electromagnet, are also described in that chapter.

A Diving Nail

A "diving nail" involves an application of the electromagnet that children may find amusing. To make one, wind bell wire into a coil around a wide test tube (or olive bottle) containing water (Fig. 18-12). (Use many more turns than are shown in the illustration.) Push an iron nail into a small cork as far as it will go. Place the cork and nail in the test tube, connect one end of the wire to one terminal of the dry cell, then touch the other end of the wire to the dry cell for a few seconds. The cork and nail will dive into the water because the coil of wire now becomes a magnet, drawing the nail down (or up, depending on the direction of flow of current).

A Dancing Spring

A "dancing spring" is a spectacular method of showing that a coil of wire acts like a magnet when it is carrying an electric current. To make one (Fig. 18-13), drive a copper nail through a cork stopper held firmly by a clamp attached to a ring stand (or a stand made of wood). Make a copper coil by wrapping some thin copper wire many times around a pencil. Have the bottom of the coil end in a straight wire. Wrap the top of the coil firmly around the pointed end of the copper nail, adjusting the straight wire at the bottom end of the coil so that it is slightly below the surface of some mercury or, if not available, a concentrated solution of salt water in a small beaker or shallow dish. Attach a copper wire from one terminal of a dry cell to the head of

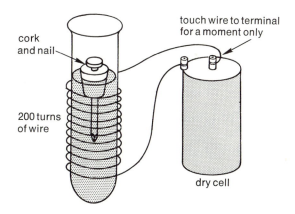

FIGURE **18-12**   A diving nail.

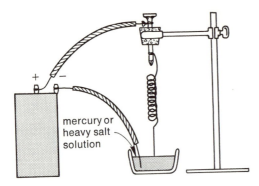

FIGURE **18-13** A "dancing spring" arrangement.

the copper nail. Then place the copper wire from the other terminal of the cell in the mercury or salt water. The coil will now dance up and down, and sparks will form at the surface of the mercury. (It may be necessary to adjust the depth of the straight wire in the mercury to get a constant dancing up and down.) When the electric current passes through the copper coil, the coil becomes a magnet with a north and south pole. Since north and south poles attract each other, the turns of the coil are pulled together. This pulls the end of the straight wire at the bottom of the coil out of the mercury or salt water. When this happens, the circuit is broken. The coil now no longer acts as a magnet and returns to its original position. The straight end of the coil touches the mercury or salt water again, and the whole process is repeated.

Magnet Games

Several games employing magnetism can be readily made. A magnetic "fishing" game can be made as follows. Have children trace and cut out 24 paper fish, each 3–4 inches long. Draw a circle on one side of each fish and give the fish a numerical value from 1 to 5. Paste a circular gummed reinforcement at the "mouth" of each fish (Fig. 18-14). Attach a paper clip to each fish, making sure that it goes through the gummed reinforcement.

Place the fish in a large fish bowl or aquarium, and tie 12–18 inches of string to each of four horseshoe magnets and attach each string to one of the four long, narrow sticks, making four "fishing poles." Have four children fish at one time. When the fish are caught, add up the values for each to determine high score.

Iron objects may be used instead of "fish." For example, nails, screws, nuts, bolts, and tacks can have numerical values assigned, and the children can fish for them as described above.

A test of skill uses iron nails with broad heads. Stand the nails on their heads about $\frac{1}{2}$ inch apart on a piece of glass. Have children take turns trying to remove one nail at a time with a horseshoe magnet without picking up or knocking over

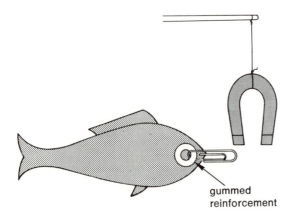

FIGURE **18-14** A fish for a magnetic "fishing" game.

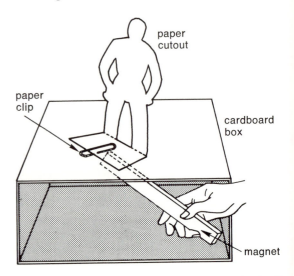

FIGURE **18-15** Figure for a magnetic "acting" game.

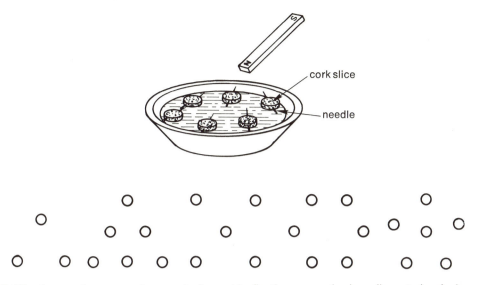

FIGURE **18-16** Geometric patterns that may be formed by floating magnetized needles acted on by bar magnet.

adjacent nails. The child who removes the most nails is the winner.

Or attach a nail or thumbtack to the underside of very small wooden boats. Place the boats in an aluminum pan supported by two piles of books, and move a magnet underneath the pan to make the boats move.

A stage with moving "actors" can be made of a cardboard box. Wings and backdrops can be added. Make actors of paper with a fold at the bottom (Fig. 18-15) to act as a stand. Insert a small paper clip on the fold. Stand the actors on the cardboard stage and move a magnet underneath each actor.

Magnetize six sewing needles so that their eyes are north poles. Cut six disks, all the same size, from cork stoppers. Push the needles through the cork disks (Fig. 18-16) and place them in a dish of water (to which a teaspoon of detergent has been added) so that the eyes of the needles are pointing up. (The dish should have sloping sides.) Bring the south pole of a bar magnet near the corks; they will all cluster around the magnet. Reverse the magnet so that the north pole is near the corks, and they will be repelled violently. Arrange these floating magnets in different geometric patterns, as shown in the lower part of the figure.

SUGGESTED PROJECTS

1. Discuss the properties of magnets in relation to toys (or parts of a machine) that utilize magnets.

2. Mix brass pins and sewing needles (or copper and iron tacks) together. Have children separate them with a magnet. Lead into a discussion of magnets, magnetic attraction, and what materials magnets will attract.

3. Test American and Canadian nickels with a horseshoe magnet. Have children find out which is mainly nickel, and discuss which metals are attracted by magnets.

4. Use a magnet to find out how many things in the school and classroom are attracted. Make a list of the materials and determine which metals can be magnetized.

5. Before class begins, magnetize the head of a small hammer by stroking it with one end of a bar magnet, stroking it many times but always in the same direc-

tion. Show children how a tack can be picked up with the head of the hammer and held in position while it is hammered into a piece of wood. Lead into a discussion of how to make temporary and permanent magnets.

6. Using a compass, locate the directions of familiar landmarks near school. Bring a magnet near the compass; initiate a discussion of magnets and how the earth behaves as a magnet. Paint cardinal compass points on floor or playground.

7. Suspend a bar magnet by a piece of thread or light string tied around its midpoint. When the magnet comes to rest, check its position with a compass. Use this phenomenon to discuss how the earth behaves as a magnet and also the lines of force of the earth's magnetic field.

BIBLIOGRAPHY

(**P** indicates recommended for primary grades, **I** for intermediate grades, **U** for upper grades.)

Behnke, Frances L., *Golden Adventure Book of Magnetism*, Golden Pr., 1962. Clear well-illustrated treatment to help develop an understanding of basic concepts. **U**

Branley, Franklyn M., and E. K. Vaughan, *Mickey's Magnet*, Crowell, 1956. Simple experiments with magnets. **P**

Knight, David, *Let's Find Out About Magnets*, Watts, 1967. Very easy book on magnets and lodestones; large print, illustrations, simple experiments are included. **I**

Parker, Bertha M., *Magnets*, Harper & Row, 1958. Simple, comprehensive treatment of magnets, their properties and uses. **U**

Pine, Tille S., and Joseph Levine, *Magnets and How to Use Them*, McGraw-Hill, 1958. Properties of magnets, together with the various kinds and their uses. **P**

Reuben, Gabriel H., and Gloria Archer, *What Is a Magnet?*, Benefic, 1959. Basic principles of magnets simply described. **I**

Sacks, Raymond, *Magnets*, Coward-McCann, 1967. Attraction and repulsion of magnetic poles, the magnetic field, and how to make a magnet. Direct and clear; large, uncluttered illustrations. **I**

Seeman, Bernard, *The Story of Electricity and Magnetism*, Harvey, 1967. Discovery of electricity and magnetism, what they are, their development and future. Many experiments. **I**

Yates, Raymond F., *The Boy's Book of Magnetism*, Harper & Row, rev. ed., 1959. Many games and tricks with magnets. **U**

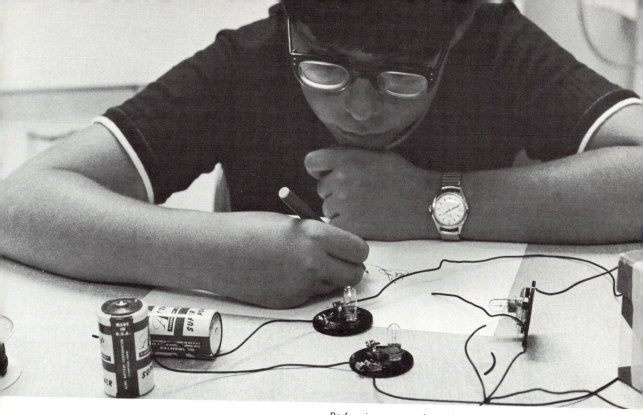

Performing an experiment in electrical circuitry in the classroom.

19 *Electricity*

Electricity exists as a stationary or as a moving charge, or quantity, of energy. The former form is called *static* electricity; the latter, dynamic or *current* electricity. All matter is made up of tiny particles called atoms (Chapter 21). Atoms contain three basic particles: electrons, protons, and neutrons. Electricity, or an electric charge, is composed of electrons and/or protons. Electrons have a negative (−) electrical charge and protons a positive (+) electrical charge. (Neutrons have no electrical charge.)

STATIC ELECTRICITY

Have children recall what happens when they walk across a deep rug on a cold, dry day and then touch a wall switch plate or other grounded metal object. A spark passes from finger to object, and they feel an electric shock. If a deep rug is available, have one child scuff his shoes the length of it and then touch another's finger or a metal radiator. Rubber-soled shoes are more effective for this because, unlike leather soles, they prevent accumulated static electricity from being discharged into the ground ("grounded") and thus help build up a larger charge.

Inflate a rubber balloon and close its neck with a string. Rub the balloon briskly with a piece of nylon, wool, or fur. Then darken the room and have a child bring his finger near the balloon. An electric spark will jump from the balloon to the finger.

Or rub a plastic water bag or plastic air pillow

(folded over itself several times) against a small aluminum pie pan to which a wooden or plastic handle has been cemented in the center. (Rub the pan vigorously.) Then lift the pan and bring a knuckle near it; a large spark will jump out. This may be done without shock if heavily insulated wire is used (instead of a knuckle), one end of which is connected to a water pipe.

Children may recall producing a spark or experiencing a shock when, on a dry winter day, they slid across the plastic seatcover of a car and then touched a door handle.

Children may also do the following experiments in a dark room: Quickly pull a piece of the black, sticky bicycle tape away from the roll. A glow will appear where the piece of tape pulls away from the roll. Or remove a nylon slipover sweater that has been worn all day. Long, crackling sparks will be produced.[1]

All the experiments above involve the production of static electrical charges by rubbing. This takes place as follows. Electrons move about freely in many substances, whereas protons and neutrons are generally stationary. Under normal circumstances, a substance will have the same number of electrons (−) and protons (+). Ordinarily, therefore, the electrons and protons will neutralize or cancel out each other, and no electrical charge will be evident.

However, when an object is rubbed, friction will transfer electrons from one object to another. Thus, a child scuffing his feet on a rug rubs electrons from the rug onto his shoe soles. In this way, his body accumulates additional electrons (negative charges). When he brings his finger near a wall switchplate or another's finger, the additional electrons leave his body in the form of an

electric spark. Similarly, when a balloon is rubbed, electrons are transferred from the fabric or fur to the balloon. The balloon then has extra electrons, which will jump from it to a finger in the form of an electric spark. Children should be able to explain the experiments described above in terms of rubbing electrons onto an object and thereby producing an electric spark.

This effect may be more dramatically demonstrated as follows. In total darkness (after the eyes have had time to adjust), rub the glass tube of a fluorescent lamp with a piece of nylon or silk. In a few seconds the lamp will glow faintly; the rubbing will have stripped some electrons from the glass, and these electrons make the white (phosphor) coating of the tube glow. (This works only on very dry days.) The same effect may be produced by touching the end of the fluorescent tube with an inflated balloon that has been rubbed with a piece of nylon, wool, or fur. Sparks from the balloon will light up the fluorescent tube.

The word "static" means "at rest" or "stationary." Thus the term "static electricity" refers to electric charges that remain on materials without running off. When a spark is formed, the moving electric charges are now called "current electricity" (see below) or an "electric current."

Attraction and Repulsion of Charged Bodies

The object that gains electrons is said to be negatively charged, and the object that loses electrons is said to be positively charged. Electrically charged objects have properties of attraction and repulsion. These properties follow a basic law, namely, that like charges repel and unlike charges attract. To demonstrate this, tie a long thread around the neck of each of two inflated balloons. Suspend the two balloons by the threads to the same point on a string stretched across a classroom above pupils' heads. Rub each balloon with nylon, wool, or fur. The two balloons will move away from (repel) each other because both picked up electrons from the nylon,

---

[1] In planning experiences in static electricity, one should keep in mind that humidity plays an important part: Experiments work best during cold and dry weather or in a heated room, which will usually be dry.

On warm, humid days in the fall and spring, experiments are often unsatisfactory because the microscopic coat of moisture that forms on the materials carries the electric charges into the ground or simply into the other particles of moisture in the air.

wool, or fur and became negatively charged. Then rub a comb (made of hard rubber) with nylon, wool, or fur and bring it near the charged balloons. The comb will repel both balloons. It, too, has picked up electrons from the nylon, wool, or fur and become negatively charged; consequently, it will repel other negatively charged objects (the balloons).

Or cut two 3 × 12-inch strips of nylon from a nylon stocking. Place both strips on white paper or cardboard and rub them briskly with the hand. Then lift the two pieces of nylon and hold them between your fingers. The two loose ends will repel each other, for electrons have been rubbed off the nylon strips, leaving both positively charged. Being alike, these charged nylon strips repel each other. A strip of the nylon brought near one of the charged balloons will show the attraction of the negatively charged balloon and the positively charged nylon.

In another demonstration, rub a glass rod with nylon or silk. (The rod from a glass towel rack will do, as will the glass handle of a coffee-maker, a long, thin glass jar or vase, or a glass drinking tube.) The friction causes the glass rod to give up its electrons to the nylon, and the glass becomes positively charged. The negatively charged balloons and the oppositely charged glass will move toward each other.

When two objects are rubbed together, both are affected because electrons are rubbed off one and onto the other. The substances listed below are arranged so that of any two rubbed together, the one higher on the list will acquire a positive charge and the other a negative charge.

glass
fur
wool
nylon
cotton
silk
Lucite
sealing wax
hard rubber
Vinylite

The farther apart on the list the two substances are, the greater will be the charge produced.

Attraction of Uncharged Bodies

Charge a hard rubber or plastic comb or a plastic coat hanger by rubbing it with nylon, wool, or fur. Bring it near some tiny pieces of thin paper and note that the paper is attracted to the comb. This attraction of uncharged (neutral) bodies takes place as follows.

As the negatively charged comb nears the neutral paper, it repels the electrons (negative charges) on the near side of the paper, pushing them to the far side of the paper. This makes the near side positively charged, and the paper is attracted to the comb.

Children may make a "kissing balloon" by inflating one (perhaps with a face painted on it) and suspending it from a string across the classroom. When the balloon is rubbed with nylon, wool, or fur, it will swing against ("kiss") the hand or face of any pupil that comes near. Children should understand that the negatively charged balloon repels the electrons in the hand and pushes them as far as possible to the other side of the hand, creating a positive charge on the side of the hand nearest the balloon. There is then an attraction between the negatively charged balloon and the positively charged side of the hand. The balloon, being lighter, moves toward the hand.

There are many more interesting experiments that demonstrate this phenomenon: An inflated balloon rubbed with a piece of nylon, wool, or fur and placed against a wall will cling to it. (The demonstration is even more spectacular to children if one simply rubs the balloon against a sleeve.) A plastic pen or pencil, a stick of sealing wax, or any nonmetallic object, rubbed with nylon, wool, or fur, will become charged enough to pick up bits of cork or paper. These same charged objects will make hair stand on end, or will attract a ping-pong ball (making it roll toward the object), or will make long cotton or nylon threads rise and weave to and fro like snakes. Or adjust a faucet so that there is a thin, steady stream of water from it. Charge a comb as described above and bring it near the stream of water, which will be attracted by the comb and bend toward it.

In another illustration of the attraction of uncharged bodies, hold a newspaper flat against a wall or blackboard and rub the entire surface briskly with a piece of cloth or fur. The paper will stay on the wall for hours. If one of the corners is pulled loose and then released, it will be attracted back to the wall. Crackling noises may be heard when the paper is pulled loose. If the room is quite dark, the many sparks produced (the source of the crackling) may be seen passing from the paper to the board.

Another graphic exercise uses a nylon stocking and a dry polyethylene fruit or garment bag. (Polyethylene can be identified by its tendency to stretch a bit before it tears.) Hold the stocking by the toe against a wall and rub it briskly with the polyethylene bag. When the stocking is taken from the wall and allowed to hang free, it will open out just as if it were being filled with air. This happens because both sides of the stocking have lost electrons and become positively charged, and thus repel each other. Note how the stocking will stick to the wall or the body.

Call children's attention to the fact that common household plastic wrap becomes very highly charged and will stick to most objects when it is drawn from the roll.

The attraction of an uncharged body and repulsion of like-charged bodies can be seen operating in the following exercise. Rub a hard rubber or plastic comb with nylon, wool, or fur, and then dip the comb into a box of puffed rice or wheat. Withdraw the comb, which will be covered with the kernels of rice, and hold it in the air. Soon the kernels will start to pop off. This is a case first of attraction, then repulsion. The comb, negatively charged by rubbing, attracts the neutral kernels of rice. The negative electrons in the comb then slowly pass into the kernels touching it. When the kernels receive enough electrons so that they, as well as the comb, become negatively charged, the comb and the kernels repel each

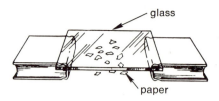

FIGURE **19-1** Dancing paper dolls.

other and the kernels drop off. The same experiment may be done using bits of cork, paper, sawdust, or other kinds of cereal. Or the bits can be placed in a plastic toothbrush container, which is then rubbed with nylon, wool, or fur. The small particles will stick to the sides of the container at first. Then, as they too become charged, they will be repelled by the container and also by the other bits of material, and will jump up and down.

Or place a pane of glass on two books resting several inches apart (Fig. 19-1). Cut paper into bits no larger than $\frac{1}{2}$-inch square. (Onionskin paper will serve well.) Place the paper bits underneath the glass pane and rub the glass briskly with a piece of nylon or silk. The paper bits will jump up and stick to the glass. After a while they will drop down, and then jump up again. Children should recognize that the glass becomes positively charged and the neutral paper bits are then attracted to it. The paper soon becomes charged positively also; the bits then are repelled by the glass, and fall back to the table where, after a while, they lose this charge and are attracted by the glass again. This process is repeated again and again. An inverted Pyrex pie dish or bowl can be substituted for the glass pane and the books. Or the same effect can be produced by using a plastic cheese container and any small, light object. Place them in the container, replace the cover, and then charge the container by rubbing.

Detection of Charge

Various devices can be made for detecting the kind of charge an object may have. A simple one can be made as follows. Apply a very thin coating of aluminum paint to two kernels of puffed rice or wheat. Pass a needle and silk thread through each grain and attach the two threads at the same point on a string stretched across a room (Fig. 19-2). Charge a rubber or plastic comb or rod negatively by rubbing it with nylon, wool, or fur. Charge the neutral kernels by touching them simultaneously with the comb. The kernels, now negatively charged, repel each other. Now, if a negatively charged object (such as the comb) is placed between the charged kernels, they will move farther apart. If a positively charged object (such as a glass rod or narrow glass tube rubbed with nylon or silk) is placed between the negatively charged kernels, they will be attracted to the oppositely charged glass. Children may want to try to explain what happens when a neutral object is placed between the kernels.

Small balloons, ping-pong balls coated with aluminum paint, and other light objects can also be used in the same way as electron detectors. One can even be made by rubbing a long strip of paper (about $15 \times 1\frac{1}{2}$ inches) with a piece of wool until it is charged and then laying it over a ruler so that equal lengths hang down on both sides.

Laboratory electron detectors are called electroscopes; most use metal "leaves" to detect the electric charges. Needed to make an electroscope are a bottle, cork stopper, long copper nail, and thin aluminum or tin foil. Some chewing gum wrappers have a layer of thin aluminum foil, which can be removed by soaking the wrapper

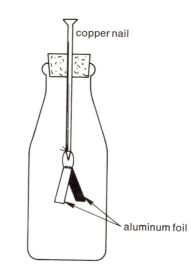

FIGURE **19-3**   An electroscope.

in rubbing alcohol and working the foil loose with the fingers. (Very fine electroscope foil is available from scientific supply houses for a modest sum.) As shown in Fig. 19-3, push the copper nail through the cork until the head of the nail is about 1 inch above the stopper. Sew together the upper ends of two strips of aluminum foil (2–3 inches long and $\frac{1}{2}$-inch wide) and tie the foil to the lower end of the nail with the remaining thread. Insert the cork firmly into the bottle. Touch the head of the nail with a negatively charged comb. Electrons from the comb will flow into the nail and down into the aluminum leaves, which will become negatively charged and will separate (because they repel each other). If another negatively charged object is brought near the nail head, the leaves will separate even further; if a positively charged object is brought near, the leaves will come together. (To neutralize the electron detectors, simply "ground" them by touching the kernels, balloons, ping-pong balls, or nail head with the fingers.)

CURRENT ELECTRICITY

Introducing the idea of invisible yet very real particles flowing through a wire can well be done by first pointing to the effects produced—for

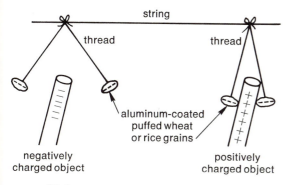

FIGURE **19-2**   Charge detector made of puffed wheat or rice grains.

example, a glowing bulb, a ringing bell, a running motor, a hot toaster. The concept of the existence of moving electrons, which are carriers of energy, can then follow.

Electric Circuits

Electricity flows only where there is an electrical *circuit*. There are at least three parts to a complete electrical circuit: (1) a source of electric current, such as a cell (battery) or generator, (2) a path for the current to travel, such as wires, and (3) an article to use the current, such as a light bulb, electric iron, toaster, bell, or motor. Needed to demonstrate a simple circuit are a No. 6 dry cell, bell wire,[2] 1.1- or 1.2-volt flashlight bulbs, and miniature porcelain bulb sockets small enough to accommodate the flashlight bulbs.

Note that the dry cell has two binding posts to which wire may be attached. The center post or terminal is called the positive terminal, while the end (side) post or terminal is called the negative terminal. (This is usually indicated at the top of the cell's cardboard or metal jacket.) To connect wire, partially unscrew the knob of the binding post, wrap the wire (from which the insulation has been stripped—see below) around the screw, and retighten the knob firmly. (One need not be concerned about electric shock when using a dry cell: The electrical pressure, or voltage, of a dry cell is $1\frac{1}{2}$ volts, the same as that of a flashlight cell. Ordinary house current usually has 110–120 volts. Point out that although the wire connected to a dry cell is safe to handle,

[2]Called also No. 18 insulated copper wire or annunciator wire. No. 20 or No. 22 wire will also serve.

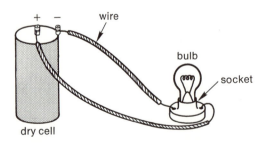

FIGURE **19-4** A simple electric circuit.

wire carrying 110 volts or more—house current—is very dangerous.)

The porcelain socket is a minature of the larger sockets used for ordinary electric light bulbs. At the base of the socket are two screws, which can be loosened with a screwdriver to serve as binding posts around which the wire can be wrapped. Tightening the screws holds the wire in place.

Remove about 1 inch of the insulation from the ends of two pieces of bell wire about 15 inches long.

Insulation can be removed by cutting with a knife, using a sawing motion all around the wire. When cut through, the insulation can be pulled off the end of the wire. (Alligator clips connected to each end of a wire can save time in disconnecting and reconnecting apparatus.)

Screw a flashlight bulb into the porcelain socket. Connect (Fig. 19-4) the end of one wire to a binding post of the dry cell (see above). (In setting up a simple electrical circuit, it makes no difference to which post one attaches the wires.) Connect the other end of the wire to either screw of the porcelain socket. Then connect one end of the second wire to the remaining binding post of the dry cell and the other end of the wire to the second screw of the porcelain socket. With the circuit completed, the bulb will light. Have children examine the circuit carefully, noting the wires and tracing the path of the electric current as it flows from one binding post, through the wire to the socket, into the bulb, back into the socket again, through the second wire, back to the other binding post, and then through the cell back to the first binding post.

It may be useful to show children how the electricity passes through the socket, pointing out that wires lead from each screw to the base of the socket where the bulb is screwed in. Have children take apart an old socket and make a large-scale drawing of it for a bulletin board. Let them also examine the bulb closely so that they see the wire filament leading in and out of it.

After pointing out that the path the current follows is called a circuit, disconnect one end (the dry cell end or socket end) of a wire leading to

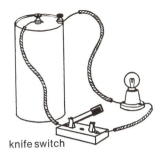

FIGURE **19-5** A simple electric circuit containing a switch.

the bulb. With the light out, reconnect the wires, but then unscrew the bulb. The light will go out again. Help children understand that the electric current will flow only if it can travel all the way around the circuit. Whenever a wire is disconnected or the bulb is unscrewed—whenever the circuit is "broken"—the electric current is unable to flow. Cutting one of the wires in two is a good way of showing how a circuit may be broken.

A closed circuit is one in which the current can flow, uninterrupted, from the cell to the socket to the bulb and back again to the cell. An open circuit is one where the current is unable to flow because the circuit is broken.

Reverse the connection of the wires to the binding posts of the dry cell. Then do the same thing with wires at the screws of the porcelain socket. Children will realize that in each case the circuit remained closed, and thus the bulb remained lit. Point out that the direction of electron flow in the dry cell or battery is from the positive to negative *inside* the dry cell; then, out the negative terminal, through the *outside* circuit, and back to the positive terminal.

Switches In the simple electric circuit described above, the only way to stop the flow of electricity is by disconnecting or cutting a wire or by unscrewing the bulb. Because this is inconvenient, not only for a simple circuit but also for electrical appliances in the home, a device is usually inserted in the circuit that can open or close the circuit easily. This device is called a switch.

With three pieces of bell wire, connect a small inexpensive knife switch and a pushbutton switch (available from a variety or hardware store) into a simple circuit containing a dry cell and one-cell flashlight bulb, as shown in Fig. 19-5. (Both switches have screws, like those in the porcelain socket, for attaching wires.) Children can turn the light off and on by manipulating the switch. Point out that the knife edge, when closed, acts as a bridge and permits the electric current to flow in an unbroken path through the circuit. When the knife edge is open, the circuit is broken. Repeat this demonstration, using a pushbutton switch. The children should be able to see how pushing the button will close the circuit.

A simple switch may be made with a wooden pencil and rubber bands. With the rubber bands, attach one wire from a dry cell binding post so that it runs the length of the pencil, as shown in Fig. 19-6. (The wire attached to the pencil should have insulation removed.) Attach one wire from the circuit to be closed to one end of the pencil quite close to the free end of the wire from the binding post. Use another rubber band to do this. The loose end of the first wire can now be used as a switch by latching it under the second wire.

A tap-key switch (Fig. 19-7), useful for turning electricity on and off quickly, may be made of a piece of smooth wood (about $5 \times 3 \times \frac{3}{4}$ inches), a piece of thin sheet copper about 1×5 inches (or metal linoleum stripping), and some tacks.

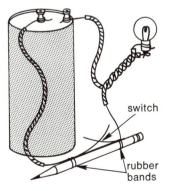

FIGURE **19-6** A simple electric circuit containing a homemade switch.

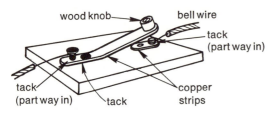

FIGURE **19-7** A tap-key switch.

The metal can be cut with ordinary scissors. (Instead of the copper, metal from a "tin" can may be used, but this requires the use of tin snips.) Cut the copper into two pieces, one 3 and the other 2 inches long. Attach a small piece of a wooden dowel to one end of the 3-inch copper strip by means of a brass screw. Place the copper strips on the wood, as shown in the figure, and tack each strip to the wood with one tack driven in as far as it will go. Then, next to these tacks, drive another tack only part way in, leaving just enough space between the strip and the tack head so that the second tack can serve as a binding post. Bend the 3-inch strip of copper so that it will not touch the other strip. Using the wooden dowel key, the copper strip can be pushed down to close the circuit.

To make a similar switch, but one that will stay down when depressed, use a block of wood and a long copper strip, as in the tap-key switch (Fig. 19-7). Attach the copper strip as shown in Fig. 19-8. Drive the tack almost all the way in, leaving just enough room so that bell wire can be connected to it and so that the copper strip (bent up slightly) is free to move sideways. At the opposite end of the wood, drive a roofing nail (with a wide head) halfway in. It, too, serves as a binding post and also to hold the copper strip when it is hooked under the head of the nail. Before driving in the roofing nail, see that it is in a position where the copper strip can be hooked under its head.

A spring-type clothespin makes a simple "on off" contact switch: Wrap bare wire around each handle and press one against the other to make contact.

A flashlight Tracing the path of the current in a flashlight can challenge children's imagina-

tion. The stage can be set by comparing the No. 6 dry cell and the flashlight cell. Point out that for both cells the center terminal is the positive terminal, and the zinc covering around each cell is the negative terminal. The dry cell has binding posts while the flashlight cell has none. The voltage (electrical pressure) of both is $1\frac{1}{2}$ volts.

Wrap the free end of a piece of bell wire firmly around the threaded base of a one-cell flashlight bulb. Tape the other end of the wire against the base of the flashlight cell; then bring the silvery button on the base of the light bulb in contact with the center terminal of the flashlight cell. The bulb will light. Have children trace the path of the electric current through the circuit. Then make a simple two-cell flashlight as follows. Cut a piece of paper the length of two flashlight cells placed end to end. Place the cells on the paper so that the positive terminal of one is touching the base of the other (Fig. 19-9). Wrap one end of a piece of bell wire around the base of a flashlight bulb. (Use a bulb made for a two-cell flashlight—about 3 volts.) Lay the wire on the paper alongside the two flashlight cells so that both ends extend beyond the paper. Roll the cells and wire up neatly with the paper, holding it in place with rubber bands. Also stretch a thick rubber band around the roll end to end to keep both cells in contact at all times so that the circuit will not be broken. Hold the loose end of the wire against the bottom of the lower cell; then bring the base of the flashlight bulb against the center terminal of the top cell. The bulb will light. Children should have little difficulty in tracing the path of the current: The electrons flow from the bottom or lower cell (negative terminal) through wire into the bulb, back to the

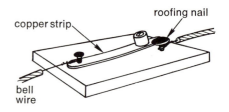

FIGURE **19-8** A homemade switch that can be kept in the on or off position.

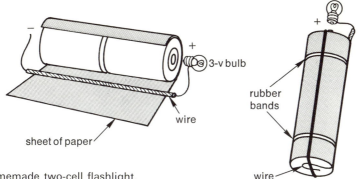

sheet of paper

FIGURE **19-9** A homemade two-cell flashlight.

3-v bulb

wire

rubber bands

wire

center (positive) terminal of the top cell and then through both cells back to the bottom of the lower cell.

Children will be quick to point out that this flashlight is different from the commercial model, the big difference being that, although the commercial flashlight has no wires, the current flows in an unbroken path when the switch is pressed or pushed. While children examine a commercial flashlight closely, display a large diagram (Fig. 19-10) on the blackboard. Point out that the bulb is at the center of a small metal bowl. The switch at the side of the case consists of a piece of metal which can be slid back and forth by pushing the button. When the switch is closed, it has been pushed forward so that the end of the metal piece touches the metal bowl. The spring at the bottom of the case ensures that flashlight cells and bulb base are touching at all times.

When the switch is closed, the current (the electrons) flow from the bottom or lower cell into the spring, along the metal case, through the switch, into the bulb, back to the center terminal of the top cell, and then through both cells back to the bottom cell. Although flashlight switches may vary, tracing the path of the current through the type of flashlight described should enable one to trace the path in any other type.

A doorbell Ringing an electric doorbell or buzzer is another example of closing a simple electrical circuit. You will note it has two binding posts, very much like those in the No. 6 dry cell. Connect with wire a dry cell, a pushbutton or knife switch, and the binding posts of an electric

doorbell (from a hardware store) so that they form a complete circuit. When the switch is closed, the bell will ring. Have the pupils trace the path of the current through the circuit. The switch opens and closes almost too fast to see, as the bell rings. (See the explanation of buzzer operation below.)

Series and Parallel Circuits

Children may have wondered why, in making a two-cell flashlight, the positive terminal of one cell was pressed against the bottom (negative) side of the other. Cells connected in this way (that is, the negative pole of one in contact with the positive pole of another) are said to be in series.

Series To show how to connect cells in series and what effect this connection has, use three No. 6 dry cells, bell wire, a knife switch, a miniature porcelain socket, and a flashlight bulb designed for a three-cell flashlight (about $4\frac{1}{2}$ volts). Set up the three cells, the switch, and the socket as shown in Fig. 19-11. Note that the center (positive) binding posts of each cell are always connected to the outside (negative) binding post

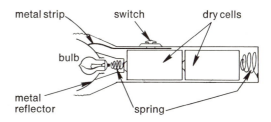

FIGURE **19-10** Diagram of a commercial flashlight.

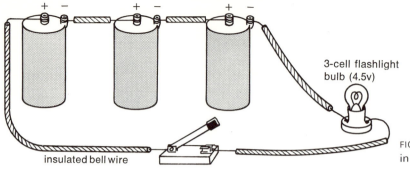

FIGURE **19-11** Cells connected in series.

of the adjoining cell. In this way a wire always leads from a positive terminal to a negative terminal. Even the outside connection to the switch and lamp is connected by wires that run from a positive to a negative terminal (or vice versa).

When cells are connected in series, the electric current flows through each cell, one after the other, making the voltage cumulative. Thus, if the voltage of one cell is $1\frac{1}{2}$ volts, the combined voltage of the three cells is three times that of a single cell, or $4\frac{1}{2}$ volts. This is why two-cell and three-cell flashlights need different bulbs from those used with one cell. If a one-cell bulb were used in a three-cell flashlight, it would quickly burn out because of the greater voltage. Automobile storage batteries have 2-volt cells. Generally, recently made cars have 12-volt batteries of six 2-volt cells; older cars have 6-volt batteries with three 2-volt cells in series.

To show this cumulative voltage, first connect the three cells in series and attach the combination to a switch and a three-cell flashlight bulb (about $4\frac{1}{2}$ volts) in a porcelain socket. Close the

switch and observe the brightness of the bulb. Now connect only two cells in series and observe how the light of the bulb is dimmed. Finally, use only one cell and note how dim the light from the bulb has become.

Parallel The other way cells may be connected is in parallel. Set up the cells, switch, and bulb as shown in Fig. 19-12. This time, use a flashlight bulb designed for a one-cell flashlight (about $1\frac{1}{2}$ volts). Note that in this setup, the center (positive) binding posts are connected to each other and the outside (negative) binding posts are likewise connected to each other.

When cells are connected in parallel, this simply increases the total surface areas of the positive and negative poles. As a result, one gets the equivalent of a single cell with greatly enlarged poles. In this case, therefore, the voltage is not cumulative, and the total voltage is the same as the voltage of one cell ($1\frac{1}{2}$ volts).

With the arrangement as in Fig. 19-12, close the switch and observe the brightness of the bulb. Then connect only two cells in parallel and close

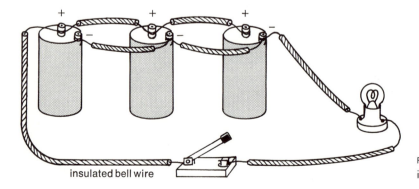

FIGURE **19-12** Cells connected in parallel.

the switch again. The brightness will not change, since no matter how many cells are connected in parallel the total amount of voltage delivered is equal to the amount delivered by just one cell.

In actual practice, cells are connected in series where a higher voltage is desired and are connected in parallel to increase current.

Lightbulbs in series and parallel Light bulbs, like cells, can be connected in series or in parallel. To demonstrate, wire together a No. 6 dry cell, a knife switch, two miniature porcelain sockets, and two flashlight bulbs designed for one-cell flashlights ($1\frac{1}{2}$ volts each), as shown in Fig. 19-13. Note that the wires lead from a screw on the left to a screw on the right. Thus, when tracing the path of the current, the pupils should be led to understand that the current flows through the cell, the switch, both sockets, and the filament of the bulb in each socket.

Close the switch and observe how both bulbs light. Unscrew one of the bulbs and note that the other also goes out because the circuit, which includes the filament in each bulb, is now broken. Children may recall the difficulty of finding a burned-out bulb in Christmas tree bulb sets (arranged in series), since all bulbs went out when one did.

To connect bulbs in parallel, wire the cell, switch, and sockets as shown in Fig. 19-14. Point out that the wires lead from left screw to left screw on the sockets, and from right screw to right screw. Thus, when tracing the path of the current, help children understand that the current flows both *through* and *across* the sockets. This means that there are branch or partial circuits for each lamp. When the current from the cell

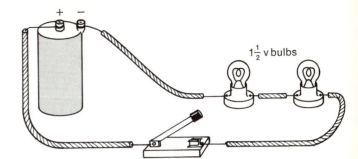

FIGURE **19-13** Light bulbs connected in series.

reaches the first socket, part of the current flows through the socket and part of the current branches off toward the second socket. At the second socket, the current branches again, part of it going through the second socket and the other part going toward the third socket.

To illustrate the effect of parallel wiring on the bulbs, close the switch. Note that all the bulbs light. Unscrew one of the bulbs and note that the other two remain lit. Repeat, unscrewing any one of the bulbs, and then any two. Point out that, when one bulb is unscrewed, the circuit is not broken. Only one branch is affected, permitting the current to flow through the other two branches, so that the other two bulbs remain lighted.

Household wiring is connected in parallel. It should now be apparent to the children that, although they cost more, strings of Christmas bulbs connected in parallel are more convenient since, when one bulb goes out, it can be seen and changed immediately because the other bulbs remain lighted.

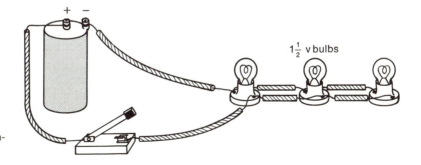

FIGURE **19-14** Light bulbs connected in parallel.

DETECTING ELECTRIC CURRENTS

It is easy to detect the electricity from a commercial cell simply by connecting it to an electrical device such as a light bulb, bell, or buzzer and noting whether the bulb lights or the bell rings, and so on.

However, when the flow of electricity is so slight that it will not activate a bulb or bell, a more sensitive device is needed to detect its presence; such instruments are called galvanometers.

Compass Galvanometer

A homemade galvanometer can be made of a compass, copper wire, a switch, and a dry cell, all available at a hardware, variety, or Army surplus store. The thinner the wire, the better the galvanometer works. Ordinary bell wire (No. 18 copper wire) is suitable, but No. 28 or 30 is best. (The higher the number, the thinner the wire.)

Wrap some wire many times around the compass and connect the wire to a switch and dry cell, as shown in Fig. 19-15. Set the compass so that the needle points north and south, and wrap the wire so that it runs parallel to the compass needle. Make as many windings as are possible without obscuring the ends of the needle. When the switch is closed (only for a moment), the electric current passing through the coil of wire will cause the compass needle to swerve sharply from its north–south position.

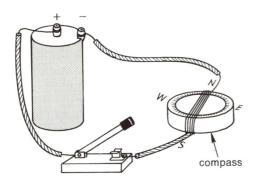

FIGURE **19-15** A compass galvanometer.

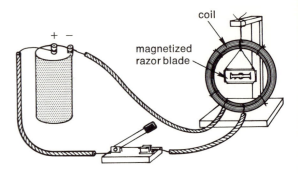

FIGURE **19-16** A razor-blade galvanometer.

Remind children that the compass needle is magnetized and that, when an electric current passes through a wire, the wire develops a magnetic field. In this case, the magnetic field of the coil of wire acts on the magnetic needle of the compass to deflect it from its usual position. The deflection is usually at right angles to the customary north–south position because the magnetic field produced in the coil is at right angles to the direction of the coil, and the compass needle tends to align with the coil's magnetic field.

Reverse the connections of the wires to the binding posts of the cell. The needle will now swerve in the opposite direction; reversing the connections will reverse the deflection as well. (See Chapter 18.)

Razor-blade Galvanometer

A more sensitive galvanometer can be made using a double-edged razor blade. Magnetize the blade by stroking it with one pole of a strong permanent magnet at least 50 times. (Always stroke the blade in the same direction.) Or magnetize the blade by wrapping a coil of bell wire around it and attaching the ends of the wire to a dry cell for a few moments.

Wrap about 50 turns of No. 28 cotton-covered copper wire neatly and compactly around a glass bottle about 3 inches in diameter, leaving about 12 inches of wire loose at each end of the coil. Slip the wire off the bottle and bind it at a few points with thread, wire, or tape so that it will not uncoil. Suspend the coil by some thread from a wooden stand so that the coil hangs freely as shown (Fig. 19-16). Also with thread, suspend the razor blade within the coil so that it can move freely.

Connect the loose ends of the coil of wire to a switch and dry cell. When the switch is closed (only for a moment), the blade will move, aligning itself with the magnetic field generated by the energized coil. The distance the blade moves depends on the strength of the current flowing through the coil of wire. Thus, this is a means not only of detecting but of indicating the strength of an electric current.

Needle Galvanometer

Another kind of galvanometer makes use of two magnetized needles instead of the razor blade. Magnetize the needles in exactly the same manner as the razor blade, holding the points in the same direction. Thread one end of a strip of cardboard (about $3 \times \frac{1}{8}$ inches) through the coil (Fig. 19-17) and suspend it from the top of the wooden stand. The opening in the coil should be large enough so that the cardboard can turn freely in it. With bent-over nails, anchor the coil upright on its side. Put both needles through the cardboard so that one is just above the top of the coil and one is within the oval made by it. The needle points should face in opposite directions, as shown in the figure. When the current flows through the coil (only a moment at a time), the needles will turn.

To explain why the needles are inserted in the cardboard with their poles opposed, recall how the deflection of the compass needle was effected by reversing the connections to the dry cell. Because of the direction of the magnetic field around the coil (Fig. 18–10), the same thing happens when the compass is moved from above to below the wire carrying the electric current (or vice versa). With the poles of the needles oriented so that the one above the coil faces in a direction opposite to that of the one below, they will move in the same direction at the same time.

Potato Tester

A novel but effective method of detecting an electric current involves the use of a dry cell, bell wire, and a potato. Slice the potato in half, attach two wires to the binding posts of a dry cell, and push the bare ends of the wires into the potato. Keep the wires fairly close together, but do not let them touch inside the potato. After a minute or two, pull out the wires. If the current is flowing, the hole made by the wire connected to the positive terminal of the dry cell will have a greenish-blue rim around it. Thus, this is a method for detecting the positive terminal as well as the flow of current.

A similar test involves the use of one third of a glass of vinegar. Dip the wires into the vinegar, holding them close but not touching. In a short time, if current is flowing, many bubbles of gas (hydrogen) appear at the wire connected to the

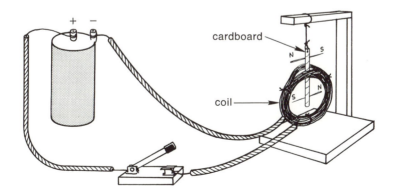

FIGURE **19-17**   A needle galvanometer, modeled after the earliest Faraday galvanometer.

negative terminal of the dry cell. None or just a few bubbles appear at the wire connected to the positive terminal. Examine the wires after a minute or two; the negative wire will still be shiny, while the positive wire will have become dull and rough.

MAKING ELECTRIC CURRENT

By Chemical Reaction

Most electricity produced by chemical reaction is electricity from batteries. Batteries are generally either "wet" or "dry" cells, though these names are somewhat misleading.

Voltaic or "wet" cell Children can make a voltaic or "wet" cell as follows. Needed are a strip of copper sheeting and a strip of zinc sheeting (available from hardware stores) 4–5 inches long and about $\frac{3}{4}$ inch wide and a quarter pound of ammonium chloride salt (available from a drugstore). Dissolve the ammonium chloride in 1 pint of water and pour the solution into a glass jar or beaker. Tack the copper and zinc strips to a narrow strip of wood about $\frac{3}{4}$ inch thick and long enough to rest on top of the jar. Punch a hole near the top of each strip, just large enough for a piece of bell wire to pass through, and fasten the bare end of a piece of bell wire to each hole. Connect the other ends of the wires to a galvanometer. When the strips (not touching each other) are submerged in the jar of ammonium chloride, the galvanometer will show the presence of an electric current, one probably strong enough to light a one-cell flashlight bulb.

Rinse the copper and zinc strips in clear water and wipe dry. Then, noting the effect on a galvanometer (and rinsing the metal strips after each test), do the following: Touch the strips together; replace the copper strip with a carbon rod (tie it to the wood strip with string or wire; wrap the stripped end of a wire around the rod and connect the other stripped end to the galvanometer); use copper for both strips; use two strips of lead, then strips of dissimilar metals such as aluminum and iron, copper and lead, zinc and iron; place the zinc and copper strips in a glass

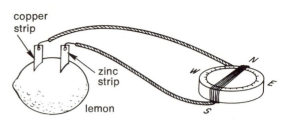

FIGURE **19-18** Producing electricity with a lemon and detecting it with a compass galvanometer.

of distilled water; repeat the last procedure using, instead of water, solutions of each of the following: vinegar, orange juice, sugar, salt, washing soda, and other common household chemicals.

After building a wet cell, children should be able to name its essential parts: the two strips of different metals and a chemical solution to help conduct electricity. Chemicals whose solutions help conduct electric currents are called electrolytes. There are acid, base, and salt electrolytes. Vinegar and fruit juices are examples of acids; ammonia is a base; and salt and baking soda are salts.

An electric current was produced because of the chemical reaction between the metal strips and the solution; the copper strip develops a scarcity of electrons, while the zinc strip accumulates electrons. This differential in charge causes the accumulated electrons to flow through the wires from the zinc strip, through the galvanometer, to the copper strip which lacks electrons, producing an electric current or flow of electricity. Electricity flows from areas having excess free electrons to those deficient in electrons.

Using the potato tester described above, children can establish that the copper strip is the positive terminal of the cell.

One can make a voltaic cell of a lemon. First, roll it firmly against a table or squeeze it in order to break up some of the inside tissue and release the juice. Cut two slits in the peel and insert a copper and a zinc strip (Fig. 19-18), making sure that the strips do not touch. Connect the metal strips to a galvanometer. Repeat the experiment using different kinds of fruit.

A voltaic cell can be made of coins. Soak a

piece of blotting paper thoroughly in salt water and place it between a penny and a nickel. Connect two wires to a compass galvanometer and touch the penny with one wire and the nickel with the other. An electric current will be detected. If the movement of the compass needle is very slight, substitute an iron washer for the nickel.

Children can "taste" electricity by placing the copper and zinc strips (cleaned thoroughly with soap and hot water) one on each side of the tongue. The tingly feeling indicates the passage of an electric current. In this case, the saliva is the electrolyte. The experiment may also be done with a clean penny and nickel.

The dry cell A dry cell is not really dry. To show this, cut an old dry cell down the center lengthwise with a hacksaw. As noted in Fig. 19-19, the dull metal can is made of zinc, which is the negative terminal. In an old cell, the zinc will have been eaten away a good deal on the inside. The rod in the center is of carbon and is the positive terminal. Carbon is used instead of copper because it is cheaper. The pasty material between the carbon rod and the zinc can contains three chemicals: ammonium chloride (white), fine carbon particles, and manganese dioxide (black).

The ammonium chloride is the chemical that, when moistened, acts as the electrolyte, which permits the chemical reaction to take place between the carbon rod and zinc can. When the cell is being used, a chemical reaction takes place and hydrogen bubbles accumulate on the carbon rod. These bubbles, which interfere with the flow of electrons (electric current), react with the manganese dioxide, which thus removes them as they are formed. In the process, water is formed.

When the cell is new, the paste is quite moist; when the cell is dead, the paste has become dry. To keep the paste moist as long as possible, the zinc can is lined with a layer of absorbent paper soaked in ammonium chloride solution (recall the ammonium chloride wet cell) and the top of the cell is sealed with pitch or sealing wax.

An almost depleted dry cell may be revived for a short while as follows. With a nail, punch a few holes into the bottom of such a cell. Place the cell in a jar. Add ammonium chloride solution until it is one third the way up the dry cell. Let the cell stand in the solution for at least a half hour, preferably longer; then try to light a flashlight bulb with the cell. If children try to light the bulb before and after soaking the cell, the result will be quite striking.

A simple storage battery Certain kinds of cells are made to be recharged when they are depleted. Many pupils will recall how the batteries in the family automobile have been recharged on occasion. The charging and discharging process can be shown quite effectively in the classroom. To do so, first make a simple storage battery as follows.

Punch a hole at one end of each of two lead strips about 6 × 2 inches (available from a plumber). Fill a glass about three quarters full

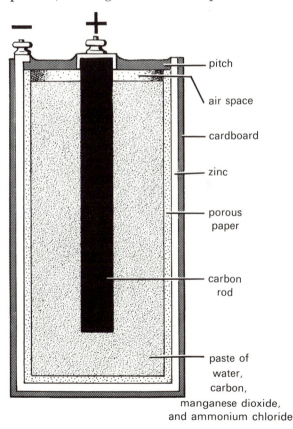

pitch

air space

cardboard

zinc

porous paper

carbon rod

paste of water, carbon, manganese dioxide, and ammonium chloride

FIGURE **19-19** Cross-section of a dry cell.

of dilute (20% concentration) acid, available from an automobile supply store. (*Should acid spatter on skin or clothes, wash it off immediately with abundant water. Never let children handle sulfuric acid solution, and cork with a rubber stopper only.*) Clean the lead strips well by sandpapering them. Bend their ends and hang over the sides of the glass, as shown in Fig. 19-20. Attach wires to the holes in the lead strips and connect the wires to a galvanometer. After it is clear that no current is indicated, charge the cell as follows: Connect three dry cells in series and attach the wires to the lead strips by means of the holes in them. The three dry cells in series will deliver about $1\frac{1}{2}$ volts each ($4\frac{1}{2}$ volts in all) to the lead cell. If a direct-current battery substitute is available, or if a child has a rectifier used for model H-O gauge trains, it may be used to charge the "storage cell." Let the current flow through the lead strips and acid for several minutes. Children can readily see that a chemical reaction is taking place: Bubbles of gas appear at both lead strips, and the strip connected to the positive terminal of a dry cell becomes brownish as it is converted to lead oxide.

After disconnecting the dry cells, connect the wires from the lead strips to a one-cell flashlight bulb in a porcelain socket. The bulb will light; each lead cell will be delivering 2 volts.

Point out that, when the battery is delivering electric current, it is said to be *discharging;* when electricity is being put into the battery, it is *charging.*

A saturated solution of baking soda (sodium bicarbonate) or of sodium sulfate may be used instead of sulfuric acid. To make a saturated solution, dissolve as much of one of the sodium compounds as possible in water at room temperature.

In a Magnetic Field

While electric current can be produced by means of chemical reaction in cells or batteries, cells can be used only for a limited time and must be replaced when depleted.

Electricity is generated commercially by a much simpler and less costly method, which requires only magnets and coils of wire.

As described in Chapter 18, and as mentioned in connection with the making of galvanometers, an electric current flowing in a wire produces a magnetic field around that wire. In a kind of reverse of this phenomenon, if one moves a wire through a magnetic field, an electric current is induced in the wire. To demonstrate, make a coil by wrapping about 50 turns of bell wire around a narrow olive jar. Slip off the coil and fasten it with thread, wire, or tape several points so that the coil won't come apart. Connect the ends of the coil to a compass galvanometer, and, holding a U-magnet (or bar magnet) motionless in one hand (as shown in Fig. 19-21), move the coil over one end of the magnet. Note that the compass needle is deflected, showing the presence of an electric current. Now remove the coil by sliding it back. The compass needle is deflected again, but this time in the opposite direction. Move the coil over the other pole of the magnet. The deflection is opposite to the one produced when the coil was moved over the first pole. Move the coil over one end of the magnet again; then stop.

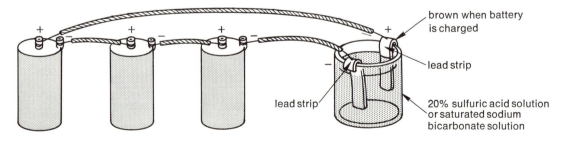

FIGURE **19-20** Charging a simple storage battery.

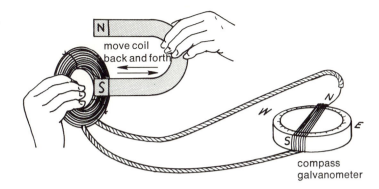

The compass needle will also stop being deflected, showing that electricity will be generated only as long as the coil is moving.

Move the magnet in and out of the coil; repeat this, moving the magnet more rapidly. Do the same after increasing the strength of the magnets by placing the like poles of two bar magnets together. Repeat these experiments after increasing the number of turns of wire to 100.

Children should realize, then, that (1) a coil of wire moving in a magnetic field generates an electric current; (2) increasing the strength of the magnet or the number of turns of the coil of wire will increase the amount of electric current produced; and (3) increasing the speed with which the coils or magnet move will increase the rate of production of the electric current.

It is these phenomena that are applied in electrical generators. Such generators, of any size and regardless of whether they are driven by steam, moving water, or a moving bicycle wheel, are essentially coils of wire moved through a magnetic field.

From Heat and Light

Under special circumstances, heat and light may produce electricity in small quantities. To do so, cut a piece of wire from a metal coat hanger. Scrape off all the paint with sandpaper. Cut a similar length of bell wire and remove all the insulation. With pliers, twist one end of the coat hanger wire together with one end of the copper

bell wire, and then connect the other ends of the wires to a compass galvanometer (Fig. 17-10). Heat the twisted ends of the wires in a candle flame or, preferably, in a hotter Bunsen burner flame. The compass needle will deflect, showing the presence of an electric current.

Photoelectric cells such as are found in photoelectric light meters produce electricity when light strikes them. The glass cell or tube is coated on the inside with a metal, such as cesium or selenium, which is sensitive to light (photosensitive). When light strikes the cell, a flow of electrons (electricity) leaves the selenium. The more intense the light, the greater the flow of electrons. Demonstration photoelectric cell units may be obtained from commercial supply houses. These can be used to turn lights off or on or ring bells.

APPLICATIONS OF ELECTRICITY

Motors

Although most children are well aware that electricity is used to operate appliances in the home, they may not understand that the heart of many of these appliances is the electric motor. An electric motor is essentially two magnets (one fixed) placed so that the interaction between their fields causes the movable one to rotate.

A simple, inexpensive, and easy-to-understand St. Louis motor can be purchased from any commercial scientific supply house, complete with instructions. Toy stores also offer a variety of electric motors. Some children may have motors that they will bring to class and whose operation they may be able to explain.

Cork-and-pin Motor

A simple electric motor can be made of three corks, some pins, two bar magnets, two small blocks of wood, a dry cell, and some insulated copper wire (No. 28 or finer). One cork should be $2\frac{1}{2}$–3 inches long. The other two corks should be shorter and wider, both the same size.

As shown in Fig. 19-22a, center a pin in each end of the large cork, so that when the cork rotates using the pins as a shaft or axle it will wobble as little as possible. Wind lengthwise about 10 inches of the fine insulated copper wire firmly around the cork as shown in Fig. 19-22b, making sure that there are equal numbers of turns on each side of both pins. Fasten the wire securely with thread, and strip the insulation from both ends, cleaning them with fine sandpaper.

Wind the wire around the cork, so that both free (bare) ends of the wire (the starting and finishing ends) are at the narrow end of the cork as shown. Bend these ends (cut so that they protrude about $\frac{1}{2}$ inch) at right angles to the coil of wire, thus making them parallel to the pin.

Push two pins criss-cross into each of the two short, wide corks. The pins from the wire-wound cork will rest on the crossed pins, which should therefore cross at approximately the same height. Do not cross the pins at a sharp angle, because the sharper the angle, the greater the friction the "motor" will have to overcome.

Set the two corks containing the crossed pins in a north–south position. Place the pins of the cork containing the coil of wire on the crossed pins. Lay the magnets on small blocks of wood, so that they are as close as possible to the cork, without touching it. Spin the cork by hand a few times to make sure the magnets are not touching it. A north pole should be on one side of the cork, and a south pole on the other.

Connect two 15-inch pieces of bell wire to a dry cell. Strip about 2 inches of insulation from the loose ends. Bend out these ends so that when

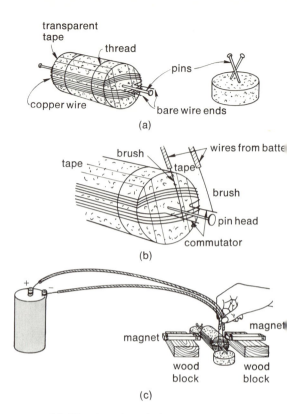

FIGURE **19-22**   A cork-and-pin motor.

the cork revolves they just touch or brush the ends of the two wires on the revolving cork.

Push the cork to start it spinning, holding the wires from the battery so that they make contact with the two wires on the cork as it revolves. Use only very light pressure—just enough to make good contact—yet avoid friction too great to permit the cork to revolve.

The cork will revolve in only one direction. Therefore, try pushing it first one way, then the other. If it is started in the right direction and the wires held with just the right pressure, the motor will keep revolving quite rapidly.

Point out the essential parts of the motor. The revolving cork with its wire wrapping is the armature; the two wires projecting from the armature, the commutator; and the wires from the dry cell, which brush against the rotating commutator, are the brushes. These latter lead the electric current into the armature. The magnets produce the necessary attraction and repulsion and are called field magnets. The dry cell supplies the electric current.

The motor operates as follows. When the electric current from the dry cell enters the coil of wire through the brushes, the coil becomes an electromagnet with north and south poles. These poles are attracted to the unlike poles of the permanent magnets, revolving the armature. When the poles of the electromagnet arrive opposite the permanent poles of the bar magnets, the wires from the armature (the commutator) have also revolved, so that each brush now touches the wire formerly touched by the other.

Thus, the current flowing from the dry cell enters first one commutator segment, then the other, reversing the flow of current and therefore the poles of the electromagnet. If this did not happen, the electromagnet would remain fixed in one position, held by its attraction to the bar magnets. Thus, the armature continues to rotate because the current entering the wire of the armature through the commutator is constantly reversed with every half turn of the armature. The reversal of current reverses the polarization of the armature, which is then alternately attracted to first one pole and then the other of the bar magnets.

The stationary magnets in a motor are usually called field magnets. Most motors use electromagnets rather than bar magnets as field magnets because they can produce greater magnetic attraction and repulsion and, consequently, a much faster-moving armature. Needed to make a motor that uses only electromagnets are a piece

of wood, preferably pine (about $6 \times 4 \times \frac{3}{4}$ inches); four 3-inch nails; two dry cells; and a piece of glass tubing slightly wider in diameter than the nail. Drive one nail though the center of the board so that its point extends into the air (Fig. 19-23).

Heat one end of the glass tubing in a hot Bunsen burner flame until the end is closed. When the glass is cool, cut the glass tubing at a point about $1\frac{1}{2}$ inches from the closed end. Ream out (with the square end of a rattail file) a hole halfway up into the wide end of a large cork. The hole should be very slightly smaller in diameter than that of the glass tubing.

Drive a nail through the upper portion of the cork so that an equal length protrudes from each side. The nail should not pass through the hole made for the glass tubing. Fit the glass tubing into the cork and let the tubing rest on the point of the nail in the board so that it acts as a bearing, turning easily on the nail. (Half of a large gelatin capsule may also be used as a bearing.)

Drive two nails into the wood spaced so that their heads just clear either end of the nail driven through the cork, as shown in Fig. 19-23. The object is to get the nails as close to the horizontal nail as possible, yet not touch it when it is spinning. These three nails should be on the same level.

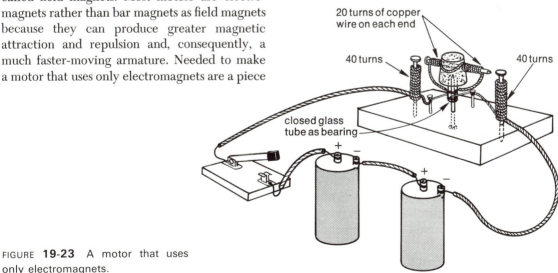

20 turns of copper wire on each end

40 turns

40 turns

closed glass tube as bearing

FIGURE **19-23** A motor that uses only electromagnets.

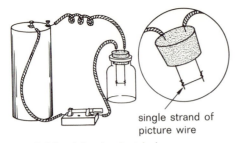

single strand of picture wire

FIGURE **19-24** A bottle electric lamp.

Wind about 40 turns of No. 22 wire around the horizontal nail (20 on each portion projecting from the cork). If necessary, wind the wires in layers. Bring the bared ends of the wire down along each side of the glass tubing. Fasten them to the glass tubing with thread or tape.

Wind about 40 turns of No. 22 wire around each vertical nail, again making layers if necessary and winding the wire around each nail in the same direction. (Children should be able to tell why this is necessary—that is, so that the flow of current will be correct.) Then strip about 3 inches of insulation from the ends of each coil of wire and wrap one end of each wire around a small nail driven into the wood so that the end of the wire projects and just touches one of the wires taped to the glass tubing, thus acting as a brush.

Connect the other ends of the wires from the vertical nails to a switch and two dry cells connected in series. Close the switch and push the horizontal nail to start the motor. (Try a push in both directions until it rotates on its own power.)

Make sure the brushes are neither too tight nor too loose. Sometimes a third dry cell (connected in series) is necessary.

A Simple Electric Lamp

Another application of electricity is the electric lamp. Let children examine a clear, unfrosted bulb and call their attention to the wire that leads in and out of it. Help them understand that this wire actually goes into the base of the bulb and that screwing the bulb into a socket and turning the switch allows the electricity to flow through the base of the bulb and into the wire inside it. Using a gooseneck lamp, have children note how the wire (filament) in the bulb glows when the switch is turned on. Point out how thin the wire is.

To make an electric light bulb, obtain a small wide-mouthed bottle, some bell wire, a cork that fits the bottle snugly, and a short piece of thin iron ("picture") wire. Make two holes in the cork wide enough for bell wire to pass through. (If the cork is rather long, cut off some of the bottom part.) Strip about 4 inches of insulation from one end of each of two pieces of bell wire, then push the stripped end of the wire through the holes in the cork.

Untwist a strand of the iron picture wire. Wind the piece of iron wire around each end of the bell wire extending through the cork; then insert the cork into the bottle. Connect the other ends of the bell wire into a circuit containing one or more dry cells and a switch (Fig. 19-24).

Close the switch. When the fine iron wire begins to glow, open the switch. Do this several times until the oxygen in the air inside the bulb combines with the filament to burn it away.

To make the filament last longer, replace the iron wire with a piece of Nichrome wire, obtainable at an electric repair shop or a radio and TV repair shop. In this case, more than one dry cell (connected in series) may be necessary.

Plating

Electricity can be used to plate metallic objects. Needed to demonstrate plating with copper are a strip of the metal about 6 × 2 inches (available

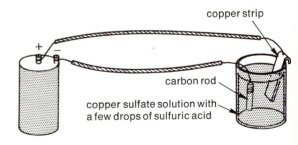

copper strip

carbon rod

copper sulfate solution with a few drops of sulfuric acid

FIGURE **19-25** Copperplating a carbon rod.

from hardware stores), some copper sulfate (blue vitriol) crystals (available from drugstores or hardware stores), a large iron nail, and some dilute sulfuric acid.

Dissolve copper sulfate in a glass or jar of water until the solution is deep blue. Because the crystals will dissolve very slowly if they are large, it is helpful to grind the crystals to a powder in a mortar and pestle, or wrap them in a clean cloth and crush them with a hammer. Add 5 drops of dilute sulfuric acid.

Punch a hole at one end of the copper strip (Fig. 19-25) and then bend this end over so that the strip will hang from one side of the glass or jar. Connect bell wire from the positive terminal of a dry cell to the hole in the copper strip; then put the strip into the copper sulfate solution. Saw open lengthwise a used-up flashlight battery or dry cell. Remove the carbon rod and wash it with soap and water to remove any chemicals or grease.

Connect bell wire from the negative terminal of the dry cell to the top of the carbon rod. Place the rod in the solution on the side of the glass opposite the copper strip. (The two must not touch.)

Soon the rod will be plated with copper. Point out that under the influence of the flow of electricity, copper leaves the solution to plate out onto the carbon, more copper from the strip dissolving to take the place of the copper that left the solution.

Try plating other objects with copper. Always connect these objects to the wire coming from the negative terminal of the dry cell.

ELECTRICAL CONDUCTORS AND NONCONDUCTORS

Children will have noted that bell wire was used in most of the experiments with electricity. On examining the wire, they will see that the conducting part is a reddish gold metal—copper. Have the children examine other wire such as that used to wire lamps in the home; this wire, also copper, consists of many thin pieces of the metal wound together. Children will recognize that copper conducts electricity quite well. They may also recall that in the wet cell, zinc also conducted electricity, as did the wire in a light bulb. To test whether all substances conduct electricity, connect a dry cell and a one-cell flashlight bulb ($1\frac{1}{2}$ volts) to a porcelain socket. Cut one wire and strip the ends. Bring the ends of the wires together and have children note that the bulb lights. Have them trace the path of the electric current through the circuit, and then hold the ends of the bell wires against a dime, again noting whether the bulb will light. Repeat the experiment using other coins, a piece of glass or a marble, a rubber eraser, an iron nail, and pieces of wood, china, porcelain, cloth, friction tape, etc. Children can make two lists, one of those materials that let electricity flow through them easily (conductors) and one of those that do not (non—or poor—conductors).

SAFETY WITH ELECTRICITY

The hazards involved in the use of electricity are so many, and the consequences so great, that it is absolutely necessary to teach safety factors and precautions as early as possible in the elementary school. The youngest children use many electrical appliances in the home, and the best way to teach safety in their use is to show correct use and the consequences of failure to follow safety rules.

Obtain two No. 2 dry cells, some bell wire, some one-cell ($1\frac{1}{2}$ volts) and two-cell (3 volts) flashlight bulbs, and miniature porcelain sockets. To illustrate a "short circuit," remove all the insulation from two pieces of bell wire, and connect them to the terminals of a dry cell and a porcelain socket containing a one-cell flashlight bulb. When the two wires are touched together, the light goes out. One can accomplish the same result by placing a screwdriver blade or other piece of metal across both wires. Point out that touching the wires together formed a new and shorter circuit, making it possible for the current to flow from one wire into the second wire at the point of contact and then back to the cell before it reached the bulb. This short cut is called a short circuit. Children should realize, then, the importance of covering the wire with insulating (nonconducting) material—to prevent the bare copper wires from touching. To duplicate everyday occurrences more realistically, one may repeat the experiment, using insulated bell wire and cutting the insulation of each wire at one point so that it is frayed and the bare wire exposed. Touch both wires together at the point where they are bare. Emphasize the importance of replacing electric cords in the home as soon as they begin to fray.

To show the danger of fire in such circumstances, make a short circuit again, using wires completely stripped of insulation. Keep the short circuit going and have children feel how the wires forming it soon become warm, even hot. Point out that if the short circuit were allowed to continue, the wires would become red hot. In buildings, where wires run through the walls, such red-hot wires could set the walls on fire. Wires may also become overheated if too many devices are used in the same circuit, causing an "overload" by using an excessive amount of electric current. To show this, connect two dry cells in series. Insert in the circuit a fuse and a two-cell flashlight bulb in a porcelain socket. Then add more two-cell flashlight bulbs in *parallel* until the circuit becomes overloaded and the fuse melts.

Fuses

To prevent short-circuited or overloaded wires from becoming red hot, circuits in buildings include a fuse. A fuse is made of a metal that melts at a lower temperature than the other parts of a circuit. When a short circuit occurs, the circuit becomes heated and the fuse melts, breaking the circuit. To illustrate the action of a fuse, cut a very thin, threadlike strip of aluminum foil or the foil in gum wrappers; fasten each end to a bare end of two pieces of bell wire projecting through a cork stopper (Fig. 19-26). This will serve as a fuse. Connect two dry cells in series; then insert into the circuit the fuse and a two-cell flashlight bulb in a porcelain socket. Remove a portion of the insulation of both wires, make the connection, and then touch both bare portions of the wires together, causing a short circuit. The fuse will melt, breaking the circuit, and the lamp will go out. If the fuse does not melt, use a thinner strip of foil. It may be necessary to experiment with different kinds of foil and different widths to devise a fuse that will permit the current to flow when connected properly, but that will melt when there is a short circuit. Lead foil makes the best fuses because of the low melting point of lead. (Lead foil may be obtained from a plumber, and scientific supply houses can provide lead fuse wire.)

FIGURE **19-26** Testing a homemade fuse.

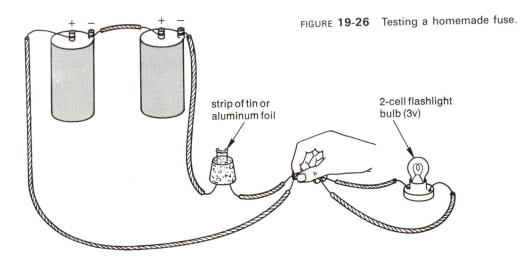

strip of tin or aluminum foil

2-cell flashlight bulb (3v)

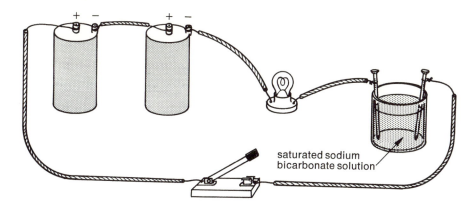

FIGURE **19-27** Demonstrating that a solution of a salt conducts an electric current.

Have children examine good fuses and burned-out fuses, and point out where the low-melting-point metal has parted in the burned-out fuses.

Point out the danger in replacing a "blown" or melted fuse with a penny, as is sometimes done: A fuse can melt but the penny cannot. Thus, wires may get too hot and cause a fire.

To show how electrical sparks can also cause fires, connect a pair of wires to a dry cell and flick the other ends together (to make a spark) just above the wick of a cigarette lighter. The wick will ignite. (This experiment should be done by the teacher.) Point out that an electrical spark can also ignite gas leaking from an appliance or vapors from gasoline, benzene, flammable cleaning fluids, paints, lacquers, and alcohol. If gas or these vapors are in a room, a spark from a switch or appliance can cause an explosion. The powerful spark produced when appliances are disconnected can be shown by plugging in and unplugging an electric iron.

Moisture on electric wiring can cause leakage of electricity, which may lead to dangerous electric shocks.

To show readily a solution of a salt carries an electrical current, fill a glass tumbler two thirds full of water and add as much sodium bicarbonate as the water can dissolve. Connect two dry cells, bell wire, a switch, a two-cell flashlight bulb (3 volts), a porcelain socket, and two long nails into a circuit with the glass of saturated sodium

bicarbonate solution (Fig. 19-27). The current flows through the solution and the bulb lights, showing a complete circuit. Point out that either an acid or an alkaline solution will conduct an electric current.

Warn children that radio and television sets operate at high voltage, and, so, should never be opened or tampered with. Holding an appliance, pull-chain, or switch in one hand while touching a radiator, water pipe, or any other metal pipe leading to the ground can make one part of an electrical circuit, which is dangerous and painful.

All electric appliances that produce heat are fire hazards if brought too close to or in contact with flammable materials. Such appliances include electric irons, stoves, heaters, toasters, etc. Even an electric bulb can cause a fire if it comes into contact with a curtain or paper shade. This can be easily shown by placing a piece of paper on a lighted 100-watt bulb. The paper will very shortly scorch. Conduct this experiment over a sheet of asbestos or on a fire-resistant pad or the stone top of a science laboratory table.

ELECTRICAL GAMES AND TOYS

Children may like to make a model of a street lighting system. For such a model, poles are made by nailing rectangular pieces of wood to a square base and then attaching small crosspieces. Two glass pushpins on each crosspiece will serve as

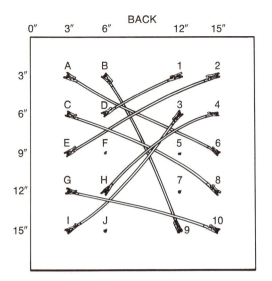

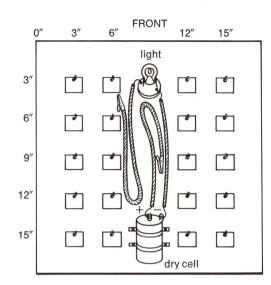

FIGURE **19-28** An electric question-and-answer board.

insulators around which bell wire is fastened. Miniature porcelain sockets containing two-cell flashlight bulbs (3 volts) become street lamps. Connect the lamps in parallel. Attach wires from the porcelain sockets to exposed portions of the bell wire, then wrap all bare portions of wire with electrical tape. A switch and two dry cells complete the circuit.

Children may prefer to wire a doll house for electricity, with miniature porcelain sockets placed in each room. If wired in parallel, separate switches in each room will light rooms individually. Some houses can be equipped with a master switch and a fuse box, with fuses made as described above.

An electric question-and-answer board can be both instructive and entertaining. To make one (Fig. 19-28), draw vertical lines at the 3, 6, 12, and 15-inch marks on a piece of thin plywood or other wood about 18 inches square. Draw horizontal lines at the 3, 6, 9, 12, and 15-inch marks. At the points where the lines intersect, screw in brass cup hooks large enough so that their screw ends protrude beyond the plywood when screwed all the way in. With a black crayon, number the two rows of protruding hook ends on the right from 1 through 10. Letter the two rows of hook ends on the left from A to J.

Cut ten lengths of bell wire, each about 20 inches long, and strip the insulation from the ends of each wire.

Attach two dozen small alligator clips (available from hardware stores) to the ends of the bell wires. Decide the number-letter combinations to be used and connect them accordingly with the wires, clamping the alligator clips to the protruding hook ends. (For example, as shown in Fig. 19-28, a wire connects Hook 2 to Hook E.) Record the ten combinations selected.

Using two metal strips, attach a dry cell to the bottom of the front of the board. Attach a porcelain socket and one-cell flashlight bulb ($1\frac{1}{2}$ volts) to the top and connect it to the dry cell, leaving two wires loose as shown in the figure. To the ends of these loose wires, attach alligator clips.

Cut in half ten 3 × 5-inch cards and punch a hole in one end of each. On ten of these half cards, write ten science questions. On the other ten, write the answers. Place the question cards on the cup hooks in the two left rows and the answer cards on the cup hooks in the two right rows according to the number-letter combinations arranged earlier.

A child attaches one alligator clip to a cup hook containing a science question and the other clip to the hook that he thinks carries the answer to the question. If the child has answered correctly, the bulb will light.

Any number of questions and answers may be used, and the combinations can be changed when children begin to learn the positions of the "right" answers.

A bell or buzzer may be substituted for the light bulb, or perhaps an owl's head cut out with two bulbs (connected in series) placed where the eyes should be; when the correct answer is selected by the player the wise old owl's eyes will light.

SUGGESTED PROJECTS

1. Have children recall experiences at home that produced sparks on a dry day. Lead into a discussion of how and why this phenomenon took place.

2. Rub a thin piece of styrofoam with wool, fur, or nylon, then place the styrofoam against the wall. It will adhere to the wall for a long time. Question why this happens.

3. Discuss what happens when children comb their hair on a dry day. Discuss the nature of the crackling sound produced and the reason hair will not lie flat. Pass a charged balloon over the heads of some pupils and ask why the hair stands on end.

4. Rub a hard-rubber comb with nylon, wool, or fur and bring the charged comb near some lengths of nylon thread. Discuss why the threads can be made to weave to and fro like snakes.

5. Discuss what causes lightning and how the charges are formed. Find out the relationship between the lightning flash and the spark produced from a charged object in a room.

6. Discuss situations where sparks can be a safety hazard. Call children's attention to the chain that usually dangles from the rear of a gasoline truck and ask the purpose of the chain.

7. Have children list electrical appliances in their homes. Plug one such appliance into an electrical circuit and trace the flow of electricity from the outlet into and out of the appliance.

8. Bring an assortment of electrical switches to class and investigate how they work. Discuss the reasons for using switches.

9. Take apart a porcelain lamp socket. (It may be necessary to break the porcelain.) Show how wires are built into the socket to conduct the electric current into and out of it. Consider the need for a completed circuit if a bulb in the socket is to light and discuss the use of porcelain for the socket. Lead into a discussion of conductors and nonconductors.

10. Explain the function of the Board of Fire Underwriters Laboratories, who set up safety standards for electrical equipment. Show electrical appliances that carry "approved" labels of the laboratory. Also show pieces of electric wire that carry a small ring of yellow paper and metal around the wire to show that it meets the laboratory specifications.

11. Consider two sets of Christmas lamps—one arranged in series and the other in parallel. Study their arrangement and observe what happens when one bulb is removed. Lead into a study of series and parallel circuits.

12. Examine a variety of lamp bulbs of different wattages and voltage ratings. Let children examine the different parts of the bulbs. Break one inside a cloth or bag (*Caution*) and observe the characteristics of the filament. Compare new and worn-out bulbs.

13. Discuss the purpose of insulation on wires that carry electricity and the reason why the ends of such wires are stripped bare when connected into a circuit. Lead into the study of electrical conductors and nonconductors.

14. Discuss why an electrical device should never be taken apart or adjusted while the current is on. Lead into a study of electrical safety. Make a list of safety rules and unsafe practices in the use of electricity.

15. Arrange for an electrician or other competent person to show small groups of pupils the master control panel, fuse boxes, electric meter, etc., in the school building. Raise the question of electrical circuits, fuses, and electrical safety.

16. Break up or take apart blown-out fuses and new

fuses. Identify the wires built into the socket and show how they serve to conduct the electric current into and out of the fuse. Examine the metal strip which acts as the fuse. Discuss the essential properties of a fuse.

17. Make a list of electrical appliances that produce other forms of energy, such as heat, light, sound, mechanical energy, etc. Study the various uses of electricity in the home and in commercial and industrial institutions.

18. Use model electric trains to study almost any aspect of electricity.

BIBLIOGRAPHY

(**P** indicates recommended for primary grades, **I** for intermediate grades, **U** for upper grades.)

Adler, Irving, *Electricity in Your Life,* Day, 1965. Application of electricity to modern life. Covers: electromagnets, electric lamp, radio, television, and radar. **U**

Beeler, Nelson, and Franklyn Branley, *Experiments with Electricity,* Crowell, 1949. Excellent experiments illustrating basic principles of electricity. **U**

Corbett, Scott, *What Makes a Light Go On?,* Little, Brown, 1966. Introductory presentation of electricity as a form of energy, the functioning of a generator, magnetic attraction and repulsion, and the working of the flashlight and light switch. Graphic diagrams and illustrations. **I**

Epstein, Sam and Beryl, *The First Book of Electricity,* Watts, 1953. Good treatment of the nature and uses of electricity. **U**

Freeman, Ira, *All About Electricity,* Random, 1957. Basic principles of electric currents, electromagnets, and their uses. **U**

Hogben, Lancelot, *The Wonderful World of Communication,* Garden City, 1957. Traces the growth of communication through art, writing, printing, motion pictures, and television. Illustrated. **U**

Michel, John D., *Small Motors You Can Make,* Van Nostrand, 1963. Directions for making electric motors from readily obtainable materials. **U**

Morgan, Alfred, *A First Electrical Book for Boys,* 3rd ed., Scribners, 1963. Updated with information on transistors, automatic switchboards, and Telstars I and II. **U**

————, *Things a Boy Can Do With Electricity,* Scribners, 1938. Contains experiments on both static and current electricity. **U**

Pine, Tillie S., and Joseph Levine, *Electricity and How We Use It,* McGraw-Hill, 1962. Children's questions answered by suggestions for simple and safe experiments. **P**

Rosenfeld, Sam, *The Magic of Electricity,* Lothrop, 1963. Concise directions for one-hundred experiments with batteries divided into experiments with electricity, electro-magnetism, electro-chemistry, and stunts with batteries. All experiments utilize easily obtainable equipment, and all are safe. Clear diagrams. **U**

Seeman, Bernard, *The Story of Electricity and Magnetism,* Harvey, 1967. The discovery of electricity and magnetism, historical development, properties, and future uses. Many experiments included. **I**

Syrocki, Boleslaus J., *What is Electricity?,* Benefic, 1960. Simple explanation of the nature of electricity, discusses circuits, conductors, insulators, switches and fuses, and some of the everyday uses of electricity. Well illustrated. **I**

Yates, Raymond F., *A Boy and a Battery,* Harper & Row, rev. ed., 1959. Experiments on electricity using a dry cell and simple materials. **U**

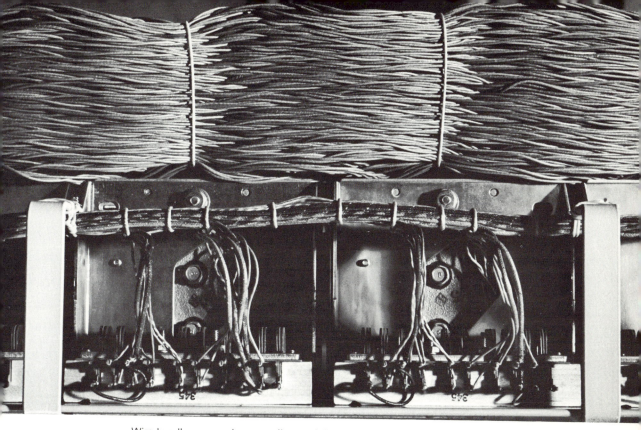

Wire bundles composing a small part of the telephone circuits in just one New York City office building.

20 *Communications*

Many devices use the principles of magnetism and electricity described in Chapters 18 and 19. Modern communications devices like the telegraph, telephone, radio, and television in particular would not exist without our knowledge of these principles.

TELEGRAPH

Children will spend hours operating a telegraph set, sending and receiving messages in Morse code or in their own secret codes. A telegraph set, which consists of a key and a sounder, can be bought in toy stores or can be quite easily made. Needed are three pieces of wood (one $6 \times 5 \times \frac{1}{2}$ inches, one about $3 \times 2 \times 2$ inches, and one $5 \times 3 \times \frac{1}{2}$ inches), two iron nails about $2\frac{1}{2}$ inches long, about 25 feet of insulated magnet wire (No. 22 or 24 bell wire), two $1\frac{1}{2}$-volt dry cells (with threaded binding posts), a tin snip or old scissors, and a "tin" can. Nail the block of wood to the larger of the flat pieces, as shown in Fig. 20-1. Drive the two $2\frac{1}{2}$-inch nails into the flat piece of wood, about $1\frac{1}{2}$ inches apart.

Using the tin snips or old scissors, cut a T-shaped strip from the tin can. (The thinner and more springy the metal, the better.) The strip should be about 5 inches long, with the body of the T about 1 inch wide and the head of the T about $2\frac{1}{2}$ inches wide. (Trim, file, or emery-cloth the edges if they are sharp.) Wind the wire

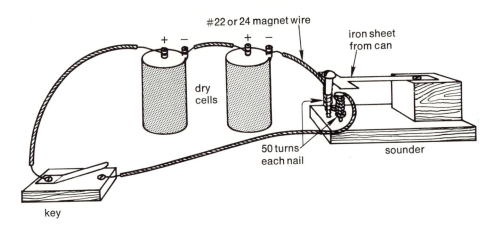

FIGURE **20-1** A homemade telegraph key and sounder.

around each nail as shown—around one nail, from top to bottom, in a clockwise direction, then around the second nail, from bottom to top, in a counterclockwise (or opposite) direction. Wind about 50 turns of wire around each nail. Then punch a hole with a nail at the long end of the T-shaped strip and screw the metal strip to the block of wood. The crossbar of the T should be about $\frac{1}{8}$ inch above the two nail heads. This distance may have to be adjusted later when the telegraph set is tried out.

To make the telegraph key, cut a strip of metal from the can about 5×1 inches and trim the edges if necessary. With a nail, punch a hole in

one end of the strip. Fasten the metal strip to the smaller flat piece of wood with a screw driven *almost* all the way in. Bend the metal strip back so that the strip is at an angle and does not touch the wood, as shown in the figure. At the other end of the piece of wood, insert a screw part way, so that the screw head extends about $\frac{1}{4}$ inch above the wood.

Connect the key and sounder to the dry cells as shown. When the metal strip of the key is pressed down, the T-shaped metal strip should hit the two nail heads with a click. With the key released, the metal T should spring back. It may be necessary to adjust the distance between the

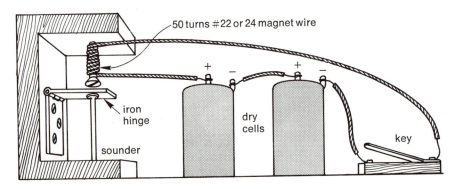

FIGURE **20-2** A hinge telegraph.

T and the nail heads in order to obtain a clear click; do this by bending the T.

Point out that the key is just a simple switch, which either opens or closes the electrical circuit. Also note that the wire-covered nails become electromagnets when electric current flows through them. Have children trace the flow of electric current when the key is closed. Help them understand that, when the key is closed, the wire-wrapped nails become electromagnets, which attract the head of the T-shaped strip. When the key is released or open, the electrical circuit is broken, the wired nails are no longer electromagnets, and the head of the metal T is released. In Morse code, a long pause between clicks is considered a dash, and a short pause, a dot.

To increase efficiency, place a long screw midway between the two wired nails (Fig. 20-1) so that the crossbar of the T just touches its underside. Now when the key is released, there will be another click when the metal T springs back and strikes the head of the screw.

Hinge Telegraph

A telegraph sounder may also be made of a door or cabinet hinge. To do so, make a U-shaped frame from three pieces of wood, as shown in Fig. 20-2. Screw an iron or steel hinge (available from hardware or variety stores) to the upright piece of wood. (The hinge should move up and down easily; if necessary, add a few drops of lubricating oil to the hinge joint.) Drive a nail into the bottom piece of wood until the loose part of the hinge just rests horizontally on the nail head. Insert a long screw into the upper piece of wood far enough so that the head of the screw is about $\frac{1}{8}$ inch above the loose part of the hinge when it rests upon the nail.

Then wrap at least 50 turns of insulated magnet wire (No. 22 or 24) around the shank of the screw. Connect the ends of the wire to two dry cells (in series) and a key. As before, when the key is closed, an electric current flows through the wire wrapped around the screw and forms

INTERNATIONAL MORSE CODE ALPHABET AND VARIOUS ABBREVIATIONS

A	. —	U	. . —
B	— . . .	V	. . . —
C	— . — .	W	. — —
D	— . .	X	— . . —
E	.	Y	— . — —
F	. . — .	Z	— — . .
G	— — .	1	. — — — —
H	. . . .	2	. . — — —
I	. .	3	. . . — —
J	. — — —	4	. . . . —
K	— . —	5	. . . . .
L	. — . .	6	— . . . .
M	— —	7	— — . . .
N	— .	8	— — — . .
O	— — —	9	— — — — .
P	. — — .	0	— — — — —
Q	— — . —	(.)	— . . —
R	. — .	or	
S	. . .		— . — . —
T	—	(,)	— . — . — . —
		(?)	. . — — . .

Abbreviation	Meaning
K	End of message; answer
R	Message received and understood
AR	Sign off—no acknowledgement necessary
Series of dots	Error, will resend word
AA	Who are you?
V	From
Single dash with light	I have received and understood the last word sent
N	Negative—no
A	Affirmative—yes
IMI	Repeat

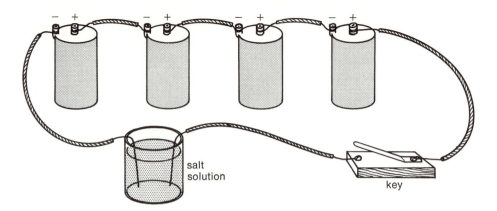

FIGURE **20-3**   A bubble telegraph.

an electromagnet, which then attracts the hinge and causes a click. When the key is opened or released, the current stops flowing, and the hinge drops back onto the nail head, producing a second click. Adjust the distance from the head of the screw to the hinge for best results.

Bubble Telegraph

A bubble telegraph, using salt water, may be made as follows. Connect four 1½-volt dry cells in series with No. 18 bell wire. Remove 6–8 inches of insulation from each end of the bell wire. Fill a clear glass tumbler about three fourths full of water. Dissolve as much table salt as possible in the water. Place the stripped ends of the wires in the salt solution so that they are about 1 inch from the bottom of the tumbler (Fig. 20-3). Insert a telegraph key or switch into the electrical circuit.

When the key is closed, an electric current flows through the solution. Bubbles of gas will be formed at one of the exposed wires. If the

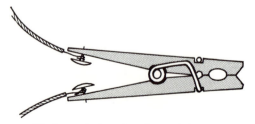

FIGURE **20-4**   A clothespin telegraph key.

key is closed a long time, a long stream of bubbles (representing a dash) will be produced.

To make a telegraph key from a spring-type clothespin, push two tacks into the inside portion of the open end, as shown in Fig. 20-4. Attach a wire to each tack and connect the wires as before in a circuit with a sounder.

Two-way Telegraph

Children may send telegraph messages from one end of the room to the other, or from one room to another, using the arrangement of two tin-can telegraph sets (sounders and keys) shown in Fig. 20-5.

Call the children's attention to the fact that if the person who is receiving does not keep his key down (closed), the electrical circuit will be broken, and no clicks will be produced. One can show this by tracing the flow of electric current through the circuit.

Because electric current becomes weaker the farther it has to flow, the electromagnet formed will also be weaker. If this happens, increase the strength of the current by connecting more dry cells in series.

BUZZER

A buzzer is, in effect, a rapidly opening and closing switch actuated by an electromagnet, the

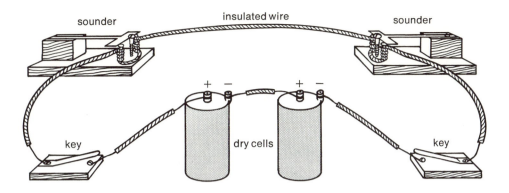

FIGURE **20-5**   A two-way telegraph system.

current to which is controlled, in turn, by that switch. To make a buzzer, first make a tin-can telegraph set (including the screw that touches the T-shaped metal strip), as described earlier and as shown in Fig. 20-1. However, now connect the wires (as shown in Fig. 20-6) so that one runs from the long screw that touches the crossbar of the metal T to a dry cell, and another runs from one of the wrapped nails to the screw that holds the metal strip to the block of wood. (Use a screwdriver to raise this screw a little so that the wire can be wrapped around it. Be sure the crossbar of the metal T is touching the underneath part of the head of the long screw.)

When the key or switch is closed, a buzzing will be produced. If the buzzer does not operate immediately, adjust the distance between the crossbar of the T and the wrapped nails, and see that the crossbar of the T is touching the screw.

Children can trace the electric current as it

flows through the circuit: from the dry cells, through the long screw, the metal T-strip, both wrapped wires, the key, and back into the cells. Call attention to the fact that the wired nails become an electromagnet when the electric current flows through them. The electromagnet then attracts the crossbar of the metal T and pulls it downward. Point out that, when pulled down, the metal strip no longer touches the screw, breaking the electrical circuit. The nails then stop acting as electromagnets, and the metal strip is released. The strip springs back, touches the screw again, and the circuit is completed once more. The nails become magnetized again, attract the metal strip, and break the circuit again. This process happens again and again, producing a rapid series of clicks, and thus making a buzzing sound.

Electric bells work the same way as an electric buzzer. To demonstrate, obtain an electric bell

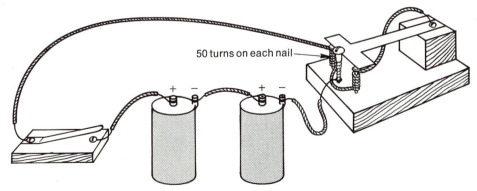

FIGURE **20-6**   A homemade buzzer.

from a hardware store, remove the cover, and examine it. Connect it to one or two dry cells and a switch. Have children watch the metal spring move back and forth very rapidly, causing the hammer to strike the bell.

TELEPHONE

Cigar-box Telephone

A simple telephone can be made of a cigar box, preferably wooden, two double-edged razor blades, about 3 feet of No. 18 bell wire, two small screws, a No. 2 pencil, a telephone earpiece or set of radio headphones, and a source of electricity (four $1\frac{1}{2}$-volt dry cells, a 6-volt storage battery, a $4\frac{1}{2}$-volt "A" battery from a portable radio, or a 9-volt transistor-radio battery). Force both razor blades into the top of the cigar box so that they stay upright (Fig. 20-7). The blades should be about $1\frac{1}{2}$ inches apart and placed along the grain of the wood.

Remove the insulation from the ends of two pieces of the bell wire and wrap one end of each wire securely around a hole of the razor blade. Insert two small screws partially into a side of the cigar box and wrap each wire around a screw to prevent tension on the wires from pulling the blades out of the box.

Split the pencil lengthwise and remove the piece of carbon or "lead." Cut two sections of carbon about 2 inches long and place them across the sharp edges of the razor blades.

Connect the wires from the blades in the cigar box to the telephone receiver and also to a source of current, as shown in the figure.

Put the receiver to an ear and roll the pieces of carbon gently over the edges of the blades. There should be a sound very much like static on a radio. Place a loud-ticking alarm clock face up on the cigar box. Listen on the receiver while adjusting the position of the pencil carbons on the blade edges. Try to find a position at which the clock ticking can be heard very loudly.

Move the receiver some distance away from the cigar box and have one child lean over the box and talk very distinctly at the pencil carbons. Another child, with the receiver to his ear, should hear the words quite distinctly. (If earphones are not being used, the child with the receiver should put his finger in the other ear if the receiver is fairly near the cigar box.)

Buzzing insects (flies or grasshoppers) placed inside the cigar box will be heard quite clearly in the receiver. To make a mouthpiece into which children can speak, cut a hole about $1\frac{1}{2}$ inches in diameter in each end of the cigar box (Fig. 20-7). Insert the cardboard tube of a paper-towel roll (or a cone-shaped paper cup with the bottom cut off) and attach it firmly with sealing wax,

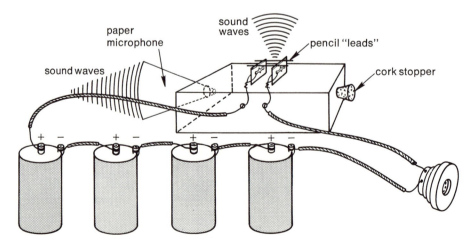

FIGURE **20-7** A cigar-box telephone.

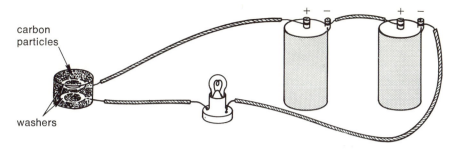

carbon
particles

washers

FIGURE **20-8** Demonstrating how pressure on carbon particles affects the flow of electricity.

chewing gum, or glue. Children may wish to place the cigar box in another room and "eavesdrop" on what is being said there.

To help children understand how the cigar-box telephone is able to reproduce the human voice and send it over a wire to the receiver, let them trace the electric current as it flows from the cells to one of the razor blades, across the pencil carbons to the second blade, then through the wire to the receiver, and back again to the cells.

The sound waves of the voice make the cigar box vibrate. (If a child rests his fingers lightly on the box while speaking, he will be able to feel the vibrations.) Explain that the vibrating of the box causes the pencil carbons to rattle or vibrate also. (Show this by rubbing the top of the cigar box with the finger.) The vibration affects the amount of contact of the pencil carbons with the edges of the razor blades. This will cause the amount, or strength, of the current flowing through them to vary.

This is essentially the basis of the telephone, although in actual commercial telephones, instead of carbon *rods,* carbon *granules* are used. If possible, obtain an old telephone transmitter (or mouthpiece) and open it. Note the tiny particles of granulated carbon present. These particles are in contact with a sheet-iron disk, called a diaphragm, that can flex, or move in and out slightly. The sound waves of the voice cause the disk to move and the resulting varying pressure against the carbon particles causes the electric current to change in strength continuously.

This can be demonstrated using a small round box, such as a thumbtack box or a pill box, two iron washers, and carbon particles. (To make

carbon particles, remove the carbon rod from a dry cell and break it into small pieces about $\frac{1}{8}$ inch in diameter.) As shown in Fig. 20-8, fasten the stripped end of some bell wire to one washer, place the washer in the bottom of the pill box, and cover it with a layer of carbon particles. Attach the stripped end of another piece of bell wire to the second washer and place it on top of the layer of carbon particles. Attach both wires to a two-cell flashlight bulb and two dry cells. Apply varying degrees of pressure to the second washer and note the effect on the brightness of the bulb.

The children should realize that the tighter the carbon is pressed together, the better the flow of electric current. Point out that in the cigar-box telephone the vibrations of the pencil carbons affect the strength of the electric current in exactly the same way.

Another demonstration of the principle uses an alarm clock, a dry cell, a set of radio earphones, and a strip of copper about $3 \times 1\frac{1}{2}$ inches. (Earphones may be obtained from a radio and TV shop, and the copper strip from hardware stores.) Break the carbon rod from an old dry cell into small pieces. Bend the copper strip at the midpoint and, with a nail, punch a small hole at one end. As shown in Fig. 20-9, lay the clock face downward and spread the small pieces of carbon rod on its metal back. Set the bent copper strip on the carbon particles and attach one end of a length of bell wire to the hole in the copper strip and the other end to one of the earphones. Connect the other earphone and one terminal of the dry cell with a second length of wire. Finally, connect the frame of the clock and the other

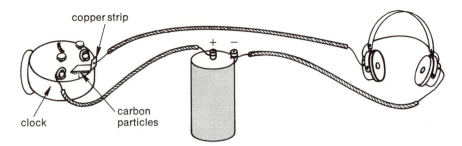

copper strip

carbon
particles

clock

FIGURE **20-9** Demonstrating a basic principle of the telephone.

terminal of the dry cell by a third length of wire. Adjust the position of the copper strip on the carbon particles until the ticking of the clock can be heard clearly in the earphones.

Point out that the device thus made is in effect a telephone transmitter. When the clock ticks, it sets up sound vibrations. The vibrations cause varying pressure against the carbon particles, which, in turn, varies the strength of the current flowing through the carbon. Thus, the electric current varies whenever the vibrations due to the sound vary. In this way, the differences in sound are transmitted to the receivers of the earphones.

If a telephone transmitter has been obtained and opened, as described above, the receiver, or earpiece, may also be available. Open it and note that sheet-iron disk and electromagnet. Test the electromagnet with some iron objects to show that it is permanently magnetized. Point out that in the telephone receiver the electromagnet is made by winding coils of wire around a permanent magnet. In this way, the iron disk is always

attracted to the magnet, but more strongly as the electric current becomes stronger, and weakly when the current is weak. This causes the iron disk to vibrate in accordance with the changes in current. The vibrations of the disk thus produce sound waves like those that entered the transmitter.

One can also demonstrate the fluctuation of the current in the telephone circuit using a galvanometer (see Chapter 19). Connect a telephone transmitter and a receiver to four dry cells in series and a compass electric current detector, or a regular galvanometer (Fig. 20-10). Use several feet of bell wire between the transmitter and receiver. While one child talks into the transmitter, have the class observe the action of the needle in the detector, noting how the deflection of the needle varies as the child talks loudly, then softly. Remove the diaphragm of the transmitter and push on the button with a pencil. Varying the pressure on the button will produce a varied deflection in the galvanometer needle.

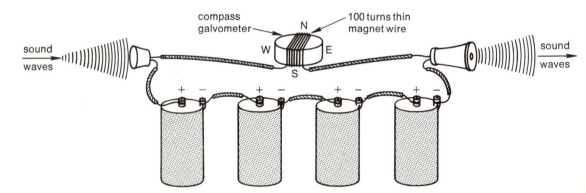

FIGURE **20-10** Demonstrating how current fluctuates in the telephone with fluctuations in volume of sound.

Children should now understand that varying pressure on the carbon particles in the transmitter causes the strength of the electric current flowing through the circuit to vary. This, in turn, affects the strength of the electromagnet in the receiver, and the iron disk or diaphragm vibrates in accordance with the change in strength of the electromagnet.

RADIO AND TELEVISION

In describing radio and television, it will be useful to recall or repeat the experiments in Chapter 18. Point out again that a wire carrying an electric current creates a magnetic field. Thus, a fluctuating or pulsating electric current traveling in a wire will send out electromagnetic impulses or waves. Also recall or repeat experiments on generating an electric current from a coil and a magnet in Chapter 19. Point out that this is a way of converting electromagnetic waves back to electricity again.

In radio, as in the telephone, sound waves are converted into a pulsating or fluctuating alternating electric current. The electric current, instead of making an electromagnet attract a metal diaphragm (as in the telephone), causes electromagnetic waves to be sent out from the antenna of the radio station. These electromagnetic waves reach the antenna in the radio set and are then converted back to electricity, which makes part of the speaker vibrate (much the way the metal disk in the telephone receiver does) and thus converts the electrical impulses to sound.

In television, light waves (instead of sound waves) are converted to a pulsating current, which sends out the electromagnetic waves that are converted by the receiver back to electricity and then to light waves again. The sound is transmitted in the same way as in radio.

One can readily demonstrate how electricity can be sent through the air without wires with an induction coil (obtainable from a scientific supply house, a radio or TV repair shop, or a high school physics teacher). The induction coil is used to develop a high voltage. Some ignition

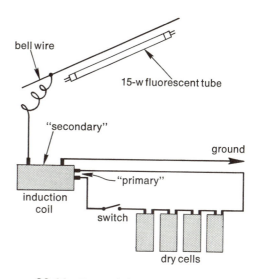

FIGURE **20-11** Transmitting electricity through the air by means of an induction coil.

coils from automobiles or tractors—such as the Fordson Model TT (tractor) or Ford Model T—will also serve.

Connect the "primary" of the induction coil to a source of direct electric current and a switch, as shown in Fig. 20-11. Four dry cells connected in series will supply enough current, as will a 6-volt storage battery or 10 volts from a model train transformer. Then connect a length of wire from one terminal of the induction coil "secondary" to a small bared spot on a length of bell wire extended across the room. (This wire should be held up at each end by a nonconductor such as wood. If the room has no wood parts, attach the ends of the wire to thick rubber bands. The object is to insulate both ends of the wire.) Attach another length of wire to the other terminal of the induction coil secondary, "grounding" the wire's other end by tying it (with the insulation removed) to a radiator or pipe.

Close the switch and hold a 15-watt fluorescent tube near and parallel to the wire strung across the room. The tube will light, indicating that electromagnetic waves are coming from the wire.

In a simpler demonstration, one can hold a portable radio (tuned away from a station) near a lighted fluorescent tube. The radio will pick up a hiss and static from the tube.

To show that a television picture is made up of electron impulses that are converted to light impulses, move a strong magnet back and forth near the screen of the television set. The magnetic field will bend the beam of electrons that is "painting" the picture on the TV screen, making the picture "wiggle" and distort.

A Crystal Radio

A crystal set may be made relatively easily and inexpensively. Needed are an $8 \times 8 \times \frac{1}{2}$-inch piece of wood and the following (all available from radio and TV repair or supply stores): a spool of No. 27 or 28 insulated copper wire, a pair of earphones, a crystal diode detector (No. IN-16 or IN-34), and a variable condenser. A piece of cardboard tube, such as that from a paper towel roll, may be used. The tube should be about 6 inches long and $1\frac{1}{2}$–2 inches in diameter.

Although not absolutely necessary, it is helpful to shellac or varnish the wood and the cardboard tubing, drying the tube first in a warm (not hot) oven. The shellac will seal the pores and prevent moisture from being absorbed, making the tube a better insulator. It will also prevent it from shrinking or expanding with changes in temperature and humidity, which would cause the wire wrapped around it to loosen.

Unwind about 50 feet of wire from the spool. With a sharp thin nail, make two holes at each end of the cardboard tube (Fig. 20-12). Push about 8 inches of the wire into one of the two holes, then loop it through the second hole to hold the wire firmly in place. Holding the tube and the end of the wire in one hand, wrap 80–100 turns side by side carefully around the core, as shown.

Cut the remaining wire, leaving about 8 inches to lace through the two holes as before. Draw both ends of the wire tight. Fasten the coil to one end of the piece of wood with a thumbtack through each end of the tube. Take care that the thumbtacks do not touch the wire.

Opposite each end of the cardboard tube, drill a hole through the wood to accommodate a bolt. Fasten the bolts with two nuts on each, making, in effect, binding posts. Position the variable condenser in front of the tube and the crystal detector in front of the condenser, as shown in the figure.

Wrap the 8-inch lengths of wire at each end of the tube around the bolts. As with the tube, drill holes opposite each end of the detector, insert bolts, and attach to them wires from the detector. Connect all the elements—earphones, coil, detector, and condenser as shown. Radio waves will travel from one binding post of the crystal detector, across the detector into the earphones, then through the earphones, and back to the binding post. Stations are selected by turning the plates of the condenser.

Needed for good reception is an antenna con-

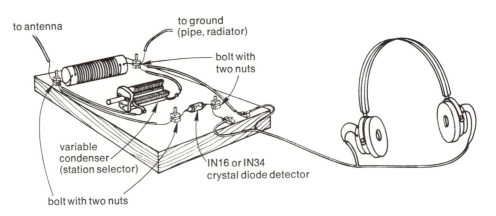

FIGURE **20-12** A homemade crystal set.

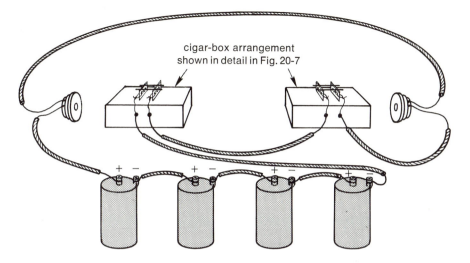

FIGURE **20-13** A two-way cigar-box telephone system.

sisting of a wire at least 100 feet long; the longer and higher, the better. Attach one end of the wire to a roof or tree and connect the other end to one of the binding posts of the detector. "Ground" the crystal set by running a wire from the other binding post to a radiator or pipe. The antenna must have insulators (nonconductors) at each end.

To operate the crystal set, turn the movable plates of the condenser, while listening carefully through the earphones. When a station is found, tune it in as with any radio.

SUGGESTED PROJECTS

1. Obtain an actual telegraph and examine its construction and operation. Lead into a study of how we communicate by telegraph.

2. Examine the construction and operation of a buzzer or bell. Lead into the study of how electricity can produce sound.

3. Examine the parts of an old telephone transmitter and receiver. Note the diaphragm and carbon particles in the transmitter and the diaphragm and electromagnet in the receiver.

4. Have children list everyday examples of electromagnetic interference—as from vacuum cleaners, airplanes, automobile ignition systems—with radio and television reception.

5. Visit a telegraph office, telephone building, radio station, or television station. Many of the larger ones offer formal tours.

6. Set up a two-way telephone system as shown in Fig. 20-13. Children will enjoy using this system in one room and between two rooms.

BIBLIOGRAPHY

(**P** indicates recommended for primary grades, **I** for intermediate grades, **U** for upper grades.)

Barr, George, *Young Scientist and the Police Department*, McGraw-Hill, 1967. Includes a very fine chapter on police communications systems. **U**

Bendick, Jeanne and Robert, *Television Works Like This*, McGraw-Hill, 4th ed. rev., 1965. Behind-the-scenes story of television. Includes pay television, closed-circuit television, and video tape. **U**

Brinton, Henry, *The Telephone*, Day, 1962. A brief

but accurate treatment with many diagrams, drawings, and a glossary. **U**

Buchheimer, Naomi, *Let's Go to the Telephone Company*, Putnam, 1958. Simple but exact explanation of the principles involved. **I**

Buehr, Walter, *Sending the Word; the Story of Communication*, Putnam, 1959. Traces man's development of methods for transmitting information. **U**

Clark, Mary Lou, *You and Electronics*, Children's Pr., 1967. Lucid presentation includes an explanation of radio waves, radar, ultra-violet radiation, X-rays, and laser beams. **U**

Coggins, Jack, *Flashes and Flags, the Story of Signaling*, Dodd, Mead, 1963. Sign language, trumpet calls, flags; telegraph, telephone, and wireless; smoke, sea, train and traffic signals; and sports signals—all briefly covered. Code flags are pictured, and the Morse Code is included.

Corbett, Scott, *What Makes TV Work?*, Little, Brown, 1965. In simple vocabulary, a logical, clear progressive description of the processes of transmission and reception, with a separate section devoted to color television. Excellent diagrams. **U**

David, Eugene, *Television and How it Works*, Prentice-Hall, 1962. The functions and operations of the television industry are explained in a straightforward text and cartoon-like drawings. Included are accounts of how television programs are developed, how television was invented and perfected, and some of the scientific principles involved. **U**

Freeman, Ira, *All About Electricity*, Random, 1957. Contains section on how the telephone, radio, and television work. **U**

Hogben, Lancelot, *The Wonderful World of Communication*, Garden City, 1959. The history of communication from cave printings and the beginning of the alphabet. Lavish illustrations. **U**

Irving, Robert, *Sound and Ultrasonics*, Knopf, 1959. Deals primarily with the nature of sound and high-frequency sounds, with a section on how sounds are recorded and transmitted. **U**

Ress, Etta, *Signals to Satellites in Today's World*, Creative Educational Society, 1965. A brief account of communication from prehistoric times to the present. Numerous photographs, diagrams, charts, and drawings. Indexed. **U**

Schneider, Herman, *Your Telephone and How It Works*, McGraw-Hill, 3rd ed., 1965. Updated with the addition of material on picturephones, touch-tone phones, card dialer phones, direct distance dialing, Telstar Satellite, and a new service called the Bellboy Personal Signalling Service. **I**

Solomon, Louis, *Telstar: Communication Break-Through by Satellite*, McGraw-Hill, 1962. Covers the building, launching, and performance of Telstar I and the operation of its sending and receiving apparatus. Fully illustrated with excellent photographs. **U**

Yates, Raymond F., *Boy's Book of Magnetism*, Harper & Row, 1959. Includes explicit instructions on how to make simple telegraph sets. **U**

Tracks of subatomic particles change course abruptly where collisions between particles occur.

21 *Atoms and Radioactivity*

Chemists have listed some 2,000,000 different substances. All are built of little more than 100 different building blocks, or elements (Chapter 10). *Elements* are synthesized into *compounds*, which contain two or more elements. With every breath, for example, the elements carbon and oxygen are combined into a compound, carbon dioxide (see below and Chapters 10 and 11). Compounds, in turn, can be broken down into elements. The smallest particle of an element still retains its characteristic properties: gold dust and gold nuggets have identical properties. The elements and compounds of elements are composed of molecules and the molecules are composed of one or more atoms (Fig. 21-1).

Because atoms are submicroscopic, and hence invisible to the naked eye, it has taken a thousand years to recognize their existence, to understand them, and to apply them to peaceful, useful work. Atoms are like the alphabet, molecules like words, a chemical equation like a sentence. In the language of chemistry, letters represent the elements, and subscript numbers indicate the number of atoms of an element present in a substance: for example, H_2O (a molecule of water) contains two atoms of hydrogen (H) combined with one of oxygen (O). Children holding placards designating them as atoms of various substances can be grouped to illustrate these relationships. Three children are needed to illustrate a molecule of water, two can illustrate a molecule of rust (FeO), three, carbon dioxide

(CO_2), and five, calcium carbonate ($CaCO_3$). Atoms composing molecules are held together by the pull and balance of their electrical charges.

ARCHITECTURE OF THE ATOM

In the nineteenth century, John Dalton, the English schoolmaster, designated as atoms particles of matter that he postulated were so small they could be divided no further. This view is no longer valid, for the atom is now known to consist of smaller—subatomic—particles such as the electron, the proton, and the neutron. (Many children will be aware of subatomic particles other than those mentioned; for the generality of elementary-grade children, however, it appears useful to narrow experience to the three basic particles named.) The proton has a positive electrical charge, the electron has a negative

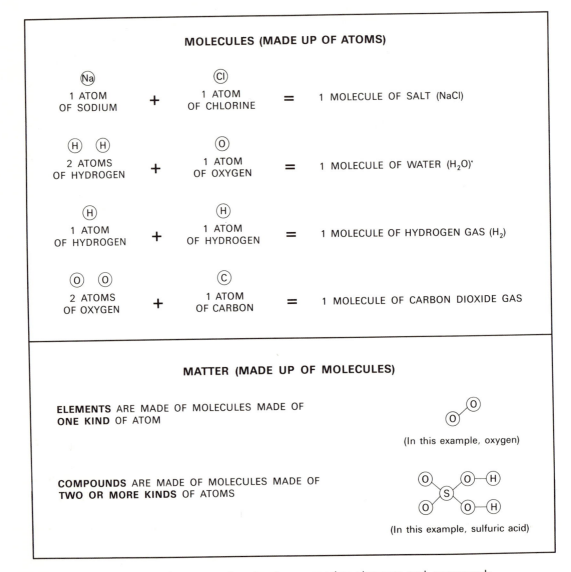

FIGURE **21-1** Relationships of atoms and molecules composing elements and compounds.

charge of the same size, and the neutron has no charge.

According to the concept of atoms as miniature solar systems (developed by Nils Bohr, the Danish physicist, and recently modified somewhat), the nucleus of the atom is made up of protons and neutrons whose total charge is balanced (Fig. 21-2) by the total charge of the electrons, which move rapidly in spherical regions around the nucleus.

Since electrical charges are basic to the architecture of the atom, in effect holding it together, children can profit from a review of the concepts of electrical energy, magnetic energy, positive and negative charges, and polarity (Chapters 18 and 19). It should also seed initial understanding of why electrons flow (Chapter 19) from minus to plus, rather than vice versa: Because the charge is negative where excess electrons gather, all electrical conductors have some free electrons.

Any classroom model of an atom is a distortion from the point of view of size and space relations alone. The electron and nucleus of a hydrogen atom are relatively no closer than a fly buzzing around the outside of a stadium is to the structure's center. Like the universe, an atom is mostly empty space, and classroom models of atoms cannot really convey the relative vastness of that emptiness.

However, scientists continually build models to help them in their understanding of the invisible world in science, and children's concepts of the invisible atoms and molecules of matter

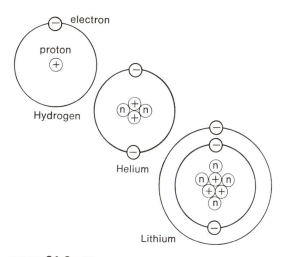

FIGURE **21-3** Diagrammatic arrangement of hydrogen, helium, and lithium atoms.

can be similarly developed through model-building. The usual three-dimensional models are not well adapted for involving a class, although individual children or the class may wish to construct them after making the simpler models described below. Needed are a 20 × 24-inch sheet of plain newsprint (for each pair of children working together) and a saucer of three kinds of seeds, macaroni, cereal grains, or other readily available materials such as paperclips, thumbtacks, or paper fasteners. (Use different materials at different times to make clear that these objects are merely symbolic of protons, electrons, and neutrons. Otherwise, through association, some children may derive false concepts.) Larger seeds such as lima beans are more easily manipulated by children. Since electrons have $\frac{1}{1840}$ the weight of protons, lighter objects should be used to represent the former.

Fold the paper into quarters, each quarter for the diagram of a different atom. Draw patterns of atoms on the blackboard; children can then reproduce these on their paper, arranging objects (seeds, paper clips, etc.) to represent protons, electrons, and neutrons in their appropriate places—the nucleus or the electron shells, or orbitals, they have drawn for each atom.

Although arrangement of electrons in circular shells is a misconception, circles may be initially

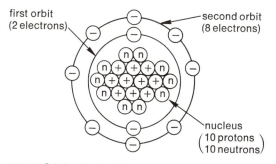

FIGURE **21-2** Typical diagrammatic arrangement of parts of an atom—in this case an atom of neon—showing balancing of electrical charges. Symbols are: n, neutron; +, proton; and −, electron.

easier for children to draw and conceptualize. If children know how to draw ellipses (p. 158), each pair will need a cardboard sheet under the newsprint to accommodate the tacks for string loops and to protect table tops.

Begin with the hydrogen atom (Fig. 21-3), designating it by its full name and/or its symbol, H. Around the symbol of a proton, draw an ellipse or circle and place the electron somewhere along this orbit. Similarly, for the next "box" on the paper, show two protons and two neutrons, representing the *nucleus* and, in a single orbit, two electrons, which will then balance the positive proton charges. (One should remind children of the rule of polarity in magnets—that like poles repel and unlike attract. Also, draw an analogy between the behavior of electrical charges and the fact that batteries—as in a flashlight—must be placed "head to tail" if their current—electrons—is to flow.) Label the neutrons with a symbol indicating absence of charge or balanced charge. The resulting diagrammatic model (Fig. 21-3) is of the structure of the helium atom. Helium is a stable gas that often replaces flammable, explosive hydrogen for inflation of lighter-than-air craft—one of its many uses. Hydrogen's *atomic number* is 1, and helium's, 2—the number of protons in their respective nuclei. Thus, to diagram the element whose atomic number is 3 (lithium), group three protons in the nucleus (with four neutrons) and three electrons, two in the first orbit or shell and one in the second or outer shell (Fig. 21–4). Lithium is a soft white metal never found free. *Atomic weight* (because an electron is but $\frac{1}{1840}$ the weight of a proton) is mainly based on the protons and neutrons in the nucleus. Make a table as follows, showing this and the other characteristics of the atoms so far diagrammed:

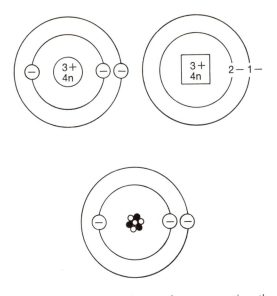

FIGURE **21-4** Three schemes for representing the structure of an atom (lithium).

At this point, some children may be able to infer some of the data for the next entry in the table—beryllium. Mental constructs can then be reinforced by having children diagram beryllium in the fourth box of their newsprint sheets, arranging the seeds or other objects to represent the four protons and five neutrons of its nucleus and the four electrons (two each in two orbits). As children come to grasp the pattern, they may profit from examination of an extended or complete list of elements (Table 21-1).

When they construct models of heavier, more complex atoms, prepare some models for the bulletin board by mounting with glue and labeling. Making atom models should help children see how some atoms can lose or gain electrons, becoming positively or negatively charged and, thus, attracting or repelling atoms of other sub-

Element	Symbol	Atomic No.	Atomic Wt.	No. of Protons	No. of Electrons	No. of Neutrons
Hydrogen	H	1	1	1	1	—
Helium	He	2	4	2	2	2
Lithium	Li	3	7	3	3	4

stances. From their models, children may be able to conclude the following rules concerning atomic architecture: (1) the atomic number is the same as the number of protons; (2) the atomic number is the same as the number of electrons; (3) the atomic weight minus the atomic number gives the number of neutrons; (4) the first orbital shell is complete with two electrons; and (5) the number of electrons in the second and third orbits does not exceed eight for the first 20 elements. On the basis of this information, children may complete the following table:

Name	Symbol	No. of Protons	No. of Neutrons	Atomic No.	Atomic Wt.
Hydrogen	H	1	0		
Carbon	C	6	6		
Oxygen	O	8	8		
Sodium	Na	11	11		
Sulfur	S	16	16		
Chlorine	Cl	17	18		
Calcium	Ca	20	20		
Iron	Fe	26	30		
Copper	Cu	29	34		
Silver	Ag	47	61		
Iodine	I	53	74		
Gold	Au	79	118		
Mercury	Hg	80	121		
Lead	Pb	82	125		
Radium	Ra	88	138		
Uranium	U	92	146		

Also on the basis of this information, and keeping in mind the significance of the subscript numbers as described above (p. 343), children may be able to substitute atomic weights in the formulas for these common substances in order to find the weight of one molecule of each: NaCl (salt), H_2O_2 (hydrogen peroxide), SO_2 (sulfur dioxide), $C_6H_{12}O_6$ (simple sugar), and C_2H_5OH (alcohol).

Children's games such as "three deep" may offer analogies with the tendency of atoms to complete orbits (Rule 5 above) and, thereby, to achieve electrical equilibrium. For example, sodium, with one outer electron, combines with chlorine's ring of seven outer electrons (Fig. 21-1) to form a stable, familiar compound—salt. Sodium, in the presence of water, is an "irritable" metallic element because it releases hydrogen from water; the hydrogen "explodes" in air. Chlorine, by itself, is a poisonous, green gas. Diagramming or modeling each of these elements will clarify the concept. Elements with complete outer shells of eight electrons turn out to be the stable, inert gases—neon, argon, krypton, and xenon. Thus, two atoms of elements with few outer electrons—such as hydrogen, sodium, and potassium—are generally active and seldom found uncombined. Although there are exceptions to the pattern, making the models develops the concept that atoms with fragmentary outer electron shells can lose electrons, lose their electrical balance, and become positively charged—as do some atoms in a balloon when it is rubbed. (See Chapter 19 for relevant experiments in static electricity and the effect of balanced and unbalanced charges.)

RADIOACTIVITY

Radioactivity was discovered by A. H. Becquerel in 1896. He accidentally placed uranium ore (pitchblende) against a light-proof covered photographic plate and found an image of the ore on the plate after developing it. This led his student, Madame Marie Curie, into the two years of research that ended with her isolation of the radioactive element, radium.

Becquerel's discovery of radioactivity and the investigations of the phenomenon by the Curies added important links to the chain of discoveries concerning the structure and uses of the atom. Radioactive elements are those whose nuclei disintegrate spontaneously, releasing energy in the form of alpha (two protons and two neutrons), beta (electrons), or gamma particles. Atoms of the top-heavy (more neutrons than protons in the nucleus) elements, which are near the end of the periodic table are continuously releasing such energy.

TABLE 21-1 THE CHEMICAL ELEMENTS
ARRANGED ACCORDING TO ATOMIC NUMBER

Atomic No.	Element	Symbol	Atomic Wt.	Electron orbit distribution*				
1	Hydrogen	H	1	1				
2	Helium	He	4	2				
3	Lithium	Li	7	2	1			
4	Beryllium	Be	9	2	2			
5	Boron	B	11	2	3			
6	Carbon	C	12	2	4			
7	Nitrogen	N	14	2	5			
8	Oxygen	O	16	2	6			
9	Fluorine	F	19	2	7			
10	Neon	Ne	20	2	8			
11	Sodium	Na	23	2	8	1		
12	Magnesium	Mg	24	2	8	2		
13	Aluminum	Al	27	2	8	3		
14	Silicon	Si	28	2	8	4		
15	Phosphorus	P	31	2	8	5		
16	Sulfur	S	32	2	8	6		
17	Chlorine	Cl	35	2	8	7		
18	Argon	Ar	40	2	8	8		
19	Potassium	K	39	2	8	8	1	
20	Calcium	Ca	40	2	8	8	2	
21	Scandium	Sc	45	2	8	9	2	
22	Titanium	Ti	47	2	8	10	2	
23	Vanadium	V	51	2	8	11	2	
24	Chromium	Cr	52	2	8	13	1	
25	Manganese	Mn	55	2	8	13	2	
26	Iron	Fe	56	2	8	14	2	
27	Cobalt	Co	59	2	8	15	2	
28	Nickel	Ni	58	2	8	16	2	
29	Copper	Cu	63	2	8	18	1	
30	Zinc	Zn	64	2	8	18	2	
31	Gallium	Ga	69	2	8	18	3	
32	Germanium	Ge	74	2	8	18	4	
33	Arsenic	As	75	2	8	18	5	
34	Selenium	Se	80	2	8	18	6	
35	Bromine	Br	79	2	8	18	7	
36	Krypton	Kr	84	2	8	18	8	
37	Rubidium	Rb	85	2	8	18	8	1
38	Strontium	Sr	88	2	8	18	8	2
39	Yttrium	Y	89	2	8	18	9	2
40	Zirconium	Zr	90	2	8	18	10	2
41	Niobium	Nb	93	2	8	18	12	1
42	Molybdenum	Mo	98	2	8	18	13	1
43	Technetium	Tc	99	2	8	18	14	1
44	Ruthenium	Ru	102	2	8	18	15	1
45	Rhodium	Rh	103	2	8	18	16	1
46	Palladium	Pd	106	2	8	18	18	0
47	Silver	Ag	107	2	8	18	18	1
48	Cadmium	Cd	114	2	8	18	18	2
49	Indium	In	115	2	8	18	18	3
50	Tin	Sn	120	2	8	18	18	4
51	Antimony	Sb	121	2	8	18	18	5
52	Tellurium	Te	130	2	8	18	18	6

TABLE 21-1 THE CHEMICAL ELEMENTS (*Continued*)
ARRANGED ACCORDING TO ATOMIC NUMBER

Atomic No.	Element	Symbol	Atomic wt.	Electron orbit distribution*					
53	Iodine	I	127	2	8	18	18	7	
54	Xenon	Xe	132	2	8	18	18	8	
55	Cesium	Cs	133	2	8	18	18	8	1
56	Barium	Ba	137	2	8	18	18	8	2
57	Lanthanum	La	139	2	8	18	18	9	2
58	Cerium	Ce	142	2	8	18	20	8	2
59	Praseodymium	Pr	141	2	8	18	21	8	2
60	Neodymium	Nd	146	2	8	18	22	8	2
61	Promethium	Pm	147	2	8	18	23	8	2
62	Samarium	Sm	152	2	8	18	24	8	2
63	Europium	Eu	153	2	8	18	25	8	2
64	Gadolinium	Gd	158	2	8	18	25	9	2
65	Terbium	Tb	159	2	8	18	27	8	2
66	Dysprosium	Dy	162	2	8	18	28	8	2
67	Holmium	Ho	165	2	8	18	29	8	2
68	Erbium	Er	166	2	8	18	30	8	2
69	Thulium	Tm	169	2	8	18	31	8	2
70	Ytterbium	Yb	174	2	8	18	32	8	2
71	Lutetium	Lu	175	2	8	18	32	9	2
72	Hafnium	Hf	180	2	8	18	32	10	2
73	Tantalum	Ta	181	2	8	18	32	11	2
74	Tungsten	W	184	2	8	18	32	12	2
75	Rhenium	Re	185	2	8	18	32	13	2
76	Osmium	Os	192	2	8	18	32	14	2
77	Iridium	Ir	193	2	8	18	32	17	0
78	Platinum	Pt	195	2	8	18	32	17	1
79	Gold	Au	197	2	8	18	32	18	1
80	Mercury	Hg	202	2	8	18	32	18	2
81	Thallium	Tl	205	2	8	18	32	18	3
82	Lead	Pb	208	2	8	18	32	18	4
83	Bismuth	Bi	209	2	8	18	32	18	5
84	Polonium	Po	210	2	8	18	32	18	6
85	Astatine	At	210	2	8	18	32	18	7
86	Radon	Rn	222	2	8	18	32	18	8

Atomic No.	Element	Symbol	Atomic wt.	Electron orbit distribution*						
87	Francium	Fr	223	2	8	18	32	18	8	1
88	Radium	Ra	226	2	8	18	32	18	8	2
89	Actinium	Ac	227	2	8	18	32	18	9	2
90	Thorium	Th	232	2	8	18	32	18	10	2
91	Protactinium	Pa	231	2	8	18	32	20	9	2
92	Uranium	U	238	2	8	18	32	21	9	2
93	Neptunium	Np	237	2	8	18	32	23	8	2
94	Plutonium	Pu	242	2	8	18	32	24	8	2
95	Americium	Am	243	2	8	18	32	25	8	2
96	Curium	Cm	247	2	8	18	32	25	9	2
97	Berkelium	Bk	249	2	8	18	32	27	8	2
98	Californium	Cf	251	2	8	18	32	28	8	2
99	Einsteinium	Es	254	2	8	18	32	29	8	2
100	Fermium	Fm	253	2	8	18	32	30	8	2
101	Mendelevium	Md	256	2	8	18	32	31	8	2
102	Nobelium	No	253	2	8	18	32	32	8	2

*First figure in series is for innermost shell or orbit; next figure next innermost and so on.

Detection

The figures of a luminous watch face, if they are of the radium chloride type, will show tiny flashes if examined in the dark with a magnifying glass (10-power). Do this in a dark closet. Wait 10–20 minutes for the eyes to become accommodated to the dark, then focus on one number of the radium dial. The tiny flashes indicate breakdown of the radioactive material. Commercial devices—spinthariscopes—that do the same thing are sold for a small sum.

With photographic film Because photographic film is sensitive to radiation, it can be used to detect radioactivity. To illustrate, remove the rim and crystal of a watch with a luminous dial. Allow the watch to run down, and then lay it face down against a piece of dental X-ray film.[1] Leave both inside a light-proof box for about ten days.

Developed, the film will show a picture of the numbers of the dial (slightly fuzzy and reversed) and of the hands. The fainter the image, the less radium chloride the dial contains. Absence of an image indicates that the dial uses a compound called a plain phosphor, which picks up light from other sources and then glows for several hours in the dark. A watch dial of this type, left in darkness for several days, will not glow. Most watch faces that glow in the dark contain phosphors as well as radium chloride or tritium, a man-made isotope of hydrogen.

The effects on film of the alpha, beta, and gamma rays given off by radioactive substances can be used to take "self-portraits" (or "radio autographs") of easily obtainable radioactive ores. (With the same materials, one can take pictures of metallic objects without using light.)

To get a self-portrait of such ore, use a new roll of No. 120 or 620 film or the next size smaller or larger. In a darkroom, slowly unroll the red or green paper wrapper until the very beginning of the actual film can be felt. Place the mineral (rock or ground-up ore specimens of uranium or radium are available at hobby shops or in children's chemistry and mineral sets) on the paper and reroll the film.

Place the film and mineral in a closed drawer for two weeks, then remove them and develop the film. The quality of the picture obtained will depend on the amount of radioactive material in the mineral used.

One can use a variety of ores: Carnotite, a yellow sandstone from the Rocky Mountains, is an easily obtainable radioactive mineral, as are radioactive sands containing thorium, which are abundant in some of the deserts of southwest United States. Dentists' X-ray film can also be used, or cut film in the $2\frac{1}{4} \times 3\frac{1}{4}$-inch size. Ordinary roll film that is not panchromatic can be cut for use in the same way under a dim, red darkroom safelight. In a darkroom, wrap each ore specimen in light-proof paper.

Radium ore and uranium ore occur together. On this continent, the main source of rich uranium ore is the Great Bear region in Canada, north of the Arctic Circle. Before the days of Geiger counters (see below), a prospector would leave unopened rolls of film on the ground in areas where he suspected the presence of uranium. Some time later the film would be retrieved, developed, and examined for the telltale tracks of gamma rays that would indicate radium and uranium ore in the rocks below. One can apply the same procedure in the classroom to rocks suspected of containing radioactive material: Simply leave the rock in darkness against a piece of film for a week or two and then develop the film.

An interesting radioautograph of thorium can be made using the mantle of a gasoline lantern (available from hardware and sporting goods stores). Mantles are made of asbestos or nylon soaked in thorium oxide, and the radioautograph will clearly show the weave of the fabric. Remove the mantle from the base, then cut it along one side with a pair of scissors (Fig. 21-5) and open it out flat. Working in the dark, unroll the red or green film wrapper (No. 120 or 620 film), as described above for testing radioactive ore. Place the mantle on the wrapper just before the begin-

---

[1] For all the demonstrations described in this section, dental X-ray film is best; it is available from dentists or their suppliers.

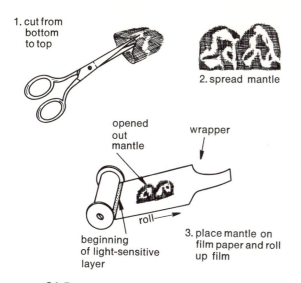

1. cut from bottom to top

2. spread mantle

opened out mantle

wrapper

beginning of light-sensitive layer

roll

3. place mantle on film paper and roll up film

FIGURE **21-5** Making a radioautograph with a gasoline lantern "mantle."

ning of the photosensitive part of the film. Roll the film tightly, fasten with adhesive tape, and let stand in darkness for a week. When developed, the film will show multiple images of the mantle that are progressively fainter (because they received less radiation) the farther the mantle from the part of the film on which they were formed. For the purpose of comparing the different images, make prints of each layer or cut up the roll of film into separate pictures.

Some orange pottery glazes, because they contain uranium oxide, are radioactive (beta particles and gamma rays) enough to make a radioautograph. Allow a dish with such a glaze to rest on a piece of covered film for two weeks. If the plate is large, allow it to cover only part of the film so that it can produce an outline of its edge. The radiation necessary to make the radioautograph is not enough to make eating from these dishes harmful. Dishes having this radioactive glaze may also be used to make photographic silhouettes of small metal objects. For example, place a flat key or any other small metal object on light-proof covered film; then put a radioactive dish over the object and let stand for several weeks. Develop the film in the usual way.

With a Geiger counter A Geiger counter is a device in which the passage of a charged parti-

cle sets up a detectable electrical current. High school physics departments may be able to provide one; they are, of course, available from scientific supply houses. The first step in experimenting with a Geiger counter of any type is to determine the "background count," which includes cosmic rays and emissions from radioactive deposits in the rocks where the device is being used. (Granite, a very common rock, always contains traces of radium and uranium sufficient to give a Geiger counter reading; the quantity present is much too small to warrant use of the granite as an ore.) Take several background counts (count the number of clicks per minute) and average them.

To test for gamma and beta rays, bring a sample of uranium ore or the radium dial of a watch near the Geiger tube. (Another good radioactive material for this purpose is thorium, present as thorium oxide in gasoline lantern mantles.) Because in ore specimens and watch dials the amount of radioactive material varies, one can expect different results for various specimens. The strong count that is produced will be for both gamma and beta rays. (Alpha particles given off by radium cannot be detected with the ordinary Geiger counter.) To separate the reading for gamma rays from that for beta rays, place a sheet of aluminum between the ore or other radioactive source and the counting tube. The reading obtained will be the gamma count. Subtracting the gamma count from the total count (without the aluminum plate) gives the beta count. The background count must be subtracted in all cases. Note the difference in total count and gamma count taken at distances of 1, 2, and 3 inches from the source.

With a cloud chamber Evidence of the existence of such subatomic entities as alpha and beta particles and secondary cosmic particles (usually mesons) can be obtained with a "cloud chamber." Such a device has as its basis the fact that, when a charged particle (ion) such as a hydrogen or helium nucleus travels through moist gas, it leaves a vapor trail much like that left in the sky by high-flying airplanes. The vapor trail of the latter is composed of condensed water vapor

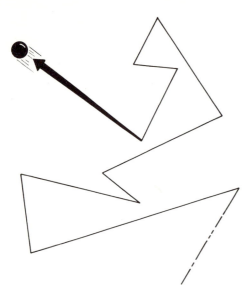

FIGURE **21-6** Hypothetical course of a molecule.

that has, as condensation nuclei, bits of matter such as dust. In the cloud chamber, in the absence of dust particles, the charged alpha or beta particles produce molecules (of the gases composing the air) with electrical charges; these molecules, which move about at random (Fig. 21-6), serve as condensation nuclei for—in the case of the cloud chamber described below—alcohol-water vapor. A light beam against a dark background illuminates the condensation trail or "fog track."

Needed to make a diffusion cloud chamber (Fig. 21-7) are the following materials: a 12-ounce to 1-pint wide-mouthed vacuum bottle and its stopper; a small, clear, plastic (thicker than $\frac{1}{16}$ inch) food container approximately 4 inches in diameter at the top, 3 inches at the bottom, and $1\frac{3}{4}$ inches deep; three small $\frac{1}{4}$-inch plastic or wood blocks; 5 inches of copper tubing with an outside diameter of $\frac{1}{2}$ to $\frac{3}{4}$ inch; a small nail; a soldering iron and solder; a disk of sheet copper $2\frac{3}{4}$ inches in diameter (must fit into bottom of plastic container); a little flat black paint; blotting paper; a 4-inch square of Lucite, $\frac{1}{16}$ to $\frac{1}{8}$ inch thick (available at hobby shops); gloves; 2 pounds of dry ice (*Do not touch with bare hands.*); 1 pint of denatured ethyl alcohol or rubbing alcohol; a piece of pure silk; a focusing flashlight or small

projector; and a luminous (radium chloride) watch dial (available from watch repairmen). (*Do not touch the radium paint with the fingers; use tweezers.*) Cut out one number from the dial or cover all but one number with a disk cut from a piece of lead foil.

Heat the copper tube and use it to melt a hole through the center of the bottom of the plastic container. The fit should be slightly loose; slight cracks in the plastic will not affect the operation. Drill or melt (as above) a hole through the stopper large enough to permit insertion of the copper tube. A loose fit is needed here also to permit the escape of carbon dioxide from the bottle; to insure such venting, use a small nail to punch a hole through the stopper halfway between the center hole and the edge. Solder the copper disk to one end of the copper tube. (A plumber or shop teacher can do this.) Paint the top surface of the copper disk with the dull black paint to provide a background against which the tracks can readily be seen. Using gloves, load the vacuum bottle with $\frac{1}{2}$-inch pieces of dry ice. Then fill the bottle with alcohol to within $\frac{1}{2}$ inch of the stopper. At first the alcohol will boil violently. (Ventilate the room well to carry off the fumes.) After a short time the dry ice will soften in the alcohol. Cut a strip of blotting paper $\frac{1}{2}$ inch wide and long enough to fit snugly within the rim of the plastic container. Dip it into alcohol and place it inside the rim of the container. Stopper the bottle tightly. Place the container on the stopper and the spacers on the bottom of the container—spaced so that they will support the copper disk firmly. Lower the copper tube through the opening and let the copper disk rest on the spacers. Rest the Lucite cover on the container.

The cloud chamber will work anywhere, but it will work best in dry places. Charge the Lucite cover by rubbing it vigorously with the silk in order to clear the field of any stray ions that might interfere with the experiment. In damp weather, the plastic top must be charged every fifteen minutes or so, and the blotting-paper strip must be soaked in alcohol every half hour. The dry ice and alcohol mixture, however, will last for many hours. Direct the beam of the flashlight or projector into the plastic container as shown in the figure. Late-afternoon sun rays may also be used. The thin whitish lines that appear moving across through the container are the tracks made by secondary cosmic particles, probably mesons, and are composed of condensed alcohol vapor. (The tracks will not be continuously visible.)

Once the children have become acquainted with the appearance of cosmic-ray tracks, one may demonstrate the tracks of alpha and beta particles, using the radioactive material of the radium watch dial as a source. Although alpha particles can be stopped by the wall of the plastic container, beta particles pass through. To demonstrate this, hold the bit of watch dial (with a pair of tweezers) close to the outside of the container, near the bottom; the beta particles will form thin, threadlike knobby tracks near the bottom of the inside of the container. If the bit of dial is placed on the copper plate inside the container, the straight, solid-looking alpha tracks will be seen moving out horizontally from the radium source, as shown in Fig. 21-7. Actually, alpha particles are sent out in all directions, but are visible only in the thin layer of vapor at the bottom of the container.

The cloud chamber promotes condensation of alcohol vapor as follows. The vapor comes (by evaporation) from the blotting paper at the top of the container and moves downward because it is heavier than air. As it moves from the near-room temperature of the Lucite cover to the copper disk, it encounters a drop in temperature (needed for condensation to occur) of about minus 103°F. (The copper tube conducts heat from the disk to the alcohol–dry ice mixture.)

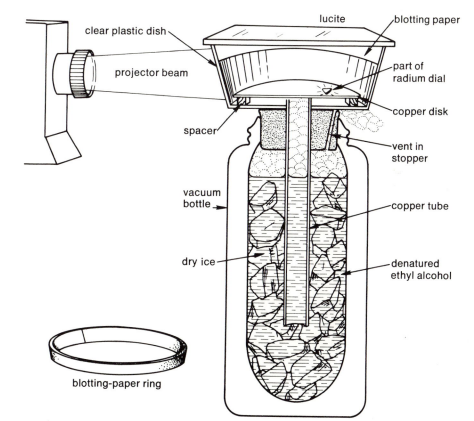

FIGURE **21-7** Homemade diffusion cloud chamber.

RADIOACTIVE DECAY AND TRANSMUTATION OF ELEMENTS

It was the dream of medieval alchemists to transmute base metals into gold. Nine hundred years later, radioactive elements were discovered to be in the process of natural transmutation to baser elements. Uranium is found throughout Earth's crust. Some of its radioactive atoms are continually decaying into lead at a minute but predictable rate. The rate of such disintegration of radioactive atoms is described as half-life; radium, for instance, has a half-life of 1620 years because the amount decreases by half in that interval (Fig. 21-8). Uranium 238 (U-238) has a half-life of $4\frac{1}{2}$ billion years. This steady, predictable breakdown is used by scientists as a kind of "uranium clock" to estimate the time of formation of the igneous rocks in which it occurs and, thus, to calculate the age of the earth. Carbon-14 (C-14), used to date more recent material, has a half-life of 5570 years. C-14 is thought to be produced by the bombardment of atmospheric nitrogen by neutrons from cosmic rays. Children may make a two-dimensional model of nitrogen to demonstrate how (through such bombardment) removal of one proton and its accompanying electron (Fig. 21-9) changes nitrogen-14 into C-14. Combined with oxygen, C-14 becomes part of plant tissue by the normal growth process. Thus, if a charred pine beam from an ancient pueblo cliff dwelling has a concentration of C-14 half that of a live pine, the structure may be tentatively dated at 5570 years old.

U-238 and C-14 are isotopes, forms of an element that differ only in the number of neutrons

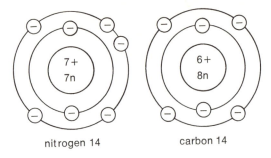

nitrogen 14   carbon 14

FIGURE **21-9** Diagrams of conversion of nitrogen-14 to carbon-14 atoms. Removal of one proton and accompanying neutron and electron from former produces carbon-14.

in the nucleus. If one considers each isotope of an element as a different element, the list of known elements totals about one thousand. Isotopes may or may not be radioactive (Fig. 21-10).

Today, nuclear reaction, as transmutation of elements is now called, is carried on under controlled conditions of timing and intensity in devices called nuclear "piles."

Nuclear Energy: Atomic Fission or Fusion

Fission In fission, an atomic nucleus is split, yielding two smaller atoms (with a total mass less

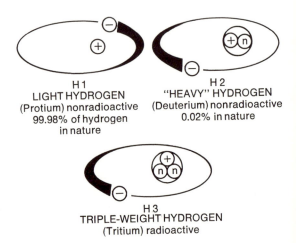

H 1
LIGHT HYDROGEN
(Protium) nonradioactive
99.98% of hydrogen
in nature

H 2
"HEAVY" HYDROGEN
(Deuterium) nonradioactive
0.02% in nature

H 3
TRIPLE-WEIGHT HYDROGEN
(Tritium) radioactive

FIGURE **21-10** Radioactive and nonradioactive isotopes of hydrogen.

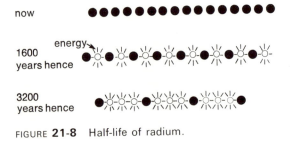

now

1600 years hence

3200 years hence

FIGURE **21-8** Half-life of radium.

than that of the original atom), neutrons, and a great amount of energy, the energy formerly employed in binding the nucleus together. Calculating Einstein's famous equation, $E = mc^2$, may give some concept of the enormous power unleashed by atomic fission. In his equation, m stands for an atom of matter, c for the speed of light squared (3×10^9 centimeters per second), and E for the energy produced by the total conversion of matter. The product is 931 million electron volts from one atom, if all its energy is released.

A dictionary lesson on the term *fission* may develop useful association of it with cell fission and with rock and ice fissures. To make clear that fission is not synonymous with halving, pound some sugar lumps and show the class the varied size of the fragments. In a chain reaction, such as occurs in an atomic bomb or in an atomic pile (where it is controlled and regulated), the neutrons produced by the splitting of a nucleus themselves split the nuclei of other atoms. To illustrate chain reaction, imbed matches in clay (Fig. 21-11) so that lighting one match sets off all of them.

Children can simulate the operation of an

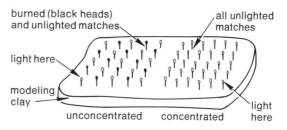

FIGURE **21-11** Arrangement of matches to illustrate atomic chain reaction. Matches should be $\frac{1}{2}$ inch apart.

atomic pile, or nuclear reactor, with a simple model (Fig. 21-12). Needed are five 12-inch squares of 1-inch wood or $\frac{3}{4}$-inch plywood, eight nails (2 inches long for wood, 1 or $1\frac{1}{2}$ inches long for plywood); a wood drill; a 15-inch piece of broom handle; black and silver paint; a thorium-saturated mantle such as are used in gasoline lanterns; a 4×4-inch piece of sheet lead or a 4-inch piece of lead pipe with an inside diameter of 1 inch; a Geiger counter with its tube on an extension wire; four $\frac{1}{2}$-inch flat-head tacks (if sheet lead is used); and a block of wood, $\frac{1}{2} \times \frac{1}{2} \times \frac{1}{2}$ inch.

Paint the five wooden squares black and mark

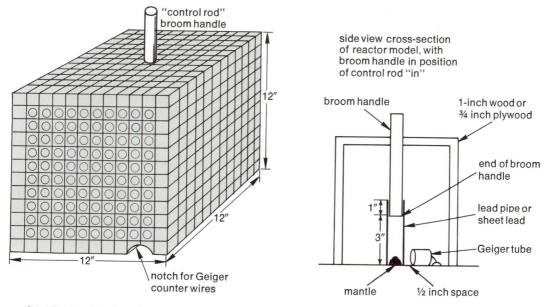

FIGURE **21-12**   Model of nuclear reactor.

them off into 1-inch squares with white chalk to represent the graphite blocks that make up the four walls and the top of the "reactor." Drill a hole in the center of each 1-inch square on one of the "walls" (or, simply draw circles on them) to represent the uranium slugs. Cut a notch at the bottom of this wall. Nail the four walls or faces of the reactor together, and stand the resulting structure on a table, which will serve as the floor of the reactor. Drill a hole in the center of the "reactor" top large enough to accommodate the broom handle.

Prepare the broom handle "control rod" by painting it silver and fastening either the sheet lead or the lead pipe over the lower end in such a way that it extends 3 inches beyond the stick end. Attach the sheet lead by wrapping it snugly around the broom handle and tacking it. If using the lead pipe, force it onto the broomstick to make a tight fit.

Place the piece of thorium mantle in the center of the floor of the reactor on the small wooden block. Place the Geiger tube (connected to a Geiger counter) on the floor of the reactor about $\frac{1}{2}$ inch from the mantle. Lead out the counter wires through the notch in the wall.

Hold the "control rod" in the "in" position by standing it on the floor of the "reactor" in such a way that it covers the mantle. Slip the top of the "reactor" over the "control rod" and let it rest on the four walls.

Fusion In fusion, as in fission, matter is converted to energy as predicted by Einstein's best-known equation. While fission results in breakdown into smaller and lighter weight atoms, in fusion there is combination of atoms of small, light elements to form larger and heavier ones, though in both cases there is a net loss in total mass (with release of energy). The enormous heat at the center of stars such as our sun fuses nuclei of four hydrogen atoms to form helium, the second simplest atom (Fig. 21-3). Hydrogen fusion is the source of stars' heat and light. Using a diagram (Fig. 21-13) of hydrogen atoms, have children note that each contains one proton nucleus and one planetary electron. Helium, on the

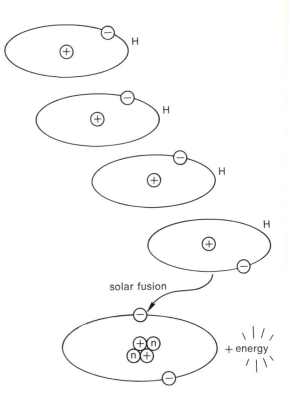

FIGURE **21-13** Diagrammatic representation of hydrogen fushion reaction.

other hand, has two protons and two neutrons in its nucleus and two planetary electrons. To make a model helium atom from the four hydrogen model atoms, take two protons from any two of the hydrogen atoms. To make two balancing neutrons, combine one proton with one electron, and a second proton with another electron. The two protons and the two neutrons form the nucleus of the helium atom. The two electrons that remain are planetary electrons.

In the actual process, the helium atom formed weighs less than the total of four hydrogen atoms. The minute amount of matter left over from this fusion reaction is converted into a tremendous amount of energy. For billions of years, hydrogen atoms in the sun have been fused into helium in a conversion that releases enough energy to warm a minor planet over 90 million miles distant.

SUGGESTED PROJECTS

1. Assign each member of class a card on which is written the name of an element. Each child carrying such a card represents an atom of the element. Call out the name of a molecule (for example, carbon dioxide), and have the "atoms" of which it is composed assemble in front of the room, showing their cards to the audience. In the many cases in which there are more than enough atoms of one element, have a child in the audience tap the shoulder of the excess "atoms," returning them to their seats.

2. Using disks of different colors to represent atoms of different elements, construct a molecule of a substance familiar to children. Have the first child to identify the molecule construct another familiar molecule, and so on.

3. Styrofoam or ping-pong balls painted colors can be used to represent atoms of different elements. Children can arrange these in individual projects to form molecules of common substances—for example, salt, sugar, water, baking soda. Use of the balls will give a conceptually useful three-dimensional effect to the project.

BIBLIOGRAPHY

(**P** indicates recommended for primary grades, **I** for intermediate grades, **U** for upper grades.)

Adler, Irving, *The Wonders of Physics*, Golden Pr., 1966. Well illustrated introduction to physics. Fundamentals are covered—mass as distinguished from weight and definition of exponential notation. Newer areas of physics are also presented—including escape velocity, electron spin and fission. **U**

Bronowski, J., and Millicent Belsam, *Biography of an Atom*, Harper & Row, 1965. The carbon cycle followed through all its stages. Clear text and helpful illustrations and diagrams. **U**

Faber, Doris, *Enrico Fermi: Atomic Pioneer*, Prentice-Hall, 1966. His personal life, his work, and his contribution to the development of the atomic bomb are described. **U**

Hamilton, Lee David, *Let's Go Aboard an Atomic Submarine*, Putnam, 1965. Illustrated with clear and meaningful drawings; includes a glossary. **I**

Hecht, Selig, *Explaining the Atom*, Viking, rev. ed., 1954. Lucid exposition for teacher or upper-grade student. **U**

Hughes, Donald J., *The Neutron Story*, Doubleday, 1959. An excellent book for the nontechnical reader. Teacher reference.

Hyde, Margaret O., *Molecules Today and Tomorrow*, McGraw-Hill, 1963. Includes a description of the role of molecules in the new "super-cold" surgical technique. Requires some background knowledge. **U**

Jaworski, I. D., and A. Joseph, *Atomic Energy*, Harcourt, 1961. A sourcebook for the student who wants to experiment safely. **U**

Kohn, Bernice, *The Peaceful Atom*, Prentice-Hall, 1963. A simplified explanation of atoms and atomic energy including summaries of the work of Curie, Fermi, Roentgen, and Becquerel, and a discussion of some of the potential uses and applications of atomic energy. **U**

McCormick, Jack, *Atoms, Energy, and Machines*, Creative Educational Society in Cooperation with the American Museum of Natural History, rev. ed., 1962. An informal introduction to physics and chemistry, including information about new explorations. **U**

Posin, Daniel Q., *What is Energy?*, Benefic, 1962. A brief introduction to such aspects as energy produced by the sun, electrical and magnetic energy, atomic and nuclear sources of energy, and possible future sources. **U**

Radlauer, Edward, *Atoms Afloat: The Nuclear Ship "Savannah"*, Abelard-Schuman, 1963. A factual, simply stated account of the design, construction, and maiden voyage of the first nuclear-powered cargo-passenger vessel. Many good photographs. **U**

Romer, Alfred, *The Restless Atom*, Doubleday. A fine reference book for teachers with no science training.

Loading ore with a large power shovel, which is essentially a system of wheels and levers.

22 *Machines and Engines*

Machines use energy to do work. Usually children will consider anything requiring physical effort as work, but in the physicist's definition of work, distance is involved as well as physical effort.

WORK

According to this definition, work is done only when a body moves—that is, *work* is the result of a *force* moving through a *distance*, and force is defined as a push or a pull.

Children will recall having pushed hard against a certain object without making it move; even though they may have become tired from the effort, no work was done in the physicist's sense, because the object did not move.

Measuring Work

To measure work, place a cardboard or wooden box on a bathroom scale. Add sand or stones to the box until it and its contents weigh 4 pounds. Tie the box firmly with strong string, insert the hook of a laundry spring balance underneath the string, and lift the box into the air. Note that the spring balance also reads 4 pounds. Help children understand that the force necessary to lift an object and overcome the pull of gravity

(Chapter 24) is equal to the weight of the object. Thus, a force of 4 pounds is needed to lift a weight of 4 pounds (discounting the effect of friction).

To find the amount of work accomplished, one multiplies the force exerted by the distance traveled. In this case, if a force of 4 pounds is moved through a distance of 1 foot, the amount of work done is 4 × 1, or 4 *foot-pounds*. Point out that the designation "foot-pounds" combines expressions of both force and distance. If the box is lifted 2 feet into the air, the work done is 4 × 2, or 8 foot-pounds.

Place the box on the table, insert the hook of the spring balance underneath the string at one end of the box, and then pull the spring balance and box across the table, holding the spring balance absolutely horizontal. Slide the box across the table as evenly and smoothly as possible (minimize friction), and while doing so, read the pointer on the spring balance. (It may be necessary to take a few readings and obtain an average.) Call children's attention to the fact that it takes less force to slide the box than to lift it. Calculate the work accomplished in sliding the box 3 feet. If the force needed was 2 pounds, then the work accomplished was 2 × 3, or 6 foot-pounds. Point out that, since the box was not lifted off the ground, it was not necessary to know weight to calculate the work. In this case, one had only to know how much force was needed to push or pull the box across the table. Therefore, for lifting, the force needed is equal to the weight of the object. For pushing or pulling, the force is just the force necessary to move the object across the surface against friction.

Children will be interested in calculating how much work they do when they walk upstairs to class from the school entrance. To do so, measure the height in feet from the entrance to the classroom floor and then multiply the child's weight by this distance. Or use a sash cord passed through a suspended, single fixed pulley. Attach some known weight to the cord, pull the other end of the cord horizontally through the pulley, and measure the distance the weights have been moved by measuring the cord drawn through the pulley. Estimate the work done in foot-pounds by multiplying the distance in feet by the weight in pounds.

One can also demonstrate the measurement of work simply by lifting an object with a known weight upward on a rope in front of a cardboard scale marked off in feet (or use a measuring tape fastened to a blackboard). A child can stand on a chair near the scale and raise the object. Then multiply the weight of the object (in pounds) by the distance in feet through which it was moved. Essentially the same thing can be done using an electric motor with a string attached to the shaft or flywheel.

ENERGY CONVERSION

The energy used in doing work can be converted from one form to another; for example, from chemical to thermal (heat) to mechanical to electrical, and so on. To show this, set a model steam engine in operation. The burning of fuel in the process represents a change from chemical to heat energy. The expansion of steam in the cylinder of the steam engine involves a change from heat to mechanical energy: Heat changed water to steam which, in turn, drives the piston (mechanical energy). Connecting the steam engine so that it drives a small bicycle "magneto" or generator demonstrates the conversion of mechanical energy into electrical energy. A light bulb connected in turn to the generator shows a conversion of electrical energy into light and heat energy.

The conversion need not follow any particular sequence. One can start with chemical energy, represented by the contents of a storage battery. This produces electrical energy, which can operate an electric motor, so that mechanical energy is obtained from electrical energy. With a tiny grindstone or some sandpaper fastened to the shaft of the motor, one can demonstrate a change from mechanical to heat energy: Simply hold a piece of metal against the spinning stone or sandpaper and have pupils note the heat generated.

Or start the sequence with nuclear energy. The gamma rays emitted by radioactive material represent a form of radiant energy into which the nuclear energy has changed; the chemical changes wrought by this energy in a film emulsion (as in the radio-autograph of a key, or the effects of uranium ore or thorium gas mantle discussed in Chapter 21) illustrate the change from radiant energy to chemical energy.

The radium dial of a watch or the action of a spinthariscope (Chapter 21) are examples of a transformation of nuclear energy to chemical energy and then to light energy.

SIMPLE MACHINES

Machines help make man's work easier primarily in four ways: All machines *transfer a force.* In sweeping a floor, one transfers a force from the hand to the floor. With a hammer, one transfers a force from the hand to the nail. In riding a bicycle, one transfers a force from the feet to the wheel. Children may show how a force is transferred when using pliers, scissors, nutcrackers, and other tools.

Most machines *increase a force.* In this way, a small force can overcome a larger force or resistance. This is easily shown by such tools as can openers, screwdrivers, and bottle openers. The class can list other tools or simple machines that help by increasing the effective force applied.

Other machines *change the direction of a force.* The small grooved wheel, called a pulley, helps this way. With a pulley, one can hoist a flag or use a clothesline. Turn the handle of an egg beater, and the gears turn the blades in opposite directions.

Still other machines *increase the speed and distance of a force.* In sweeping, the upper part of the broom handle moves back and forth a short distance, but the lower part of the broom moves farther and much more quickly. When one swings a tennis racket or a baseball bat, the same thing happens.

Children may want to know why a machine cannot increase both force and distance at the same time. If a machine could do both, it would save work—its output of work would now be greater than the work put into it. But this is not so, and machines deliver more force at the expense of distance, or vice versa. The experiments described below will offer many opportunities to show that one cannot increase both force and distance at the same time.

All the machines that man uses are composed of one or more of a few simple machines: these are the lever, the wheel and axle, the pulley, and the inclined plane, of which the wedge and the screw are special forms.

The Lever

The seesaw or teeter-totter is a classic example of a lever. A teeter-totter in a school playground may be used for a lesson on the lever. Call children's attention to the place in the center where the board turns or pivots; this is the fulcrum. With two children of equal weight at opposite ends of the pivot, or fulcrum, the teeter-totter, of course, will balance, and with two children of different weight, the teeter-totter will go down on the side of the heavier child. Have the heavier child move toward the pivot or fulcrum until the balance is restored. Point out that for the lighter child to balance the heavier, he must be farther from the fulcrum. In other words, a smaller weight is used to balance a larger weight, but the smaller weight had to be a larger distance away from the fulcrum to do it, making, in effect, a longer lever.

To emphasize this, show how one of three children of identical weight can balance the other two. Do this by placing two children halfway between one end of the teeter-totter and the fulcrum while one child is at the opposite end. Point out that in this fashion one child is able to balance twice his weight. The relationship between one force or weight and the force or weight that it lifts or balances is *mechanical advantage.* Note also that the distance of the one child from the fulcrum was twice the distance

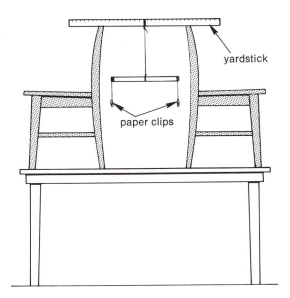

FIGURE **22-1** A classroom teeter-totter.

of the two children from the fulcrum. This relationship between distances is another way to find the mechanical advantage.

If a teeter-totter is unavailable, one can be made in the classroom as follows. Place two chairs on top of a table or desk back-to-back about 30 inches apart (Fig. 22-1). Rest a yardstick on the backs of the chairs. With a string, suspend a stick of uniform thickness, as shown, from the yardstick. If the stick does not balance, slide it through the loop of string until it does. Using paper clips as weights, repeat the experiment of the teeter-totter. Suspend the clips by tying a thread to the clip and making a loop at the other end. Try hanging a weight on just one side, moving the supporting string (which is really the fulcrum) toward the weight until the stick is level.

The principle of the lever can also be shown in a pair of pliers. Point out the long handles and the short jaws, and the fulcrum, which, in this case, is round. The long handles and short jaws make it possible for a small force applied to the handles to produce a large force at the jaws. This is analogous to the single child balancing twice his weight because his side of the

teeter-totter is twice as long. Children should be able to understand readily the mechanical advantage in the pliers.

Effort is the force applied at the handles of the pliers. The distance from this effort to the fulcrum is called the *effort-distance*. The large force produced at the jaws is called the *resistance* because at this point a resistance is presented to the effort exerted. The distance of this resistance to the fulcrum is called the *resistance-distance*.

Demonstrations of the lever that involve more readily quantifiable results can be performed with the simple apparatus shown in Fig. 22-2. This can be made by drilling $\frac{1}{8}$-inch holes at intervals along a yardstick which may then be supported on a nail as a fulcrum. (Pivoted stick supports may be purchased from scientific supply houses.) Two other supports (nails) are needed for suspending (by wires) the weights. The larger of the two stands shown provides stability and an arm from which to suspend the spring balance.

First-class levers Levers like the teeter-totter and the pliers are called first-class levers. In first-class levers, the fulcrum is between the two forces. Scissors are another example of a first-class lever, as is a tack-puller. In the tack-puller, the point at which it is bent is the fulcrum; a force exerted at the handle results in a larger force at the claws. If the distance from the handle to the fulcrum is 12 inches, and the distance from the tack to the fulcrum is 3 inches, the mechanical advantage is 12 divided by 3, or 4.

The yardstick device described above (under *The Lever*) may be used to demonstrate the action of first-class levers, as shown in Fig. 22-2a, in which the products of the arm (or lever) length and the attached weight are equal on both sides. For example, a 3-ounce weight placed 20 inches from the fulcrum will balance a 30-ounce weight located 2 inches from the fulcrum on the opposite side. In this instance, the mechanical advantage of the lever is ten, since only 3 ounces were required to balance 30. The mechanical advantage can also be calculated from the lengths of the lever arms: 2 inches is $\frac{1}{10}$ of 20 inches.

Second-class levers In a second-class lever, the fulcrum is at one end and the resistance is

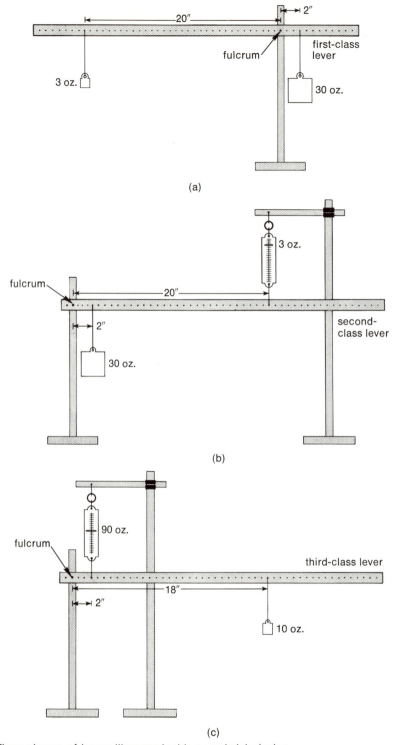

FIGURE **22-2**   Three classes of levers illustrated with a yardstick device.

between the fulcrum and the effort. A nutcracker is a second-class lever. Have children try to crack some filberts between their hands; even if they are successful, the force required will be great. Then use the nutcracker machine, calling attention to the fulcrum, which is, in this case, at the end. The filbert, or resistance, is between the fulcrum and the handles where the force or effort is exerted. Compare the distance between the filbert and the fulcrum with the distance between the ends of the handle and the pivot. If the former is 2 inches and the handle distance is 6 inches, the mechanical advantage is 6 divided by 2, or 3.

A door is a good example of another second-class lever. The hinges are the fulcrums, the door itself is the resistance, and the effort is applied at the doorknob. Point out that the doorknob is located as far from the hinges (fulcrums) as possible in order to give the best possible mechanical advantage. A classroom paper-cutter is also a second-class lever.

Help the children understand that first- and second-class levers enable a small force to apply a larger force. However, to do so, the small force must move through a larger distance than the larger force.

To use the yardstick device described above to demonstrate second-class levers, set it up as shown in Fig. 22-2b. In the arrangement shown in the illustration, the reading of the balance will be 90 ounces.

Third-class levers Sometimes one wants a machine to help increase the speed and distance of a force even if a larger effort or force is necessary to do so. A broom is an example of this type of machine. By exerting a strong force at the midpoint of the broom handle, one can make the lower part move farther and more quickly. The fulcrum in this case is the hand nearer the top of the broom. Thus, in this third-class lever the fulcrum is at one end (the top), the resistance is at the other end (the bottom), and the effort is between them (Fig. 22-3).

It may interest children that their arms are third-class levers. To demonstrate, place an apple in a child's outstretched hand and have him bring his hand to his shoulder and back again. In this case, the forearm is the lever and the elbow is the fulcrum. The apple, the weight or resistance to be raised, is at the other end of the forearm. The muscle in the forearm is the effort that exerts the force to raise the apple.

Another example of third-class levers is a pair of sugar tongs. All third-class levers have a mechanical advantage less than one. This means exerting a greater force at the start, but the advantage gained is an increase in both distance and speed. Remind children that it is not possible to increase both force and distance at the same time.

To demonstrate third-class levers with the yardstick device, arrange the weight and balance as shown in Fig. 22-2c. Here the resistance arm is 20 inches and the effort arm is 2 inches, so that the mechanical advantage is $\frac{1}{10}$, and the effort that must be expended is greater than the weight lifted rather than less.

The Wheel and Axle

The wheel and axle machine is like the lever, except that the wheel and the axle travel in circular distances. To demonstrate this, tie two fairly heavy books together with a string. Have children lift the books with the string, noting the force needed to overcome the force of gravity (weight) pulling on the books. Then remove the

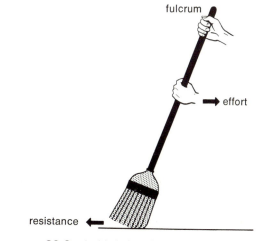

FIGURE **22-3** A third-class lever.

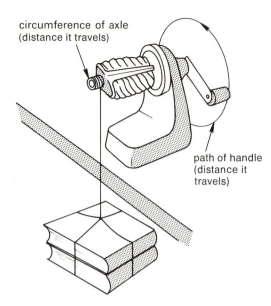

circumference of axle
(distance it travels)

path of handle
(distance it
travels)

FIGURE **22-4**   A classroom wheel and axle.

cover from a pencil sharpener and tie the other
end of the string very tightly around the protruding shaft of the sharpener (Fig. 22-4). (If the
string is not tied tightly to the shaft, it will slip
when the shaft is rotating.) Turn the handle and
point out how much less force is now needed to
lift the books.

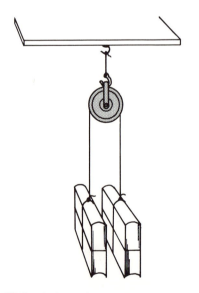

FIGURE **22-5**   A single fixed pulley.

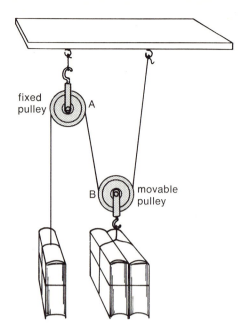

fixed
pulley

A

B

movable
pulley

FIGURE **22-6**   A combination fixed and movable
pulley.

The handle of the sharpener is, in effect, a
wheel, and the shaft is the axle. Point out that
although one complete revolution of the wheel
produces one complete revolution of the axle, the
wheel covers more distance during one revolution
than the axle; this difference in circular distances
is responsible for the mechanical advantage of
the wheel and axle.

Repeat the experiment with the wheel and
axle, using the pencil sharpener. After the books
have been raised, release the crank handle and
pull down on the books, noting how rapidly the
handle turns.

Another good example of a wheel and axle is
the doorknob. Point out that the round knob
is the wheel and the square shaft the axle. To
show the mechanical advantage, remove a doorknob from its shaft (axle) and have pupils try to
open the door by turning just the axle. Then put
the knob back and note how easy it is to open
the door. Here again is an example of a small
force being used to apply a larger force.

Use string to find the circumference of the
knob and of the axle. If the circumference of the

knob is 6 inches and that of the axle 1 inch, the mechanical advantage of the machine is 6 divided by 1, or 6. Using the diameters of the knob and axle will give the same result. Other wheels and axles children can explore are the rotary can opener, the egg beater, and the steering wheel of an auto.

The Pulley

A pulley is also like a teeter-totter, or lever. In this case, the fulcrum is the pulley axle. Place two chairs back-to-back about 3 feet apart on a table. Screw one of two medium-sized cup hooks into a soft pine board about $48 \times 6 \times \frac{1}{2}$ inches and place the board across the backs of the chairs. Suspend one clothesline pulley (available at hardware stores) from the cup hook with a piece of cord and pass another piece of cord through the groove of the pulley, attaching a book at each end of the string (Fig. 22-5). (The

books should be of equal weight.) The books do not move because they are in balance.

Since the length of each cord from the book to the pulley axle is the same, there is no mechanical advantage to a single pulley arranged this way. To show how such a pulley is used, have a child pull down on one of the books. The other book will go up; thus, in this case the pulley machine is a convenient way of changing the direction of a force. To make one book go up, we must exert the same force as the weight of the book. The book going up will travel at the same speed and over the same distance as the book going down. Although there will probably be some friction in the pulley, so that a slightly larger force downward will be needed to raise the book, the aim in using the pulley is only to change direction.

Attach another cup hook about 6 inches away from the first, and arrange two pulleys as shown in Fig. 22-6. Hang one of three books of equal weight from the top pulley and the other two from the bottom pulley. One book will now support two. Point out that there are two cords supporting the two books, each supporting half the total weight of the two books. The weight (one book of the two) supported by the string, AB, is balanced by the single book at the end of the cord.

The top pulley is called a *fixed pulley*, and the bottom one a *movable pulley*. Pull on the single book to show the origins of these names.

Pulleys can be made in the classroom of two spools, two nails to fit loosely through the spools, and pieces of wire. (If a wire cutter is available, use pieces of lightweight clothes hangers as the wires.) Pass the wires through the spool holes and attach them as shown in Fig. 22-7. Repeat the previous experiment, using one and two books.

Fasten two spools of different sizes to a piece of wood about $8 \times 4 \times \frac{1}{2}$ inches with two loosely fitting nails through the spool holes. The spools should be about 3 inches apart. Slip a rubber band around both spools (Fig. 22-8). The rubber band should grip the spools rather tightly. Turn the larger spool once and note that the smaller spool makes more than one full turn and thereby moves

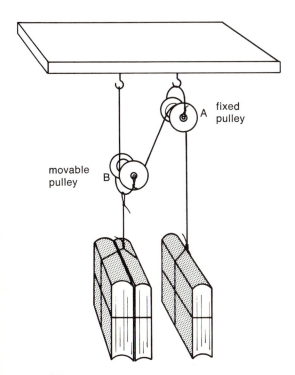

FIGURE **22-7** Homemade spool pulleys.

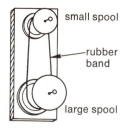

FIGURE **22-8** Wheels can change the speed or direction of a force.

faster. Also point out that both spools move in the same direction, and then turn the rubber band so that it makes a cross between the spools. Turn either spool and note that the other now turns in the opposite direction.

To show graphically how things are lifted with pulleys, arrange the pulleys as shown in Fig. 22-9. Attach four books (of five books of the same size) to the bottom pulley and one book to the free end of the cord. Children can count the number of cords supporting the bottom pulley: There are four, each one supporting one fourth of the total weight. The fourth is balanced by the single book at the end of the cord. In this case, the mechanical advantage is four, because one book balances

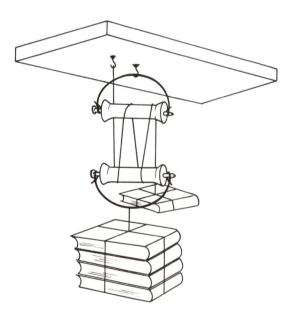

FIGURE **22-9** Arrangement of pulleys in which one book can lift four.

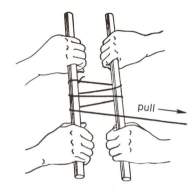

FIGURE **22-10** Illustrating pulley action by a tug-of-war with broomsticks.

four. Note how quickly the four books are lifted when one pulls on the string holding one book.

This is the way heavy objects are lifted with relatively little expenditure of energy. This can be shown quite dramatically by a tug-of-war in which one child balances four of the same weight and strength. To do this, tie a strong rope to the end of one of two broomsticks or mop handles. Then loop the cord around both sticks two complete turns, keeping the loops evenly spaced from stick to stick (Fig. 22-10). Have the single "strong man" wrap the free end of the rope around the palm of his hand. While he pulls have the four others holding the broomsticks pull in opposite directions. The "strong man" pulls also and is able to balance the pull of the four others. Children will note that there are four ropes, but that each carries the force of only one fourth the "strong man's" pull. The pull on the end rope is balanced by the pull of the "strong man." If two boys drop out, leaving one for each stick, the "strong man" will be able to bring the sticks closer together.

The Inclined Plane

Set one end of a board $48 \times 6 \times \frac{1}{2}$ inches on a stack of books or a block of wood. Tie three books to a roller skate or toy truck. Lift the roller skate and books with a laundry spring balance or scale of the type that measures from 0 to 30 pounds (Fig. 22-11). Record the weight on the scale.

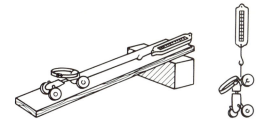

FIGURE **22-11** Demonstrating that it takes less force to pull a load up an inclined plane than to lift it.

Then place the roller skate and books on the inclined board and draw them up the board with the spring balance as shown. Try to hold the balance so that it is parallel to the board at all times. Have a pupil read the scale while this is being done and record the value.

Children will see that it takes less force to pull the load up the hill than it would to lift it through the same vertical distance. However, they should also understand that the load travels a longer distance uphill than it would if it is simply lifted straight up to that height. Thus, though less force is used, the load must travel a longer distance.

Have children measure the length of the board, and then the height of the stack of books supporting the end of the board. The load must travel the length of the board in order to reach the height of the books. Dividing the length of the board by the height of the books gives the mechanical advantage of the inclined plane machine.

Repeat the experiment, using inclines at different angles and recalculating the mechanical advantage in each case. Simply adding to or subtracting from the stack of books that support the incline will change the angle. Children will note that the steeper the angle, the greater the pull required. On the other hand, the gentler the hill (or angle), the less the force required. For this reason, hills on highways are made as gentle as possible.

The wedge Almost all cutting tools and kitchen cutting utensils are inclined planes that are forced into an object. These simple machines are called wedges. A wedge is another form of an inclined plane. The only difference is one of

procedure. With the inclined plane, the incline remains stationary and we move the object up the incline. With the wedge, the body remains stationary and we force the wedge into the body.

Borrow a wedge from a carpenter or cut one from wood. Place the narrow end of the wedge under a table leg, then tap the broad end with a hammer. The wedge will lift the table. Children can examine the inclined plane that makes up the edges of a chisel. Show the inclined plane or wedge of a knife blade. Needles, pins, and nails are also wedges.

The screw Another important simple machine is the screw, which is also a form of inclined plane—in this case one that is wrapped in the form of a spiral. To show this, draw a right triangle on a piece of white paper. Make the height 5 inches and the base 8 inches. Cut out the triangle and color the hypotenuse with red crayon. Roll the paper around a pencil (Fig. 22-12). Lay the height of the triangle against the pencil and wrap the triangle around the pencil. Children will see the spiral formed by the colored edge. Unroll the paper triangle and show how it returns to the form of an inclined plane. Compare the

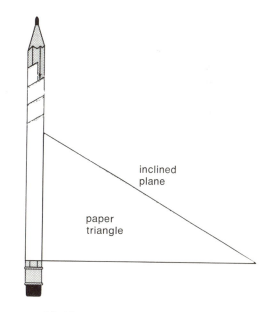

FIGURE **22-12** Demonstrating that a screw is a spiral inclined plane.

paper spiral with the spiral in a wood screw.

If possible, show children (at a local automobile service station) how an automobile jack of the screw type can jack up a car. Children will see how little effort is required to lift a 3000–4000-pound automobile as the screw helps a very small force lift a very heavy object. Point out that the screw jack has to turn many times to raise the automobile only a few inches. In this case, a small force is used to lift a very large force, but the small force must travel a large distance to do so.

In school woodworking shops, the vise that holds the wood for sawing or planing has a similar screw, used to apply great force to hold the wood in place.

Gears and Wheels—Changing Speed or Direction

Gears are most commonly used to change speed or direction. Actually, gears are no more than wheels with teeth. Some children may have a metal construction set with which they can set up a large and a small gear wheel so that one can turn the other. If the large wheel is turned, the small one will move many times as fast. Point out that the gears turn in opposite directions. Children can count the number of teeth in each gear and recognize that if the large gear has, for example, ten teeth and the small gear five teeth, then for each revolution of the large gear the small gear will revolve twice. A diagram on the

board will help make clear that because the smaller gear travels twice as far, a 1-pound force applied at it becomes a 2-pound force at the larger gear.

In Fig. 22-13a, the large gear has 30 teeth, the middle gear ten, and the small gear five teeth. Help children understand that the speeds, forces, and directions are not the same at all wheels. If the 30-tooth gear revolves once, the ten-tooth gear revolves three times and the five-tooth gear makes six turns. A 1-pound force applied at the five-tooth gear becomes a 2-pound force at the ten-tooth gear. This, in turn, becomes a 6-pound force at the 30-tooth gear. All three wheels turn whether a force is applied to the 30-tooth gear or to the five-tooth gear. If the large gear is made to rotate in a clockwise direction, the middle gear will turn counterclockwise, and the small one clockwise. In the diagram, arrows indicate the direction in which the gears move if the largest moves clockwise.

This is how gears are used in an automobile to change the speed during shifting. When the driver shifts to "low" or "first" gear, the power from the motor is transmitted to the wheels through the largest gear. In this case, the automobile moves slowly but has much force or power. In "second" gear, now that the car is under way, a smaller gear is used to get less force and more speed. "Third" or "high" gear is the smallest and gives maximum speed and minimum power. In a car with an automatic shift or transmission, the gears shift automatically.

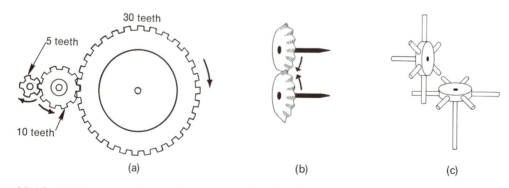

FIGURE **22-13**   (a) How gears change the speed or direction of a force; (b), (c) homemade gears.

Needed to make a simple set of gears are five bottle caps that have not been twisted out of shape by a bottle opener. With a hammer and nail, make holes precisely in the center of each cap. Place two caps on a small block of wood so that their toothed projections mesh (Fig. 22-13b) and, holding the caps in place, fasten them down with tacks, making sure that the caps will turn easily. Point out that when one of the caps turns, the other turns in the opposite direction and, since each cap has the same number of projections, both revolve at the same speed; all that changes is the direction. Repeat the experiment using three caps and have children note the direction that each turns.

Figure 22-13c shows simple gears made with a wooden construction toy of the Tinkertoy type. The "teeth" of these gears mesh at right angles. In another demonstration, stand a bicycle upside down, turn the pedal wheel exactly one turn, and note the number of turns made by the rear wheel (exclusive of turns made while coasting). Count the number of teeth in the gear attached to the pedals and compare it with the number of teeth in the gear fastened to the rear wheel.

Or operate an egg beater or hand drill, noting the speed of the drill or beaters. Then compare the number of teeth in the gears involved in the operation. Another useful exercise would be examination of a broken wristwatch or clock. Remove the back so that children can observe the gears, count the teeth, and note which produce what changes in speed, direction, and force. Turn the knob that controls the minute hand so that the gears that drive the minute hand and the hour hand can be seen.

Children can make a working model of an elevator, which will help show change in direction. To do so, place six small wooden spools on a sheet of plywood or heavy cardboard about 24 × 12 inches, as shown in Fig. 22-14. Use nails or long spread-type paper fasteners to hold the spools in place. For the elevator car use a small cardboard matchbox.

Pass a string through a hole in the center of the "car" at A. Knot the string so that it cannot slip out. Pass the string down and around spool

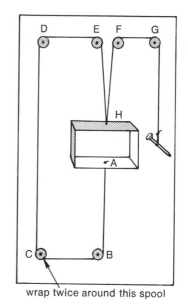

wrap twice around this spool

FIGURE **22-14**   A homemade elevator.

B, then to spool C (making two turns around it), then over spools D and E. At H, the center top of the "car," make two holes about $\frac{1}{4}$ inch apart. Put the string into the box through one hole and back out through the other. Then pass the string over spools F and G and tie a nail (or other weight) to its end. This weight should counterbalance the weight of the car plus any objects placed inside the car. To counterbalance properly may require some experimentation with lighter or heavier nails.

Turning spool C will cause the car to move up or down. Point out that the force of gravity will help the car descend, but will hinder it when the car has to go up. With enough counterweight, the car can ascend by itself. In an actual elevator, the part corresponding to spool C is turned by an electric motor.

COMMON MACHINES IN THE SCHOOL AND HOME

Children will be surprised to find what a number of common machines are used in the average classroom and school: for example, window fasteners, pulleys, faucets, radiator valves, hinges, closet fasteners, pencil sharpeners, and so on.

A multitude of tools, utensils, and devices in the home are either simple machines or combinations of simple machines, providing an opportunity to show how familiar objects function as machines.

Examples of first-class levers in the home are: scissors, garden shears, plier, wire cutter, tin or metal snips, tack-puller, crowbar or pinch bar, forceps, and beer- or soda-can opener. Children should be able to identify the fulcrum in each case—the point where the small force is applied, and the point where the larger force is exerted or overcome. Compare the distances of both these forces from the fulcrum and note the effects when the distances are large or small. If possible, compute and compare mechanical advantages of the various devices. Do this as well for the other machines listed below.

Second-class levers include: nutcracker, lemon squeezer, bottle opener, can opener (hand), crowbar, door, and rowboat oars. Examples of third-class levers are: sugar tongs, tweezers, broom, spoon, baseball bat, tennis or badminton racket, golf club, fly swatter, pitchfork, and mouse trap. All the third-class levers aim for more speed and distance rather than more force.

The wheel and axle uses a small force to overcome a much larger force. They include: rolling pin, meat grinder, screwdriver, doorknob, rotary can opener, egg beater, pencil sharpener, hand drill, bicycle wheel and pedal, auto steering wheel, and all gear combinations. Pulleys are used with flag poles, clotheslines, old-fashioned window sashes, and blocks and tackles.

Inclined planes include the staircase, the escalator, a hill, and a winding mountain road. Wedges include: knife, chisel, saw (has many chisel edges), pin, needle, nail, ax, and the blade, or circular wedge, used in delicatessen and grocery stores to cut thin slices of meat. Examples of the screw are: lifting jack, wood screw, bench vise, nut and bolt, mechanical pencil, and piano stool.

Compound Machines

The combination of two or more simple machines is called a compound machine. Most machines are in this group. With careful examination, children should have little difficulty in identifying the various components of compound machines and understanding how each one functions. For example, the handle of the shovel, hoe, or ax is a lever, while the blade is a wedge. Hand-operated hair clippers are a lever and many shearing wedges.

The rotary can opener is a combination wheel and axle and wedge. The crank handle of the pencil sharpener is part of a wheel and axle; it turns two screw-like or spiral wedges which cut the wood. A lawn mower operates the same way. A meat grinder is a combination wheel and axle, screw, and wedge: the crank handle turns a screw; the meat is caught in the screw and pushed against wedge-shaped threads which rend the meat. The hand drill and water faucet contain a wheel and axle and a screw. The Stillson (pipe) and the "monkey" wrench use a screw to open and close the jaws, and then act as turning levers (wheel and axles).

The egg beater is particularly interesting to observe: the handle turns two gears that turn two blades. This is a combination of wheel and axle and gears (which are modified wheels and axles).

Children may be able to identify the combination of simple machines in such familiar items as the typewriter, hand vacuum cleaner, sewing machine, alarm clock, spring- or electric–motor-operated toy, bicycle, automobile, tractor, airplane, and locomotive.

COUNTERACTING FRICTION IN MACHINES

Have children slide a block of wood over a board, both with rough surfaces. Call attention to the resistance the surfaces offer each other. This resistance is called friction.

Examine the surfaces of the block and board with a magnifying glass, and point out the uneven places in the wood. Children can see and feel the bumps and hollows, which make it difficult for the block to slide. Then slide a smooth block of wood and board (or sand the rough pieces smooth) and note how much less effort is required. To reinforce the point, have children feel the texture of some fine sandpaper, a rough stone, smooth and rough wood, and a mirror or pane of glass. Then rub pieces of fluffy cotton over each surface and note the amount of cotton left behind. The smoother the surface, the less the cotton will catch and tear. Or, in another demonstration, put a screw eye into one end of a block of wood and attach a spring to the screw eye. Place three books on the block of wood, then draw the block over a board with a rough surface, a board with a smooth surface, and a large pane of glass. Note the difference that smoothness makes in the amount of force required to pull the block of wood. The force may be measured by attaching the string to a laundry spring balance and pulling horizontally on the spring balance.

Repeat the experiment with six books on the block of wood. Point out that the greater the pressure between two surfaces rubbing together, the more friction there is.

That friction produces heat can be shown by having children rub their hands together briskly or rub a pencil eraser briskly on a table. Their hands and the eraser will become quite warm. When wood is sawed or a hole is bored through a thick board, the metal tool used also becomes quite hot, as do automobile tires after they have been running for a while. Children should realize that friction wears things out: shoe soles, rugs, and carpets become thin, lead pencils become dull, rubber erasers wear away, rubber tires become thinner and lose their tread—all for the same reason.

Friction can also be helpful and necessary. Sand on icy streets and automobile tire chains are used to increase friction and prevent skids. One could not walk without friction. All objects would have to be fastened in some way to prevent their sliding, but one would have nothing with which to fasten them: without friction, nails and screws would pull right out of the material into which they were inserted; ropes would slide, and one would not even be able to unscrew a jar top. To demonstrate, have children wet their hands with soapy water or rub them with cold cream; then have them try to unscrew the metal cover from a glass jar.

When machines work, some of their parts also rub against each other. Although metals may feel and look much smoother than wood, they have tiny bumps and hollows that are visible under magnification.

Because friction produces wear and heat which can interfere with the operation of a machine, it is useful to reduce the friction as much as possible; in machines this is usually done by the use of lubrication and/or roller or ball bearings.

Lubrication

Children should now realize that one way of reducing friction is to have smooth surfaces; another way is to put some slippery material like oil or grease between the surfaces. To show this, try to slide two pieces of metal over one another. Then add a few drops of oil to the surfaces and try again. The friction is reduced, and the pieces of metal slide quite easily.

Lay two mirrors or panes of glass side by side. Place a few drops of oil on one mirror. Have the children rub with their fingers first the dry glass, then the oiled one. Children should understand that the oil helps reduce friction because the particles of oil make the surface smoother by filling in the holes in the surface and also form a liquid (hence, mobile) molecular film, which keeps the surfaces apart and on which an object can slide.

In another demonstration of the effect of lubricants, rub two pieces of sandpaper together and note the friction produced. Then put a thick layer of grease between the two pieces of sandpaper and rub again. (Cooking oil or fat will also serve the purpose.) One can get the same effect with two pieces of cold toast and a generous supply of butter.

Certain materials all but eliminate friction. Children who ice-skate will recall the ease with which the skate blade moves across the ice. This is because the pressure of the skate melts the ice slightly, forming a thin film of water between it and the skate blade. The film of water is a very effective liquid lubricant. To demonstrate this, remove the dividers from an ice cube tray so that a single slab of ice will form. Show how freely this moves on a piece of plate glass (provided the glass is at room temperature or warmer) or even a smooth table top. Blocks of wood or bricks can be set on top of the ice to add mass. A block of Dry Ice will produce a similar effect, but for a different reason: In this case the material (solid carbon dioxide) sublimates, rather than melts, so that it slides on millions of "ball bearings" of the subliming gas. (*Caution: Use tongs or wear gloves when handling Dry Ice.*)

There are many everyday examples of lubricants used in machines to reduce friction. Automobiles are greased regularly for this reason. A useful exercise is to examine tools and machines for parts that rub together—for example, in a rusty hinge, bicycle wheel, or roller skate that either squeaks or does not turn easily. Apply a few drops of oil and point out the difference. Children can time how long a bicycle wheel, cart wheel, or roller skate turns before and after oiling.

Oil and grease are not the only lubricants. Soap works quite well with desk drawers or wooden window frames that stick as will the wax or paraffin from a candle. Powdered graphite will help a door catch that sticks. If powdered graphite is not available, rub the catch with the "lead" (largely graphite) of a soft pencil.

Bearings

A second method of reducing friction is the use of bearings, which are essentially wheels, rollers, or balls. Roller-skate wheels usually have such ball bearings, which usually can be heard to rattle

when the skate is shaken. Children may bring beginner's skates and ball-bearing skates to class for comparison; the beginner's skate has only a simple bearing, while the ball-bearing skate has a ring of balls around the axle, on which the load tends to roll rather than slide, thus reducing friction. Children can note which wheels turn longer with the same applied force—those with or those without ball bearings.

A simple demonstration of the principle involved can be done as follows. Slide a large book across the table. Then place a few round pencils under the book and notice how much easier it is to move. Call children's attention to the fact that rolling has been substituted for sliding. Rolling friction is much less than sliding friction because, in rolling, the bumps on one surface are lifted out of and away from the hollows on the other.

A rimmed coffee can lid and a handful of marbles can also be used to show this. First try spinning a book on a table top. The book will not spin easily because the friction between the book and the table top impedes it. Then put the marbles on the table and cover them with the lid (Fig. 22-15). Place the book on top of the lid and try spinning the book again. This time the book will spin easily.

INERTIA

Rest a coin on a small square of heavy cardboard placed on a drinking glass or empty milk bottle. If flicked with the finger, the card will fly out from under the coin and the coin will drop into the tumbler. Or stack four checkers and put a fifth 2 or 3 inches away. With the finger, flick

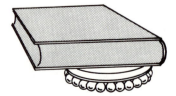

FIGURE **22-15** Ball bearings reduce friction.

the fifth checker at the bottom checker in the pile. The bottom checker will fly out while the rest of the pile remains behind.

Bodies at Rest

In the experiments, the coin and the checker are following Newton's law of inertia, one part of which states that a body at rest tends to stay at rest. This tendency is called inertia. If a body at rest is to be moved, the force of inertia must be overcome by additional forces.

Attach a rubber band to a toy truck. (Weight it if it is very light.) Place the truck on a table so that it is at rest. Carefully stretch the rubber band until the truck begins to move. Note how much the rubber band had to stretch. Once the truck is moving, keep pulling it along at a steady rate of speed. Now the band will be stretched considerably less. Children should realize that it took extra force to overcome the tendency of the truck to remain at rest.

Or rest a metal or plastic tumbler half full of water on a sheet of typewriter paper. Place the tumbler about an inch from one end of the paper. With one hand, grasp the center portion of the other end of the paper and, with a horizontal movement, quickly jerk the paper toward you. The paper will come out from under the tumbler while the tumbler remains in its original position. Help children understand that when the paper was jerked, the inertia of the paper was overcome, but not that of the tumbler. Repeat the experiment, but pull slowly and steadily on the paper. By pulling slowly, one is able to overcome the inertia of the tumbler as well, and both glass and paper move.

Tie two medium-sized stones with thread so that the stone has a length of thread above and below it. Tie one end of each thread to a door knob (Fig. 22-16a). Pull slowly and steadily downward on the bottom of the thread of one stone. The upper thread will break (Fig. 22-16b), as the force exerted overcame the inertia of both the lower thread and the rock. Then grasp the bottom thread of the second stone and pull downward with a quick jerk. Only the bottom

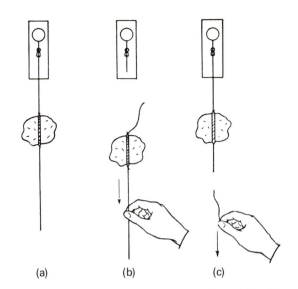

(a)　　　　　　(b)　　　　　　(c)

FIGURE **22-16**　Demonstrating the effect of inertia.

thread will break (Fig. 22-16c), for only the inertia of the lower was overcome.

Bodies in Motion

Newton's law of inertia also states that a body in motion tends to remain in motion. To show this, cut away one end of a long cardboard box such as a shoe box or milk container. Place a small rubber ball inside the box. Slide the box quickly along the table. The ball will remain at the closed end of the box until the box is brought to a sudden stop. When this happens, the ball will keep traveling at its original speed and will roll out the open end. The ball was in motion and continued to stay in motion because there was nothing to stop it.

Children may recall what happens in an auto when it starts suddenly. The occupants seem to fall back against the seat, for they are at rest when the car starts and tend to stay at rest. The car moves quickly forward and so does the lower part of the body, because of friction between it and the seat. The upper part of the body, hinged at the hip, remains in its original position and so seems to be thrown back. If the moving car were to stop suddenly, the children would now seem to be thrown forward because they tend to continue in motion. Remind children that a force was required to put both the car and its occupants in motion, and another force was required to stop them.

Children should now understand that a body at rest tends to remain at rest, and a body in motion tends to continue in motion. Furthermore, a force is required in both cases to change this condition. That is, a force is needed to put a stationary object in motion, and a force is needed to stop a moving object.

SIMPLE ENGINES

Almost all engines depend on the same basic principles. Most convert chemical into mechanical energy. In all engines it is ultimately the mechanical energy of gas molecules that moves a piston, drives a turbine, or produces the jet that results in motion.

The first engine was a reaction engine (see below) and was probably made in Alexandria more than 2000 years ago by the Greek scientist, Hero. His aeoliphile, as he called it, consisted of a hollow sphere suspended over a fire pot. As steam escaped from two angled nozzles on the sphere, it revolved in the opposite direction.

Commercial Hero engines made of glass or metal are sold by scientific supply houses. These are heated by means of a burner, an electric test tube heater, or several candles. The glass engines are very fragile.

A homemade Hero engine can be made from a thoroughly cleaned can with a friction cover. If the can is round, punch holes at opposite points in the can wall near the top. Into the holes place metal or glass tubes bent at a right angle and each pointing in the same rotational direction—that is, clockwise or counterclockwise. Solder metal tubes in place, being certain that the tubes are clear and not clogged. If glass tubes are used, wrap them in rubber electrician's tape so that they fit snugly into the holes. Attach two thin wires about 18 inches long with a piece of tape encircling the can or to a wire wrapped around the can just under the top rim. Attach the wires to a piece of fishing line or a piece

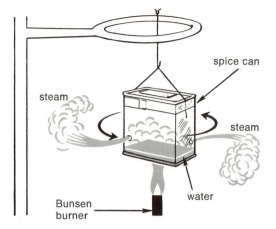

FIGURE **22-17**   A homemade Hero engine.

of pull-chain from an old electric socket and suspend the whole arrangement so that it can turn freely. Place an ounce of water in the can, close the cover, and heat the can. When the water boils and steam forms, the steam will escape from the tubes, causing the can to rotate in a direction away from that of the steam jet.

A simpler variation uses a rectangular spice can. Punch two holes at points diagonally opposite each other (Fig. 22-17) and hang the can from a fishing line swivel or pull-chain, as above. This oldest type of engine known is a reaction engine which was a forerunner of the jet engine and the rocket engine (see below). Another way to show reaction, or propulsion by reaction, uses a tank-type vacuum cleaner. Place only the cleaner (no accessory parts) on a well-oiled, ball-bearing roller skate on a very smooth floor. Remove the dirt-collecting sack and reclose. Turn on the cleaner. The air rushing out the back of the cleaner will act as a jet, and the reaction will cause the vacuum cleaner and the roller skate to move forward.

Steam Engine

The cannon, which provided mechanical energy from burning gunpowder, suggested the next idea in the development of engines—the steam engine. The French physicist Papin demonstrated that the principle of the cannon could be used to lift a weight and devised a means to use steam to move a piston—the basis of all steam engines.

From this Newcomen developed his engine, which depended on the condensation of steam and atmospheric pressure. Watt developed this engine into the high pressure steam engine that made its adaptation to transportation possible.

To show the conversion of steam to mechanical energy—the basis of the steam engine—place about an inch of water in a heavy Pyrex test tube set in a clamp attached to a stand (Fig. 22-18). Fit the test tube with an ordinary cork. (Do not use a rubber or plastic stopper.) Aim the tube at the ceiling. Heat the water and, a few seconds after it begins to boil, the cork will be expelled and hit the target. (*Caution: To prevent shattering, wrap the test tube in a layer of ordinary metal window screening, securing it with wire tied about the tube.*)

Some students will have model steam engines, most of which are electrically heated. Point out that fuels such as coal or oil are normally used to heat the boiler in actual engines.

A more realistic effect may be had with a model engine by replacing the electrical heating unit with a Bunsen burner or alcohol lamp. Some model steam engines use alcohol as a fuel. A can

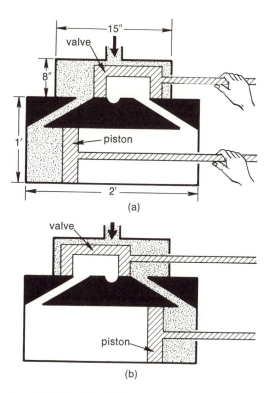

FIGURE **22-19** Model illustrating the action of a valve and piston.

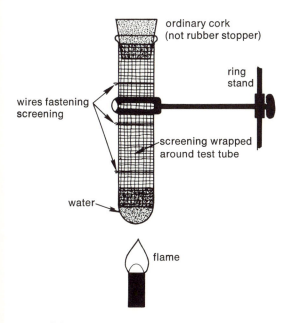

FIGURE **22-18** Demonstrating conversion of steam to mechanical energy.

of Sterno (alcohol in paraffin) also makes a good source of heat.

To demonstrate the action of the valves and pistons of a steam engine, make a large model of a single valve and piston as shown in Fig. 22-19. Use 1 × 1-inch wood or heavy cardboard. Draw on the blackboard (or on a large sheet of paper) the cross-section of the steam engine cylinder as shown in the figure and have one child hold the piston and rod in position against the diagram and another the valve rod. As one child simulates the motion of the piston, the other moves the valve rod to the correct position for the next stroke. In the upper drawing of Fig. 22-19, the piston is shown as it would be positioned when the steam begins to enter the cylinder. After the pressure of the steam has pushed the piston (the fuel stroke), the valve shifts to the position (lower drawing) in which the steam enters behind the piston face to help move it back to its original position.

Turbines

To show the principle of the turbine, direct a jet of steam (from a glass nozzle connected by rubber tubing to a steam generator or tea kettle) at an ordinary toy plastic pinwheel or one cut from lightweight aluminum sheet metal. The steam presses against the vanes of the wheel just as does the air.

Internal Combustion

Internal combustion (largely gasoline) engines also operate by the conversion of heat to mechanical energy. Instead of steam, the gases resulting from the explosion of an air-fuel (gasoline, kerosene, diesel oil, and so on) mixture thrust the piston of the engine (Fig. 22-19) in its stroke. Model-airplane engines may be used to demonstrate the operation of internal-combustion engines. (*Caution: Fuel for these engines may be toxic and require careful handling.*)

Reaction Motors

The enormous speed of modern jets is achieved without the use of either propellers or piston engines. The principle of a jet engine was based on Sir Isaac Newton's third law of motion: for every action there is an equal and opposite reaction. Try picking up a heavy boulder and throwing it as far as you can. The weight of the boulder may even force you off balance. This is one of the reasons people are cautioned not to throw things from high places.

Children know what happens when they try to throw a ball or other sizable object while standing on roller skates. As the ball leaves the hand, they are forced backward. The same effect may be seen by throwing a ball while sitting in a swing. Newton's third law of motion is in evidence everywhere.

Children may have watched firemen lean against their hoses to keep the recoil from the jet of water from flinging the nozzle into the air. Modern plastic hoses are so light that they tend to recoil in the hand when the water is turned on. Children may see many examples of ac-

tion-reaction in nature. Squids, octopi, sea urchins, and other marine animals move through about by squirting water through an orifice in their bodies.

A few other action-reaction occurrences are as follows:

Action	Reaction
Stepping ashore from skiff or canoe	Craft bobs away
Frog jumping off lily pad or float in tank	Lily pad or float bobs under
Water passing through a rotating lawn sprinkler	Nozzle revolves, pushed away by force of water
Bullet fired from gun	Gun recoils or "kicks"

How the rotary lawn sprinkler works can be illustrated easily. With a nail, punch two holes opposite each other near the bottom of a can about the size of a soup can. Also punch two holes near the top of the can so that the can may be suspended by a string (Fig. 22-20). In each of the bottom holes, twist the nail sideways (in the same direction for both holes) while holding it parallel to the bottom. When water is poured into the can, as shown in the figure, jets of water

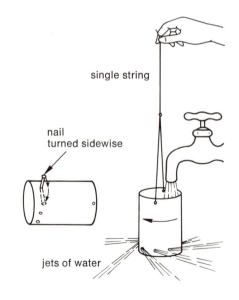

single string

nail turned sidewise

jets of water

FIGURE **22-20** Illustrating how a rotary lawn sprinkler works.

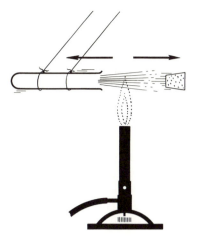

FIGURE **22-21** A test tube recoils (action-reaction) as its cork is forced out by steam.

emerging from the bottom holes in one direction make the can spin in the opposite direction. Repeat the experiment, doubling or tripling the number of angled holes, and note how much faster the can turns.

Action-reaction can be shown simply by heating, slowly and carefully, 1 teaspoonful of water in a small stoppered test tube that is lightly suspended by thin wires. Observe the tube's movement when the cork is forced out by the steam (Fig. 22-21). Wrap the test tube in metal window screening as described for arrangement shown in Fig. 22-18.

Another good demonstration of action and reaction uses two loops of track such as those for wind-up trains. Place one loop on the floor or a table and set four cars of the same height (preferably flatcars) on the tracks. Lay a circle of stiff cardboard or pressed wood on the four flatcars and place the second loop of track on it. Wind the locomotive and place it on the upper track. As the engine goes one way, the tracks move in the opposite direction.

To show the reaction of a playground swing support to the swing seat and ropes, place a small working model of a swing on a wood base that rests on a few ball bearings or on glass rods placed so their long axes are at a right angle to the direction of the swing. Then attach a small

weight to the swing and set it in motion. As the swing moves in one direction, the support slides back over the rollers in the opposite direction.

Balloon as motor   The easiest way to illustrate jet and rocket propulsion is with a balloon. To soften the rather stiff synthetic rubber balloons used today, first stretch the balloon in all directions. Inflate; then release suddenly. It will whirl around until all the air has escaped. As air rushes out, the balloon—really a little jet or rocket engine—rushes in the opposite direction. The air in the balloon presses equally on all parts of the inner surface. When an opening is made at one point, the equilibrium of forces is upset and the balloon moves in the direction opposite that of the opening (Fig. 22–22). The balloon flies about erratically because it has no control surfaces; oblong balloons therefore work better than round ones.

Fasten the balloon to a lightweight toy auto. Escaping air should jet-propel the toy. Or glue paper wings and rudder to a sausage-shaped balloon. Scotch-tape the balloon to a drinking straw, fore and aft (Fig. 22-23) and run a long thin wire through the straw. Stretch the wire across a room

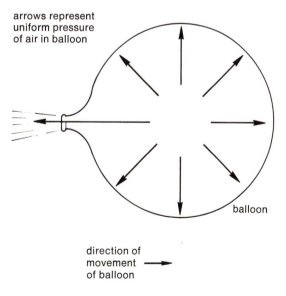

arrows represent uniform pressure of air in balloon

balloon

direction of movement → of balloon

FIGURE **22-22** How opening in balloon upsets balance of forces and sends balloon in direction opposite opening.

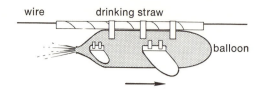

FIGURE **22-23** A model jet airplane with a balloon motor.

or other space. Inflate the balloon and release it. The air jet will move it rapidly along the wire.

In another demonstration of action-reaction, make a waxed cardboard (milk carton) or lightweight wood boat and drill or burn a small hole in the stern (Fig. 22-24). Fit a medicine dropper or small plastic tube cut from a plastic drinking straw to the back of the boat by running it through the hole in the stern, and slip a balloon over the tube, securing its mouth to the tube with string or a rubber band. Inflate the balloon through the plastic tube. Then place the boat in a large aquarium or a large tray of water and release the air. The boat will move as the air escapes from the balloon, thus producing a jet-propelled boat. If one had a boatload of stones, and threw them overboard one by one, the boat would keep moving in the opposite direction; in the case of the balloon-motor boat, millions of air molecules, rather than stones, are being "thrown overboard."

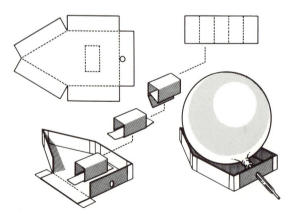

FIGURE **22-24** A jet-propelled boat with a balloon motor.

Carbon dioxide cartridge motor Toy jet-operated cars that can travel 60 miles per hour can be made from a piece of balsa wood and a carbon dioxide cartridge (sold by drugstores, department stores, mail order houses, and hobby shops). Carve or drill a hole in the wood to receive the cartridge. Wheels must be lightweight and spin freely. These can be made of disks, with a nail or heavy wire pushed through them and the balsa body, or can be taken from a simple plastic car and the axle taped to the bottom of the balsa block. The cartridge may also be simply taped to a lightweight toy car. To guide the jet car, place small screw eyes in the top and pass a long thin wire through them. Attach the ends of the wire wherever convenient and so that the wire is taut. Race the cars down a corridor or across a gymnasium floor. To set the carbon dioxide cartridge into action, use a small carbon dioxide cartridge "gun" (sold by hobby shops) or puncture the lead seal at the mouth of the cartridge with a very sharp nail struck with a hammer. (*Caution: The end of the jet car's run should be cushioned. Keep children back.*)

Essentially the same method can be used to make a carbon dioxide model rocket ship. In this case, stretch the wire between two posts 60–100 feet apart and fashion the balsa wood in the form of a rocket or use a small plastic toy rocket model. Fix the carbon dioxide cartridge securely into the tail.

A flying model airplane can be made to fly for a short time with a carbon dioxide cartridge attached under the center of balance with tape. The airplane can also be made to ride a wire like the model rocket or car.

Oil-can motor Another action-reaction motor employs a small oil can mounted on a boat at 30° to the horizontal, the spout extending through a hole in the boat's flat bottom (Fig. 22-25). Put an ounce of water into the can and place a small can of Sterno under it as a heat source. After a short time, the water will boil and steam will emerge from the can spout in a jet, causing the boat to move forward.

This can be done without using heat by putting vinegar and sodium bicarbonate (baking soda) in

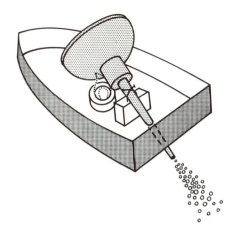

FIGURE **22-25** A jet-propelled boat with an oil-can motor.

the can. (See fire extinguishers in Chapter 16.) Bubbles of carbon dioxide gas will form and go out the spout as a jet. Toy plastic boats are sold that operate on this principle. Sodium bicarbonate tablets are better than the powder since the reaction then proceeds at a slower and more regular rate.

Jet engines and rockets Many schemes for jet propulsion of aircraft had appeared in the years following World War I. The successful development of jet-propelled airplanes came, as a product of World War II, with the first British air-borne jet engine in 1941. Of course, the principle of jet propulsion as applied to a vehicle goes back over 700 years to the rockets devised by the Chinese.

Rocket and jet engines are alike in that their principle of propulsion is based on Newton's third law of motion. Thus, in both cases, expanding gases from the burning fuel travel out from the rear and kick the rocket or jet forward.

There is one basic difference between the rocket engine and the jet engine. The rocket carries not only its own fuel but also its own supply of oxygen. (This is necessary for travel into space where there is no air, and therefore no oxygen, for the burning of the fuel.) Jets carry the fuel alone, and use the oxygen from the air to burn the fuel. Since the jet needs a great deal

of oxygen quickly, a powerful blower is used to compress the air before it reaches the fuel chamber.

To help children understand the compression action in a jet engine, inflate a balloon and then release the air against a small pile of oatmeal, puffed rice, or sand. Repeat, this time squeezing the balloon as the air goes out. Children can decide which method blew away more material.

To illustrate the expansion of gases due to heating in a jet engine, fit a balloon over the mouth of a Pyrex baby bottle or other heatproof glass. Set the bottle in a saucepan of hot water and watch the balloon fill. Point out that the balloon was filled by heated air expanding in the bottle. The fierce heat in a jet engine causes sudden and enormous expansion of the air entering it.

Using a rough blackboard sketch of a jet engine (Fig. 22-26), have children help label the parts and decide what each part does.

Air enters the front end of a jet engine and, under enormous pressure, passes into a combustion chamber into which kerosene or other fuel is sprayed into the air. The mixture is ignited, and the burning gases expand in all directions and blast their way out the only opening, at the rear. The steady burning of air and kerosene sounds very much like a blowtorch, magnified in intensity many times.

In some rockets (liquid fuel) the fuel and the oxygen supply are stored separately. When they are combined in the combustion chamber, the resulting gases roar astern at speeds of thousands of miles per hour. As noted above, because a rocket does not depend on outside air, it is at present the only practical device developed which can negotiate outer space.

Rockets have been known for a long time. The Chinese used gunpowder for firing rockets during a siege in 1232. During the fifteenth century, an Italian architect, Joannes de Fontana, suggested a rocket-driven boat. Two hundred years ago, an Indian prince used bamboo rockets with feathers at the end to guide their flight. In 1806, a British colonel, Sir William Congreve, developed rockets with a range of 3000 yards. And it was Con-

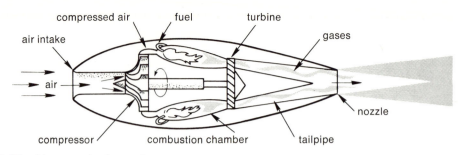

compressed air   fuel   turbine
air intake   gases

air

compressor   combustion chamber   tailpipe   nozzle

FIGURE **22-26**   Diagram of a jet engine.

greve's rockets that inspired the familiar line in our national anthem, "the rocket's red glare," written during the 1812 bombardment of Baltimore. The U. S. Army had a rocket brigade until 1862, but rockets were discontinued in favor of the much more accurate cannon. Modern rocketry really began with the inventions and experiments of Robert Goddard, head of the physics department at Clark University. The antitank bazooka used in World War II was a ground-to-ground rocket, as were the German rockets used to bombard England.

Toy rockets that use compressed air and water should be operated outdoors. For the more intrepid, hobby shops sell small, dry-fuel rocket engines called "Jetex," which are attached to small flying model planes. (*Caution: Follow to the letter all precautions and instructions given with this rocket engine.*) Also available are rockets using non-poisonous non-explosive Freon gas.

SUGGESTED PROJECTS

1. Bring different types of shears to class—those for cutting paper, metal, etc. Ask the class why the blades and handles are of different lengths. Lead into the study of levers and wedges and their uses.

2. Remove the handle or knob from a door and have children try to turn the shaft with their hands. Repeat the experiment with a water faucet. Lead into the study of the wheel and axle and how it makes work easier.

3. Set up several pulleys: simple ones which merely change direction, and combinations of fixed and movable pulleys which make work easier as well. Lead into the study of pulleys as machines, and how machines help us.

4. Have children bring lists of devices that use pulleys. They can see pulleys on a wrecking truck, a derrick, a steam shovel, elevators, and a barn hoist.

5. Place a heavy child on a rotating piano stool. Measure the height of the seat from the ground. Have another child rotate the seat slowly but steadily, then

measure the height again. Lead into the study of the screw, inclined plane, and wedge.

6. Have children make a list of devices that are used to make things go faster. Discuss and study the use of machines to increase speed. Do the same for machines that change direction.

7. Children may have the chance to study the block and tackle devices on painter's scaffolds and those used by riggers or movers of heavy equipment.

8. Invert a bicycle and make a chalk mark on the rear tire. Have a child slowly turn the large gear attached to the pedal until it makes one complete turn. Note the number of turns the rear wheel makes while this is happening. Lead into a study of gears and their uses.

9. Carefully examine a compound machine such as a typewriter, bicycle, alarm clock, or mechanical toy. Make a list of all the simple machines in it. Note how they operate as simple machines, and how they combine to form a compound machine.

10. Show household tools and appliances that represent all six simple machines. Observe how they function, and lead into the study of machines and mechanical advantage.

11. Have a child list household tools or appliances that make work easier at home.

12. Children may visit a machine shop or auto repair shop and list the tools and machines they see.

13. Examine an automobile brake drum or a picture of one. (A garage man will be glad to cooperate.) Point out how the brake shoe uses friction between it and the brake drum to stop an auto. Hold a glass tumbler in one hand. Let it represent a brake drum.

14. Have children list ways that friction is harmful or useful. Study and try different methods of reducing friction.

BIBLIOGRAPHY

(**P** indicates recommended for primary grades, **I** for intermediate grades, **U** for upper grades.)

Bergaust, Erik, *Rockets of the Armed Forces*, Putnam, 1966. A simple listing, illustrated with photographs of 42 current rockets. **U**

Coombs, Charles, *Lift-Off: the Story of Rocket Power*, Morrow, 1963. The history of rocketry, different types of rocket motors—function, operation, and uses. Clear text and diagrams. **U**

Corbett, Scott, *What Makes a Car Go?*, Little, Brown, 1963. An explanation of the functions of different parts of an automobile—carburetor, transmission, battery, axles, steering wheel, and brakes. Well illustrated with drawings and diagrams. **U**

Epstein, Samuel and Beryl, *All About Engines and Power*, Random, 1962. Brief historical background on the use of power from wind and moving water, with an explanation of different kinds of energy and the machines used to produce it. **U**

Huey, Edward G., *What Makes the Wheels To Round?*, Harcourt, 1952. Describes how many machines and other work-saving devices operate. **U**

Huntington, Harriet E., *Cargoes*, Doubleday, 1964. The complex machinery and techniques used to load and unload cargoes described. **I**

Johnson, Ryerson, *Upstairs and Downstairs*, Crowell, 1962. Simple explanation of the principle of the inclined plane and how it works with stairways. Illustrated. **P**

Liberty, Gene, *The First Book of Tools*, Watts, 1960. A succinct account of the development of twelve important cutting, pounding, and piercing tools and simple machines. Clearly illustrated with drawings and diagrams. Indexed. **U**

McCormick, Jack, *Atoms Energy, and Machines*, Creative Educational Society in cooperation with the American Museum of Natural History, rev. ed., 1962. An informal introduction to physics and chemistry, with information about new explorations. **U**

Meyer, Jerome S., *Machines*, World, 1958. Clear explanation of the lever, wheel and axle, wedge, and screw. **U**

Milgrom, Harry, *Adventures with a Party Plate*, Dutton, 1968. How an ordinary rippled-edge paper plate can be used to study the principles of wheels, turbines, gravity, and other aspects of simple mechanics. **I**

Podendorf, Illa, *The True Book of Energy*, Children's Pr., 1963. Subject presented in short sentences, easy vocabulary, and many simple diagrams. **P**

Saunders, F. Wenderoth, *Machines for You*, Little, Brown, 1967. Informative introduction to the huge machines utilized in building industries and in maintaining cities and towns. **I**

Schneider, Herman and Nina, *Now Try This*, W. R. Scott, 1947. Simple, effective explanation of machines. **U**

Schwartz, Julius, *Go On Wheels*, McGraw-Hill, 1966. A picture-science book showing how and why wheels accelerate locomotion and encouraging readers to perform simple experiments. Cartoon illustrations. **P**

Sharp, Elizabeth, *Simple Machines and How They Work*, Random, 1959. Simple explanation of the lever, wheel, inclined plane, wedge, screw, and how they make man's work easier. **I**

Stockard, Jimmy, *Experiments for Young Scientists*,

Little, Brown, 1964. Simple experiments (with safety rules and illustrations) that demonstrate scientific principles concerning air, water, light, sound, simple machines, and electricity. **I**

Ubell, Earl, *The World of Push and Pull*, Atheneum, 1964. An introduction to force and motion, explaining pendulums, gravity, friction, buoyancy of matter, leverage, centrifugal force, and kinetic energy. Illustrated. **I**

Valens, E. G., *Motion*, World, 1965. Applications in daily life and excellent photographs, encourage the reader to follow some of the same patterns of critical thinking which led to the formulation of the three classical laws of motion. A provocative book which treats well-established scientific material in an original, creative manner. **U**

Victor, Edward, *Machines*, Follett, 1962. The princi-ples governing simple machinery accurately but prosaically presented. **I**

Wyler, Rose, and Gerald Ames, *Prove It!*, Harper & Row, 1963. Simple, safe experiments, clearly explained and carefully illustrated. **P**

———, *What Makes It Go?*, McGraw-Hill, 1958. Discusses the operation of cars, locomotives, planes, and other types of machines. **U**

Zaffo, George J., *The Giant Nursery Book of Things That Work*, Doubleday, 1967. Large cartoon-like drawings fill this over-size picture book which presents basic concepts of work, tools, and machines as they evolved from prehistoric to modern times. **P**

Ziner, Feenie, *About Wonderful Wheels*, Melmont, 1959. Easy book about wheels and how man uses them to get work done. **P**

An exceptionally large kite presents enough surface to lift a man.

23 *Flight*

For centuries men watched and envied and sought to imitate the free flight of birds. Flying has been compared to swimming. Children who swim may be able to describe the freedom one gains from the three-dimensional character of movement in water as opposed to the largely two-dimensional locomotion to which we are confined on land. Understanding of flight may be aided by thinking of air as a fluid, though one that is lighter than water. Encourage children to observe the flight of air-borne seeds and insects, and of birds and airplanes. A bulletin board and a three-dimensional table exhibit might include examples and pictures of some of these.

BIRD FLIGHT

Even the city child may have opportunities to observe such birds as the common rock dove or pigeon. Point out how birds use the wing as a lever to raise the whole body. The downstroke lets as little air as possible through the feathers; the upstroke lets through as much as possible. Have children push their fingers through the wing feathers of a bird wing—even a chicken's—from the top down and then from below up to see how well the wing cover is adapted for "swimming" in the air. Note how the leading or front edge of a long wing feather (a primary) is soft and wide. On the upstroke, air slips easily through this flexible part of the feather. On the downstroke, the surface resists the air. Emphasize the relationship between anatomy and function in bird bones—how the keel or breastbone, for example, offers a place for attachment of the big wing muscles (the white meat). Children may discover by observation that bird wings, like many airplane wings, are tilted slightly at the point of attachment to the body (fuselage).

Birds change their line of flight by movements of feathers in the tail and wing tip; children can see how pigeons use tail feathers to "brake," or reduce their speed, when landing.

Those who live near the ocean or desert or any height of land can observe how gulls, buzzards, hawks, and ravens soar with motionless wings on thermal currents (updrafts of warmer air). Gulls or other sea birds often do the same thing by trailing ferries and riding the warm currents that rise from them. Watch for bird flight, too, where warmed air rises against the face of a cliff or along a mountain range. Glider pilots prefer places where the geography offers such thermal currents in combination with topography that is good for taking off and landing.

Children who own roller skates or ice skates

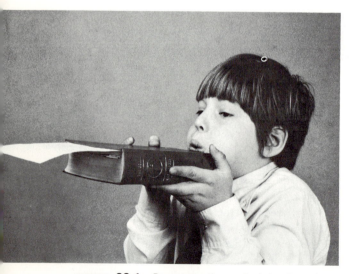

FIGURE **23-1** Demonstrating principle that, in a flowing fluid, pressure decreases as the speed of the fluid increases.

may have already tried a kind of flying by paddling themselves forward with a piece of cardboard in each hand. On a windy day, they may have used a larger single cardboard as a sail.

PRINCIPLES OF AERODYNAMICS

Whether bird, propeller-driven airplane, jet plane, or rocket, a body traveling through air is acted on by four forces: gravity, lift, thrust, and drag.

Gravity pulls down on everything (see Chapter 24). *Lift* pushes up—that is, it opposes the force of gravity. *Thrust,* such as is given by a bird's wing beat, a turn of a propeller, the exhaust from a rocket or jet engine, pushes forward. *Drag,* caused by air resistance and air friction, holds back.

Lift

The basis of any "plane" surface riding the air is air resistance. Children can be shown this by having them hold out horizontally, at arm's length, a sheet of notebook paper while pirouetting. Or hold the paper slightly curved so that it doesn't droop, then quickly push it forward. The leading edge lifts. If one pulls one end of a strip of paper through the air quickly, the unsupported end of the strip will rise. The reason is the same: Air molecules are crowded under the leading portion of the paper, so that they push up, countering the pull of gravity and the pressure of air above. Chapter 5 discusses other means of demonstrating air resistance.

The preceding demonstrations were of dynamic lift. To demonstrate negative lift, have children blow down the length of a paper strip about 2×10 inches. Note that if one blows *under* the paper, it will rise. Yet if it is held just under the lower lip, and one blows *over* it, the strip will also rise and flutter in the air stream.

About 200 years ago, Bernoulli, a Swiss physicist and mathematician, observed that, in a flowing fluid, pressure decreases as the speed of the fluid increases. The same principle applies to

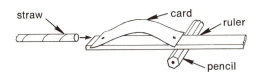

FIGURE **23-2** An air stream lifts a ruler.

flowing air. To illustrate this, close a book on a piece of paper so that it extends from between the pages (Fig. 23-1). (The sheet of paper should be close to the cover.) Lay the book flat and blow across it. The tail end of the paper will rise until it is level with the air stream. As the air flows quickly across the top, it reduces the pressure, allowing the relatively greater pressure of air molecules under the paper to raise it.

Or tape or tack a card to one end of a ruler so that the card curves up like the top of an airplane wing (Fig. 23-2). Balance the ruler across a six-sided pencil so that it very lightly tips down at the card end. Through a soda straw, direct an air stream parallel to the ruler's length and across the curved top of the card. The low end of the ruler will rise. (Be sure to use the soda straw in directing the air stream. Finding the ruler's point of balance may require some patience.) Even without the curved card, an air stream along the balanced ruler will cause it to rise. However, the curved surface produces a more pronounced effect.

For a very simple demonstration, fold down the ends of a card. Blow straight at it; the card will not blow over but will hug the table top because of decreased air pressure on the under surface. Similarly, a piece of notebook paper laid across two books a few inches apart (Fig. 23-3) will sink into the space between the two books if one blows under the paper. Repeat the experiment varying the space between books or placing the paper across two piles of a half dozen books each. Directing the moving air across the top surface of the paper makes it rise. Many other demonstrations of the Bernoulli principle are given in Chapter 5; a few others follow.

Try to blow a ping-pong ball out of a thistle tube or glass funnel. Even held open-end down, the ball will not fall out as long as one continues to blow through the stem. In fact, it should be possible to pick up the ball from a table by laying the open end of the tube over the ball while blowing through the stem of the funnel. The phenomenon may also be shown with two spoons, bowls back to back, held under a running faucet. Hold the handle of one spoon between the second and third fingers, and the other between the fourth and fifth fingers of the same hand. As water attains the proper force, the spoons will move together. Substitute a stream of air for the water by suspending the spoons back to back and blowing between them through a straw until they touch with a click.

FIGURE **23-3** Demonstrating how an air stream under a sheet of paper causes it to fall.

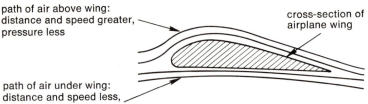

path of air above wing: distance and speed greater, pressure less

cross-section of airplane wing

path of air under wing: distance and speed less, pressure greater

FIGURE **23-4** Air flow over an airplane wing.

Bernoulli's principle is also operative in throwing a ball that follows a horizontally curving path. To demonstrate, throw a ping-pong or tennis ball out of a mailing tube to induce the ball to spin as it flies through the air. The effect is the same as that obtained when a pitcher spins the baseball as he throws it. As the ball moves through the air, the air, in effect, moves past the ball. As the ball spins, the friction of the air against the cover of the ball increases the effective air velocity around that portion of the ball that is turning in a direction the same as the movement of the air. Because the pressure is reduced on the side where the air velocity is greater, the ball curves toward the side of greater effective air flow.

Airfoils

An airfoil is anything designed so that the air will act on its surfaces in the ways demonstrated above. To make a crude airfoil, double under a piece of thin copy paper or onion skin paper. Do not crease the paper at the bend. Hold or paste the edges together. The resultant airfoil will show all the characteristics described above and explained by Bernoulli's principle. If one blows *against* the underside of the paper, it rises; under and more or less parallel to the paper it dips; and if one blows across the *top*, it rises.

Make a loop from a 10 × 1-inch strip of paper. Crease the loop at one point so that it resembles a plane wing in cross section, with flat under-surface and curved top. Slip the loop, curved surface outward, over a pencil and hold just under the lips. Blowing downward along the curved surface should bring the whole up to a nearly horizontal position.

Children can examine a chicken or pigeon wing and note that it is neither flat nor straight, but curved. The front or leading edge is much thicker, especially when the wing is spread, than the trailing edge. Plane wings, like those of birds, are not flat; they are slightly curved, with the top usually having a greater curvature. Even a quarter of an inch change in the curvature can make a significant difference in the way an airplane flies.

In flight, an airplane wing with a shape like that shown in Fig. 23-4 has an average air pressure on its top surface that is 10 pounds per square foot less than the average air pressure on its undersurface.

The knowledge used today in designing the shape of airplane wings comes from years of study of air flow in wind tunnels. However, much of the knowledge should be credited to early students of gliding who found, for example, that air streaming over a flat wing swirled in eddies and reduced lift, while curved wings allowed air to flow smoothly over the top but had eddies underneath. A wing curved on top and much less curved below allowed a smooth flow of air over both surfaces. Modern wings are curved on both surfaces for high-speed flight. Only the wing of a very light plane has a flat undersurface.

Areas of low pressure, such as develop on the upper surfaces of an airplane wing, may be shown as follows. Set a lighted candle behind a 3 × 5-inch card. Have a child blow hard toward the card. Point out that the flame bends *toward* the card because the air movement created low pressure behind the card, and the surrounding air moved in toward it, moving the flame in the process. Or set a lighted candle inside a quart-size tin can near a window cut in one side. Blow hard against the side of the can opposite the window and note how the flame bends toward or even out of the window.

Wind Tunnels

The first necessity for the study of how air moves past airfoils is a steady stream of air. An electric fan is not good without modification because it produces a whirling stream of air. This may be shown by passing smoke from a smoldering dampened newspaper through a running fan; the smoke will be seen to whirl.

A demonstration wind tunnel has four basic parts: a fan; a honeycomb or grid to make the stream of air move in a straight line; a means for mounting the model planes, airfoils, and other objects in the air stream; and a source of fog or smoke, which will make the moving air visible. The grid may be a criss-cross partition from an egg carton or from a box used to ship bottled products. One can be made from strips of cardboard slotted at regular intervals to fit into and across each other to form a pattern of squares.

Smoke or fog can be produced in a number of ways. Fog can be generated with Dry Ice and warm water in a bottle with a one-hole stopper. (Do not stopper the bottle tightly.) Or the Dry Ice can simply be put in a pan of warm water. Turpentine-soaked tufts of cotton on wires mounted in corked bottles (see Fig. 23-5) and ignited will provide smoke. One can also use smoldering punk or damp cardboard tubes or rolled paper.

Fix the honeycomb or grid arrangement on a board in front of and close to the smoke source and the electric fan (Fig. 23-5). A wooden honeycomb can be attached with corner braces, and cardboard one with tape and/or tacks placed in the lowest horizontal strip of the honeycomb. This will provide a fairly straight stream of smoky air.

Objects can be mounted in the air stream on a piece of coat hanger bent and nailed to the board (as shown in the figure) or pushed into a cork either glued or nailed to the base or in a bottle containing counterweighing water or sand. A piece of wood dowel in a lump of modeling clay will also serve. The model can be wired, tied, or glued to the mounting support.

The wind tunnel is more effective inside an empty aquarium or a box with one side replaced with cellophane or glass taped in place and the ends removed. When setting up the wind tunnel, experiment with various positions of the parts, speed of fan, positions of models, and so forth.

Children can make an airplane wing of balsa wood—curved on top and flat on the bottom—which can be mounted or hung in the air stream. Mount and hang objects of other shapes such as a ball, a cube, a flat wing, a toy glider.

If an airplane model with movable ailerons, elevators, and rudder is available, set these control surfaces in various positions, mount the plane

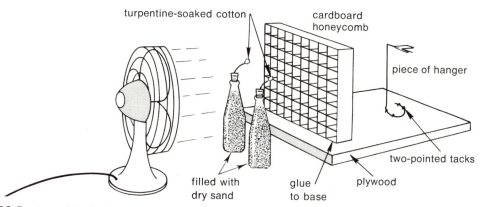

FIGURE **23-5** A model wind tunnel.

on the holder, and start the smoke and the fan. The movement of the smoke will show how these parts affect the flow of air. A more graphic demonstration can be made by suspending the model from a thread through a screw eye inserted at its point of balance (often the center of the wing), attaching another thread to a lightly stretched rubber band as shown in Fig. 23-6. The airplane will take certain attitudes in response to different aileron, elevator, and rudder positions. A simple model can be made of cardboard as shown in Fig. 23-14.

KITES AND PARACHUTES

Kites were man's first flying machines. From these, gliders evolved, which were ultimately developed into engine-powered aircraft. Before the Wright brothers could invent their first plane (1903), they had to learn to use gliders. And before that, like most boys, they learned to fly kites. The forepart of the Wrights' plane was really a huge, curved box kite. When the Niagara Falls suspension bridge was begun, the first line was carried across the gorge by kite. Today, kites are sometimes used to carry weather instruments and life-raft radio antennas.

Most children know that if there is little or no wind, one runs with a kite to make it rise.

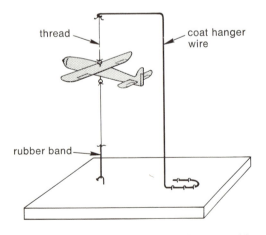

FIGURE **23-6** A suspended model for use with a wind tunnel.

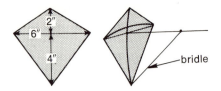

FIGURE **23-7** A miniature bow kite.

They also know that a kite will not stay aloft if there is no wind, and the stronger the wind, the better. Children will be able to show where to tie a kite string or "bridle." Point out how this allows the wind to *push up* on the kite's undersurface.

Children can learn much about the motion of kites by flying miniatures in front of a fan or outdoors. A miniature bow kite can be made of two 6-inch heavy broomstraws crossed as shown in Fig. 23-7. Notch slightly the ends of the sticks and soak one in water for a few minutes so that it will bend easily. Flex it into a bow, and tie a string from one end to the other. Lay the midpoint of the bow (horizontal piece) on the spine 2 inches from the spine's top. Bind the sticks together with coarse thread where they cross. Make a number of turns with the thread, first through one diagonal of angles and then the other.

Beginning at the top of the spine, string the kite by connecting all the points—from upper tip of spine to tip of bow to lower tip of spine to the other bow tip and back to the upper tip of the spine. Wind string around the ends of the sticks to hold the framework string in place and to reinforce the ends of the sticks. Brush glue on the string at the ends of the sticks and at the point where the spine and bow meet.

Lay the framework on tissue or thin paper and cut along the path of the string, allowing an extra inch of paper all the way around. Fold this extra inch of paper over the string and glue it. Allow the glue to dry.

Make a very small hole in the paper at the crossing point of the bow and spine. Run thread through the hole and tie it securely to the crossing point. The length of the bridle string should be the distance from the crossing to the end of the bow plus the distance from the end of the bow to the bottom of the spine.

To make a miniature box kite, use a $6 \times 8\frac{1}{4}$-inch piece of typing paper. Cut out the areas shown untinted in Fig. 23-8, and fold on the dashed lines. Fasten the edges of the sheet together with mending tape, rubber cement, or glue, using the $\frac{1}{4}$-inch overlap as an anchoring strip. Fasten the bridle and string (midway along the bridle) as shown in the figure; the length of the bridle is equal to two thirds of the length plus the width of one side—6 inches. (A triangular box kite is made like the four-sided box kite, but with only three sides.)

Tailless kites, like a box kite, are able to fly upright because any two sides form a 90° or right angle. This "dihedral" angle (an angle formed by the intersection of two planes or surfaces) can be seen at the junction of the wings and fuselage of small planes. Air moving against the two planes of the kite keeps it in position. If the wind shifts, the kite tends to turn end over end in a self-correcting movement that then exposes two other dihedral surfaces to the wind.

Full-sized kites can be made by following the same patterns described above for the miniature kites, with the dimensions increased proportionately. Stronger sticks are needed, such as bamboo strips. For the box kite, first make a form of the strips in the shape of the miniature and then cover with tissue paper. Full-sized kites are common and inexpensive items in variety stores.

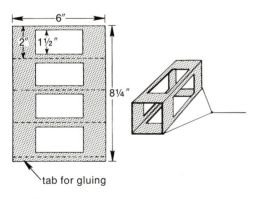

FIGURE **23-8** A miniature box kite.

Like airplanes, kites are heavier than air and, therefore, will remain aloft only if the air pressure on undersurfaces is greater than that on other surfaces. The kite string and bridle, like the sail and mast of a sailboat, can be adjusted to make an angle of deflection that serves to move them. In other words, when a kite is held so that the top part leans into the wind, the air molecules crowded up under the kite will create the difference in air pressure needed to keep it aloft. On a windless day, children may try flying a kite by running with it or towing it behind a bicycle to produce the same effect of air molecules crowded against the kite's undersurface.

Parachutes are devices that use air resistance to slow descent. To reinforce the idea, drop a flat piece of paper. It flutters slowly to the floor. Repeat, wadding paper into a ball. Point out that the sheet, with more surface, offered more resistance to the air and so fell more slowly.

To make a model parachute, tie strings about 6 inches long from the four corners of a large silk handkerchief to a cork. Fold carefully so that the strings do not tangle, throw as high as possible, and watch the descent. Children may jump off a low stool with and without an open umbrella and feel the pull of the umbrella against the air.

The seeds of dandelion, milkweed, or sycamore travel by a kind of natural parachute.

Just as a rubber life belt supports a man in water, a parachute utilizes the buoyancy and resistance of air to save man's life in the air. A man falling unimpeded would increase his speed 32 feet every second. After falling one fourth of a mile, he would be falling at a rate of 3 miles a minute.

A. J. Garnerin, an early investigator in the nature of air travel, made a parachute which had a diameter of 24 feet and whose shape was convex when open. The passenger rode in a wicker basket fastened to the parachute by cords.

For his exhibition leap (1797), the inventor was carried aloft in a balloon. When he started his drop, the parachute opened, but the basket began to swing violently from side to side. The air trapped in the dome of the chute could not get out and acted like a pivot on which the chute

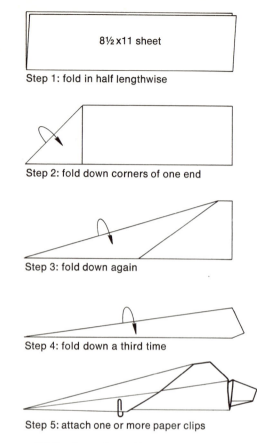

8½ x 11 sheet

Step 1: fold in half lengthwise

Step 2: fold down corners of one end

Step 3: fold down again

Step 4: fold down a third time

Step 5: attach one or more paper clips

FIGURE **23-9** Steps in making a paper dart glider.

could swing like a pendulum. The hole in the top (to allow some air to escape) which Garnerin made in subsequent parachutes is still used in parachute design.

GLIDERS

Manned gliders are sometimes launched by a tow from a car or an airplane or even a windlass. Sometimes gliders are catapulted into flight by giant slingshot-like mechanisms. Gliders can cover astonishing distances and remain aloft for hours, depending on pilot skill and the number and strength of "thermals," updrafts or currents of heated air that rise from the earth's surface as a result of heating by the sun or from other sources.

To make a very simple glider, fold an $8\frac{1}{2} \times 11$-inch piece of paper as shown in Fig. 23-9. A paper clip slipped over the center fold, as indicated in the figure, changes the center of gravity in such a way that the glides are long and graceful.

Inexpensive balsa wood gliders are available at variety stores. After using them, children may want to make their own out of tagboard or, better, manila folders according to the pattern shown in Fig. 23-10. Cut through both layers of the folder (keeping the fold at the bottom). The positioning of the paper-clip weights has a great effect on how well the glider glides, as does the way it is thrown. The object of the weights is to shift the glider's center of gravity so that it is approximately on the center line of the wing. By trying to balance the glider with the wings on the tips of the forefinger and thumb, one can readily estimate the center of gravity. Or lay the glider on a ruler and nudge it forward slowly until the point is reached where it just begins to fall off. Add paper clips until the center shifts to roughly the wing's center line.

Reinforcing the wings with simple, durable braces may help provide more stable flight characteristics. To do so, staple or glue two thin

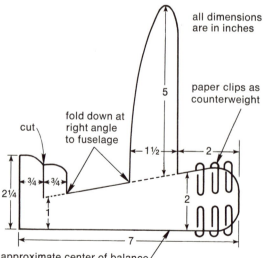

all dimensions are in inches

paper clips as counterweight

fold down at right angle to fuselage

cut

5

1½

2

¾ ¾

2¼

2

1

7

approximate center of balance

FIGURE **23-10** Pattern for a small model glider of tagboard or other stiff paper.

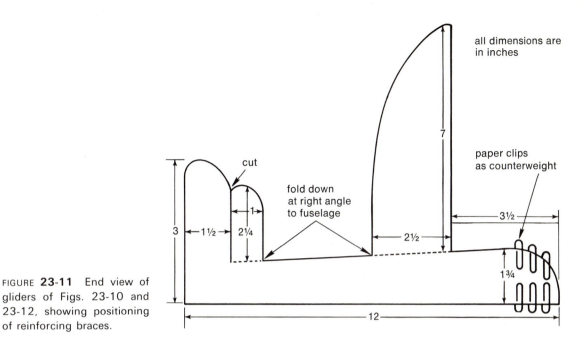

all dimensions are
in inches

cut

fold down
at right angle
to fuselage

paper clips
as counterweight

FIGURE **23-11** End view of gliders of Figs. 23-10 and 23-12, showing positioning of reinforcing braces.

rectangular pieces of tagboard between the fuselage and the undersides of the wing, as shown in Fig. 23-12. Do the same with the stabilizer (rear wings).

The glider whose shape and dimensions are given in Fig. 23-11 is considerably larger than the glider described in Fig. 23-10. This size may be handy as a demonstration model. In general, the bigger the glider, the longer its glide and the slower its shifts in direction.

A carefully made large glider can be modified (Fig. 23-13) to show some of the means by which airplanes are able to turn, climb, and descend. Children can note that changes in the glider's flight when the elevators (on the stabilizer) are bent in various combinations: both up; one up

and one down; and one up and one level. The ailerons (on the wing) may also be tried in various positions.

Gliders, in general, can be adjusted and manipulated in many ways. For instance, if the surface (size) of the stabilizers is increased, it is likely that the nose will need less weight. Narrowing the wing or shortening it (reducing its surface) will increase the speed needed to "take-off".

The glider should be held at the center of gravity. When released, it should be tilted slightly upward but not tipped to the side. The force of the throw should be gently firm, not with a sharp snap of the wrist. The object is to make the glider float out of the hand.

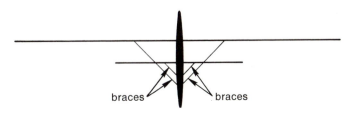

braces   braces

FIGURE **23-12** Pattern for a large model glider of tagboard or other stiff paper.

AIRPLANES

For centuries, men tried to imitate bird flight. The Wright brothers were successful because of their epochal invention of a mechanism which allowed control of the rudders and the elevators with one lever: Changes in both control surfaces had to be simultaneous.

The addition of a small gasoline engine to their glider enabled them to fly by providing the power necessary to pull (by means of the propeller) the whole aircraft forward with a force that exceeded the drag caused by air resistance and air friction. A collection or exhibit of airplane models covering a span of years should illustrate the decrease in wingspread as engine power has increased. Reduction of surface reduces resistance to air and, therefore, drag. Doubling the speed quadruples the lift. But double speed may require eight times the power—hence the enormous fuel consumption of newer, faster planes.

Ultimately, what keeps an airplane aloft is the same thing that keeps any heavier-than-air craft (kites and gliders included) aloft—a greater air pressure on its undersurfaces than on the other surfaces. As pointed out under *Principles of Aerodynamics*, an airplane wing, shaped like the one in Fig. 23-4, has an average pressure on its upper surface 10 pounds less than that on its undersurface. This is the product of dynamic lift,

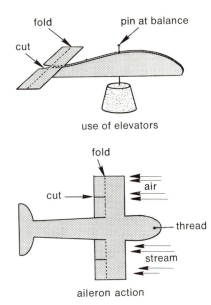

use of elevators

aileron action

FIGURE **23-14** Models for illustrating the action of the control surfaces of an airplane.

from the planing action of the wing (which crowds air molecules under it), and of lift achieved because the fast-flowing air decreases the pressure (Bernoulli's principle) on the upper surface of the wing.

Children will already have learned much about plane controls by making and studying paper darts or gliders (above).

An airplane turns when the ailerons are moved. It is a common misconception that the rudder steers an airplane the way a rudder steers a boat; actually, the rudder prevents sideslipping in the turn. To find out how a plane climbs, dives, or banks, make tagboard models of the fuselage, ailerons, and elevators (Fig. 23-14). For demonstrating elevator action, cut two patterns and glue them together, except for stabilizer pieces, which are folded down as shown. Pin through the balance point of the model into a cork. Push the corks into bottles and set in a wind tunnel (see *Wind Tunnels*) or blow air over the surfaces with a straw. Observe action with elevators up, elevators down.

To show how a plane banks for turning, hold the third tagboard model (Fig. 23-14) in an air stream by a thread attached to the nose. Action

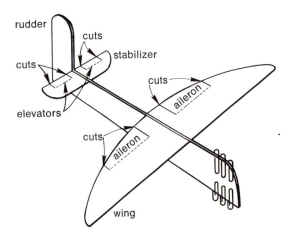

FIGURE **23-13** A large model glider, showing control surfaces.

of the ailerons controls banking left or right. An aileron always moves in a direction opposite the other aileron; thus, with the right aileron down, the left aileron is up and the plane banks to the left, as a result of pushing the control stick to the left. If the control stick is pushed to the right, the right aileron is up, the left down, and the plane now banks to the right. In both cases, the side with the aileron down has the greater lift, thus tilting the wing of the airplane.

PROPELLERS AND HELICOPTERS

The plane's propeller pushes the air back just as a jet does. The equal and opposite reaction pushes the plane forward. Have children examine model plane propellers and various kinds of common screws and note the similarity of form. Point out that some seeds are, in effect, equipped with "propeller blades"—for example, maple, ash, elm, and linden. Children can stand on a chair and watch the helicopter-blade action as they drop the dry seeds.

To make a model propeller, draw the pattern shown (Fig. 23-15) on cardboard and cut out. Punch three holes where shown in the figure and then roll the cardboard around a pencil until the three holes are aligned. Push a hat pin or wire through the three holes and the overlapping parts of the cardboard to form a shaft. Slip some buttons or washers over the shaft, push it through one wall of a cardboard box, and then bend the wire or the point end of the pin to form a hook; if a wire, form a head at the other end by bending it into a ball. A heavy rubber band slipped over the hook will serve as the motor. Pass the other end of the rubber band through a small hole in the opposite wall of the box, and anchor it on the outside of the box with a small stick or dowel. Simple, inexpensive flying model airplanes that use this system of propulsion may be bought in novelty stores.

In an airplane, the propeller's job is not to blow a stream of air over the wings, but to push air back so that the airplane is pushed forward, just

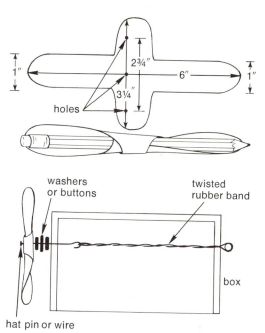

FIGURE **23-15** A working-model propeller.

as a rowboat moves in a direction opposite that of the oars as they are pulled through the water. Jets send exhaust gases backward so that the reaction (Chapter 23) forces the airplane forward. Propeller action may be illustrated using a fan mounted on roller skates, on a wheeled cart, or on a wood block, box, or desk drawer on rollers. If the fan has more than one speed setting, children can see how the higher speed produces a greater reaction.

The principle of helicopter flight may be demonstrated with simple devices such as those shown in Fig. 23-16, 17, and 18. To make the simple rotor shown in Fig. 23-16, cut a filing card along

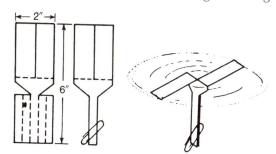

FIGURE **23-16** A card model helicopter.

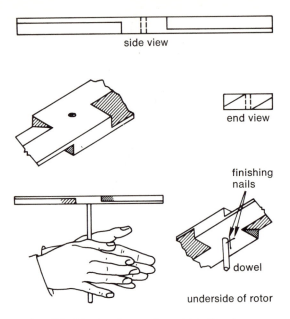

FIGURE **23-17** A soft wood model helicopter.

directional motions of bird wings in flight. The helicopter rises because the rotor blades push down against the air. A rotor blade (or wing) also develops lift by acting as an airfoil as the helicopter moves horizontally.

Another model to show the action of the helicopter rotor may be made of two spools, a model airplane propeller blade, dowel, string, and a wood block as shown in Fig. 23-19. Hammer two finishing nails into the spool end, and drill two small holes in the propeller to accommodate them. The dowel should be slightly smaller than the spool hole to allow the spool to rotate freely and may be fixed to the base by forcing it into a hole drilled in a larger dowel, which is in turn nailed to the flat base. Wind the string around the spool and pull it quickly. The blade should spin rapidly and rise several feet. Similar toys are sometimes found at variety or hobby shops.

the solid lines and fold along the dashed lines, holding the folded portion together with a paper clip or staples. Bend the two "blades" in opposite directions. To make the soft (or balsa) wood model, shape a piece of wood (about 9 × 1 inches) as shown in Fig. 23-17. Drill a hole at the center slightly larger than a $\frac{1}{4}$-inch dowel and insert a small finishing nail in the dowel and the "rotor" as shown.

Throw the card device into the air and observe the spin. The spin in this case will not lift the device (because there is no input of power, as from an engine) but will reduce the rate of fall. The balsa wood model (Fig. 23-17) *will* rise when the dowel is spun quickly between the hands; the rotating propeller blades force the model up by pushing the air down.

Helicopters are really airplanes with moving wings. Toy helicopters or models can be used to show how the usual airplane wing and propeller are replaced by a large horizontal rotor. The ability to change the pitch of the rotor blades— that is, the angle the blade makes with the horizontal (or in relation to the position of the rotor shaft)—approximates the flexibility and multi-

LIGHTER-THAN-AIR CRAFT

Man's first trip in the air was made not in an airplane but in a balloon. Two Frenchmen, the Montgolfier brothers, deserve the main credit for this adventure. The sons of a papermaker, they experimented for years in making balloons that would rise when filled with hot air from a bonfire.

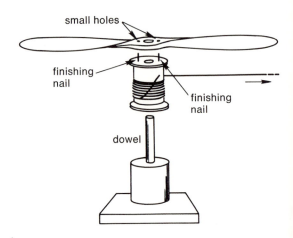

FIGURE **23-18** A model helicopter using wood propeller.

Warmed air rises because volume-for-volume it weighs less than the surrounding air (Chapter 5). The Montgolfiers built a balloon that carried a sheep and two barnyard fowl 1500 feet aloft. The balloon floated two miles and came down with the passengers unharmed.

Most balloons used today, such as a dirigible, rise because they are filled with a gas lighter (less dense) than air. Early balloons of this kind used hydrogen, which is a very explosive gas when removed from its quiet partnership with other elements, as in such compounds as water (Chapter 10). The great number of fires and explosions with hydrogen balloons led to the use of helium, an inert gas, which is also lighter than air though less so than hydrogen.

Just as the buoyancy or lifting power of water holds up ships in the ocean, the buoyancy of air holds up planes and balloons in the ocean of air. A hundred cubic feet of helium weighs 2.2 pounds, whereas the same amount of air weighs 8 pounds. Therefore, each 100 cubic feet of helium can lift 5.8 pounds. A balloon filled with 100,000 cubic feet of helium can therefore lift 1000 × 5.8 or 5800 pounds.

Hot-air ballooning has achieved a new popularity in recent years. The air in balloons used today is heated by means of a burner suspended just below the mouth of the bag and uses propane gas as its fuel. The balloonist uses the burner to regulate ascent and descent.

Children may enjoy their own miniature balloon ascension. To make the balloon, cut a central circular piece and six elliptical sections of tissue as shown in Fig. 23-19. Paste together the edges of the sections and lap the ends over onto the middle circle. Different colors of tissue can be used, and the pieces can be larger, so long as the proportions of the dimensions remain the same. Reinforce and weight the mouth of the balloon with a 1-inch collar of masking tape. Fill with hot air rising from a heater or electric plate. Collect (as shown in Fig. 23-19b) through a cylinder or chimney made by cutting the top and bottom off a tin can. Tie 12-15 feet of light cotton string to the mouth of the balloon. When the

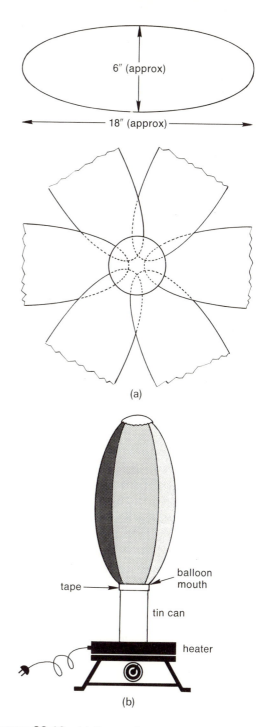

FIGURE **23-19** (a) Pattern for a hot-air balloon; (b) filling the completed hot-air balloon.

balloon is filled with hot air, children will be able to feel its pull on the line, which should then be payed out gradually.

To make a model dirigible, tie $\frac{3}{16}$-inch reeds or canes together at one end and tie (or glue) them along their length to balsa wood hoops (the largest at the midpoint and smaller toward the ends); then tie together the free ends to form a typical blunt-nosed, streamlined dirigible shape.

Cut gores (about six) from tissue paper and paste to ribs. Insert empty balloons, small ones in nose and tail, larger ones in mid-section, and fill with a lighter-than-air gas. Natural or illuminating gas will lift a balloon, but these gases are explosive. Helium is sometimes available from local commercial firms or from toy or novelty stores in cans with a convenient valve top. The model dirigible has been constructed to keep weight minimal, and if balloons are fully inflated, it should rise. To keep the model on an even keel, attach light mooring lines (made from thread) to front and rear.

SUGGESTED PROJECTS

1. Encourage reading about hurricanes and tornadoes and their effects on buildings. Often the roof is blown off and the shell left standing because the flow of air over the roof creates lift, as on an airplane wing, and the higher air pressure inside the house pushes upward.

2. Children may cut out a model airfoil and mount it on a flannel board with arrows to denote air pressure above and below.

3. Aircraft panel instruments may be available at airfield repair shops. Children can do research and/or construct simple models to explain the basic principles involved.

4. Children may be encouraged to read and report on new parachute designs such as the Rogallo wing and others under test. Similarly researched work may be done on advances in helicopter design.

5. Aerodynamic principles as embodied in the hydrofoil and VERTOL vehicles may be research as an avenue of special interest to some children.

BIBLIOGRAPHY

(**P** indicates recommended for primary grades, **I** for intermediate grades, **U** for upper grades.)

Allison, Dorothy K., *Helpful Helicopters*, Melmont, 1954. About their many peacetime uses. Illustrated with photographs. **P**

American Heritage, *The History of Flight*, adapted by Sarel Eimerl, Golden Pr., 1964. Beginning with the myths and legends of flight through aviation's decisive role in World War II, and culminating in the monumental achievements in outer space. Large art program supplements the text. **U**

Beeler, Nelson, *Experiments with Airplane Instruments*, Crowell, 1953. Children learn the use of plane instruments through problem exercises. **I**

Bendick, Jeanne, *The First Book of Airplanes*, Watts, 1958. Basic concepts for small children. Brief history of aeronautics included. Well illustrated. **P**

Cooke, David C., *Helicopters that Made History*, Putnam, 1963. Traces the development of the helicopter. **U**

Coombs, Charles, *Skyhooks*, Morrow, 1967. A compact overview of the historical and modern use of helicopters. Striking photographs, open format. **U**

Corbett, Scott, *What Makes a Plane Fly?*, Little, Brown, 1967. The principles of flight are well explained as are the functions of different parts of a plane. Many illustrations, diagrams, an index and a glossary add to the text. **U**

Delear, Frank, *The New World of Helicopters,* Dodd, Mead, 1967. The past, present, and future of helicopters. **U**

Elting, Mary, *Aircraft at Work,* Harvey, 1964. Crop dusting, smoke jumping, water bombing, and flying lessons are described in addition to the transportation of passengers and freight. **I**

Freeman, Mae, *When Air Moves,* McGraw-Hill, 1968. Explanations are built on everyday experiences. Clear and simple experiments help the reader to understand the functions of airplanes, rockets, jets, air trains, and Hovercraft. **I**

Jacobs, Lou, Jr., *SST Plane of Tomorrow,* Golden Gate, 1967. Story of the plane that will revolutionize air travel. Photographs and diagrams. **U**

Kettelkamp, Larry, *Kites,* Morrow, 1959. Much information on atmosphere as well as on kite construction. **I**

Knight, Clayton, *The Big Book of Real Helicopters,* rev. ed., Grosset & Dunlap, 1963. A historical account of the aircraft in commercial and military use. **I**

Lidstone, John, *Building with Balsa Wood,* Van Nostrand, 1965. Examples of children's work in designing planes and model building and suggests possibilities for space air projects. **U**

Loomis, Robert D., *All About Aviation,* Random, 1964. From the Wright brothers' first plane to the supersonic transports now being developed; a smoothly written text supported with clear drawings and diagrams. **U**

Richards, Norman, *Giants in the Sky,* Children's Pr., 1967. An account of man's attempt to fly with balloons from 1785 to the present. Many historical photographs. **U**

Schneider, Leo, and Maurice U. Ames, *Wings in Your Future,* Harcourt, 1955. Principles of flight; jets, helicopters, gliders, rockets in space exploration. Simple experiments. **I**

Settle, Mary Lee, *Story of Flight,* Random, 1967. Historical approach from the times when men dreamed of flying to the current space race. **I**

Verral, Charles, *Jets,* Prentice-Hall, 1962. An interestingly presented, well-illustrated introduction to jet propulsion, organized chronologically. Good index and glossary appended. **U**

Wells, Robert, *Wonders of Flight,* Dodd, Mead, 1962. A well written explanation of the principles of flight by birds and men including problems of thrust, lift, drag, gravity. Appendix with definitions, and an index. Illustrated with photographs and diagrams. **U**

An astronaut walks on the moon during the Apollo 11 expedition. At right is a leg of the lunar module.

24 *Gravity and Space Travel*

Most of us go about our daily activities oblivious of the effects on our bodies, and on all matter, of a force—the force of gravity—that is ever-present and crucial. Children may be surprised that every step they take, every movement of every machine, every grain of sand is to some extent being acted on at every moment by gravity.

GRAVITY

Gravity can be simply defined as the amount of attraction, or pull, one mass has for another. Only very massive bodies have it in an easily measurable amount. Even though unmeasurable in small bodies, all possess gravity. Newton's theory holds that all bodies in space attract or pull on each other. The amount of the attraction depends on the mass of the bodies and the distance between them. The larger the mass, the greater the gravitational attraction; the closer the bodies involved, the greater the attraction. If the distance between two bodies is doubled, the gravitational attraction between them is one fourth its original value; at three times the distance, it is one ninth, and so on.

Without being aware of it, everyone knows something about gravity and the effect of this force—for example, the weight of a person. This weight is the measure of the pull of gravity upon the atoms or molecules that make up his body.

The sum of the number of these atoms is called mass. Mass does not change. At the North Pole or at the top of a mountain, where gravity is slightly less (see below), the pull on the mass of atoms is less, and one will weigh less, but one's mass (the number of atoms of which one is composed) does not change. Deep in a mine, the pull on the same mass is greater, and one weighs more. Since the pull of gravity on the moon is one-sixth that on the earth, one would have the same mass as on the earth but would be one-sixth his earth weight.

Gravity pulls all bodies toward the center of the earth. To show this, separate a small cardboard geography globe at the seam. Glue small magnets to the inside of the globe's surface. (The greater the number of magnets, the better.) Reassemble the globe, seal the seam with cellophane tape, and return the globe to its stand. Using tin snips, cut from the end of a tin can a simple outline figure of a man 1 inch high. Leave a section of metal below the legs and bend it underneath to act as a stand. Place the figure on the globe near one of the magnets, which will hold it in place. Move the model about to show that the figure is pulled toward the center when it is both at the North Pole and at the South Pole. By moving the little man, children should readily see that "up" simply means away from the earth, while "down" always means toward its center.

If a cardboard geography globe is unavailable, use a grapefruit and toothpicks. Insert the toothpicks into different points of the grapefruit so that they all stick out straight. Then fasten tiny paper figures to the protruding ends of each toothpick.

When a ball is thrown straight up into the air, the earth's gravity is pulling on the ball even as it leaves the hand, so that it begins to slow down as soon as it is no longer being pushed by the hand; it slows, stops it ascent, then is pulled back toward the earth. Help children understand that gravity is always acting on the ball. If the ball had been thrown out horizontally instead of vertically, gravity would immediately begin to pull it down even while it was traveling horizontally. In fact, it would not take any longer for the ball

to fall than if it had been just dropped from the hand at the same level from which it was thrown.

This can be shown quite effectively as follows. Place a 12-inch ruler obliquely across one corner of a table top so that one end just projects over the edge of the table and the other lies about 1 inch from the edge (Fig. 24-1). Place a penny on top of the projecting end of the ruler. Place a second penny on the table, between the other end of the ruler and the edge of the table. With the flat part of another ruler, strike the projecting end of the first ruler sharply, using a horizontal motion, so that it slides quickly out from under one penny as it knocks the other penny from the table. One penny will fall straight to the floor while the other travels in a long arc. Have children listen to the sounds of both pennies as they hit the floor. Both will hit at the same time. It may be necessary to practice a few times to acquire the knack of releasing both coins at the same time.

The sun, the moon, the planets, and the stars all have their own forces of gravity. Each has a gravitational force different from that of the earth, depending on its composition and density. A wonderful way to show the effect of the moon's gravity on the earth is to study the tides. Also, the sun's gravity holds the planets in their orbits, while the earth's gravity holds the moon in its orbit.

To escape the earth's gravity completely and move off into space, an object, such as a rocket, must travel at a speed of about 25,000 miles per hour; this is called the escape velocity.

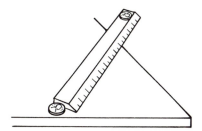

FIGURE **24-1** Arrangement to demonstrate that objects falling from the same height will strike the floor at the same time.

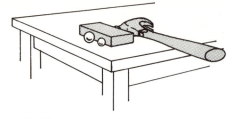

FIGURE **24-2** Demonstrating that the weight of an object does not affect its rate of fall.

Rate of Fall

Size and weight have no effect on the time it takes two bodies to fall the same distance. Needed to show this are two marbles of different size, a wooden block, and a hammer. Set the block near the edge of the table and place the marbles against the side of the block nearer the table's edge (Fig. 24-2). Tap the center of the block moderately with a hammer. (The block must be hit in the center for proper results.) Both marbles will reach the floor at the same time. Children should understand that gravity pulls each ounce of matter with a constant and equal force of 1 ounce. There is no summation of forces that would make heavier things fall more quickly. Thus, size and weight have nothing to do with the time it takes for objects to fall in a vacuum. The resistance of the air, however, does make a difference. To show this, hold a flat piece of aluminum foil and a marble (one in each hand) at arm's length and let them drop simultaneously. The foil will float down, taking longer to fall. Then fold the foil very tightly and compactly, hold it and the marble at arm's length, and again let them fall. Both will hit the ground at the same time. Point out that when the foil was dropped as a flat sheet, the air resisted its movement more than it did that of the marble because the sheet offered more surface against which the air could press. The second time the air resistance was reduced because the amount of foil surface was smaller. (One can also use two sheets of typing paper, one rolled into a ball, the other flat, for this demonstration.)

One can also demonstrate this with a "guinea and feather" tube and a hand vacuum pump. If a commercial tube is not available, fit 3 feet of strong glass or plastic tube 2 inches in diameter with a solid stopper at one end and a one-hole stopper at the other. The one-hole stopper carries a glass or metal tube which leads to a hand vacuum pump by means of a pressure hose. Place a dry coin and feather inside the tube. Evacuate the tube and invert it (Fig. 24-3a). Observe that the coin and feather fall with the same acceleration. Next release the vacuum and invert the tube again to show that the resistance of the air present in the tube slows the fall of the feather more than that of the coin (Fig. 24-3b).

The rate of acceleration of falling bodies is uniform—32 feet per second per second. To show this, attach steel balls or lead sinkers about $\frac{1}{2}$ inch in diameter to a fish line at the following distances from the floor (in inches): 3, 12, 27, 48, 75, 108, 144, and 192. Suspend the line in a gymnasium or other high-ceilinged room. Place a large sheet of metal under the point of suspension and release the line by cutting or burning it at the top. The metal balls will be heard to strike the metal sheet at a constant frequency—about every eighth of

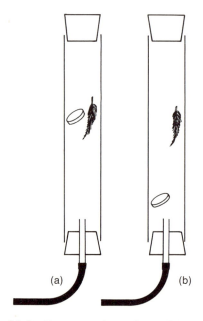

FIGURE **24-3** Demonstrating effect of gravity on falling objects (a) in a vacuum and (b) with interference from resistance to air.

a second. This occurs because the longer a ball has to fall, the faster it will be falling at impact. Thus, the speed of a ball tends to reduce the space between it and the next lower ball on the string.

In a variation of this demonstration, the weights are spaced at equal intervals along the line. Then when the line is dropped, the weights will strike the metal sheet at an increasing frequency. (*Caution: Keep pupils back from the point of impact.*)

That weight is simply the measure of the pull of gravity can be given impact by asking each child his weight by saying: How much does gravity pull on you?

Show how a box suspended on a rubber band or spring (from a window shade roller or screen door) stretches the band or spring more and more as weights are added to the box. The stretch of the rubber band clearly shows the pull of gravity. Replace the rubber band with the spring from an old window-shade roller and repeat the experiment. Suspend the spring from a cup hook screwed into the underside of the ruler. If a window-shade roller is unavailable, use a light porch-door spring (available at hardware stores).

As examples of measuring the pull of gravity, weigh various objects on a laundry scale or other spring balance. Point out that the laundry scale and other such balances make use of a spring much as in the experiment above.

One can make a simple spring balance as shown in Fig. 24-4. With the box empty, mark the point where it aligns with the scale; this is the zero point. Add one or more marbles at a time, making a mark at each new position of the box. Label each mark to denote the number of marbles needed to bring the box to this point. Thus the balance scale is marked with marbles as the unit of weight. If the box does not return to the zero mark when all the marbles are removed, adjust the thread supporting the box until the box does reach the zero level. Then add a stone or other object to the box and determine how many "marbles" it weighs.

Children are intrigued by the idea that their weight would be different on the moon, on the

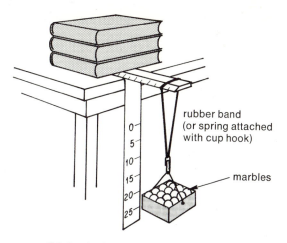

FIGURE **24-4** A simple spring balance.

sun, and on Mars or any other planet. For example, the moon's pull of gravity is about one-sixth that of the earth, so that a person would be only one-sixth his weight on the earth. On Mars the pull of gravity is one-third that on the earth. But on the sun, one would find a force of gravity 26 times that of the earth, so that one would weigh 26 times more on the sun. Children should be able to calculate their weights on the other planets, given the pull of gravity in those planets. They may be surprised that on top of a high mountain they weigh a minute amount less than they do at its foot. The higher one goes (that is, the farther from the center of the earth), the less the force of gravity. At an altitude of 8000 miles above the earth's surface, a person's weight is only one-fourth as much as at sea level; at 12,000 miles, one-ninth as much; and at 16,000 miles, one-sixteenth as much. Have children calculate their weights at these altitudes.

Children may have heard or read about the force called a "g," particularly with respect to rockets and jet planes. A g is a force equal to the earth's gravity; thus, 1 g on a 30,000-pound airplane equals 30,000 pounds. Each child can tell what the g force is on himself (his own weight). A 5-g force on a child who weighs 90 pounds is five times 90, or 450 pounds.

The g forces increase when speed is increased or direction changed. This can be shown with an inexpensive balsa wood glider. Fasten a weight to the wing with a thread and have a child move the glider first in level "flight," then in a dive, ending suddenly by leveling off. The wing will snap off because the g's increased sharply when the direction of the dive was changed suddenly to level flight. (See the discussion of *inertia* in Chapter 22.) Test pilots find out how many g's a plane can withstand by diving rapidly and then suddenly flattening out to level flight.

The U.S. Air Force tests the effect of increased g's on a man by swinging him in a circle in a closed cockpit. One can show this by using a ball attached to a rubber band and swinging it in a circle. The faster one swings the ball, the larger the circle its path makes because the ball acts as if it is heavier.

The Center of Gravity

To demonstrate the center of gravity, cut a piece of cardboard in an irregular shape like that shown in Fig. 24-5. With a thin nail, puncture the cardboard at random at four fairly widely separated points. Label the points A, B, C, and D. Suspend the cardboard from a bulletin board on a small nail or long tack pushed part way through point A. (It is important that the cardboard swing freely on the nail.) Then tie a thread to a small stone or other weight, making a loop at the other end of the thread. Pass the loop over the end of the nail and let the stone and thread hang down. Draw a line on the cardboard directly underneath (and, therefore, showing the direction of) the thread. Repeat the procedure with points B, C, and D. Point out that the point at which the resulting four lines intersect is the center of gravity. Suspended on a pin through this point (cg on the figure), the cardboard will be perfectly balanced in any position—that is, it will remain at rest and will not rotate to a new position.

Help children understand that the center of gravity of an object is the center of the object's mass. To show this graphically, cut out a cardboard rectangle and determine its center of gravity as described above. Make a pinhole through the center, turn the cardboard over, and draw

the two diagonals of the rectangle (from corner to corner). They should cross at the pinhole. Point out that for regular-shaped or uniform objects the center of gravity is at the midpoint.

Have one child balance a yardstick on his finger, and show that the point of balance is on or about the halfway mark, or 18 inches. Because the yardstick is uniform in shape, the center of gravity is at the midpoint. Then tie a jackknife or any similar object to one end of the yardstick, and try to balance it. This time the stick will balance—the center of gravity will be—at a point much closer to the heavier end.

Or stand a large soda bottle on its base and note that the bottle does not tip very easily because the center of gravity is located nearer the heavier end, *below* the middle of the bottle (stable equilibrium). Then stand the bottle upright on its narrow mouth and note that it tips very easily (unstable equilibrium), because the center of gravity is now located *above* the middle.

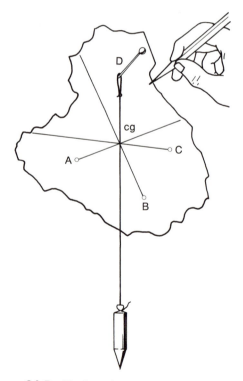

FIGURE **24-5** Finding the center of gravity of an irregular shape.

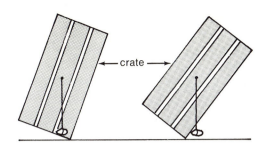

FIGURE **24-6** Demonstrating that an object's stability depends on the relationship between the center of gravity and the base of an object.

An object in this position is usually denoted "top-heavy." With the bottle resting on its side, the center of gravity is always at the same height, no matter how much the bottle rolls and, thus, is in neutral equilibrium.

Some children may point out that the base of the bottle is broad, while the mouth is narrow, and that this seems to make a difference. This observation provides an opportunity to show the relationship between the center of gravity and the base of an object as follows. Obtain a wooden crate (from a grocery or market) with the original cover. Nail the cover back on in order to have a uniformly rectangular object. Find the center of gravity by drawing two diagonals and locating the midpoint. Place the crate on its narrow end, drive a nail halfway into the midpoint, and loop, over the head of the nail, a black thread attached to a rock. (See that the thread and stone can swing freely.) The thread should be long enough so that the rock almost touches the floor (Fig. 24-6). Tilt the crate at various angles and point out that as long as the vertical line of the thread falls within the limits of the base, the crate will not tip.

Repeat the experiment, placing the crate on its broad side. (It will be necessary to shorten the thread.) Note how difficult it is to tip the crate this time. The crate must be tilted quite some way before it will topple. Have children measure the distance between the center of gravity and the ground when the crate is on its narrow side and on its broad side. They should now readily understand that there are two ways

of making an object stable: by lowering its center of gravity or by broadening its base. Automobile designers have used these principles to achieve stability: modern cars have wide bases, and their weight is concentrated at a low point.

Many toys and stunts make use of a low center of gravity or a broad base to create startling effects. Children will enjoy making some of the following. Open the large blade of a jackknife so that it is at right angles with the handle. Push the point of the blade into a pencil at a point near the sharpened end. Balance the knife and pencil on the edge of a table (Fig. 24-7). When the pencil is balanced, a gentle push on the knife

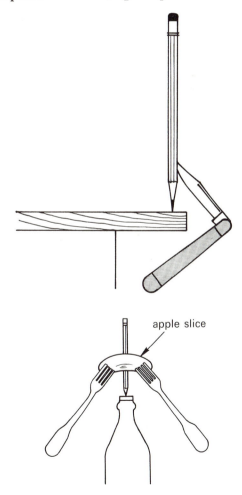

apple slice

FIGURE **24-7** Two examples of how a low center of gravity makes a narrow base stable.

will make both knife and pencil rock back and forth.

Remove the stem of an apple and in its place push a 3-inch nail until all but $\frac{1}{2}$ inch is in the apple. Press two forks into the apple (Fig. 24-7) and balance the point of the nail on a cork stoppering a soda bottle. Give the top of the apple a gentle twirl, and the device will spin.

Cut a slice of apple about 1 inch thick. Push the point of a sharpened pencil through the piece of apple until it protrudes about 1 inch on the other side. Insert a fork and balance the arrangement on the edge of a table as shown in Fig. 24-8. Push down the eraser end of the pencil slightly. The pencil will bob up and down.

SPACE TRAVEL

Flying through space has for centuries been one of man's persistent dreams. Cyrano de Bergerac (1619–1655), later the hero of the nineteenth-century French play by Edmond Rostand, wrote of a space ship made like a huge box with holes at each end. Air heated by lens-focused sunlight was to rush out one of the holes and drive the box ahead. Although Jules Verne's books have been read as fantasy, travel under the sea, envisioned in his *20,000 Leagues Under the Sea*, has come to full reality. And space travel, also foreseen by him (in *From the Earth to the Moon*, written in 1865), is now fact.

The Wright brothers' "contraption" flew 120 feet in a few seconds, or about 31 miles per hour. Within 50 years, airplane builders had produced propeller-driven planes which flew nearly 600 miles per hour. And that was as far as they could get. With the development of jet engines, speeds increased to approximately 1800 miles per hour, at which speed, it was found, the plane was severely buffeted. This speed is the same as that of sound and is thus called the "sound barrier."

The Sound Barrier

The mechanism behind the "sound barrier" is as follows. A plane engine warming up is sur-

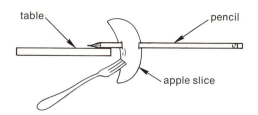

FIGURE **24-8** Balancing an object by use of a low center of gravity.

rounded by a sea of sound waves kicked up by its propeller. As the blade cuts into the air, every particle of air in its path is compressed or bunched, and then rarefied or thinned as it falls behind the plane.

At over 700 miles per hour, the sound waves from a plane overhead pour from it in all directions. As it increases its speed, the compression waves in front are crowded closer and closer together and the plane has to push harder and harder as it approaches the speed of sound.

In laboratory wind tunnels, scientists found that ordinary plane models were wrenched apart when air speed approached that of sound. The special kinds of sound waves piled up in front of objects traveling at or above the speed of sound are called *shock waves* (Fig. 24-9). The crack of a whip is an example of such a super-squeezed compression wave.

With the power of jet engines, designers saw the possibility of getting the push needed to drive a plane past the sound barrier into the world of silent and smooth flying beyond.

Satellites

Newton wondered why the moon, under the influence of Earth's gravity, did not fall into the earth. On the other hand, he knew the moon was moving: Then why didn't it simply fly off into space? From observation he calculated that each second the moon moves two-thirds of a mile. During this time, it falls toward the earth one-twentieth of an inch. These two motions produce an orbit that is a nearly perfect circle about the earth. Thus, two major forces act upon the moon—its forward momentum and the pull of the earth's gravitation.

When a ball is thrown, the line it describes through the air is a curve. However, the curve is much steeper than the curvature of the earth, and thus the ball falls back to the surface. If the earth were smooth and there was no air and one could throw a ball at the necessary speed, its curve of falling would exactly correspond to the curvature of the earth, and, like the moon, the ball would fall perpetually. Yet the earth is not smooth and does have an atmosphere. In essence, what we have had to do to orbit satellites is to throw them hard enough so that they escape the earth's atmosphere. A series of rocket "stages" (each of which is discarded after it is used) provide the necessary force to boost the satellite into space. Above the atmosphere there is relatively little friction to slow the satellite once it is moving at a speed at which the curve of its fall toward the earth is such that it does not hit the earth.

Children can throw a ball or any object and observe how it follows a curved path, called trajectory. Have children observe how speed determines trajectory: An object thrown slowly describes a steeper curve than one thrown fast.

A useful way of illustrating this uses the rubber ball and long rubber band of a paddle tennis game. Whirl this around the head just fast enough so that the ball and elastic string are nearly horizontal. The ball represents the moon, and the rubber band the earth's gravitational pull on the moon. The force pulling the ball inward (centripetal force) is the gravitational pull; the whirling ball exerts a pull outward (centrifugal force). When the ball is whirled at just the right speed, one force balances the other. If it is whirled too slowly, the ball moves inward. Help children make the analogy between this and the speed required to orbit an artificial satellite. Point out that the band stretches (that is, the length of the orbit increases) when the force put into the whirling is increased. If the length of the band is suddenly shortened, the number of revolutions sharply increases: The moon circles the earth once in 28 days, while artificial satellites, which are only a few hundred miles from Earth as against the moon's distance of 240,000 miles, revolve about the earth many times a day.

A student especially interested in space might point out that the orbits of the artificial satellites are not circular but elliptical (oval-shaped). This is explained as follows. When a satellite is sent up, the last stage may travel at a speed that is too great, so that it swings out further—that is, the curve of part of its orbit is a little greater than the curve of the earth. As it curves out, it loses speed, and as it loses speed, the curve approaches that of the earth. Once a satellite is set on a particular orbit, it will keep to that orbit. If the error occurs in the direction in which the last-stage rocket points the satellite, the same kind of oval orbit can result. If the error is too great, the satellite curves out sharply and then curves back to the earth in a sharper curve than the earth's surface. If this curve is too sharp, the satellite descends into the earth's atmosphere and burns up from friction. The opposite can also occur: If the satellite is sent aloft with a speed greater than 18,000 miles per hour, the curve of the orbit is so shallow that it never comes back on itself; thus, the satellite swings off into space, never to return. In order to put a satellite into orbit, its curve must never be so steep as to

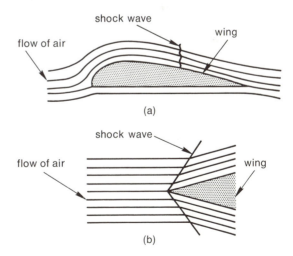

FIGURE **24-9** Shock waves (a) created by a normal airplane wing at subsonic air speed; (b) created by a supersonic airplane wing at supersonic air speed.

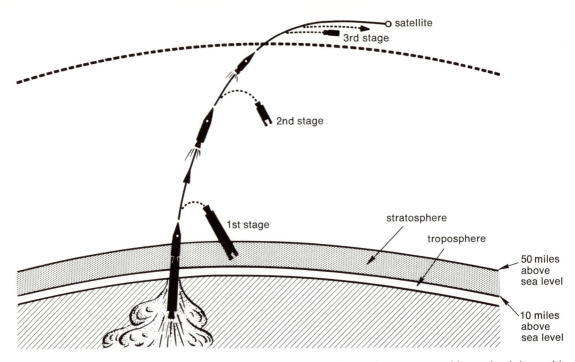

FIGURE **24-10** Typical sequence in launching of a satellite, showing rocket stages used in putting it into orbit.

plunge it into the earth's atmosphere, nor so shallow that it does not come back on itself. In other words, a satellite orbit can either be a circle or an ellipse, but not a parabola.

Launching a Satellite

Rockets that carry satellites into space also carry a huge load of fuel used to achieve the speed to orbit the satellite. Thus, moving a rocket from Earth into space is somewhat like climbing an enormous hill that gets easier to climb the longer one climbs (as the load of fuel is decreased by being consumed and as the pull of gravity decreases with distance from the Earth).

The solution to the problem was piggyback rockets (Fig. 24-10). As each stage burns out, it drops off, thereby reducing the overall weight and permitting an increase in speed.

Once the satellite is in an orbit beyond the earth's atmosphere, it requires no further fuel; it merely obeys Newton's law that a body in motion tends to remain in motion (Chapter 22).

The Atmosphere as a Barrier

We live at the bottom of an ocean of air. Just as there are different layers of water at different depths of the oceans, there are different layers of air in the atmosphere. As far back as 1730, Dr. Edmund Halley theorized that the air above Earth was divided into layers.

In 1900 a French meteorologist, Léon Teisserenc de Bort, used instrument-carrying balloons in research that expanded Halley's theories. Teisserenc de Bort named the lowest layer the *troposphere*. In this layer occur major weather phenomena. The depth of the layer varies seasonally and latitudinally, being deeper over the poles than at the equator. Teisserenc de Bort named the second layer the *stratosphere*, because its relatively constant temperatures permitted horizontal layers of wind currents, now called jet streams. Since his time, scientific research has delineated two other layers: the *ionosphere*, where the air is electrically charged by the sun, and the *exosphere*, the outermost layer, which contains single atoms of nitrogen and oxygen, all circling the earth like microscopic satellites. Nearly all the molecules in the earth's atmosphere are within 23 miles of the ground. Up about 100 miles, a molecule travels a mile before colliding with another.

Getting the satellite through the atmosphere and beyond is difficult. Anyone who has pedaled a bicycle against the wind knows what a significant factor "air resistance" can be. A child who has slid down a rope knows the heat that friction can generate. Point out that, during a launch, *tons* of air rub against a rocket, which is why satellites (and meteors) burn up when they enter the earth's atmosphere at high speeds.

As fast as a launching rocket rises, it does not begin to attain orbital speed until it is above most of the earth's air. If, in the first few hundred feet, it attained full speed, a good deal of the energy of the rocket's fuel would be wasted pushing against air and gravity.

Uses

Not all the uses of space satellites are known. Some obvious benefits are noted below.

Acquisition of new knowledge From the shape of satellite orbits, we have been able to learn the exact shape of the earth: Slight deviations from the spherical give it a very slightly pear-like shape. Also determined (by instruments inside satellites) is information radioed back to Earth, such as the nature of radiation in space, the number of meteors, temperature, and so on. These data are recorded and studied. At present we are planning to mount a telescope in space as an Earth satellite so that we can, for the first time, see the universe without the shimmering, hazy, filter of the atmosphere intervening. Medical and other research needing an environment free of microbes will be possible in space.

Weather forecasting With respect to the weather, man has been, until recently, in the position of trying to talk about something which he has seen only in pieces. Satellite-mounted cameras, however, can take and transmit to Earth photographs or TV images of huge areas so that we can see, at a glance, the weather pattern of the world. This, in turn, may be related to solar flares, sunspots, and other phenomena so that it may some day be possible to predict weather months in advance. Typhoon, hurricane, tornado, and other warnings well in advance of their advent will be possible, with potential savings (in property damage) of hundreds of millions of dollars a year.

Communication Satellites whose speed and direction match the speed and direction of the

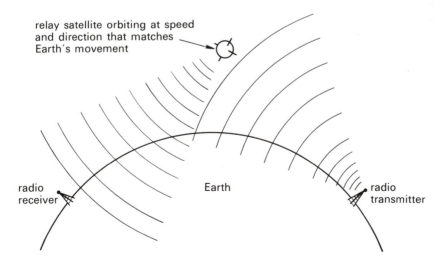

FIGURE **24-11** How satellites help send radio signals long distances.

earth's rotation hang, in effect, motionless over the earth. Such satellites are used to send television, radio, and telephone signals great distances by providing a relay station high above the horizon (Fig. 24-11).

MANNED SPACE TRAVEL

As formidable as are the problems behind the successful launching of a satellite, getting a man to the moon and back is much more difficult, for wherever man goes, he must take a miniature of his world with him. He must have food, water, suitable pressure and temperature, oxygen, and protection against meteors and radiation. Speeds of acceleration and deceleration must be low enough to avoid crushing him, and he must be able to cope with weightlessness.

Food and Water

Condensed and concentrated foods are now used by astronauts in space capsules. When space ships are larger, plants such as algae may actually be grown aboard. This would be exceptionally economical since, besides providing food, the growing plants would use carbon dioxide (a human waste product) while producing oxygen, a necessity of human life. Other wastes could be used to fertilize the plants.

Fuel cells (which use oxygen and hydrogen gas to make electricity for the space ship or capsule) produce water as a by product. This water is consumed by astronauts.

Pressure

Crossing the ten-mile limit was really man's first step into outer space, for, above an altitude of ten miles, man (unprotected) would explode because of the difference between the pressure on the inside and on the outside of his body. In such a low-pressure environment, water, and therefore blood, would boil at the normal body temperature of 98.6°F. Thus, the space traveler must take pressure with him—either by means of an airtight room (or cabin) or by means of a pressurized suit. Both of these have been used.

Oxygen

People who drive over high mountain passes sometimes feel the lack of oxygen. In the ascent of Mount Everest, the climbers, Tensing Norkay and Edmund Hillary, carried oxygen tanks. Children see the similarity to deep-sea divers and their oxygen tanks. At an altitude of 18,000 feet, there is just half as much oxygen as at sea level. Above 50,000 feet, there is not enough oxygen for man to live more than fifteen seconds. This is only ten miles up, or on the lower edge of the stratosphere. Airplanes flying at altitudes of 8000 to 40,000 feet have pressurized interiors or provide individual oxygen masks. Because of the pressure differential, the plane windows must be very thick and the openings carefully sealed to prevent internal pressure from blowing them out. Anything falling out of a plane at high altitude is pulled out as though by giant suction.

Thus, oxygen compressed in tanks is carried on space vessels. (As mentioned, it may someday be provided by growing plants.) The air in space compartments is filtered and treated to remove carbon dioxide and water vapor. Because a coasting or orbiting space ship has no weight, fans are needed to circulate the air; otherwise, a man could suffocate. The nature and cause of convection currents, discussed in Chapters, 7, 13, and 17, should clarify why such currents would not occur under weightless conditions.

Radiation and Meteorite Protection

If a fish in the ocean considered such things, he would probably regard the air above his world as "empty," in that there is (relatively) little or no water in it. Space may seem, in that way, empty to us; but it is not empty, although it is airless.

Space is flooded with intense radiation—X-rays, radio, infrared, visible, ultraviolet, cosmic. Recent evidence indicates that there is also a very tenuous presence of free hydrogen. Affecting all this in various ways are the forces of the planets and stars. Gravitational and magnetic attractions fluctuate in intensity according to location. At times the sun eruptively flares up, throwing out streams of hydrogen and helium nuclei and other elements. Bands of electrons (the Van Allen Belt), great streams of moving electrons, encircle the earth. In short, space may be described as filled with energy.

A space suit or space cabin must also protect the astronaut from such cosmic and other radiations. Early unmanned-satellite investigation furnished valuable and unexpected information on the kinds and intensities of radiation present in space.

Our atmosphere is, in effect, the earth's space suit, acting as a shield against cosmic particles, life-destroying ultraviolet and X-rays, and so on. In space, man must carry his shield.

Meteors may also bombard man, although space flights thus far have shown little danger from meteors.

Acceleration-deceleration

Men traveling inside a space ship must also be able to cope with enormous changes in speed during takeoff and landing. Some men can endure the pull of a force many times their ordinary weight. Test pilots can black out under only $2\frac{1}{2}$–5 g's (see p. 401), unless special precautions are taken. Experiments have shown that a man is much less apt to black out if he is reclining. The special pressurized suits that prevent blood from leaving the brain have been used for years by pilots of high-speed airplanes. These suits are forerunners to the special suits (Fig. 24-12) designed for astronauts, which provide radiation-protection and oxygen, as well as pressure. For short periods, properly suited and positioned, a man can stand a stress of many gravities.

FIGURE **24-12** An astronaut in a space suit, which provides the oxygen, radiation protection, and pressures necessary for man to exist in space.

Temperature

Two sources of heat extremes beset space exploration—friction and radiation. Friction from air molecules, which can melt metal and burn a meteorite, can kill the inhabitants of a space ship. This problem exists, for the most part, only at the beginnings and endings of voyages. Special materials have been developed that withstand great heat or melt and flow in a controlled fashion that helps dissipate heat. The heat shield of U.S. space capsules (Fig. 24-13) uses such materials. Also, special techniques of moving in and out of the atmosphere are being explored.

Heat from solar radiation, however, lasts through an entire voyage. Without air to disperse and absorb radiated heat, objects in space could boil one moment and freeze the next. In a space ship, the surface facing the sun is very hot; the side in shadow is well below freezing.

Children should review the relation of dark and light colors to temperature (Chapters 13 and 17). Space suits reflect the sun's rays from their surface and have devices for heating the inside. Space ships use a special white reflecting paint or checkerboard design.

Undiminished solar radiation in space, while a problem, is also a boon to space travelers, since special devices (Fig. 24-14) are used to convert it directly to electricity. Some day the slight pressure radiation exerts may drive a space ship.

Being airless, space presents another problem, a seeming contradiction. Although the light of the sun is intense, most of the rest of space is jet black. On Earth, light flows all about us because dust particles and the molecules of the air scatter light, sending it off in every direction. Shadows are dark, but not so black that nothing can be seen in them. In space there is only the incredible glare of the sun and impenetrable shadows—no grays, no shadings. Stars do not twinkle, but are unblinking, sharp, and bright in an eternity of black velvet. It is the effect of air molecules and of dust that give us the blue sky and the colors of sunset respectively. It is air that makes it possible to walk about without special

FIGURE **24-13** An Apollo spacecraft shortly after its flight. The heat shield, partially melted and burned away, is the large dark disk being touched by the man at the center of the picture.

shielding against the sun's intensity. In space, special glass and lenses are necessary for survival.

Weightlessness

Children may be able to sense weightlessness at the top of a jump. Those who have been in a quickly descending elevator will recall momentary experiences of near weightlessness. Anyone who has been in a small plane during a "nose-over" will never forget how unattached objects momentarily floated in air.

This feeling of weightlessness can be very confusing to our posture sense—our sense of balance. However, there is much evidence that most people can, with training, learn not only to deal with weightlessness, but actually to enjoy being freed from the tyranny of gravity. It has offered little in the way of physiological problems to astronauts. During long voyages, however, unused muscles—those used on Earth to hold us up against the pull of gravity—may become weak and flabby. Consequently, such voyagers may have to exercise frequently if they are not to become so weak they cannot stand or walk once they return to Earth. Point out that even a few weeks spent confined to bed can make it hard to walk about.

SPACE AND TOMORROW

Undoubtedly what has been done so far is only a beginning. So far no impenetrable barrier has been found which would forever bar man from space beyond the moon. Even though radiation is intense and there are giant steps yet to be made before an efficient, economical motor for space is perfected, the host of problems is within man's capacity to solve.

We have intentionally been very general in our review of getting man into space. All science and technology are growing rapidly, but the pace of space knowledge is breath-taking. Today all attempts to reach and probe beyond the atmosphere use the rapid-thrust rocket. Speed is ac-

FIGURE **24-14** A meteorological satellite, showing the large panels at right and left that contain the cells that convert solar radiation to electricity.

quired in the first few minutes of flight, and the rest of the rocket's trip is coasted—negotiated by momentum, except for small rockets used to reduce speed and for navigation course correction. To escape the earth's attraction, a rapid-thrust rocket or group of rockets arranged piggyback must acquire a speed of 25,000 miles per hour in the first few minutes. Yet it may be that the final answer will lie with space ships whose takeoff is relatively slow but which maintain a slow but steady acceleration. A space ship can get to the moon—and to Mars or Venus by going 25,000 miles per hour. But one can also make the trip by the application of low but continued thrust. We have avoided describing particular rockets, particular technological methods, since these change rapidly. Many of the current space handbooks (often in paperback editions) provide specific and valuable data. New books of this sort are published frequently. See also the bibliography.

SUGGESTED PROJECTS

1. Have children make two lists: one that contains ways in which gravity may help man, and the other of ways in which it may hinder man. Lead into the study of gravity and its effects.

2. Have children consider why racing cars, which are required to make sharp turns at high speeds, are extremely low and use wide-tread tires. Lead into discussion of center of gravity, inertia, and friction.

3. A library research project in the investigation of gravity by men not thought of as scientists (for example, Leonardo da Vinci) may interest an older child.

4. Many children may have heard the report made by airplanes as they penetrate the sound barrier. Lead into discussion of that and shock waves.

5. Children may be able to list sources of radiation similar to that in space—for example, the X-ray devices used by doctors and dentists, heat and "ultraviolet" lamps, and nuclear reactors.

6. Consider the effect of rapid acceleration in an automobile or train and lead into the cause of the greater but similar effects experienced by astronauts at launching of the space craft.

BIBLIOGRAPHY

(**P** indicates recommended for primary grades, **I** for intermediate grades, **U** for upper grades.)

Asimov, Isaac, *Satellites In Outer Space*, rev. ed., Random, 1964. Simple explanations of gravity, orbits, and natural and manmade satellites. Emphasizes how the latter are used to further scientific knowledge. Well illustrated and indexed. **U**

Bergaust, Erik, ed., *Illustrated Space Encyclopedia*, Putnam, 1965. Definitions of aerospace terms not likely to be found in a standard dictionary. Photographs and drawings of aerospace devices, installations, and activities. **U**

Branley, Franklyn M., *Book of Astronauts for You*, Crowell, 1963. Discusses selection and training of astronauts, their duties, and the capsule's limited capacity. Illustrated with drawings and diagrams. **I**

———, *Experiments in the Principles of Space Travel*, Crowell, 1955. Well-designed experiments showing the principles of space travel. **U**

Bruce, Lois, *Space ABC*, Bobbs-Merrill, 1967. Excellent compilation of photographs about space, with a description of each using many space terms. **U**

Carona, Philip B., *Magic Mixtures: Alloys and Plastics*, Prentice-Hall, 1963. Historical approach to the creation of improved materials. One chapter deals with the importance of alloys and plastics to the space program. **U**

Chester, Michael, *Rockets and Spacecraft of the World*, Norton, 1964. Information on rockets, missiles, and satellites, the history and potential of each vehicle and an explanation of the various types of fuel and guidance systems. Many graphs and comparative tables, 90 photographs, bibliography, and an index. **U**

Colby, Carroll B., *Our Space Age Jets*, Coward-McCann, 1959. Describes and gives statistics on different kinds of jet aircraft. **U**

Coombs, Charles, *Aerospace Power*, Morrow, 1966. A pictorial guide to recent aerospace achievements, with 362 photographs of all types of aircraft, missiles, and satellites. **U**

———, *Project Apollo: Mission to the Moon*, Morrow, 1965. Simple, yet accurate coverage of Apollo from take-off to lunar landing and return to Earth. Well illustrated. **U**

Crosby, Alexander, *The World of Rockets*, Random, 1965. A brief historical survey of rocket travel and a projection into the future. Well illustrated. **I**

Englebrektson, Sune, *Gravity at Work and Play*, Holt, Rinehart and Winston, 1963. A simple, easily understood presentation of the concept of gravity and its effects. Meaningful color illustrations. **I**

Feravolo, Rocco, *Wonders of Gravity*, Dodd, Mead, 1965. Clearly presented material on such aspects of the subject as the relationship of gravity to

weight, falling bodies, pendulums, projectiles, orbits, and space stations. Simple but effective experiments and meaningful illustrations. **U**

Fischer, Vera, *One Way is Down: A Book About
Gravity*, Little, Brown, 1967. The concept *gravity*
is developed from the concrete to the abstract using
many examples. The word *force* is explained and
used with great clarity. **I**

Freeman, Mae, *A Book of Real Science*, Four Winds,
1966. A simply written guide to a few basic physical
science concepts. The format of concluding each
chapter with a question provides a stimulus for the
reader. The subjects discussed are atoms, molecules,
sound, gravity, and the utilization of these concepts
in space exploration. **I**

———, *You Will Go to the Moon*, Random, 1959.
Simple but effective treatment of how an actual
trip to the moon feels. **P**

Gallant, Roy A., *Man's Reach into Space*, Doubleday,
1964. A profusely illustrated, oversize volume with
a detailed index, describes some space flights. **U**

Goodwin, Harold L., *All About Rockets and Space
Flight*, Random, 1964. A description of the major
space vehicles of today, their history and operation,
and the exploration of outer space. Glossary and
illustrations. **U**

Gottlieb, William P., *Jets and Rockets and How They
Work*, Doubleday, 1959. Many interesting and instructive experiments on all phases of aeronautics. **U**

———, *Space Flight and How It Works*, Doubleday, 1963. Pictures and text give a step-by-step
explanation of space flight, and simple experiments demonstrate the principles involved. **U**

Joseph, Alexander, *Rockets into Space*, Science Research Associates, 1962.

Kane, Elmer R., *What is Space?*, Benefic, 1962. A brief
discussion of space and space technology with color
illustrations, including drawings, diagrams, and
charts. **I**

Keen, Martin, *The Wonders of Space Rockets, Missiles
& Spacecraft*, Grosset & Dunlap, 1967. Emphasis
is on recent achievements in astrodynamics and the
problems involved in space travel. Excellent photographs and diagrams. **U**

Lauber, Patricia, *Big Dreams and Small Rockets: A
Short History of Space Travel*, Crowell, 1965. Explains the development of rocketry and its uses,
including some information on the men who discovered and developed the principles. Illustrated
with photographs and drawings. **U**

Lewellen, John, *You and Space Travel*, Children's Pr.,
1958. Describes the principles of flight and their
application to space travel. **U**

Parker, Bertha, *Gravity*, Harper & Row, 1959. Simple,
well-defined explanation of gravity. **U**

Pondendorf, Illa, *The True Book of Space*, Children's
Pr., 1959. Beginning book on satellites, space,
travel, and rockets. **I**

Posin, David, *Exploring and Understanding Rockets
and Satellites*, Benefic, 1967. Explains how a rocket
generates thrust and a satellite stays in orbit. A
number of questions, problems, and experiments
conclude each chapter. **U**

Posin, Daniel Q., *What is Energy?*, Benefic, 1962. A
brief introduction to such aspects of the subject
as energy produced by the sun, electrical and magnetic energy, atomic and nuclear sources of energy,
and possible future sources. **U**

Sparks, James C., Jr., *Gyroscopes: What They Are and
How They Work*, Dutton, 1963. Basic material on
the workings of the gyroscope, its uses at sea, the
first automatic pilot, in rockets and missiles, how
they are used by astronauts and X-15 pilots, and
some possible uses of gyroscopic instruments. **U**

Verral, Charles S., *Go! The Story of Outer Space*,
Prentice-Hall, 1962. An introduction to the subject
that includes a short history of rocketry, information
about U.S. astronauts, and scientific principles involved. **U**

Vries, Leonard de, *The Second Book of Experiments*,
Macmillan, 1964. Seventy two simple experiments
requiring only readily obtainable materials divided
into the following groups: force, sound, gases, liquids, and heat. For each experiment the author lists
the necessary materials, gives a clear explanation,
and presents the underlying scientific principle. **U**

Wells, Robert, *Electronics, Key to Exploring Space*,
Dodd, Mead, 1964. An analysis of the role electronics plays in the conquest of space, with emphasis
on current studies, and possible future applications. **U**

Reference Information

METRIC SYSTEM

Length

1 centimeter (cm) = 10 millimeters (mm)
1 decimeter (dm) = 10 centimeters
1 meter (m) = 10 decimeters
1 dekameter (dkm) = 10 meters
1 hectometer (hm) = 10 dekameters
1 kilometer (km) = 10 hectometers

Area

1 square centimeter (cm^2) = 100 square millimeters (mm^2)
1 square decimeter (dm^2) = 100 square centimeters
1 square meter (m^2) = 100 square decimeters
1 are (a) = 100 square meters
1 hectare (ha) = 100 ares
1 square kilometer (km^2) = 100 hectares

Volume

1 cubic centimeter° (cm^3) = 1000 cubic millimeters (mm^3)
1 cubic decimeter (dm^3) = 1000 cubic centimeters
1 cubic meter (m^3) = 1 stere (st) = 1000 cubic decimeters

Capacity

1 centiliter (cl) = 10 milliliters (ml)
1 deciliter (dl) = 10 centiliters
1 liter (l) = 10 deciliters
1 dekaliter (dkl) = 10 liters
1 hectoliter (hl) = 10 dekaliters
1 kiloliter (kl) = 10 hectoliters

Weight

1 centigram (cg) = 10 milligrams (mg)
1 decigram (dg) = 10 centigrams
1 gram (g) = 10 decigrams
1 dekagram (dkg) = 10 grams
1 hectogram (hg) = 10 dekagrams
1 kilogram (kg) = 10 hectograms
1 metric ton (t) = 1000 kilograms

° 1 milliliter = 1.000027 cubic centimeters. For all practical purposes they are equivalent.

EQUIVALENTS OF METRIC AND COMMON OR ENGLISH SYSTEMS

Length and Area

1 millimeter (mm) = 0.03937 inch (in)

1 centimeter (cm) = 0.3937 inch

1 meter (m) = 39.37 inches = 3.2808 feet (ft)

1 kilometer (km) = 0.6214 mile

1 inch = 2.54 centimeters

1 foot = 30.48 centimeters

1 yard (yd) = 91.44 centimeters
= 0.9144 meter

1 mile = 1.6093 kilometers

1 square centimeter (sq cm) = 0.155 square inch (sq in)

1 square meter (m²) = 1550.0 square inches
= 10.764 square feet (sq ft)
= 1.196 square yards (sq yd)

1 square inch = 6.4516 square centimeters

1 square yard = 0.8361 square meter

Volume and Capacity

1 cubic centimeter (cc) = 0.0610 cubic inches (cu in)

1 cubic meter (m³) = 35.3145 cubic feet (cu ft)
= 1.3079 cubic yards (cu yd)

1 cubic inch = 16.3872 cubic centimeters

1 cubic yard = 0.7646 cubic meter

1 milliliter (ml) = 0.2705 fluid dram (fl dr)
= 0.0338 fluid ounce (fl oz)

1 liter = 33.8148 fluid ounces
= 2.1134 pints (pt)
= 1.0567 quarts (qt)
= 0.2642 gallon (gal)

1 fluid dram = 3.697 milliliters

1 fluid ounce = 29.573 milliliters

1 quart = 946.332 milliliters

1 gallon = 3.785 liters

1 cubic inch (cu in) = 16.387 milliliters

1 cubic foot (cu ft) = 28.316 liters

Weight

1 gram (g) = 15.432 grains (gr)
= 0.03527 avoirdupois ounce (avdp oz)
= 0.03215 apothecaries' or troy ounce

1 kilogram (kg) = 35.274 avoirdupois ounces
= 32.151 apothecaries' or troy ounces
= 2.2046 avoirdupois pounds (avdp lb)
= 2.6792 apothecaries' or troy pounds

1 grain = 64.7989 milligrams (mg)

1 avoirdupois ounce = 28.3495 grams

1 apothecaries' or troy ounce = 31.1035 grams

1 avoirdupois pound = 453.5924 grams

1 apothecaries' or troy pound = 373.2418 grams

EQUIVALENTS OF KITCHEN AND OTHER MEASURES

1 small test tube ≅ 30 milliliters (ml)

1 large test tube ≅ 70 milliliters

1 tumbler or 1 cup = 16 tablespoons (tbsp)
= 8 fluid ounces (fl oz)
= ½ pint (pt)
≅ 240 milliliters

1 teacup ≅ 4 fluid ounces = 120 milliliters

1 tablespoon ≅ ½ fluid ounce ≅ 16 milliliters

1 teaspoon (tsp) ≅ 4 milliliters
≅ 60 drops (depending on bore of medicine dropper)

1 milliliter ≅ 25 drops (depending on size of bore)

1 dime° ≅ 2.5 grams

1 penny ≅ 3.25 grams

1 nickel ≅ 5.0 grams

1 quarter ≅ 6.5 grams

1 half dollar ≅ 13.0 grams

1 silver dollar ≅ 26.0 grams

° About 1 mm thick.

FORMULAS FOR VOLUME OR SURFACE

$\pi = 3.1416$
Circumference of a circle $= \pi d = 2\pi r$
Area of a circle $= \pi r^2$
Surface area of a cylinder $= \pi dh = 2\pi rh$
Volume of a cylinder $= \pi r^2 h$
Surface area of a sphere $= 4\pi r^2$
Volume of a sphere $= \frac{4}{3}\pi r^3$

POWERS OF TEN

$10^0 = 1$	$10^0 = 1$
$10^1 = 10$	$10^{-1} = 0.1$
$10^2 = 100$	$10^{-2} = 0.01$
$10^3 = 1000$	$10^{-3} = 0.001$
$10^4 = 10,000$	$10^{-4} = 0.0001$
$10^6 = 1$ million	$10^{-6} = $ one millionth
$10^9 = 1$ billion	$10^{-9} = $ one billionth

WAVELENGTHS OF VARIOUS RADIATIONS

Radiation	Ångström units (Å)°
Cosmic rays	0.0005 and under
Gamma rays	0.005–1.40
X-rays	0.1–100
Ultraviolet	2920–4000
Visible spectrum	4000–7000
Violet	4000–4240
Blue	4240–4912
Green	4912–5750
Yellow	5750–5850
Orange	5850–6470
Red	6470–7000
Limit of human vision	5560
Infrared	over 7000

° To convert to inches, multiply by 3.937×10^{-9}; to convert to centimeters, multiply by 1×10^{-8}.

GREEK ALPHABET

Capital	Lower Case	
A	α	alpha
B	β	beta
Γ	γ	gamma
Δ	δ	delta
E	ϵ	epsilon
Z	ζ	zeta
H	η	eta
Θ	θ	theta
I	ι	iota
K	κ	kappa
Λ	λ	lambda
M	μ	mu
N	ν	nu
Ξ	ξ	xi
O	o	omicron
Π	π	pi
P	ρ	rho
Σ	σ	sigma
T	τ	tau
Υ	υ	upsilon
Φ	ϕ	phi
X	χ	chi
Ψ	ψ	psi
Ω	ω	omega

SPECIFIC GRAVITY* OF SOME COMMON MATERIALS (grams per cc at 20°C)

Acetone	0.79	Magnesium	1.74
Agate	2.5–2.6	Marble	2.7
Alcohol (95%)	0.81	Mercury	13.6
Aluminum	2.7	Milk	1.03
Brass	8.5	Mortar	1.44–1.6
Butter	0.86	Nickel	8.8
Brick (common)	1.79	Opal	2.1–2.3
Carbon tetrachloride	1.6	Osmium	22.5
Celluloid	1.4	Paraffin	0.82–0.94
Cement	2.8	Plaster of Paris	1.18–1.28
Clay	1.92–2.4	Platinum	21.4
Coal (anthracite)	1.5	Polystyrene	1.06
Coal (bituminous)	1.3	Porcelain	2.38
Concrete	1.92–2.24	Quartz	2.6
Copper	8.9	Rock salt	2.1–2.2
Cork	0.22–0.26	Rubber (gum)	0.92
Diamond	3.1–3.5	Sand	1.44–1.76
Earth (loose)	1.15–1.28	Sea water	1.03
Earth (packed)	1.44–1.76	Silver	10.5
Gasoline	0.68	Slate	2.72–2.88
German silver	8.4	Steel	7.8
Glass (common)	2.5	Sulfur (roll)	2.0
Gold	19.3	Tile	1.76–1.92
Granite	2.7	Tin	7.3
Graphite	2.2	Tungsten	18.8
Gravel	1.6–1.92	Wood	
Gypsum	2.32	balsa	0.16
Human body (normal)	1.07	red oak	0.67
Human body (when lungs are filled)	1.00	rock elm	0.76
Ice	0.92	southern pine	0.56
Iron	7.9	white pine	0.4
Lead	11.3	Zinc	7.1
Limestone	2.7		

*The ratio of the weight of any volume of a substance to the weight of an equal volume of water, taken as 1—thus, the ratio of the density of a substance to the density of water. Values differ for substances of variable composition.

TEMPERATURE CONVERSION

To convert Fahrenheit into centigrade temperatures (and vice versa), all that need be remembered is that $0°C = 32°F$ (the freezing point of water) and that each Fahrenheit degree is only $\frac{5}{9}$ of a centigrade degree. Thus to convert Fahrenheit to centigrade temperature, subtract 32 and take $\frac{5}{9}$ of the remainder. To convert centigrade to Fahrenheit, multiply by $\frac{9}{5}$ and add 32. Conversions can be read directly from the illustration on this page simply by reading directly across from one thermometer scale to the other. The simple formulations for conversion are as follows:

$$°F = °C \times \tfrac{9}{5} + 32$$
$$°C = °F - 32 \times \tfrac{5}{9}$$

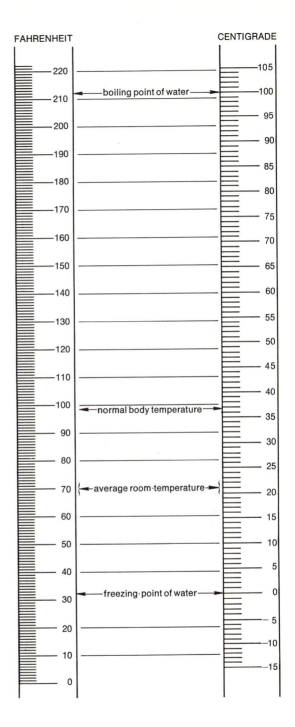

Directory of Manufacturers, Distributors, and Supply Houses

Several companies provide general supplies and equipment for all areas of science; others specialize in one or another area, as noted. All suppliers will send catalogs on request; many also offer useful free or inexpensive booklets, charts, films, filmstrips, etc. To avoid discontinuation of these services because of overuse, the teacher should discourage their use by students.

DIRECTORY

Allied Radio Corp., 833 N. Jefferson Boulevard, Chicago, Ill. 60610. Radio and electronic equipment, meters, etc.

America Basic Science Club, 501 E. Crockett, San Antonio, Tex. 78202. Kits and manuals on physics projects.

Baker Science Packets, 650 Concord Drive, Holland, Mich. 49423. Card file of 153 indexed science experiments.

Cambosco Scientific Co., 37 Antwerp Street, Brighton, Mass. 02135. General.

Carolina Biological Supply Co., 2700 York Road, Burlington, N.C. 27215. Biological apparatus, supplies, living and preserved specimens, models, charts.

Castolite Co., Woodstock, Ill. 60098. Plastics for imbedding and molding.

Central Scientific Co., 2600 S. Kostner Road, Chicago, Ill. 60613; 79 Amherst Street, Cambridge, Mass. 02143; 6446 Telegraph Road, Los Angeles, Calif. 90022. Hobby kits for electronics, medicine, geology, optics, weather. General.

John Cunningham, 23280 Mobile Street, Canoga Park, Calif. 91304. Monthly packets containing equipment, specimens, chemicals.

Denoyer-Geppert Co., 5235–39 Ravenswood Avenue, Chicago, Ill. 60640. Biological models, charts on biology and astronomy.

Difco Laboratories, Inc., 920 Henry Street, Detroit, Mich. 48201. Culture media and reagents.

Eastman Kodak Co., Rochester, N.Y. 14608. Photographic supplies, equipment, and literature.

Edmund Scientific Co., 555 Edscorp Bldg., Barrington, N.J. 08007. Optical apparatus and supplies.

Ronald Eyrich, 1091 N. 48th Street, Milwaukee, Wisc. 53208. Alnico permanent magnets.

Fisher Scientific Co., 711 Forbes Street, Pittsburgh, Pa. 15219; 635 Greenwich Street, New York, N.Y. 10014. Molecular models.

General Biological Supply House, 8200 S. Hoyne Avenue, Chicago, Ill. 60620. Biological apparatus, supplies, living and preserved specimens, models, charts.

A. C. Gilbert Co., New Haven, Conn. Toy microscope sets, tool cabinets, model telephone and electric construction sets, chemical laboratories.

C. S. Hammond Co., Maplewood, N.J. 07040. Space and weather kits, color maps.

Heath Co., Benton Harbor, Mich. 49022. "Build-it-yourself" electronic instrument kits.

"Industrial America," Inc., Merchandise Mart Plaza, Chicago, Ill. 60654. Educational hobby kits on physiology, light, meteorology, mineralogy, electronics.

Los Angeles Biological Laboratories, 2977 W. 14th Street, Los Angeles, Calif. 90006. Biological apparatus, supplies, living and preserved specimens, models, charts.

Macalaster-Bicknell Co., 253 Norfolk Street, Cambridge, Mass. 02139. General.

Models of Industry, Inc., 2100 Fifth Street, Berkeley, Calif. 94710. Three handbooks and 200 essential pieces of equipment for 80 activities beginning in primary grades. In three parts, for use in three separate classrooms.

Mountcastle Map Co., 1437 E. 12th Street, Cleveland, Ohio 44114. Markable maps and charts.

National Audubon Society, 1130 Fifth Avenue, New York, N.Y. 10028. Inexpensive nature charts and bulletins.

Nature Games, 8339 W. Dry Creek Road, Healdsburg, Calif. 95448. Card games using colorful, authentic pictures.

A. J. Nystrom and Co., 3333 Elston Avenue, Chicago, Ill. 60618. Biological models, charts on health, biological sciences, general science, atmosphere, and weather.

Plastics Center, 138 S. Alvarado, Los Angeles, Calif. 90057. Plastic materials including beads suitable for making simple microscopes.

Product Design Co., 2769 Middlefield Road, Redwood City, Calif. 94063. Kits for teaching electricity, chemistry, physics, conservation. Working models for student experiments.

Revell Co., Venice, Calif. 90291. Models of atomic power plants, nuclear submarines, space stations.

Ross Allen's Reptile Institute, Silver Springs, Fla. 32688.

Harry Ross, 61 Reade Street, New York, N.Y. 10007. Microscopes and telescopes, science and laboratory apparatus.

Hy Ruchlis' Book-Lab, Inc., 144 37th Street, Brooklyn, N.Y. 11218.

Sargent–Welch Co., 4647 Foster Avenue, Chicago, Ill. 60630. General.

Science Associates, P.O. Box 230-S, Princeton, N.J. 08540. Instruments and teaching aids for meteorology, astronomy, optics, and earth sciences.

Science Electronics, Inc., P.O. Box 237, Huntington, N.Y. 11743. "Breadboard"-type kits for teaching radio, electricity, electronics.

Science Kit, Box 69, Tonowanda, N.Y. 04150. Standard laboratory equipment, teacher's manual, astronomy manual and star chart.

Standard Oil of Calif., Public Relations, 225 Bush Street, San Francisco, Calif. 94104. Teaching materials and services.

Stansi Scientific Co., 1231 N. Honore Street, Chicago, Ill. 60622. Teaching kits in electricity and elec-

tronics. Science kits for use in elementary grades. General.

Taylor Instrument Co., 95 Ames Street, Rochester, N.Y. 14601. Weather and temperature instruments.

Things of Science, Science Service, 1719 N Street, N.W., Washington, D.C. 20036. Monthly kits on various subjects.

Tracerlab, Inc., 130 High Street, Boston, Mass. 02110. Radioactivity apparatus.

Training Aid Studio, 2121 S. Josephine, Denver, Colo. 80210. Felt-O-Graph classroom aids: geology, coal and oil mining, airplane and rocket parts, biological cells.

Ward's Natural Science Establishment, Inc., P.O. Box 24, Beechwood Station, Rochester, N.Y. 14609. Teaching aids, charts, equipment, geology specimens, and other materials for teaching biological, natural, and earth sciences.

Weston Electrical Instrument Corp., 614 Frelinghuysen Avenue, Newark, N.J. 07114. Electrical instruments.

Wilkens-Anderson Co., 4525 W. Division Street, Chicago, Ill. 60651. Semimicro apparatus and equipment for chemistry.

REFERENCE AIDS

Many compilations of free and inexpensive materials have been published; a few follow.

Beuschlein, Muriel, *Free and Inexpensive Materials for Teaching Conservation and Resource-Use*, National Association of Biology Teachers, P.O. Box 2073, Ann Arbor, Mich. 48106. 1954. 50 pp.

———, and J. Sanders, "Free and Inexpensive Teaching Materials for Science Education," *Chicago Schools Journal*, Vol. 34, Nos. 5, 6, 1953. Available as reprint.

Cardoza, P., *A Wonderful World for Children*, Bantam, 1956. $1.50.

Choosing Free Materials for Use in the Schools, National Education Association, Washington, D.C., 1955. 24 pp., 50¢. Issued by the American Association of School Administrators. Avoids those that contain obvious advertising or biased information.

Conservation Teaching Aids, Michigan Dept. of Conservation, Education Division, Ann Arbor, Mich., 1951.

Educators' Progress Service Annual, Educators' Progress Service, Randolph, Wisc. 53956. Yearly revision.

Guide to free curriculum materials.

Fowlkes, John G., et al., *Elementary Teachers' Guide to Free Curriculum Materials*, Educators' Progress Service, Randolph, Wisc. 53956. 348 pp., $6.50.

Free and Inexpensive Instruction Aids, Bruce Miller Publishers, Box 369, Riverside, Calif. 92502.

Free and Inexpensive Learning Materials, George Peabody College for Teachers, Nashville, Tenn. 37203, 1960. $1.50.

General Motors Aids to Educators, General Motors Corp., Willow Run, Mich. 48197, 1956.

Health Materials and Resources for Oregon Teachers, State Dept. of Education, Salem, Ore., 1955.

Hobby Publications, Superintendent of Documents, U.S. Govt. Printing Office, Washington, D.C. 20401.

Holland, C., *Free and Inexpensive Teaching Aids for High Schools*, National Association of Secondary School Principals, NEA, 1201 Sixteenth Street, N.W., Washington, D.C. 20036. 1949. $1.00.

Hough, John B., ed., *Something for Nothing for Your Classroom*, Curriculum Laboratory, Div. of Secondary Education, Temple Univ., Philadelphia, Pa. 19122, 1957. $1.00.

Phillips, Brose, *Index to Free Teaching Aids*, Free Teaching Aids Co., Harrisburg, Ill. 62946.

Salisbury, Gordon, and Robert Sheridan, *Catalog of Free Teaching Aids*, P.O. Box 943, Riverside, Calif. 92502, $1.50.

Science Service Aids to Youth, Science Service, 1719 N Street, N.W., Washington, D.C. 20036.

Sources of Free and Inexpensive Educational Materials, Field Enterprises, Merchandise Mart Plaza, Chicago, Ill. 60654, 1958. $5.00.

Sources of Free and Inexpensive Materials in Health Education, Curriculum Laboratory, Teachers College, Temple Univ., Philadelphia, Pa. 19122, 1954. 25¢.

Sources of Free and Inexpensive Pictures for the Classroom, Bruce Miller Publishers, Box 369, Riverside, Calif. 92502, 1956. 50¢.

Sources of Free and Low-Cost Materials, Civil Aeronautics Administration, U.S. Dept. of Commerce, Washington, D.C. 20428.

Sponsors Handbook, Science Service, 1719 N Street, N.W., Washington, D.C. 20036. 1957. 25¢.

Teaching Aids, Westinghouse Electrical Corp., School Service, 306 4th Avenue, Pittsburgh, Pa. 15222.

Thousands of Science Projects, Science Service, 1719 N Street, N.W., Washington, D.C. 20036. 1957. 25¢.

Using Free Materials in the Classroom, Association of Supervision and Curriculum Development, NEA, 1201 Sixteenth Street, N.W., Washington, D.C. 20036. 1953. 75¢.

Vertical File Index, H. W. Wilson Co., New York, N.Y. Monthly listings of inexpensive materials.

Weisinger, M., *1001 Valuable Things Free*, Bantam, 1957.

Williams, C., *Sources of Teaching Materials*, Bureau of Educational Research, Ohio State Univ., Columbus, Ohio, 1955.

Wittich, W. A., and G. L. Hanson, *Educators' Guide to Free Tapes, Scripts and Transcriptions*, Educators' Progress Service, Randolph, Wisc. 53956.

Worksheets for Use in Constructing Science Equipment, Los Angeles County Superintendent of Schools, January, 1955. 40 pp. Illustrated worksheets with lists of materials and construction directions.

Using the Classroom

BULLETIN BOARDS

Grade-school children can often carry on the work, planning, and execution of bulletin board displays. It is hard but rewarding labor to think out and collect the material for a good display and change it often enough to keep it from becoming "wallpaper." Some teachers use more than one kind of bulletin board: one may summarize the results of some particular study, so that the group can realize its accomplishments; another may be the children's own board to be arranged as *they* wish. A classroom teacher° described the latter kind (as well as a third type) as follows:

> To the children it is not a clutter; rather it is filled with vastly interesting items that are not propounded by the school. Perhaps there is something psychological about this; perhaps that's what keeps the interest high. At any rate, the standards are theirs, both in methods and materials.
>
> The little fellow who can't bring himself to stand before the group to "show and tell" will draw a picture and pin it on this board, probably when nobody is watching him. Some youngsters cut from magazines and newspapers pictures and articles about special interests that are never mentioned in class—subjects that may be a far cry from the curriculum outlined for the grade. Yet a little imagination and ingenuity can pull these unlikes into interesting relationships. For example, a sixth grade I knew was studying Greece, but

Peter had disoriented himself from the group for days. His contributions to the clutter board had been several star maps and an article about a planetarium. A book containing star myths by the ancients was the tie that once more bound him to the group. (This sort of thing happens when one takes time to look at the children's board and to note who offered the materials on display.)

Neatness of the clutter board will vary according to age and ability. Middle graders have a strong sense of design as well as fair play. They will not allow monopolies. Sometimes children will choose a class member they look up to for fair play and quiet leadership. They are occasionally quicker than the teacher to see in someone an aptitude for neat lettering and effective arrangements. Or it may be the teacher who will choose a child for this type of ability not yet recognized by his classmates who may excel him in other things. Primary children need a helping hand— when they ask for it. A committee or manager may have to be chosen to keep things under control and see that old items are removed and reclaimed by their owners. I find this works better when instigated as a result of difficulties. If too many restrictions are set up in the beginning and it becomes a chore, the clutter board will be short-lived and unproductive. Duration of display, spacing, mounting, and labeling offer opportunities for problem solving and group work. The children are brought together by sharing interests, and often are stimulated to discover and develop new ones.

Type three is my own board, and I am as jealous of it as the children are of theirs. Here I can do

° Patricia Adams, *Schoolroom Science Center*, Cornell Rural School Leaflet, Teacher's Number, Vol. 49, No. 1, Fall, 1955, pp. 28–30.

what I wish, from some "terribly clever" review of an old and troublesome lesson, to ideas for modern art or stimulus for a new science project. I can be formal or informal; I can arrange it myself or assign it to a class committee who will work under my direction. I prefer to have my board at or near the front of the room, where the wandering eye comes to rest most often; for I like to think, at least, that this silent teaching has several effects; that it gives a sense of orderliness of color and arrangement (I sometimes go so far as to measure distances) and that it stimulates thinking. I can use every trick of the trade from peep shows to 3-D to create interest. A shoe box with a window cut in it may harbor anything from a small living creature to an important notice I want everybody to read. Small shelves can be built of oak tag or construction paper to hold "real" objects, or they can be wired or pinned on. Questions and captions can be devised to lead to experiments, to observations, or to the use of books available close by. Often a series lesson can be taught with nothing more than good pictures and captions: papermaking from the forest to the mill, with a follow-up study of paper products. (I have found follow-up lessons useful and rewarding, for they tell me who has done the work in this particular field, and how much understanding has been gained.) This bulletin board has offered a satisfying way to deal with questions that arose from small groups and which could not be handled adequately in class time. Maple syrup from tree to pancakes, milk from cow to dinner table, a letter from mailbox to mailbox—social studies, science, arithmetic, spelling—all find a place on my board and appeal to some in the group. To try to reach everybody every time is to court despair. Certain things everyone must do, such as march in a fire drill and learn the multiplication tables; but bulletin boards to be fun must have strong interest appeal. If they look like fun and lead to individual activities, most of the children will be interested most of the time. The bulletin board is often the answer for "What shall I do when I have nothing to do?"

Good ideas on my board often carry over to the clutter board. Through the year choice of materials, labels, use of colors for mounting, and effectiveness in arrangement improve. Indeed I have found more than once that some of the best ideas for display do not emanate from my board. I have found, above all, that "easy does it" in preparing a board. If it is as important as I think to have a fresh, new display often, then I cannot be a perfectionist in all things. It is important for me to be neat and accurate because my work must be a model in writing, lettering, spelling, and all the skill subjects I teach. I want to develop good taste insofar as I understand good taste. But I cannot and do not reletter an entire poem if one letter blurs, or send for a new ream of paper if one corner of the last sheet is torn. Neither do I ink over carefully penciled letters; I start with ink or crayon or whatever medium I have chosen. I find a kit handy, so that tools and materials can be kept in order, apart from the general classroom supplies. Mine was a cardboard box that contained a long-bladed scissors, a box of crayons, an alcohol pen, a ruler, some cut-out letters, thumb tacks, Scotch tape, and a small, firm brush I especially prefer for lettering. The kind of stapler that opens up flat cuts mounting time to almost nothing.

DISPLAYS AND EXHIBITS

A display may be anything from a few sea shells on a table to an elaborate exhibit in a glass case. The important thing is not the medium but the display. Generally it should be the child's work and appropriate to the current science unit. However, a wise teacher often makes room for irrelevant material because of its status value for the child who brought it. A real space saver for exhibiting such offerings is a vertical display case such as an old bookcase. Children can paint the shelves different colors in light shades. (Use rubber-base paints, for they dry quickly and are fireproof, odorless, washable, and the paint brushes can be washed out in warm water.) One shelf may be for shells, one for bird nests, one for rocks, one for reference books on science, and so on. Fasten cellophane sheets at the top to form windows that will protect the shelves from dust and still permit handling of the exhibits. Outline the objects in place on the shelves so that the children will know where to replace them and so that they will notice whether anything is missing. Appoint a team of rapid learners as junior curators of the "science corner." In the beginning, work with children to establish high standards of arrangement and labeling of materials. The writing of labels can be a valid and valuable group practice in language. Strive to encourage observation and accuracy by asking for labels that tell where and when the object was found and that, if possible, give a tentative classification pending conclusive identification. Use a section of a marked highway map to pinpoint the place of origin and add interest to the exhibit. Related science news and notices may be mounted on a piece of Cellotex or Bristol board set in an old picture frame repainted in bright colors.

Most children are collectors. A teacher's problem is not to get them to bring in materials for a science exhibit, but to help them select and organize their treasures. In East and West Coast schools, for example, the usual autumn flood of sea shells from summer beachcombing can be overwhelming and useless from an educational viewpoint. Permit only perfect specimens or one of a kind in an exhibit. Use cardboard egg cartons to exhibit up to twelve small shells. (The box cover is a good place for the labels.) Or spread sand on one exhibit shelf and put shells in the sand. Attach a strip of cardboard or wood to the edge of the shelf to prevent sand leakage. Children may want to paint a diorama background of summer sky.

Beware lest all exhibits illustrate biological science only. To avoid this one can encourage collections of other items—for example, electric light bulbs that illustrate the history of lighting. Many school systems have school service museums. State departments of education or conservation may have loan exhibits. Such material can be used to stimulate children to make their own exhibits, rather than to serve as the science exhibit per se. One teacher goes to a county museum every two weeks to borrow a stuffed bird or animal, an unusual shell or rock. This he exhibits with a slotted question box entitled "What is it?" to stimulate research and discussion that often are the most valuable by products of the device. At the end of the week the class examines the children's written answers and learns what the object really is.

Living displays such as fish and turtles may need window space for health as well as visibility. In any case, the owner and a responsible alternate should be appointed to give such exhibits the best of care. And it is better to change exhibits too frequently than too seldom. The same old dusty rocks in the "science corner" and half-dead plants in the window belie the living quality of interest that science should have for children. The spate of insects in glass jars, which often follows the sea shells in children's fall collections, can very quickly become worthless. The insects can teach the children only as long as the children are interested in them—a week or two at most; then the insects should travel home or outdoors in plastic rather than glass containers. Information for collectors of rocks, insects, feathers, leaves, and small animals is summarized on the following two pages.

THE SCIENCE DISCOVERY TABLE

Many classrooms today have a large work table with multiple uses. When there is a need to use it for science, plastic will preserve the finish. Orange crates at the corners may provide storage space for simple science equipment. A slightly remodeled cafeteria cart may afford storage space below and work or demonstration space on top, all on four wheels. Here again, linoleum or a similar protection for the top will prove of value. Small items—for instance, electric plugs, switches, doorbells, and so on—tend to disappear unless they are fastened to stiff, heavy cardboard that can be stored vertically until needed.

Some teachers store materials for related areas of investigation in shoeboxes—one for magnets, one for flight, one for insects, and so on. One scientific supply house markets a mobile science lab table. It is about the size and shape of a cafeteria cart. The inner cupboards are filled with plastic hydrator boxes, each holding a different kind of equipment.

A rack made of dowels attached to a board at about a 45° angle permits the drying and storage of glassware as soon as it has been washed clean.

Some schools use central storage closets; one such was described as follows.°

> Just off the office is a supply room. The ditto machine is kept there, and many teachers use the room. Above the machine are shelves which hold the science books.
>
> As the teacher takes a book, she signs the card and drops it in a file box, replacing the card and book when she is through with it. The file box lists all the books arranged alphabetically by topic.
>
> Next to the ditto machine are many shelves which hold the science materials. Different types of materials are placed together. Materials for measuring will be on one shelf. Another shelf has all the electrical materials. Another has tools, and so on.
>
> Each object is marked with nail polish. If misplaced, it is easy to know where it belongs. On the front of the shelf there is a label for each object. It can be replaced in the right spot. At the side of each label is a hook with a string tag. This is also labeled. When the teacher takes a piece of equipment, she also removes the string tag with the name on it. This she hangs on a board by her name. When the equipment is returned, it and its tag are replaced on the proper shelf. If someone needs a piece of equipment that is not on the shelf, it is easy to check the board to see who has it.
>
> Partial list of science apparatus and materials:

> Electric hot plate
> Teakettle
> Sauce pans
> Cake pans
> Cookie sheet
> Pie tins
> Batteries (many)
> Sockets (many)
> Switches (many)
> Light bulbs (many)
> Thermometer (F, C, candy)
> Scales (spring, balance)

> Tape measure
> Measuring cups (various sizes)
> Measuring spoons (various sizes)
> Compass
> Magnets (horseshoe, bar—several)
> Lamp chimneys
> Flasks
> Beakers
> Rubber stoppers (with and without holes)
> Glass tubes
> Soda straws
> Bunsen burner or alcohol burner
> Prisms
> Magnifying glasses
> Microscope
> Plastic container (to hold water)
> Corks
> Sponges
> Pipe cleaners
> Balloons
> Rubber bands
> Tools
>> Hammer
>> Saw
>> Screwdrivers
>> Tin snips
>> Square
>> Paring knife
> Marbles
> Wheels
> Gears
> Springs
> Egg beater
> Scrap materials
> Spools
> Mailing tubes
> Wire
> Candles
> Vinegar
> Soda
> Limewater
> Food coloring
> Salt
> Sugar

In other schools one teacher and one class are designated the science distribution center for the school. The duties involved are often challenging to the children who learn and finish other work

---

° Marjorie Pursell, Oak Grove School, La Canada, California.

readily. One school has a room available for individual activities. The following description was contributed by a nonteaching observer:[*]

> The children sit at tables in the lab. The teacher has earlier listed on the blackboard the activities . . . leaving space for names under each entry. First she asks the children whether they wish to add any other activities to the list. . . . Then she asks who wishes to do what. Some activities, of course, are limited to a certain number of children. As each child indicates his choice, she writes his name under the particular heading on the board. Then she assigns tables for work. Before the work begins, the teacher invites questions concerning anything that the children do not understand. When their questions have been answered, the children go to work. They all know where the supplies are kept, and they obtain them before working and put them away afterward.

SAFETY SUGGESTIONS

1. Set an example by being careful.
2. When using matches, have a special place to dispose of them. (A large coffee can filled with sand is good.)
3. When heating objects, have tongs, pot holders, and asbestos pads close at hand.
4. When heating materials in test tubes, point the tubes away from *all* observers.
5. Heat evenly by rotating or moving the vessel being heated.
6. Use Pyrex or other heat-resistant glassware.
7. Place hot plate or burner where it cannot be knocked over.
8. Do not use cracked, chipped, or broken apparatus.
9. Use common sense to anticipate accidents.
10. Leave *nothing* (not even water) in an unmarked container.
11. Put away or dispose of all materials as soon as they have been used.
12. Smell or taste substances carefully—by wafting toward the face with the hand across the top of the container, or, with weak substances, by a quick pass under the nose.
13. Place a chair over extension cords so that no one will trip or step on the cord.

---

[*] Anna Greve, Elementary Science Supervisor, Bronxville Public Schools, Bronxville, N.Y.

SUMMERTIME SCIENCE COLLECTIONS

Rocks	Where to Look	Equipment Needed
	Around home, road cuts, excavations, quarries, hills, mountains	Hammer (geologist's or carpenter's), chisel, newspapers, cloth bag, notebook and pencil, compass, guidebook.
Insects	Almost everywhere—around home, fields, gardens, beaches, woods, ponds	Long-handled cloth net, flashlight, small glass bottles with covers, envelopes, pencil and paper, tweezers, magnifying glass, a glass bottle partly filled with 80–90% ethyl alcohol (killing jar), large sieve, cigar boxes, guidebook.
Feathers	Almost everywhere—fields, gardens, woods, near pools of water, places where birds dust themselves, and bird nests	Magnifying glass, envelopes, gummed tape, colored construction papers, guidebook.
Leaves	Almost everywhere—streets, woods, parks	Flat board, books, newspapers, gummed tape, colored construction papers, guidebook.
Animals (other than insects) in and near a pond	Near small ponds	Kitchen sieve or butterfly net, old sneakers, glass jars with covers, guidebook.

Chart adapted from *Singer Science News*, Vol. XII, No. 9, May 1959, pp. 2–3. Reproduced by permission of L. W. Singer Co.

How to Collect

Use hammer and chisel to collect samples about the size of walnuts. Be careful of flying chips. Do not collect too many specimens. Be selective. Number the sample with a numbered piece of adhesive tape, then wrap rock in newspaper. In a notebook, write the number, date, place collected, and kind of rock. Place samples in cloth bag.

Care of the Collection

Place specimens in compartmentalized trays. Use egg cartons or plastic trays. Number samples. Show the number of the rock, date, place collected, kind of rock, and name of collector on 3 × 5 index cards.

Use net for pursuing butterflies and other airborne insects and sieve for scooping insects from shallow pond water. Flashlight and glass jars are for collecting insects at night. Gather as wide a variety as possible. Place most insects in killing jar (see guidebook for directions for killing moths and butterflies). Remove with tweezers and store in envelopes until ready to mount. During collection, observe movements and feeding habits of live insects.

House insect collections in cigar boxes. Push a pin through the body of insect into cardboard placed on the bottom of the box. Arrange the pins in an orderly fashion. Make small cards which give information about the sample. Pierce the cards with the pin, and mount with the insect. Mount butterflies and moths on cotton in cigar boxes. Cover these mounts with cellophane or glass for permanence.

Store feathers in envelopes before mounting.

Mount feathers on colored construction paper with gummed tape. Label each sample.

Try to find leaves that have not been partly eaten by insects or damaged.

Place leaves on a thick layer of newspapers on a board. Cover the leaves with another layer of papers and then place about three heavy books on top. When the leaves are thoroughly dried, remove them from the paper press and with gummed tape attach them to sheets of colored paper. Record the names of the leaves and any other information on the papers.

Salamanders, turtles, snakes, et cetera can be found around and under logs and rocks near a pond's edge. Tadpoles, minnows, fairy shrimp, crayfish, et cetera are found in shallow water. Use hands or sieve or net to collect. Wear sneakers in the water to prevent cuts from rocks and debris. Place animals such as minnows, crayfish, and fairy shrimp in water in glass jars; place other animals in glass jars without water.

Place animals collected from the water in the pond in an aquarium, and animals collected near the pond's edge in a terrarium. (See text for instructions on how to make and maintain aquariums and terrariums.) When the animals have been studied, they should be returned to their natural homes.

Bibliography:
Books for a Science Library

STANDARD REFERENCES

Encyclopedias: General

Britannica Junior Encyclopedia (15 volumes). Chicago: Encyclopedia Britannica Educational Corp., 1968 edition.

Collier's Encyclopedia (24 volumes). New York: Collier-Macmillan International, 1967 edition.

Compton's Pictured Encyclopedia and Fact Index (15 volumes). Chicago: Encyclopedia Britannica Educational Corp., 1969 edition.

Encyclopedia Americana (30 volumes). New York: Grolier Educational Corp., 1969 edition.

Encyclopedia International (20 volumes). New York: Grolier Educational Corp. (reviewed annually).

New Book of Knowledge: The Children's Encyclopedia (20 volumes). New York: Grolier Educational Corp., 1967 edition.

World Book Encyclopedia (20 volumes). Chicago: Field Enterprises Corp., 1970 edition.

Encyclopedias: Science

Book of Popular Science (10 volumes). New York: Grolier Educational Corp., 1969 edition.

Harper Encyclopedia of Science (4 volumes). New York: Harper & Row, 1968.

McGraw-Hill Encyclopedia of Science and Technology (15 volumes). New York: McGraw-Hill Book Co., 1966.

Moments of Discovery (2 volumes). New York: Basic Books, Inc., 1958.

Our Wonderful World (18 volumes). New York: Grolier Educational Corp., 1968 edition.

Van Nostrand's Scientific Encyclopedia (1 volume). Princeton, N.J.: D. Van Nostrand Co., Inc., 1958, third edition.

Young People's Science Encyclopedia (20 volumes). Chicago: Children's Press, Inc., 1962.

Yearbooks

Educator's Guide to Free Science Materials. Randolph, Wisc.: Educator's Progress Service. A guide to selected films, filmstrips, slides, charts, bulletins, pamphlets, exhibits, posters, and books available free.

Information Please Almanac Atlas and Yearbook. New York: Simon and Schuster.

National Council for the Social Studies. "Science and the Social Studies," by Glen O. Blough. 27th Yearbook, Chapter 8. Washington, D.C.: National Education Association, 1957. 271 pp. A national authority's effort to develop a point of view on the issue of whether or not to fuse science and social studies.

National Society for the Study of Education. *Rethinking Science Education*. 59th Yearbook, Part I. Chicago: University of Chicago Press, 1960. 338 pp. National authorities discuss the role of science and give the directions and designs of modern thinking in science education.

Science Year: The World Book Science Annual. Chicago: Field Enterprises Educational Corp. 433 pp. Reviews the latest happenings in the world of science.

U.S. Department of Agriculture, *Yearbook of Agriculture*. Washington, D.C.: Superintendent of Documents: 1949, *Trees;* 1952, *Insects;* 1963, *A Place to*

430

Live; 1965, *Consumers All;* 1966, *Protecting Our Food;* 1967, *Outdoors USA.*

World Almanac and Book of Facts. New York: Newspaper Enterprise Association, Inc.

PERIODICALS AND JOURNALS

American Biology Teacher. National Association of Biology Teachers, 1420 N Street, N.W., Washington, D.C. 20005. Eight issues per year, $10.00.

American Journal of Physics. American Association of Physics Teachers and the American Institute of Physics, American Institute of Physics, Inc., 335 E. 45th Street, New York, N.Y. 10017. Monthly, $12.50 per year.

Audubon Magazine. National Audubon Society, 1130 Fifth Avenue, New York, N.Y. 10028. Bi-monthly, $5.00 per year.

Chemistry. American Chemical Society, 1155 Sixteenth Street N.W., Washington, D.C. 20036. Eight issues, $3.00 per year.

Current Science (Grades 7–9). American Education Publications. Education Center, Columbus, Ohio 43216.

Journal of Chemical Education. American Chemical Society, Division of Chemical Education, 1155 Sixteenth Street N.W., Washington, D.C. 20036. Monthly, $4.00 per year.

Journal of Research in Science Teaching. Official journal of the National Association for Research in Science Teaching and the Association for the Education of Teachers in Science, John Wiley & Sons, 605 Third Avenue, New York, N.Y. 10016. Quarterly, $10.00 per year.

Junior Natural History. American Museum of Natural History, Central Park West at 79th Street, New York, N.Y. 10024. Ten issues per year, $1.50.

Natural History. American Museum of Natural History, Central Park West at 79th Street, New York, N.Y. 10024. Ten issues per year, $7.00. (Incorporates *Nature Magazine*).

Nature and Science. American Museum of Natural History, Central Park West at 79th Street, New York, N.Y. 10024. Eighteen issues per year, $3.50.

Pacific Discovery. California Academy of Sciences, 2057 Center Street, Berkeley, Calif. 94704. Bi-monthly, $4.00 per year.

Physics Today. American Institute of Physics, 335 E. 45th Street, New York, N.Y. 10017. Monthly, $4.00 per year.

Popular Mechanics. Popular Mechanics Magazine, 200 E. Ontario Street, Chicago, Ill. 60611. Monthly, $4.00 per year.

Popular Science Monthly. Popular Science Publishing Co., Inc., 355 Lexington Avenue, New York, N.Y. 10017. Monthly, $5.00 per year.

Scholastic Magazines, Inc. Publishers of *Science World* (Grades 7–9) and *Senior Science* (Grades 10–12). Weekly student publications accompanied by teacher editions. 902 Sylvan Avenue, Englewood Cliffs, N.J. 07632.

School Science and Mathematics. Central Association of Science and Mathematics Teachers, P.O. Box 108, Bluffton, Ohio 45817. Nine issues per year, $7.00.

Science. American Association for the Advancement of Science, 1515 Massachusetts Avenue, N.W., Washington, D.C. 20005. Weekly, $12.00 per year.

Science and Children. National Science Teachers Association, 1201 Sixteenth Street, Washington, D.C. 20036. Eight issues per year, $4.00.

Science and Math Weekly (Grades 7–12). American Education Publications. Education Center, Columbus, Ohio 43216. Weekly.

Science Digest. Science Digest, Inc., 250 W. 55th Street, New York, N.Y. 10019. Monthly, $5.00 per year.

Science Education. Science Education, Inc., University of Tampa, Tampa, Fla. 33606. Five issues per year, $8.00.

Science News Letter. Science Service, Inc., 1719 N Street, N.W., Washington, D.C. 20006. Weekly, $6.50 per year.

Science Teacher. National Science Teachers Association, 1201 Sixteenth Street, N.W., Washington, D.C. 20036. Nine issues per year, $8.00.

Scientific American. Scientific American, Inc., 415 Madison Avenue, New York, N.Y. 10017. Monthly, $8.00.

Sky and Telescope. Sky Publishing Corp., Harvard College Observatory, 60 Garden Street, Cambridge, Mass. 02138. Monthly, $6.00 per year.

UNESCO Courier. UNESCO Publications Center, 801 Third Avenue, New York, N.Y. 10022. Monthly, $5.00 per year.

Weatherwise. American Meteorological Society, 45 Beacon Street, Boston, Mass. 02108. Bi-monthly, $4.00 per year.

Welch Physics and Chemistry Digest and *Welch General Science and Biology Digest.* W. M. Welch Scientific Co., 1515 N. Sedgwick Street, Chicago, Ill. 60610. Free.

BOOKS AND PAMPHLETS FOR TEACHERS

American Association of School Administrators. *Conservation—In the People's Hands.* Washington, D.C.: The Association, 1964. 330 pp. Positive steps that can be taken toward using natural resources in a more effective manner.

Arey, Charles K. *Science Experiments for Elementary Schools.* New York: Teachers College Press, Columbia University, 1961 Rev. Ed. 110 pp. Simple experiments (requiring little equipment) with plants, the atmosphere, the earth in space, magnetism and electricity, heat, light, and sound.

Ashley, Tracy H. et al. *An Administrator's Guide to the Elementary-School Science Program.* New York: Association of Public School Systems, 525 W. 120th Street, N.Y. 10027. 30 pp. Suggestions for administrators who want to improve science programs.

Asimov, Isaac. *Building Blocks of the Universe.* Eau Claire, Wisc.: E. M. Hale & Co., 1957. 256 pp. The 101 chemical elements so far discovered—their importance and place in the periodic table, how they were discovered, by whom, and how they are used.

Association for Childhood Education International, 3615 Wisconsin Avenue, N.W., Washington, D.C. 20016. *Children's Books—For $1.50 or Less.* 1967. 48 pp. A classified list of inexpensive, approved books for use by teachers or parents.

———. *Science for the Eights-to-Twelves.* 1964. pp. A guide to ways of helping children learn how to continue learning about science throughout their lives.

———. *Young Children and Science.* 1964. 56 pp. A discussion of *what* and *how* the young child should learn about science.

Aylesworth, T. G. *Planning for Effective Science Teaching.* Columbus, Ohio: American Education Publications, 1964.

Baker, Emily V. *Children's Questions and Their Implications for Planning the Curriculum.* New York: Bureau of Publications, Teachers College, Columbia University, 1945. 172 pp. More than 9000 unstructured questions from 1500 children throughout the country, grouped and analyzed. Approximately 30 pp. on the natural sciences.

Berger, Melvin, and Frank Clark. *Science and Music.* New York: McGraw-Hill Book Co., 1961.

Berman, W. *Experimental Biology.* New York: Sentinel Books Publishers, Inc., 1963. Techniques and procedures for conducting research in selected areas of biology, including suggested investigations.

Blackwood, Paul E. "Science and Humanities," in *The Humanities and the Curriculum.* Washington, D.C.: National Education Association, 1967. Papers from a conference sponsored by the Association for Supervision and Curriculum Development Commission on Current Curriculum Developments.

Science Teaching in the Elementary Schools, A Survey of Practices. U.S. Office of Education Publication 29059. Washington, D.C.: Government Printing Office, 1965. 104 pp. A thorough report on science teaching in elementary schools in the United States.

Blough, Glen O. *It's Time for Better Elementary-School Science.* Washington, D.C.: National Science Teachers Association, 1958. 48 pp. Characteristics of a good elementary-school science program, ways of developing it, and how to provide in-service experiences for teachers.

———, and Marjorie Campbell. *Making and Using Classroom Science Materials in the Elementary Schools.* New York: Holt, Rinehart & Winston, Inc., 1954. Clear, well-illustrated suggestions for constructing demonstration materials for various areas of science.

———, and Julius Schwartz. *Elementary School Science and How to Teach It.* New York: Holt, Rinehart & Winston, Inc., Third Edition, 1964. 655 pp. Science subject matter and methods, the former exceptionally well written and comprehensive.

Brandwein, Paul F. *Building Curricular Structures for Science—With Special Reference to the Junior High School.* Washington, D.C.: National Science Teachers Association, 1967. 23 pp.

———. *Elements in a Strategy for Teaching Science in the Elementary School.* New York: Harcourt, Brace and World, Inc., 1962. 40 pp. The Burton Lecture for 1961, delivered at Harvard University by the author. He proposes that elementary science be organized according to major "conceptual schemes."

———. *Substance, Structures, and Style in Teaching of Science.* New York: Harcourt, Brace and World, Inc., 1965. A version of a lecture given at the General Motors Annual Conference for High School Teachers of Science and Mathematics.

Burnett, R. W. *Teaching Science in the Elementary School.* New York: Holt, Rinehart & Winston, Inc., 1960. The place of science in the elementary-school program, with a comprehensive account of science content and activities.

California Association for Supervision and Curriculum Development. *Leadership for Science in the Elementary Schools.* Burlingame, Calif.: The Association, 1960. 88 pp. For teachers, administrators, consultants, and supervisors: Practical suggestions for the science program, science experiences, developing attitudes and problem-solving abilities, materials and equipment, and continuous professional growth. Excellent photographs.

California State Department of Education. *Implementing the Science Program in California, Grades K–8.* 1968. Hayward, Calif. 94544: Alameda County School Department, 224 W. Winton Avenue, Room 186. Five booklets of information to assist teachers in implementing a science program and improving their professional role: Series 1, *Science Materials and Equipment, Grades 7–8;* Series 2, *Science Materials and Equipment, Grades 1–6;* Series 3, *Library and Audiovisual Materials, Grades K–8;* Series 4, *Guidelines for Implementation—Including Examples of District and County In-Service Activities;* Series 5, *Science Resource Guide—Including Information to Extend and Correlate the Basic and Supplementary Textbooks.*

———. *Looking Ahead in Science.* Sacramento: The Department, 1960. 88 pp. Outline report of the Production Seminar and Conferences on the Improvement of Science Education in the Elementary School: purposes, appropriate experiences and content, equipment and materials, scheduling, evaluation, and pre- and in-service education.

———. *Planning a Continuous Science Program for All Junior High School Youth.* Riverside, Calif.: Office of the Superintendent of Schools, 1967. 155 pp. Guidelines for designing and implementing contemporary science curricula for grades 7–9.

———. *Science Curriculum Development in the Elementary School.* Sacramento, Calif.: The Department, 1964. 37 pp. Defines the structure and nature of science; describes the processes of scientific inquiry; and presents in broad terms an organizational plan for the science curriculum.

Carin, Arthur, and Robert B. Sund. *Teaching Science Through Discovery.* Columbus, Ohio: Charles E. Merrill Books, Inc., 1964. 542 pp. A methods book stressing the "discovery method" with more than half the book devoted to lesson plans grouped into basic areas of science.

Challand, Helen J., and Elizabeth Brandt. *Science Activities from A to Z.* Chicago: Children's Press, Inc., 1963. 221 pp. Experiments as activities for anyone curious about why and how things happen—from "Absorption" to "Zygote."

Compton's Dictionary of the Natural Sciences. Chicago: Encyclopedia Britannica Educational Corp., 1966.

Compton's Illustrated Science Dictionary. Chicago: Encyclopedia Britannica Educational Corp., 1969. Approximately 3500 words from 14 fields of science defined and used in a sentence, with about 1500 illustrations.

Comstock, Anna. *Handbook of Nature Study.* Ithaca, N.Y.: Cornell University Press, Rev. Ed., 1962. For inexperienced teachers, the most useful reference for identifying most of the natural objects children bring to school.

Conant, James B. *Science and Common Sense.* New Haven: Yale University Press, 1951. 344 pp. An attempt to provide the non-scientist with some understanding of the way scientists operate.

Craig, Gerald S. *Certain Techniques Used in Developing a Course of Study in Science for Horace Mann Elementary School, N.Y.* New York: Teachers College, Columbia University, 1927. 73 pp. The dissertation that was a turning point in the development of elementary science from nature study to its present scope.

———. *Science for the Elementary-School Teacher.* Waltham, Mass.: Blaisdell Publishing Co., Inc., Rev. Ed., 1966. 894 pp. A good reference volume, the most comprehensive book available on elementary science education.

———. *Science in the Elementary School: What Research Says to the Teacher Series, No. 12.* Washington, D.C.: Department of Classroom Teachers, National Education Association, 1957. 33 pp. Teaching practices in elementary science as indicated by research.

Deason, H. J. *AASA Science Book List for Young Adults.* Washington, D.C.: American Association of School Administrators, National Education Association, 1964. An excellent listing (according to specific disciplines) of books for general and specific reference.

———. *Guide to Science Reading.* New York: New American Library, Signet (T3003), Rev. Ed., 1966. An annotated catalog of over 1000 paperbound science and mathematics books.

DeVries, Leonard. *Book of Experiments.* Trans. by Eric G. Breeze. London, England: John Murray Publishers, 1959. Delightful descriptions and diagrams of experiments with air, force, sound, heat, water, electricity, light, chemistry, and other phenomena. Good for the gifted pupil. (Distributed by Macmillan.)

Dunfee, Maxine. *Elementary School Science: A Guide to Current Research.* Washington, D.C.: Association for Supervision and Curriculum Development, National Education Association, 1967. 77 pp. A revision of the 1957 publication by Dunfee and Greenlee that offers a comprehensive survey of more recent research developments and current thinking in elementary science.

Educational Policies Commission. *Education and the Spirit of Science.* Washington, D.C.: The Commission, National Education Association, 1966. 27 pp. An attempt to define the spirit of science and to relate it to education.

Education for the Age of Science. Statement by the President's Science Advisory Committee, the White House. Washington, D.C.: Superintendent of Documents, May 24, 1959. 36 pp. The place of science and technology, the major tasks, national goals, opportunities for the gifted student.

Elementary Science Advisory Center. *Science Equipment in the Elementary School.* Boulder, Colo.: University of Colorado, 1967. 36 pp. One long list of materials to be used in teaching elementary-school science, with photographs and suggestions for using the materials.

Fitzpatrick, Frederick L., Ed. *Policies for Science Education.* New York: Teachers College, Columbia University, 1960. 219 pp. Various authorities suggest policies for the improvement of science education at all levels.

Freeman, Kenneth, and T. I. Dowling. *Helping Children Understand Science.* New York: Holt, Rinehart & Winston, 1954. 314 pp. Planning and organizing science instruction, community resources, equipment, and audiovisual aids.

Gantert, Robert L. *Practical Classroom Science Experiments.* Minneapolis, Minn.: T. S. Denison & Co., 1967. 85 pp.

Gega, Peter C. *Science in Elementary Education.* New York: John Wiley & Sons, Inc., 1966. 451 pp. How to teach science in elementary schools. Part I introduces the basic methods; Part II applies them within the typical subject-matter fields of elementary science.

Haney, Richard E. *Changing Curriculum: Science.* Washington, D.C.: Association for Supervision and Curriculum Development, National Education Association, 1966. 44 pp. First in a series devoted to the study of specialized areas in the curriculum. Details the current developments in science teaching.

Heffernan, Helen, and V. E. Todd. *Kindergarten Teacher.* Boston, Mass.: D. C. Heath and Co., 1960. Excellent chapter on science.

Heller, Robert L., Comp. *Geology and Earth Sciences Sourcebook for Elementary and Secondary Schools.* (American Geological Institute.) New York: Holt, Rinehart & Winston, Inc., 1962. An excellent sourcebook in geology, with a large bibliography, list of filmstrips, and reference materials.

Hennessy, David E. *Elementary Teacher's Classroom Science Demonstrations and Activities.* Englewood Cliffs, N.J.: Prentice-Hall, Inc., 1964. 308 pp. For teachers who are not specialists in science, demonstrations and student activities for designated grade levels.

Hubler, Clark. *Working with Children in Science.* New York: Houghton Mifflin, 1957. 425 pp.

Hurd, Paul DeHart. *Science Teaching for a Changing World.* Chicago: Scott, Foresman and Co., 1965.

——— and J. Gallagher. *New Directions in Elementary Science Teaching.* Belmont, Calif.: Wadsworth Publishing Co., 1968. 166 pp.

Hutchinson, Margaret M. *Children as Naturalists.* New York: Hillary House Publishers, Ltd., Second Edition, 1966. 193 pp. Part One deals with the scope of nature study; Part Two attempts to answer briefly questions teachers may face on a nature walk. Conservation is emphasized.

Johnson, June. *838 Ways to Amuse a Child.* New York: Collier-Macmillan International, 1960. Crafts, hobbies, nature lore, travel ideas for the child from 6 to 12.

Jordan, E. L. *Hammond's Guide to Nature Activities.* New York: Macmillan Co., 1958. 64 pp. Collecting rocks, minerals, and shells; terraria and aquaria; plants and bird hobbies; collecting insects; nature photography; fishing and hunting. Excellent illustrations.

Joseph, A., and Paul F. Brandwein et al. *Teaching High School Science: A Sourcebook for the Physical Sciences.* New York: Harcourt, Brace & World, Inc., 1961. 674 pp. An anthology of demonstration and laboratory procedures together with ideas for experiments and projects. Thoroughly illustrated.

Kambly, Paul E., and John E. Suttle. *Teaching Elementary School Science, Methods and Resources.* New York: Ronald Press Co., 1963. 492 pp. Methods, comprehensive resource units, and a detailed listing of source materials.

Karplus, Robert, and Herbert D. Thier. *New Look at Elementary School Science.* Chicago: Rand McNally & Co., 1967. 204 pp. Current information about the Science Curriculum Improvement Study for elementary-school teachers.

Kuslan, Louis I. *Teaching Children Science: An Inquiry Approach.* Belmont, Calif.: Wadsworth Publishing Co., 1968. 464 pp.

———— and A. H. Stone. *Readings on Teaching Children Science.* Belmont, Calif.: Wadsworth Publishing Co., 1969. 333 pp.

Laboratories in the Classroom: New Horizons in Science Education. New York: Science Materials Center, 1960. 96 pp. Contributions from outstanding educators and creative classroom teachers on basic aims, new curricula, and new plans and procedures.

Laybourn, K., and C. H. Bailey. *Teaching Science to the Ordinary Pupil.* New York: Philosophical Library, 1957. 415 pp.

Lewis, June E., and Irene C. Potter. *Teaching of Science in the Elementary School.* Englewood Cliffs, N.J.: Prentice-Hall, Inc., 1961. 381 pp. Emphasizes the kinds of problems that interest children, ways to use the techniques of problem-solving, and methods for helping children develop science understandings and concepts.

McGavack, John, Jr., and Donald P. LaSalle. *Guppies, Bubbles and Vibrating Objects.* New York: John Day, 1968. 156 pp.

Mathematics Through Science. Palo Alto, Calif.: School Mathematics Study Group, 1963.

Milgrom, Harry. *Explorations in Science: A Book of Basic Experiments.* New York: E. P. Dutton & Co., Inc., 1961. 127 pp. Ways to help students and teachers enjoy science. Simply written and illustrated.

Miller, D. F., and G. W. Blaydes. *Methods and Materials for Teaching Biological Science.* New York: McGraw-Hill Book Co., Inc., 1962. Part II includes a wealth of information on collecting, culturing, and preserving, as well as suggestions about techniques.

Morholt, E., Paul F. Brandwein, and A. Joseph. *Teaching High School Science: A Sourcebook for Biological Sciences.* New York: Harcourt, Brace & World, Inc., 1958. 506 pp. Techniques, demonstrations, projects, experiments, and references for teaching and learning biology, general sciences, health, botany, and zoology at the high-school level. Heavily illustrated.

Munzer, Martha E., and Paul F. Brandwein. *Teaching Science Through Conservation.* New York: McGraw-Hill Book Co., 1960. Selected and practical classroom, laboratory, and field study procedures for teaching science as a phase of conservation.

National Science Foundation. *Science Course Improvement Projects,* Second Edition. NSF 64-8. Washington, D.C.: The Foundation, 1964. 77 pp. Information on course improvement projects supported by the National Science Foundation.

National Science Teachers Association. Washington, D.C.: The Association, National Education Association. *Bibliography of Textbooks and Courses of Study for Science Teaching—Elementary Level.* 1968. 68 pp. (471-14298). Textbooks available for science for the elementary grades (and junior high) and listing of courses of study in science that are available from state and local school departments.

————. *Building Curricular Structures for Science.* 1967. 23 pp. (471-14542)

————. *Helping Children Learn Science.* 1966. 192 pp. (471-14498) A collection of articles from "Science and Children," 1966.

————. *How to Care for Living Things in the Classroom.* 1965. 16 pp. (471-14288)

————. *How to Individualize Science Instruction in the Elementary School.* 1965. 12 pp. (471-14294)

————. *How to Record and Use Data in Elementary School Science.* 1965. 12 pp. (471-14292)

————. *How to Teach Science Through Field Studies.* 1965. 12 pp. (471-14290)

————. *How to Use Photography as a Science Teaching Aid.* 1968. 8 pp. (471-14560)

————. *How to Utilize the Services of a Science Consultant.* 1965. 6 pp. (471-14286)

————. *Ideas for Science Investigations.* 1966. 64 pp. (471-14500). A source of ideas for research-type science investigations. Primarily for high school students, but useful to the classroom teacher.

————. *Ideas for Teaching Science in the Junior High School.* 1963. 256 pp. (471-14184). From "The best of *The Science Teacher,*" articles giving guidance and teaching suggestions for junior high school science.

————. *Improving Objective Tests in Science.* 1967. 24 pp. (471-14432)

————. *Investigating Science with Children Series.*

1964. Six booklets each 96 pp. Entire set (478-14280). 1. *Living Things.* (479-14266) 2. *The Earth.* (479-14268) 3. *Atoms and Molecules.* (479-14272) 4. *Energy in Waves.* (479-14274) 5. *Motion.* (479-14276) 6. *Space.* (479-14278) Developed for elementary science teachers in cooperation with the National Aeronautics and Space Administration, each well-illustrated book contains up to 120 scientific activities, keyed to varying student abilities, as well as an extensive bibliography.

——. *Learning and Creativity with Special Emphasis on Science.* 1967. 51 pp. (471-14544)

——. *Science Seminars: Elementary and Junior High School.* 1966. 29 pp. (471-14502). Summaries of four subject-matter seminars that covered in depth ten frontier topics in science, each presented by an outstanding scientist in the field. Included are oceanography, meteorology, interdependence of living things, and a matter-energy cycle.

——. Teaching Tips From TST: *Biological Science.* 1967. 224 pp. (471-14526) *Earth-Space Science.* 1967. 128 pp. (471-14350) *Physical Science.* 1967. 144 pp. (471-14348)

——. *Theory into Action in Science Curriculum Development.* 1964. 48 pp. (471-14282). Guidelines for K–12 curriculum improvement.

——. *You and Your Child and Science.* 1963. 28 pp. (181-05424). Discusses the nature of the elementary-school science program and describes the ways in which parents and teachers can help young children develop scientific attitudes.

Navarra, John G., and Joseph Zafforoni. *Science Today for the Elementary-School Teacher.* New York: Harper and Row, 1960. 470 pp. Developmental approach to evaluation, and current content and methods in nine major areas—air, weather, aviation, space, time, earth, matter, energy, and life.

Nedelsky, Leo. *Science Teaching and Testing.* New York: Harcourt, Brace & World, 1965. 368 pp.

Nelson, L. W., and G. C. Lorbeer. *Science Activities for Elementary Children.* Dubuque, Iowa: Wm. C. Brown & Co., Rev. Ed., 1959. 178 pp. Two hundred and forty-nine activities on typical areas of science organized into general and specific area problems and grade levels. Information on materials, procedures, and results.

Nelson, Pearl A. *Elementary School Science Activities.* Englewood Cliffs, N.J.: Prentice-Hall, 1968. 210 pp.

New School Science: *A Report to School Administrators on Regional Orientation Conferences in Science.* Washington, D.C.: American Association for the Advancement of Science, 1963. 92 pp. Report on dramatic new developments in the various science disciplines and the growing unity of science.

New York State Department of Education. *General Science Handbook, Part I, Part II, and Part III.* Albany, N.Y.: The University of the State of New York, The State Department of Education, 1951–1956. Part I is for grade 7; Part II for grade 8; Part III is for grade 9. Aid for schools in developing a program of science instruction in harmony with the needs of the times. Each part includes experiments, demonstrations, teaching techniques, and other activities covering living things, health, electric circuits, gravity and friction, fire, light, seasons, rocks, seeds. Excellent line drawings.

Parker, Bertha M. *Science Experiences: Elementary School.* New York: Harper & Row, 1963. Directions for simple experiments and construction of apparatus and toys illustrating various principles. Primarily for the middle grades.

Piltz, Albert. *Creative Teaching of Science in the Elementary School.* Boston, Mass.: Allyn and Bacon, Inc., 1968. 217 pp.

Prentice-Hall Education Series. Englewood Cliffs, N.J.: Teachers Practical Press, Prentice-Hall, Inc. *Enriching the Science Program* by Berger and Baumel. 1964. 56 pp.

——. *Successful Science Teaching* by Lesser. 1961. 62 pp.

——. *Science Experiences for Elementary School Teachers* by Salem. 1961. 64 pp.

Reid, Robert W. *Science Experiments for the Primary Grades.* Palo Alto, Calif.: Fearon Publishers, Inc., 1959. 40 pp.

Renner, John W. *Teaching Science in the Elementary School.* New York: Harper & Row, 1968. 359 pp.

Report of the International Clearinghouse on Science and Mathematics Curricular Developments. College Park, Md.: American Association for the Advancement of Science and the Science Teaching Center, University of Maryland, 1967. 413 pp. An annual report dealing with curriculum developments in science and mathematics.

Research in Education. Bloomington, Ind.: Phi Delta Kappa, Inc. Annual review with subject and author index and bibliography.

Romey, William D. *Inquiry Techniques for Teaching Science.* Englewood Cliffs, N.J.: Prentice-Hall, Inc., 1968. 342 pp. Material useful for selecting a style of teaching science.

Roy, Mary M., Comp. *Probe: A Handbook for Teach-*

ers of Elementary Science. Benton Harbor, Mich.: Educational Service, Inc., 1964. 284 pp. A handbook of games, activities, and experiments to motivate the learning of elementary science.

Rublowsky, John. *Nature in the City.* New York: Basic Books, Inc., 1967. 152 pp. An account of the plant and animal life of the city, as well as a brief history of living things in cities.

Ruchlis, H. *Discovering Scientific Method.* New York: Harper & Row, 1963. Twenty-two "science puzzle pictures" that present natural phenomena. The reader is challenged to formulate questions about the phenomena.

Schwab, Joseph J., and Paul F. Brandwein. *Teaching of Science as Enquiry* with Brandwein's *Elements of Strategy for Teaching Science in the Elementary School* in *Teaching Science.* Cambridge, Mass.: Harvard University Press, 1962.

Schmidt, V. E., and V. N. Rockcastle. *Teaching Science with Everyday Things,* New York: McGraw-Hill Book Co., 1968. 167 pp.

"Science Education," *Nation's Schools,* February, 1960, pp. 65–118. Special issue reports on three surveys. Includes 36 illustrations by editorial staff and science educators.

Science Manpower Project Monographs. New York: Teachers College Press, Columbia University. Monographs designed as references are part of a large-scale attempt at formulating a unified science program for grades K–12.

———. *Earth in Space: A Source Book for Elementary-School Teachers.* 1965. 265 pp.

———. *Modern Elementary-School Science: A Recommended Sequence.* 1961. 127 pp.

———. *Modern Junior High School Science: A Recommended Sequence of Courses.* 1961. 127 pp.

———. *Problem-Solving Methods in Science Teaching.* 1960. 88 pp.

Sheckles, Mary. *Building Children's Science Concepts Through Experiences.* New York: Teachers College Press, Columbia University, 1958. 138 pp. Experiences with rocks, soil, air, and water.

Suchman, J. Richard. *Elementary School Training Program in Scientific Inquiry.* Urbana, Ill.: University of Illinois, 1962. 150 pp. The culmination of five years of work on the development and evaluation of a technique by which teachers can make inquiry a regular classroom activity.

Syrocki, B. John. *Science Activities for Elementary Grades.* Parker Publishing Co., 1968. 213 pp.

Tannenbaum, Harold E. *Evaluation in Elementary School Science.* Washington, D.C.: U.S. Office of Education, 1964. 75 pp.

——— et al. *Science Education for Elementary-School Teachers.* Boston: Allyn and Bacon, Inc., 1965. 349 pp. Methods of science teaching, with excellent material on relation of child development to science education.

Thaw, Richard, and John E. Morlan. *Experiences and Demonstrations in Elementary Physical Science.* Dubuque, Iowa: Wm. C. Brown & Co., 1964. 187 pp. Designed to give teachers a variety of science experiences that can be used either as teacher demonstrations, or as pupil activities and projects. Simple and well illustrated.

UNESCO. *700 Science Experiments for Everyone.* (Grades 1–4) New York: Doubleday & Company, Inc., 1958. 221 pp. A compilation of the work of experienced science teachers from many countries.

———. *UNESCO Source Book for Science Teaching.* New York: UNESCO Publications Center, USA, Second revised edition, 1966.

U.S. Department of Health, Education, and Welfare. Washington, D.C.: Superintendent of Documents. *Evalatuion in Elementary School Science.* Circular No. 757, by Harold E. Tannenbaum et al, 1964. Help for supervisors, administrators, and teachers in evaluating the effectiveness of the total elementary science program.

———. *Research in the Teaching of Science.* Bulletin 1965, No. 10, by Lloyd K. Johnson et al. Biennial reports summarizing research in the teaching of science. (Annual from 1950 until 1960.)

———. *Science Equipment and Materials: Science Kits.* Bulletin 1963, No. 30, by Albert Piltz and William J. Gruver. Aims to clarify issues concerning the instructional value of science kits and to suggest criteria for their classification and evaluation.

———. *Science Teaching in the Elementary Schools: A Survey of Practices.* Circular No. 749, by Paul E. Blackwood, 1965. Information about procedures, policies, practices, and conditions affecting science teaching in the public elementary schools.

———. *Science Teaching in the Public Junior High School,* by Lola E. Rogers, 1967. Focuses on science teaching, instructional resources, organization for instruction, course offerings and enrollments, extra-instructional activities, and teaching personnel.

Vessel, Matthew F. *Elementary-School Science Teaching.* New York: Center for Applied Research in Education, 1963. 119 pp. The organization and improvement of programs of instruction in elementary science.

———— and Herbert Wong. Palo Alto, Calif.: Fearon Publishers, Inc.

————. *How to Stimulate Your Science Program.* 1957. 32 pp.

————. *Science Bulletin Boards.* 1957. 48 pp.

————. *Teaching Science Through Holidays and Seasons.* 1959. 40 pp.

Victor, Edward. *Science for the Elementary School.* New York: Macmillan Co., 1965. 772 pp. Methods and activities for teaching science, with an extensive presentation outline of subject matter.

———— and Marjorie E. Lerner. *Readings in Science Education for the Elementary School.* New York: Macmillan Co., 1967.

Visner, Harold, and Adelaide Hechtlinger. *Simple Science Experiments for the Elementary Grades.* Palisades, N.J.: Franklin Publishing Company, Inc., 1960. 232 pp. Designed to acquaint elementary school children with the basic principles of science by the easiest, most enjoyable method—doing things themselves.

Wensberg, Katherine. *Experiences with Living Things: An Introduction to Ecology for Five- to Eight-Year-Olds.* Boston: Beacon Press, 1966. 143 pp. Planned as a guide for the teacher who undertakes backyard exploration with children of kindergarten and early primary age.

Woodburn, John H., and Ellsworth S. Osbourn. *Teaching the Pursuit of Science.* New York: Macmillan Co., 1965.

BOOKS AND PAMPHLETS FOR TEACHERS AND STUDENTS

"All about . . ." Books. New York: Random House, Inc. Authentic, easy-to-read books covering a great variety of science topics, such as: *All about Birds, All about Electricity, All about Rockets and Jets, All about Whales.* (Complete list available from the publisher.)

American Education Publications. Columbus, Ohio: Education Center. Inexpensive science unit books, such as: *Exploring the Universe, What Insect is That?, Probability and Statistics.*

Animal Welfare Institute. *First Aid and Care of Small Animals.* Bethesda, Md.: The Institute, 7035 Wilson Lane, Bethesda, Md. 20034, 25¢.

————. *How to Raise and Train Gerbils.* By D. G. Robinson, Jr. Bethesda, Md.: The Institute.

Ann Arbor Science Library. Ann Arbor, Mich.: University of Michigan Press. Paperback editions, each on a scientific subject, such as: *The Senses* (Broddenbrock), *Light* (Ruechardt), *Ebb and Flow* (Defant). (Complete list available from the publisher.)

Audubon Nature Charts. *Twigs, Simple Leaves, Compound Leaves, Evergreens.* New York: National Aubudon Society. Help in identification of trees. Good for bulletin boards.

Barnard, J. Darrell et al. *Science for Tomorrow's World* Series. (Grades 1–6.) New York: Macmillan Co., 1966. Each book presents interrelated science learnings to contribute to the pupil's understanding of ten key concepts that encompass all of man's scientific achievements.

Basic Science Education Series. (Science Unitexts, Grades 1–9.) New York: Harper & Row. Eighty-eight 36-page booklets on single, specific, topics in biological and natural sciences, space travel, and the solar system. Grouped appropriately for primary, intermediate, and junior-high reading levels. Some titles: *Fall is Here, Birds in Your Back Yard, Water Appears and Disappears, Magnets, You as a Machine, Superstition or Science.* (Complete list available from the publisher.)

Beauchamp, Wilbur L. et al. *Basic Science Program.* (Curriculum Foundation Series, Grades 1–6.) Glenview, Ill.: Scott, Foresman and Co., 1968. Work for each grade is developed around problem units related to children's interest in their natural environment.

Beginning Knowledge Books by Amy Clampitt. New York: Macmillan Co. Answers to children's own questions. Big, colorful, simply written and scientifically accurate, with such titles as: *Backyard Birds, Snakes, Turtles.* (Complete list available from the publisher.)

Bond, Guy L. et al. Developmental Science Series. (Grades 1–6.) Chicago: Lyons and Carnahan, 1963.

"Book About. . . ." Books. Chicago: Maxton Publishing Corp. Cover a great variety of science topics, such as: *Book about Insects, Book about Rivers, Book about Life Under the Microscope, Book about Sea Shells.* (Complete list available from the publisher.)

Booth, Ernest S. *Birds of the West* and *Western Bird Guide for Youth.* Escondido, Calif. Identification Handbooks.

Brandwein, Paul F. et al. Concepts in Science Series. (Grades K–9.) New York: Harcourt, Brace and World, Inc., 1968. Puts "theory into action" by structuring a comprehensive science curriculum so that children grow, grade by grade, in their ability to perceive the basic ideas of science.

Branley, Franklyn M. *Reader's Digest Science Readers.* (Grades 3–6.) Pleasantville, N.Y.: Reader's Digest Services, Inc., 1961–1964.

Community of Living Things Series. *Field and Meadow, Fresh and Salt Water, Desert, Parks and Gardens, Forest and Woodland.* Mankato, Minn.: Creative Educational Society, Inc., 1967.

Cooper, Elizabeth K. *Science on the Shores and Banks.* New York: Harcourt, Brace & World, Inc., 1960.

Corrington, J. D. *Exploring with Your Microscope.* New York: McGraw-Hill Book Co., 1957. Explores the uses of the microscope and the techniques of the microscopist in several branches of science.

Craig, Gerald S. Science for You Series. (Grades 1–6.) Boston: Ginn and Company, 1965.

———. Science Today and Tomorrow Series. (Grades 1–8.) Boston: Ginn and Company, 1961.

Creative Science Series 1. *Plants, Stars, and Space; Atoms, Energy, and Machines; Earth's Story; Way of the Weather.* Mankato, Minn.: Creative Educational Society, Inc., 1962–1967.

Creative Science Series 2. *Ocean Laboratory, Food and Life, Lives of Animals, Man from the Beginning.* Mankato, Minn.: Creative Educational Society, Inc., 1962–1967.

Exploring and Understanding Series. (Grades 4–9.) *Exploring and Understanding Magnets and Electromagnets, Exploring and Understanding Rockets and Satellites.* Westchester, Ill.: Benefic Press. Each booklet explores a subject in depth, with special emphasis on science processes. (Complete list available from the publisher.)

Farris, E. J., Ed. *Care and Breeding of Laboratory Animals.* New York: John Wiley & Sons, 1950. Each chapter contains a thorough discussion of a particular laboratory animal.

"First Book of . . ." Books. New York: Franklin Watts, Inc. Cover a great variety of science topics, such as: *First Book of Air, First Book of Caves, First Book of Fishes, First Book of Stones.* (Complete list available from the publisher.)

Fischler, Abraham S. et al. Science: A Modern Approach Series. (Grades K–6.) New York: Holt, Rinehart and Winston, Inc., 1966. Reveals the processes of science in a carefully planned sequence of activities and emphasizes the activities through which the pupil learns to depend on his observation and experience for arriving at basic concepts of science.

Follett Beginning Science Books. (Grades 1–8.) Chicago: Follett Educational Corp. Forty books that contain authentic, up-to-date scientific facts with controlled vocabularies. A few titles are: *Air, Ants, Robins, Rockets.* (Complete list available from the publisher.)

Foundations of Science Library. Boston: Ginn and Company, 1966. Thirty-one volumes comprise a complete elementary-level introduction to the fundamental concepts of science. Titles such as: *The Natural World* (4 vol.), *The Chemical Sciences* (4 vol.), *The Biological Sciences* (6 vol.), *Technology* (5 vol.), *The Physical Sciences* (9 vol.), *History and Reference* (3 vol.). (Complete list available from the publisher.)

Goldstein, P. *How to Do an Experiment.* New York: Harcourt, Brace & World, Inc., 1957. Comprehensive and practical analyses of scientific methods that can apply to problem-solving.

Goodwin, Harold R. *Space: Frontier Unlimited.* Princeton, N.J.: D. Van Nostrand Company, Inc., 1962. An excellent introduction to the entire space program.

Gray, Charles A. *Explorations in Chemistry.* New York: E. P. Dutton & Co., Inc., 1965. Chemical experiments.

Great Mysteries of Science Series. (Age 10-up.) New York: Basic Books, Inc. Titles such as: *Secret of The Mysterious Rays: The Discovery of Nuclear Energy.* (Complete list available from the publisher.)

Growing Up with Science Books. Chicago: American Library Association. A bibliography issued annually.

Heffernan, Helen, and George Shaftel. Man Improves His World Series. New York: L. W. Singer Company. Seven booklets emphasizing conservation: *Fisheries Story, Forestry Story, Wildlife Story, Energy Story, Soil Story, Water Story, Minerals Story.*

Holt Library of Science. New York: Holt, Rinehart & Winston, Inc. Paperbacks covering many science topics, such as: *General Science Series* (14 titles), *Biology Series* (14 titles), *Science and Engineering Series* (14 titles), *Space Science Series* (14 titles). (Complete list available from the publisher.)

Jacobson, Willard J. et al. Thinking Ahead in Science Series. (Grades K–6.) New York: American Book Company, 1968. Through inquiry the pupil deals with both the processes of science and the conceptual structure of science in an integrated manner.

Jacques, H. E. "How to Know the . . ." Books. Dubuque, Iowa: Wm. C. Brown & Co. Presents picture keys for identification, and techniques in curating and collecting. Titles such as: *How to Know the Insects, How to Know Beetles, How to Know Spiders, How to Know Cacti.* (Complete list available from the publisher.)

Johnson, B., and M. Bleifeld. *Hunting with the Microscope.* New York: Sentinel Books Publishers, Inc., 1963. How to use magnifying lenses and microscopes, with techniques for slide preparation.

Junior Science Books Series. (Grades 2–5.) Champaign, Ill.: Garrard Publishing Co., 1960–1966. Twenty-four 64-page booklets in simple, clear language with many suggestions for activities and experiments to make the concepts more significant to young readers. Some titles are: *Junior Science Book of Bacteria, Junior Science Book of Beavers, Junior Science Book of Heat, Junior Science Book of Flying.* (Complete list available from the publisher.)

Kalmus, H. *101 Simple Experiments with Insects.* Garden City, N.Y.: Doubleday & Co., Inc., 1960. Directions for many techniques in solving problems are included.

Leavitt, Jerome, and John Juntsberger. *Fun-Time Terrariums and Aquariums.* Chicago: Children's Press, Inc., 1961.

Life Nature Library by Editors of *Life.* Morristown, N.J.: Silver Burdett Company. Descriptive, thoroughly illustrated monographs with such titles as: *The Poles, Ecology, The Universe.* (Complete list available from the publisher.)

Life Science Library by Editors of *Life.* Morristown, N.J.: Silver Burdett Company. Colorful, illustrated popular texts with titles such as: *Matter, Energy, The Cell, The Body.* (Complete list available from the publisher.)

MacCracken, Helen D. et al. Science Through Discovery Series. (Grades K–6.) New York: L. W. Singer Company, 1967.

Mallinson, George G. et al. *Science Program.* (Grades K–6.) Morristown, N.J.: Silver Burdett Company, 1968. A series that embraces the biological, earth, and physical sciences and provides a wealth of activities to develop skills.

Mason, George F. *Animal Appetites,* and *Animal Baggage.* New York: William Morrow & Company, Inc. Two of many books on science topics of interest to pupils in Grades 4–6. (Complete list available from the publisher.)

McClung, Robert M. *Caterpillars and How They Live, Ladybug,* and *Luna, The Story of a Moth.* New York: William Morrow & Company, Inc. Three of many books on science topics of interest to pupils in

Grades K–6. (Complete list available from the publisher.)

Munch, Theodore W., and B. John Syrocki. Science for a Changing World Series. (Grades 1–6.) Westchester, Ill.: Benefic Press, 1967. Uses a combination of process and concept in its approach.

National Audubon Society. *Audubon Aids in Natural Science.* A wide variety of material for outdoor and classroom science programs. New York: National Audubon Society, 1130 Fifth Avenue, New York, N.Y. 10028. (Free.)

Natural History Library. New York: Doubleday & Company. A paperback series including: *Dwellers in Darkness, Modern Science, Nature of Life, Life and Death of Cells.* (Complete list available from the publisher.)

Navarra, John G. et al. Today's Basic Science Series. (Grades K–8.) Evanston, Ill.: Harper & Row, 1967. Through experimentation, observation, and investigation, students are encouraged to explore science in depth by significant concept blocks. Emphasizes science process.

Novak, Joseph D. et al. World of Science Series. (Grades 1–6.) Indianapolis: Bobbs-Merrill Co., Inc., 1966.

Oddo and Carini. Exploring Science. New York: Holt, Rinehart & Winston Inc. An activity-centered discovery approach to science using ten books and corresponding boxes of materials to provide children with the incentive and direction to explore. Some titles: *Exploring Balance, Exploring Motion.* (Complete list available from the publisher.)

Our Living World of Nature Series. New York: McGraw-Hill Book Co. Covers important life communities in the United States. Well illustrated with full-color and black and white photographs. Titles include: *The Forest, The Seashore, The Desert.* (Complete list available from the publisher.)

Owl Book Series. New York: Holt, Rinehart & Winston, Inc. An individualized reading program designed to supplement and extend children's learning activities in the four primary areas of instruction: science, mathematics, literature, and social studies. Kin/Der Owl Books: Science. 1967; Little Owl Books: Science. 1963, Grades K–2; Young Owl Books: Science. 1964, Grades 2–4; Wise Owl Books: Science. 1965, Grades 4–6. (Complete list available from the publisher.)

Palmer, Nelson P., and W. B. Herron. Science and You Series. (Junior High School.) Chicago: Lyons and Carnahan, 1967.

Peterson Nature Field Books. Boston: Houghton Mifflin Company. A well-indexed and illustrated series made popular by its simplified identification of species. One title: *How to Know the Birds.* (Complete list available from the publisher.)

Putnam's Nature Field Books. New York: G. P. Putnam's Sons. Illustrated pocket-size handbooks with accurate and authoritative descriptions. Handy for field trips and usable for science students of all ages. Some titles: *Field Book of Nature Activities and Conservation, New Field Book of American Wild Flowers.* (Complete list available from the publisher.)

Robinson, D. G., Jr. *Gerbils America's Newest Pets.* Fort Leavenworth, Kansas 66027: The Author, 320–3 Doniphan Drive.

Rosenfeld, S. *Science Experiments with Water.* Irvington-on-Hudson, N.Y.: Harvey House, Inc., 1965. Experiments related to water phenomena lead the way to further questions and investigations.

Schneider, Herman and Nina. *Science Series.* (Grades K–6.) Boston: D. C. Heath and Co., 1965. Encyclopedia-type content with many suggested demonstrations.

Science I Can Read Books. Grades 1–3. Evanston, Ill.: Harper & Row, 1960–1966. Help children explore specific areas of scientific interest and provide a well-balanced selection of materials for enriching understanding of basic science topics. Some titles: *Let's Get Turtles, Plenty of Fish, Prove It!* (Complete list available from the publisher.)

Science Study Series. New York: Doubleday and Company, Inc. More than 44 paperback in-depth studies prepared under the direction of the Physical Science Study Committee of Educational Services Incorporated. Included are: *Life in the Universe, Bird Migration, Edge of Space.* (Complete list available from the publisher.)

"See Through . . ." Books. (Grades 3–4.) Evanston, Ill.: Harper & Row Publishers. Included: *See Through the Sea, See Through the Lake.* (Complete list available from the publisher.)

Selsam, Millicent E. *Birth of a Forest* (1963), *Birth of an Island* (1959). Evanston, Ill.: Harper & Row. Two of many books by this author on science topics of interest to pupils in grades 3–8.

————. *How Animals Live Together* (1963), *Language of Animals* (1962), *Underwater Zoos* (1961). New York: William Morrow and Co. Some of several books on science by this author. (Complete list available from the publisher.)

Smith, Herbert et al. *Science Series.* (Grades 1–6.) River Forest, Ill.: Laidlaw Brothers, 1966. Through personal involvement the pupil learns the techniques of the scientist as science concepts and their relations are presented in an open-spiral organization.

Speck, G. E., and Bernard Jaffe, Eds. *Dictionary of Science Terms.* New York: Hawthorn Books, 1965.

Stone, G. K., and L. W. Stephenson. Science You Can Use. Englewood Cliffs, N.J.: Prentice-Hall Inc., 1964. Emphasis on biological science and nature study.

Tannenbaum, Harold, and Nathan Stillman et al. Experience in Science Series. (Grades 1–3.) New York: Webster/McGraw-Hill Book Company, 1966.

Thurber, Walter A. et al. Exploring Science Series. (Grades 1–8.) Boston: Allyn and Bacon, Inc., 1966. Activity is emphasized in the "let's find out" approach to problem-solving.

"True Book of . . ." Books. Chicago: Children's Press. Some of many titles: *True Book of African Animals, True Book of Bacteria, True Book of Insects, True Book of Automobiles.* (Complete list available from the publisher.)

University of Illinois Astronomy Project. (Grades 5–10.) Evanston, Ill.: Harper and Row, 1968. Six books produced by The Elementary School Science Project at the University of Illinois explore astronomy in depth and provide a basic understanding of astronomy through language and activities that the average pupil will find provocative.

Vessel, Matthew F., and Herbert H. Wong. *Introducing Our Western Birds.* (Grades 4–6.) Palo Alto, Calif.: Fearon Publishers, Inc., 1965.

————. *Seashore Life of Our Pacific Coast.* (Grades 4–6.) Palo Alto, Calif.: Fearon Publishers, Inc., 1968.

Viorst, Judith. *Projects: Space.* New York: Washington Square Press, Inc., 1962. A paperback that relates the story of space exploration by the United States along with reports of fourteen student projects in space science.

Vistas of Science Series. Englewood Cliffs, N.J.: Scholastic Book Services. Produced by the National Science Teachers Association in cooperation with Scholastic Book Services. Includes current and accurate data in specialized fields, and project suggestions developed by classroom teachers. Some of the twelve titles available: *Challenge of the Universe, Frontiers of Dental Science, Microbes and Man.* (Complete list available from the publisher.)

Walt Disney's True-Life Adventures Series. New York: L. W. Singer Company. Vivid and motivating paperback nature stories illustrated with color photographs. Some titles: *Beaver Valley, Vanishing Prairie, Living Desert*. (Complete list available from the publisher.)

Watts, May T. *Tree Finder*. (Leaf characteristics). Naperville, Ill.: Nature Study Guide. A very good key for elementary grades or for a person with no experience with such keys.

Webster Beginner Science Series. (Grades 2–4.) New York: Webster/McGraw-Hill Book Company. Many physical and natural science topics, carefully written and illustrated, are dealt with in twelve books such as: *We Read about Airplanes and How They Fly, We Read about Earth and Space*. (Complete list available from the publisher.)

Webster Classroom Science Library. (Grades 4–8.) New York: Webster/McGraw-Hill Book Company. Material on more than 700 different topics provides a source of science enrichment, in 24 books such as: *Let's Read about Prehistoric Animals, Let's Read about Space Travel, Let's Read about Time*. (Complete list available from the publisher.)

What Is It Series. (Grades 1–8.) Westchester, Ill.: Benefic Press. Specific elementary science areas treated in a factual, thought-provoking manner, with emphasis on basic facts, not oddities. Some of 40 titles are: *What Is a Frog?, What Is Light?, What Is a Rock?* (Complete list available from the publisher.)

Wonderful World of Science Series. The McGraw-Hill Library for Young Scientists. (Grades 4–6.) New York: McGraw-Hill Book Co. Accurate information on a wide variety of science topics, in 25 illustrated books such as: *What Makes it Go? Your Telephone and How It Works*. (Complete list available from the publisher.)

Zim, Herbert S. *Fishes, Photography, Zoology*, New York: Golden Press Inc.; *Comets, Corals, Sharks*, New York: William Morrow & Co., Inc. Some of many books on science by this author on topics of interest to elementary-school pupils. (Complete list available from the publishers.)

PRINCIPAL PUBLISHERS OF ELEMENTARY-GRADE SCIENCE TEXTS

Allyn and Bacon, Inc.
470 Atlantic Avenue
Boston, Mass. 02110

American Book Co.
Van Nostrand-Rheinhold Books
450 W. 33rd Street
New York, N.Y. 10001

Ginn and Company
Statler Bldg.
125 Second Avenue
Boston, Mass. 02154

Harcourt Brace Jovanovich, Inc.
757 Third Avenue
New York, N.Y. 10017

D. C. Heath and Co.
285 Columbus Avenue
Boston, Mass. 02116

Holt, Rinehart, and Winston, Inc.
383 Madison Avenue
New York, N.Y. 10017

Laidlaw Brothers
Thatcher & Madison Avenues
River Forest, Ill. 60305

J. P. Lippincott Co.
E. Washington Square
Philadelphia, Pa. 19105

The Macmillan Co.
Sub. of Crowell, Collier, and Macmillan
866 Third Avenue
New York, N.Y. 10022

Rand McNally & Co.
P. O. Box 7600
Chicago, Ill. 60680

Scott, Foresman & Co.
1900 E. Lake Avenue
Glenview, Ill. 60025

Charles Scribner's Sons
597 Fifth Avenue
New York, N.Y. 10017

Silver Burdett Company
Park Avenue & Columbia Road
Morristown, N.J. 07960

L. W. Singer Co., Inc.
501 Madison Avenue
New York, N.Y. 10022

Audio-Visual Materials

Each item in this list gives the distributor's name in abbreviated form (e.g., *FilmAssoc.*); the name in full and the address are given under *Principal Distributors* at the end of this section (pp. 451–453). All films have a sound track unless otherwise indicated; film loops are silent. Materials were selected for their success in development of science concepts and investigative processes, scientific accuracy, and interest, but should be evaluated by school or district staffs before purchase since needs vary.

INVESTIGATIVE TECHNIQUES OF SCIENCE

The Aquarium: Classroom Science. (Grades 1–6) Film. Color, $135. 1967. FilmAssoc. The techniques and procedures for setting up a classroom aquarium with some attention to the variety of living things that can inhabit it.

Classification and Natural History. (Grades 3–7) Six filmstrips. Color, $40. 1966. Wards. The principles of classification treated through the use of symbols and common objects. Three deal with what classification is, and three with animal and plant classification.

Experimenting with Animals: White Rats. (Grades 4–6) Film. Color, $135; B/W, $70. 1966. EBE. Students do library research and laboratory work in an investigation of white rats. Care in the treatment of the animals is manifest.

Learning with Your Eyes. (Grades 1–3) Film. Color, $120; B/W, $60. 1968. Coronet. How to develop observational skills that use our eyes more effectively.

Mathematics of the Honeycomb. (Grades 7–10) Film. Color, $120. Moody. A historical and analytical approach to the honeycomb problem stresses the value of problem-solving, research, and scientific processes.

The Microscope and Its Use Series. (Grades 5–10) Four filmstrips. Color. Series, $18; each, $5. 1962. SVE. The functions and uses of the microscope. How to prepare slides for investigating algae, protozoa, and stem sections.

The Processes of Science: Classifying. (Grades 1–6) Four filmstrips. Color. Series, $26; each, $6.50. 1968. FilmAssoc. Size, shape, color, and ways of grouping.

The Question Tree. (Grades 7–12) Film. Color, $60. 1961. IBM, available Strauss. The ways in which man "questions" and how this has furthered development of science. Investigative techniques for research and experimentation.

Science for Beginners. (Grades 1–4) Film. Color, $120; B/W, $60. 1964. Coronet. A boy investigates bread mold; scientific techniques on an elementary level.

ANIMALS—VARIETY AND FORM

Animal Babies. (Grades 1–3) Filmstrip. Color, $4.75. 1964. SVE. How care and training of the young differs with each animal; the effect of heredity.

Animals and Pam. (Grades K–3) Film. Color, $160. 1968. Cahill. Pam's jungle animals are treated by her father, an animal doctor.

Animals Hear in Many Ways. (Grades 1–4) Film. Color, $135. 1968. FilmAssoc. Emphasizes sounds produced by vibrating objects and how animals receive these messages. Illustrative animals include dogs, birds, frogs, grasshoppers, snakes, and fish.

Animals without Backbones Series. (Grades 3–7) Filmstrips. Color. Series, $30; each, $6. 1964. EBE. One-celled animals, worms, the snail, the sea star, the lobster, and related animals.

Beetles: Backyard Science. (Grades 2–6) Film. Color, $125. 1967. FilmAssoc. The characteristics and adaptations of helpful and harmful species. How to raise mealworm beetles to observe the changes they undergo.

Birds: How They Live Where They Live. (Grades 1–5) Film. Color, $120. 1967. FilmAssoc. Differences among birds related to food supply and environment. Narrow focus, simple language, and photography enhance educational value.

Birds of the Sandy Beach: An Introduction to Ecology. (Grades 3–6) Film. Color, $120. 1965. FilmAssoc. How different birds hunt their food in different places and different ways, making it possible for many kinds to live together.

Birds that Migrate. (Grades 4–9) Film. Color, $120; B/W, $60. 1968. Coronet. How 27 species use the four great migratory flyways across North America. The Blue-Winged-Teal is traced from Manitoba down the Mississippi flyway to Southern Mexico.

Brine Shrimp. (Grades 1–7) Two film loops. Color, super-8 mm., $14.50 each; 8 mm., $13 each. ESS. The development, activities, and life cycle of the brine shrimp.

Butterflies. (Grades 4–8) Six film loops. Color, super-8 mm., $14.50 each; 8 mm., $13 each. ESS. The parts of the life cycle of a Black Swallowtail butterfly.

The Fish in a Changing Environment. (Grades 5–8) Film. Color, $135; B/W, $70. 1966. EBE. How the fish has survived through its ability to adapt slowly to changing environments. Encourages viewer to observe, draw inferences, and make predictions from fossil evidence and known conditions.

Flight of Birds. (Grades 4–8) Film. Color, $160. 1966. FilmAssoc. The two mechanisms that are the basis of many different kinds of flight, each adapted to the needs of the bird.

The Grizzly Bear: A Case Study in Field Research. (Grades 7–12) Film. Color, $265. 1967. EBE. The behavior, habitat, and relationship of the grizzly bear to man. Produced by National Geographic Society.

Life Science: Invertebrates. (Grades 4–9) Six film loops. Color, super-8 mm., $22 each; 8 mm., $20 each. FilmAssoc. Close-up photography of the external anatomy and life cycle of the ant and dragonfly, the garden snail and water snail.

Mister Moto Takes a Walk. (Grades K–2) Film. Color, $150. 1965. Sterling. Mr. Moto, a mischievous Macaque monkey, conducts an alphabetical tour of the zoo from aardvark to zebra.

Moose Baby. (Grades K–2) Film. Color, $150. 1966. Barr. The life story of a moose from birth to maturity in the Rocky Mountains.

My Chick. (Grades K–2) Filmstrip. Color, $5. 1965. Eye Gate. The growth and development of a pet chick illustrate the process for all newborn animals.

Nature's Strangest Creatures. (Grades 3–8) Film. Color, $170. 1963. Disney. Some of the most unusual animals in the world in their habitat—Australia and Tasmania.

Of Cats and Men. (Grades 2–6) Film. Color, $150. 1968. Disney. An animated story of the cat, its history and usefulness to man.

The Robin. (Grades K–6) Film. Color, $65. 1966. Gibson. The sight and sounds of robins. Absence of narration encourages observation of their life cycle.

Tad, the Frog. (Grades K–2) Film. Color, $120; B/W, $60. 1965. Coronet. Tad as he hatches from a tiny egg and develops into an adult. Science concepts are combined with language arts activities.

Tuffy, the Turtle. (Grades K–2) Film. Color, $120; B/W, $60. 1965. Coronet. Animals of the pond observed by way of a story about Tuffy and his shell.

What Is a Mammal? (Grades 7–12) Film. Color, $167.50; B/W, $86. EBE. The basic structural and behavioral characteristics of mammals and their successful adaptation to a wide variety of ecological niches is shown. Reptilian and mammalian characteristics are compared.

What Is a . . . ? Series. (Grades 1–3) Four filmstrips. Color, $25. 1966. Wards. What a living thing is, how animals and plants differ, and the nature and significance of fossils.

PLANTS—VARIETY AND FORM

The Cultured Christmas Tree. (Grades 4–8) Film. Color, $250. 1968. Moyer. How trees are planted, nurtured, harvested, and marketed in the Pacific Northwest. Illustrates conservation practices.

Flowering Plants and Their Parts. (Grades 4–8) Film. Color, $200; B/W, $102.50. 1966. EBE. The typical structure and functions of the flowering plant. Emphasizes the food-carrying process and simple investigations of osmosis and chlorophyll.

Growing Seeds. (Grades K–3) Two film loops. Color, super-8 mm., $14.50 each; 8 mm., $13 each. ESS. Detailed time-lapse views of bean plant growth.

Life Story of a Plant: About Flowers. (Grades 2–5) Film. Color, $100; B/W, $52.50. 1966. EBE. The life cycle of a flower. Encourages observation and generalization about the life processes of a plant.

Microgardening. (Grades 4–7) Seven film loops. Color, super-8 mm., $14.50 each; 8 mm., $13 each. ESS. Microscopic observation of four molds (one per loop) and unenlarged views of two other molds and a small mushroom (three loops).

Plants Around Us Series. (Grades K–3) Twelve filmstrips. Color. Series with hand-viewer, $19.90. 1963. EBE. Broad concepts about plants in nature—from their variety to the many ways plants serve man.

Plants Around Us. (Grades 1–3) Six filmstrips. Color. Series, $31.50; each, $5.75. 1964. JamHandy. The world of green plants, the factors of plant growth, and the parts of the plant and the role each plays in plant growth and development.

Plants that Have No Flowers or Seeds. (Grades 4–6) Film. Color, $120; B/W, $60. 1967. Coronet. Plants that have neither flowers nor seeds—fungi, algae, mosses, ferns. The various ways such plants reproduce and obtain food.

Trees—Our Plant Giants. (Grades 3–6) Film. Color, $150. 1960. Academy. Basic information on trees—their growth and value to man.

Why Plants Grow Where They Do. (Grades 1–3) Film. Color, $120; B/W, $60. 1966. Coronet. Plant growth, environment, and ecology in four types of plant communities: the open field, woodland, desert, and pond.

Wildflowers of the West. (Grades 3–8) Film. Color, $135. 1967. Barr. The habitats and needs of the many wildflowers in various ecological environments.

ECOLOGICAL COMMUNITIES

An Island in Time: The Point Reyes Peninsula. (Grades 5–12) Film. Color, $285. Sierra. The rich variety of wildlife and geologic features at Point Reyes National Seashore in Northern California.

Chaparral—The Elfin Forest. (Grades 7–10) Film. Color, $120. 1964. Barr. The chaparral as a brushland community: interdependence of its plant and animal life, its importance as a watershed cover, and how its destruction affects man.

Conservation in the City; Forest Conservation; Soil Conservation; Water Conservation. (Grades 5–8) Four film loops. Sound, color, $36 each, 1968. Harper. The environmental problems of the urban and rural areas.

Conserving Our Natural Resources. (Grades 4–8) Film. Color, $190; B/W, $110. 1966. FilmAssoc. Methods of conserving nonrenewable resources, such as oil, as well as renewable resources. Emphasizes that misuse and increasing demand make conservation essential.

Discovering the Forest. (Grades 3–8) Film. Color, $135; B/W, $70. 1966. EBE. The atmosphere, sounds, and living things found on a trip through the forest. Absence of narration encourages observation and interpretation.

Flowering Desert (2nd Edition). (Grades 4–8) Film. Color, $120. 1968. Bailey. The nature and characteristics of desert climate and topography, and the value and uses of the desert.

Forest Murmurs. (Grades 1–8) Film. Color, $100. 1963. Interlude. The effect of littering on a natural forest. Absence of commentary enhances the impact and encourages observational awareness.

The Giant Forest. (Grades 4–9) Film. Color, $150; B/W, $80. 1966. PtLobos. A view of California's sequoia forests in the 1800's as recalled by an early settler, the role of the forest in the history of the area, and a survey of the parks and facilities today.

Hot Dry Desert. (Grades 3–8) Film. Color, $170. 1964. Bailey. Close-up photography of desert life.

A Land Betrayed: Ugly America. (Grades 4–8) Film. Color, $120. Higgins. The land misused and made ugly in city and country, and what can be done to beautify America's landscape.

Learning About Living Things Series. (Grades 1–5) Six filmstrips. Color. Series, $36; each, $6. 1965. EBE. Where things live, what they need to survive, and how they relate to each other and their environment.

Life in a Vacant Lot. (Grades 4–7) Film. Color, $135; B/W, $70. 1966. EBE. The interrelationships of organisms in a vacant city lot. Comparison is made with other natural communities.

Living Things Are Everywhere. (Grades 2–6) Film. Color, $135; B/W, $70. 1963. EBE. The discovery of a variety of living things along a river bank and in the woods. Offers an opportunity to test children's powers of observation.

Plant and Animal Relationships Series. (Grades 5–8) Six filmstrips. Color. Series, $36; each, $6. 1965. EBE. Examines ecological communities of the seashore, grasslands, desert, swamp, forest and pond.

Plant-Animal Communities: Ecological Succession. (Grades 7–12) Film. Color, $150; B/W, $75. 1968. Coronet. Ecological succession as a predictable pattern that can be traced from either a bare rock stage or a water environment to the appearance of a climax forest.

Spring Comes to the City. (Grades 1–6) Film. Color, $120; B/W, $60. 1968. Coronet. The wonderful and exciting signs of spring—melting snow, warm weather, gardens being planted, animals reappearing.

MATTER—FORMS AND CHANGES

Experiments in Physical Science Series. (Grades 6–12) Twelve filmstrips. Color. Series, $59.50; each, $6. 1966. SVE. Twelve experiments on measurement, simple machines, heat transfer, light, and color.

How Little, How Big. (Grades K–2) Film. Color, $120. 1964. EdHorz. Common animals and objects used to convey beginning concepts of large-small, near-far, shape-size.

Introduction to Matter and Energy Series. (Grades 2–6) Five filmstrips and recordings. Color, $34.25. 1967. SVE. Familiar objects and operations introduce simple machines, heat, light, electricity, and sound.

Kitchen Physics. (Grades 5–8) Three film loops. Color, super-8 mm., $14.50 each; 8 mm., $13 each. ESS. Water flow from a faucet and capillarity in a blotter in close-up.

The Nature of Solids. (Grades 4–8) *The Nature of Liquids, The Nature of Gases.* (Grades 7–12) Three filmstrips. Color, $4 each. 1967. Budek. The nature of matter.

Physics and Chemistry of Water. (Grades 7–12) Film. Color, $230. FilmAssoc. A basic explanation of the chemical bonding of water as a solid, liquid, or gas. How life on earth depends on some of water's unusual properties.

Water and What It Does. (Grades 1–5) Film. Color, $135; B/W, $70. 1962. EBE. The mechanisms of dissolving, evaporation, condensation, freezing, and expansion.

ENERGY—FORMS AND CHANGES

Electric Power Generation in Space. (Grades 7–12) Film. Color, loan. 1967. NASA. The wide range of power requirements for space. Examines power generation devices such as batteries, solar cells, and fuel cells.

Electricity: How to Make a Circuit. (Grades 1–6) Film.

Color, $135; B/W, $70. 1958. EBE. Basic concepts about electric current introduced through use of a dry cell.

First Experiences with Heat. (Grades 1–3) Six filmstrips. Color. Series, $31.50. 1963. JamHandy. Heat—the sources, how it affects and changes things, and how it travels.

Food: Energy from the Sun. (Grades 3–6) Film. Color, $120. 1966. FilmAssoc. Food as an energy source needed by all living things. How plants make food using the energy in sunlight.

Gravity and What It Does. (Grades 1–3). Film. Color, $120; B/W, $60. 1966. Coronet. Common experiences used as examples of gravity. Vocabulary is simple, examples realistic.

The Laser: A Light Fantastic. (Grades 7–12) Film. Color, $225. FilmAssoc. How the laser is used in making precise measurements, in melting and welding, communication, surgery, and to produce holograms. Produced by CBS News.

The Laser Beam. (Grades 7–12) Film. Color, $190. Handel. The basic properties and uses of the laser. Largely animated.

Light—On the Subject of Light. (Grades 4–9) Film. Color, $120. 1965. Cahill. A survey of concepts of light; includes the characteristics and sources of natural and manmade light.

Magnetism of Magnets. (Grades 1–3) Film. Color, $120. 1966. Cahill. A boy temporarily exchanges his pet frog for a magnet, with which he experiments in a casual way. Encourages careful observation, questioning, and self-discovery.

Making Things Move. (Grades 1–3) Film. Color, $135; B/W, $70. 1964. EBE. Examples of forces that make things move and forces that keep things from moving.

Pendulums. (Grades 4–6) Five film loops. Color, super-8 mm., $14.50 each; 8 mm., $13 each. ESS. A sand pendulum is used to record the motion of a pendulum on stationary and moving surfaces.

Simple Machines at Sea. (Grades 4–8) Film. Color, $175; B/W, $90. 1965. Cahill. Simple machines make it possible for a few men to sail a large clipper ship. Such basic forms as the wheel and axle, pulley, inclined plane, screw, wedge, and lever are defined and explained.

Simple Machines Help Us Work. (Grades 1–6) Six filmstrips. Color. Series, $31.50. 1964. JamHandy. Pulleys, inclined planes, levers, screws, wedges, wheels, and axles.

Sound and How It Travels. (Grades 1–5) Film. Color,

$135; B/W, $70. 1964. EBE. Sound is defined and shown to be caused by vibrations. Enhances observational skills.

Sounds and How They Travel. (Grades 7–12) Film. Color, $120. 1965. Academy. The mechanics of transmission, reflection, and absorption of sound in air. Animation and photography.

The Story of Electricity—The Greeks to Franklin. (Grades 5–9) Film. Color, $150; B/W, $75. 1968. Coronet. Key advances in man's knowledge of electricity re-enacted and told in the words of the discoverers.

Toys at Work. (Grades 1–2) Filmstrip. Color, $4.75. 1964. SVE. Toys demonstrate some simple machines and their work.

ATOMIC ENERGY

A Is for Atom (Revised) (Grades 6–12) Film. Color, $120. 1964. GE. The radioactive elements and their basic atomic structure. Peaceful applications of atomic energy in medicine, agriculture, and power production. Animated.

The Accelerator: A Tool of Atomic Research; Nuclear Reactors: A Source of Atomic Power; Radioactivity; The Structure of the Atom. (Grades 6–8) Four film loops. Sound, color, $36 each, 1968. Harper. The basic structure of the atom, its destructive force, and its use in peaceful activities.

The Atom and Its Nucleus. (Grades 7–12) Seven filmstrips. Color. Series, $42; each, $6.50. 1965. JamHandy. The atom, radioactivity, radioactive transmission, isotopes, and nuclear energy.

The Atom: Man's Servant Series. (Grades 6–9) Four filmstrips. Color. Series, $36; each, $6. 1964. EBE. Diagrams and action photography point out the diverse uses of the atom in textile mills, power plants, medicine, and agriculture.

Atom Smashers. Rev. Ed. (Grades 7–12) Film. Color, $120. 1967. Handel. Basic principles of "atom smashers," with theory, historic background, and present-day experiments.

Atomic Energy for Space. (Grades 7–12) Film. Color, $195. 1966. Handel. Research in nuclear rocketry and power systems for spacecraft and artificial satellites. Animation and photography.

Atomic Power Production. (Grades 6–12) Film. Color, $150. 1967. Handel. The production of electricity by nuclear power plants. Includes reactors in use and in preparation. Animated.

BWR: The Boiling Water Reactor. (Grades 7–12) Film. Color, loan or purchase, $120. GE. How the heat of nuclear fission is used in modern power stations to generate electricity. Animation and photography.

ELEMENTS OF CHEMISTRY

Chemistry for Today, Groups 1 and 2. (Grades 7–12) Twelve filmstrips. Color. Complete series, $61.20; each, $6. 1961–63. SVE. The fundamentals of chemistry developed simply. Some suitable for lower grades.

Combustion: An Introduction to Chemical Change. (Grades 5–12) Film. Color, $190. 1967. FilmAssoc. The nature of chemical change and the conservation of matter. Illustrates a number of fundamental chemical principles.

Crystals and Their Growth. (Grades 7–12) Film. Color, $120; B/W, $60. 1967. Coronet. The nature of crystals and how they grow, including industrial uses and methods for growing several types.

Finding Out How Things Change. (Grades 1–3) Filmstrip. Color, $4.50. 1963. SVE. Changes in state of matter explained in terms of heat. Simple investigations of heat and cold, evaporation, and chemical change.

Gases and "Airs." (Grades 5–8) Four film loops. Color, super-8 mm., $14.50 each; 8 mm., $13 each. ESS. Variations on candle burning in a closed system raise questions on the available oxygen in the air.

Introducing Chemistry: Formulas and Equations. (Grades 5–8) Film. Color, $120; B/W, $60. 1966. Coronet. Explains and demonstrates the basic language of chemistry, the symbols used in formulas and equations. Acids, bases, and salts are defined.

THE CELL

Cracking the Code of Life. (Grades 6–12) Film. Color, loan. 1967. AmerCancer. The story of DNA told by use of a large DNA model, imaginative animation, live classroom scenes.

Eggs and Tadpoles. (Grades K–8) Eight film loops. Color, super-8 mm., $14.50 each; 8 mm., $13 each. ESS. The continuous development of a frog egg in time-lapse photographs. Natural pairing, egg laying, and fertilization are illustrated.

The Protist Kingdom. (Grades 7–12) Film. Color, $150. 1965. FilmAssoc. The Kingdom of Protists is presented as those living things not divided into cells. Includes microscopic closeups of groups such as sarcodina, sporozoa, and bacteria.

Small Things. (Grades 5–8) Eleven film loops. Color, super-8 mm., $14.50 each; 8 mm., $13 each. ESS. Details of structure, shape, and movement of microorganisms. Included are the paramecium, euglena, amoeba, rotifer, and volvox.

Water and Life. (Grades 5–8) Film. Color, $175. 1967. FilmAssoc. Water as a vehicle for transporting substances between living cells by osmosis. Other needs for water by living organisms are explored.

HUMAN BODY

Bones. (Grades 4–8) Five film loops. B/W, super-8 mm., $13 each; 8 mm., $11.50 each. ESS. X-ray motion pictures of living human bones (in the head, neck, shoulder, knee, elbow, hand, and foot).

Bones and Muscles of the Upper Arm; Exploring the Human Heart; Gas Exchange in the Respiratory System; The Human Brain; Human Reproduction. (Grades 5–8) Five film loops. Sound, color, $36 each. 1968. Harper. The functions and interrelation of parts and processes of the human body.

How a Hamburger Turns Into You. (Grades 6–9) Film. Color, loan or purchase. 1968. NatDairy. Metabolism of protein traced from digestion through re-synthesis in cells according to DNA direction.

Human Body: The Brain. (Grades 7–10) Film. Color, $180; B/W, $90. 1968. Coronet. Basic functions of the brain shown in laboratory demonstrations, X-ray footage, specimens and animation.

Human Physiology Series. (Grades 5–10) Seven filmstrips. Color. Series, $37.80; each, $6. 1965. SVE. The functions and structure of the human body: systems, framework, and sense organs.

Learning with Your Senses. (Grades 1–3) Film. Color, $120; B/W, $60. 1968. Coronet. What we can learn through the five senses, and why we use several together.

A Thousand Eyes. (Grades 2–5) Film. Color, $120; B/W, $60. 1967. Stanton. The position and general use of the human eye as well as the eyes of insects, birds, fish, and mammals.

Your Body and You. (Grades 2–5) Filmstrip. Color, $4.75. 1965. SVE. The skeletal, muscular, and digestive systems.

Your Body Grows. (Grades 4–8) Film. Color, $120; B/W, $60. 1967. Coronet. Growth of cells: different cells grow in different ways and not at the same time or speed.

HEALTH AND DISEASE

The Big Dinner Table. (Grades 1–3) Film. Color, loan or purchase. 1968. NatDairy. Family mealtime in 35 worldwide locations. Emphasizes the "big dinner table" idea of eating various foods from the four food groups.

Biology—Disorders in Humans. (Grades 7–12) Six filmstrips. Color. Series, $36; each, $6.50. 1964. JamHandy. Disorders that may affect the human body presented with detailed art work.

Eat to Your Heart's Content. (Grades 7–12) Film. Color, loan or $100. 1968. AmerHeart. How to eat well but wisely to prevent heart attacks. Emphasizes low saturated-fats and cholesterol diet.

Finding Out How You Grow. (Grades 1–3) Filmstrip. Color, $4.50. 1962. SVE. The need for food, play, rest, and cleanliness. The five senses are introduced.

Food for Fun. (Grades K–3) Film. Color, $120; B/W, $60. 1967. Stanton. The basic food groups shown through the diets of domestic and zoo animals. The value of each food is related to human needs.

Food for Life. (Grades 7–12) Film. Color, loan or purchase. 1968. NatDairy. Compares the food practices and problems of four teenagers—two Americans, a South American, and an Asian.

Microbes and Their Control. (Grades 1–6) Film. Color, $140; B/W, $75. 1963. FilmAssoc. Microbes seen through the microscope. The control of both helpful and harmful varieties is explored.

Phagocytes: The Body's Defenders. (Grades 7–12) Film. Color, $110. 1964. Sterling. The body's first and second lines of defense—phagocytes and macrophages. Microphotography shows the circulatory and lymphatic systems, and the process of mitosis.

Smoking and Heart Disease. (Grades 7–12) Film. Color, loan or purchase, $45. 1967. AmerHeart. The effect of smoking on the lungs, blood pressure, circulation, and as one of the contributing causes of heart attacks and emphysema. Recovery powers of the body are illustrated. Animated.

The Time to Stop Is Now. (Grades 7–12) Film. Color, loan. 1967. AmerCancer. The effects of smoking on the human body and how the body repairs itself after smoking stops. Animated.

Vitamins from Food. (Grades 4–8) Film. Color, loan or purchase. 1968. NatDairy. The role of vitamins in body regulation, and food sources for these nutrients. Reenacts the drama surrounding discovery of vitamins.

What's Good to Eat. (Grades 4–8) Film. Color, loan or purchase. 1968. NatDairy. A 12-year-old boy learns to use the four food groups to get needed nutrients.

RESEARCH AND TECHNOLOGY

Automation: What It Is and What It Does. (Grades 7–9) Film. Color, $150; B/W, $75. 1966. Coronet. Automation, feedback, use of computers, and how automation affects us. Illustrations from the steel industry, banking, and rocket designing.

Charles Proteus Steinmetz: The Man Who Made Lightning. (Grades 7–12) Film. B/W, loan or purchase, $80. 1966. GE. Biography of the mathematical and electrical genius whose work was a basic contribution to the growth of the electrical industry.

Food for a Modern World. (Grades 9–12) Film. Color, loan or purchase. 1968. NatDairy. Developments in U.S. food technology and agriculture over the past 50 years.

Forest and Forest Products. (Grades 4–8) Five filmstrips. Color. Series, $30; each, $6. 1966. Bailey. Aspects of the Pacific Coast lumber industry, from growing trees on tree farms to the end products of finished lumber, plywood, and paper.

Steelmaking Today. (Grades 5–12) Film. Color, loan. BurMines. How iron ore is processed into the many structural shapes and forms of steel. Automation and research aspects are included.

Technicians in Our Changing World. (Grades 7–12) Film. Color, $150; B/W, $80. 1965. Stanton. Requirements for becoming a successful technician. The need for technicians in science, industry, medicine, and the armed services.

Underwater Search. (Grades 6–12) Film. Color, loan. Shell. The research and technology needed for offshore oil drilling in different parts of the world.

THE EARTH

Archaeologists at Work. (Grades 5–8) Film. Color, $140; B/W, $75. 1962. FilmAssoc. Archaeologists find artifacts that are clues to the lives of ancient people in the Southwest.

Earth in Motion. (Grades 5–9) Film. Color, $120; B/W, $60. 1963. Cenco. The motions of the earth and their effects.

Erosion—Leveling the Land. (Grades 4–12) Film. Color, $167.50; B/W, $86. 1965. EBE. The surface processes of weathering, erosion, and deposition. Narration and questions.

Evidence for the Ice Age. (Grades 7–12) Film. Color, $232.50; B/W, $119. 1964. EBE. The activity of modern glaciers proves that glacial moraine deposits, polished and striated rock, stray boulders, and abandoned drainage channels were fashioned by large ice sheets.

Geomorphology Series. (Grades 5–9) Six filmstrips. Color, $40. 1963. Wards. The origin and development of land forms. Includes weathering and erosion, streams and rivers, glaciers, mountain building, volcanism, lakes and oceans.

The Grand Canyon: Living River, Living Canyon. (Grades 7–12) Film. Color, $285. 1967. Sierra. The Grand Canyon, including a trip down the Colorado River. The geological formations and the living things along the canyon encourage appreciation of natural surroundings.

An Introduction to Fossils Series. (Grades 7–12) Six filmstrips. Color, $40. 1965. Wards. The fossil record and the life of the past.

Materials of the Earth's Crust Series. (Grades 5–9) Six filmstrips. Color, $40. 1961. Wards. Rocks and minerals.

Rocks and Minerals. (Grades 2–5) Filmstrip. Color, $4.75. 1962. SVE. The principle types of rocks and how they are formed.

Rocks that Form on the Earth's Surface. (Grades 5–12) Film. Color, $200; B/W, $102.50. 1965. EBE. How sediments are produced, transported, accumulated, and hardened into sedimentary rock.

Rocks that Originate Underground. (Grades 7–12) Film. Color, $265; B/W, $135. 1966. EBE. How igneous and metamorphic rocks are formed within the earth's crust.

Stream Table Series. (Grades 5–12) Twelve film loops. Color, super-8 mm., $225; 8 mm., $210. 1968. Hubbard. Natural geologic building processes shown by means of a special stream table. Includes alluvial fans, deltas, development of shorelines, sedimentation, and stream erosion.

Why Do We Still Have Mountains? (Grades 5–12)

Film. Color, $265; B/W, $135. 1965. EBE. Examining the nature of mountains by means such as photography and bench-mark measurements over a 40-year period.

OCEANOGRAPHY

The Beach—A River of Sand. (Grades 5–12) Film. Color, $265; B/W, $135. 1965. EBE. Analysis of currents produced by waves demonstrates that the beach is a river of sand between land and breaking waves.

Desalinization: Fresh Water from the Sea. (Grades 5–8) Film loop. Sound, color, $36 each. 1968. Harper. The use of ocean water to solve world-wide water problems. Includes the methods of purifying ocean water and operating installations.

Mysteries of the Deep. (Grades 7–12) Film. Color, $265. 1961. Disney. Life on the surface and in the mysterious deep waters of the sea.

Plankton: Pastures of the Ocean. (Grades 4–8) Film. Color, $135; B/W, $70. 1965. EBE. Plankton as a vast source of food for all marine life as well as a possible food source for man.

Primary Oceanography. (Grades K–3) Film. Color, $120. 1966. Gateway. Simple concepts of oceanography. Child-like "drawings."

Sealab II. (Grades 4–8) Filmstrip and recording. Color, $9. 1968. Merrill. The recent underwater exploration and research of aquanauts housed in Sealab II, 205 feet beneath the ocean surface. Part animation.

Underwater Acoustics. (Grades 4–8) Filmstrip and recording. Color, $9. 1968. Merrill. Current research and technology concerned with exploring sound in the ocean.

Waves on Water. (Grades 7–12) Film. Color, $200; B/W, $102.50. 1965. EBE. Large experimental tanks help explain how waves are created; the effect of high-energy waves.

METEOROLOGY

Clouds: A First Film. (Grades 1–3) Film. Color, $120. 1966. FilmAssoc. Observations a child can make about clouds.

Exploring the Upper Atmosphere; The Formation of Clouds; Weather Fronts; Weather Satellites. (Grades 5–8) Four film loops. Sound, color, $36 each. 1968.

Harper. The atmosphere: air masses, fronts, clouds, and weather forecasting.

Lightning and Thunder. (Grades 4–6) Film. Color, $150; B/W, $75. 1967. Coronet. A summer rainstorm illustrates the causes of lightning and thunder. Simple experiments with static electricity show the origin of lightning.

Thermometers, How They Help Us. (Grades 1–3) Film. Color, $100; B/W, $55. 1964. Sigma. The principles of a thermometer explained through the construction of one.

Weather—Air in Action (3 parts). (Grades 4–8) Film. Color: Pt. I, $100; Pt. II, $120; Pt. III, $120; Series, $320. 1965. Cahill. Weather formation: temperature and wind, pressure and humidity, and fronts and storms. Stop-action techniques, and animation.

What Makes Clouds? (Grades 5–10) Film. Color, $232.50; B/W, $119. 1965. EBE. What makes clouds. Includes material on fog, water vapor, and condensation.

What Makes the Wind Blow? (Grades 5–10) Film. Color, $200; B/W, $102.50. 1965. EBE. Possible causes of a typical on-shore breeze are tried out in the laboratory and then checked in nature.

Wind and What It Does. (Grades 1–3) Film. Color, $135; B/W, $70. 1963. EBE. What wind is, what it can do, and how it affects man.

Winds and Their Causes (Second Edition). (Grades 4–8) Film. Color, $120; B/W, $60. 1967. Coronet. What wind is, what causes wind, and what causes unequal heating of the earth's surface. Local and global wind belts are illustrated.

FLIGHT AND SPACE EXPLORATION

Airplanes: How They Fly. (Grades 4–8) Film. Color, $135; B/W, $70. 1959. EBE. A light airplane in flight and a large model aircraft being constructed demonstrate basic concepts of flight.

Airplanes: Principles of Flight. (Grades 4–9) Film. Color, $120; B/W, $60. 1960. Coronet. Animation and actual in-flight photography demonstrate the aerodynamic principles of flight.

Apollo: From Moon to Earth; Apollo: Mission to the Moon; Apollo: The Spacecraft. (Grades 5–8) Film loops. Sound, color, $36 each. 1968. Harper. Relates to the most recent space flights.

Jets and Rockets: How They Work (Grades 4–8) Film. Color, $150; B/W, $75. 1967. Coronet. The principles of the jet engine shown by animation and a simple experiment.

Rockets: Key to Space Age. (Grades 6–9) Filmstrip. Color, $4. 1965. Budek. The fundamentals of space travel.

Our Class Explores the Moon. (Grades 2–5) Film. Color, $120; B/W, $60. 1968. Coronet. Two students take an imaginary trip to the moon.

ASTRONOMY

Basic Astronomy Series. (Grades 5–9) Filmstrips. Color. Series, $40. 1966. Wards. Understanding the earth in space, including rotation and revolution.

Finding Out About Day and Night. (Grades 1–3) Filmstrip. Color, $4.50. 1965. SVE. Light from the sun and moon. Suggests simple investigations.

Light and Shadow. (Grades 1–3) Film. Color, $75. 1967. Sterling. Where the earth gets its light, and the concepts of day, night, and shadows.

Position of the Moon. (Grades 1–3) Film. Color, $75. 1967. Sterling. The moon and its location, how it rotates and revolves, and how it gets its light.

Size of the Moon. (Grades 1–3) Film. Color, $75. 1967. Sterling. The changes in the size and phases of the moon. Includes their relation to the calendar.

The Star Seekers. (Grades 5–8) Film. Color, $110. 1966. Sterling. The history of astronomy from the Babylonians and Greeks to the present.

The Stars at Night. (Grades 1–3) Film. Color, $120; B/W, $60. 1967. Coronet. The stars and some familiar constellations.

A View of the Sky. (Grades 7–12) Film. Color, loan. 1967. NASA. The major scientific ideas of Ptolemy, Copernicus, and Newton and their impact on the development of science.

PRINCIPAL DISTRIBUTORS*

AEC U.S. Atomic Energy Commission, Division of Public Information, Washington, D.C. 20545 (Apply to regional office for information.)

Academy Academy Films, 748 N. Seward, Hollywood, Calif. 90028

° Since prices vary, it is useful to obtain catalogs from distributors.

Almanac Almanac Films, Inc., 29 E. 10th Street, New York, N.Y. 10003

AmerCancer American Cancer Society, Inc., 219 E. 42nd Street, New York, N.Y. 10017. (Apply to local or state office for information.)

AmerDental American Dental Association, Bureau of AV Services, 222 E. Superior Street, Chicago, Ill. 60614

AmerHeart American Heart Association, Film Library, 267 W. 25th Street, New York, N.Y. 10001. (Apply to local or state office for information.)

AmerMuseum American Museum of Natural History, Central Park West at 79th Street, New York, N.Y. 10024

Assoc Association Films, 347 Madison Avenue, New York, N.Y. 10017

Audubon National Audubon Society, Photo and Film Department, 1130 Fifth Avenue, New York, N.Y. 10028

Avis Avis Films, 2408 W. Olive Avenue, Burbank, Calif. 91506

Bailey Bailey Films, Inc., 6509 DeLongpre Avenue, Hollywood, Calif. 90028

Barr Arthur Barr Productions, 1029 N. Allen Avenue, Pasadena, Calif. 91104

BellTel Bell Telephone System. (Apply to regional offices for information.)

Brandon Brandon Films, Inc., 221 W. 57th Street, New York, N.Y. 10019

Budek Herbert E. Budek Company, Inc., 324 Union Street, Hackensack, N.J. 07601

BurMines U.S. Bureau of Mines, 4800 Forbes Avenue, Pittsburgh, Pa. 15213

Cahill Charles Cahill and Associates, Inc., P.O. Box 3220, Hollywood, Calif. 90028

CanNFB National Film Board of Canada, 680 Fifth Avenue, New York, N.Y. 10019

Carolina Carolina Biological Supply Company, Burlington, N.C. 27215

Cenco Cenco Educational Films, 1700 Irving Park, Chicago, Ill. 60613

Churchill Churchill Films, 662 N. Robertson Boulevard, Los Angeles, Calif. 90069

Coronet Coronet Films, Coronet Building, Chicago, Ill. 60601

Disney Walt Disney, 16 mm Films, 800 Sonora Avenue, Glendale, Calif. 91201

Ealing The Ealing Corporation, 2225 Massachusetts Avenue, Cambridge, Mass. 02140

EBE Encyclopedia Britannica Education Corporation, 425 N. Michigan Avenue, Chicago, Ill. 60611

EdHorz Educational Horizons. Distributed by Encyclopedia Britannica Education Corporation

EducTest Educational Testing Service, 20 Nassau Street, Princeton, N.J. 08540

EDC Educational Development Center, Inc., 39 Chapel St., Newton, Mass. 02160

ESS Elementary Science Study, 55 Chapel Street, Newton, Mass. 02160. Distributed by McGraw-Hill Book Company, The Ealing Corporation, Kaydee Films, Macalaster Scientific Company, Modern Talking Picture Service, Universal Education and Visual Arts, Popular Science Publishing Company, and Association Instructional Materials.

EyeGate Eye Gate House, Inc., 146-01 Archer Avenue, Jamaica, N.Y. 11435

FH Filmstrip House, Inc., 432 Park Avenue South, New York, N.Y. 10016

FilmAssoc Film Associates, 11559 Santa Monica Boulevard, Los Angeles, Calif. 90025

Ford Ford Motor Company, Film Library, 3000 Schaefer Road, Dearborn, Mich. 48122

Gateway Gateway Productions, 1859 Powell Street, San Francisco, Calif. 94133

GE General Electric Educational Films, 60 Washington Avenue, Schenectady, N.Y. 12305

Gibson Dan Gibson Productions, 196 Bloor Street West, Toronto, Ontario, Canada

GM General Motors Corporation, Film Library, 3044 W. Grand Boulevard, Detroit, Mich. 48202

Grover Grover Film Productions, P.O. Box 303, Monterey, Calif. 93940

Handel Handel Film Corporation, 8730 Sunset Boulevard, Los Angeles, Calif. 90069

Harper Harper and Row Publishers, 49 E. 33rd Street, New York, N.Y. 10016

Heath D. C. Heath and Company, 285 Columbus Avenue, Boston, Mass. 02116

Higgins Alfred Higgins Productions, 9100 Sunset Boulevard, Los Angeles, Calif. 90069

Hubbard Hubbard Scientific Company, P.O. Box 105, Northbrook, Ill. 60062

IFB International Film Bureau, 332 S. Michigan Avenue, Chicago, Ill. 60604

IndU Indiana University, AV Center, Bloomington, Ind. 47401

Interlude Interlude Films. Distributor: H. Newenhouse, 1017 Longaker Rd., Northbrook, Ill. 60062

JamHandy Jam Handy Organization, Inc., 2821 E. Grand Boulevard, Detroit, Mich. 48211

JohnsonHunt Johnson Hunt Productions. Distributed by Modern Learning Aids

Journal Journal Films, Inc., 909 W. Diversey Parkway, Chicago, Ill. 60614

Kaydee Kaydee Films, Ltd., National Instructional Films, 58 E. Route 59, Nanuet, N.Y. 10954

Macalaster Macalaster Scientific Company, 186 Third Avenue, Waltham, Mass. 02154

McGraw McGraw-Hill Text Films, 330 W. 42nd Street, New York, N.Y. 10018

Merrill Charles E. Merrill Books, Inc., 1300 Alum Creek Drive, Columbus, Ohio 43216

MLA Modern Learning Aids, 1212 Avenue of the Americas, New York, N.Y. 10036

ModernTP Modern Talking Picture Service, 1212 Avenue of the Americas, New York, N.Y. 10036

Moody Moody Institute of Science, 12000 E. Washington Boulevard, Whittier, Calif. 90606

Moyer Martin Moyer Productions, 900 Federal Avenue, Seattle, Wash. 98102

NASA National Aeronautics and Space Administration, Washington, D.C. 20546. (Apply to national office for address of regional center.)

NatDairy National Dairy Council, Chicago, Ill. 60606. (Apply to state dairy council for information.)

NEA National Education Association, 1201 Sixteenth Street, N.W., Washington, D.C. 20036

NET NET Film Service, Indiana University, AV Center, Bloomington, Ind. 47401

PopSc Popular Science Publishing Company, AV Division, Inc., 355 Lexington Avenue, New York, N.Y. 10017

PtLobos Point Lobos Productions, 20417 Califa Street, Woodland Hills, Calif. 91364

Shell Shell Film Library, 450 N. Meridian Street, Indianapolis, Ind. 46204

Sierra Sierra Club, 1050 Mills Tower, 220 Bush Street, San Francisco, Calif. 94104

Sigma Sigma Educational Films, P.O. Box 1235, Studio City, Calif. 91604

SoilConsService Soil Conservation Service, U.S. Department of Agriculture, South Building, Washington, D.C. 20250. (Apply to state or local office for information.)

SRA Science Research Associates, Inc., 259 E. Erie Street, Chicago, Ill. 60611

Standard Standard Oil Company, 39 Rockefeller Plaza, New York, N.Y. 10020

Stanton Stanton Films, 7934 Santa Monica Boulevard, Los Angeles, Calif. 90046

Sterling Sterling Educational Films, 241 E. 34th Street, New York, N.Y. 10016

Strauss Henry Strauss Productions, 31 W. 53rd Street, New York, N.Y. 10019

SVE Society for Visual Education, Inc., 1345 Diversey Parkway, Chicago, Ill. 60614

Thorne Thorne Films, 1229 University Avenue, Boulder, Colo. 80302

UnivEd Universal Education and Visual Arts (formerly United World Films) 221 Park Avenue, New York, N.Y. 10003

USAgric U.S. Department of Agriculture, Motion Picture Services, Washington, D.C. 20250

VisualSc Visual Sciences, Suffern, N.Y. 10901

Wards Ward's Natural Science Establishment, Inc., P.O. Box 1712, Rochester, N.Y. 14603

Credits and Acknowledgments for Illustrations

Key to Credits

AMNH	American Museum of Natural History
GSH	*General Science Handbook*
HBJ	Harcourt Brace Jovanovich, Inc.
MUSM	*Making and Using Classroom Science Materials in the Elementary School*
NAS	National Audubon Society
PW	*The Physical World*
SPS	*A Sourcebook for the Physical Sciences*
USB	*UNESCO Source Book for Science Teaching*

Chapter 1

1: courtesy of Education Development Center, Newton, Massachusetts. **6**: (top) AMNH; (center) George Porter from NAS. **8**: (right) Isabelle Hunt Conant. **10**: reprinted from M. Cosgrove, *Eggs and What Happens Inside Them.* Copyright © 1966 by Margaret Cosgrove. Reprinted by permission of Dodd, Mead and Company, Inc. **12**: (bottom) Harbrace photo. **13**: AMNH. **14**: Alvin E. Staffan from NAS.

Chapter 2

21: George Porter from NAS. **24**: both, redrawn from G. O. Blough and M. H. Campbell, *MUSM.* Copyright 1954 by Holt, Rinehart and Winston, Inc. Redrawn by permission of Holt, Rinehart and Winston, Inc. **26**: reprinted from G. O. Blough and M. H. Campbell, *MUSM.* Copyright 1954 by Holt, Rinehart and Winston, Inc. Reprinted by permission of Holt, Rinehart and Winston, Inc. **27**: AMNH. **28**: (top left) Bildarchiv Croy, Munchen, © Dr. Otto Croy; (top right), Hugh Spencer. **30**: (bottom, both) Hugh Spencer. **31**: (top right) Dade Thorton from NAS. **32**: (top) reprinted from H. E. McMinn and E. Maino, *Manual of Pacific Coast Trees,* 1963. Originally published by

the University of California Press; reprinted by permission of The Regents of the University of California; (bottom right) Allan Roberts. **33**: photo courtesy Ward's Natural Science Establishment, Inc., subsidiary of KDI Corp. **34**: (top left) reprinted from A. B. Comstock, *Handbook of Nature Study.* Copyright 1911 by Anna Botsford Comstock. Used by permission of Cornell University Press; (top right and bottom) Hugh Spencer. **35**: (both) Hugh Spencer. **37**: (top left) U.S. Department of Agriculture; (top right) Manuel dos Passos from NAS. **38**: (bottom left) Stephen Collins from NAS; (right) AMNH. **39**: (left) Grace A. Thompson from NAS; (right) L. G. Kesteloo from NAS. **40**: (top, both) Hugh Spencer; (center) Alexander Klots; (bottom) AMNH. **42**: (top, left and center) Louis Quitt from NAS; (top right) Robert H. Wright from NAS. **43**: (center) Hugh Spencer; (bottom) Jennie Lea Knight from NAS. **44**: (top left) Hugh Spencer; (top right) John H. Gerard from Monkmeyer; (bottom left) U.S. Department of Agriculture; (bottom right) (a) & (b), AMNH, (c), Hugh Spencer. **45**: (bottom left) Harold V. Green; (bottom right) Jeanne White from NAS.

Chapter 3

49: Helen Cruickshank from NAS. **61, 62** (top): reprinted from E. Morholt et al., *A Sourcebook for the Biological Sciences,* 2nd Edition, 1966, by permission of HBJ. **63**: (bottom, both) Bildarchiv Croy, Munchen, © Dr. Otto Croy. **65**: (top) reprinted from H. E. McMinn and E. Maino, *Manual of Pacific Coast Trees,* 1963. Originally published by the University of California Press; reprinted by permission of The Regents of the University of California; (bottom left) both Harbrace photos. **65** (bottom right), **66**: courtesy CCM; General Biological, Inc., Chicago. **67**: (top) Bildarchiv Croy, Munchen, © Dr. Otto Croy. **67** (bottom), **68** (top left): Hugh Spencer.

Chapter 4

71: courtesy of Education Development Center, Newton, Massachusetts. **73**: (bottom) courtesy of Bausch & Lomb, Rochester, New York. **74**: (top) redrawn from E. Morholt et al., *A Sourcebook for the Biological Sciences,* 2nd Edition, 1966, by permission of HBJ. **75**: (top right) (a) reprinted from G. F. Atkinson, *Botany*, 1905, by permission of Holt, Rinehart and Winston, Inc.; (b) reprinted from E. Morholt et al., *A Sourcebook for the Biological Sciences*, 2nd Edition, 1966, by permission of HBJ; (c) reprinted from W. H. Brown, *The Plant Kingdom*, Blaisdell Publishing Co., 1935. Copyright by Mary Angus Brown. Reprinted with the permission of Mary Angus Brown. **76**: (bottom) Dr. Dan O. McClary, Southern Illinois University. **77**: (top) reprinted from E. Morholt et al., *A Sourcebook for the Biological Sciences*, 2nd Edition, 1966, by permission of HBJ; (bottom) courtesy CCM: General Biological, Inc., Chicago. **79**: (top left) courtesy of Bausch & Lomb, Rochester, N.Y.; (center left) Bildarchiv Croy, Munchen, (c) Dr. Otto Croy; (right, both) Harbrace photos.

Chapter 5

82: United Press International. **83**: (bottom) reprinted from *USB*, 1962. Reproduced with the permission of UNESCO. **84**: adapted from F. C. Consolazio et al., *Physiological Measurements of Metabolic Functions in Man*, © 1963 by McGraw-Hill, Inc. Used with the permission of McGraw-Hill Book Company. **85**: from R. W. Burnett, *Teaching Science in the Elementary School*. Copyright 1953 by R. Will Burnett. Reprinted by permission of Holt, Rinehart and Winston, Inc. **86**: (both) redrawn from A. Joseph et al., *SPS*, 1961, by permission of HBJ. **91**: (top right and bottom left) Harbrace photos; (bottom right) redrawn from A. Joseph et al., *SPS*, 1961, by permission of HBJ.

Chapter 6

96: Gordon Smith from NAS. **103, 106** (bottom): reprinted from A. Joseph et al., *SPS*, 1961, by permission of HBJ.

Chapter 7

112: courtesy of NASA. **117**: (bottom) reprinted from A. Joseph et al., *SPS*, 1961, by permission of HBJ.

Chapter 8

127: courtesy of the Amoco Production Company, Oklahoma. **129**: (left) Robert J. Poirier; (right) *Los Angeles Times* photo. **130**: (bottom) adapted from R. Langley, *Teaching Elementary Science: Teacher's Guide to Effective Classroom Activities*, by permission of Parker Publishing Company, Inc. **131**: (bottom) reprinted from A. Joseph et al., *SPS*, 1961, by permission of HBJ. **137**: Hugh Spencer. **139, 140, 141**: reprinted from Cornell Rural School Leaflet V. 49 #4 Spring 1956, courtesy of the New York State College of Agriculture, Cornell University.

Chapter 9

145: photo courtesy Hale Observatories. **146**: reprinted from R. Brinckerhoff et al., *PW*, 1958, by permission of HBJ. **147**: (top) adapted from *USB*. Reproduced with permission of UNESCO; (bottom) reprinted from G. O. Blough and M. H. Campbell, *MUSM*. © 1954 by Holt, Rinehart and Winston, Inc. Redrawn by permission of Holt, Rinehart and Winston, Inc. **148**: adapted from the Cornell Rural School Leaflet V. 46 #3 Winter 1952–53, courtesy of the New York State College of Agriculture, Cornell University. **150**: (top) redrawn from R. W. Burnett, *Teaching Science in the Elementary School*. Copyright 1953 by R. Will Burnett. Redrawn by permission of Holt, Rinehart and Winston, Inc.; (center), reprinted from *GSH, Part III*, New York State Education Department, 1956; (bottom) redrawn from R. W. Burnett, *Teaching Science in the Elementary School*. Copyright 1953 by R. Will Burnett. Redrawn by permission of Holt, Rinehart and Winston, Inc. **152**: redrawn from R. Brinckerhoff et al., *PW*, 1963, by permission of HBJ. **153**: AMNH. **156**: (top) redrawn from *GSH, Part II*, New York State Education Department, 1952. **158**: reprinted from *GSH, Part II*, New York State Education Department, 1952. **160**: reprinted from R. Brinckerhoff et al., *PW*, 1963, by permission of HBJ. **162**: redrawn from R. Brinckerhoff et al., *PW*, 1963, by permission of HBJ. **163**: redrawn from *GSH, Part II*, New York State Education Department, 1952. **164**: (both) reprinted from R. Brinckerhoff et al., *PW*, 1963, by permission of HBJ. **167**: (top) British Information Service; (bottom) redrawn from R. Brinckerhoff et al., *PW*, 1963, by permission of HBJ. **168**: (bottom left) reprinted from *USB*, 1962. Reproduced with the permission of UNESCO. **169**: W. S. Warren.

Chapter 10

173: Carol Ann Bales.

Chapter 11

188: © Max Yves Brandily, Paris. **192**: reprinted from G. Simpson et al., *Life*, Shorter Edition, 1969, by permission of HBJ. **195**: Hugh Spencer. **198**: reprinted from Biological Sciences Curriculum Study, Yellow Version, *Biological Science: An Inquiry Into Life*, 1963, by permission of HBJ.

Chapter 12

205: courtesy of United Nations. **206**: reprinted from P. Brandwein et al., *Science for Better Living*, 1952, by permission of HBJ.

Chapter 13

212: Vernon Merritt from Black Star.

Chapter 14

222: Bill Anderson **225**: (top) reprinted from *GSH, Part II*, New York State Education Department, 1952. **226**: redrawn from A. Joseph et al., *SPS*, 1961, by permission of HBJ. **229**: courtesy of Bell Laboratories. **230**: (bottom right) redrawn from *USB*, 1962. Reproduced with the permission of UNESCO.

Chapter 15

233: courtesy of Education Development Center, Newton, Massachusetts. **234:** (top) reprinted from A. Joseph et al., *SPS*, 1961, by permission of HBJ. **239:** (right) reprinted from R. Brinckerhoff et al., *PW*, 1963, by permission of HBJ. **242:** (both) Harbrace photos. Mirrors courtesy of the Fabrite Metals Corp. **251:** (top) reprinted from A. Joseph et al., *SPS*, 1961, by permission of HBJ; (bottom) adapted from A. Joseph et al., *SPS*, 1961, by permission of HBJ.

Chapter 16

255: courtesy of U.S. Department of Agriculture. **257, 260, 261, 262** (bottom), **265:** reprinted from A. Joseph et al., *SPS*, 1961, by permission of HBJ.

Chapter 17

268: Marc and Evelyne Bernheim from Rapho-Guillumette Pictures. **269:** (top) reprinted from G. O. Blough and M. H. Campbell, *MUSM*. Copyright 1954 by Holt, Rinehart and Winston, Inc. Reprinted by permission of Holt, Rinehart and Winston, Inc. **276:** reprinted from A. Joseph et al., *SPS*, 1961, by permission of HBJ. **282:** (top and bottom) from *USB*, 1962. Reproduced with the permission of UNESCO. **286:** (bottom) redrawn from A. Joseph et al., *SPS*, 1961, by permission of HBJ.

Chapter 18

290: courtesy of United States Steel Corporation. **292:** (bottom) reprinted from R. Brinckerhoff et al., *Exploring Physics*, 1959, by permission of HBJ. **294:** (top center) reprinted from *GSH, Part II*, New York State Education Department, 1952; (bottom, both) courtesy Bell Laboratories. **301:** (top left) redrawn from *USB*, 1962. Reproduced with the permission of UNESCO; (top right) adapted from A. Joseph et al., *SPS*, 1961, by permission of HBJ. **302** (bottom right), **303:** adapted from *GSH, Part II*, New York State Education Department, 1952.

Chapter 19

305: courtesy of Education Development Center, Newton, Massachusetts. **308, 309** (bottom): reprinted from *GSH, Part II*, New York State Education Department, 1952. **309:** (top) adapted from A. Joseph et al., *SPS*, 1961, by permission of HBJ. **311:** (both) adapted from *USB*, 1962. Reproduced with the permission of UNESCO. **319:** reprinted from R. Brinckerhoff et al., *Exploring Physics*, 1959, by permission of HBJ. **324:** (top) redrawn from *USB*, 1962. Reproduced with the permission of UNESCO.

Chapter 20

331: Harbrace photo.

Chapter 21

343: Lawrence Radiation Laboratory, Berkeley, California. **353:** redrawn from I. Janorski and A. Joseph, *Atomic Energy*, 1961, by permission of HBJ.

Chapter 22

358: David L. Crofoot from Design Photographers International, Inc. **362, 363:** reprinted from A. Joseph et al., *SPS*, 1961, by permission of HBJ. **364:** (top left) adapted from *USB*, 1962. Reproduced with the permission of UNESCO. **366:** (top left) redrawn from *USB*, 1962. Reproduced with the permission of UNESCO; (top right) reprinted from *USB*, 1962. Reproduced with the permission of UNESCO. **367:** redrawn from *USB*, 1962. Reproduced with the permission of UNESCO. **368:** reprinted from A. Joseph et al., *SPS*, 1961, by permission of HBJ. **374:** reprinted from P. Brandwein et al., *You and Science*, 1960, by permission of HBJ. **375:** (top) redrawn from A. Joseph et al., *SPS*, 1961, by permission of HBJ. **376:** redrawn from C. J. Lynde, *Science Experiments with Home Equipment*. Copyright 1941 by Litton Educational Publishing Co. Used by permission of D. Van Nostrand. **377:** (top) reprinted from A. Joseph et al., *SPS*, 1961, by permission of HBJ. **378:** (top) redrawn from A. Joseph et al., *SPS*, 1961, by permission of HBJ; (bottom) reprinted from G. O. Blough and M. H. Campbell, *MUSM*. Copyright 1954 by Holt, Rinehart and Winston, Inc. Reprinted by permission of Holt, Rinehart and Winston, Inc. **380:** redrawn from R. Brinckerhoff et al., *PW*, 1963, by permission of HBJ.

Chapter 23

383: Franz Kraus from Design Photographers International, Inc. **384, 385** (bottom, both): Harbrace photos. **385:** (top) redrawn from G. O. Blough and M. H. Campbell, *MUSM*. Copyright 1954 by Holt, Rinehart and Winston, Inc. Redrawn by permission of Holt, Rinehart and Winston, Inc. **393:** (bottom) reprinted from *GSH, Part II*, New York State Education Department, 1952. **394:** (top) redrawn from *GSH, Part II*, New York State Education Department, 1952; (bottom) redrawn from G. O. Blough and M. H. Campbell, *MUSM*. Copyright 1954 by Holt, Rinehart and Winston, Inc. Redrawn by permission of Holt, Rinehart and Winston, Inc.

Chapter 24

398: courtesy of NASA. **402:** redrawn from R. Brinckerhoff et al., *Exploring Physics*, 1959, by permission of HBJ. **403** (bottom), **404:** adapted from *USB*, 1962. Reproduced with the permission of UNESCO. **405:** redrawn from E. A. Bonney, *Engineering Supersonic Aerodynamics*. Copyright 1950 by McGraw-Hill, Inc. Used with the permission of McGraw-Hill Book Company. **406:** redrawn from R. Brinckerhoff et al., *PW*, 1963, by permission of HBJ.

Index

Index

Page numbers in italics indicate illustrations; related text on the same page is not listed separately.

Mars, 156, 159
Mass, gravity related to, 398, 402
Matter, forms of, 176–177
Maximum-minimum thermometer, 275, *276*
May fly, *44*
Mayonnaise, as emulsion, 177
Maze, for ants, *26*
Meal worm, 33
Measurement, of precipitation, 121
of work, 358–359
Mechanical advantage, 260
Mechanical energy, 359
Medicine dropper, 94
action of, 87
Megaphone, *230*
Mercator, 169
Mercerizing, 205
Mercury (metal), in freezing demonstrations, 279
thermometer, 273–274
Mercury (planet), 151, 156, 158
Meridian, 170
Metal-can barometer, *115*
Metal thermometer, *275*
Metals, as heat conductors, *280, 281*
as insulators, *216*
and magnetic attraction, 290–291
sound transmitted by, 226
transmutation of, 354–356
Metamorphic rock, 133
Metamorphosis, of ant, 27
of praying mantis, 31
in rock, 132
of woolly bear, 34
Meteor, 159–160
Meteorite, space travel and, 409
Mica schist, 131
Microprojector, 73, *74*
Microscope, 73
glass-bead, 72
selection of, 72–73
use of, 73–79
See also Microscopy
Microscopy, of fibers, 205, *206*
of leaf stomata, 196
Milk, protein test with, 189
Milk of magnesia, 4
Milk-carton barometer, *115*
Milk-carton constellation finder, *165*

Milkweed, 41, *42*
Milky Way, 160
Mineral(s), 131–133
in food, 190–191
in sea bottom, 137
in water, 108–109
Mining, of sea bottom, 137
Mirror, curved, 241
and distorted images, 241, *242*
and light reflection, 236–239
multiple images in, 240
reversal of images in, 241
spectrum made with, 248
Mixtures, 174
Molds, 67
microscopic examination of, 76
Molecules, 343
atoms of, *344*
hypothetical course of, *352*
Molybdenum, in food, 191
Monarch butterfly, 41, *42*
life cycle of, *42*
Moon (Earth satellite), 154–156
color of, 155–156
distance from earth, 152
eclipses of, 156
gravity of, 401
line of sight to, *156*
phases of, 154, *155*
rotation and revolution of, 155
size of, 155, *156*
and solar eclipses, 152–153
Moons (of other planets), *158*
Morse Code, International, 333
Mosquito, 43
larva of, *195*, 196
Moss, 66, *75*
microscopic examination of, 75
Moth, 39–41
clothes, 41
Mothballs, 98
for insect mounting, 24
volatility of, 178
Motion, laws of, 373–374
Motors, balloon as, *377, 378*
carbon dioxide cartridge, 378
electric, 301
internal combustion, 376
oil-can, 378, *379*
reaction, 376–380
Mountains, 128, *129*, 130–131
Mounting, of insects, 23, *24*
Mud-dauber wasp, 38, *39*
Mulberry leaves, *32, 33*, 64
Muscle, 195

Museum of Natural History, 159
Mushroom, 67
spore prints with, *76*
Music, 227–228
Myriophyllum, 11
Myrmeleonidae, 28
Myths, about stars, 162–163

N

National Dairy Council, 194
Navigation, celestial, 169–170
Nearsightedness, 243
correction of, *245, 246*
Nebulas, 162
Needle galvanometer, *317*
Neon, 82
Neptune, 157
Nest, of mud wasp, 39
Nest box, 4
Net, insect, 23
Newcomen, 375
Newton, Sir Isaac, 373, 376, 404
Nicotine spray, 177
Night-day alternation, 146, 148
Nitella, 44
Nitrogen, atomic model of, 354
Nitrogen-14, conversion to carbon-14, *354*
Nomads, 212
Nonconductors of electricity, 325
Nongreen plants, 66–68
Nomogram, *84*
North Star (Polaris), 163, *169*, 170
Nuclear energy, atomic fission and, 354–356
Nuclear reactor, *355, 356*
Nucleus of atom, 346
Nutcracker, 363
Nutrition, 188–195
calorie requirements in, 193
carbohydrates in, 189–190
and digestion, 191–193
fats in, 190
minerals in, 190–191
proteins in, 188–189
standards, 194–195
See also Diet; Food
Nutrition guide sheets, 194
Nylon, 205
Nymph, grasshopper, 30

Tree cricket, 30
Tree study, 60–61, 64–65
Trees, coniferous, 62, 64–65
  decidious, 65
Tree toad, 7
Troposphere, 406
Tug-of-war, in demonstration of
  pulley action, *366*
Tuning fork, 223, 225, *226*
Turbines, 7
Turtle, 7
  growth rings of, *8*, 61
20,000 Leagues Under the Sea,
  404
Two-way telegraph, 334, *335*

U

United States Department of Ag-
  riculture, 139
Uranium, 354–356
"Uranium clock," 354
Uranium ore, 350
Uranium oxide, 351
Uranus, 157
Utricularia, *13*, 44

V

Vacuum, 85–87
  demonstrations of, 87–90
  partial, *85*, *86*, *87*
Vacuum cleaner, 91
Vallisneria, 76
Valve action, 375
Vaporization, of dry ice, 176
Vega, 152
Ventilation. *See* Air, circulation of
Ventilation box, *219*
Venus, 156, 159
Verne, Jules, 404
Vibration, sound caused by, 222–
  223, *224*, 225–226
  sympathetic, 226–227
  ultrasonic, 223
  See also Sound waves
Violin, 227
Vision, "blind spot" in, 247
  corrective lenses for, 244, *245*
  persistence of, 247
Vitamins, 4, 190
  sources and functions of, 194
  tests for, 190

Vocal cords, 228, *229*
  vibrations of, 222
Voice, telephone reproduction of,
  337
"Voices of the Night," 6
Volatility, 177–178
Volcano, and igneous-rock forma-
  tion, 132
  model of, 129, *130*
Voltaic cell, 318–319
von Guericke, Otto, 85
Vorticella, *13*, 78, *79*

W

Warm front, 122, *123*
Walker, Ernest, 9n
Walking-stick beetle, 22, 31
  cage for, *22*
Walls, of house, 214
Warfare, rockets in, 379–380
Wasp, 38, *39*
Watch, gears of, 369
Water, air in, 94
  in air, 98
  air pressure effect on, 84–87,
    88, *89*, 90
  for amphibian eggs, 6, 7
  for animals in classroom, 1, 2
  for aquarium, 11
  boiled, 101–102
  boiling point of, 97, 278
  buoyancy of, 103–106
  capillarity of, *106*, 107
  cohesion of molecules of, 106–
    107
  composition of, 174–175
  condensation of, 97–98
  convection in, 109
  density of, 104
  dissolving action of, 108
  distillation of, 99–100
  effects of temperature on, 277–
    278
  electrolysis of, 174, *175*
  erosion by, 134–137
  evaporation of, *97*, 98
  expansion on freezing, 100–101
  expansion on heating, 271–272
  in fire-prevention, 261
  freezing point of, 97
  of guttation, 99
  heat absorption capacity of, 98
  and heat convection, 282

  in household products, 108
  in human body, 101
  in living organisms, 101
  for lizard, 9
  as lubricant, 372
  for manned space travel, 408
  in nutrition, 191
  oxygen test in, 196
  for plant terrariums, 56
  for plants, 51, 54
  properties of, 96–97
  "pure," 108
  purification of, 99, *100*, 101–
    102
  and refraction of light, 242–243
  in soil, 140, *141*
  as solid, liquid, and gas, 176
  stagnant, 43
  in summer, 98
  surface tension of, 106–108
  and weather changes, 109
  work done by, 102–109
  See also Water cycle; Water
    pressure
Water beetles, 45
Water boatman, 45
Water clock, 169
Water cycle, 98–99
Water flea, *15*
Water fountain, for pet cage, 3
Water lily, 15, 66, *67*
Water milfoil, *68*
Water plantain, *68*
Water plants, *13*, 14–15, 44,
  65–66
Water pressure, 102–103
  and depth of water, *103*
  device for measuring, *105*
  problems of, 104–105
Water spider, 45
Water strider, 45, 106
Water table, 130
Water thermometer, *274*
Water turtle, 7
Water vapor, in air, 82
Water wheel, *102*
Water drop lens, 71, *72*
Water-holding characteristics, of
  soil, *53*
Watermite egg, *13*
Waterproofing, 219–220
Watt, 375
Wear resistance of fabrics, *208*
Weather, and air masses and
  front, *122*, *123*

1
B 2
C 3
D 4
E 5
F 6
G 7
H 8
I 9
J 0